Pidgins, Creoles and Mixed

Creole Language Library (CLL)

ISSN 0920-9026

A book series presenting descriptive and theoretical studies designed to add significantly to the data available on pidgin and creole languages.
All CLL publications are anonymously and internationally refereed.

For an overview of all books published in this series, please see
http://benjamins.com/catalog/cll

Volume 48

Pidgins, Creoles and Mixed Languages. An Introduction
by Viveka Velupillai

Pidgins, Creoles and Mixed Languages

An Introduction

Viveka Velupillai

Justus Liebig University Giessen

John Benjamins Publishing Company

Amsterdam / Philadelphia

The paper used in this publication meets the minimum requirements of the American National Standard for Information Sciences – Permanence of Paper for Printed Library Materials, ANSI Z39.48-1984.

DOI 10.1075/cll.48

Cataloging-in-Publication Data available from Library of Congress:
LCCN 2015001370 (PRINT) / 2015002125 (E-BOOK)

ISBN 978 90 272 5271 5 (HB)
ISBN 978 90 272 5272 2 (PB)
ISBN 978 90 272 6884 6 (E-BOOK)

John Benjamins Publishing Co. · P.O. Box 36224 · 1020 ME Amsterdam · The Netherlands
John Benjamins North America · P.O. Box 27519 · Philadelphia PA 19118-0519 · USA

Till Mange
da kine jackpot

Table of contents

Acknowledgements

I am indebted to a great many friends, colleagues and students for their help and support during the writing process of this book. In alphabetical order I would like to thank Andrei Avram, Marlyse Baptista, Angela Bartens, Tabea Behr, Jennifer Bielek, Hugo Cardoso, Michel DeGraff, Geneviève Escure, Bart Jacobs, Vijay John, Christine Jourdan, Claudia Lange and her students, Yasim Lieberum, Hannah McCulloch, Pieter C. Muysken, Mikael Parkvall, Peter L. Patrick, Mona Rinn, Charlotte Schaengold, Armin Schwegler, Rachel Selbach, Eeva Sippola, M. Anissa Strommer, Margot van den Berg and Craig Volker for sharing data and sources, helping with the snapshots, and giving general comments and encouragement. Special thanks to Kimberly J. Gilbert for getting me started on R-maps.

I wish I could properly thank Thomas Klein, who prematurely passed away in the autumn of 2014. He will be much missed.

I am extremely grateful to Peter Bakker and Ian Hancock for their enormous help with sources and snapshots, to Christine Stuka for her tireless help in hunting and gathering literature and to Damaris Neuhof for her proofreading help.

Special thanks to Umberto Ansaldo, Anthony Grant and Miriam Meyerhoff for their generous and helpful comments on the manuscript of the book.

Very special thanks to Philip Baker for his comments and help with the manuscript, as well as his incredible generosity in not only sending me loads of data, sources and literature, but also life-saving chutney from across the ocean.

Very special thanks also to Sarah J. Roberts and Sandra Götz not only for invaluable comments and help with the manuscript, but also for their constant support and patience during my writing process.

Last but foremost my thanks go to my husband Magnus Huber, to whom this book is dedicated.

List of abbreviations

–	affix boundary
*	ungrammatical/nonexistent form
//	passage break
=	clitic boundary
≤	equal to or less than
1, 2, 3	first, second, third person
$1\rightarrow 3$	1 subject, 3 object (etc)
4	inanimate singular ("it")
ABIL	ability
ABL	ablative
ABS	absolutive
ACC	accusative
ACCOMP	accompaniment
ACT	action marker
ADD	additive
ADJ	adjective
ADL	adlative
ADV	adverb
AFF	affirmative
AG	agent/agentive
AGR	agreement marker
AI	animate intransitive verb
ALL	allative
ANIM	animate
ANT	anterior
APiCS	*The Atlas & Survey of Pidgin and Creole Languages*
ART	article
ASS	associative plural
AUGM	augmentative
AUX	auxiliary
B	(in statistics) amount of replicas
BEN	benefactive
CAUS	causative
CIS	cislocative
CL	classifier
COM	comitative
COMP	complementizer
COMPAR	comparative
COMPL	completive
COND	conditional
CONJ	conjunction
CONT	continuative/continuous
COP	copula
COP$_i$	individual-level copula
CP	conjunctive participle
CRS	currently relevant state
CTPL	contemplative
DAT	dative
DEF	definite article
DEM	demonstrative
DEM$_d$	distal demonstrative
DEM$_p$	proximate demonstrative
DET	determiner
DETR	detransitivizer
df	degrees of freedom
DIM	diminutive
DIR	directional
DIST	distal
dO	direct object
DS	different subject
DU	dual
DUB	dubitative
DUR	durative
EGN	empty generic noun
EMPH	emphasis
ENCL	enclitic

ERG	ergative
EVID	evidential
EXCL	exclusive
EXCLAM	exclamation
EXIST	existential
F	feminine
FAM	familiar
FIN	finite
FOC	focus
FT	Foreigner Talk
FUT	future
G	likelihood ratio (value)
GEN	genitive
GENER	generic
GER	gerund
GHN	general human noun
H	high
HAB	habitual
HL	highlighter
HON	honorific
HORT	hortative
IDEO	ideophone
IL	Interlanguage
IMM	imminent
IMP	imperative
INANIM	inanimate
INCL	inclusive
INDEF	indefinite
INF	infinitive
INSTR	instrumental
INTENS	intensifier/intensive
INTENT	intentional
INTERJ	interjection
INTERROG	interrogative
INV	inverse
iO	indirect object
IPFV	imperfective
IRR	irrealis
L	low
L1	first language
L2	second language
LBH	Language Bioprogram Hypothesis
LINK	linker
LOC	locative
M	masculine
MOD	modal
MULT	mulitple
N	neuter
NCOMPL	noncompletive
NEG	negation
NFUT	nonfuture
NMLZ	nominalizer
NOM	nominative
NPST	nonpast
O	object
OBJ	objective
OBJPER	objective perspective marker
OBL	oblique
p	probability (value)
p_{sim}	simulated probability (value)
PART	particle
PASS	passive
PAT	patient
PAUC	paucal
PCL	particle
PFV	perfective
PL	plural
PM	predicate marker
PN	proper name
POL	polite
POSS	possessive
POT	potential
PRED	predicative
PREP	preposition
PRES	present
PREST	presentative
PREV	previous
PRF	perfect
PRO	pronoun
PROB	probability
PROG	progressive
PROHIB	prohibitive

PROP	proprietive
PROSP	prospective
PROX	proximate
PST	past
PTCP	participial
PURP	purposive
Q	question marker
QUOT	quotative
REAL	realis
RED	reduplication
REFL	reflexive
REL	relative (particle)
REP	reportative
REQ	requestative
RES	resultative
S	subject
SEQ	sequential
SG	singular
SIMIL	similative
SOC	sociative
SRC	source
SS	same subject
STATM	statement marker
SUB	subordinate
SUBJ	subjunctive
SUBORD	subordinated
SUPERL	superlative
TA	a verbal prefix in Malay varieties; in Michif: animate transitive verb
TAG	tag (question)
TERM	terminative
TI	transitive inanimate verb
TOP	topic
TR	transitive
V	verb
WALS	*World Atlas of Language Structures*
X	inserted segment (for pronunciation)
χ	chi-square (value)

General introduction

Pidgin and especially creole languages have for the last century been a focus of interest because of how they challenge various theories of language. They do not fit the concept of family trees, that is, the idea that languages descend from one parent, since pidgins, creoles and mixed languages clearly have more than one ancestor. They also raise questions about what they might tell us about the interaction of language and the mind and the process of acquisition. Since the inception of pidgin and creole studies major questions have therefore been how these languages emerged, whether they form a structural group of their own and what they may tell us about the nature of language. The remainder of this introductory chapter will give a very short overview of some key milestones in the history of the field, a brief mention of the purpose of this book, a short explanation of the general conventions used, and, finally, a brief outline of the structure of this book.

A brief note on the history of the field

Creoles have generally received more attention than pidgins. Systematic and scientific study of creole languages started in the second half of the 19th century. The first comparative study is Addison van Name's (1869–1870) 'Contributions to creole grammar', where he highlights their relevance for linguistics:

> The Creole dialects which have grown out of different European languages grafted on African stock, though inferior in general interest to even the rudest languages of native growth, are in some respects well worth attention. The changes which they have passed through are not essentially different in kind, and hardly greater in extent than those, for instance, which separate the French from the Latin, but from the greater violence of the forces at work they have been far more rapid, and, what constitutes the peculiar interest of the case, the languages from which they have sprung are still living and are spoken side by side with them. Under ordinary conditions these changes proceed at so slow a pace as to become appreciable only at considerable intervals of time, but here two or three generations have sufficed for a complete transformation.
> (van Name 1869–1870: 123)

van Name goes on to compare a selection of creoles, most of them French, and proposes that their similarities lie in the sociohistory of their emergence: the fact that the slaves brought to the colonies were adults (and thus were not as capable as children to acquire new languages) and that they outnumbered the European population would have led to a broken version of the colonizer's language, which would then have developed into a "well defined Creole" (van Name 1869–1870: 124). He goes on to state that the continued influence of the European metropolitan language has affected the creole and that "the standard of Creole purity is to be sought at the farthest remove from the French, where the Creole tendencies are most fully developed" (van Name 1869–1870: 128).

Another important pioneer of creole studies was Adolpho Coelho, who attempted a broad comparative study of Portuguese-lexified creoles in several instalments of the *Boletim da Sociedade de Geografíea de Lisboa* in 1880–1882, under the general title 'Os Dialectos Romanicos ou Neo-Latinos na Africa, Asia e América' ('The Romance or Neo-Latin dialects in Africa, Asia and America'). Coelho argued that the creoles were outcomes of universal principles of the acquisition of foreign languages.

Contemporary with Coelho was yet another important pioneer of creole studies, Hugo Schuchardt, who was inspired by Coelho's early work. Schuchardt has in fact been called the 'undisputed father of pidgin-creole studies' (DeCamp 1977: 9). He produced some 700 pages of descriptions and discussions on various creole languages (all of them available online at the *Hugo Schuchardt Archiv*, hosted by the University of Graz, at http://schuchardt.uni-graz.at/home, accessed 6 February 2015). Schuchardt challenged the concept of family trees and the at the time prevailing idea of the so-called Neogrammarians that languages were like a natural organism that followed natural laws of change and development.

Studies on creole languages became more frequent in the first half of the 20th century and important contributions were made by Dirk Christiaan Hesseling, specifically working on Afrikaans and Negerhollands, Suzanne Sylvain, specifically working on Haitian, and many others. Another scholar who has been called the 'father of modern creole studies' (cf. Holm 2000: 38) is John E. Reinecke, whose comprehensive PhD dissertation on what he called 'marginal languages', covered jargons, pidgins and creoles. In his dissertation Reinecke not only discussed the theories of development for these languages and the problem of their classification, but he also gave a survey of over 40 languages, discussing their sociohistorical backgrounds and their linguistic characteristics as well as giving a full bibliography for each of them.

Yet another milestone for the field of pidgin and creole studies was the *First International Conference on Creole Language Studies* held at Mona, Jamaica in 1959. This was the first time that almost all the known specialists of pidgins and creoles from different parts of the world convened and during the discussions "the participants began to think of themselves more as 'creolists' than just as students of Haitian French or Jamaican English" (DeCamp 1977: 12). By the time of the second conference, held nine years later, the field had grown. The conference proceedings, *The pidginization and creolization of languages*, edited by Dell Hymes, were published in (1971) and "[m]ore than any other, this was the book that brought pidgins and creoles to the wider attention of linguists" (Kouwenberg & Singler 2008: 3).

Because the present book is meant for those who have a basic linguistic background but are new to the studies of pidgins and creoles, the path of development of the field, however fascinating, may be difficult to follow before having any real idea of what the field is about in its current state. I will therefore refrain from examining the history of pidgin and creole studies further. For a very thorough overview of the epistemological routes of the discipline, see Holm (2000: 14ff).

The purpose of this book

There are a large number of introductions to pidgins and creoles available and it would be impossible to list them all here. A very early general introduction is Hall (1966). Todd (1974) is another early and very accessible introduction to pidgins and creoles, which appeared as a revised second edition in 1990. Romaine (1988) is a very thorough and oft-referred to introduction, as is Mühlhäusler (1997), a classic by now. Holm's (1988) two volumes are almost encyclopaedic, and were condensed into Holm (2000) as a general introduction. Arends et al. (1994b), Sebba (1997) and Winford (2003) are all very accessible introductions indeed for those new to the field. Arends et al. (1994b) also contains an extremely useful annotated language list where over 500 languages and dialects are classified (Smith 1994).

This introduction is in a sense a second generation of Arends et al. (1994b) and owes much to its parent in spirit. However, new tools have become available since the publication of the previous introductions to pidgin and creole studies. They all appeared before the publication of the groundbreaking *World Atlas of Language Structures* (Haspelmath et al. 2005; henceforth WALS[1]) and *The Atlas and Survey of Pidgin & Creole Languages* (Michaelis et al. 2013b; henceforth APiCS). The former is a typological database covering almost 200 linguistic features, while the latter is the first large-scale collection of information on 78 pidgins, creoles and mixed languages, covering both their sociohistorical background, their sociolinguistic situation and some 130 linguistic features. This has contributed considerably to the possibility to empirically test various assumptions about pidgins, creoles and mixed languages, such as whether they are internally similar and in how far they differ from other languages. Part II in this book is therefore devoted to the empirical testing of linguistic features from all levels of the linguistic system, ranging from contrastive segments (phonology) over morphological and syntactic features to pragmatic features.

1. Unless otherwise specified, the acronym WALS refers to the 2011 edition of WALS Online.

In spirit with Arends et al. (1994b), I have included holistic overviews of selected pidgin, creole and mixed languages in order to give the reader access to collected language data in addition to isolated examples. However, this introduction differs from the previous volume in that here each chapter contains three language sketches ("snapshots"), bringing the total to 45 language sketches for the book, the highest collection of holistic language overviews of pidgins, creoles and mixed languages after APiCS. Each chapter features one pidgin, extended pidgin, creole or mixed language with English (or an English-lexified language) as a major input language, one with Romance as a major input language and one with some other language as a major input language. This will allow for cross-comparison within as well as between lexifier languages. I have made every effort to spread the languages regionally, also within each chapter. I have also made every effort to strike a balance between including well-known and lesser-discussed languages. Furthermore, while a considerable overlap with the languages in APiCS is unavoidable, 18 of the 45 "snapshots" are in fact of languages that do not appear in APiCS.

With the exception of Arends et al. (1994b) and Winford (2003), mixed languages tend to be neglected in general introductions to contact languages. This book seeks to remedy that by devoting one whole chapter to mixed languages in Part I of the book, and by consistently including mixed languages for each of the linguistic features discussed in Part II of the book, as well as by providing nine different "snapshots" of mixed languages, the largest collection of holistic overviews of mixed languages after Bakker & Mous (1994).

The purpose of this book is first and foremost to serve as a course book introducing the reader to the field of pidgin, creole and mixed language studies. It is directed towards those readers who have a basic linguistic background, i.e. have at the minimum done introductory courses in general linguistics and phonetics/phonology, but have not studied pidgins, creoles or mixed languages before. The book thus seeks to provide an overview of what pidgins, creoles and mixed languages are, as well as of the various issues that have received specific attention in the debate about contact languages.

Although a general linguistic background is presupposed, short definitions and explanations are given for even the most basic linguistic concepts when they appear in the discussion, in order to make the book as self-contained as possible. The glossary at the end of the book also serves to increase the autonomy of the book.

It is important to keep in mind that this book in no way claims to be exhaustive. Rather, it should be seen as a glimpse into the rich and multifaceted nature of contact linguistics and the study of pidgins, creoles and mixed languages, which will hopefully be intriguing enough to spur the reader into further investigation. Every effort has therefore been made to provide a starting point for further study in the form of reference tips for each issue or field discussed.

The book attempts to be self-contained enough to be used on its own as a course book. While the chapters build on each other, they are written so that each of them can be used in isolation. Each chapter contains a map of the languages mentioned in the chapter, suggestions for further readings, and three "snapshots". The further reading references are by force a selected few that are intended to serve as starting points for more information; priority has been given to more recent literature and literature that I believe will be accessible for those who are not familiar with the topic at hand.

It is hoped that this book will not only whet the appetite of the newcomer to the study of pidgin, creole, and mixed languages, but also serve the linguistic community in general as a guide to the current state of knowledge of the field. Every effort has therefore been made to trace down the primary sources of any given quote or piece of information, in order to try to avoid the risk of perpetuating possible typos and misquotes in secondary literature.

Conventions

Most of the terminology needed will be defined in the context where they first appear. Nevertheless there are some terms and conventions that the reader will have to be familiar with from the start.

Some general terminology

In any field which studies contact between languages on some level it is necessary to distinguish between what position the language has for the speaker or the speaker community. An **L1** is a **mother tongue**, that is, a **native language** for an individual (or, by extension, an entire community). A mother tongue is thus a language that an individual acquires in his or her early childhood, and is most typically a language that at least one of the caretakers speaks. The term 'mother tongue' should not be taken to mean that it is the language of an individual's mother only. People can have two or more mother tongues, in which case they are **bilingual** (two mother tongues or L1s) or **multilingual** (more than two mother tongues or L1s), as opposed to those who are **monolingual** (have only one mother tongue or L1) – in fact it is more common in the world that people grow up bi- or multilingual than that they grow up monolingual, although monolingualism is often portrayed as the natural state of affairs, probably due to its dominance in the Western world.

An **L2** is a **second language**, i.e. an additional language that an individual learns. A second language (L2) is per definition not a mother tongue; anyone who acquires a second language (L2) already has at least one mother tongue (L1) as his or her native language. Research on L1 acquisition and L2 acquisition indicates that the mechanisms at play differ between the two, partly precisely because of the L1 basis available for anyone acquiring an L2.

A **target language** is that language which an individual is aiming to acquire, or is presupposed to be aiming to acquire. The L1 of an individual can in that process be viewed as a **substrate language** (from *sub* 'below' and *stratum* 'layer'), that is, the linguistic system which is already established for the individual and which may in various ways influence the outcome of the acquisition of the L2. For example, Germans learning English might import various German strategies into their English (without necessarily being aware of the fact), such as ways of pronunciation, ways of organizing the units in a sentence or ways of expressing things. More generically the term substrate language is used to refer to that language or variety which has influenced the structure and/or use of a more dominant language or variety in a community.

Languages that emerge out of contact situations of various kinds have various **input languages**, that is, the different languages that were part of the contact situation and/or contributed to the contact language that emerged in that situation. In analogy with the idea of substrate languages we also distinguish between superstrate and adstrate languages. A **superstrate language** (from *super* 'above' and *stratum*) is essentially the counterpart of a substrate, i.e. a superstrate language is that language which is imposed over another. Superstrate influence does not necessarily mean that the language has replaced the substrate. In many cases substrate and superstrate languages have different social statuses and are associated with different levels of power, where the substrate is not infrequently a stigmatized language or variety and/or a language associated with lesser power, while the superstrate is not infrequently a prestigious language or variety and/or a language associated with higher power. For example, after the Norman conquest of England in 1066, English carried low prestige and French came to exert a high degree of superstrate influence on English even though the population did not stop using English. An **adstrate language** (from *ad* 'beside' and *stratum*) is a language or variety which has influenced some other language or variety of roughly equal prestige, i.e. where the population groups are of roughly equal power. A **lexifier language** is that language from which a contact language derives the bulk of its lexicon. Often, though not always, the lexifier language is identical with the superstrate language.

A ***lingua franca*** (also called a **bridge/vehicular language** or an **interlingua**) is a language which is systematically used to enable communication between groups of people who speak different native languages. The term derives from the actual language Lingua Franca (now extinct), which was used as a language of intercultural communication in the Mediterranean Basin (see further 5.3.1).

A note on language names

Pidgins, creoles and mixed languages have a long history of stigmatization and most of them were until recently not even recognized as languages in their own right. This is often reflected in the names given to these languages, especially in earlier sources, where they were not infrequently referred to as *Broken English/French/Portuguese*/etc. or *Bastard English/French/Portuguese*/etc. and so on. In this book I have for the most part followed the naming conventions of APiCS where possible, or adhered to the name of the language used in the primary sources. Very often these languages are academic and do not match the **autoglossonyms**, i.e. the names by which the speakers themselves call their languages. This is usually for pragmatic reasons: very often pidgins and creoles have similar names, such as *Broken*, *Dialect* or *Pidgin*. In order to be able to distinguish, for example, between *Broken* in the Torres Straight (an English-lexified creole spoken on the Torres Straight Islands) and *Broken* in Ghana (an English-lexified extended pidgin spoken in Ghana), we tend to disambiguate by giving the location and type of the language, sometimes also the lexifier of the language, as in *Torres Straight Creole* and *Ghanaian Pidgin English* respectively. I have in this book also labelled the languages as English-lexified, Dutch-lexified, French-lexified and so on, to give an at-a-glance indication of the language from which most of the vocabulary derives in each case. I stress that this should only be viewed as a simplification and a shortcut and that it in no way implies that these languages are dialects of the lexifier language rather than languages in their own right. Furthermore, it should also in no way be taken to imply that the lexifier languages were the standard varieties of today, rather than the respective regional varieties at the time of contact.

A note on the examples

Even though many of the examples in this book are from English-lexified languages, which might seem quite close to English and thus might be considered accessible to the reader, I have consistently provided each example with morpheme-by-morpheme analyses and glosses, a practice called **interlinearization, interlinearized morpheme translation** or **interlinearized glossing**, among other terms. This is for two reasons: first of all, many of the examples are from languages that only few readers will have first-hand knowledge of; secondly, I consider pidgins, extended pidgins (pidgincreoles), creoles and mixed languages as languages in their own right and the fact that most of their vocabulary etymologically derives from languages that are in general commonly known, such as English, may give the false impression that the syntax and meaning of any given example is easily accessible to the reader, when in fact both the structure and semantics differ considerably. The wide-spread and unfortunate practice of generally refraining to give morpheme-by-morpheme glossing for pidgins and creoles, especially the English-lexified ones, thus not only risks perpetuate the impression that these are simply somewhat odd versions of the lexifier language (rather than languages in their own right), but also risks obfuscate what the examples actually show.

A **gloss** is essentially an analytical explanation of the unit in question. For example, the English sentence *The birds are chirping in the trees* could be interlinearized as follows:

English (Indo-European (Germanic): UK)

(1)	the	bird-s	are	chirp-ing	in	the	tree-s
	DEF.ART	bird-PL	be.PRES.PL	chirp-PROG	in	DEF	tree-PL

In (1) each word is provided with at least one gloss. The grammatical information is given as abbreviations (for a full list of the abbreviations and their full forms, see List of Abbreviations) and in small caps, while the bare form of the lexical information is given in full and in lower case. Thus the first word in the sentence is glossed as a definite article (DEFinite.ARTicle), the second word in the sentence is segmented into its lexical stem *bird* and the grammatical suffix *s* indicating plural number, which is shown in the glossing by separating the two units with a hyphen. If a unit is not easily segmentable, the lexical information is given first, with the grammatical information following. Each component of the non-segmentable analysis is separated with a full stop; cf. *the* and *are* in the example above.

The glosses generally follow the principles set up in the Leipzig Glossing Rules (http://www.eva.mpg.de/lingua/resources/glossing-rules.php, accessed 6 February 2015). Different authors may use different terms and abbreviations; while I have in almost all cases followed the analyses of the sources, I have streamlined the terms and glosses to be consistent throughout this book, in order to make the examples more cross-compatible with each other.

It is very important to keep in mind that the **translations** given for each example are only the closest idiomatic equivalences to English. That is, a translation should never be seen as an analysis of data, but merely the closest approximation of language A into English. Languages may differ radically from each other with respect to their characteristics, which means that various kinds of information may be lost in translation. It would thus be highly questionable to draw conclusions about the structure of a language based on translations only. For example, the French *le* and *la* both translate into English 'the'; without the glossing and based on the translation only we would lose the gender information that is implied in the two French articles, but which does not carry over to English. Likewise, the German *der*, *den*, *dem* and *des* all translate into English 'the' and without the glossing we would not see the fact that both gender and case are implicit in each of the German forms, since that does not carry over to English. In other words, the glossing is essential in order to provide the analysis of the data and show its actual structure, while the translation is merely an idiomatic translation into English and only serves to give an idea of what the example means. Notice also that the glossing is not the data itself, but an analysis. Different researchers might analyse the same data differently and/or to different degrees of detail.

In order to make each example immediately accessible, I have consistently given the language name and some macro-data (such as 'English (Indo-European (Germanic): UK)' in Example (1) above), irrespective of whether the macro-data has already been provided in the text. For the contact languages in this book the macro-data provided is the type of language (pidgin, extended pidgin, creole or mixed language), the lexifier or, for mixed languages, the main input languages, and the location where it is spoken. For other kinds of languages I have given the genetic affiliation (language family and genus; see further the Introduction to Part II below) and the location where it is spoken. For each example the source of the example is given, allowing the reader to make further inquiries about the language or example in question. Where I have not been able to go back to the primary source myself, I have still included a reference to it in order to allow the reader to trace the data. In those cases where I have based the example on my own knowledge or my own fieldwork of the language, this is indicated by the source reference 'personal knowledge' or 'own fieldwork' respectively.

The structure of this book

There is no set standard according to which an introduction to the study of pidgin, creole and mixed languages should be organized and different introductory books will organize their discussions differently. The motivation for my structure is first of all to introduce issues gradually and in such a way that the discussion can lean on previous chapters and sections. At the same time chapters are structured so that they are independent enough to be used in isolation or in any chosen combination. On occasion this may lead to some repetition, a compromise which I have chosen to retain in order to make the chapters independent of each other. Secondly, since this book is a course book, I have tried to make the chapters of roughly comparable lengths, although different topics by necessity demand different treatments and amounts of space. The chapters in Part I are on average somewhat longer than those in Part II, due to the nature of the topics discussed in the respective parts.

The chapters have a largely uniform format: they start with a short overview of what the chapter is about, then deal with the topic at hand, then give "snapshots" of three languages that were mentioned in the chapter, before concluding with a summary. For each chapter a map of the languages cited in that particular chapter has been provided, as well as a list of key topics relevant for the chapter at hand and some exercises.

The "snapshots" also have a largely uniform format: I first give a short sociohistorical and sociolinguistic background, then give a short overview of the structure of the language, then provide a short text and finally give a few primary sources of the language, as a starting point for the reader to investigate the language further. Unless otherwise specified the sources given are a selection of material rather than an exhaustive list of everything available. The sketches are by necessity condensed, though every effort has been made to make the "snapshots" maximally informative, both with respect to the sociohistorical background and with respect to the structure of the language, as well as with respect to providing as much primary data as possible. As mentioned, two fifths of the "snapshot" languages do not appear in APiCS.

In the same way as the book can be read as a whole or piecemeal in that individual chapters can be used on their own according to the reader's interest or area of focus, the "snapshots" can either be used as a complement to any given chapter, or can be used on their own for cross-comparisons (ignoring the chapter texts) or can be ignored completely without any loss of context within the chapter text itself.

Chapter 1 gives a definition of what pidgin languages are and lists the linguistic features assumed to be typical for them. Similarly **Chapter 2** focuses on creole languages and their assumed linguistic characteristics. **Chapter 3** provides a definition of mixed languages and brings up various formation processes that have been proposed for them.

The rest of **Part I** deals with various theoretical issues associated with the study of pidgins and creoles. **Chapter 4** discusses the sociohistorical contexts of pidgins and creoles, with a focus on creole languages. **Chapter 5** introduces the main theories of genesis that have been put forth for pidgin languages, while **Chapter 6** deals with the main theories of genesis that have been put forth for creole languages. **Chapter 7** brings up the notion of variation and change in pidgin and creole languages, such as the issues of lectal continua and diglossia. Finally in Part I, **Chapter 8** looks at the position of these languages in society, including sociological issues such as language policy and planning, as well as cultural issues such as different types of literature in pidgin and creole languages.

Part II systematically and empirically tests a selection of the features that were given in the lists of typically assumed characteristics for pidgins and creoles (in Chapters 1 and 2) by checking samples of pidgins and creoles for the features in question, as well as by comparing the distribution of the features in the respective samples with that in non-pidgins and non-creoles. Each linguistic feature is also discussed for extended pidgins and mixed languages. Such systematic empirical testing of assumptions on the characteristics of pidgins and creoles has not been made in any previous introduction to pidgin and creole studies. Furthermore, the creation of separate samples for pidgins on the one hand and creoles on the other, as well as treating extended pidgins as a separate group, allows the reader to establish in how far these languages (or language types) differ from or align with each other. Moreover, a separate section on mixed languages has been included for each linguistic feature.

The chapters in Part II start with the smallest linguistic unit and gradually move to larger units. **Chapter 9** investigates the consonant and vowel inventories, syllable structures and tone, while **Chapter 10** discusses morphological synthesis and reduplication in contact languages. **Chapter 11** brings up nominal plurality as well as definite and indefinite articles and **Chapter 12** discusses tense, aspect and mood. **Chapter 13** investigates word order and passive constructions, while **Chapter 14** examines relative clauses and serial verb constructions. Finally in Part II, **Chapter 15** discusses strategies for negation and polar questions.

The **glossary** at the end of the book gives short definitions of those terms that appear in boldface in the text.

Part I

General aspects

Languages cited in Chapter 1

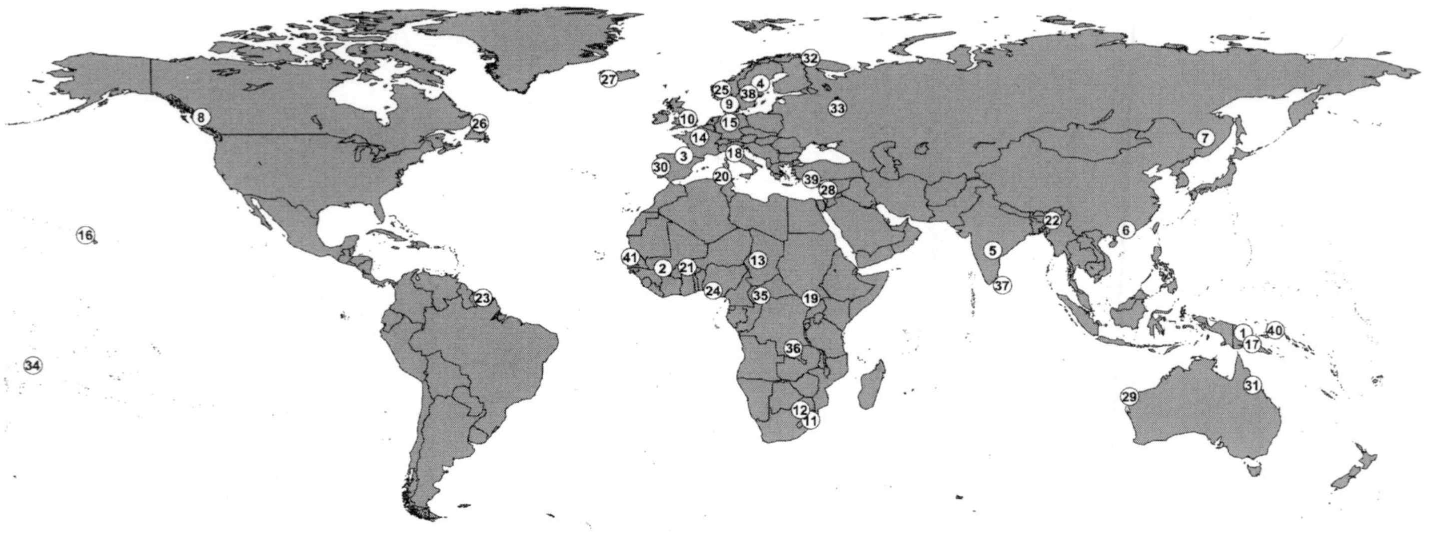

1. Arafundi; Yimas; Yimas-Arafundi Pidgin; Yimas-Alamblak; Yimas-Karawari
2. Bambara
3. Basque; Spanish
4. Borgarmålet; South Sami
5. Butler English
6. Chinese Pidgin English
7. Chinese Pidgin Russian
8. Chinuk Wawa
9. Danish
10. English
11. Fanakalo
12. Flaaitaal
13. Français Tirailleur
14. French
15. German
16. Hawai'i Pidgin English; Pidgin Hawaiian
17. Hiri Motu; Tok Pisin
18. Italian; Todesche
19. Juba Arabic
20. Lingua Franca
21. Mòoré
22. Nagamese
23. Ndyuka-Trio Pidgin
24. Nigerian Pidgin
25. Norwegian
26. Pidgin Basque
27. Pidgin Basque
28. Levantine Arabic; Pidgin Madame
29. Pidgin Ngarluma
30. Portuguese
31. Queensland Plantation Pidgin
32. Russenorsk
33. Russian
34. Samoan Plantation Pidgin
35. Sango
36. Shaba Swahili
37. Sinhala
38. Swedish
39. Tarzanca
40. Tolai
41. Wolof

Chapter 1

Pidgins

Pidgins are languages that emerged in situations of intense contact, in which speakers of mutually unintelligible languages needed a medium for communication. This chapter will first give definitions of some key concepts, such as various levels of stability of the contact situation, the social status of pidgins, and the etymology of the word 'pidgin' (Section 1.1). Section 1.2 discusses some typical situations where pidgins emerged. Section 1.3 lists the linguistic features that are most commonly assumed for pidgins. Section 1.4 gives short sketches of three different languages: Borgarmålet (an extinct Swedish-lexified trade jargon), Français Tirailleur (an extinct French-lexified military pidgin) and Tok Pisin (an English-lexified extended pidgin/'pidgincreole').

1.1 Definitions

This section will give some brief and very simplified definitions of what pidgins, jargons and extended/expanded pidgins ('pidgincreoles') are, as well as a short note on the possible etymology of the word *pidgin*. It is by no means an exhaustive discussion of the various issues related to the topic. There is a large body of literature dealing with possible definitions of what pidgins are and what the various stages might be that lead to the emergence of a pidgin, as well as what further developments of pidgin languages might lead to. For concise definitions of what pidgins and jargons are, see, for example, Bakker (1994, 2008), both of which this chapter relies heavily on, as well as Sebba (1997). For more detailed definitions, see Mühlhäusler (1997) and Parkvall & Bakker (2013).

A **pidgin** is, very simplified, a language that emerges when groups of people are in close and repeated contact, and need to communicate with each other but have no language in common.

There are many situations when a communicative need arises, but where each party speaks mutually unintelligible languages and therefore has to resort to some kind of communicative bridge. Trade, for example, is one such situation. If speakers of different languages repeatedly meet to negotiate, they will need to have some kind of tool for communication. This tool only needs to serve the immediate function of the situation, and is typically only used in that particular situation; for everything else the parties have their own respective languages. If this tool or communicative bridge is used systematically, a new linguistic variety, a pidgin, may emerge.

It is important to keep in mind that pidgins are not *ad hoc* languages, but that they have a linguistic structure that has to be learned. There are thus a few crucial elements to the definition given above.

First of all the contact needs to be repeated or extended. A spontaneous communicative bridge between, for example, a Swedish tourist who only speaks Swedish and an Italian fruit vendor who only speaks Italian, involving many gestures and efforts to understand each other, is not a pidgin but rather a **jargon** (see further below).

Second, in a contact situation that gives rise to a pidgin, the languages of each party are typically not mutually intelligible. Danish and Swedish, for example, are two very closely related languages that to a great extent are mutually intelligible. A Danish tourist speaking a kind of temporarily stilted and "Swedified" Danish when negotiating with a Swedish fruit vendor is not speaking a pidgin. If this kind of situation occurs systematically it might give rise to a **koineization** or **dialect levelling** of the two language varieties, where each party makes his or her variety more similar to that of the other's.[2] For more on koineization or dialect levelling, see, for example, Kerswill (2002) with further references.

Third, a pidgin is not simply an imperfectly learned second language. For example, speakers that are trying to learn a new language will be at various levels of competence in it while they learn it and might simplify the target language in various ways. Or immigrants may be imperfectly competent in the language of their host country. In neither of these situations are the speakers using a pidgin, but rather what is called an **interlanguage** (sometimes also called a **broken language**).[3] For accessible introductions to second language acquisition studies, see, for example, Ortega (2009) and Gass (2013). For more on the possible role of interlanguage in the emergence of pidgin languages, see 5.1.3.2.

2. But see Mufwene (2001), who argues that koineization is essentially a case of restructuring, where contact between different language varieties gives rise to a (or several) new, unique variety (or varieties).

3. A possible exception to this would be situations like that found in Stockholm, where speakers – most commonly, although not exclusively, second or third generation immigrants – who are fluent in Swedish will use a kind of interlanguage Swedish in certain neighbourhoods or situations. This variety was coined Rinkeby Swedish (*rinkebysvenska*) by the speakers themselves after an area in Stockholm; the name caught on and is now generally known. It is, by now, a variety of its own (cf., for example, Kotsinas 1989) which may even be acquired and used by speakers with no immigrant background. Since Rinkeby Swedish forms a target for second language learning, it could possibly be argued to constitute a pidgin (Bakker 1994: 26).

Fourth, the communicative bridge, the pidgin, is typically used in specific situations. For example, the pidgin will be used by its speakers in the marketplace, in the harbour, on the ship, or on plantations, but not at home, and usually not for social purposes. Furthermore, the pidgin needs to be used by two or more language groups:

> If a form of broken language is used only by group A in their contacts with group B, and not by B in their contacts with A, it is probably not a pidgin but either a form of foreigner talk or an imperfectly learned second language. (Bakker 1994:26)

The term **foreigner talk** used in the quote above was coined by Charles Ferguson (1971) and refers to a special register[4] where the speaker will simplify his or her own language when speaking with someone with little proficiency in that language. This essentially refers to "attempt[s] to improve communicative efficiency by mimicking the speech of the foreigner" (Snow et al. 1981:90). See also Gass (2003). Foreigner talk and its possible role in the emergence of pidgin languages will be further discussed in 5.1.3.3.

Finally, most often "a pidgin is a secondary language in a speech community" (Jourdan 1991:196), that is, a pidgin is typically not the mother tongue of its speakers, although there are situations where pidgin languages acquire native speakers, especially in urban environments.[5]

In sum and very simplified, a pidgin, then, is a structured language that emerges through the need of a communicative bridge between speakers of mutually unintelligible languages; it is usually learned as a second language and is typically used in specific situations or as a *lingua franca* across communities.

---

4. By register I mean a language variety that is appropriate for a specific situation or purpose. A formal register will be the variety a speaker is likely to choose for formal settings, while an informal register will be chosen for informal settings, and so on (see further Section 7.1). For more on style and register, see, for example, Biber & Conrad (2009).

5. It should be noted that not all languages which lack native speakers are pidgins. Artificial or constructed languages, for example, such as Klingon or Quenya, do not tend to have native speakers. Klingon, the language of the warrior race in Star Trek, was originally invented by James Doohan and subsequently extended into a full-fledged language by Marc Okrand (see, for example, Okrand 1992). Quenya (or Quendi) is one of the Elvish languages constructed by J. R. R. Tolkien for his epic fantasy novel *Lord of the Rings*. I am not aware of any native speakers for either Klingon or Quenya. However, Esperanto, a language constructed by Ludwig Lazarus Zamenhof in the late 1880s, is claimed to have about 1,000 native speakers by now (Lindstedt 2006). Constructed languages will not be further discussed in this book. For more on Klingon, see, for example, The Klingon Language Institute (http://www.kli.org/, accessed 6 February 2015). For more on Elvish languages, see, for example, The Elvish Linguistic Fellowship (http://www.elvish.org/, accessed 6 February 2015). For more on Esperanto, see, for example, The World Esperanto Association (Universala Esperanto-Asocio, http://uea.org/, accessed 6 February 2015).

1.1.1 Levels of stability

What may start out as *ad hoc* solutions by individuals in specific situations may, if the situations occur repeatedly, crystallize into a ready-to-use communicative tool that the parties continue using when dealing with speakers of different languages. This would essentially be a jargon stage. If this tool is then used systematically enough, it may crystallize further into a language variety which has its own system and which must be learned. This would essentially be a pidgin stage. It is important to keep in mind that there are no sharp boundaries between the stages, rather it is a continuum where on the one end there is no structured language for the communicating parties to fall back on and everything is temporary where individual solutions are created for that particular situation, and on the other end of the continuum there is a structured language (a pidgin) which the communicative parties have learned and which is systematically used for a variety of situations and with a variety of language groups.

1.1.1.1 *Jargons*

There are various definitions of what a jargon is and I will here essentially follow that given in Bakker (2008; cf. also Drechsel 1999). A **jargon** (also called **unstable/early/primitive/incipient/rudimentary pidgin** or **pre-pidgin**, among other terms) is, as mentioned, essentially a contact variety that is highly variable and lacks a stable set of norms.[6] The crucial fact about a jargon is "whether or not it is useful in a given context" (Good 2012:7), that is, there is no structured language to learn which, consequently, could be imperfectly used. Rather, jargons are "individual solutions to the problem of cross-linguistic communication and hence subject to individual strategies" (Mühlhäusler 1997:128). In other words, 'correct' jargon is simply that which is understood by all parties that need to communicate with each other (cf. Thomason 1993) – levels of proficiency and issues of 'correctness' are essentially irrelevant. That means that the communicative tool, the jargon, is structurally highly variable; users typically import a lot from their own mother tongues and experiment with words and phrases in order to get their message across.[7]

6. A separate, unrelated, definition of 'jargon' is a set of words or expressions used by a particular group of people, such as the kinds of words and expressions used by those in the medical profession ('medical jargon'), and so on.

7. This definition differs from, for example, Clark (1990), who considers jargons fairly structured linguistic systems that are used in intra-ethnic communication, as opposed to pidgins that are "the regular means of communication *used by non-native speakers among themselves*" (106; emphasis in original).

> In informal terms, we can think of a jargon as being akin to a traveler's phrasebook: [i]t comprises descriptions of utterances that do something rather than a system for generating and interpreting an open-ended set of utterances expressing an open set of conceptualizable meanings as found in a full grammar. (Good 2012: 7)

Anyone who has used a traveller's phrase book will know that they can be helpful in providing words, phrases and expressions for specific situations, such as ordering food in a restaurant or getting medical help. They are, however, rarely useful for those who would like to have a conversation covering a limitless amount of topics. In a similar way, jargons are useful tools for communication between speakers of different languages, but they are typically limited in what a speaker can express with them.

A jargon is therefore by definition an unstable communicative tool, which essentially has to be reinvented for each situation and by every user. There may be many ways of saying the same thing – what is important is only that both parties manage to understand what the other is trying to express. For instance, someone who wants to know what an item costs may point at the item and ask 'how much does this cost?' or 'how much?' or 'cost?' or 'pay what?' or 'pay?'. Someone who needs directions to the harbour may ask 'where is the harbour?' or 'where harbour?' or 'where boat place?' or 'harbour?' or 'boats?' or anything else that gives the desired information. An individual who finds that a particular manner of expression works is likely to use the same solution again in similar situations. However, it remains an individual solution which is not typically passed on to others. Jargons thus do not generally get transmitted across generations.

1.1.1.2 *Pidgins*

If a jargon is used regularly enough it might stabilize into a conventional means of communication. This process typically entails that the communicative tool acquires a set of structural norms (it 'normalizes') which can be learned as a second language more or less perfectly – it has become a new language, a pidgin. We can thus define **pidgins** (also called **stable pidgins**) as "normative systems of communication that have to be acquired, but which are not yet mother tongues" (Bakker 2008: 131). That is, a pidgin is a language that has to be learned – as opposed to the *ad hoc* solutions of a jargon – and can therefore be learned to a higher or lesser degree of proficiency. In other words, as opposed to a jargon, where whatever gets understood by all parties is the most 'correct' (or rather, the most functional; 'correctness' is essentially irrelevant for a jargon, as mentioned above), a person can be more or less fluent in a pidgin language.

Furthermore, more often than not – but by no means always, as shall be seen – a pidgin language is not anybody's mother tongue. More commonly, the pidgin is a secondary language for the speakers, typically used in certain contexts, or as a *lingua franca* when communicating with speakers of other languages than their own. That means that most of those who use a pidgin will have some other primary language that they, for example, use at home or for more expressive functions, such as story telling or poetry.

Pidgins may exist for long periods of time, even several centuries. Typically they will survive, that is, they will continue to be transmitted through the generations, for as long as the contact situation exists. If the contexts where they are used cease to exist for any reason, the pidgin is likely to go extinct. For example, the 19th century saw an intensive whaling industry, which led to a number of contact varieties that were used with and among the whalers on the ships and in the ports. Once this industry faded out, the need for those varieties subsided.

It may also be that the contact situation remains, but that one contact variety gets replaced by another. For example, on the islands of Hawai'i intense contact initially due to the Pacific trade and the whaling industry, but very soon also due to missionary work and the agricultural industry on the islands, led to a Hawaiian-lexified pidgin (Pidgin Hawaiian). The contact situation remained and intensified, leading to import of labourers. At the same time English-language schools were set up on the islands. With this development English gained in prestige and a new, English-lexified, pidgin emerged (Hawai'i Pidgin English) and replaced the first pidgin that had been used on the islands. For more on the contact situation in Hawai'i, see 6.4.1 and 11.4.1.

1.1.1.3 *Extended pidgins ('pidgincreoles')*

If a pidgin becomes the main means of interethnic communication, it may come to be employed in more domains than it was originally used in. Such pidgins have been called '**extended**' or '**expanded**' **pidgins** (also called **stable pidgins**[8]), a term, originally suggested by Loreto Todd, meant to indicate that the language "proves vitally important in a multilingual area, and (…), because of its usefulness, is *extended* and used beyond the original limited function which caused it to come into being" (Todd 1974: 5, emphasis mine). More recently the term **pidgincreole** was suggested (Philip Baker via Bakker 2008: 131) to indicate that these kinds of languages carry affinities with both pidgins and creoles (for more on creoles, see Chapter 2).

The main difference between pidgins and extended pidgins (pidgincreoles) is that the latter has become a main language for its community, regularly employed in a large number of situations, maybe even within the immediate community or family. Another important difference is that once the language has become such an important means of communication, it may become a mother tongue for some of

8. The fact that the term 'stable pidgin' has been used both to denote pidgins and to denote extended/expanded pidgins (pidgincreoles) is an indication of how terms and concepts have not been universally agreed upon in the literature. I will refrain from using the term 'stable pidgin' altogether.

its speakers. This is especially true in urban environments, and is happening with, for example, Tok Pisin (Papua New Guinea) and Nigerian Pidgin. Recall that neither jargons nor pidgins are anybody's mother tongue. The fact that an extended pidgin (pidgincreole), on the other hand, may indeed be an L1 places it somewhere between the languages we call pidgins and those we call creoles.

Extended pidgins (pidgincreoles) are typically more stable than pidgins. They are typically used in a wide variety of situations, from the everyday market dealings to official national functions and media. Just like pidgins they have structural norms that have to be learned and that can be learned to a greater or lesser degree of proficiency. However, more often than not, the extension of function of the language to cover more domains than it initially was used in brings with it a larger set of rules to be learned. In other words, as the language becomes an increasingly central tool for communication in a larger number of situations, it has to be able to cater for more and more communicative needs. If it was at one point sufficient to be able to use the language to barter for fish with, once the language comes to be used in conversations with the neighbour, it will have to fill new functions. This causes the structure of the language to alter and expand. With a pidgin, a learner might only have had to master the rules for buying, selling, refusing and accepting goods; the learner of an extended pidgin (pidgincreole), however, might have to master how to talk about the weather, or the upcoming election or a funny story they just heard, and so on. In other words, a pidgin has a set of structural norms but only rather limited utility. An extended pidgin (pidgincreole) has a larger set of structural norms and an – in principle – unlimited use.

1.1.2 The social status of pidgin languages

The pidgin languages known to us vary radically in terms of size: number of speakers may range from none at all (the language is extinct) to several million. Nigerian Pidgin, for example, is an English-lexified extended pidgin currently spoken by about 75 million people in Nigeria and among the Nigerian diaspora. It is widely used as a *lingua franca* and is at the moment the fastest growing language in Nigeria; for many users it is the main language in their daily communication (Faraclas 2013a).

Pidgins are usually not recognized as languages in their own right in the societies where they are used. Very often a pidgin language will be seen as "lazy" or "broken" talk with no overt prestige and which may even reflect badly on the user. In many cases the autoglossonyms are (or were) something like "broken X". Chinese Pidgin Russian, for example, was called *lomanəj jazyk* 'broken language' or *lomanəj ruskij* 'broken Russian' (Perekhvalskaya 2013a, cf. also Shapiro 2012). It was used in far eastern Russia towards and on the border to China, mainly for trading purposes and in the Russian colonization of southern Siberia (which for the most part involved trade and tax-collection): "[t]he Europeans regarded Pidgin as a primitive means of communication solely reserved for 'Asians'. The latter were Chinese in the cities and trading centres, and also Tungusic people in the countryside" (Perekhvalskaya 2013a: 70).

There are notable exceptions to this stigmatization. Sango, for example, is, together with French, one of the two official languages in the Central African Republic (Samarin 2013a). Two of the three official languages of Papua New Guinea are (extended) pidgins, namely Tok Pisin and Hiri Motu (the third official language is English; Smith & Siegel 2013a). Languages do not have to be made official for a certain country or region in order to acquire a positive status: Nagamese, for example, is the common *lingua franca* for Nagaland in the extreme North-East of India on the border to Myanmar. It is widely used in all levels of society, both in private, such as in mixed households, and in public domains, such as in media, governmental announcements, and as a medium of instruction in schools (cf. Boruah 1993 and Sreedhar 1985; for more on Nagamese, see 8.3.1). Pidgins may also have a positive status as identity markers: Juba Arabic has come to symbolize a "super-tribal South Sudanese identity" (Manfredi & Petrollino 2013a: 55) and Chinuk Wawa has acquired a sense of 'cool' in the Pacific Northwest of USA (Grant 2013a).[9]

Pidgins are typically oral, not written languages. In the Central African Republic, for example, despite its official status, Sango is not used in formal settings. Instead French is the language of the media, of the education system and of official institutions (Manfredi & Petrollino 2013a). But again there are notable exceptions to this general tendency. There is a lot of material available online for Chinuk Wawa.[10] Tok Pisin is used as a medium of instruction in schools (Smith & Siegel 2013a). And most of our information on Chinese Pidgin English stems from various written sources (see further 5.3.2).

1.1.3 The etymology of 'pidgin'

Various etymologies have been proposed for the word 'pidgin' and it is beyond the scope of this section to give more than a very short overview of some of the more commonly discussed theories. For accessible and detailed discussions on various theories for the etymology of 'pidgin', see Hancock (1979) and Todd (1990), both of which this section relies heavily on.

An early theory which has largely been rejected by now is that 'pidgin' represents a "South Seas pronunciation of English 'beach' (*beachee*) for the location where the language was typically used" (Mühlhäusler 1997: 1).

9. It is worth noting that all these listed exceptions, apart from Chinuk Wawa, are listed as extended pidgins (pidgincreoles) in Smith (1994).

10. See, for example, http://chinookjargon.wordpress.com/ (accessed 10 February 2015) with further links.

Another theory which has largely been rejected was brought forth by Kleinecke (1959:271f). He proposes that *–pidian* 'people', used for various language names around the Oyapock basin (along the border of French Guyana and Brazil), can be traced back to the early 1600s to denote local people in general. The colonizers of the Oyapock area might therefore have termed the variety used when dealing with the indigenous people as 'pidian English'. However, this theory rests on one single mention of 'Pidians' (Wilson 1625:1260) in a text that makes several mentions of 'Indians' and that otherwise contains many spelling inconsistencies. It is not unlikely that 'Pidians' is a misprint for 'Indians'. Furthermore, the theory does not explain why the term then disappears completely for two centuries, until it resurfaces on the Chinese coast in the early 1800s.

Various Portuguese sources have been proposed for 'pidgin'. It should be noted that the Portuguese were very early explorers and traders in both the Americas, West Africa and Asia; it was the Portuguese who first discovered a sea route from Europe to Asia which took them along the West African coast. There is evidence for Portuguese contact varieties along this route which might have influenced later contact varieties. Leland (1876), for example, proposed that 'pidgin' is a corruption of the Portuguese *ocupação* 'business, affair, occupation'. Holm (1988:9) suggests the Portuguese *baixo* 'low' as the origin of 'pidgin' and points to the fact that there was a Portuguese trade language referred to as *baixo português* ('low Portuguese') on the Chinese coast that predated Chinese Pidgin English. Hancock (1972) cites the theory proposed by Moser (1969:87) that the Portuguese *pequeno* 'small, little; child' might be the origin for 'pidgin' on the basis that *pequeno português* (ridiculed as *pretoguês* "blackiguese") denoted a contact variety of Portuguese in Angola.

Yet another theory is that 'pidgin' derives from *pidjom* which is claimed to have signified 'trade, barter, exchange; redemption' (cf. Todd 1990:13 and Mühlhäusler 1997:1, among others) but which actually goes back to the Hebrew *pidyon* (פִּדְיוֹן) 'ransom' – a rather large leap semantically from 'trade'. There was indeed a large Jewish population in the New World from the 17th century onwards. However, this does not explain why the first attestation for the term 'pidgin' is found on the southern Chinese coast in 1807.[11] Nevertheless, the term *pidjom* seems to have been in use in connection with a kind of English and Jewish people: "*Pidjom English nannte man das von Londoner Ghetto-Juden gesprochene eigenartige Idiom*" ("The peculiar vernacular spoken by the Jews of the London Ghetto was called Pidjom-English"; my translation. Winterstein 1908:24 quoted in Hancock 1979). The question is what came first here – *Pidgin English* or *Pidjom English*:

11. Furthermore, the phonological change from [ˈpɪʤəm] to [ˈpɪʤɨn] "is inconceivable for Cantonese speakers" (Shi 1992:354).

> There is the possibility too that the residents of the Jewish districts (scarcely ghettoes) of east London coined the expression themselves as a pun on 'Pidgin English', though one would need to know the meanings of both *pidgin* and *pidjom* to have been able to do this. (Hancock 1979: 87)

The most widely accepted theory is that 'pidgin' derives from the Chinese Pidgin English pronunciation of *business*. Baker & Mühlhäusler (1990) have provided the first known attestation of *pidgin* (spelled *pigeon*) in the sense of 'business': "Tingqua led me into a Poo Saat Mew, a temple of Poo Saat. 'This Jos', pointing to the idol, said he 'take care of fire 'pigeon', fire 'business'" (Morrison 1807: entry 21 September). Subsequently the word *pigeon* or *pidgin* appeared repeatedly in the sense of 'business' in connection with the English contact variety of the Chinese coast (Ansaldo et al. 2012). The first attestations of 'Pidgin English' (spelled either *pigeon English*, *pigeon-English* or *Pigeon Englese*) are all from 1859 and all by Anglophones referring to Chinese Pidgin English (Baker & Mühlhäusler 1990: 93; see also Ansaldo et al. 2012).

It is not unlikely that 'pidgin' has its origin in a number of different sources which all reinforced each other to produce what has become a widely used term.

1.2 Types of pidgins

There are several types of situations that may have involved intense multilingual communications and the need for a common communicative bridge, and it would be beyond the scope of this section to list them all. However, there are some very typical situations in which pidgins arose and were or are used, and according to which pidgins may be classified by social criteria. This section gives a short overview of some such situations but makes no claims whatsoever to be an exhaustive list. It is very important to keep in mind that there are no sharp boundaries between these types; a given pidgin could have been used in any or all of these situations. Rather, the classifications given in this section should only be seen as very rough indications of the kinds of situations that might have led to the emergence of a pidgin.

1.2.1 Trade and nautical pidgins

As mentioned, trade was instrumental in the emergence of pidgins: repeated situations where people of different linguistic backgrounds had to be able to communicate with each other. Trade often involved ships as a crucial means of transport and communication – usually this meant seafaring, but trading by waterways also includes lakes and rivers. Therefore it is not always possible to give neatly delineated categories of maritime or nautical pidgins versus trade pidgins. Some typically maritime or nautical pidgins were predominantly used as a trade language. On the other hand, not all trade was dependent on waterways, so not all trade pidgins are or were maritime or nautical.

1.2.1.1 *Maritime/nautical pidgins*

A number of pidgins emerged as a result of interethnic communication between sailors of different linguistic backgrounds on board ships and between ships, as well as between seamen and coastal people, for example during their dealings in ports.

An example of an early known **maritime** or **nautical pidgin** – in fact the earliest known recorded pidgin – is Lingua Franca (sometimes also called Sabir), which was spoken from the time of the Crusades, if not earlier, and used in ports along the Mediterranean coast until the 19th century (see further 5.3.1).

Fishing has led to a number of maritime pidgins. The Basque, for example, were early and very skilled seafarers. Their shipbuilding techniques were highly advanced and they were among the first Europeans to engage in whale hunting and open sea cod fishing. This took them to northern Atlantic and Arctic fishing grounds, which brought them into contact with the people living along those coasts. There is evidence of Basque-lexified pidgins along the eastern coast of North America as well as on Iceland in the 16th and 17th centuries (cf., for example, Bakker 1989). Fishing was also the reason for intense contact between Norwegian and Russian ships around the North Cape in the 19th and 20th centuries, which led to the mixed pidgin Russenorsk (see further 12.4.1).

Chinese Pidgin English is an example of a trade pidgin spoken mainly in those ports where trading with Europeans was permitted. It emerged in southern China and survived for more than two centuries; it is now effectively extinct, though there are still some rememberers left (Matthews & Li 2013). For more on Chinese Pidgin English, see 5.3.2.

1.2.1.2 *Trade pidgins*

Trade pidgins are or were used predominantly for the purpose of trading. While seafaring has for many centuries been central to trade, it should be noted that not all trade is dependent on it. The population of villages along the Arafundi River in Papua New Guinea, for example, speak two unrelated languages, Yimas and Arafundi. Those men who had clan-based rights to engage in trade between the villages would use Yimas-Arafundi Pidgin, one of several Yimas-lexified pidgins in the area.[12] The language, which was employed exclusively in trading contexts, is now highly endangered or, more probably, already extinct (Foley 2013a).

An example of a trade pidgin that arose in the interior is Chinese Pidgin Russian, which was spoken between the end of the 18th century and the middle of the 20th century and was, as mentioned above (1.1.2), primarily used in trade and tax collection

12. Williams (2000: 42ff) lists four Yimas-lexified pidgins: two types of Yimas-Arafundi trade pidgins (with different Arafundi dialects) as well as Yimas-Alamblak trade pidgin and Yimas-Karawari trade pidgin.

situations. It is now extinct, although around 50 "elderly (over 70 years old) representatives of Siberian minorities can still be considered semi-speakers" (Perekhvalskaya 2013a: 69).

Chinese Pidgin Russian is also an example of the fact that, while trade pidgins arose primarily for the purpose of trade, they may come to be used for other purposes: with further colonization and mass contact, Chinese Pidgin Russian became the main means of communication between the Russian and Chinese communities during the first three decades of the 20th century in the bigger Far-Eastern Russian urban centres (Shapiro 2012, Perekhvalskaya 2013a). Another example of a trade pidgin that has acquired other domains of use is Ndyuka-Trio Pidgin. It arose about 200 years ago as a contact language for the trade between speakers of Ndyuka and speakers of Tiriyó and Wayana along the Tapanahoni and Palumenu Rivers in south-eastern Suriname. Today, however, it is not only used for trade, but also in general conversation between Ndyuka and Tiriyó or Wayana speakers (Huttar & Velantie 1997). For more on Ndyuka-Trio Pidgin, see 13.4.1.

1.2.2 Workforce pidgins

Apart from trade and seafaring, another type of situation where contact languages arose were workforces of various kinds. These can be divided into two major types of situations: the first kind saw interaction between foreigners and local workers, such as between colonial people and their interaction with locals, who typically made up the domestic staff in colonial households. The second kind saw multilingual workforces, such as on plantations, in mines and on construction sites.

1.2.2.1 *Domestic workforce pidgins*

An example of a **domestic workforce pidgin** is Butler English in India, which emerged some 200 years ago and was originally used by local domestic staff when speaking to their colonial masters (Hosali 2000); it is still spoken in the "domestic work-sphere domain, fixed locales like those of hotels, clubs and household, during fixed working hours to indicate the role-relationship of master and servant and to discuss limited topics" (Hosali 2004: 1032).

Another example of a domestic workforce pidgin is Pidgin Madam (or Maid's Arabic), used in Lebanon between Arab employers (typically female) and their Sinhala domestic workers (typically female) (Bizri 2010).[13] Notice that this contact situation is

13. Interestingly enough, the Filipino workforce, which in Lebanon is also significant, typically speaks English with their employers (Bizri 2009). Pidgin Madam is thus based on only two languages, Sinhala and Arabic, and could possibly be argued to be a 'mixed pidgin' (or 50/50 pidgin; cf. Bakker 1994), similar to Russenorsk and Ndyuka-Trio.

in a sense a mirror image of that which gave rise to Butler English: with Pidgin Madam the locals are the employers and the foreigners make up the workforce.

A somewhat related phenomenon might be so-called **tourist pidgins** (cf. Sebba 1997:31), a rather poorly studied area. Here repeated interaction between the tourist industry workforce and the tourists may lead to a pidgin variety, provided that the contact between the input languages is consistent enough. An example might be Tarzanca in Turkey, with Turkish and English as its input languages (Hinnenkamp 1982), although it should be noted that it has by now evolved into an urban cool youth language (Acar 2004). There might have been a very early Italian-lexified tourist pidgin used primarily by German mercenaries in the 15th and 16th centuries, but maybe also by pilgrims to Rome. The variety was distinctive enough to have a name, Todesche, and seems to also have been used in songs for comic effect. Very little data is available for Todesche, though a handful of references can be found in Reinecke et al. (1975:73). It is not unlikely that any given popular tourist destination may develop contact varieties.

1.2.2.2 *Plantation pidgins*

An important type of multilingual workforce pidgin is the **plantation pidgin**, which arose in connection with the large-scale agricultural enterprises that were one of the many effects of European expansion and colonization. The need for a large and constant workforce for the plantation, coupled with the harsh conditions, led to mass importation of labour to plantation sites, with workers from a variety of linguistic backgrounds. This kind of pidgin has received special attention because of the fact that many of the contact languages we know of today have their origin in plantation contexts.

An example of a plantation pidgin is Tok Pisin, which was at first primarily used on the plantations in the German territories of New Guinea. There are various theories about the exact origin of Tok Pisin: it may be that Tok Pisin is an offspring of Samoan Plantation Pidgin (cf., for example, Mühlhäusler 1976 and Mosel & Mühlhäusler 1982, largely echoed in Smith & Siegel 2013a), essentially brought back by New Guinean plantation workers returning home and using it on New Guinean plantations. However, German colonial archival evidence may suggest that there were also workers on the German New Guinea plantations who had acquired a pidgin English while working in Queensland (Huber & Velupillai 2009), in which case Tok Pisin might be a partial offspring of Queensland Plantation Pidgin. Whatever the exact origin of Tok Pisin may be, it is fair to assume that the language (or rather, its predecessors) emerged as a consequence of multiethnic plantation workforces.

On the islands of Hawai'i two separate pidgins developed: first a Hawaiian-lexified pidgin, then an English-lexified pidgin. Neither of them emerged as a result of plantations, though both of them came to be the main means of communications on plantations. Pidgin Hawaiian was at first specifically used between Hawaiians and foreigners; by the end of the 19th century, it had become the main language used between plantation workers of different origins. A couple of decades later Hawaiʻi Pidgin English, which originally emerged in urban centres and in interaction with Anglophones, gained in prestige and rapidly replaced Pidgin Hawaiian also on the plantations (Roberts 2013a).

1.2.2.3 *Mine and industry pidgins*

An example of a **mine pidgin** is Shaba Swahili (also called Lubumbashi Swahili), which emerged sometime between 1920 and 1940 as a consequence of Belgian copper mining in Shaba (formerly Katanga) in what is now the south-east of the DR Congo. Labour was recruited from all over Central Africa, leading to a multilingual workforce (de Rooij 1994a). Shaba Swahili has by now become an extended pidgin (pidgincreole) and is widely used in all spheres of the Shaban society (Kapanga 1998).

Another language typically cited as a mine pidgin is Fanakalo in South Africa. It originated about 200 years ago and was originally used in workforce situations, such as on farms, in mines, in domestic employment, and so on. It is still a widely spoken language, although in decline, and is used in labour situations "as well as in 'transactional' communications such as in petrol stations, shops, markets, and rural trade stores, in which one of the interlocutors is black and the other Indian or white" (Mesthrie & Surek-Clark 2013: 34).

An example of an industry pidgin is Pidgin Ngarluma which was used around the last few decades of the 19th century in the North West Cape area of Australia "as a contact language between Aboriginal people, and perhaps to a limited extent between Aborigines and Europeans, in the early years of the Pilbara pearling industry" (Dench 1998: 57).

1.2.3 Military pidgins

Military pidgins arose in situations where the troops or forces consisted of members from diverse linguistic backgrounds. An example of a military pidgin is Juba Arabic (called *arabi juba* by its speakers), a Sudanese Arabic-lexified extended pidgin (pidgincreole) spoken in South Sudan. It emerged in the Egyptian military camps in Southern Sudan to which soldiers of a variety of ethnic backgrounds had been recruited. It has survived as a *lingua franca* and is currently spoken by the majority of South Sudanese people, and has even acquired a considerable number of mother tongue speakers, particularly in the capital, Juba (Manfredi & Petrollino 2013a). For more on Juba Arabic, see 15.4.1.

1.2.4 Urban pidgins

An example of an **urban pidgin**, that is, a pidgin that emerged due to intense interethnic contact in an urban environment, is Hawai'i Pidgin English, which actually initially arose in urban areas: it was "used by non-native speakers of English but its use was initially limited to Honolulu and other communities with large numbers of Anglophones" (Roberts 2013a: 120). It very rapidly spread to other domains and became the main means of interethnic communication on the plantations.

Flaaitaal (also called Tsotsitaal or Iscamtho) is sometimes called an urban contact vernacular. It arose in urban and town-ship communities of South Africa in the 20th century as an "in-group result of social and linguistic interaction among equals, or those sharing similar sociocultural values and perspectives" (Makhudu 2002: 399) and is most typically used by African adult males. However, Flaaitaal is not a pidgin *per se* but rather an in-group sub-culture identity marker (see, for example, Slabbert & Myers-Scotton 1996 and Mesthrie 2008).

1.3 Assumed typical linguistic features of pidgins

There has been a long history of viewing pidgins as simplified versions of their lexifier languages and it is commonly stated that a typical characteristic of pidgins is their lack of complexity: "the grammars of pidgins were characteristically less complex than the grammars of their source languages. Relative grammatical simplicity is thus one of the distinguishing marks of a pidgin" (Sebba 1997: 37). What exactly is meant by simplification and lack of complexity can at times be somewhat opaque and also depends on how the concept of 'linguistic complexity' is defined; the implication is generally that 'simplification' and 'lack of complexity' means reduced overt morphological inflection and variation, as well as an increase in regularity. It should also be noted that whether 'simplification' is an accurate description or not for pidgins depends on what input language is assumed to have been available to the speaker (see the various theories on this point in Chapter 5). This section will bring up some linguistic features that tend to be presented as typical features for pidgin languages. It makes no claims whatsoever to presenting an exhaustive list of assumed pidgin features, but should rather be seen as a general sketch of what is commonly cited as pidgin features. For lengthy discussions on the linguistic features of pidgins, see Bakker (1994, 2008), Mühlhäusler (1997), Parkvall & Bakker (2013), Romaine (1988) and Sebba (1997), on which this section is based.

The following summary starts with the smallest linguistic units and moves towards the bigger ones. A selection of these assumed typical pidgin features will then be further investigated in the relevant chapters of Part II in this book. I stress that it is at this stage left entirely open whether or not these assumed features do in fact apply to the pidgin languages we have data for.

1.3.1.1 *Phonology*

Pidgins are typically described as having fewer phonemes than their input languages, typically only five vowels and no contrastive length. The phoneme inventories are typically described as lacking typologically unusual sounds. The syllable structure is typically described as CV, that is, consisting of only one consonant and one vowel, in words that typically have two syllables (giving a CVCV structure). Furthermore, pidgins are typically described as lacking tone contrasts.

1.3.1.2 *Morphology*

Pidgins are typically described as having few or no morphological inflections and little or no derivational morphology. They are described as mainly using analytic morphological strategies, where grammatical relationships are indicated with free rather than bound morphemes. They are described as lacking the morphological process of reduplication. Allomorphy is typically not expected in pidgins, neither is agreement: "there is a tendency for each grammatical morpheme to be expressed only once in an utterance, and for that morpheme to be expressed by a single form" (Romaine 1988: 28).

1.3.1.3 *The noun phrase*

Pidgins are typically described as lacking case, gender and number. They are also described as lacking definite and indefinite articles (as in *the book* versus *a book*).

1.3.1.4 *The verb phrase*

Pidgins are typically described as lacking tense marking, with time optionally indicated either through context or through various adverbials (such as *yesterday*, *now*, *tomorrow*, *later*, and so on). Aspect is typically not expected in pidgin languages.

1.3.1.5 *Simple sentences*

Pidgins are typically described as having fixed word order, where the subject, verb and object tend to appear in the same order relative to each other. They are also typically described as having the same word order for declarative sentences as for questions, with the only difference between them being in intonation (questions have a rising intonation). Pidgins are often described as having question words consisting of two morphemes.

Pidgins are described as using a free and invariant form to negate sentences (a so-called negator), which is placed before the verb.

Pidgins are typically described as lacking passive sentences.

1.3.1.6 *Predication*

Pidgins are typically described as lacking the copula, i.e. the connector between the noun phrase and its predication. In English, for example, a sentence like *The house is red* or *The man is a teacher* contains the copula *is*, which essentially functions as a connector between the noun phrase (*the house* or *the man*) and its description (*red* or *a teacher*).

1.3.1.7 *Complex sentences*

Pidgins are often described as lacking complex sentences, or, if clauses combine, to express complex clauses by way of juxtaposition (i.e. merely placing the two clauses next to each other without any added marking).

1.3.1.8 *The lexicon*

Pidgins are typically described as having a lexicon that first of all is mainly derived from one input language, and secondly that is smaller than that of the source language. The words are typically assumed to be short and the vocabulary to contain few compounds. Furthermore, the words are typically described as being multifunctional, that is, as being used as, for example, both verbs and nouns. Synonyms are typically not expected and words are typically less specific and more general in their meanings. That is, words tend to be both semantically and grammatically ambiguous.

Pidgins are typically described as having fewer function words than their input languages, for instance fewer adpositions.

1.4 Snapshots

By their very nature, jargons are elusive languages: the fact that they are essentially *ad hoc* solutions means that they rarely are (or were) recorded. However, some very scanty material of a trade jargon in northern Sweden, Borgarmålet, exists.

Pidgins are, as mentioned, more stable as linguistic systems than jargons, though they are also typically used in specific contexts. An example of a pidgin is Français Tirailleur, a military pidgin used in West Africa.

Extended pidgins (pidgincreoles) have come to be used in a wide variety of contexts. Hand in hand with the extension of their domains of use, their linguistic systems both expand and stabilize further. An example of an extended pidgin is Tok Pisin, a language in Papua New Guinea, which originated in plantation contexts but which is now widely used in all domains of society.

1.4.1 Borgarmålet: An extinct trade jargon in northern Sweden

Borgarmålet was used in the trade between the Sami population and the Swedish merchants in the northern Swedish coastal towns. The latter were called *borgare* 'townsmen' in the southern Sami areas. There is only one single source available that mentions Borgarmålet, an account from 1747 of the Sami areas that belonged to Sweden (Högström 1747). In his account Högström describes how, while a great deal of the Sami population understands Swedish, and a great deal of the Swedish population in the Swedish Southern Sami areas understands Sami, particularly those Swedish tradesmen and merchants who regularly deal with the Sami in the yearly markets have come to use "a language which is according to the ways of neither the Swedish nor Lapp tongues" ("som hwarken med Swenska eller Lapska tungomålens art är enligit" 1747:77; my translation). The only surviving examples of this variety are the five sentences that Högström provides (1747:77):

Borgarmålet

(2) a. Du stick uti mäg din skin så ja sätt uti däg min bränwin
2SG.S put out 1SG.O 2SG.POSS fur then 1SG.S place out 2SG.O 1SG.POSS brandy
'(If) you give me your furs, then I'll give you brandy.'
(Högström: *Du gifwer mig dina skinwaror, så gifwer jag dig bränwin igen.*)

b. Du släpp din räf uti min wåm, så få du din bak den pelsomesak.
2SG.S leave DEF turnip out 1SG.POSS rumen then get 2SG.S 2SG.POSS back DEF fur.wristlet
'(If) you give me this root/turnip for my stomach, then you'll get back your fur wristlet.'
(Högström: *Du ger denna rot eller rofwa åt min maga, så gifwer jag dig tilbaka detta muddskin.*)

c. Den Lapman kast sin renost bak i den borgar
DEF Lapp throw 3SG.POSS reindeer.cheese back in DEF townsman
'The Sami is giving the cheese (from reindeer milk) to the townsman.'
(Högström: *Lappen ger renosten åt Borgarn.*)

d. Som du wara rätt stin.
that 2SG.S be right fat
'You are very expensive.'
(Högström: *Du är mycket dyr.*)

e. Hur sit din heit?
how way 2SG.POSS be.called
'What is your name?'
(Högström: *Huru heter du?*)

Based on this scanty data, it seems as if the lexicon in Borgarmålet was predominantly Swedish (compare the translations given by Högström himself, but bear in mind that they represent 18th century Swedish); the only non-Swedish word in these examples is *pelsomesak* 'fur wristlet'. The lexicon seems highly variable: the verbs *stick* 'put', *sätt* 'place', *släpp* 'leave', *kast* 'throw' are all used for 'give'. It seems as if the lexicon has been reduced and generalized: for instance, instead of using a specific word for 'expensive', the word *stin* 'fat' was used, possibly indicating that *stin* had acquired a general meaning of "big amount". The little morphological inflection that Swedish has is completely gone in these sentences: the Swedish present tense marker *-(e)r* is absent from all examples; there is no plural marking at all (for instance *din skin* '2SinGular.POSSessive fur', which in Swedish would have been *dina skin* '2PLural.POSSessive fur'); and the Swedish definite marking, which is a suffix *-(e)n/-(e)t* (depending on gender) has been replaced by a general function word *den* 'the/this/that'. As examples of the latter, notice that *din räf* 'DEFinite turnip' is translated by Högström as *denna rot/rofwa* 'DEMonstrative.common turnip', *Den Lapman* 'DEFinite Lapp' is translated as *Lapp-en* 'Lapp-DEFinite.common' and *den borgar* 'DEFinite townsman' is translated as *Borgar-n* 'townsman-DEFinite.common'. The latter also indicates that the two-gender distinction found in Swedish (common versus neutral gender) has been dropped. Furthermore, the monomorphemic Swedish question word *hur* 'what' has been replaced by the bimorphemic *hur sit* 'what way'. Finally, the politeness distinction that was made in Swedish until very recently has been dropped: rather than the polite *han* '3SINGULAR.MASCULINE' or *hon* '3SINGULAR.FEMININE' (which modern Swedish changed to *ni* '2PLURAL' and was eventually abandoned; cf., for example, Bergman 1984 and Wessén 1992) all reference to a second person is done with the second person singular pronoun *du*.[14]

It is worth noting that each party seems to have been well aware of the fact that they were communicating in a jargon. Högström specifically states that the Samis are aware of the fact that the language is not 'proper' Swedish and that, when asked if they are knowledgeable in the Swedish tongue, they will reply that they know nothing but Borgarmålet or whatever they have learned from the townsmen (*"Och, emedan Lapparna tagit i akt at detta språket icke är rätt Swenska, så swara de gemenligen, då man frågar dem om de äro det Swenska tungomålet mägtige, at de kunna ej annat än Borgarmålet, eller sådant som de lärdt af Borgerskapet"*; 1747:77).

We thus have a glimpse of what was probably a trade jargon, functional enough for the yearly market dealings, but otherwise highly unstable and not passed on to new generations.

1.4.2 Français Tirailleur: An extinct French-lexified military pidgin in West Africa[15]

1.4.2.1 *A brief background sketch of Français Tirailleur*

Français Tirailleur (also called *français-tirayou, français tiraillou, tirailleur, tiraillou, foro fifon naspa, forofifon naspa*) was a French-lexified pidgin used by African troops in the French army, predominantly during the first half of 20th century (but speculations have been made to the fact that the origins of Français Tirailleur go as far back as the 17th century and the first French settlements in Senegal; cf. Wilson 1999).

The Tirailleur troops were recruited from the entire French West Africa, as well as French Equatorial Africa, an area of great ethnic and linguistic diversity, although it seems as if especially Bambara, Mòoré and Wolof were dominating languages among the troops. While smaller units may have been ethnically homogenous (Lunn 1988), the generally heterogeneous composition of the troops led to the need either for interpreters or for *lingua francas*. The use of interpreters was not deemed practical; rather, one of the generals argued, "linguistic unity can only be usefully and easily achieved with the teaching of simplified French, which is already widely spoken among the indigenous population and by a great number of *Tirailleurs*" (*"l'unité de langue ne peut être utilement et facilement poursuivie que par l'enseignement du français simplifié, déjà parlé par*

14. It may have been the case that there was an issue of status involved, in that the townsmen might have addressed the Sami with the familiar *du* '2SINGULAR' because they considered the Sami of a lesser status. However, as far as can be made out from the examples, the exchange could be two-way, implying that townsmen in that case tolerated that the Sami also used the familiar *du*-form when addressing them.

15. All data and information in this section was provided to me by Mikael Parkvall, whose generosity and helpful comments are here gratefully acknowledged.

tous les gradés indigènes et par un grand nombre de tirailleurs"; letter by General Mordacq 23 March 1918, quoted in Avenne 2005:140; my translation).

It seems reasonable to assume that Français Tirailleur was used not only between African troops, but also between French officers and their African soldiers. An indication for this is the manual for Français Tirailleur anonymously published in 1916 (*Le français tel que parlent nos tirailleurs sénégalais*[16]). Here the author(s) give a grammatical outline of the language, including grammaticality judgements. The manual is clearly directed to those with French as a mother tongue; the text refers to the structures of the indigenous languages and discusses certain typically French expressions that may lead to misunderstandings. In other words, the manual is directed to the French officers.

The mere existence of the abovementioned manual and its outline of what was and was not grammatical indicates that this was a variety that had stabilized enough to have norms. It could thus be learned as a second language to a higher or lower degree of proficiency. This was therefore not a jargon, but a pidgin language.

1.4.2.2 *A short linguistic sketch of Français Tirailleur*

The phoneme inventory of Français Tirailleur seems to have differed from that of the lexifier, with some phonemes dropped or altered and others that might have been added, possibly due to substratal influence from Bambara, Wolof and/or Mòoré. Consider the following examples:

(3)	séri	'dear'	/seri/	(cf. French: chère	/ʃɛʁ/)
	ngazer	'enlist'	/ngazer/	(cf. French: engager	/ɑ̃gaʒe/)
	sénéral	'general'	/seneral/	(cf. French: général	/ʒeneʁal/)
	pà'ce que	'because'	/paske/	(cf. French: parce que	/paʁsk(ə)/)
	moussié	'Mister'	/musie/	(cf. French: monsieur	/məsjø/)
	doulé	'milk'	/dule/	(cf. French: du lait	/dylɛ/)
	pilivoir	'(to) rain'	/pilivwar/	(cf. French: pleuvoir	/pløvwaʁ/)
	piti	'small'	/piti/	(cf. French: petit	/pəti/)

In Example (3) we see that the French postalveolar fricatives /ʃ/ and /ʒ/ seem to have been realized as /s/ and /z/ respectively (they were depalatalized), or, in some cases, only as /s/ (meaning that /ʒ/ was both depalatalized and devoiced): *séri* 'dear', *ngazer* 'enlist', *sénéral* 'general'. The uvular fricative /ʁ/ seems to either have been altered to an apical /r/ or dropped altogether: in *pà'ce que* 'because' the orthography indicates that the *r* has been dropped; Cousturier (1920:210) explicitly states that the *r* was apical and uses a special spelling (*rr*) to indicate as much: *grrande* 'big' (French *grand(e)* /gʁɑ̃(d)/). The French front rounded vowels /y/ and /ø/, which are very rare cross-linguistically (cf. Maddieson 2013b), seem to have been altered in various ways: *moussie* 'Mister', *doulé* 'milk', *pilivoir* '(to) rain'. Notice that in the latter the consonant cluster /pl/ has been broken up by a vowel, turning the single moderately complex syllable /plø/ into two simple syllables /pi/ and /li/. Furthermore, the French /ə/ (schwa) seems to have been raised and fronted to an /i/: *piti* 'small'. Notice that the second item in Example (3) contains the consonant cluster /ng/. French does not allow so-called NC-onsets, that is, syllable initial consonant clusters that consist

16. *Sénégalais* was commonly used to refer to anyone of West or Equatorial African origin.

of a nasal and some other consonant. However, as NC-onsets are very common in West African languages, this might be an indication of substratal influence.

The language seems to have overwhelmingly made use of analytic constructions and there seems to have been very little, if any, inflection at all. While the language seems to have lacked any articles, the French articles sometimes fused with the noun to form a single unit. Thus *lebras* 'arm' and *lajambe* 'leg' derive from the French *le bras* 'DEFinite.ARTicle arm' and *la jambe* 'DEFinite. ARTicle leg', but the article has fused with the noun and the definiteness has been lost, as also indicated in Example (4):[17]

(4) ça y en a mon laroute
DEM LOC.COP my way
'This is my way/route.' (Anonymous 1916: 18)

The French masculine/feminine gender distinction was dropped, as was the French singular/ plural number distinction. There was one set of personal pronouns irrespective of whether they functioned as subjects or objects (notice the lack of gender distinctions in the third person forms):

1SG	*moi*	'I; me'	1PL	*nous*	'we; us'
2SG	*toi*	'you'	2PL	*vous*	'you'
3SG	*lui, ça*	's/he, it; him, her'	3PL	*eux, ça*	'they; them'

There were possessive pronouns for the singular:

1SG	*mon*	'my; mine'
2SG	*ton*	'your(s)'
3SG	*son*	'his, her(s), its'

Possession could also be expressed by juxtaposition only or the possessive marker *pour*:

(5) a. tirailleur fusil
sharp-shooter rifle
'The sharp-shooter's rifle.' (Anonymous 1916: 14)
b. case pour lui
house POSS 3SG
'His house.' (Anonymous 1916: 9)

As for the verb phrase, the unmarked form, which was not inflected for person or number, seems to have been used for present and future time reference, while past time reference was optionally marked with *ya* (which was also used as a copula).

(6) a. moi parti(r)
1SG leave
'I am leaving.' / 'I will leave.'
b. moi ya parti(r)
1SG PST leave
'I left.' (Anonymous 1916: 12)

17. This is very common for French-lexified contact languages. See, for example, the sketches on Mauritian Creole (4.3.2) and Haitian Creole (6.4.2).

Sentences were negated with the invariant *pas* (this is also common in colloquial French):

(7) ya pas boucou manger
COP NEG much eat
'There wasn't much to eat.' (*The Baba Diarra Letter*)[18]

The word order was rather rigidly subject-verb-object (as in both French and the main substrate languages). Modifiers, such as adjectives, numerals or adverbs, seem to have followed the modified unit:

(8) ça tirailleur dix
DEM sharp-shooter ten
'These ten sharp-shooters.' (Anonymous 1916:11)

Polar questions seem to typically have been formed by raised intonation, without any inverted word order (Anonymous 1916:16). Relative clauses were formed with the relativizer *yena*:

(9) tirailleur yena àgenou
sharp-shooter REL kneeling
'The tirailleur who is kneeling' (Anonymous 1916:22)

1.4.2.3 *Short text*

(Excerpt from *The Baba Diarra Letter*)

1912 moi ngasi volontaire partir la guerre Moroco pasqui mon commandant mon
1912 1SG enlist volunteer leave war Morocco because 1SG.POSS commander 1SG.POSS

cercle li promi boucou bons quand moi y a bien travailler pour Lafranci tuer
district 3SG promise much good when 1SG PST well work for France kill

boucou Morocains. Moi venir 2e régiment Kati, Ayéyé! moi boucou maloré plus
much Moroccan 1SG come second brigade Kati INTERJ 1SG much unhappy more

que esclave. Caporani y a frapper moi, sergent y a toujours manigolo et yettenan
than slave corporal PST beat 1SG sergeant PST always cudgel and lieutenant

même sosi. Y a pas bon, y a pas boucou manger.
just.like COP NEG good COP NEG much eat

'In 1912 I enlisted as a volunteer to go to the war in Morocco, because the local commander promised a lot of rewards if I worked well for France and killed many Moroccans. I came to the 2nd regiment in Kati. Boy, I was more miserable than a slave! The corporal hit me, the sergeant always had a cudgel, and the lieutenant was the same. It was bad, there was not a lot to eat.'

1.4.2.4 *Some sources of data*

Some sources of primary data include Anonymous (1916), essentially a short grammar of the language with a section on example sentences; Cousturier (1920), where quotes by Africans are in Français Tirailleur; and the Baba Diarra Letter (1927), which is entirely in Français Tirailleur. Delafosse (1904) is a brief description of the Ivorian variety of Français Tirailleur.

18. *The Baba Diarra Letter* was written by a Mali (probably Bambara) *Tirailleur* and printed in the periodical *La Race Nègre* in (1927).

1.4.3 Tok Pisin: An English-lexified extended pidgin (pidgincreole) in Papua New Guinea[19]

1.4.3.1 *A brief background sketch of Tok Pisin*

Tok Pisin (sometimes also called *New Guinea Pidgin* by scholars) is an English-lexified extended pidgin (pidgincreole) spoken by some 3–5 million people in Papua New Guinea, which makes it the most widely spoken language in the country (Smith & Siegel 2013a). It is recognized as one of the three national languages of Papua New Guinea (together with English and Hiri Motu). For most of its speakers, Tok Pisin is a second language, although there are by now up to 500,000 mother tongue speakers of Tok Pisin and it is likely that the number will continue to grow (Smith & Siegel 2013a). Tok Pisin is one of the closely related Melanesian pidgins, together with Solomon Islands Pijin (see 12.4.2) and Bislama.[20]

What became Tok Pisin first came to the Bismarck Archipelago (the group of islands off the northern coast of Papua New Guinea) in the second half of the 19th century with the return of labourers who had spent time on plantations on Samoa and/or in Queensland, where they had encountered Samoan Plantation Pidgin and/or Queensland Plantation Pidgin. The need for large-scale plantation labour arose in Papua New Guinea with the German rule: in 1884 Germany took possession of Kaiser Wilhelmsland (the northern part of modern Papua New Guinea) and the Bismarck Archipelago. While archival evidence indicates that the labour force on the German plantations in Kaiser Wilhelmsland (on the mainland) initially either spoke indigenous languages or Malay (cf. Huber & Velupillai 2015+a),[21] the newly imported pidgin English had currency among the plantation workers in the Bismarck Archipelago. This pidgin English was subsequently introduced to the plantations in Kaiser Wilhelmsland and was rapidly adopted as a *lingua franca* in other domains of use.[22]

---

19. This section relies heavily on Smith & Siegel (2013a). I am very grateful to Craig Volker for his helpful comments on this snapshot.

20. The three Melanesian pidgins are so closely related that they are mutually intelligible and could be argued to be dialects of the same language (Craig Volker, p.c.).

21. Otto Schellong (1934: 34), for example, recounts how he in the 1880s communicated on the plantations in Malay and Carl von Beck describes how in the 1890s "all immigrated Coloureds (not the indigenous workers) soon get used to the Javanese customs and languages, so that they after about one year can communicate with each other in the Malay vernacular; it is also not difficult for the Europeans to learn this language, it is therefore, once each party has got used to it, the bond for the communicative needs of the business" ["*An die javanischen Sitten und an deren Sprache gewöhnen sich alle engewanderten Farbigen (nich so die eingeborene Arbeiter) bald, so daß sie sich in malaiischer Mundart nach etwa einem Jahr untereinander verständigen können; auch dem Europäer bietet die Erlernung dieser Sprache wenig Schwerigkeiten, sie ist daher nachdem man sich gegenseitig eingewöhnt, der Kitt für das Verkehrsleben der Unternehmung.*"; (von Beck 1903: 558) my translation]. There were even some who proposed to make Malay the official *lingua franca* in German New Guinea, though this did not catch on (Huber & Velupillai 2015+b).

22. But see Keesing (215–229) for a discussion on how Tok Pisin developed on multiethnic ships before becoming the language of the plantations.

Tok Pisin plays an important role in modern Papua New Guinea. It is used in printed media and radio broadcasting, and is also gaining currency in formal situations, for instance being used in parliamentary debates. And although English is the official language of education, Tok Pisin is used as a medium of instruction in the first three school years (Elementary School) in many communities, "especially in urban areas and certain rural areas, such as the Sepik" (Smith & Siegel 2013a: 215).

Although English is the major lexifier of Tok Pisin, the roughly three decades of German rule left its traces, notably in the lexicon of the language. The major substrate languages are various Austronesian languages on Papua New Guinea, especially those of the Bismarck Archipelago, in particular Tolai (Craig Volker, p.c.).

1.4.3.2 *A short linguistic sketch of Tok Pisin*

This section uses the standard orthography initially developed by Mihalic (1971).

There is a great deal of variation in the Tok Pisin phonology, partly due to influence from the mother tongue of the speakers. However, in general the phoneme inventory has been reduced compared to the lexifier. The highly complex 13-vowel system of English has been reduced to five: /i, e, a, o, u/. There are 18 consonants: /p, b, m, w, f, v, t, d, n, r, s, ʤ, l, j, k, g, ŋ, h/ (cf. Mihalic 1971, Laycock 1985 and Smith 2004). Consider the following examples:

(10)	samting	/samtiŋ/	(cf. English: something	/sʌmθɪŋ/)	
	dispela	/dispela/	(cf. English: this	/ðɪs/)	
	sain	/sain/	(cf. English: shine	/ʃaɪn/)	
	resa	/resa/	(cf. English: razor	/ɹeɪzə(ɹ)/)	
	senis	/senis/	(cf. English: change	/ʧeɪnʤ/)	
	ensin	/ensin/	(cf. English: engine	/enʤɪn/)	(Smith 2004: 718)

The morphology is predominantly analytic, although it should be noted that some affixation occurs, such as the adjectival suffix *-pela* and the transitive marker *-im*:

(11) a. haus i bikpela
house PM big
'the house is big.'

b. dedi blo(ng) mi pait-im em
father POSS 1SG hit-TR 3SG
'My Dad smacked him.' (Smith & Siegel 2013a: 216, 221)

There is no grammatical inflection on the nouns, no grammatical gender and no definite article. Plural is marked with the particle *ol*, which "is becoming increasingly obligatory in first language speech" (Smith & Siegel 2013a: 216):

(12) dok 'dog' ol dok 'dogs' (Dutton 1985: 68)

The word for 'one' (*wanpela*) may be used as an indefinite article and the demonstrative *dispela* 'this' is prolific. Possession is indicated with the possessive marker *bilong*, as in Example (11b).

The Tok Pisin personal pronoun system is quite complex, with three – occasionally even four – number distinctions, as well as inclusive and exclusive forms. The forms are invariant irrespective of whether they function as subjects or objects in the clause.

	SINGULAR	DUAL	TRIAL	PLURAL
1-EXCL	–	*mitupela*	*mitripela*	*mipela*
1-INCL	*mi*	*yumipela*	*yumitripela*	*yumi*
2	*yu*	*yutupela*	*yutripela*	*yupela*
3	*em*[23]	*emtupela*	*emtripela*	*ol*

The dual number means that two and exactly two people or things are referred to, while the trial means that three and exactly three people or things are referred to. Exclusive means that the addressee is not included, something like 'we but not you' and inclusive means that the addressee is included, something like 'we including you'.

The particle *i* is usually referred to as a predicate marker, although it seems that it may have other functions than merely marking a unit as a predicate (for example, in Faraclas 2007 it is glossed as a subject referencing pronoun):

(13) a. ai blong-en i pas nau
eye POSS-3SG PM closed now
'His eye was closed.'

b. brata blo(ng) mi i bin kam na i kam koros
brother POSS 1SG PM PST come and PM come cross
'My brother came and was angry.' (Smith & Siegel 2013a: 217, 221)

The transitive marker *-im* (see Example (11b)) may be used to indicate transitivity. Future tense is indicated by the marker *bai* and past tense may be indicated with the marker *bin*. There are several aspect distinctions: the completive marker *pinis* denotes completed action, while *laik* may denote imminent action. Habitual action is denoted by the marker *sa(ve)*; the shorter form is more common with fluent speakers. Progressive or continuous action may be indicated with *wok long* or *i stap*. The modal markers *mas* (obligation/epistemic, from 'must'), *ken* (permissive, from 'can') and *(i)nap* (ability, from 'enough') are common.

The word order is typically subject-verb-object and polar questions are typically formed by raised intonation, without inverted word order. Question words are generally bimorphemic.

Relative clauses may be formed in a variety of ways of which only a few will be mentioned here. For more details see, for example, Bradshaw (2007), Dutton (1985), Sankoff & Brown (1976), and Smith (2002). Although a relative clause may be formed by simple juxtaposition, it is more common to use a personal pronoun:

(14) mi luk-im dok em i ran-im pik bilong mi
1SG see-TR dog 3SG PM run-TR pig POSS 1SG
'I saw the dog that chased my pig.' (Dutton 1985: 140)

A rather recent phenomenon is to use the question words *husat* 'who' and *we* 'where' as relativizers:

(15) em papa bilong em we help-im em
3SG father POSS 3SG REL help-TR 3SG
'It was his father who helped him.' (Smith & Siegel 2013a: 220)

23. This can also be expressed with the suffix *-en* in connection with *long* 'about, along, at, for, from, in, on, to' and *bilong* 'possessive'.

1.4.3.3 *Short text*

(From Dutton 1985: 53)

Pikinini meri	bilong	mi	em	i	ranawe	long	taun.	Em	i	tok,	em	i	laik	go	stap
daughter	POSS	1SG	3SG	PM	run.away	to	town	3SG	PM	say	3SG	PM	want	go	be

wantaim	pren	bilong	em.	Em	i	ranawe	nating.	Em	i	no	tok-im	mi.	Mi	save
one	friend	POSS	3SG	3SG	PM	run.away	nothing	3SG	PM	NEG	tell-TR	1SG	1SG	know

nau	tasol	long	boipren	bilong-en.	Emtupela	i	stap	wantaim.	Emtupela	i	bruk-im
now	only	about	boyfriend	POSS-3SG	3DU	PM	be	together	3DU	PM	break-TR

bikpela	lo.	Dispela	pasin	em	i	nogut	tru.
big	law	DEM	behaviour	3SG	PM	bad	very

'My daughter ran away to town. She said she wanted to go and stay with a friend. She ran away for no reason. She didn't tell me. Just now I have got to know about her boyfriend. The two of them are living together. The two of them have broken an important law. This behaviour is very bad.'

1.4.3.4 *Some sources of data*

There is a wealth of information on Tok Pisin. A source of primary data is, for example, the popular *Wantok Niuspepa* (http://wantokniuspepa.com/), which publishes articles, reports, stories and folk tales, as well as letters to the Editor in Tok Pisin. There are radio broadcasts in Tok Pisin, for example *redio tok pisin* (http://www.youtube.com/channel/UCau_6QfTRE_VFdolZVgjZmA), *Radio Australia – Tok Pisin Service* (http://www.radioaustralia.net.au/tokpisin/) and *Yumi FM*. The Bible has been translated into Tok Pisin (for example available at https://www.stepbible.org/version.jsp?version=TPI, accessed 6 February 2015.). Text collections can be found in Romaine (1992) and Smith (2002). Volker (2008) is a very helpful bilingual dictionary.

1.5 Summary

Pidgins are languages that arose in situations of intense contact, where speakers of mutually unintelligible languages needed to communicate with each other. What might start out as individual *ad hoc* solutions in individual situations (jargons), may, if contact is sustained, stabilize to a system of norms that can be learned as a second language (a pidgin). A pidgin is typically used only in a limited set of contexts and is typically not the mother tongue of its speakers. However, speakers may come to use the contact variety in a wide, possibly unlimited, set of contexts, thereby extending its function and its linguistic system (forming an extended pidgin/pidgincreole). An extended pidgin may gradually spread as a first language of its speakers.

Pidgin languages have a long history of stigmatization. They have generally been viewed as corrupt, bad or lazy versions of other languages. While most pidgins are still stigmatized, extended use in society may lead to increased status, and a number of extended pidgins even enjoy the formal status of national language in their countries.

The word 'pidgin' most likely derives from the Chinese Pidgin English word for 'business'.

There are a number of different situations which typically led to the emergence of pidgin languages. These include trade and maritime activities, mixed workforces, and urban settings.

Pidgins are typically assumed to have a reduced linguistic system compared to their input languages, with fewer inflections, fewer and more regular rules, and a smaller vocabulary.

1.6 Key points

- **Jargons are individual ad hoc solutions to individual situations.**
- **Pidgins are stable linguistic systems used as secondary languages in a limited set of contexts.**
- **Extended pidgins (pidgincreoles) are stable linguistic systems used in potentially any kind of context and may have a growing number of native speakers.**
- **There are no sharp boundaries between the fluid scale of jargons, pidgins and extended pidgins (pidgincreoles).**
- **Pidgins may arise in a variety of situations, all of which involve repeated contact between speakers of different languages.**
- **There are no sharp boundaries between the types of situations that pidgins may arise in; a given pidgin may be used in several kinds of situations.**
- **Although they are languages in their own right, pidgins tend to be stigmatized.**
- **Pidgins may have anything from zero to many million speakers.**
- **Pidgins tend to be viewed as simplified versions of their lexifier languages.**

1.7 Exercises

1. In what way is stability related to the differences between jargons, pidgins and extended pidgins (pidgincreoles)?
2. Why do pidgins tend to be stigmatized languages?
3. What is the accepted etymology of the word 'pidgin'? Why is this etymology preferred over other proposed etymologies?
4. What are the most common types of situations known where pidgins have emerged?
5. Why are pidgins often viewed as simplified versions of their lexifier languages?

Languages cited in Chapter 2

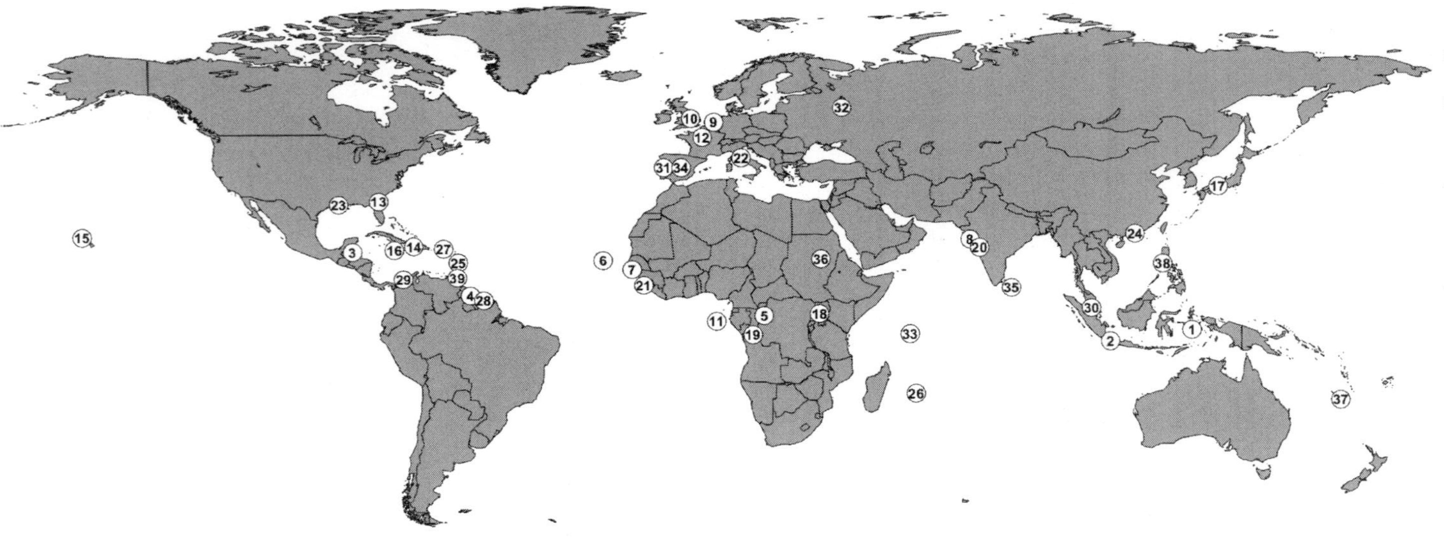

1. Ambon Malay
2. Batavia Creole
3. Belizean Creole
4. Berbice Dutch
5. Bobangi; Lingala
6. Cape Verdean Creole
7. Casamancese; Guinea Bissau Kriyol
8. Diu Indo-Portuguese
9. Dutch
10. English
11. Angolar; Fa d'Ambô; Santome
12. French
13. Gullah
14. Haitian Creole
15. Hawai'i Creole English; Hawaiian
16. Jamaican
17. Japanese
18. Kinubi
19. Kikongo-Kituba; Kongo
20. Korlai
21. Krio
22. Italian; Latin
23. Louisiana Creole
24. Macau Creole
25. Guadeloupean Creole; Martinican Creole
26. Mauritian Creole; Reunion Creole
27. Negerhollands
28. Nengee; Saramaccan
29. Palenquero
30. Papia Kristang
31. Portuguese
32. Russian
33. Seychelles Creole
34. Spanish
35. Sri Lanka Portuguese
36. Sudanese Arabic
37. Tayo
38. Ternate Chabacano
39. Trinidad English Creole

Chapter 2

Creoles

Creoles are natural languages that arose in situations where people of diverse ethno-cultural and linguistic backgrounds were brought together and formed distinct communities. They are full-fledged languages on par with any other language. This chapter will first give some background information on the etymology of the word 'creole' and the social status of creole languages (2.1). Section 2.2 gives some definitions of types of creoles based on the kinds of situations they arose in and Section 2.3 briefly summarizes the linguistic features that are most commonly presented as typical for creole languages. In Section 2.4 short sketches are given of three creole languages: Negerhollands (an extinct Dutch-lexified plantation creole), Nengee (an English-lexified maroon creole) and Diu Indo-Portuguese (a Portuguese-lexified fort creole).

2.1 Definitions

A **creole** is, extremely simplified, a natural language spoken as a mother tongue by an entire community that arose due to situations of intense contact. Creoles are full-fledged languages on par with any other natural language in the world, and are capable of fulfilling any linguistic need of the relevant speech community. In other words, whatever can be talked about, thought about, and conducted in, for example, Japanese, Italian, Russian or any other language of the world spoken as a mother tongue by an entire community, can also be talked about, thought about and conducted in any given creole language.

It is a matter of intense debate how to define more exactly what a creole language is. Some argue that creoles can be identified by the linguistic structure that they have, i.e. that they form a special type of language (among others, for example McWhorter 2005, Bakker et al. 2011 and Bartens 2013a, with further references). Others argue that there is no (or not enough) evidence for the claim that creoles form a distinct typological class and that the motivation for treating some languages as creoles lies in the sociohistorical settings in which they emerged (among others, for example Mufwene 2000, DeGraff 2003 and Ansaldo & Matthews 2007, with further references). However, the fact that creole languages are fully adequate natural languages that may serve any and all linguistic needs of the speakers is not questioned by any serious linguist.

2.1.1 The etymology of 'creole'

The etymology for 'creole' is less opaque than that for pidgin. For thorough discussions on the origin and the path of semantic shift for 'creole', see, for example, Todd (1990) and Bartens (2013a).

The term 'creole' was initially used for those Europeans who were born in the colonies, especially the Caribbean colonies. It seems as if the word entered English via the French *créole*, which in turn derives from the Portuguese *crioulo* (diminutive of *criado* '(a person) domestically raised, brought up, bred') and/or the Spanish *criollo* 'native'. Both the Portuguese and Spanish forms derive from *criar* 'breed, raise, bring up', which in turn derives from the Latin *creare* 'create, produce'. The term then came to be used for any person, animal or plant that had been born, bred or grown in the colonies (especially the Caribbean colonies), as opposed to those of indigenous origin or recent import (cf. *Oxford English Dictionary* 2013 *sv*: Creole). Gradually 'creole' came to be used to refer to the culture(s) and language(s) of those who came to form the bulk of the population in the colonies.

The first known use of 'creole' to refer to a language is from a travel account by the Portuguese Francisco de Lemos Coelho in 1684 (*Description of the coast of Guinea*), where he writes about the "creoulo de Cacheu" (in present-day Guinea-Bissau; cf. Bartens 2013a:70 citing Couto 1994:35). According to the *Oxford English Dictionary*, the first known English use of 'creole' to refer to a language is from 1726; the passages in question refer to the Cape Verde Islands.

> …and as soon as they ceas'd heaving Stones, I look'd up again, and in the *St Jago* [i.e. Santiago – VV] *Creole* Tongue ask'd them the Reason of using us so roughly?
> (…)
> I thanked him, and assisted him with my Advice all I could, and served as Linguist [i.e. interpreter – VV] for him; for neither he, nor any on Board, could speak either the *Creole* of the Islands or *Portuguese*, either of which, would have been sufficient to trade with. (Defoe & Roberts 1726:319, 367, emphasis in the original)

Currently the term is in English chiefly used to refer to the languages that grew out of especially the European expansion and colonization of the world – although I stress that there are a number of known creole languages that are not related to any European languages.

2.1.2 The social status of creole languages

Languages known to us as creole languages may vary radically in terms of size, ranging from no known speakers (the language is extinct) to several million speakers. Berbice Dutch of Guyana, for example, recently went extinct (Kouwenberg 2011). Batavia Creole, which was once spoken in Batavia (present-day Jakarta) on the Indonesian island of Java, went extinct during the 19th century (Maurer 2011). By contrast, Haitian Creole has some 11 million speakers, including the Haitian diaspora (Fattier 2013).

The vast majority of languages that we know as creoles today have suffered a long history of condescension and stigmatization, a situation which is far from over today. The languages have been viewed as "broken", "lazy", "debased", or in other ways highly inadequate versions of their European lexifiers. Speakers of creole languages were made to understand that their mother tongues were in every way inferior to what was considered the "proper" European languages, which were usually spoken by a minority population of the society. Creole languages have been assumed to be obstacles for economic and intellectual growth; only a few decades ago, this attitude could, astonishingly, even be found in academic discourse:

> ...modern linguists may have been dangerously sentimental about creole languages, which, with only a few notable exceptions, constitute in most communities a distinct handicap to the social mobility of the individual, and *may* also constitute a handicap to the creole-speaker's personal intellectual development.
> (...)
> ...from what we know of the role of language in intellectual development, one would expect the speakers of these primitive creoles [i.e. at an early stage of creolization – VV] to be intellectually handicapped. ... linguists do not have the evidence to assert with confidence that speakers of creole-languages are not handicapped by their language... (Whinnom 1971: 110, emphasis in the original)

Needless to say, such attitudes are no longer held by any serious scientist, irrespective of his or her theoretical background.

Creole languages have, typically, not been accepted for use as languages of education or media, and rarely have official status in the societies where they are spoken. Instead, the languages of the former colonizers are advocated as the only desirable and acceptable languages – in short, that the only route to individual and collective well-being is to acquire the European language of the former colonizer. This attitude still prevails in many societies; for example, in many cases the creole will not be listed among the official languages. Angolar, for instance, was not listed as a national language for the Democratic Republic of São Tomé and Príncipe in the 2006 census (Maurer 2013a). Likewise, the official languages of Hawai'i are English and Hawaiian, but not Hawai'i Creole English,[24] which is the mother tongue of half of the population.

---

24. The islands of Hawai'i saw contact languages emerge from two different lexifiers, Hawaiian and English. Since Hawai'i Creole English, Hawai'i Pidgin English as well as Pidgin Hawaiian are discussed in this book, the fuller name Hawai'i Creole English rather than the shortened Hawai'i Creole is used here for reasons of disambiguation. I stress that the use of the fuller name does not in any way imply that the language is considered a dialect of English rather than a language in its own right. For more on Hawai'i Creole English and Pidgin Hawaiian, see 6.4.1 and 11.4.1 respectively.

Education in Hawai'i is done in Standard (American) English and the language of the media is also Standard (American) English, except for such items as cartoons and advertisements. Hawai'i Creole English is typically seen as an obstacle to advancement. For more on Hawai'i Creole English, see 6.4.1.

Such attitudes have made many creole speakers regard their own language as backwards or inferior, leading many to deny the fact that they have a creole language as a mother tongue. These kinds of situations also commonly lead to **diglossia**, where speakers use specific language varieties in specific situations, typically using the creole in familiar or informal situations while using the officially recognized language(s) in official or formal situations (see further 7.1). Ambon Malay, for example, has been spoken on the island of Ambon (Indonesia) for many centuries and has about 200,000 mother tongue speakers, and is also used as a *lingua franca* by as many as a million speakers on the central and southern Maluku Islands. However, the speakers of Ambon Malay "often view it as an inferior variety of Indonesian" (Paauw 2013a: 94). The two languages stand in a diglossic relationship to each other, with Indonesian used in formal settings (government administration, media, education, etc.) and Ambon Malay used at home or in informal interaction in the community (Paauw 2013a). For more on Ambon Malay, see 7.3.2.

Nevertheless, the last couple of decades have brought a certain degree of reversal of such attitudes to varying degrees in many societies where creole languages are spoken. In Hawai'i, for example, attitudes are slowly changing to allow recognition of the fact that Hawai'i Creole English is a fully functional language like any other, thanks to, for instance, targeted awareness programs by the University of Hawai'i at Mānoa, as well as speakers starting to assert the validity of the language. Palenquero, spoken by a couple of thousand people in the village of El Palenque in Colombia, was until recently heavily stigmatized, which led the younger generations to shift to Spanish. However, the last decade has seen a reversal of attitude: "[m]any adolescents now take great pleasure in learning the creole, and gone are the days when Palenquero (and with it local culture) was shunned" (Schwegler 2013a: 182). For more on Palenquero, see 12.4.3.

Societies have also started accepting creole languages in education. In Trinidad, for example, Trinidad English Creole has been accepted in schools at the primary level since 1975 (Mühleisen 2013a).[25] Haitian Creole, along with French, is an official language of Haiti (although most administrative texts are in French) and was accepted as a medium of education in 1979 (Fattier 2013). Even so, French is still typically seen as the preferred language. For more on Haitian Creole, see 6.4.2.

25. This may possibly have contributed to the change in attitude towards the language in the last quarter of the 20th century, which has seen increased acceptance of Trinidad English Creole in the media, especially the radio (cf. Mühleisen 2013a).

Despite this stigmatization and despite the fact that creoles have, because of this, until recently, mainly been oral and not written languages, many of the societies where creole languages are spoken have seen vibrant literary use of the languages. A number of creole languages are used for poetry, drama, in novels (very commonly for dialogues, less commonly for the narration), column writing and so on (see further Chapter 8).

2.2 Types of creoles

The exact sociohistorical setting for any given language is unique, including any given creole language. Nevertheless, a few typical situations can be distinguished for the languages we today know as creoles. The following will give the most commonly distinguished types of situations that led to creole languages. It is meant only as a brief overview; for a more detailed discussion on different sociohistorical contexts where creoles emerged, see Chapter 4.

The most fundamental divide between types of creoles in terms of their sociohistorical backgrounds is whether or not the speakers were indigenous to the region. With exogenous creoles none of the population groups that were in contact with each other were indigenous to the area, while with endogenous at least some of the population groups in contact were native to the region (Chaudenson 1977). The different types of situations may lead to different amount of influence from the various input languages.

It is very important to notice that there are no sharp boundaries to the types given in this section. A creole may have arisen in a situation where the bulk of the population were immigrants to the area, but where an indigenous minority not only contributed to the language but has remained in contact with it throughout its history, as is the case with Hawaiʻi Creole English: while immigrant settlement saw massive depopulation and led to mass importation of labour, the Hawaiian indigenous population remained on the islands (albeit as a minority) and the Hawaiian language has continued to exist alongside the creole and Standard American English. Other creole languages may be spoken in areas indigenous to various possible substrate languages, but the creole itself was initially imported from elsewhere, as may be the case with Krio in West Africa, which might have its origins in Gullah and Jamaican (Huber 2000, Huber 2004). The Spanish-lexified Ternate Chabacano, now spoken in the Philippines, possibly originated on the Indonesian Maluku island of Ternate near Sulawesi and was then transported around 1660 when the Spanish relocated their garrison to Manila in the Philippines (Sippola 2013b; see further 7.3.3). I therefore stress that the types given in this section should be seen as simplified typical examples of different situations that may have led to what we today call creole languages. It is by no means an exhaustive list of all known contact situations that led to what we today identify as a creole language.

2.2.1 Exogenous creoles

Exogenous creoles are those which arose in a setting where none of the groups involved were indigenous to the area. Here we essentially have a situation where different degrees of migration brought people of different languages into contact. This typically involved colonial settlements in either previously uninhabited areas or in areas where the indigenous population rapidly declined after colonial settlement (most commonly due to imported diseases in combination with harsh working conditions and/or genocide). Both situations typically led to mass importation of labour, typically of people from diverse backgrounds. This in turn led to a linguistically heterogeneous labour force. With exogenous creoles, then, both the speakers of the superstrate languages and the speakers of the substrate languages were immigrants to the area where the creole arose. The colonial settlers were typically numerically in the minority but dominated socioeconomically and subjugated the labour force, despite the numerical majority of the latter. Crucial for exogenous creoles is that after resettlement, especially of the labour force, continued contact with the substrate languages was minimal.

2.2.1.1 *Plantation creoles*

The most typical example of an exogenous creole is a **plantation creole**, which arose in the context of the colonial plantation economy. As mentioned above (Section 1.2), the European expansion saw a multitude of plantation societies. The harsh conditions on the plantations as well as imported diseases almost invariably caused rapid depopulation in previously populated areas. This led to large-scale importation of labour, either in the form of slave labour (especially in the Atlantic) or in the form of indentured labourers (especially in the Pacific). The workforce was typically linguistically heterogeneous, meaning that the labourers needed a common communicative bridge. The European settlers were typically in the numerical minority, but dominated the societies politically. The labour force typically had to be able to function in the language of the plantation owners; that fact, and the fact that the labour force had no common language of their own, typically led the European language to become the principal communicative bridge within the workforce. Furthermore, access to the various substrate languages of the different ethnic groups that made up the workforce was limited once the labour force (especially slaves) had been transported to the colonies. Because of this, some scholars have suggested that substratal influence on creoles that grew out of exogenous plantation economy societies was restricted.

A number of creole languages arose in exogenous plantation societies. Most of the creoles in the Caribbean originated as plantation creoles, such as – to mention only a few – the English-lexified Jamaican in Jamaica, Belizean Creole in Belize and Trinidad English Creole in Trinidad; the French-lexified Haitian Creole in Haiti, Guadeloupean Creole on Guadeloupe and Martinican Creole on Martinique; the Dutch-lexified

Negerhollands on the islands of St. John, St. Croix and St. Thomas (present-day US Virgin Islands) and Berbice Dutch in Guyana, both of which are now extinct. Plantation creoles emerged in other areas than the Caribbean, such as in southern North America, with, for example, the English-lexified Gullah along the south-eastern US coastline, as well as, from the second half of the 18th century, the French-lexified Louisiana Creole in the US state of Louisiana (although this was a homestead society for the first 80 years of settlement, during the French rule; Chaudenson 2001: 55f);[26] off the West African coast, with, for example, the Portuguese-lexified Cape Verdean Creoles (a group of three closely related creole varieties) in the Republic of Cape Verde, Santome on the island of São Tomé in the Democratic Republic of São Tomé and Príncipe, and Fa d'Ambô on the island of Annobón (the latter two in the Gulf of Guinea); in the Indian Ocean with Reunion Creole on the island of Réunion (which belongs to France), Mauritian Creole in the Republic of Mauritius and Seychelles Creole in the Republic of the Seychelles, all French-lexified.

2.2.1.2 *Maroon creoles*

Maroon creoles also form a type of exogenous creole, as these languages were also creoles that arose in areas which none of the principal population groups were indigenous to. The term 'maroon' derives from the Spanish *cimarrón* 'wild, untamed; fugitive' and refers to "slaves who had run away from plantations and formed settlements based on common ethnic origin, or on having escaped from the same plantations" (Bartens 2013a: 67). These Maroons would form their settlements in regions difficult to access, such as densely forested mountain areas. The Maroon settlers subsided on farming and hunting, as well as by raiding plantations. Some Maroon communities grew strong enough to pose a threat to the plantation societies. Palmares, for example, in Eastern Brazil (in the present-day Alagoas state), was a state formed by Maroons which existed for almost the whole of the 17th century. It was "a centralized kingdom with an elected ruler" (Kent 1996: 187) founded no later than 1605/6 and lasting until its destruction in 1694 after two decades of war with Dutch and Portuguese plantation owners (Kent 1996). Towards the end of the 17th century it measured about 1100 square leagues[27] (Ennes 1948) and had a population of many thousands (Kent 1996). For a detailed overview of the history of Palmares, see Kent (1996).

---

26. With 'homestead society' a society with smaller farms and small "semi-isolated social and economic units" (Chaudenson 2001: 12) are meant. Here the socially dominating group, the French in this case, would have been numerically more or less on par with, or even have outnumbered, the labour force (typically slaves). The slaves would have had intense interaction with the French settlers and thus have constantly been exposed to the lexifier. See further Chapters 4 and 6.

27. Some 6000 square kilometres.

Because the Maroons escaped from slavery and set up their own societies, the question arises whether this may in some way have consequences linguistically. First of all, similar to the plantation creoles, it may be the case that substratal influence would be restricted, since the speakers were displaced from their ancestral areas; however, it could also be the case that substratal features were given more space to evolve once the pressure of the lexifier had been removed. Maroon creoles may also have had a different level of influence from the lexifiers, since the communities were to varying degrees removed from areas settled by the European colonizers. Maroon societies cannot be assumed to have been linguistically static, given that the initial Maroon settlers in many cases were of linguistically diverse backgrounds and given that new members would continuously join the societies (either having escaped themselves, or having been freed by raiding Maroons, or even having been captured as slaves by the Maroons). However, it may possibly be that removal from the immediate dominance of the European colonizers and their languages, i.e. the lexifiers, may have had an effect on the outcome of the Maroon languages (cf. Arends 1994b: 16), for instance that they may be less similar to the lexifiers than other exogenous creoles.

Most of the known Maroon communities were eventually "absorbed into the mainstream culture of the societies within which they existed" (Arends 1994b: 16) by various means. However, several have survived. Suriname is home to two Maroon creoles, the English/Portuguese-lexified Saramaccan, (with the Saramaccan and Matawai dialects), with about 50,000 speakers (Aboh et al. 2013a), and the English-lexified Nengee (with the Ndyuka, Aluku and Paramaccan dialects), the latter also in French Guiana, with about 65,000 speakers (Migge 2013a). The Spanish-lexified Palenquero is still spoken by a couple of thousand people in the village of El Palenque de San Basilio in northern Colombia (Schwegler 2013a). In West Africa the Portuguese-lexified Angolar is spoken by about 5,000 people on the island of São Tomé. The Maroon communities of interior Jamaica do not (any longer) speak a separate language from other Jamaicans, but as late as in the 1980s reports were made of a "Maroon spirit possession language" (called "deep language" by the community) used in *Kromanti* ceremonies where certain participants are possessed with ancestor spirits.

> …the ancestors have their own form of speech, quite different from that of living Maroons. (…) When the living – those who are not possessed by spirits – speak to one another during Kromanti ceremonies, they employ the normal creole [i.e. Jamaican – VV]. When they address those in possession, they attempt to talk "deep," so that the visiting ancestors will understand them. The possessed themselves, either when addressing the unpossessed or others in possession, use only the "deep language".
>
> (Bilby 1983: 38)

2.2.2 Endogenous creoles

Endogenous creoles (often also called **fort creoles** as a reference to the trading posts set up by the European explorers and colonizers) typically developed through contact between immigrant settlers, usually engaged in systematic trade, and the indigenous population of the areas. A typical scenario along the West African as well as the Indian coasts was that the European merchants set up trading centres for their activities in the area. This is especially true for the early Portuguese colonial activities, but the practice was continued by the later English powers. It is important to keep in mind that, contrary to the plantation societies, the eventual colonizers of these areas did not form large agrarian settlements, but that their colonization was commercially based. In this kind of situation the trading partners, as well as the domestic labour force, would not only be exposed to a European lexifier language, but would also be continuously exposed to the vernacular languages of the areas. However, it cannot be automatically assumed that the labour force (typically slave labour) of the European fort colonies was indigenous to the area of the fort or trading centre: in both West Africa and India the workforce was often displaced from one region to another – forts sometimes even "swapped" labour with each other, thus displacing the labourers from their native areas. There was, in fact, on the Gold Coast (present-day Ghana) an

> established policy of importing labour from other places on the Guinea Coast. Foreign slaves were apparently thought less likely to identify with the local population, to mutiny or run away. The Europeans therefore endeavoured to keep the proportion of foreign slaves at their factories [i.e. trading centres – VV] high, and to achieve this sometimes even exchanged slave populations between factories on different parts of the Guinea coast. (Huber 1999a: 92)

For instance, in 1721 Robert Plunkett, Chief Merchant in Sierra Leone, got the following request from his bosses:

> We desire you will send one of your Sloops with 30. or 40 of the Slaves of your parts to Mess:rs Glynn, Ramsey, & Cox Our Chiefe Merch:ts at Gambia, who will have orders to return you a like Numb:r of theirs.
> (Letter from African House, 31 October 1721; *PRO* T/70/60: 32)

In other words, the vernacular(s) of the area the forts or trading centres were located in may not have been the native languages of the labour force. In such cases it seems likely that the lexifier language would have had a greater influence on the creole than the local indigenous languages, even though adstratal influence from local vernaculars also seems likely.

Examples of endogenous creoles still spoken today can be found in both West Africa and Asia and are often, though not always, Portuguese-lexified. In West Africa, the Portuguese-lexified Guinea-Bissau Kriyol is spoken as a mother tongue by about

600 people (and as an L2 by another 600,000) in Guinea Bissau and southern Senegal (Intumbo et al. 2013) while Casamancese in Lower Casamance Province in Senegal has about 10,000 speakers (Biagui & Quint 2013). In India the Portuguese-lexified Diu Indo-Portuguese still has around 180 speakers on the island of Diu in the west (Cardoso 2013) and Korlai is spoken by some 800 people in the Korlai village south of Mumbai (Clements 2013). There are still some speakers left of Sri Lanka Portuguese in Trincomalee and Batticaloa on the eastern coast of Sri Lanka (Smith 2013a). Papía Kristang, also Portuguese-lexified, is spoken by some 800 people, primarily in Malacca in western Malaysia (Baxter 2013a). Kinubi is an example of a fort creole based on a non-European language, with Sudanese Arabic as its major lexifier. It is spoken in Kenya and Uganda, as a mother tongue by the Nubi and as a *lingua franca* by other ethnic groups (Luffin 2013a).

While the above examples could be argued to be fort creoles due to the fact that they all had their beginnings in trading centres, not all endogenous creoles are fort creoles. An example of an endogenous creole that is neither a fort creole nor Portuguese-lexified is Tayo (French-lexified), with some 3,000 speakers in Saint-Louis in New Caledonia (Ehrhart & Revis 2013). Saint-Louis was founded as a centre for "religious instruction and education for Melanesian and mixed Kanaka/European children" (Speedy 2007: 225) in a previously inhabited (albeit sparsely) area; it was also an agricultural centre, with a plantation-like sugar industry. Lingala and Kikongo-Kituba are examples of endogenous creoles that are not lexified by any European language.[28] The Bobangi-lexified Lingala is the mother tongue of some 15 million and the *lingua franca* of another 10 million people in the western and northern parts of the DR Congo, the central and northern parts of the Republic of Congo, and in northern Angola, as well as of the Congolese and Angolan diaspora (Meeuwis 2013a). Kikongo-Kituba, which has Kikongo-Kimanyanga as its major lexifier, is spoken in south-western DR Congo, southern Republic of Congo, and in northern Angola by about 6–8 million people. Both these languages have their origins in "population movements and contacts associated with labour migrations" (Mufwene 2013: 3) rather than trading forts.

2.3 Assumed typical linguistic features of creoles

As mentioned above, it is a matter of intense debate whether creole languages can be identified by purely linguistic means. A number of attempts have been made at setting up lists of linguistic features that are typical for creole languages as opposed to non-creole languages. Not infrequently the general assumption behind the lists is

28. Notice that both Lingala and Kikongo-Kituba are listed as extended pidgins (pidgincreoles) in Smith (1994: 357). This shows that there are no sharp borders between the various categories.

that creoles are less complex, morphosyntactically, than non-creoles (but again, what exactly 'simple' and 'complex' means may remain opaque, cf. 1.3 above). Another not uncommon tendency seems to be that those linguistic features which seem to set a given creole apart from its lexifier will be assumed to be typical for creole languages as opposed to non-creoles – essentially leaning towards the assumption that what sets creoles apart as a group of languages is whatever makes them different from their lexifiers (which in turn indirectly assumes that the lexifier languages are structurally similar to other non-creole languages).

This section will attempt to summarize the features that are commonly brought up in the discussion of the possible uniqueness of creole languages. It is beyond the scope of this section to provide the motivations for why the individual features should be specific to creole languages and should thus be seen only as a general sketch of what is commonly presented as potentially typical creole features. For summaries and thorough discussions of the linguistic features associated with creoles, see, for example, Romaine (1988), Mühlhäusler (1997) and Bartens (2013a), the latter of which this section relies heavily on.

As in Section 1.3 above, the following summary starts with the smallest linguistic units and moves towards the bigger ones. A selection of these assumed typical creole features will then be further investigated in Part II of this book. I stress once again that it is at this stage left entirely open whether or not these assumed features do in fact apply to the creole languages we have data for.

2.3.1.1 *Phonology*

Creole languages are prototypically described as having dropped the typologically unusual phonemes (both consonants and vowels) of their lexifier languages, while to some extent retaining some typologically rare consonants of the substrate languages (cf. e.g. Bartens 2013a).[29] They are prototypically described as preferring a CV syllable structure. Furthermore, tone is assumed to be of marginal relevance for creole languages, and, if present at all, to have only two contrasts and to be restricted to the lexicon (rather than have a grammatical function).

2.3.1.2 *Morphology*

Creoles are typically described as having reduced morphology, both in terms of inflectional and in terms of derivational morphology. This "morphological simplicity" (Crowley 2008:77) is typically described as regularization, avoidance of redundancy, avoidance of portmanteau morphemes (i.e. such morphemes that encode several pieces of grammatical information at the same time), avoidance of multiple affixes

29. Cf. Smith (2008), who also states that "[t]he vowel systems of creole languages tend to resemble those of their superstrates more than their consonant systems do" (2008:103).

and, if multiple affixes do occur, preference for concatenation (i.e. that morphemes are fused linearly to the stem or root, making the word straightforward to segment). Creole languages are described as having predominantly analytic morphological constructions. Reduplication is described as being particularly common in creole languages.

2.3.1.3 *The noun phrase*

Creoles are typically described as lacking case. Number distinction is described as optional and expressed analytically (often with a third person plural form such as *dem* 'them'). Grammatical gender is described as only marginally relevant (e.g. in the pronoun system), if at all.

Possession is described as either being indicated through juxtaposition, or with a preposition, or with a possessor (i.e. an invariant form marking possession).

Creoles are described as having an indefinite article which derives from and is identical to the numeral word for 'one'.

2.3.1.4 *The verb phrase*

Creoles are described as having preverbal and invariant tense, mood and aspect (TMA) markers that combine in a fixed order. In fact, it is not uncommonly assumed that creole languages will have only one tense marker (for the anterior tense), one aspect marker (for the progressive aspect) and one mood marker (for the irrealis mood). Lexical aspect is described as affecting the reading of the base form of the verb (with stative verbs getting a present tense reading and dynamic verbs getting a past tense reading), as well as for the form marked for the anterior (with stative verbs getting a past tense reading and dynamic verbs getting a past-before-past reading).

Creoles are often described as lacking non-finite verb forms.

2.3.1.5 *Simple sentences*

Creoles are described as having a fixed word order, typically subject-verb-object, for declarative, interrogative as well as imperative sentences. Polar questions are described as differing from declarative sentences only by way of intonation (with rising intonation for questions). Creoles are described as typically having bimorphemic (i.e. consisting of two morphemes) question words.

On the phrasal level, creoles are typically described as having the demonstrative, definite article and possessive pronoun precede the noun.

Creoles are described as having a free and invariant form for negation (negator), which occurs before the verb and the TMA markers. Creoles are also described as having negative concordance (as in, for example, *I didn't see nobody*).

Creole languages are often described as lacking the passive voice.

2.3.1.6 *Predication*

Creole languages are typically described as lacking the copula in predicate nominal (such as *The man is a teacher*) and predicate adjectival clauses (such as *The man is tall*). Creoles are also typically described as having the same form for existential constructions (as in *There is a fly in my soup*) and possessive constructions (as in *John has a cat*) which is distinct from the form for locative constructions (as in *The fly is in my soup*).

2.3.1.7 *Complex sentences*

Subordination is often described as infrequent for creole languages.

Serial verbs, where two or more verbs function as one unit, are described as being particularly common in creole languages.

2.3.1.8 *The lexicon*

First of all, creoles are described as deriving the bulk of their lexicon from one language. Creoles are also, however, often described as having incorporated other, or additional meanings in various lexical items, so that what sounds like a word from the lexifier may, in fact, have new or additional semantic and symbolic connotations.[30]

Creoles are described as having fewer adpositions than their lexifier languages, in turn leading them to derive new ones from nouns. Creoles are also sometimes described as using the same word for 'with' (comitative) as for 'and' (coordinating conjunction). Creoles are often described as lacking relative pronouns, and reflexives are described as being expressed with 'my body' (as in *I hear my body* meaning 'I hear myself').

2.4 Snapshots

Exogenous creoles typically arose in areas where neither the colonizer nor the labour force was indigenous. Negerhollands is an example of an exogenous creole that arose in a plantation context of the Caribbean, while Nengee is an example of an exogenous creole that was formed by Maroons (escaped slaves) in Suriname.

Endogenous creoles typically arose in areas where at least part of the population that formed the creole was indigenous. Diu Indo-Portuguese is an example of an endogenous creole that had its origin in Portuguese trading forts in India.

30. What could be viewed as a combination of semantic shift and so-called "multi-level syncretisms" (Mühlhäusler 1997:206).

2.4.1 Negerhollands: An extinct Dutch-lexified plantation creole on the Virgin Islands[31]

2.4.1.1 *A brief background sketch of Negerhollands*

Negerhollands is a now extinct Dutch-lexified creole that was spoken on the islands of St. John, St. Thomas and St. Croix in what today is the US Virgin Islands in the Caribbean. It had been spoken for close to three centuries when the last speaker, Mrs. Alice Stevens, died in 1987.

The Virgin Islands were "discovered" by Columbus in 1493 (who gave them their present name) which subsequently led to the depopulation of the Taínos, indigenous to the island of St. Croix, through genocide and diseases. From 1600 the Virgin Islands were settled by Europeans of various origins and their African slaves. The Danish West-Indian Company acquired monopoly over St. Thomas in 1671 after which Danish settlers started colonizing the island. Soon after that Dutch settlers arrived, possibly bringing slaves with them. By 1688 the 422 slaves outnumbered the 317 Europeans. It is important to bear in mind that the European settlers were of mixed origins: the 1688 census shows 66 Dutch, 32 English, 20 Danish, 8 French, 3 German, 3 Swedish, 1 Holstein (present-day Germany on the border to Denmark) and 1 Portuguese households (Arends & Muysken 1992: 51). In other words, while the Dutch (and the language they spoke) dominated numerically, the slaves were exposed to a number of other European languages too. Especially English and Danish is likely to have had an influence on what would become Negerhollands. The early Dutch settlers may have brought with them slaves who may already have spoken some variety of Dutch (Goodman 1985). Interestingly, the birth rate of the slave population was so high that by 1692 a fifth of the slave population was locally born (Sabino 1990).[32] This kind of population increase probably balanced the need for labour import, reducing the influx of newly arrived speakers of various West African languages. This might in turn have sped up the formation of the creole language.

The island of St. John was colonized by Danes in the early 1700s but Dutch households rapidly increased and outnumbered the other European planters. Here too the slaves spoke Negerhollands.

The first decades of the 19th century saw an increase in use and prestige of English, especially in the urban areas. By 1850 an English-lexified creole was replacing Negerhollands among what had been the slave population, possibly aided by the 1848 abolition of slavery and subsequent migration from the plantations to the urban centres, where English dominated. By the end of the 19th century Negerhollands could only be found in remote areas.

2.4.1.2 *A short linguistic sketch of Negerhollands*

Negerhollands had nine vowels: /i, e, ɛ, ə, ɑ, a, u, o, ɔ/, which could, except for /ə/ and /u/, optionally be nasalized before a nasal consonant. The typologically very rare front rounded vowels of Dutch, /y/ and /ʏ/, were most commonly realized as /i/ and /u/ respectively. There were 20

31. This section relies primarily on van Rossem & van der Voort (1996) and van Sluijs (2013b).

32. It should be noted that a high proportion of the Europeans were also locally born: in 1692 about a quarter (109 of 464) of the Europeans were born on the Dutch owned Caribbean islands (Sabino 1990).

consonants: /p, b, m, f, v, ʋ, t, d, n, r, s, z, l, ʃ, ʤ, j, k, g, ŋ, h/. Word stress seems to have been predominantly word-initial.

The morphology was predominantly analytic, although compounding could occur, for example with natural gender using the words *man* 'man' and *frou* 'woman':

(16) di manroto sini
DET man.rat 3PL
'the male rats' (van Sluijs 2013b: 268)

The indefinite article *ēn* was identical to the numeral 'one': *ēn mes* 'a/one knife'. The definite article *di/də* 'the' was also used in generic contexts and combined with the adverbs *hi(so)* 'here' and *dā* 'there' to form the demonstratives *di/də hi(so)* 'this' and *di/də dā* 'that'.

Possession could be indicated in three different ways: by juxtaposition (as in (17a)), with the possessive pronoun (as in (17b)) or with the preposition *fa(n)* 'of' (as in (17c)):

(17) a. di kui bik
DET cow stomach
'the cow's stomach' (van Sluijs 2013b: 268 citing de Josselin de Jong 1926: 28, line 33)

b. di mēnši ši coach
DET girl 3SG.POSS coach
'the girl's coach' (van Sluijs 2013b: 268 citing de Josselin de Jong 1926: 60, line 35)

c. di kaptein fan di bōt
DET captain of DET boat
'the captain of the boat' (van Sluijs 2013b: 268 citing de Josselin de Jong 1926: 43, line 36)

The personal and possessive pronouns were identical except for the third person singular:

	PERSONAL	POSSESSIVE
1SG	*mi*	*mi*
2SG	*ju*	*ju*
3SG.ANIM	*am*	*ši*
3SG.INANIM	*di*	*ši*
1PL	*ons*	*ons*
2PL	*jen*	*jen*
3PL	*sinu*	*sinu*

As can be seen in the table above, the third person singular personal pronoun had animacy but not gender distinctions. There was a great deal of allomorphy with the pronouns; the forms given in the table above were the most common ones.

The present tense was expressed with the base form of the verb, while past tense was marked with *(h)a* and future with *lō* (or *lō lō*) or *sa(l)*. There were three aspect markers: *kā* denoted the perfective, completive or resultative, *kan* the habitual and *lō* (homophonous with the future marker) the durative. There were also three modal markers: *kan* (homophonous with the habitual marker) denoted ability, possibility and permission, *ha fo* necessity (also epistemic) and *mańkē (fo)* the desiderative. There was no specific passive form.

Negation was expressed with a preverbal negation particle (which took the forms *no, na, nu, nə, ni* or *ne*).

There were several copulas used in a variety of predicative clauses.

Word order was subject-verb-object and polar questions were distinguished only by intonation, as in (18). With content questions the question word occurred sentence initially, as in (19).

(18) di man sē, ju wel di kabái?
DET man say 2SG want DET horse
'The man said: "Do you want the horse?"'
(van Sluijs 2013b: 271 citing de Josselin de Jong 1926: 21, line 26)

(19) wa bagin ju kā mā?
what bargain 2SG PFV make
'What bargain did you make?' (van Sluijs 2013b: 271 citing de Josselin de Jong 1926: 11, line 22)

There were serial verb constructions with *gi* 'give', *kō* 'come' and *lō* 'go', as in (20):

(20) am a flig lo mi di flut
3SG PST fly go with DET flute
'He flew away with the flute.'
(van Sluijs 2013b: 271 citing de Josselin de Jong 1926: 40, lines 21f)

Negerhollands had the conjunctions *en* 'and', *mi* 'with' and *ma* 'but'. Adverbial clauses were introduced with *weni* 'when, if', *tē* 'until' and *astər* 'after'; purpose clauses with *fo* 'for'. Complement clauses were typically merely juxtaposed, though occasionally subordinated with *dat* 'that' or *se* 'to say'. Relative clauses were either juxtaposed or subordinated with the invariant *wa* 'what'.

2.4.1.3 *Short text*

(From van Rossem & van der Voort 1996: 3 citing de Josselin de Jong 1926: 59, lines 12–14 with modified orthography.)

Am a ko a hus. Am a sē a ši šiši, ju kā trou ēn man, am mi ēn
3SG PST come PREP house 3SG PST say PREP 3POSS sister 2SG PRF marry INDEF man 3SG COP INDEF

bēfergi! Nu ši šiši a sē nu a wā! Di jung a sē am: jā, as ju nu
boar.pig now 3SG.POSS sister PST say NEG COP true DET boy PST say 3SG yes if 2SG NEG

glō mi sa wis ju wapi ju kā trou ēn
believe 1SG FUT show 2SG where 2SG PRF marry INDEF

'He came home. He told his sister, you married a man who is a pig! Then his sister said it is not true! The boy said to her: yes, if you don't believe me, I will show you where you married one.'

2.4.1.4 *Some sources of data*

An excellent and highly accessible source of primary data for Negerhollands is, for example, van Rossem & van der Voort (1996), who provide an anthology of a wide variety of glossed and translated texts spanning from different periods and an extensive list of manuscripts and further sources. A forthcoming source which is likely to provide a lot of data is the Negerhollands Database (NEHOL; http://www.clarin.nl/node/162#NEHOL, accessed 7 February 2015).

2.4.2 Nengee: An English-lexified maroon creole in Suriname and French Guiana[33]

2.4.2.1 *A brief background sketch of Nengee*

Nengee (by scholars also called *Eastern Maroon Creole* or *Ndyuka* in English; *takitaki* or *businenge tongo* in French; or *Auccaans* in Dutch) is an English-lexified maroon creole spoken by about 65,000 people in Suriname and French Guiana, as well as diaspora communities. The speakers themselves call their language *Nenge*, *Nengee* or *Businenge Tongo*. There are three varieties (dialects): *Ndyuka* (also called *Aucan* or *Okanisi*), with about 32,000 speakers in Suriname, 14,000 in French Guiana and 4,500 in the Netherlands, *Aluku* (also called *Boni*), with about 6,000 speakers in French Guiana, and *Pamaka* (also called *Paramaccan* or *Paramakan*), with about 3,000 speakers each in Suriname and French Guiana.

Suriname was settled in 1651 by English farmers and their Barbadian slaves. By the mid 1660s sugar plantations had grown significantly, which led to an increased import of labour and a decreased interaction between the Europeans (who were either plantation owners or indentured labourers) and the slaves imported from West Africa. Around the same time Suriname saw a significant immigration of Portuguese Jews (either coming from the New World or the Old) who probably also brought some of their slaves with them, in which case those slaves were likely to have been Portuguese-speaking (Smith 1999). The bulk of the Jewish immigrants settled along the upper Suriname River in an area that was called *Joden Savanne*. Suriname became Dutch in 1667, but Dutch was not widely used and the contact language(s) on the plantations continued to be English-lexified. Economic growth saw a rapid increase in slave importation and by the end of the 18th century the slave population vastly outnumbered the European population: the ratio in 1652 was 1:1, in 1679 1:2 and in 1695 1:12, showing a sudden growth of the slave population towards the end of the century; another hundred years later, in 1783, the ratio was 1:24. This sharp increase of the slave population, with the bulk being imported from West Africa, led to a steep decrease in interaction between the Europeans and the Africans, which in turn affected the formation of the Surinamese creoles. The slaves were imported from various regions along the West African coast, which means that several West African languages can be assumed to have been substrates for Nengee, but Kwa languages (especially Gbe) seem to have played a particularly prominent role.

Maroonage (the act of resisting slavery, particularly by desertion) had been going on throughout the history of the colonial settlement. The first decade of the 1700s saw an intensification of slave flights. The Maroons settled in remote and inaccessible rainforest areas and organized raids and attacks on the plantations. The Ndyuka signed a peace treaty with the colonial government in 1762 while the Aluku continued their battles until they were able to settle under the protection of the French Guianese colonial governor at the end of the 18th century.

33. This section is based almost exclusively on Migge (2013a).

Six Maroon communities have survived until today: the Saamaka (also called Saramaccans), the Matawi, the Kwinti, the Ndyuka, the Aluku and the Pamaka. The first two speak varieties of Saramaccan, the other Maroon creole of Suriname, the others speak varieties of Nengee.

The Maroon languages have no official recognition in Suriname and have endured a long history of stigmatization, though this has lessened somewhat since the civil war ended in 1987. In French Guiana the Maroon languages have gained the status of *langue de France*, which means they receive official recognition and may be incorporated in school curricula.

2.4.2.2 *A short linguistic sketch of Nengee*

Nengee has five vowels, /i, e, a, o, u/, which contrast phonemically in length (cf. *fo* /fo/ 'four' versus *foo* /fo:/ 'bird') and are nasalized when followed by a nasal consonant. There are 18 regular consonants, /p, b, m, w, f, t, d, c, s, ʧ, ʤ, l, ɲ, j, k, g, ŋ, h/, and 8 rare consonants, /^{m}b, v, kp, gb, ^{n}z, z, ^{n}ʤ, ^{ŋ}k/^{ŋ}g/, that mainly occur in ideophones or a small number of African words.

The morphology is predominantly isolating, though there is morphological reduplication, and most constructions are analytical. Word formation is typically done by compounding.

Nouns are morphologically invariant (cf. *wan bofoo* 'one tapir' versus *dii bofoo* 'three tapirs') and plural is indicated with the definite article *den* (e.g. *den bofoo* 'the tapirs') or by a quantifier. Grammatical gender is not relevant in Nengee, though natural gender may be indicated with *man* 'male' or *uman* 'female' (e.g. *man/uman foo* 'male/female bird').

There is a definite article, differentiated by number (*a* 'the.SinGular' and *den* 'the.PLural'), and an indefinite article *wan* (identical with the numeral 'one'). Demonstratives are formed by combining the definite article with *ya* 'here', *de* 'there' or *anda* 'over there'.

Possession is either formed by juxtaposition, as in (21a), or with the preposition *fu* 'for', as in (21b):

(21) a.

a	kownu	pikin
DET.SG	king	child

'the king's child'

b.

a	pikin	fu	a	kownu
DET.SG	child	POSS	DET.SG	king

'the king's child' (Migge 2013a: 42)

With description items comparison is done with *moo* 'more': the comparative is typically expressed with a postposed *moo* and the superlative typically with *a moo* 'the more', as in (22a) and b respectively:

(22) a.

en	osu	bigi	moo	du	fu	Saafika
her	house	nice	more	the.one	POSS	Saafika

'Her house is nicer than Safika's.'

b.

en	osu	na	a	moo	moy	osu	fu	a	konde
her	house	COP	DET.SG	more	nice	house	POSS	DET.SG	village

'Her house is the nicest in the village.' (Migge 2013a: 42)

There is one set of pronouns, used both as personal pronouns (subject and object) and possessive pronouns, most of which can be shortened:

1SG	*mi/m*	1PL	*wi/u*
2sg	*yu/i*	2PL	*u*
3SG	*en/a*	3PL	*de(n)*

The second person plural *u* may be used as a polite singular form.

The base form of the verb implies present tense and perfective aspect. There are two preverbal tense markers: *be* is an optional (relative) past tense and *o* the future; two aspect markers: the preverbal *e* denotes the imperfective aspect and the postverbal *kaba* the completive; and three preverbal modality markers: *mu* denotes necessity, *sa* the positive potential, and *man* (in the Aluku and Pamaka dialects) or *poy* (in the Ndyuka dialect) denote the negative potential. The TMA markers may be used in combination with each other. Verbs of any lexical aspect may combine with any of these markers. There is no specific passive form.

There are two preverbal negators, *ná* (used before a vowel) and *á(n)* (used before a consonant).

There are two copulas: *de*, which can combine with any of the TMA markers, and *(n)a*, which is identical to the locative and focus marker and which can only combine with *be* 'past'. In equative and attributive constructions (as in *mi na Baa Sima uman* 'I'm Mr. Sima's wife', lit. '1SINGular COPula Mr. Sima woman') *(n)a* is used; in any other construction, or equative/attributive constructions that need to be marked for TMA (other than past), *de* is used.

The word order is invariant and predominantly subject-verb-object. Polar questions are typically only distinguished by rising intonation. In content questions the question word occurs sentence-initially.

There are a number of serial verb constructions.

Coordination may be formed either through juxtaposition or overt coordinating conjunctions. Complements are introduced with the complementizer *taki* (also a quotative marker):

(23) u be yee taki a teki M. man, B.
1PL PST hear COMP 3SG take M. man B
'We heard that she had an affair with M's husband, B.' (Migge 2013a: 46)

Purpose clauses are introduced with *fu* 'in order to', as in (24), or *bika* 'because' and temporal clauses with *di* or *te* 'when', as in (25a) and b respectively:

(24) a go a busi fu sukuu wan baafu
3SG go DET forest COMP search INDEF sauce
'He went to the forest to find meat to make a sauce.' (Migge 2013a: 46)

(25) a. di den subi, a de anga den S.
when 3PL go.upriver 3SG COP with DET.PL S.
'When they went upriver, she came together with S. and his family.'
b. te i go gi den odi gi mi baa
when 2SG go give 3PL greeting from 1SG POL
'When you go to meet them, greet them from me.' (Migge 2013a: 46)

Relative clauses are typically marked with the relativizer *di* or with *san* 'what'.

2.4.2.3 *Short text*

(From Migge 2013a: 47)

A ten de, den kumalu be sani fu soso. Den toko en so tjo tjo tjo tjo. A e
DET.SG time there DET.PL fish PST thing for nothing 3PL dirty 3SG so IDEO 3SG IPFV

kon ya bub bub bub. He, a de ete! A Baa, a Baa B. án de fi en, a fa a
come here IDEO OK 3SG exist still FOC Mr, FOC Mr B. NEG COP for 3SG FOC how 3SG

du lon komoto a patapata. A kisi, a o kisi en, papa.
do run come.out LOC IDEO 3SG get 3SG FUT get 3SG elder

'At that time, the salmons were plentiful. They made it full of mud. It is swimming toward us with high speed. It's still there! Mr B. doesn't look, how did he manage to run out of that mud. He will manage to get it, elder.'

2.4.2.4 *Some sources of data*

A large number of sound files available online are listed in the Open Language Archives Community (OLAC) entry for Nengee (http://www.language-archives.org/language/djk, accessed 7 February 2015). Huttar & Huttar (1988) is a longer published text in the Pamaka dialect. Migge (2013a) gives a transcribed and glossed text as well as examples and Huttar & Huttar (1988) is an extensive grammar, including a large number of glossed and translated examples. The SIL International page (http://www.sil.org/, accessed 7 February 2015) gives a long list of primers and readers in Nengee under the entry 'Eastern Maroon Creole' in the Language and Culture Archives.

2.4.3 Diu Indo-Portuguese: A Portuguese-lexified fort creole in India[34]

2.4.3.1 *A brief background sketch of Diu Indo-Portuguese*

Diu Indo-Portuguese (by scholars called *Norteiro*, *Português dos Norteiros* or *Indo-Português* in Portuguese) is a Portuguese-lexified creole spoken by about 180 people on the island of Diu in western India. The language is called *purtəgez də diw*, *līg də diw* or *purtəgez* by the speakers themselves. The dominant language in the region, including the island of Diu, is the indigenous Gujarati, which the Diu Indo-Portuguese speakers are fluent in. Hindi, English and Konkani are other languages used by the Diu Indo-Portuguese community.

Diu is an ancient city that had long been a major port in western India when the Portuguese traders began arriving. In 1535 the Portuguese were given permission to build a fort on the island, to which they were initially confined. In 1554 they gained control of the island, which marked the beginning of Christian settlements outside the fort. This soon led to a community of mixed descendants ('Euroasians') and to the start of Christian missionary activities. At the same time settlers arrived from Portuguese communities in southern India. The Portuguese also had African slaves in their forts and settlements (Cardoso 2010). This led to a rather heterogeneous Catholic community.

34. This section relies almost exclusively on Cardoso (2013). I am very grateful to Hugo Cardoso for his helpful comments on this snapshot.

The commercial activities on Diu declined from the 17th century onwards. With this the Portuguese settlers diminished and slave import halted, all of which led to a reduced ethnic and linguistic diversity on the island. Diu Indo-Portuguese came to be used primarily by the locally born Catholics.

Diu, together with Goa and Daman, were integrated into the Republic of India in 1961, which led to the decolonization of the island by the Portuguese.

Despite its small number of speakers, Diu Indo-Portuguese still remains relatively vital and is transmitted to children. All Diu Indo-Portuguese speakers live in a multilingual environment: they are all fluent in Gujarati, many are proficient in English and many can also function in Hindi and Konkani. Many are also fluent in Portuguese "which retains great prestige and still exerts a considerable normative pull" (Cardoso 2013: 91). However, the language has no official support and is also under considerable pressure from English.

2.4.3.2 *A short linguistic sketch of Diu Indo-Portuguese*

Diu Indo-Portuguese has eight vowels: /i, e, ɛ, ə, a, ɔ, o, u/, only five of which can be nasalized (/ĩ, ẽ, ã, õ, ũ/). There are 20 consonants: /p, b, m, f, v, w, t, d, n, r, s, z, l, ʃ, ʧ, ʤ, j, k, g, ŋ/. The language allows both simple and complex syllables, where the complex syllables may have a maximum of two adjacent consonants. Words can have one, two or three syllables and stress falls on the final syllable.

There is considerable morphological inflection in the verb phrase. Nouns are invariant (cf. (26a)). Plural number may optionally be marked with *tud* 'all', as in (26b); reduplication, as in (26c), is by now a largely obsolete strategy for pluralization and is only sporadically found with some of the oldest speakers, although reduplication is still productive with other functions, such as the distributive.

(26) a. makak vey
monkey come.PST
'The monkey/monkeys came.'

b. ikəl tud koyz
DEM all thing
'those things'

c. muyɛ-muyɛr də ɔrlãd
woman-woman of Orlando
'the women of Orlando('s family)' (Cardoso 2013: 93)

The personal and possessive pronouns are clearly related to each other, with the possessives prefixed with *d* (<*də* 'of') in all forms except the first person (singular and plural):

	PERSONAL	POSSESSIVE
1SG	*yo*	*mĩ*
2SG	*use*	*duse*
3SG	*el* (M), *ɛl* (F)	*del* (M), *dɛl* (F)
1PL	*nɔs*	*nɔs*
2PL	*usez*	*dusez*
3PL	*e(l)z*	*de(l)z*

Object pronouns are formed by preposing *a* or *pə* to the subject pronouns, except in the case of the first person, which has the oblique specific form *mĩ*. A male/female gender distinction is made in the third person singular.

There are two invariant demonstratives, *es* 'this' and *ikəl* 'that', both of which also function as definite articles:

(27) a. aki aki, nə es igrej
here here LOC DEM church
'Here, here, in this church.'
b. es tud ɔn foy raprig?
DEM all where go.PST girl
'Where did the girls go?' (Cardoso 2013: 93f)

Indefiniteness is expressed by *ũ* 'one'.

Adjective comparison is carried out by *mays* 'more':

(28) galiŋ ɛ mays barat ki də karner
chicken COP.NPST more cheap COMPAR of mutton
'Chicken is cheaper than mutton.' (Cardoso 2013: 93)

The verbal system is morphologically complex. There are three conjugational classes, marked with the thematic vowels *-a-*, *-e-* and *-i-*. The form of the inflectional suffixes depends on conjugation class. There are four different verbal forms for each conjugation class: the infinitive, the nonpast, the past and the participle. The infinitive forms may combine with various tense, aspect and mood auxiliaries: *tə/te* 'nonpast imperfective', *tiŋ* 'past imperfective', *a/ad* 'nonpast irrealis', *vidi* 'past irrealis', *pɔd/pəd* 'nonpast potential', *pudiŋ* 'past potential', *ti ki* 'nonpast obligation', *tiŋ ki* 'past obligation', *(a) kere* 'obligation, predictive'.

There is an invariant preverbal negator *nã/nə*.

There are two copulas: *ɛ/ɛr* (nonpast/past) and *te/tiŋ* (nonpast/past). The former is used for essentially permanent states, while the latter is used for impermanent states, as a locative, and also as an existential and possessive.

Nouns can be verbalized by using *faze* 'make':

(29) nɔs kwɔn fez fon a elz, elz ain t-iŋ durmid
1PL when make.PST phone to 3PL 3PL still IPFV-PST asleep
'When we called them, they were still asleep.' (Cardoso 2013: 96)

Word order is rather flexible in Diu Indo-Portuguese, but is most commonly subject-verb-object:

(30) yo tə kuziŋ-a aroz ku pex
1SG IPFV.NPST cook-INF rice with fish
'I am cooking rice and fish.' (Cardoso 2013: 96)

Polar questions may either be formed through rising intonation only, or with the requestative particle *nə*, as in (31).

(31) ikəl tud koyz ki lɛvo nə museum father Marian ki lɛv-o, nə?
DEM all thing REL take.PST LOC museum Father Mariano REL take-PST REQ
'Wasn't it Father Marino who took those things to the museum?' (Cardoso 2013: 93)

Content questions are formed with question words preceding the verb phrase.

Clauses may be coordinated with the conjunction *i* 'and', the disjunctive *o* 'or' or the adversative *may* 'but'. Complement clauses are indicated with the complementizer *ki*:

(32) yo sab ki use foy Una
1SG know.NPST COMP 2SG go.PST Una
'I know that you went to Una.' (Cardoso 2013: 98)

Relative clauses are very frequently formed with the relativizer *ki* but may also be formed with a relative pronoun.

2.4.3.3 *Short text*

(From Cardoso 2009b: 325)

Ũ di ũ rey də jungle t-iŋ i ũ piken rat t-iŋ vay nə d-el kamiŋ.
one day one king of jungle EXIST-PST and one small mouse IPFV-PST go.INF LOC of-3SG way

I rey də jungle fal-o use ɛ tãt piken, use uki a faz-e? I ũ jungly
and king of jungle say-PST 2SG COP$_{i}$.NPST so small 2SG what IRR.NPST do-INF and one jungly

jat vey i amər-o pɛ d-ikəl lion. Ɛ-r pə kum-e a el. I rat kir-iŋ
jat come.PST and tie-PST leg of-DEM$_{d}$ lion COP$_{i}$-PST PURP eat-INF DAT 3SG and mouse want-PST

salv-a a el. I rat foy, murde-w murde-w pikəl-iŋ, sult-o. I dəpəy lion
save-INF DAT 3SG and mouse go.PST bite-PST bite-PST bit-DIM release-PST and after lion

fal-o ki muyt ubrigad. Istɔr kab-o.
say-PST COMPAR much thanks story finish-PST

'Once upon a time there was a king of the jungle, and a little mouse was going about his way. And the king of the jungle told him: "you are so small, what are you going to do?". And then a wild man came and bound the lion's leg, he intended to eat him. And the mouse wanted to save him. So the mouse went and gnawed and gnawed [at the rope] and set him free. And then the lion said: "thank you very much". The story is finished.'

2.4.3.4 *Some sources of data*

There is not much primary data available for Diu Indo-Portuguese. Cardoso (2009b) offers an excellent grammatical description of the language and provides numerous examples as well as some longer texts, all glossed and translated. An early source of data is Schuchardt (1885). Cardoso (2012) provides songs in Diu Indo-Portuguese.

2.5 Summary

Creoles are languages that arose in situations of intense contact. They are mother tongue languages of entire communities and can fulfil any and all functions of human language. They typically derive the main part of their lexicon from one or a few languages, typically that (or those) which was spoken by a politically dominant minority in the settlements.

Creole languages have endured a long history of stigmatization and condescension, typically with the view that they were inadequate and corrupt versions of their lexifier languages.

The term 'creole' derives from the Iberian *criar* 'breed, raise, bring up' (from Latin *creare* 'create, produce') and originally meant 'native, domestically raised'.

Creoles may be divided into various types depending on the contact situation that gave rise to the language. Exogenous creoles are those where neither the colonizers nor the labour force (whether slave or indentured) were indigenous to the area where the creole arose. Examples are plantation creoles, which arose in plantation settings, and maroon creoles, which were formed by escaped slaves who set up their own communities away from the institution of slavery. Endogenous creoles are those which arose in areas where at least part of the population that formed the language were indigenous. Fort creoles have their origin in trading centres where the colonial settlers (mainly engaged in trade) were foreigners and at least part of the workforce was indigenous.

Creoles are typically assumed to be less complex than their input languages, with a simplified phonemic and morphological system and a semantically more transparent grammar and lexicon.

2.6 Key points

- **Creoles are mother tongues to communities that emerged due to intense contact; they are full-fledged languages on par with any other natural language in the world.**
- **Creoles may have anything from zero to many million speakers.**
- **Most creole languages have endured a history of condescension and stigmatization, and have long (and unfairly) been viewed as inadequate versions of their lexifier languages.**
- **Exogenous creoles are those that emerged in areas to which none of the population groups involved were indigenous, such as plantation and maroon creoles.**
- **Endogenous creoles are those that emerged in areas which at least some of the population groups involved were indigenous to, such as fort creoles.**
- **There are no sharp boundaries between the types of situations that creoles may arise in.**
- **It is a matter of debate whether creoles can be identified by purely linguistic criteria (i.e. form a special linguistic type of language) or whether they can only be identified through the sociohistorical setting they arose in.**
- **Creoles are often assumed to be less complex than non-creoles.**

2.7 Exercises

1. What is the etymology of the word 'creole'?
2. What is the difference between endogenous and exogenous creoles? How might this difference have influenced the outcome of the creole?
3. What is the difference between plantation and maroon creoles? How might this difference have influenced the outcome of the creole?
4. In what way are creoles often assumed to be different from non-creoles?
5. Why do creoles tend to be stigmatized languages?

Languages cited in Chapter 3

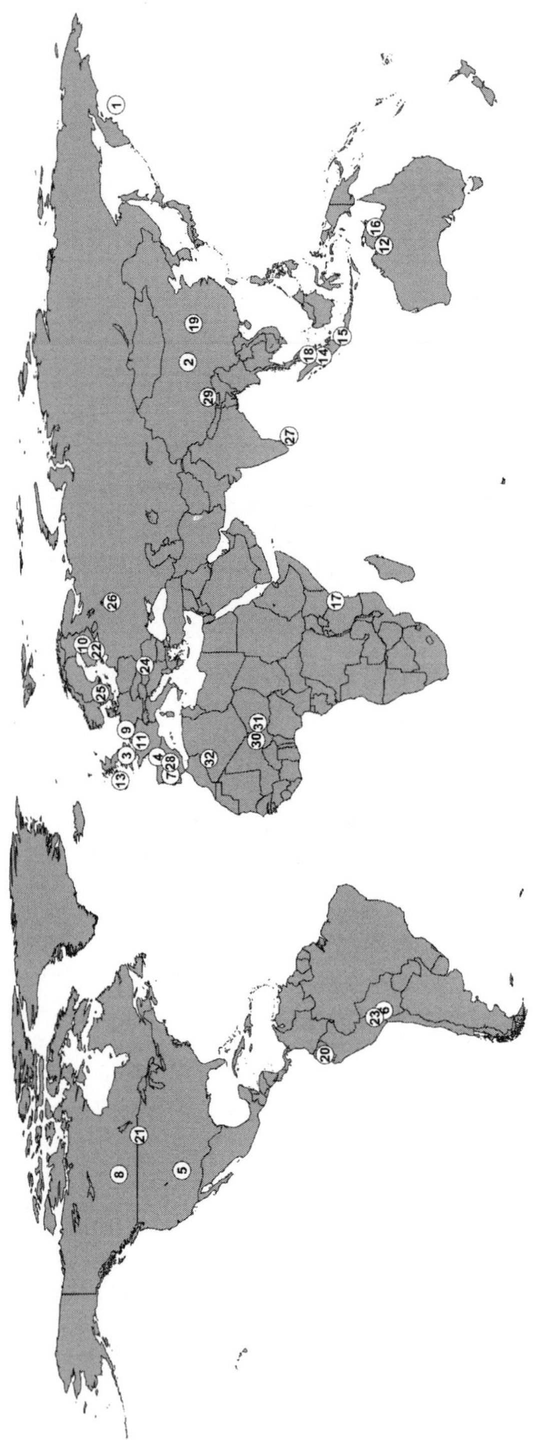

1. Aleut; Mednyj Aleut
2. Amdo Tibetan; Wutun
3. Angloromani; English
4. Basque; Errumantxela
5. Bilingual Navajo; Navajo
6. Callahuaya
7. Caló
8. Cree, Plains
9. Dutch
10. Finnish
11. French
12. Gurindji; Gurindji Kriol
13. Irish; Shelta
14. Javanese
15. Javindo; Petjo
16. Kriol
17. Ma'a/Mbugu
18. Malay; Singapore Bazaar Malay
19. Mandarin Chinese
20. Media Lengua; Quechua, Ecuadorian
21. Michif
22. Old Helsinki Slang
23. Puquina
24. Romani, Vlax
25. Rommani; Swedish
26. Russian
27. Sinhala; Sri Lankan Malay; Tamil
28. Spanish
29. Tibetan, Central
30. Tadakshak
31. Tagdal; Tasawak
32. Korandje

Chapter 3

Mixed languages

Mixed languages came about through the fusion of two or a few identifiable source languages and typically represent identity markers that emerged through expressive rather than communicative needs. They take part of their linguistic system from one source and the other part from the other source. This chapter will first give an overview of the main structural and sociolinguistic types of mixed languages (Section 3.1) before very briefly mentioning some of the theories on possible formation processes for mixed languages (Section 3.2). In Section 3.3 short sketches are given of three mixed languages: Bilingual Navajo (a grammar/lexicon mix as a marker of a retained identity), Michif (a noun phrase/verb phrase mix as a marker of a new identity) and Sri Lankan Malay (a form/structure mix as an effect of a new identity).

3.1 Definitions

Mixed languages are languages with split ancestry, that is, languages that have two (or a few) identifiable parent languages, and that typically emerged in situations of community bilingualism. This section will give a brief overview of the main kinds of social conditions that may lead to the emergence of mixed languages as well as a brief sketch of the main structural types of mixed languages that have been identified. It is beyond the scope of this chapter to do justice to the full discussion about mixed languages. For an accessible chapter-length overview of mixed languages, see Bakker & Muysken (1994). Matras & Bakker (2003) is a whole volume dedicated to the study of mixed languages and Bakker & Mous (1994) is a collection of 15 sketches of different mixed languages. For an up to date and very thorough discussion on mixed languages, see Meakins (2013c), which this chapter relies heavily on.

It is only in the last few decades that mixed languages have received closer attention. Thomason & Kaufman (1988) identified these as contact languages in their own right (cf., for example, the discussion on pages 103–109 and the case studies of Ma'á, Michif and Mednyi Aleut). Since then data on a number of mixed languages have been made available, facilitating the study of this group of languages.

Mixed languages are, like pidgins and creoles, contact languages. However, pidgin and creole languages typically have several input or source languages and most commonly it is only the source of the lexicon that is known with any degree of certainty.

Mixed languages typically only have two source languages and more often than not the source of both the lexicon and for the structure of the language are identifiable. Furthermore, most often both source languages are spoken in the same area, alongside the mixed language. Like creoles, mixed languages are associated with specific communities, which arose due to contact. Unlike creoles, mixed languages are not necessarily the first language of the community and often the community is proficient in one, or sometimes even both, of the source languages. And while creoles might have emerged due to a need for a means of communication, mixed languages did not, since the communities in question already had common languages. Rather, mixed languages emerged due to social conditions that fostered a desire for an in-group identity marker which took the form of a mixed language.

It is important to keep in mind that mixed languages form autonomous linguistic systems; they are languages in their own right. In other words, these are not varieties of the source languages which are then individually modified through, for example, code-switching or borrowing. It is likely that code-switching and borrowing were instrumental factors in the formation of any given mixed language (cf., for example, Thomason & Kaufman 1988, Auer 1999, Muysken 2000, Thomason 2001, Matras 2003, Myers-Scotton 2003). It is also possible that "the mixed language and code-switching may continue to co-exist within the same speaker population" (Meakins 2013c: 198). Even so, mixed languages are autonomous languages for a variety of reasons. For example, mixed language speakers tend to exhibit a high level of uniformity with respect to both the lexicon and the structure of their languages. That is, as with any other language, the structures are predictable between the speech of different individuals as well as within the speech of the same individual. Furthermore, mixed languages and their source languages do not necessarily follow the same patterns of change; the source languages may change in various ways without the mixed language being affected, or, conversely mixed languages may adopt new functions which are not reflected in any of the source languages.

The following will give brief overviews of the kinds of situations where mixed languages have emerged and the kinds of structural patterns mixed languages tend to have. It is by necessity a superficial sketch and should in no way be taken as a comprehensive list of mixed language types.

3.1.1 Structural types of mixed languages

Very broadly and simplified, we can distinguish between two main structural types of mixed languages: intertwined languages and converted languages (Bakker 2003a). Within these two major categories we find a number of diverse languages, all with their own unique composition. Each of these types will be discussed in turn.

3.1.1.1 *Intertwined languages*

Intertwined languages are essentially languages that are composed of two mutually dependent components that form a unique whole. Each of the components has its origin in a different source language and none of the components are sufficient on their own. Most commonly the two components follow a grammar versus lexicon divide, in that most of the grammar originates from one of the parent languages while most of the lexicon originates from the other parent language. These are sometimes called *G-L mixed languages* (Bakker 2003a, Meakins 2013c) for 'grammar-lexicon mixed languages'. However, some intertwined languages follow a different divide, where the nouns and those grammatical functions that are associated with the noun phrase originate with one of the source languages, while the verbs and those grammatical functions associated with the verb phrase originate from the other source language. These are sometimes called *N-V mixed languages* (Bakker 2003a, Meakins 2013c) for 'noun-verb mixed languages'. It is important to notice that these are not absolute divides, but rather more or less strong tendencies. In other words, G-L languages may derive some of the grammar from the source language which provided the bulk of the lexicon and some lexical items from the source language which provided most of the grammar. Likewise in N-V mixed languages some of the nominal items or structures may originate from the source language which provided most of the verbs and verbal grammar, and some of the verbal items or structures may originate from the source language which provided most of the nouns and nominal grammar. However, in both cases the general trend of the divide is rather clear.

G-L MIXED LANGUAGES. The most common type of mixed language known to us today is the G-L mixed language, where the grammar originates from one source language and the lexicon from the other. Angloromani is an oft-cited example of a language with a rather sharp grammar/lexicon divide, where the grammar is English and the lexicon is Romani. It is still spoken in Great Britain and the USA (and perhaps also other English-speaking countries, such as South Africa); the exact number of speakers is not known, though the language seems to be in decline in Great Britain (Matras et al. 2007: 158) but is vibrant in the USA (Ian Hancock, p.c.). It is an intimate, in-group language that is in general not used for entire conversations but rather for individual utterances "usually triggered either by reactions to outsiders or by the emotive content of a speech act" (Matras et al. 2007: 159). This is not unlike other mixed Romani languages of Europe, for example Rommani (Swedish/Romani) in Sweden, Caló (Spanish/Romani) in Spain and Errumantxela (Basque/Romani) in the Basque region of France and Spain, to mention only a few (for an overview of eight different mixed Romani languages, mainly located in Europe, see Boretzky & Igla 1994). Example (33) shows the same sentence in Angloromani (a) and Rommani (b), with the Romani elements underlined, as well as Swedish (c) and Romani (d):

Angloromani (English/Romani: UK)

(33) a. will we putch the mush if he=ll atch and suti to-rati?
FUT 1PL ask ART man if 3SG=FUT stay and sleep to-night

Rommani (Swedish/Romani: Sweden)

b. ska vi puttja dålle mossj om han vill suta palla i rati?
FUT 1PL ask DEM man if 3SG want sleep behind in night

Swedish (Indo-European (Germanic): Sweden)

c. ska vi fråga den där karl-en om han vill ligga kvar inatt?
FUT 1PL ask DEM man-DEF if 3SG want lie remain tonight

Romani (Indo-European (Indic): larger Europe)[35]

d. phuč-as i murš-este te ačel te sovel aka-rat?
ask-1PL ART man-LOC COMP stay.3SG COMP sleep. 3SG DEM-night
'Shall we ask that fellow if he'll stay and sleep tonight?' (Hancock 1992: 45)

As can be seen in Example (33) the structure of the Angloromani sentence follows that of the English translation exactly, while the structure of the Rommani sentence follows that of the Swedish sentence. In both Angloromani and Rommani the content words derive from Romani while the function words derive from the other source language. They both differ in terms of structure from the Romani equivalent. For more on Angloromani, see 15.4.3. For more on Caló, see 14.4.3.

Media Lengua is another example of a G-L mixed language, where the grammar is Quechua and the lexicon Spanish. It is spoken natively by about 200 people near Salcedo in Central Ecuador, but other varieties have been discovered elsewhere (Muysken 2013a). It is an in-group language not used and not understood outside the communities where it is spoken; that is, while speakers of Media Lengua tend to be proficient in either Spanish or Quechua or both, outsiders (whether Spanish or Quechuan) do not understand Media Lengua. Unlike Angloromani, Media Lengua is used for "ordinary, day-to-day community-level communication" (Muysken 2013a: 145). Example (34) shows a sentence in Media Lengua (a), with the Spanish elements underlined, as well as the Quechua (b) and Spanish (c) equivalents:

Media Lengua (Quechua/Spanish: Ecuador)

(34) a. yo-ga awa-bi kay-mu-ni
1SG-TOP water-LOC fall-CIS-1SG

Quechua (Quechua (Quechua): Ecuador, Peru, Bolivia)

b. ñuka-ga yaku-bi urma-mu-ni
1SG-TOP water-LOC fall-CIS-1SG

35. The interlinear glossing for the Romani example is done by myself, based on Matras (2002).

Spanish (Indo-European (Romance): Spain)

c.	vengo	despues	de	ca-er	en	el	agua
	come.1SG.PRES	after	PCL	fall-INF	in	ART.SG.M	water

'I come after falling into the water.' (Muysken 2013a: 144)

Again the structure in (34) clearly follows that of one of the source languages (Quechua) while the lexicon is derived from the other (Spanish): the Media Lengua and Quechua sentences look exactly the same in the glossing line, only the lexical roots (but not the suffixes) differ. For more on Media Lengua, see 10.4.3.

Javindo, on Java in Indonesia, was spoken by the descendants of Dutch/Indonesian mixed marriages. The grammar is essentially Javanese while the lexicon is Dutch. It is an identity marker for the separate ethnic identity of the speakers. The language and its speakers (i.e. people of mixed European/Indonesian ancestry) used to be referred to as Krontjong, Krõtjo or Kroyo, but these terms have derogatory connotations (de Gruiter 1994). In Example (35) the Dutch elements are underlined:

Javindo (Javanese/Dutch: Indonesia)

(35)	als	ken-niet	ja	di-ken~ken-a	wong	so	muulek	kok	sommen-nja
	if	can-not	IMP	PAT-can~RED-IRR	EMPH	for	so	difficult	sum.PL-DEM

'If it is not possible, try to get them done, for the sums are hard.'

(de Gruiter 1990: 44f)

N-V MIXED LANGUAGES. A different type of intertwined language is the N-V mixed language, where the divide between what originates from the source languages is not along a grammar/lexicon split, but rather along a noun/verb split. In these languages the part of the lexicon and grammar that has to do with the noun phrase tends to originate from one source language, while the part of the lexicon and grammar which has to do with the verb phrase tends to originate from the other source language. Michif is a well known N-V mixed language. It is spoken by between 50 and 200 people in Métis communities in Canada (Manitoba and Saskatchewan) and USA (North Dakota and Montana) by the descendants of French and Plains Cree mixed marriages (Bakker 2013a). The language, which is no longer transmitted to children, was an in-group language for those with a new, separate mixed ethnic identity, and it had remained unknown to outsiders for about a century before it was first mentioned in writing in the 1930s (Bakker 2013a: 158). Michif has its nominal system from French and its verbal system from Cree: nearly all the nouns and the grammar of the nominal system are almost exclusively French, while nearly all verbs and the grammar of the verbal system are almost exclusively Cree (Bakker 1997a). In Example (36) the French items are underlined:

Michif (French/Cree: Canada, USA)

(36)	ahkIkI-n	la	mus	ita	li	salɛj	e:ka	e:-wa:še:n-lke-t
	grow-4	ART.SG.F	moss	where	ART.SG.M	sun	NEG	COMP-shine-DETR-3

'Moss grows where the sun doesn't shine.' (Bakker 1997a: 97)

In Example (36) those elements which belong to the noun phrase (the articles and the nouns) derive from French, while those elements that belong to the verb phrase (the verbs, the verbal inflection and the negator) derive from Cree. For more on Michif, see Section 3.3.2.

Another N-V mixed language is Gurindji Kriol, with about 1000 speakers among the Gurindji people in northern Australia. It is by now the first language of the younger generation, while the older generations speak Gurindji amongst themselves (Meakins 2013a). The dominant language in the area is Kriol, an English-lexified creole, which most Aboriginal groups in northern Australia have shifted to. Gurindji Kriol thus "represents the maintenance of Gurindji" (Meakins 2008: 85) under pressure from Kriol. The Gurindji Kriol nominal system is predominantly from Gurindji while the verbal system predominantly derives from Kriol, although there are Kriol nouns (with Gurindji morphology) and Gurindji verbs (with Kriol tense, mood and aspect marking). In Example (37) the Gurindji elements are underlined:

Gurindji Kriol (Gurindji/Kriol: Australia)

(37)	nyawa=ma	wan	karu	bin	pleibat	pak-ta	deya	warlaku-yawung=ma
	this=TOP	a	child	PST	play	park-LOC	there	dog-PROP=TOP

'There was a kid playing with his dog in the park.' (Meakins 2011: 275)

In Example (37) most of the nominal items originate with Gurindji while most of the verbal items originate with Kriol. Notice that the Kriol noun (*pak* 'park') takes a Gurindji case marker (*ta* 'LOCative'). For more on Gurindji Kriol, see Section 9.5.3.

A language which carries affinities with both G-L mixed languages and N-V mixed languages is Mednyj Aleut. It is a moribund (i.e. nearly extinct) language: in the early 1990s there were only some 10 native speakers left, all middle aged or elderly (Golovko 1994: 113).[36] It was spoken on Mednyj, one of the Russian Commander Islands in the Bering Strait, by the descendants of mixed marriages between Russians and Aleuts (these mixed heritage descendants were referred to as "creoles" from early on; Thomason 1997b: 451). Mednyj Aleut has almost all its lexicon from Aleut, but the grammar follows an N-V divide in that the nominal system has an Aleut structure while the finite (i.e. inflected) verbal system is Russian (here underlined):

Mednyj Aleut (Aleut/Russian: Mednyj Island, Russia)

(38)	on	hixtaa-yit	ni	but	timas	agiital	txin	ayx'a-chaa-t
	3SG	say-PRES.3SG	NEG	FUT	1PL	together	REFL.3SG	go-CAUS-INF

'He says he will not go with us.' (Golovko 1994: 115)

For more on Mednyj Aleut, see 13.4.3.

36. Wikipedia states that there were five speakers in 2004, without, however, giving the source of that information (cf. http://en.wikipedia.org/wiki/Medny_Aleut_language, accessed 8 February 2015).

3.1.1.2 *Converted languages*

Converted languages are languages that have adopted the grammar of another language (or other languages) more or less wholesale without changing the lexicon. With these kinds of languages the entire lexicon and all grammatical morphemes come from one source language, while the formal and syntactic structure – that is, how the morphemes and lexical items are employed and arranged – come from a different source language (or a different few source languages). These are sometimes called *F-S mixed languages* (Bakker 2003a) for 'form-structure mixed languages'.

An example of an F-S mixed language (or converted language), which is based on three rather than two languages, is Sri Lankan Malay, spoken in various parts of the island of Sri Lanka as well as among the diaspora. There are to date no exact figures for the number of speakers and the language vitality varies for different regions: while Sri Lankan Malay is mildly to heavily endangered in most communities, it is still fully vibrant and used as a mother tongue in Kirinda in the south-east of the island (Ansaldo 2008). The Sri Lankan Malays are descendants of immigrants, mainly political exiles and soldiers, who were brought to the island from various parts of Indonesia and Malaysia by the Dutch and the British in the 17th and 18th centuries. All words and forms in Sri Lankan Malay derive from Bazaar Malay, but the language is not intelligible to other Malay speakers. That is because the structure is Tamil and Sinhala (the latter having assimilated considerably to Tamil in terms of structure):

Sri Lankan Malay (Malay/Tamil, Sinhala: Sri Lanka)

(39)	a.	baapa	derang=pe	kubbong=ka	hatthu	pohonh	nya-poothong
		father	3PL=POSS	garden=LOC	INDEF	tree	PST-cut
		S				O	V

'My father cut a tree in their garden.' (Nordhoff 2009: 273)

b.	Farida	Tariq=nang	duit=yang	tər(ə)-kasi
	Farida	Tariqa=DAT	money=ACC	NEG.FIN-give
	S	iO	dO	V

'Farida does not give Tariqa the money.' (Slomanson 2013a: 80)

As Example (39) shows, Sri Lankan Malay makes use of morphological concatenation, with segmentable case and tense/mood/aspect markers fused to the nominal and verbal stems. This is similar to Tamil and Sinhala:

Tamil (Dravidian (Southern Dravidian): India, Sri Lanka)

(40)	Kumaar	appaa·v-ukku	oru	paṭa-tt-ai·k	kaaṭṭ-iṉ-aaṉ
	Kumar	father-DAT	a	picture-OBL-ACC	show-PST-3SG.M
	S	iO		dO	V

'Kumar showed father a picture.' (Lehmann 1993: 31)

Sinhala (Indio-European (Indic): Sri Lanka)

(41)	Kumar	thaththa-ta	pinthooray-ak	pennuwa
	Kumar	father-DAT	picture-INDEF.SG	show.PST
	S	iO	dO	V

'Kumar showed father a picture.' (Dilini Algama, p.c.)

Compare this with the largely isolating structure of Singapore Bazaar Malay,[37] where both lexical and grammatical units are free morphemes:

Singapore Bazaar Malay (Pidgin (Malay-lexified): Singapore)

(42)	Mary	punya	Aunty	ada	kasi	dia	baju
	PN	POSS	aunty	have	give	3SG	dress
	S			V	iO	dO	

'Mary's aunt did give her a dress.' (Aye 2005: 65)

Notice also that Sri Lankan Malay shows a subject-(indirect object)-object-verb structure, as do Tamil and Sinhala, while Singapore Bazaar Malay shows a subject-verb-(indirect object)-object structure. The examples above thus show that the structure of Sri Lankan Malay follows that of Tamil and Sinhala, even though the lexicon and morphemes have a Bazaar Malay origin. For more on Sri Lankan Malay, see Section 3.3.3.

Wutun is another example of an F-S mixed language (but see Janhunen et al. 2008 for a discussion on why Wutun should not be classified as a mixed language but a Sinitic (Sino-Tibetan) language). It is spoken by about 4,000 people in three villages along the Longwu river in Qinghai Province in China (Janhunen et al. 2008: 19). In Wutun the lexicon and morphemes largely derive from Mandarin, while the structure is essentially Amdo Tibetan. For instance, Wutun has the concatenative structure of Amdo Tibetan:

Wutun (Mandarin/Amdo Tibetan: China)

(43)	ggaiggan	lhokang-li	huaiqa	kan-di-li
	teacher	classroom-LOC	book	read-PROG-OBJ
	S		O	V

'The teacher is reading books in the classroom.' (Janhunen et al. 2008: 58)

Example (43) shows that Wutun has concatenative case markers (e.g. *-li* 'LOCative; OBJective') and tense/mood/aspect markers (e.g. *-di* 'PROGressive'). Furthermore, the word order is subject-object-verb. This contrasts with the largely isolating nature as well as the subject-verb-object word order of Mandarin:

---

37. While Singapore Bazaar Malay is not likely to have been the source of Sri Lankan Malay, it may serve as an example of a vehicular Malay variety.

Mandarin (Sino-Tibetan (Chinese): China)

(44) wǒ zài mǎi shū le
1SG DUR buy book CRS
S V O
'I am buying a book.' (Li & Thompson 1981: 21)

Compare this with the concatenative subject-object-verb structure of Tibetan as shown in Example (45):

Standard Spoken Tibetan (Sino-Tibetan (Bodic): Tibet)

(45) _tandə _ŋa ¯kjeraŋ-gi ¯tsa-lə _jʊŋ-gy-jø:
now 1SG 2SG-GEN place-LOC come-LINK-AUX
S O V
'I'm coming to your place now.' (Denwood 1999: 152)

Examples (43) and (45) show that Wutun has a Tibetan structure, even though the lexemes and morphemes are etymologically Mandarin.

The Northern Songhay languages constitute a group of four languages (Tadakshak in Mali, Tagdal and Tasawak in Niger, and Korandje in Algeria) that have been argued to form a subgroup of essentially F-S mixed languages, where, extremely simplified, the form has essentially been taken over from various non-Songhay sources (predominantly Berber) and the structure derives from Songhay (cf. e.g. Benítez-Torres 2009 with further references, cf. also the work of Robert Nicolaï, e.g. 1979 & 1997; for a recent and detailed discussion of Tadakshak, see Christiansen-Bolli 2010).

3.1.2 Sociolinguistic types of mixed languages

Both creoles and mixed languages are languages associated with a specific population group. However, they arose under different social circumstances in that while creoles are in many cases believed to have arisen through a need for a communicative bridge between groups of people with no language in common, mixed languages arose through a need to express a specific identity. Mixed languages typically arise "in situations where a common language already exists and communication is not an issue" (Meakins 2013c: 180). In other words, a mixed language is an identity marker (cf. Croft 2003 for a discussion on mixed languages as expressions of acts of identity).

Very simplified, there are two sociolinguistic types of mixed languages: those spoken by new ethnic groups and those spoken by minority ethnic groups who have "clung to their old cultural identity, resisting total linguistic assimilation to a dominant group" (Thomason 2003: 25).[38] In both cases we are dealing with in-group languages.

38. But see (Benítez-Torres 2009) for a discussion on how Tagdal emerged as a result of intentional language shift.

Typically, but not always, the mixed language is the first language of the community, while the source languages are also used to varying degrees. Those mixed languages which exist alongside one or more of their source languages and which are not the only language of its speakers are sometimes called **symbiotic mixed languages** (cf. Smith 1994 and 2000) to indicate their "symbiotic and dependent relationship with (dominant) unmixed languages" (Smith 1994: 333).

It is important to notice that not all mixed languages have to come about through new or threatened ethnic identities. Media Lengua, for example, is not spoken by descendants of mixed ancestry, nor by an ethnic group that is under pressure from some other culturally dominant group, but by Quechua people who identify to a degree with urban Spanish society (Muysken 2013a). The following should therefore not be taken as hard and fast categories, but rather as examples of typical situations that have led to mixed languages. Furthermore, the following will only bring up a few representative examples and should by no means be taken as an exhaustive list of mixed languages.

3.1.2.1 *Mixed languages as markers of a new identity*

A number of mixed languages are spoken by people who form new ethnic groups in the societies they belong to. This not infrequently comes about due to mixed marriages, where the descendants form a new ethnic identity. The speakers of Michif, for example, who call themselves Métis, are the descendants of French-speaking traders and indigenous North American (mainly Cree) women. The speakers of Mednyj Aleut were descendants of mixed marriages between Russian traders and Aleut women. The speakers of Javindo were descendants of the mixed marriages between Dutch colonial settlers and Javanese women. Another mixed language in Indonesia, or rather a group of mixed languages, is Petjo, which was spoken by the so-called Indos, that is, descendants of Dutch colonial settlers and Asian women of different ethnicities. Typically the members of the new ethnic group, the descendants of mixed ancestry, identified with neither of the ancestor ethnicities. Instead, they formed a unique, new, identity, which had as one of its markers a new, mixed, language.[39] In many cases the mixed language would be used only among the mixed descendants, while the ancestor languages would be used with others. Petjo, for example, was only used on the street with peers, typically among boys (girls were generally not allowed to play on the streets), and has been called "the broken language of the playground" (van Rheeden 1994: 225). At school and at home Petjo speakers would use Dutch or the language of the mothers (which was often Malay). In fact, Michif is the only mixed language known where the speakers are not proficient in the source languages.

39. The speakers of Mednyj Aleut, however, consider themselves Aleut and consider their language "the right Aleut language" (Golovko 1994: 117).

New identities can come about in other ways than through mixed marriages. Sri Lankan Malay, for example, is spoken by what is now a separate ethnic group, namely Sri Lankan Malays, who identify neither with the Sinhala or Tamil, nor with the Malay. Another example of a mixed language spoken by a group with a new, separate identity, but that did not involve descendants of mixed marriages, is Old Helsinki Slang, which could be classified as a G-L mixed language, with a Swedish vocabulary and Finnish grammar. It was spoken around 1890–1950 by gangs with both Swedish and Finnish members in the Swedish-Finnish bilingual working class areas of Helsinki and became a marker for a new urban identity (Jarva 2008, de Smit 2010).

3.1.2.2 *Mixed languages as markers of a retained identity*

A number of mixed languages emerged as a consequence of outside pressure from some other, dominating, group. In other words, these mixed languages typically emerge because of ethnic minorities who resist outside pressure to assimilate into the mainstream society and wish to retain their ethnic identity. The mixed language then becomes a marker for that retained identity. An example of that is Gurindji Kriol, where the speakers

> continue to identify as Gurindji and also call their mixed language Gurindji, despite the Kriol content. The strong maintenance of Gurindji lexicon and noun phrase structure in this mixed language marks the Gurindji as separate from other Kriol speakers, and indeed the encroaching and assimilative non-Indigenous world.
>
> (Meakins 2013c: 184)

Another example of a mixed language that emerged through an effort to maintain an old identity is Ma'á/Mbugu, spoken by some 7,000 people in the Usambara Mountains in Tanzania and called Inner Ma'á or Inner Mbugu by the speakers themselves. It could be called a G-L mixed language, with its grammar from the surrounding Bantu languages and the lexicon mostly from Cushitic ancestor languages. The Mbugu were originally from the Cushitic area further north but had to resettle due to persecution. They have retained their Cushitic culture and economy, as well as their appearance. The mixed language forms part of this separate ethnic identity (Mous 2013).

Bilingual Navajo, also called Navglish by some of the speakers (cf. Webster 2008), is another example of a mixed language that has emerged as an effort to retain an old identity. It could be called a G-L mixed language, with the grammar from Navajo and the vocabulary of content words from English. Bilingual Navajo initially arose among Navajo children who, from the early 1900s until World War II, were forcibly sent to boarding schools where they were required to speak English and punished for speaking Navajo (Schaengold 2003: 236). As a result, children would speak a kind of "boarding school Navajo" in secret, "filling in English words where their native vocabulary failed them" (Schaengold 2004: 8). This code would also be used back home with other boarding school students and graduates, and became an in-group solidarity code for bilingual Navajos. At present Standard Navajo is declining, with English gaining ground due to the complete dominance of English in the American society. Few children learn Navajo natively nowadays, though they do encounter it, as it is still actively used among adults, especially the elderly. However, most of those who have difficulties with Standard Navajo are proficient in Bilingual Navajo. While this mixed language is still stigmatized as inferior to Standard Navajo, it is, for many of the young generation, the only variety of Navajo they can speak (Schaengold 2004: 145). As such it functions as a Navajo identity marker and a means for maintaining Navajo under the heavy pressure and dominance of English. For more on Bilingual Navajo, see Section 3.3.1.

A number of mixed languages are labelled secret languages because their primary function seems to have been that of group-internal communication "deliberately used to exclude outsiders" (Croft 2003: 65). The use of these languages may also be seen as acts of identity of various kinds, for example acts of retaining a threatened ethnic identity, or to otherwise delimit oneself from mainstream society as an act of in-group solidarity – what Croft (2003) terms 'negative acts of identity'. The various Romani-based mixed languages of Europe, such as Angloromani, can be seen as secret languages used as an in-group act of maintaining a threatened ethnic identity under pressure from the outside community, which is then excluded from the communication.

Shelta, called Shéldru (/ʃeldru:/) by the speakers themselves, is an example of a secret language. It is claimed to have about 6,000 speakers in Ireland and about 86,000 speakers worldwide, mostly in the English-speaking areas (Lewis et al. 2014). Shelta is spoken by so-called Travellers,

> a generally endogamous group of (traditionally) itinerant craftsmen, small traders, musicians and beggars, sharing a number of cultural traits, such as common patterns of livelihood, customs relating to birth, marriage and domestic affairs, and adherence to Roman Catholicism, who were formerly known as Tinkers. (Grant 1994: 123)

Shelta is mainly derived from Irish (which has provided most of the lexicon) and English (which has provided most of the structure) and is not meant to be revealed to 'Buffers' (non-Travellers). Indeed it remained unknown until 1876. It is an in-group language used for any kind of conversation and will take different forms depending on the situation: in the presence of Buffers, for example, the structure will be such that users are able to disguise their speech in such a way that they will not draw attention to the fact that they are using a secret language. For more on Shelta, see 11.4.3.

Another example of a secret language is Callahuaya, also called Machaj Juyay, which is spoken in northwest Bolivia. The structure of the language is mostly Quechua, while the vocabulary is drawn from different sources, predominantly from Puquina, which is by now extinct. It is one of the identity markers of the Callahuayas, who constitute a separate ethnic group of about 2,000 and who are descendants of itinerant healers (Muysken 1994). Callahuaya is a secret language that was used during healing rituals. Today only a minority of healers know and use the language, all belonging to the older generation (Muysken 1997a).

3.2 A very brief note on mixed language formation processes

There is general agreement that mixed languages emerge as in-group identity markers rather than through the need for a communicative bridge between population groups. However, it is a matter of debate what the actual formation processes involved in the emergence of a mixed language are. The following will give a very brief sketch of some of the most common theories. It is beyond the scope of this section to do anything more than to scratch the surface of the discussion. For an accessible overview of the theories of mixed language formation, see Meakins (2013c: 185ff). For more in-depth discussions on various aspects of mixed languages, see the chapters in Matras & Bakker (2003).

Very broadly, theories on the formation of mixed languages fall into one of two major approaches: (i) unidirectional, which propose a one-way shift from an ancestor (source) language to an introduced (target) language, and (ii) fusional, which propose that the two source languages merge (or fuse) to form a third, new, language. In both cases large-scale community bilingualism is a necessary condition.

It should be noted that none of these approaches are mutually exclusive and can – and, in fact, are in some of the cases mentioned below – be combined. Rather, any given approach may more or less strongly emphasize various processes.

3.2.1 Unidirectional formation processes

Very simplified, the unidirectional approaches to mixed languages propose that speakers of one language, the ancestor (or source) language, were in the process of shifting to another, introduced (and typically socially dominant) language. This **language shift** was, however, never fully completed; the mixed language is the result of this incomplete shift. This shift can take a variety of forms, such as borrowing, code-switching, relexification or paralexification.

3.2.1.1 *Mixed languages as a result of borrowing*

It is very common for languages to **borrow** elements from other languages.[40] However, the types of elements that languages tend to borrow and the scale of the borrowing may differ radically, depending on the nature and length of the contact between the

40. A more accurate term than 'borrowing' would be '(code) copying', since what actually happens is that a language copies a feature or element from another language, rather than that the speakers of one language temporarily use, and then "return", a feature or element from a different language. Cf. the discussion in Johanson (2008).

languages. On one end of the scale, population groups of roughly equal status may have casual contact with each other and may borrow scattered lexical items from each other's languages. On the other end of the scale, a population group may be severely dominated by another population group; this may lead to one-sided influence where the dominated group takes over not only lexical items but also structural patterns from the dominating language. For extensive discussions on borrowing, see, for example, Thomason & Kaufman (1988), Curnow (2001), Aikhenvald (2006a) and Matras (2009:146ff), to mention only a few, as well as Matras & Sakel (2007) for a volume dedicated to kinds of borrowings in different languages.

Some theories argue that large-scale community bilingualism may lead to different scales of borrowing as a path towards language shift. However, the shift stops along the way, leading to a situation where the ancestor language has borrowed so extensively from the target language that it resembles neither of the two and a new, mixed language has emerged. According to this approach mixed languages would thus have their origin in extensive linguistic borrowing (cf., for example, Thomason & Kaufman 1988, Thomason 2001 and Matras 2003).

3.2.1.2 *Mixed languages as a result of code-switching*

A common phenomenon with bi- or multilinguals is **code-switching**, which essentially means that a speaker uses more than one language or variety in the same utterance. This is not unrelated to borrowing in the sense that linguistic borrowing effectively is a language level outcome of systematic code-switching in a speech community. Code-switching may take place at any level of the linguistic structure, from the word unit to larger units such as entire sentences or even across sentences. For extensive discussions on code-switching, see, for example, Myers-Scotton (1993, 2002), Muysken (2000), Poplack (2001), as well as the chapters in Auer (1998a), to mention only a few.

Some theories argue that mixed languages are the outcome of systematic code-switching that has stabilized into a set of norms, essentially that mixed languages originate in the "gradual fossilization of code-switching" (Meakins 2013c:189). This would come about in stages, where the initial stage would be individual code-switching via conventionalized community code-switching to a new, mixed, linguistic system (cf., for example, Auer 1998b & 1999, Maschler 1998 and Myers-Scotton 2003). Gurindji Kriol is an example of a mixed language for which there indeed is evidence that code-switching was a relevant factor in its emergence: what was adult code-switching in the 1970s had, one generation later, crystallized into a stable mixed linguistic system (McConvell & Meakins 2005).

3.2.1.3 *Mixed languages as a result of relexification*

Relexification is essentially a phenomenon whereby a language replaces most or all of its lexicon with that of another language, but retains its original structure. In other words, with relexification a language takes over the forms from another language, and superimposes them onto the grammatical and semantic structure of the ancestor language. For more on relexification, see Section 6.1.2.

Some theories argue that mixed languages are the outcome of relexification where the lexicon of the introduced language is mapped onto the structure of the ancestor language (cf., for example, Brenzinger 1987 and Muysken 2013a).

3.2.1.4 *Mixed languages as a result of paralexification*

Paralexification essentially denotes a phenomenon where a speech community has access to two parallel lexicons, one from the ancestor language and one from the introduced or target language. This would be a situation where a speech community is on the verge of shifting, or perhaps has already shifted, to a dominant language. However, the lexicon of the ancestor language is still available as a **lexical reservoir** (Matras et al. 2007) to the speech community and speakers would then, in this scenario, consciously choose to insert vocabulary from the ancestor language. For more on paralexification and language reservoirs, see, for example, Mous (2001 & 2003a) and Matras et al. (2007).

Some theories argue that mixed languages are the outcome of paralexification in that a community consciously attempts to reverse a language shift by reintroducing lexical items from the ancestor language. This would in particular be relevant for severely dominated ethnic groups and for speakers of secret languages, where the mixed language is used specifically to exclude the outsiders and is thus "disguised" with a vocabulary from the ancestor language.

3.2.2 Fusional formation processes

Fusional approaches to mixed languages propose that the two source languages merged and thus formed a new language, rather than that speakers were in the process of shifting from one language to another and stopped along the way. This merging may come about through language intertwining or through language competition.

3.2.2.1 *Mixed languages as a result of language intertwining*

With **language intertwining** a process is meant where speakers combine aspects of the two source languages and thereby form a new, mixed language. In this process there is no direction from one language to another, rather, the two linguistic source systems contribute a component each, which intertwine to form an organic whole. The two components are thus mutually dependent and of equal importance (Bakker & Muysken 1994). For more on language intertwining, see, for example, Bakker (1997a, 2000 and 2003a).

3.2.2.2 *Mixed languages as a result of language competition and evolution*

Very simplified, theories about **language competition** investigate language change in general, both with respect to internally motivated factors and to external factors such as contact. The principles largely follow those of biological evolutionary natural selection (see, for example, Labov 2001 & 2010) as well as biological replication (Croft 2000). Genes are constantly copied (replicated) in natural reproduction; these replicated genes may come out identical or may mutate or rearrange. Similarly, every speaker produces utterances in which linguistic structures are replicated from previous utterances; these linguistic structures (termed *linguemes* by William Croft) may come out identical or not. Mutated linguemes, that is, new linguistic structures, may catch on and spread (propagate) – that is, out of a pool of available linguemes (linguistic structures), a few are selected and propagate due to their higher competitive value. For more on language competition and evolution, see, for example, Labov (1994, 2001, 2010), Croft (2000) and Mufwene (2001). Section 6.1.4 discusses lingueme (feature) pools further.

Some theories argue that mixed languages are the outcome of a high level of bi- or multilingualism and code-switching, which would lead to a feature pool of competing linguemes from the source languages. Out of this feature pool certain linguistic structures are selected and end up forming the system of the new, mixed language (cf., for example, Croft 2003, Ansaldo 2008, Meakins 2011).

3.3 Snapshots

Mixed languages are in-group languages that serve as identity markers. There are two major types of identity that mixed languages tend to be a symbol of: (i) those that represent new ethnic groups, such as descendants of mixed marriages and descendants of a displaced population, here exemplified by Michif and Sri Lankan Malay respectively; and (ii) those that represent an original ethnic identity which is somehow threatened by various social conditions, here exemplified by Bilingual Navajo.

Mixed languages may be classified according to their structural properties. With intertwined languages one component of the language typically originates with one of the source languages, while the other component originates with the other source language. In G-L languages the components are more or less consistently structured according to a grammar/lexicon divide (as is the case in Bilingual Navajo), while N-V languages are more or less structured according to a noun phrase/verb phrase divide (as is the case in Michif). With converted languages the form originates from one source language while the semantic and syntactic structure originates with the other source language (as is the case in Sri Lankan Malay).

3.3.1 Bilingual Navajo: A G-L mixed language as a marker of retained identity[41]

3.3.1.1 *A brief background sketch of Bilingual Navajo*

Bilingual Navajo, also called *Vernacular Navajo* by scholars and sometimes called *Navglish* by the speakers themselves (Webster 2008), is a mixed language spoken in the Navajo Nation, which is located in the area where the US states of Utah, Colorado, New Mexico and Arizona meet. The Navajo population numbers some 200,000 and there is a generational divide as to language use: while the older generation tends to be monolingual in Navajo, the school-aged children are considered to be monolingual in English. The majority of the adult population is bilingual and a number of them are speakers of the mixed language Bilingual Navajo, which to English speakers is indistinguishable from Standard Navajo. However, Bilingual Navajo is its own language code, which monolingual speakers of Standard Navajo are not able to understand. The exact number of speakers for Bilingual Navajo is not known. It is a G-L mixed language where English content words are mapped onto a Navajo morphosyntactic frame.

While the Navajo Nation is located within the United States and the Navajo people are US citizens, many Navajos "consider themselves to be a separate people oppressed by the dominant Anglo culture and economy" (Schaengold 2004:10).[42] This may well be due to the history and nature of the contact between the Navajo and English population. The first contact between the two was in the 1860s, during the "Long Walk", when the population that remained of the conquered Navajo tribe was forced by the US Army to march to Fort Sumner in New Mexico. The purpose of the relocation was to convert the Navajo population to an agricultural lifestyle, but when that attempt failed the Navajo population was again relocated, roughly to the area they had originally occupied. This treatment left the Navajos unwilling to learn English or assimilate into mainstream society.

Indian boarding schools were set up from the 1880s onwards and when school became compulsory in 1887 many Navajo children were taken and sent away to the boarding schools during the school year, often against their or their parents' will. This practice continued up until World War II. At these schools speaking English was obligatory and speaking Navajo a punishable offense. Because of this many bilingual children in secret spoke a code which was essentially Navajo with an English vocabulary where they had not had a chance to learn the Navajo equivalents. This code became an in-group language for the children when they were back home for vacations, as well as for boarding school graduates who had moved back to the Navajo Nation. Eventually this code stabilized and by the 1950s–70s had become a fully formed mixed language. It is by now the only kind of Navajo spoken by many of the younger generation. Standard Navajo, English and Bilingual Navajo are thus all part of the linguistic repertoire of the Navajo Nation and some speakers are fluent in two or all three of the languages.

41. This section is based largely on Schaengold (2004). I am very grateful to Charlotte Schaengold for her helpful comments on this snapshot.

42. 'Anglo' denotes "the English-speaking non-Indian, non-Hispanic population, and what are seen as the worst values associated with it, such as materialism, greed for power, and disregard for family and friends" (Schaengold 2004:19).

3.3.1.2 *A short linguistic sketch of Bilingual Navajo*

The phonological system of Bilingual Navajo is essentially an amalgamation of Navajo and Navajo English (the non-standard variety spoken on the Navajo Reservation), since the language consists of elements from both these languages. Navajo has 35 consonants: /b, m, w, t, t^{x}, t', ʦ, ʦ^{h}, ʦ', s, z, n, ʧ, ʧ^{h}, ʧ', ʃ, ʒ, tɬ, tɬ^{h}, tɬ', ɬ, l, ç, j, k, k^{x}, k', x, ɣ, ɰ, k^{w}, k^{xw}, ɣ^{w}, ʔ, h/ and 4 vowels: /i, e, a, o/, which have contrastive length and nasalization (McDonough 2003). The way consonants may combine in Bilingual Navajo is influenced by how they may combine in Navajo. Thus 'clock' is pronounced /tɬoʔ/ and 'glasses' /dlases/. Because in Navajo the glottal stop is the only voiceless consonant that can occur word finally, Bilingual Navajo may drop final consonants or assimilate final consonant clusters, as in 'test' /tes/ or spit /spiʔ/ (Schaengold 2003: 240). There is no /ŋ/. The large vowel system of English has been adjusted to that of Navajo, where length is distinctive rather than the point of articulation.[43] Navajo is a tone language, which affects the suprasegmental pattern of Bilingual Navajo.

There is considerable morphological inflection, taken over from the Navajo system. Inflection is typically concatenative, or, in the verbal system, non-linear (i.e. involving stem changes). Case and gender are not relative in Bilingual Navajo. Plural is not marked in Navajo, but obligatorily marked in English. In Bilingual Navajo, the given noun is typically the inflected English word:

(46) a. shi-relative-s
1SG.POSS-relative-PL
'my relatives'

b. bi-dlasses
3SG.POSS-glass.SG
'her glasses' (Schaengold 2004: 47, 49)

Notice that the inflected English form may be a fossilized form, as in (46b), where the English plural form *glass-es* has fossilized into the unsegmentable Bilingual Navajo singular form *dlasses*. Example (46) also shows that possession is marked with the Navajo possessive pronouns.

Articles are largely irrelevant, but the demonstrative may be used as a definite article and the word for 'one' may be used as an indefinite article. Both are carried over from Navajo:

(47) a. Bertha hádą́ą́ lá éiyá take picture ánihilaa?
Bertha when.PST EMPH.DEM take picture 3SG.PFV.make
'When did Bertha take the picture?'

b. bookshelf ɬa' shá save áni-lééh
bookshelf one for.me save 2SG-make
'Save me a/one bookshelf.' (Schaengold 2004: 53, 55)

Nouns may be marked with the Navajo direction suffixes:

(48) a. town-góó déyá
town-towards 1SG.go
'I am going to town.'

43. That which is commonly termed a contrast between long and short vowels in Standard English is, in fact, a contrast of both length and point of articulation. The difference between feet /fi:t/ and fit /fɪt/ or fool /fu:l/ and full /fʊl/, for example, is not only length, but also the vowel quality.

b. tɫinic-di check-up biniyé all day sédá.
clinic-at check-up 3SG.because all day 1SG.PFV.wait
'I went to the clinic for a check-up (and) waited (there) all day.'
(Schaengold 2004: 47, 50)

Adverbs are formed by adding the Navajo subordinate suffix *-go* to English noun phrases.

When English verbs are used the sentence requires an inflected form of the Navajo *áshɫéeh* 'to make' as an auxiliary, in order to accommodate for the clausal syntactic information that is carried on the Navajo verb. In other words, the Navajo syntax is expressed through the auxiliary while the semantic content is carried by English lexical verbs in their base form:

(49) a. áádóó nihi-room tɫiin áda-hw-ii-l-nééh
and then 1PL.POSS-room clean REFL-X-1DU/PL-CL-make
'And then we clean our room.'
b. bi-'éé' change íí-ɫééh
3SG.POSS-clothes change 1DU/PL-make
'We are changing her clothes.' (Schaengold 2004: 54f)

The Bilingual Navajo word order largely follows that of Navajo, which is ordered according to pragmatic roles (topic and focus) rather than syntactic roles. Overt discourse markers are carried over from Navajo, such as in Example (50), where *yę́ę* marks a previously mentioned item.

(50) [record player]-yę́ę
record player-PREV
'the previously mentioned record player' (Schaengold 2004: 60)

As Navajo is a tone language, intonation plays little role in marking sentence types. This has carried over to Bilingual Navajo. Polar questions are formed with a question particle (as in Example (51a)) rather than through intonation. Content questions are formed with Navajo question words (as in Example (51b)):

(51) a. book-ísh?
book-Q
'Is it a book?'
b. ha'át'íí bibiiyé tape recorder yilwoɫ?
what.3SG because.of tape recorder 3SG.run
'Why is the tape recorder running?' (Schaengold 2004: 47, 60)

An innovation in Bilingual Navajo is to use repetition for emphasis, typically once in Navajo and once in English:

(52) dį́į́'-go June fourth góne
four-SUB June fourth 3SG.inside
'on June fourth' (lit. on the fourth of June fourth in it) (Schaengold 2004: 61)

3.3.1.3 *Short text*

(From Schaengold 2004:71)

Diyin	God	bi-diné'é-nt'éé'	breastplate	jó	ałk'idą́ą́'	priest-s	danilǫ́	jó
holy	God	3SG.POSS-people-PST	breastplate	(you see)	long.ago	priest-PL	3PL.be	(you see)

Aaron	éí	dahoolzhiizh.	The	priest	wore	a	breastplate;	bikáa-gi	éiyá	precious
Aaron	DEM	3SG.happened	DEF	priest	wear.PST	INDEF	breastplate	3SG.on-at	DEM	precious

stone-s	dabi'dii'ní	gold	is	one	of	them	óola	wolyé-hígíí.
stone-PL	1PL.recount.PST	gold	be.3SG.PRES	one	of	3PL	gold	3SG.is called-NMLZ

'A long time ago God's people, the ones who were priests, you see, like Aaron (wore) a breastplate. The priest wore a breastplate with precious stones on it, we said that about it, gold was one of them.'

3.3.1.4 *Some sources of data*

There is as yet very little collected primary data on Bilingual Navajo. Schaengold (2004) provides numerous examples, many of them glossed, as well as some further references.

3.3.2 Michif: An N-V mixed language as a marker of a new identity[44]

3.3.2.1 *A brief background sketch of Michif*

Michif, also called *Mitchif*, *Métchif*, *Mitif*, *Cree* and *Turtle Mountain Chippewa Cree* by scholars, is called either *Michif* or *(aan) krii* by the speakers themselves. It is spoken by 50–200 people (Peter Bakker, p.c.), called Métis, in Western Canada (specifically Manitoba and Saskatchewan) and USA (in North Dakota and Montana). It is an N-V mixed language where French noun phrases combine with Cree verb phrases.

The Métis have their origin in mixed marriages between French-speaking fur traders and indigenous, or First Nations, women. This became common from the second half of the 18th century on. By the turn of the 19th century and the first decade of the 1800s a new identity had formed, where mixed people were identified as a separate ethnic group who called themselves *La Nouvelle Nation* ('The New Nation'). This may partly have come about as a form of resistance against new settlers who were brought in by fur trading companies in the first decades of the 19th century. There is evidence of Métis songs, a Métis flag and political manifestos. From then on, this new ethnic group had a distinct culture, such as a distinct economy, music and dance, art, clothing, cuisine, mythology and religion, with elements from both ancestor cultures as well as innovations.

Michif has always been used as an in-group language. It is likely that it emerged around the time in which the new ethnic identity emerged. However, it remained unknown for about a century before it was first mentioned in writing in 1946 by Anne de Mishaegen, who visited western Canada in the 1930s and who recognized Michif as a separate language:

44. This section is primarily based on Bakker (1997a) and (2013a). I am very grateful to Peter Bakker for his helpful comments on this snapshot.

> The Métis do not live in the middle of the woods like the Indians. They settle in the outskirts of the towns of the Whites, or they form true colonies, a separate little world, like, for example in Camperville on Lake Winnipegosis, where an extraordinary language is spoken consisting of Cree and French.
> (de Mishaegen 1946: 106, quoted and translated from French in Bakker 1997a: 165)

The fact that the language remained unknown for so long is an indication that the language was used only among the Métis and that other languages, such as French or Cree, were used with outsiders.

The Métis are typically a minority group in their communities and those who speak Michif are a minority within the Métis. In general the Métis are shifting to English. While there are conscious efforts both within the communities themselves and among academics to keep the language alive, Michif is declining. All of the speakers are middle aged or above and the language is not being transmitted to children, although grandparents may speak it with their grandchildren, which may lead to a limited, passive, knowledge.

3.3.2.2 *A short linguistic sketch of Michif*

It is a matter of debate whether Michif has one unified phonological system (cf., for example, Rosen 2007 and Prichard & Shwayder 2013) or whether it is stratified according to the source languages (cf., for example, Bakker 1997a & 2013a, Papen 2003). Irrespective of whether the phonemes are stratified according to etymological origin, Michif has the following 25 consonants: /p, ʰp, b, m, f, v, t, ʰt, d, n, r, s, z, ʃ, ʰʃ, ʧ, ʒ, ʤ, l, j, k, ʰk, g, kʷ, h/. The vowel system is very rich, with 11 short oral vowels: /i, y, ɪ, e, ɛ, œ, a, ɑ, ɔ, o, u/; 4 long oral vowels /iː, eː, aː, oː/; and 4 nasal vowels: /æ̃, ɑ̃, õ, ũ/. Words up to three syllables long have their primary stress on the final syllable, while words of four syllables or more have their primary stress on the antepenultimate (i.e. the third to the last) syllable. This pattern holds irrespective of the etymological origin of the words (Rosen 2006).

Michif has a rather mixed morphology due to the fact that the elements belonging to the noun phrase are essentially of French origin, while the elements belonging to the verb phrase are essentially of Cree origin. The largely isolating nature of the French nouns is thus carried over in the noun phrase while the largely concatenative nature of the Cree verbal system is carried over in the verb phrase. That is, Cree roots typically get Cree morphology, while French roots typically get French morphology.

Articles are obligatory. Gender and definiteness is distinguished only in the singular:

		SINGULAR	PLURAL
DEFINITE	M	*li*	*li:*
	F	*la*	
INDEFINITE	M	*æ̃*	
	F	*ɛn*	

It should be noted that the definite article is used in more contexts in Michif than in French:

(53) a. kahkɪja:w awljak la pwi dawe:stam-wak
all somebody DEF.SG.F rain want.it-3PL→4
'All the people want rain.'

b.	li	ste:k	si	la	ply	mijœr	vjãd
	DEF.SG.M	steak	be.3SG.PRES	DEF.SG.F	more	best	meat

'Steak is the best meat.' (Bakker 1997a: 87, 107)

Number is expressed analytically and obligatorily with the plural article *li:* preceding the noun, also in clauses with numerals:

(54)	a.	atɪht	manɪša	li:	brãš	da	li	za:br	uhčl
		some	cut.off.IMP.T12	ART.PL	branch	LOC	DEF.SG.M	tree	from

'Cut off some of the branches from the tree.' (Bakker 1997a: 110)

b.	trwa:	gi:wa:pama:wak	li:	fa:m
	three	saw.1SG→3PL	ART.PL	woman

'I saw three women.' (Bakker 2013a: 161)

Number may also be optionally indicated with demonstratives, which are derived from Cree and are inflected for gender (animate/inanimate), number (singular/plural), distance (close/intermediate/far) and pragmatic role (emphatic/non-emphatic).

Personal pronouns are derived from Cree and are only used for emphasis, as person agreement on the verb otherwise indicates the syntactic roles in the clause. There is no gender distinction in the third persons.

	SINGULAR	PLURAL
1-EXCL	–	*nɪjana:n*
1-INCL	*nɪja*	*kɪjana:n*
2	*kɪja*	*kɪjawa:w*
3	*wɪja*	*wɪjawa:w*

Possession is marked with possessive pronouns, which are derived from French, although Cree nouns are marked with Cree possessive affixes.

	SINGULAR		PLURAL
	M	F	
1SG	*mu/mũ*	*ma*	*mi*
2SG	*tu/tũ*	*ta*	*ti*
3SG	*su/sũ*	*sa*	*si*
1PL	*nɔt/nut*		*nu*
2PL	*vɔt/vut*		*vu*
3PL	*lœ*		*lœ:/ly*

Properties are either expressed by French-derived adjectives or by Cree verbal clauses (which function roughly like a relative clause).

The verb phrase follows the Cree system. Verbs agree with the subject of the sentence, as well as with the object in transitive sentences (as in *The man saw the dog*) and the indirect, or recipient, object in ditransitive sentences (as in *The man gave the girl a puppy*). The animacy of the subject and object affects the verbal morphemes chosen, as does the sentence type (such as main versus subordinate clauses and clauses containing a pragmatic focus). Tense, mood, aspect, voice, valency and conditionality are coded on the verb through affixation. Verb stems are derived "and contain at least two morphemes, traditionally called initials (expressing a state) and finals (expressing the way this came about and the grammatical status of the verb)" (Bakker 2013a: 161).

Word order is essentially free in Michif in the sense that it does not depend on the syntactic roles of the elements in the clause (which is indicated on the verb) but on pragmatic factors such as topic and focus. Polar questions are formed with the Cree question particle *čĩ* (or *či*), as in Example (55a). Content questions are formed with Cree question words which appear clause initially, as in Example (55b).

(55) a. ki:-ki:mučɪ-natustaw-a:w-ak ti: zami: čĩ?
2SG.PST-secretly-listen-3O-PL your.PL friend Q
'Did you eavesdrop on your friends?'
b. ta:nlnl li: livr ka:-utlnam-a:n?
which.PL ART.PL book COMP-take.it-TI1→4
'Which books shall I take?' (Bakker 1997a: 91f)

There is no copula in Cree, but there is one in French. In Michif predication can either be through juxtaposition of the noun phrase and the descriptive element (typically a verb phrase), or through verbalization of the noun, or with a fossilized form of the French *être* (*ili* < Fr. *il est* or *si* < Fr. *c'est*).

Complex sentences may be formed through subordinating affixes that attach to the verb.

3.3.2.3 *Short text*

(From Bakker 1997a: 78f)

Kaja:š ma:na li: šava:ž ki:pe:kɪjoke:wak ni:gɪna:hk. Wɪjawa:w ušta:čɪk
long.time.ago usually ART.PL Indian 3PL.came.to.visit 1PL.EXCL.POSS.house 3PL make.3PL

li: suji: mũ. Pi la vjãd ki:pa:šamwak. E:gwanɪgi li: sava:z ki:pa:šamwak
ART.PL shoe soft and DEF.SG.F meat 3PL.dry.by.heat 3PL.EMPH ART.PL Indian dry.PST

la vjãd. La vjãd ɔrɪja:l, la vjãd šovrœ, tut ki:pa:šamwak. E:gwanlma
DEF.SG.F meat DEF.SG.F meat moose DEF.SG.F meat.of deer all dry.3PL→3SG.PST that

e:gwa ki:šɪkwahamwak. Da:dibčca:k ki:a:šta:wak ma:na. Egwanɪma pɛmikɑn
now mash.3PL→3SG in.little.bags put. 3PL→3SG usually that pemmican

ka:šnɪhka:tahkɪk. Li: sava:z gi:kanawa:pama:nɪk e:ušɪta:čɪk ma:na.
call.1PL→3SG ART.PL Indian watch.PST. 1PL→3PL making.3PL→3SG usually

'A long time ago the Indians used to visit us at our house. They made moccasins and they dried meat. These Indians dried the meat. Moose meat, deer meat, they dried it all. This then they mashed. They used to put it in little bags. We called it pemmican. We used to watch the Indians when they made it.'

3.3.2.4 *Some sources of data*

There is a reasonable amount of primary data available for Michif, apart from the numerous glossed and translated examples in Bakker (1997a). Bakker & Fleury (2004) is an audio CD with accompanying text aimed at teaching Michif. The site *Learn Michif* (http://www.learnmichif.com/, accessed 8 February 2015) provides some lessons, videos of narratives and dialogues, as well as information on the Métis culture. An extensive annotated bibliography of Michif language resources can be found at http://www.metismuseum.ca/media/db/11686.

3.3.3 Sri Lankan Malay: An F-S mixed language as a marker of a new identity[45]

3.3.3.1 *A brief background sketch of Sri Lankan Malay*

Sri Lankan Malay, called *Ja basawa* in Sinhala and *Java mozhi* in Tamil and called *Melayu*, *Sri Lanka pe Melayu* or *Java* by the speakers themselves, is spoken in Sri Lanka and among the Sri Lankan diaspora. There are currently some 40,000 people listed as ethnic Malays in Sri Lanka. This figure, however, is not an indication of number of speakers for Sri Lankan Malay, since not all fluent speakers categorize themselves as Malay and, conversely, not all those that do categorize themselves as Malay are fluent speakers of Sri Lankan Malay. The language is in decline, as the younger generation of speakers is shifting to Sinhala, especially in the urban areas. The only area where Sri Lankan Malay remains vigorous and where most children grow up monolingual in the language is in and around the fishing village of Kirinda at the very south-east of the island. Sri Lankan Malay is unintelligible to other Malays speakers.

The origins of the Sri Lankan Malays are quite heterogeneous, which means that the ethnic and linguistic backgrounds of those termed 'Malays' that resettled in Sri Lanka are highly diverse, and mainly came from present-day Indonesia.[46] They were brought to Sri Lanka by the Dutch from the mid-1600s onwards. These were political exiles and convicts, as well as soldiers – the latter forming the largest group – who came from different places in a large area from Northern Malaysia to easternmost Indonesia. Many of the political exiles, typically nobility, were resettled with their families. This was also common for the soldiers, especially under British rule.

Despite their different origins, the 'Malay' seemed to have formed a rather cohesive community, held together by a common religion (the 'Malays' were typically Muslim) and by army ranks: while the social status of the deportees ranged from nobility to convicts and a large intermediate group of soldiers, the army may have provided a common basis for interrelations, since the Malay noblemen were frequently employed as military officers. Malay every-day life would thus to a high degree have evolved around military bases. Given this cohesion despite the different linguistic backgrounds, it seems reasonable to assume that the common language among the 'Malays' was some kind of vehicular Malay, possibly Bazaar Malay, which had, by then, already been widely used as a *lingua franca* in Southeast Asia for a considerable period.

It is a matter of debate to what extent the Malays intermarried with Sri Lankans, especially the Tamil Muslims, and to what extent such intermarriages were instrumental in the formation of Sri Lankan Malay. However, it seems without doubt that this rather cohesive Malay community was a minority in an area of Tamil and Sinhalese dominance. It is important to keep in mind that Sri Lanka was a multilingual (and multiethnic) society also under colonial rule. The absolute majority in Sri Lanka are Sinhalese, which in itself is likely to have led to widespread use of Sinhala

45. This section is based on Ansaldo (2008), Nordhoff (2009) and Slomanson (2013a).

46. Records mention the Moluccas, the Lesser Sunda Islands, Java, Bacan, Tidore, Timor, Madura and Sumatra as the origins of the first immigrants, among whom the immigrants from the Moluccas and Lesser Sunda Islands dominated; the other main group of immigrants were the soldiers, who were Batavian (Jakarta), Ambonese, Bandanese, Balinese, Buginese, Javanese, Madurese and Malay (Nordhoff 2009: 11ff).

by the Malays when dealing with non-Malays. The same would hold for the Tamil-dominated areas of the island. A possible source of Tamil influence, especially Sri Lanka Muslim Tamil, is likely to have been common religious practices. It is likely, then, that the language ecology of the Malay communities would have been their common Malay, as well as Sinhala and Tamil, with widespread and extended trilingualism.[47]

3.3.3.2 *A short linguistic sketch of Sri Lankan Malay*

Sri Lankan Malay has 25 consonants, /p, b, ^{m}b, m, (f), ʋ, t, d, ^{n}d, n, s, (z, ʃ), l, r, c, ɟ, ɲɟ, ɲ, j, k, g, ^{ŋ}g, ŋ, h/, three of which, /f, z, ʃ/, are only used in loanwords. The dental and retroflex stops (/t̪, d̪, ʈ, ɖ/) as well as the palatal affricates (/tɕ, dʑ, ^{ɲ}dʑ/), are allophonic to the apical and palatal stops. There are 6 vowels, / i, e, a, ə, ɔ, o, u/. All vowels except /ə/ may be lengthened, although vowel length is not contrastive but is conditioned by position in the word. Sri Lankan Malay allows moderately complex syllables, with maximally three onset consonants. Clusters do not occur in codas. Roots may have up to three syllables. Stress and tone are not relevant linguistic features.

The morphology of Sri Lankan Malay is complex. Stems consist of an obligatory root and optional additional roots (compounding) or derivational suffixes. To these stems optional inflectional affixes and clitics may be added. Concatenation, especially of clitics, is thus prolific. Quantifiers, adjectives and verbs may reduplicate.

There is no grammatical gender. Sri Lankan Malay has four cases, nominative (the base form), accusative (*=(n)ya(ng)*), dative/allative (*=na(ng)*) and ablative (*=dəri(ng)*):

(56) itthu baathuN=yang incayang SeelongN=dering laayeng
DEM$_{d}$ stone=ACC 3SG.POL Ceylon=ABL other
nigiriN=nang asà-baapi
country=DAT CP-bring
'These stones, he brought them from Ceylon to other countries.' (Nordhoff 2009: 199)

Plurality may optionally be marked with the invariant plural marker *pada*:[48]

(57) bannyak mlaayu (pada) Hambanthota=ka arà-duuduk
much Malay PL Hambantota=LOC NPST-exist.ANIM
'There are many Malays in Hambantota.' (Nordhoff 2009: 639)

There is no definite article, but there is an indefinite clitic *(h)a(t)thu*, which may cliticize on either side of the noun.

(58) a. hathu=haari, hathu=oorang [thoppi mà-juval]=nang kampong=dering
INDEF=day INDEF=man hat INF-sell=DAT village=ABL
kampong=nang su-jaalang pii
village=DAT PST-walk go
'One day, a man walked from village to village to sell hats.'

47. For a thorough discussion on the linguistic history of Sri Lankan Malay, see Nordhoff (2009).

48. But see Slomanson (2013b) for a different analysis, where nominal plural is considered obligatory and *pada* is analyzed as a suffix.

b. giini criitha=hatthu=le aada
like.this story=INDEF=ADD exist
'There is also a story like that.' (Nordhoff 2009: 319, 429)

There are two deictics, *ini* 'proximal' and *itthu* 'distal'. Possession is marked with the possessive clitic *=pe*.

(59) kithang=pe baapa=pe naama Mahamud
1PL=POSS father=POSS name Mahamud
'Our father's name is Mahamud.' (Nordhoff 2009: 345)

The personal pronouns inflect for three cases and have two politeness distinctions in the singular. Possessive pronouns are formed by adding the possessive clitic *=pe* to the nominative forms of the personal pronouns.

		NOMINATIVE	ACCUSATIVE	DATIVE	POSSESSIVE
1SG	FAM	*go*	*gonya/goyang*	*goḍang*	*goppe*
	POL	*se*	*senya/senyang*	*seḍang*	*seppe*
2SG	FAM	*lu*	*lunya/luyang*	*luḍang*	*luppe*
	POL	*lorang*	*loran(g)nya/lorangyang*	*lorangnang*	*lorangpe/lompe*
3SG	FAM	*de*	*denya/deyang*	*deḍang/dianang*	*deppe*
	POL	*incian*	*incianya(ng)*	*incenang/inciannang*	*incepe/inciampe*
1PL		*kitang*	*kitangyang/kitan(g)nya*	*kitanang*	*kitampe*
2PL		*lorang/lorampəḍə*	*lorangna(ng)*	*lorana(ng)*	*lorampe/lompe*
3PL		*derang/dempəḍə*	*deran(g)nya/dempəḍəyang*	*dempəḍəna(ng)*	*derampe/dempəḍəpe*

Adjectives may take verbal morphology, such as tense inflection and negation (compare (60a) with (60b & c)), as well as nominal morphology. The superlative may be expressed with *anà-* (as in Example (60d)):

(60) a. aanak thiiňğgi
child tall
'The child is tall.'

b. aanak arà-thiiňğgi
child NPST-tall
'The child is growing tall.'

c. aanak thàrà-thiiňğgi
child NEG.NPST-big
'The child is not growing tall.'

d. Seelon=ka anà-bìssar pohong
Ceylon=LOC SUPERL-big tree
'The biggest tree in Sri Lanka.' (Nordhoff 2009: 211ff)

Affirmative verbs are obligatorily inflected for one of three tenses: past (*s(u)-/s(i)-* or *anà-*), non-past (*a(rə)-/ar(à)-)* or future/irrealis (*a(n)t(h)i-)*. The perfect affix *-abbis-* is prefixed to a non-finite verb form and suffixed to a finite verb form. There is a progressive marker *ambe(l)*. The infinitive is marked with *mə-*. Finite verbs are negated with *thàr(à)-* (past) or *thama-* (nonpast) and non-finite verbs with *jamà-*. There are a number of modal particles and prefixes.

Word order is free, although the pragmatic topic tends to be clause initial. Polar questions are indicated with the clitic *=si*, which attaches to that portion of the clause that is being questioned:

(61) a. se=pe uumur masà-biilan=si?
1=POSS age must-tell=Q
'Do I have to tell my age?'
b. daging baabi=si anà-bìlli?
pork=Q PST-buy
'Did you buy pork?' (Nordhoff 2009: 512)

Content questions are formed with question words that remain *in situ* (i.e. at the position where the element questioned about would have been in a declarative clause). The imperative is marked with the particle *mari* and may also be marked for two politeness distinctions, indicated by suffixes on the verb: *la-* for polite imperatives and *-de* for informal imperatives. The prefix *jamà-* specifically denotes prohibitive.

There is an optional copula *(asà)dhaathang(apa)* derived from the verb *dhaathang* 'come'.

The quotative marker *kata* functions as a complementizer. Relative clauses are formed with a gap or the optional relativizer *=(n)ya(ng)*, which is homophonous with the accusative clitic.

3.3.3.3 *Short text*

(From Nordhoff 2009: 730ff)

Hathu hari Andare=le aanak=le mliiga=nang anà-pii. Incayang mliiga=nang kapang-pii,
INDEF day Andare=ADD child=ADD palace=DAT PST-go 2SG.POL palace=DAT when-go

Raaja hathu thiikar=ka guula asà-siibar mà-kirring simpang su-aada. Andare raaja=ka
king INDEF mat=LOC sugar CP-spread INF-dry keep PST-exist Andare king=LOC

su-caanya inni mà-kìrring simpang aada aapa=yang katha. Andare=yang mà-enco-king=nang
PST-ask DEM$_p$ INF-dry keep exist what=ACC QUOT Andare=ACC INF-fooled-CAUS=DAT

raaja su-bilang itthu paasir katha. Thapi=le Andare thàrà-jaadi enco. Andare
king PST-say DEM.DIST sand QUOT but=ADD Andare NEG.PST-become fooled Andare

[[bale-king=apa] raaja=yang mà-enco-king=nang] su-iingath. Andare aanak=nang su-biilang:
turn-CAUS=after king=ACC INF-fooled-CAUS=DAT PST-think Andare child=DAT PST-say

Aanak, [[[lu=ppe umma su-maathi] katha bitharak=apa] asà-naangis] mari! Suda
child 2SG.FAM=POSS mother PST-die QUOT scream=after CP-cry come.IMP thus

Andare=pe aanak=le baapa anà-biilang=kee=jo asà-naangis ambel su-dhaathang
Andare=POSS child=ADD father PST-say=SIMIL=EMPH cry take PST-come

Itthu=nang blaakang Andare guula thiikar=ka asà-lompath lu=ppe muuluth=ka=le
DEM$_d$=DAT after Andare sugar mat=LOC CP-jump 2SG.FAM=POSS mouth=LOC=ADD

paasir, se=ppe muuluth=ka=le paasir katha biilang~biilang baaye=nang baapa=le
sand 1SG=POSS mouth=LOC=ADD sand QUOT say~RED good=DAT father=ADD

aanak=le guula su-maakang
child=ADD sugar PST-eat

'One day Andare and his son went to the castle. When he was going to the palace, the King had sprinkled sugar in a mat and had left it to dry. Andare inquired from the King what it was that had been left (on the mat) to dry. To tease Andare the King said (that) it was sand. But Andare was not fooled. Andare thought that he should fool the king instead. Andare told his son: "Son, cry loudly and come towards me saying that your mother died!" So, Andare's son did exactly what he was asked to do and came crying (to the king). And then, Andare jumped on to the mat of sugar and crying out "Your mouth is filled with sand, my mouth is also filled with sand," repeating this over and over again they both ate sugar well.'

3.3.3.4 *Some sources of data*

Nordhoff (2009) is an almost encyclopaedic grammar of Upcountry Sri Lankan Malay, containing a vast amount of glossed and translated examples, as well as texts of different lengths. Bichsel-Stettler (1989) provides a number of texts from the Colombo area.

3.4 Summary

Mixed languages are languages that arose due to widespread community bi- or multilingualism and represent the fusion of two or a limited amount of identifiable source languages. They did not arise due to a need for a communicative bridge, but rather due to a need to express a unique identity. They may be the mother tongue of a community, or an auxiliary language. Typically the speakers of mixed languages are also proficient in one or both of the source languages.

Mixed languages are in-group languages. They are either markers of a new ethnic identity, for example descendants of mixed ancestry or descendants of a displaced population, or a marker of a retained ethnic identity, for example a minority group severely dominated socially and economically by some other ethnic group.

Mixed languages are typically intertwined in the sense that the grammar originates from one of the source languages and the lexicon from the other, or that the noun phrase and related components originate from one source language and the verb phrase and related components from the other. Converted mixed languages are those where the forms originate from one of the source languages and the structure from the other.

Theories on the formation processes of mixed languages vary. Unidirectional theories assume that the new language is a result of a speech community partly shifting to another language through code-switching or relexification. With paralexification an attempt is made to reverse a shift. Fusional theories assume that mixed languages came about due to the merging of the linguistic forms and functions of two or a few languages, but do not assume any directional shift from any given language to another.

3.5 Key points

- **Mixed languages are languages in their own right that emerged through the fusion of two or a few identifiable source languages in situations of large-scale community bilingualism.**
- **Speakers of mixed languages are often proficient in one or both/all of the input languages.**
- **Mixed languages are identity markers that arose due to expressive rather than communicative needs.**
- **Mixed languages usually arise as markers of a new identity or markers of a retained identity.**
- **Intertwined mixed languages are those where two/a few systems have fused to form a new system: G-L languages take their grammar from one source and their lexicon from the other while N-V languages take their noun phrase from one source and their verb phrase from the other.**
- **Converted (F-S) mixed languages are languages that have adopted the grammar of one language while retaining the lexicon of another.**
- **The types of mixed languages are not absolute divides but (strong) tendencies.**
- **The formation processes of mixed languages may be either unidirectional or fusional or a combination of both.**

3.6 Exercises

1. What is the difference between mixed languages and creoles?
2. In what way are mixed languages autonomous linguistic systems rather than just varieties of their source languages with instances of code-switching or borrowing?
3. What is the difference between intertwined and converted mixed languages?
4. What are the main sociolinguistic types of mixed languages?
5. What are the different theories on formation processes for mixed languages and how do they differ from each other?

Languages cited in Chapter 4

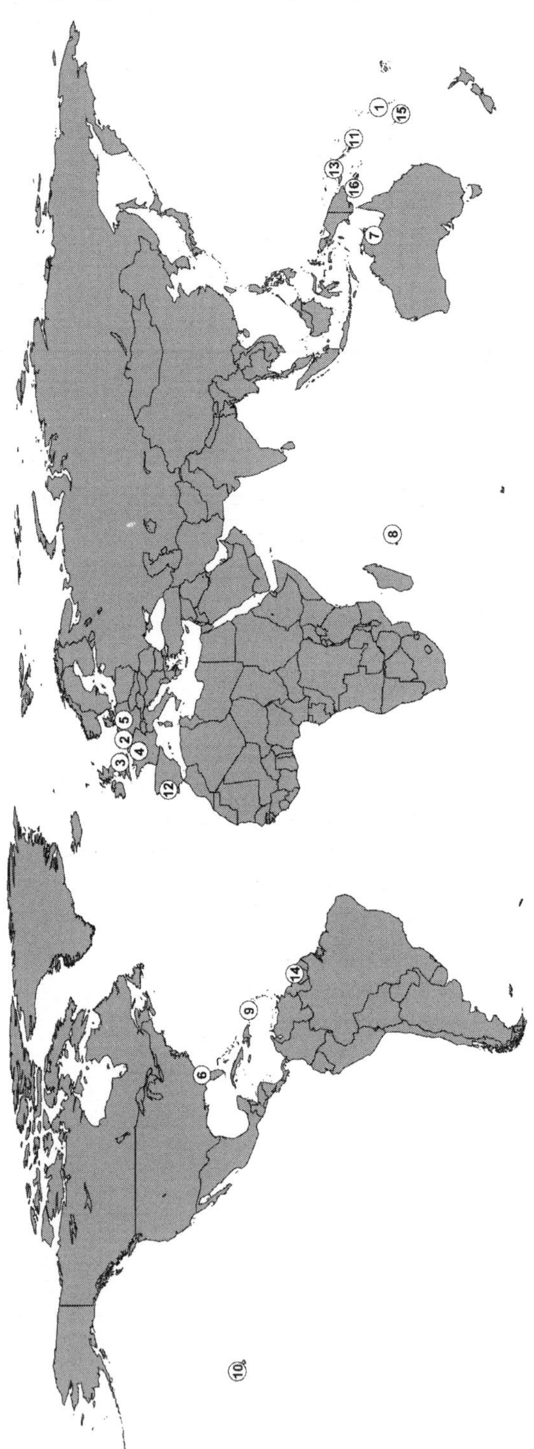

1. Bislama
2. Dutch
3. English
4. French
5. German
6. Gullah
7. Kriol
8. Mauritian Creole
9. Negerhollands
10. Pidgin Hawaiian
11. Pijin
12. Portuguese
13. Rabaul Creole German
14. Sranan
15. Tayo
16. Tok Pisin

Chapter 4

Sociohistorical contexts of pidgins and creoles

The majority of the languages we know today as pidgins, creoles or mixed languages emerged as a consequence of migration, colonization or slavery. This chapter will give a very brief overview of the European expansion, its motivations and consequences (Section 4.1) before bringing up a few demographic (4.2.1) and sociolinguistic (4.2.2) factors that are likely to have influenced the outcome of the contact languages. The role of diffusion is briefly mentioned (4.2.3). Section 4.3 gives short sketches of three creoles that emerged as an effect of European plantation colonies: Gullah (an English-lexified Atlantic creole), Mauritian Creole (a French-lexified Indian Ocean creole) and Rabaul Creole German (a German-lexified Pacific creole).

4.1 The European expansion

While there are a number of contact languages that are not related to any European languages, the vast majority of the languages that we today call pidgins, creoles and mixed languages emerged as a result of the European exploration and exploitation of the world. This section will give a very brief overview of the **European expansion** and its consequences. It is by no means possible to here do justice to such an immense topic and the following serves only as a very superficial background sketch. For a very accessible article-length overview of the European colonialism and imperialism, see, for example, Stuchtey (2011) with further references. An accessible introduction for the complete beginner to the European maritime exploration of the world and its consequences is Love (2006).

European trade had, until the end of the 15th century, mainly been dependent on land routes for such goods as spices, gems and cloth from Asia and, for example, gold from sub-Saharan Africa. With improved technology of ships, navigation instruments and maps it became possible for the Europeans to navigate the oceans. The Portuguese were the first to sail along the West African coast, initially with the aim of finding the mouth to the Niger in order to be able to find a ship borne passage to the gold mines of the Upper Volta region. The Portuguese were also the first to discover a sea route to Africa's southern tip in 1488 and then later rounding it in 1498, which opened up a sea route to Asia. This led to commercial operations whereby the Portuguese set up trading centres at strategic spots along the western African coast as well as along the South and Southeast Asian coasts. It is important to keep in mind that these were not territorial colonies, but simply centres for trading that were dependent on the local population and entered agreements of various kinds with them.

Spain was the first to discover a route to the Americas, with Christopher Columbus' 1492 voyage. This opened up new possibilities for trade and led to territorial occupation, initially of the Caribbean islands, but soon also on the American continent. The aim of the occupation was to amass riches, specifically heavy metals such as gold and silver.

The Dutch, English and French powers entered the colonial enterprise in the 17th century and made territorial claims of new areas as well as challenging those of Spain and Portugal.

This expansion spurred the economic revolution that had already started in Europe before the discoveries and settlements of the colonies. The gold from the colonies created a money economy and fostered **mercantilism**, which held that wealth can only truly be measured in gold and silver. Very simplified, according to this theory the purpose of the European colonies was to bring economic profit to the 'mother country' by providing raw materials (such as sugar, cotton, and so on) to Europe as well as acting as a market for the European manufactured goods (such as textiles) in order to strengthen the power of the 'mother country' (cf., for example, Magnusson 2003 and LaHaye 2008).

4.1.1 From homestead to plantation economy

In general, the main purpose of the colonial territories was, as mentioned, to produce raw material, such as crops of various kinds (e.g. cotton, sugar, tobacco, coffee, etc.), timber, and minerals, for the European colonizing power, the **metropole** or 'mother country'. Colonial territories also came to be of strategic value, not only because of the potential of resources, but also because their location might allow control of trade routes.

In the majority of cases acquired colonies were initially settled by small groups of people and their households. The settlers would claim and clear farmland for themselves, and set up farms for various kinds of crops, especially crops that could be exported, such as rice, tobacco, corn, and so on (Petitjean-Roget 1980). These farms, or **homesteads**, were typically smaller "semi-isolated social and economic units" (Chaudenson 2001: 12). In these homesteads the European farmers typically interacted with the labour force, which typically consisted of some slaves and/or European indentured labour and servants.

With the switch to labour intensive crops, such as sugar and cotton, farms grew into **plantations**, that is, large-scale agricultural units that produced goods in industrial, factory like conditions. On these plantations the European owners typically did not interact directly with the labour force, but employed middlemen.

The plantations demanded a high number of labourers; initially that might in previously populated regions, such as in Brazil, have meant indigenous labour. However, very soon plantations were dependent on labour import – in previously uninhabited areas this was of course the state of affairs from the start, and in previously inhabited areas labour import soon also became a necessity: European colonization almost invariably caused drastic population decimation, due to introduced diseases (such as smallpox, cholera, measles, tuberculosis, syphilis, influenza, and so on), which the indigenous population did not have any natural immunity to, as well as due to warfare during territorial expansion. Harsh working conditions on the plantations constituted an added cause of the depopulation. Plantation owners thus had to import labour in large numbers, which, depending on region, took the form of either slave labour (predominantly in the Atlantic and Indian Oceans) or indentured labour (predominantly the Pacific and Indian Oceans).

4.1.2 Plantations and mass migration

4.1.2.1 *European colonialism and slave labour*

Slavery has been a common phenomenon throughout history. In Europe it had decreased by the time the European explorations of the oceans started. With colonization, however, it was revived. The early Portuguese settlements on the Cape Verde Islands, Bioko (formerly Fernando Po) and São Tomé, for example, were largely established with West African slaves, a number of which were then brought to Portugal (Fernández-Armesto 1987).

The large-scale and systematic colonial slave trade coincided with the introduction of the plantation economy, especially the highly labour intensive sugar crop.[49] With the indigenous population decimated or extinct, the labour shortage was remedied through the import of slaves. In the Atlantic Ocean the **triangular trade** developed, where raw material, such as cotton, sugar, tobacco, coffee and so on, would be shipped from the plantations in the New World colonies to Europe, where it would be traded for manufactured goods, such as weapons, textiles, liquor and so on. The

49. While sugar had successfully been produced in, for example, Madeira and the Castilian Canary Islands with sharecroppers working the land, the prototype of what would later become the agricultural industries of the colonial plantation societies began on the Cape Verde Islands in the 1460s, with a "slave-based plantation economy, unprecedented in European experience since the ancient *latifundia*" (Fernández-Armesto 1987: 200).

manufactured goods would be shipped from Europe to West Africa, where it would be traded for slaves, who would be shipped across the so-called **Middle Passage** to the colonies in the New World and traded for raw material.

Approximately 11 million people were shipped as slaves from West Africa to the New World between about 1500 and 1900 (Eltis et al. 1999, Rawley 2005).[50] This trade involved the cooperation between the European trading forts and the West African kingdoms the European forts were located in (Baku 2011); since the Europeans were not able to make any territorial expansions due to the military power of the West African kingdoms, as well as due to the threat of diseases, they were completely dependent on African sellers of slaves (cf. Klein 1999, Rawley 2005).

Colonial slave trade was not confined to the Atlantic Ocean, but also took place in the Indian Ocean and to some degree in the Pacific Ocean. Slaves were shipped from West Africa, East Africa, Madagascar and India to the Indian Ocean island plantations.

4.1.2.2 *European colonialism and indentured labour*

Indentured labour is a form of contract labour where a person is bound per contract to work for someone else for a set amount of time (very often this bondage includes heavy debts that have to be paid off, for example debts for the travel costs of the migration). After the abolition of slavery, indentured labourers became the main workforce of the plantations (Northrup 1995). The plantations in the European Pacific colonies emerged due to the restructuring of the North American society after the Civil War, which led to the collapse of the sugar and cotton production (Brown 2007). These Pacific plantations were populated with indentured labour from the South Sea Islands (mainly Melanesia), Papua New Guinea, and insular as well as mainland Southeast and East Asia. In most cases these were young men who would sign up for three to five years' work on plantations, after which they could either sign on for another set amount of years or leave. While indentured labour is, in theory, not slavery, it is important to know that the conditions on the plantations were often slave-like. Furthermore, a number of labourers were "recruited" through so-called **blackbirding**, that is, trickery or even kidnapping (cf. Mortensen 2000, Brown 2007).

Indentured labour on the European plantations was not confined to the Pacific. After the abolition of slavery a number of European colonies in both the Indian and Atlantic Oceans recruited indentured labour, predominantly from Asia. For a very thorough discussion on the move from slavery to indentured labour in the European colonies, see, for example, Northrup (1995).

---

50. Another estimated 7 million were "shipped into the Indian Ocean or across the Sahara to the slave markets in the East" (Klein 1999:129). See further Klein (1999) and Rawley (2005) for a discussion on the demographic effects of the Atlantic slavery and its consequences for the West African kingdoms.

4.2 Contact languages as a result of the European expansion

One of the effects of the European expansion and exploitation of both the New and the Old World was relocation of peoples on a massive scale. This meant that people with different ethnic and linguistic backgrounds were brought together in situations where they had to be able to communicate with each other. Most of the languages that we today identify as pidgins, creoles or mixed languages are the result of these heterogeneous contact situations.

It is a matter of great debate how exactly these languages emerged. One important aspect of the emergence of these languages is to trace the demographic history of the region where they emerged, in order to establish which input languages were involved in the formation of the pidgin or creole, and, if possible, what degree of influence the input languages may have had. Those languages that arose as a result of the European expansion tend to have somewhat similar histories. This section will give a brief overview of some salient points that are typically brought up in connection with the sociohistory of pidgins and creoles, with focus on the earlier, formative, period. For thorough discussions on the sociohistorical and cultural contexts of the formation of pidgins and creoles, see, for example, Chaudenson (2001), Faraclas et al. (2007), Arends (2008), Jourdan (2008) and Singler (2008), to mention only a few. For a very thorough discussion on the sociohistorical and cultural circumstances of the formation of pidgins and creoles in the Asian context specifically, see Ansaldo (2009).

4.2.1 Demographic factors in creole formation

The plantation societies were highly unstable demographically, with high mortality and low growth rates. Continuous and large-scale immigration was therefore necessary in order to keep the plantations productive. This means that there would constantly be a high number of recently arrived people who would need to acquire some kind of communicative bridge. At the same time there would be a growing local population for whom this communicative bridge had become a standard means of communication. In other words, there is likely to have been a combination of L2 acquisition and L1 acquisition of the contact language in this heterogeneous setting. Relevant demographic factors for the formation of contact languages include information on the origins of the labourers, their life expectancy and age distribution, the ratio of men versus women and children versus adults, as well as the ratio of locally versus foreign born people in the colonies. Furthermore, the kind of access labourers had to the lexifier and linguistic role models is also likely to have affected the outcome of the contact language. This kind of information can only be gleaned through thorough archival research. For a very helpful guide on Dos and Don'ts in demographic research of plantation populations, see Arends (2008).

4.2.1.1 *Life expectancy, age distribution and population growth of the labourers*

The exceptionally harsh working and living conditions on the plantations, coupled with insufficient nutrition and exposure to new diseases, led to extremely low life expectancies for the plantation labour. Population growth was very low, with a low birth rate and high child mortality.

The preferred ages for the labour was between 15 and the mid-thirties (cf., for example, Moore 1981 and Postma 1990), that is, people at the height of their physical strength. However, children were also part of the labour trade, even though they were generally less profitable for the traders, since they cost as much to transport but fetched less in takings (Klein 1999).[51]

Mortality was high on the ships to the destinations, both in the slave trade and in the indentured labour trade, with the transatlantic slave trade showing the worst figures. Overcrowded ships, insufficient nutrition and lack of hygiene allowed for aggressive diseases; children and infants were the worst affected. It is fair to assume that the labourers, whether slaves or not, reached their destination in a state of exhaustion and severe trauma.

Once they had arrived they had to cope in an unfamiliar environment. Housing was crude, typically just makeshift and crowded shacks. The food was unfamiliar, the water could be contaminated and sanitation was poor, all of which again posed new threats of diseases. On top of this came overwork: "[t]he tasks were unfamiliar, the workday long, and the pace enforced by overseers and managers a test to their strength and stamina" (Northrup 1995: 104).

Coupled with this high mortality was the fact that birth-rates in the plantation societies were low and infant and child mortality was high (Arends 2008). The population therefore grew at a slow pace, which fuelled the need for labour immigration. We thus had societies where a constant stream of newcomers from different linguistic backgrounds were arriving, who had to learn the contact language as soon as possible to be able to function, while at the same time the local population, which would already be using the contact language, was growing only slowly. The implication of this would be that there would be a large population using an L2 variety, while the population using the contact language as an L1 variety would be growing at a slow rate. This might have affected the kinds of language models that were available in the society and how the emerging language might have developed.

4.2.1.2 *Men to women ratio of the labourers*

The ratio of men to women seems to have differed between the slave labour plantations and those worked by indentured labour. While men outnumbered women in all

51. For a discussion on the effect of the lack of the older generation and their acquired knowledge of tradition and history, see, for example, Jourdan (2008).

labour populations, the slave population of the colonies typically showed a less imbalanced ratio between the sexes than the indentured labour populations. In Haiti, for example, the ratio of women was around 40%, while it was about 45–50% in Martinique (Singler 1995: 215), French Guiana (Jennings 2009: 376), Brazil (Postma 1990: 230) and Mauritius (Baker 1982: 14, 26). Most slave traders in fact aimed for a 2:1 ratio of men versus women, because male slaves fetched higher prices (Postma 1990: 229, Moitt 2001: 26).[52] While the exact numbers would differ for different periods, the overall picture confirms that a 2:1 ratio was in fact achieved, with about 65% male to 35% female slaves in the transatlantic slave trade figures collected by Eltis et al. (1999).

In the Pacific, however, where indentured labour was the main type of workforce, the ratio of male to female immigrants to the plantations was initially much more unequal than that in the slave plantations. In Queensland, for example, women made up only 6% of the labour immigrants (Northrup 1995: 76), in Fiji only 8% (Siegel 1985: 54) This may partly have been due to the expectation that the men would return home after serving their contracts, after which plantation owners would recruit new workers. In other words, plantation owners with indentured labourers may not have had much interest in trying to secure a steady population growth; women were typically not desired as workers. Partly it may have been due to discouragement from their home societies as well as from the migrating men, for whom it was taboo to live in such close proximity with women as the intimacy of shared ship space entailed (Moore 1981: 105). However, once plantation owners started to aim for long-term labour forces, the number of immigrant women and families typically increased.

Very simplified, the relevance of male to female ratios of labourers lies in the potential for children being born to the immigrants in the plantation societies. The fewer women of child-bearing age, the slower the proportion of locally born children with two immigrant parents would have increased. This is likely to have had an effect on the rate of L1 acquisition of the emerging contact language.

4.2.1.3 *European to non-European ratio and locally versus foreign born population*

While the plantation societies were typically ethnically (and thus, presumably, linguistically) heterogeneous, the population would in the majority of cases consist of two major groups: the European population and the non-European population. Most typically the societal hierarchy saw European plantation owners and officials at the top, followed by merchants and small farmers, followed by European contract labourers, followed by slaves or, later, non-European indentured labourers.

52. But see Klein (1999: 165):

> The sexual imbalance in the departing Africans was especially determined by African supply conditions. African women, both free and slave, were in high demand within Africa, and it was this counterdemand that explains why fewer women entered the Atlantic slave trade.

However, as mentioned above, the colonies seldom started out as plantation economies. During the initial settlement the colonies were typically homestead societies, with smaller farms. During this period the ratio of Europeans typically outnumbered or was equal to the non-Europeans. The two groups, Europeans and non-Europeans, typically interacted intensely with each other. For instance, settlers and labourers would share space and work on the farmsteads together (cf., for example, Gautier 1985, Chaudenson 2001, Singler 2008). This was the case for Réunion in the Indian Ocean, Louisiana and the southern Atlantic Coast states in present-day USA (Chaudenson 2001, Klein 2013a), as well as for São Tomé in the Gulf of Guinea (Hagemeijer 2013a), and Trinidad, the Bahamas, and the present-day US Virgin Islands in the Caribbean (Mühleisen 2013a, Hackert 2013, van Sluijs 2013b), to mention only a few examples. The implication is that the non-Europeans had close and intense access to potential linguistic models for European languages.[53]

With the change to plantation economy and the increasing demand for labour the ratio of Europeans to non-Europeans typically decreased dramatically. With this demographic change the level of interaction between Europeans and non-Europeans changed. Now the majority of labourers would not interact directly with Europeans, thus removing them from the potential linguistic models of European languages.

Although population growth was slow, eventually the locally-born labour did grow in numbers. In the Caribbean a difference was made between '**Creoles**', i.e. those slaves who were born in the colonies, and '**Bozals**', i.e. those slaves who were born in Africa. As the locally born population increased, the linguistic models for the newcomers would increasingly be the locally-born labourers, who were increasingly likely to have grown up with the contact language as one of their first languages.

At this stage it is important to also point out that these societies were multilingual. It is reasonable to assume that the substrate languages, the ancestor languages of the labour immigrants, continued to be spoken where possible. It is also reasonable to assume that children born to the labour population would grow up multilingual, acquiring the language of the plantation society as well as the language(s) of their caretaker(s) – as pointed out by Singler, "for African children born in the Caribbean, I do not assume the creole to be the only first language or, particularly in the child's first few years, necessarily the primary one" (1995: 218). It is thus fair to assume that the shift from ancestor languages to the contact variety went through stages of speaker bi- or multilingualism (Muysken 2008), as indeed was the case in Hawai'i (Roberts 2000).

53. It should, however, also be kept in mind that not all households had slaves, which means that ratios of Europeans to non-Europeans are only rough indications of potential interaction. If, for example, a newly established colony had 100 Europeans and 100 non-European slaves, but only 1/3 of the Europeans owned slaves, the non-Europeans would outnumber the Europeans on the slave-owning farms (Baker 2002).

These demographic changes are events that redefine the speech community and thus may have an effect on the development of the contact language. Baker (1982) and Baker & Corne (1986) set out a framework for how important events may shape the formation of a given creole language. **Event 0** (cf. Arends 1994b) is when the colony is founded. **Event 1** is when the number of substrate speakers (slaves or indentured labourers) surpasses the number of superstrate (or lexifier) speakers. From now on the non-Europeans have reduced access to Europeans as linguistic models, in proportion to the ratio of Europeans to non-Europeans. This means that new labour arrivals increasingly have to learn the lexifier language from other substrate speakers, i.e. the linguistic models of the L2 learners were themselves not native speakers of the lexifier language. **Event 2** is when the number of locally-born substrate speakers surpasses the number of superstrate speakers (whether foreign- or locally-born). At this stage access to superstrate speakers is further reduced and the contact variety may stabilize into a separate language, a creole. Furthermore, the contact language may at this stage acquire a function as an identity marker, as a language belonging to the locally born labour class as opposed to foreign born labourers, as well as opposed to the ruling class (cf. Jourdan 2008, Singler 2008). **Event 3** is when mass labour immigration stops. From now on there are no large-scale arrivals of people speaking the substrate languages, reducing the potential influence of L1 transfer from the ancestor (substrate) languages to the contact language. Typically the substrate population would shift from the ancestor languages to the contact language within a few generations. **Event X** (cf. Roberts 2000), which may occur at any stage between Event 0 and until after Event 3, is when the number of locally born substrate speakers surpasses the number of foreign-born substrate speakers. From now on the ancestor languages are increasingly replaced with the contact language.[54] The Events are summarized in Table 4.1:

Table 4.1 Demographic events that may influence the formation of a contact language.

Stage	Characterization
EVENT 0	Colony is founded.
EVENT 1	Substrate population surpasses superstrate population.
EVENT 2	Locally-born substrate population surpasses total superstrate population.
EVENT 3	Mass-importation of labour stops.
EVENT X*	Locally-born substrate population surpasses foreign-born substrate population.

* Event X may occur at any time between Event 0 and until after Event 3, but typically occurs between Events 1 and 3.

54. It's important to notice that Event X may occur at different points for different ethnic groups. In Hawai'i, for example, the Portuguese were the first to nativize, i.e. where the locally-born proportion of Portuguese exceeded that of the foreign-born Portuguese. This happened almost 30 years before the overall proportion of the locally-born substrate population outnumbered the foreign-born one (Roberts 2000).

Table 4.1 shows the landmark demographic transitions that may affect the formation of a creole. It is postulated that the relative timing between the Events has linguistic consequences for the emergence of a contact language. Arends (2008:317f) tentatively puts forth that the later Event 1 occurs, the less chance there is of a creole emerging; the later Event 2 occurs, the less chance of an emerging creole stabilizing; the later Event 3 occurs, the greater the chance that a given creole remains an autonomous language variety; and, finally, the later Event X occurs, the more a given creole will differ from its lexifier (cf. Singler 1992).[55]

4.2.1.4 *The origins of the population groups*

The input languages are of fundamental importance to the outcome of the contact language. A way of trying to gauge the input languages and their relative influence on the pidgins or creoles is to investigate the origins of the colonizers as well as the labourers, assuming that the origins of the populations involved gives an indication on the languages they spoke.

When it comes to the superstrate population, it is important to notice that colonies were often settled by people from different European backgrounds: "the fact that a colony belonged to a particular European nation does not mean that that nation's language was the only, or even the major, European language spoken in the colony" (Arends 2008:314). In the Dutch Virgin Islands, for example, just over half of the households were non-Dutch (see Section 2.4.1 on Negerhollands). Likewise, in 1678 only just over half of the European population in the British colony of St. Kitts was English (Parkvall 1998:66). In 1737, half of the plantations in the Dutch colony Suriname were owned by non-Dutch Europeans (van den Berg & Smith 2013). In 1803 more than two thirds of the Europeans in the British colony of Trinidad were non-British (Mühleisen 2013a).

It is also important to keep in mind that the Europeans, whether settlers or labourers, may not have spoken the standard, or metropolitan, varieties of the European languages, and they certainly did not speak the standard varieties of today. Rather, it is more likely that the Europeans spoke the dialects of the regions of their origins, which were likely to have been economically disadvantaged regions. Chaudenson (2001:66), for example, has shown that the French settlers in the French colonies primarily came from the western and central areas of France, and are likely to have spoken the dialects of those regions. Furthermore, many of them, both settlers and labourers typically came from "modest social backgrounds" (Chaudenson 2001:67), which means that it was likely that they spoke nonstandard varieties of French and would have different levels of literacy in the given regional variety. Where possible, census data might be an

55. Notice, however, that this ignores the relative size of the superstrate population, which is also likely to affect the outcome of the contact language (Roberts 2000:263).

indication of the origins of the settlers, and thus what languages and language varieties they may have spoken.

When it comes to the substrate population, archival information on where labour embarked on the ships has been taken as an indication of the ethno-linguistic origins of the slaves and indentured labourers. Detailed information on the ports of embarkation, the number of slaves taken on, and where they were shipped to has been collected for the Transatlantic slave trade (see, especially, Eltis et al. 1999), as well as for the Indian Ocean (see, especially, Baker 1982 and Chaudenson 2001). However, it should be kept in mind that the location of the forts and the points of embarkation for the ships are not likely to coincide with the origins of the slaves that those forts traded with. It is not feasible to assume that Europeans were able or even willing to go on slave raids around their trading forts, given their exposed position: they were dependent on the goodwill of the kingdoms in which the trading forts were located, who, for example, demanded taxes for their trading privileges. Moreover, the military power of the host kingdoms as well as the high mortality of the Europeans, due to malaria and other diseases, would have further prevented the Europeans from any kind of systematic slave raiding. They therefore had to rely on African slave traders, whose slaves were typically from the interior rather than the coastal areas: "[s]laves in numbers sufficient to fill the holds of the slave ships only arrived to the coast via African merchants willing to bring them from the interior" (Klein 1999: 106). The languages spoken today around the slave forts and points of embarkation should therefore not automatically be taken as substrate languages. Rather we must try as well as possible to establish the likely interior areas that would supply certain forts and ships, and which languages were likely to have been spoken in those interior areas at the time. It should be noted, however, that even if we were able to establish those facts, we would have extremely limited access, if any, to the kinds of varieties spoken in the given areas at the time.

The indentured labour trade occurred mainly in the 19th and 20th centuries, a period for which archival information is generally more available. Detailed investigations on the origins of the indentured labour during the colonial era as a whole can be found in Northrup (1995).

Very broadly stated, the general assumption is that, all else being equal, the substratal input language(s) with many speakers had more influence on the outcome of the contact language than the substratal input language(s) with few speakers.

4.2.2 Sociolinguistic factors in creole formation

We should never forget that language is used in interaction between people in the societies they populate. Each time interaction takes place a host of issues are involved, such as the relationship between and the identities of the interlocutors. Sociolinguistic factors such as power, prestige and identity are thus also important to consider in the context of the emergence of contact languages. As mentioned, these were highly multilingual societies, where it is fair to assume that, for an extended period of time, a large part of the population was multilingual (Muysken 2008). Different groups of people would have had different levels of interaction with each other, which may have affected not only the outcome of the contact language, but also the choice of language variety used.

4.2.2.1 *Levels of interaction*

The plantation societies had a multilayered social stratification. As pointed out by Arends, these were not simply severely dichotomized societies, "with a small number of whites holding power over large numbers of African slaves" (Arends 1994b: 19), but more complex in structure. This means that different groups of people would have different levels of interaction with each other, which is likely to have had an effect on the type of register or linguistic variety used, as well as access to various linguistic models.

As mentioned above, plantation colonies typically saw a hierarchy among the Europeans, with officials and large planters at the top, then merchants, then small farmers, then European labourers. Within the plantation the owner would be at the top of the hierarchy, followed by plantation managers, followed by European plantation overseers, followed by the European skilled labourers. Figure 4.1 shows a schematic representation of the plantation hierarchy, based on Arends (1994b: 19).

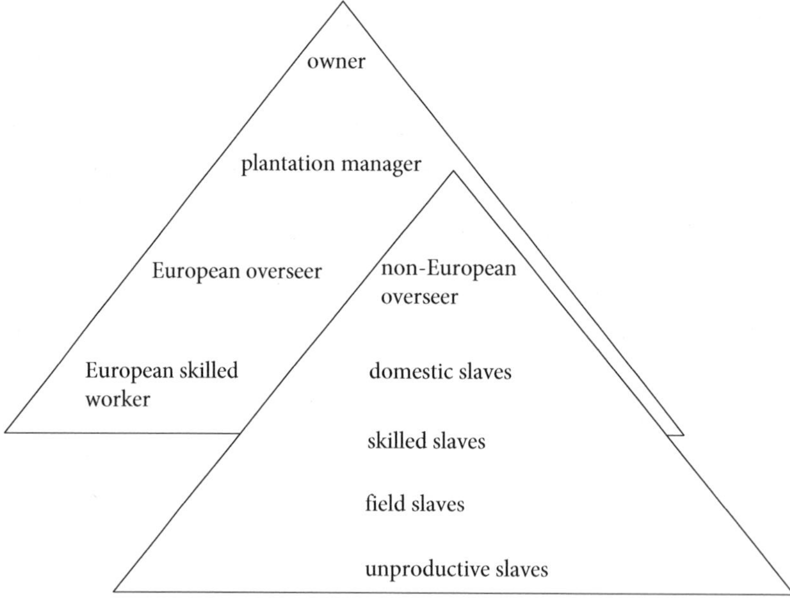

Figure 4.1 A schematic representation of the plantation hierarchy of the Atlantic colonies. From Arends (1994b: 19).

Within the slave population on the plantations the non-European overseer(s) would be at the top of the hierarchy, occupying roughly the same position as the European overseer. These non-European overseers thus had a high status; they were in charge of the running of the slaves, such as allocating tasks, meting out punishments, determining whether a slave was fit for work or not, and so on. This was therefore a position of considerable power. It is likely that the slave overseers had a considerable amount of interaction with both the Europeans and the slaves, since they were intimately involved in the running of daily affairs. One step down in the hierarchy from the non-European overseer were the domestic slaves, who were servants to the Europeans. They occupied roughly the same social position as the European skilled labour and would have had considerable interaction with the Europeans. Within the domestic slave labour the 'creole mama' occupied a special position. She, usually an elderly woman, took care of the younger European children and is therefore likely not only to have had considerable interaction with the Europeans, but also to have had an influence on the language acquired by these children. Lower down the social scale were, in descending order, skilled slaves (craftsmen such as carpenters, coopers, and so on) and field slaves (working the field; this typically made up about half of the slave labour population) and, at the bottom, so-called 'unproductive slaves' (who did various tasks, for instance hunting and fishing). The skilled slaves would have had some interaction with the Europeans, but the field slaves and the 'unproductive slaves' are likely to have had minimal interaction with the superstrate population.

We now also need to take into account that these multistratal organizations are likely to have involved a number of linguistic varieties. For example, a British plantation owner might have spoken one regional variety of English. The manager might have spoken some other variety, or maybe even a different European language. The European overseer might have spoken yet another variety of English or maybe yet another European language. The white labourers are likely to have spoken different varieties, possible even different European languages. The slaves would have had different linguistic backgrounds. To assume that (metropolitan) English would have been the target because the plantation owner was from the British Isles risks simplifying the picture considerably.

While there is no evidence for exactly how much interaction there was between different social groups, and what kind of interaction this would have been, it seems reasonable to assume that the differences in status and tasks would have had an effect on the amount of access people had to various linguistic models. It also seems reasonable to assume that these multilingual and multistratal societies saw a number of different linguistic registers, i.e. that, depending on the linguistic backgrounds of the people at the various levels in the hierarchy, there was a fair amount of **lectal diversity** or **diglossia** (see further Chapter 7), where speakers would use prestigious language varieties in certain situations and less prestigious varieties in other situations. This is very often the case in multilingual societies today. For example, it does not seem far-fetched to assume that a non-European overseer could have used one linguistic variety when discussing affairs with the plantation management and European overseers, while using another variety when talking with the slaves.

4.2.2.2 *Levels of prestige*

We might also do well in exerting some caution about what exactly the target language was. The tacit assumption is generally that a metropolitan variety of the colonizing language was the linguistic target for all population groups involved in the settlement and that any aberration from that target was due to various factors beyond the control of the speakers. This disregards several sociolinguistic aspects.

First of all, we have seen that the origin(s) of the superstrate population was or were typically mixed, and often associated with non-standard varieties of the European languages. If these settlers functioned as linguistic models for the immigrant labour population, then we should expect the outcome to deviate from any standard European language variety.

Secondly, it presupposes that the labour population tried, and failed, to properly acquire the European languages of the colonizers. This may or may not have been the case. Baker, for example, proposes that "participants in contact situations, motivated by the desire to solve the problem of interethnic communication, set about creating a new language and succeeded in that endeavour" (Baker 1995:13).

Third, it ignores the potential role of identity. It does not seem unreasonable to assume that the language associated with the superstrate population, the power holders, would have carried with it **overt prestige**. However, as pointed out by Singler,

> language is not simply about communication; it is also about identity and membership. The cost of sounding more like one's superiors, i.e. one's colonial masters, is that one also sounds less like one's fellows. ... In the circumstances of race-based enslavement on the plantation, the notion that everyone wanted to talk as white as possible is, to say the least, improbable. (Singler 2008:344).

It therefore also does not seem far-fetched to suggest that the labour population might have attached **covert prestige** to a language variety of their own, one that was common to the entire workforce – thus solving the problem of communication between different ethno-linguistic groups – but was different enough from the language of the power holders to serve as a solidarity marker among the labourers (cf. also Milroy 1987, 2002 for discussions on the social value of non-standard or stigmatized language varieties).

Fourth, it ignores the potential of the contact language as an expression of a new cultural identity (cf. also Jourdan 1991 and Muysken 2008:291). Jourdan (2008) argues that the contact languages may not only have functioned as a marker for a new social identity, but also as a form of resistance against hegemony, essentially serving as a form of empowerment for its creators.

> For not only did pidgins[56] allow for communication to take place among workers and cause the breaking down of their linguistic isolation, but the developing pidgins also allowed for the crystallization of a nascent cultural identity, different from, yet in relative continuity with, that of the European cultures found locally and that of the vernacular cultures of the workers. … Resistance to hegemony is not limited to the use of force; it often has to do with seizing whatever space is devoid of controls and claiming it. In this case, the void was linguistic. All the while, pidgin makers were developing a new cultural identity that could now be expressed in words. (Jourdan 2008: 373)

The contact language could therefore have carried its own (covert) prestige as an expression of solidarity with a new, unique culture, which resisted the authority of the power holders, making it a desirable linguistic target in its own right.[57]

4.2.2.3 *Missionaries and education*

A further factor that is likely to have influenced the outcome of the contact language is European missionary activity and European schools.

Missionary activity accompanied the European expansion from very early on. While there is evidence that many missionaries attempted to learn the indigenous languages of the populations they came into contact with, there is also evidence for missionaries conducting their work and dealing with their congregations in the colonizers language or even in the contact language.[58] As such they are likely to have functioned as linguistic models for the converted. In Suriname, for example, the Moravian Missionaries began using a form of Sranan in church around 1780, and this variety of Sranan, "Church Sranan" became more prestigious than the "common creole" (Voorhoeve 1971).[59] The first missionaries to Hawai'i learned and used a jargon version of what would become Pidgin Hawaiian (Roberts 2013a). The Saint-Louis

56. Notice that Jourdan (2008) uses 'pidgin' as a cover term for both pidgins and creoles.

57. As pointed out by Philip Baker, by automatically assuming a European target language for the speakers in these contact situations "the linguist is helping to perpetuate the widespread belief, which underlies the negative attitudes toward these languages often held by educationists, that pidgins and creoles came into being because of human failure to achieve something 'better'" (Baker 1990: 117).

58. For a discussion on the different roles and ideologies of the Catholic versus the Protestant/Puritan Churches in the European colonies, see, for example Faraclas et al. (2007: 242ff).

59. Christian Ludwig Schumann produced one of the earliest Bible translations in a creole language (Sranan): *Tori va wi Massra en Hepiman Jesus Christus. Die Geschichte unsers Herrn und Heilandes Jesu Christi, aus den vier Evangelisten zusammengezogen* (1781), MS (EBG Suriname 12/617), Moravian Archives, Utrecht.

settlement which led to the emergence of Tayo in French Caledonia was founded by French Marist missionaries (Ehrhart & Revis 2013).

In a number of colonies schools were set up and conducted in the colonizer's language. However, it may not necessarily have been the case that the teachers, who would have taught in the colonizer's language and who are likely to have been linguistic models, were themselves native speakers of that language. Furthermore, it is also likely that the language that was spoken in the classrooms was not necessarily the language that the peers spoke with each other in the school setting outside the classrooms. In Hawai'i, for example, Standard English was the required language for the classrooms, very often taught by L2 speakers of Standard English. On the playgrounds, however, the creole was the norm (Sato 1985). It is possible that the school environment was influential in the development of Kriol, with the boarding school of the Anglican mission at Roper River near Ngukurr in northern Australia (Schultze-Berndt et al. 2013). However, it would again have been a case of children using the contact language among themselves, rather than in the classrooms. Likewise, Rabaul Creole German was created and used by the children of immigrant labourers to the German colony plantations and their local wives at the German boarding schools they were sent to. While German was used in the classrooms, the creole was used among the children in all other communication (Volker 1989a). For more on Rabaul Creole German, see 4.3.3.

4.2.3 Diffusion

Another important factor in the history and development of pidgin and creole languages is the role of **diffusion**. As has been mentioned repeatedly, the colonial societies were dynamic and typically in a constant state of fluctuation. There was intense contact between the colonies and regions.

The European powers competed for and fought over colonial territories, meaning that a particular region could change hands between nations. Whether due to change of power or for other reasons, it was not uncommon for settlers to move to new (colonial) locations, more often than not bringing their slaves with them. It is likely that this also meant that whatever contact language had been used in the old location would be brought to the new location and either served as a potential role model for other settlers and their slaves, or blended with whatever existing contact language(s) that was encountered in the new location, or a combination of both. St. Kitts was an early European colony in the Caribbean, shared by the English and French. Starting towards the end of the 17th century, Kittitians migrated to other parts of the Caribbean, such as Barbados, Antigua, Suriname, Jamaica, Guyana, St. Vincent and what would become the Gullah-speaking area of USA (Baker 1998).

An important role for diffusion was played by the Sephardic Jews who had fled the inquisition on the Iberian Peninsula and settled in what was then the Dutch colony of Pernambuco in the northeast of Brazil. When the Portuguese reconquered the colony in the mid-17th century, the Sephardic Jews resettled in other regions of the New World, including the Caribbean. They brought with them their slaves, as well as the knowledge and technology of large-scale sugar cultivation, which had been practiced in Brazil for several decades. This was one of the main triggers for what has come to be termed the sugar revolution, which saw the wide-spread shift from homestead to plantation economy and which boosted the triangular trade.[60]

Ship crews as well as indentured labourers are likely to have relocated repeatedly, taking whatever contact variety they may have acquired with them and spreading them to new locations. In the Pacific plantation labourers frequently changed plantations, bringing the contact language they had acquired with them. Also, in a number of cases the contact language that plantation workers brought back home with them became a useful communicative bridge between people of different linguistic backgrounds, and the contact languages gained ground and became major languages in the home region too. This, for instance, was the case with Tok Pisin in Papua New Guinea (cf. Section 1.4.3), as well as Bislama in Vanuatu (Meyerhoff 2013a) and Solomon Islands Pijin (Jourdan & Keesing 1997, Jourdan & Selbach 2004; cf. Section 12.4.2).

There was thus a fair amount of contact between these heterogeneous societies and settings, as well as between regions of contact languages. Baker & Huber (2001), for example, investigated 302 features in 13 English-lexified Atlantic and Pacific contact languages and found that 75 were attested both in the Atlantic group and in the Pacific group.

4.3 Snapshots

Most of the Atlantic creoles emerged in European colonial plantation societies that relied on slave labour and the triangular trade between the New World, Europe and West Africa. Gullah is an example of such a language. The Indian Ocean creoles emerged in colonial societies which typically started out with slave labour from both Africa and South Asia, then relied heavily on indentured labour, primarily from South Asia, once slavery had been abolished. Mauritian Creole is an example of such a language. The European colonies in the Pacific typically relied on indentured labour from the start.

60. As shown by Higman (2000), it was not simply sugar as a crop that caused this economic and agricultural change; other labour-intensive crops, such as indigo, did not lead to an equivalent of the sugar revolution. In fact, sugar could be, and was, cultivated profitably by various other systems, such as land leasing, shareholders and small farmers with cooperative central mills, or other systems, such as mobile crushing mills and boiling equipment. Rather, it was a combination of the crop and "the incipient pre-sugar concentration of land holding, the existence of an enslaved population, and the moral acceptability to the colonial state of the status of the enslaved" (Higman 2000: 229) that led to what would become the industrial-like monoculture of the colonial plantation societies.

All European colonial societies saw missionary activities of various Christian denominations. Rabaul Creole German is an example of a language that emerged as a result of a German missionary boarding school in German colonial Papua New Guinea, where the children of immigrant fathers and local mothers were taught and housed.

4.3.1 Gullah: An English-lexified Atlantic creole[61]

In memory of Thomas Klein

4.3.1.1 *A brief background sketch of Gullah*

Gullah, sometimes also called *Sea Island Creole* by scholars, is spoken in the US Atlantic coastal belt from the south-eastern corner of North Carolina, stretching over South Carolina and Georgia down to north-eastern Florida, as well as on the Sea Islands. The exact number of speakers is not known; a high estimate is a maximum of about 10,000 monolinguals (Klein 2013a). The speakers themselves call their language either Gullah, or, in Georgia and some areas of South Carolina, *Geechee* (in these areas 'Gullah' usually refers to the people than the language).

What would become the rice-growing area in the coastal south-eastern US began as the South Carolina colony, settled in 1670 from the British colony of Barbados by small groups of whites and their black slaves. The first black slaves to be settled on the south-eastern US Atlantic coast were thus from the Caribbean and for the first 25 years they were in a clear minority, outnumbered by about 3:1 by whites. However, from about 1695 slaves arrived from Africa in such high numbers that by 1710 blacks outnumbered whites (Wood 1974: 131). By the end of the 1700s the ratio was about 1:100 whites to black. With the expansion to Georgia slaves were initially brought from South Carolina, but, again, very soon the number of slaves from Africa increased and by 1776 the black and white population of Georgia had reached numerical parity (Klein 2013a).

Slaves newly arrived from Africa were taken straight to the plantations and put through a learning process of about two years. They were assigned "teachers" (called "drivers") who spoke mutually intelligible varieties of West African languages and who were experienced in the ways of the plantation. The newcomers were expected to learn English – food was used as an incentive: lack of progress was punished by withholding it – and, after a while, various labour tasks. Their language models were thus other slaves who spoke the same or similar varieties of West African languages as the newcomers. It is worth noticing that that the groups assigned to each "driver" would all speak mutually intelligible varieties and presumably spoke with each other in this new environment. This fact, coupled with the uneven ratio of whites to black, means that substrate influence is likely to have been high at this stage.

Importation of slaves continued well after the abolition of slavery in 1808, with the last cargo arriving in Georgia in 1858. The land acquired by freedmen after the Civil War was "a foundation for Gullah and Geechee homesteads up to the present" (Klein 2013a: 140).

61. This section is based primarily on Klein (2013a). I am very grateful to Thomas Klein for his helpful comments on this snapshot. His premature departure in the autumn of 2014 is a great loss for us all and he will be much missed as a very dear friend and colleague. This snapshot is dedicated to his memory.

Most speakers of Gullah are proficient in other American English varieties (African American Vernacular English, Southern American English and/or Standard American English). There is concern that the language is endangered and that younger speakers are shifting to other American English varieties. Gullah has typically been a spoken language only, but written works have started appearing and the Gullah/Geechee Nation produces bilingual media. In 2006 the US Congress designated the Gullah-Geechee Heritage Corridor, which may also help curb the current shift from Gullah.

4.3.1.2 *A short linguistic sketch of Gullah*

Gullah has 21 consonants, /p, b, m, ɸ, β, t, d, n, s, z, ɹ, l, ʃ, c, ɟ, ɲ, j, k, g, ŋ, h/, and 12 vowels, /i, ɪ, e, ɛ, a, ə, ʌ, ɑ, ɔ, o, ʊ, u/. The bilabials /ɸ/ and /β/ are nowadays often realized as /f/ and /w/. Gullah is non-rhotic. Tone is not a relevant feature. Syllable structure can be complex, with up to three consonants in the onset and two in the coda, as in *strens* 'strength', although the final *-t*/*-d* is often elided (Klein 2013a: 142).

The morphology is predominantly analytical. There is some reduplication, denoting intensity:

(62) *ɲam* 'to eat' → *ɲamɲam* 'to eat, to devour'
dɛ 'there' → *dɛdɛ* 'exactly there, correct' (Turner 2002 [1949]: 235)

Gender is largely irrelevant in Gullah, although natural gender for animals may occur through compounding with 'man' and 'woman', as in *ʊmə cɪkɪn* 'hen' (lit. 'woman chicken') and *man cɪkɪn* 'rooster' (lit. 'man chicken') (Turner 2002 [1949]: 230). Plural is optionally marked with the English forms (*-s* or irregular) or with a postposed plural marker *dem*:

(63) a. piece-s
piece-PL
'pieces'

b. twenty-four bed
'24 beds'

c. de leader dem
ART leader PL
'the leaders' (Klein 2013a: 142)

The plural marker *dem* may also indicate associative plural, as in *Sarah dem* 'Sarah and those associated with her'.

Generic NPs are not marked (e.g. *Dog eat scrap* 'Dogs eat scrap') while specific NPs are marked with either the definite article *de* (in both singular and plural) or the indefinite article *a* (singular only).

There is no gender distinction in the pronominal system and the subject and object personal pronouns differ only in the first person singular and the third persons (but notice Example (65a) and the text below, where object forms are used in subject position). Number distinction is relevant for all forms, although the third person singular object pronoun may also be used in plural contexts:

	SUBJECT	OBJECT
1SG	*a*	*me*
2SG	*ya*	*ya*
3SG	*e*	*um*
1PL	*we*	*we*
2PL	*oona*	*oona*
3PL	*dey*	*um/dem*

The possessive pronouns are identical to the object personal pronouns, except in the third person plural, which is *dey* (as the subject form). Reflexives are formed by adding *-se(l)f* to the possessive pronoun forms.[62]

Possessive constructions may be expressed by juxtaposition only (e.g. *Sister Campbell house* 'Sister Campbell's house') or with the English analytical *of*-construction (e.g. *foot of de tree* 'foot of the tree').

Adjective forms are invariant. The comparative may be formed with *mo na* 'more than':[63]

(64) a. i big mo na ʊnə
3SG.S big COMPAR 2PL.O
'He is bigger than you.' (Turner 2002 [1949]: 215)

The superlative may be formed with *di moɹɪs* 'the morest'. Both the comparative and the superlative may be formed with the English forms *ə* (<*er*) and *ɪs* (<*est*).

All tense, aspect and mood markers are preverbal and may combine in various ways. There are two tense markers: *been/bin* 'ANTerior/PAST' and *going/g(w)ine/ga* 'FUTure'. There are four aspect markers: *done* 'PERFective', *duh/da* for various imperfective connotations (or, with stative verbs, even a perfective reading), *duhz* for repeated activities and *be* for repeated states of affairs. There are several modal markers. Lexical aspect is significant in that an unmarked form indicates past tense or habitual for non-stative verbs, but the present tense for stative verbs (Mufwene 2004).

Negation may be expressed with *nə*, *ə̃* (<*ain't*), *dõ* (<*don't*) or *-n* (<*n't*). There is negative concord (as in (65a, b)):

(65) a. mi nə gwɒin fə no flɒwə
1SG.O NEG going for NEG flour
'I'm not going for any flour.'
b. ɒɪ ẽ gɒɪn go pɪk nʌn dɛ
1SG.S NEG FUT go pick none there
'I won't go and pick any there.'
c. ɒɪ dõ kəmplen
1SG.S do.NEG complain
'I don't complain.' (Turner 2002 [1949]: 210, 219, 264)

The word order is subject-verb-object for both declaratives and polar questions; the latter may be indicated through either level or rising intonation (Turner 2002 [1949]: 253). There is a question marker (*ɛnti* <*ain't it*), which may appear either at the beginning or the end of the clause. An interrogative inverted word order only seems possible with *ain't*. Of these three options, marking

62. This pronominal system reflects the one represented in *De Nyew Testament* (Sea Island Translation Team 2005).

63. Turner also listed *pas* 'surpass' as a possible comparative form, though this seems actually to have been a mistake, since none of his texts contain the construction. Also, it is not found in Seminole Creole, which is archaic compared to Gullah (Ian Hancock, p.c.).

polar questions with interrogative intonation seems the most common (Klein 2013b). Question words appear sentence initially in content questions. The predicative and equative copula may be expressed through a form of *be*, while the locative copula is expressed by *dɛ*.

Clauses are coordinated with the coordinating conjunctions *and*, *but* and *or*. There is a quotative sɛ (<*say*), which is identical to the complementizer. There are a number of subordinators. Relative clauses may be formed with *weh* or *wa/what*:

(66) da gyal (weh) Clinton duh look at
ART girl REL Clinton IPFV look at
'The girl (that) Clinton is looking at.' (Mufwene 2004: 364)

Serial verb constructions are prolific:

(67) a. i tɛk stɪk kɪl əm
3SG.S take stick kill 3SG.O
'He killed it with a stick.'

b. dɛm gɒɪn tɛk əm go bak
3PL FUT take 3PL go back
'They are going back in company with them.' (Turner 2002 [1949]: 211)

4.3.1.3 *Short text*

(From Turner 2002 [1949]: 262ff, retranscribed and glossed in Klein 2013a: 146; this is an excerpt of a text recorded by Lorenzo Dow Turner in 1932. The speaker, Diana Brown of Edisto Island, SC, was 88 years old at the time.)

Aɪ bɪn ʌp sɪstə kʲaməl hɐʊs, ən ə pil sʌm pətetə pʊt an do. Sɪstə kʲaməl,
1SG.S PST up Sister Campbell house and 1SG.S peel some potato put on door Sister Campbell

a sɛ, ju ɛβə si kʲat it ɹa tetə skɪn? Sɪstə kʲaməl sɛ, sɪstə, sʌpm
1SG.S say 2SG.S ever see cat eat raw potato skin Sister Campbell say Sister something

də kʌmɪn. It ɪz staβeʃən dɛ, bʌt dɛm pipl nə no. A sɛ, dɛm bʌkɹə sɛn
IPFV coming HL is starvation LOC but them people NEG know 1SG.S say them buckra send

φi ʝa φə φid βi, ɛn dɛm kʲa əm gi dɪ ɲaŋ pipʊ βɛ də βʌk dɛ an
feed here for feed 1PL and 3PL.O carry 3SG.O give ART young people REL IPFV work LOC on

dɛm ples. De en də gʲi əm no βɪdʌ.
3PL.POSS place 3PL.S NEG IPFV give 3SG.O NEG widow

'I was up at Sister Campbell's house, and I peeled some potatoes and put them on the door. 'Sister Campbell,' I said, 'have you ever seen cats eat raw potato skins?' Sister Campbell said, 'Sister, something is happening. There is starvation there, but those people don't know.' I said, 'those white people [from the Red Cross] sent food here to feed us and they carried it to the young people who were working there on their place. They wouldn't give any to a widow.''

4.3.1.4 *Some sources of data*

The Gullah New Testament (*De Nyew Testament*, Sea Island Translation Team 2005) gives 900 pages of written data. It includes the English version. The Gullah/Geechee Nation (http://gullah-geecheenation.com/, accessed 8 February 2015) has a bilingual blog, ezine and newsletter (*De Conch*), as well as links to bilingual TV (Gullah/Geechee TV Nayshun Nyews) and radio (Gullah/Geechee Riddim Radio) broadcasts. Various materials, including a selection of beautifully narrated and illustrated tales in Gullah, can be found at the *WatchKnowLearn* site (http://www.watch-knowlearn.org/, accessed 8 February 2015).

4.3.2 Mauritian Creole: A French-lexified Indian Ocean creole[64]

4.3.2.1 *A brief background sketch of Mauritian Creole*

Mauritian Creole, usually called *Kreol* by the speakers themselves, is also known as *Morisyen* (pronounced /moɣisjẽ/) by those who promote the language and *Patois* (pronounced /patwa/) by its detractors. It is the first language of most of the 1,300,000 inhabitants of Mauritius (including its dependencies of Rodrigues and Agalega), located east of Madagascar in the Indian Ocean, as well as of the Mauritian diaspora in Europe and Australia.

The Dutch occupied Mauritius in 1598, but the colony did not prosper and was abandoned altogether by 1713. French occupation began in 1721. Less than a decade later, non-Francophones already formed a majority of the population. By 1736 there were slaves from Madagascar, North and South India, Senegal, Benin and East Africa, as well as Tamils paid to work as artisans. By the latter part of the 18th century the dominant plantation crop was sugar.

Mauritius came under British rule in 1812, giving English exclusive official status, but without seriously diminishing the position of French. Slavery was abolished in 1835, although many had freed their slaves before that. Freedmen were required to remain on the plantations for several years, but most ex-slaves refused to work for the low wages offered and abandoned the plantations. This, combined with expansion in sugar production, led to the importation of Indian indentured labour on a truly massive scale; within 30 years people of Indian descent formed two thirds of the population, adding Bhojpuri as a major language in rural areas.

With the advent of free primary education in the 1950s, Mauritian Creole became the main language on playgrounds, while children were exposed to English and French in the classrooms. French was the dominant language of the media and formal situations, whereas English was primarily used in education and the government.

Mauritius became independent in 1968, since when there has been a slow improvement in the status of Mauritian Creole. French remains dominant in the media, while English, the only official language, is largely limited to government and education.

64. This snapshot is contributed to Philip Baker.

4.3.2.2 *A short linguistic sketch of Mauritian Creole*

The transcription of the Mauritian Creole examples in this section follows that outlined in Baker & Hookoomsing (1987): vowel+*ṁ*/*ṅ* indicate a nasal vowel; the acute accent (´) marks potentially stressed syllables; vowel+*r* in word-final or pre-consonantal position indicates an elongated vowel or centring diphthong.

Mauritian Creole has five vowels, /i, e, a, o, u/, three of which can be nasalized (/ẽ, ã, õ/). The schwa (/ə/) is becoming increasingly frequent in words where this French vowel had originally been replaced by /i/ (as in /dəlo/ 'water', traditionally /dilo/) and is also heard in some words from English (e.g. /ɣəgbi/ 'rugby'). There are 18 consonants, /p, b, m, f, v, w, t̪, d̪, n, l, s, z, ɲ, j, k, g, ŋ, ɣ/, plus /ʧ/ and /ʤ/ which now occur in many words of non-French origin and have phonemic status for some speakers. Except in word-final position, /ɲ/ varies freely with /nj/. The reverse is also true: /maɲeə/ (< Fr. *manière*) 'manner'. The voiced velar fricative /ɣ/ only occurs in pre-vowel position. Mauritian Creole differs from most other French-lexified creoles in that many etymologically nasalized vowels have become denasalized, particularly in word-final position, as in, for example, *píma* (< Fr. *piment*) 'chilli', *lamé* (< Fr. *la main*) 'hand'.

Mauritian Creole is a stress-timed language.[65] Most words contain one syllable that is normally stressed, but if two such syllables occur in close proximity, one of them may lose its stress. Certain high frequency words are unstressed in all circumstances, such as subject pronouns, tense/aspect markers, conjunctions and articles. Stress placement is contrastive:

(68) a. *refér* 'to recover' ~ *réfer* 'to make/do again'
b. *en* 'INDEFinite ARTicle' ~ *én* 'one' (Baker & Kriegel 2013: 253, 255)

The morphology is typically analytic, although reduplication may be used with adjectives to indicate augmentation or intensification (preposed adjectives with word-initial stress) or attenuation or diminution (postposed adjectives with word-final stress):

(69) a. *en gráṅ lakáz* 'a big house' → *en gráṅgraṅ lakáz* 'a very big house'
b. *en simíz rúz* 'a red shirt' → *en simíz ruzrúz* 'a reddish shirt'
(Baker & Kriegel 2013: 254)

If both occurrences of a reduplicated verb retain their stressed vowel, the interpretation is augmentative, whereas if only the second bears stress, it has a diminutive or more casual interpretation:

(70) *márse* 'walk'
márse-márse 'walk a long way/for a long time'
mars-márse 'go for a little walk' (source: Philip Baker, p.c.)

65. In stress-timed languages stressed syllables fall at approximately regular intervals. Unstressed syllables are thus shortened to fit the rhythm.

All nouns have a single, invariable form; plurality may be optionally marked with the invariable *ban*. There is no grammatical gender. The indefinite article is preposed *en*. Postposed *la* is generally described as the definite article, but it can also be regarded as a demonstrative. An unusual feature of this is that it can only occur as the final item in an NP:

(71) zom ki met en sapo la
man who wear a hat *la*
'The (that) man who is wearing a hat.' (source: Philip Baker, p.c.)

The presence of *sa* before the noun and with *la* as the final element in the NP gives an unambiguous demonstrative reading (but this is far less frequent than *la* alone).

In the pronominal system the subject forms are identical to the object forms, except in the first and (familiar) second person singular:[66]

	SUBJECT	OBJECT
1SG	*mo*	*mwa*
2SG.FAM	*to*	*twa*
2SG.POL	*u*	*u*
3SG	*li*	*li*
1PL	*nu*	*nu*
2PL	*zot*	*zot*
3PL	*zot*	*zot*

Notice that number distinction is made in the second person, but that the second and third persons plural have identical forms. The possessive pronouns are identical to the dependent subject pronouns except in the third person singular, which is *so*.

Possession may be expressed either through juxtaposition or with the possessive pronoun:

(72) lisyeṅ Sesil / Sesil so lisyeṅ
dog Cécile Cécile 3SG.POSS dog
'Cécile's dog' (Baker & Kriegel 2013: 255)

The great majority of the Mauritian Creole verbs have two forms: a long form usually with a final *-e* (which occurs clause-finally), as in (73a), and a short form without the *-e* (which is found when an NP immediately follows the verb), as in (73b):

(73) a. Moník ti sáṅte
PN PST sing
'Monique sang.'
b. Moník ti sáṅt en zóli sáṅte
PN PST sing INDEF nice song
'Monique sang a nice song.' (source: Philip Baker, p.c.)

66. It should be mentioned that *mwa* and *twa* were also subject pronouns; *mo* and *to* are unstressed abbreviations of these which emerged slowly in the 19th century.

There are five tense and aspect markers: *ti* 'PAST', *a/va/ava* 'INDEFinite FUTure', *pu* 'DEFinite FUTure', *pe* 'PROGressive' and *fin* 'PERFECT'. The base form may indicate present tense or, once a past context has been established in a narrative, the past tense. There are a number of modal auxiliary verbs. The invariant negator *pa* precedes all verbal markers.

The word order is subject-verb-object. Polar questions are formed through rising intonation or with the tag *nóṅ?* 'no?'. Content questions are formed with the question word *ki* or *(ki) senla ki* 'who, what'. There is no change in intonation. There is no overt copula in declarative sentences.

Clauses may be coordinated through juxtaposition or with conjunctions, such as *e* 'and', *avek/ek/ar* 'and; with', *me* 'but', *ubyeṅ* 'or'. There are a number of subordinators.

Relative clauses are formed with the optional *ki* 'who(m), that'. The demonstrative/definite article *la* must occur at the end of the NP:

(74) Mári ti zwàn tifí (ki) Gásen pu màrye la
Marie PST meet girl REL Gassen FUT marry DEF
'Marie met the girl (who) Gassen is going to marry.' (Baker & Kriegel 2013: 254)

As with the majority of the French-lexified creoles, the first consonant or syllable of many Mauritian Creole nouns derives from the French article, such as in *zóm* 'man' (<French *les hommes*), *laví* 'life' (<French *la vie*), *lezó* (<French *les os*). It is important to notice that these are the base forms of the nouns; the initial consonant or syllable does not indicate definiteness.

4.3.2.3 *Short text*

(Text supplied by Philip Baker)

Éna dé dók; en sél láṁbilaṅs. Letáṁ u labá, li dír u láṁbilaṅs
have two dock INDEF single ambulance time 2SG.POL over.there 3SG tell 2SG.POL ambulance

pa lá. Li'n práṅ lót, li'n ále. Letáṁ sá, dimún la pe mór ísi. Párfwa,
NEG there. 3SG.PRF take other 3SG.PRF go time that person DEF PROG die here sometimes

mísye Vyé bízeṅ práṅ so masín. En bláṅ li rézone. Zis lí tu sél
Mr Wiehe must take 3SG.POSS machine One white 3SG be.reasonable Just 3sg all alone

fér sa ísi. Mísye Vyé... dimún gréne aṅba bál, mór, sipa kát-seṅk táse aṅba
do that here Mr Wiehe person collapse under bale die if.NEG four-five trapped under

bál, lí, li práṅ par kát-seṅk, li mét daṅ so lóto, li ále. Li p'éna okén
bale 3SG 3SG take by four-five 3SG put in 3SG.POSS car 3SG go 3SG NEG.have any

obzéksyoṅ lí, li pa fyér, li pa naryéṅ, mísye Vyé. Li aksépte, li práṅ li,
objection 3SG 3SG NEG proud 3SG NEG nothing Mr Wiehe 3SG accept 3SG take 3SG

kaṅmém ar so páke disáṅ tú. Li mét daṅ so lóto. Me, éna lezót,
even.though with 3SG.POSS quantity blood all. 3SG put in 3SG.POSS car but have others

zot pa fér li. Éna ínyoraṅ daṅ zót. Disáṅ nwár pu fán daṅ zot lóto...
3PL NEG do 3SG have uncivilized in 3PL blood black for spread in 3PL car...

'There are two docks; only one ambulance. When you get there, you are told that the ambulance isn't there. It has taken someone else, it has left. Meanwhile the injured person is dying here. Sometimes Mr Wiehe has to take his vehicle. He's a reasonable Franco-Mauritian. He's the only one who behaves like that here. Mr Wiehe… If someone collapses under a bale and dies, with perhaps four or five trapped under the bale, he will take the four or five, put them in his car, and set off. He would have no objection. He isn't haughty, he isn't anything bad, Mr Wiehe. He would agree to take him even if he was bleeding profusely. He would put him in his car. But others wouldn't do that. Some are uncivilized [and wouldn't let] black blood spoil their car…'

4.3.2.4 *Some sources of data*

A wealth of primary data can be found in Anonymous (1980). Baker & Fon Sing (2007) lists 60 texts, many of them reproduced, from the period 1734–1929; the texts as well as a concordance of all the words of the 60 texts (100,000+ words) have been made available online by Guillaume Fon Sing (http://concordancemmc.free.fr/, accessed 8 February 2015). Baker (1972) is a grammar of Mauritian Creole, containing numerous examples. Syea (2013) is also a grammar and also contains numerous glossed and translated examples.

4.3.3 Rabaul Creole German: A German-lexified Pacific creole[67]

4.3.3.1 *A brief background sketch of Rabaul Creole German*

Rabaul Creole German, called *Unserdeutsch* ("Our German") by the speakers themselves, is a moribund (nearly extinct) German lexified creole spoken by up to 100 people in Papua New Guinea (around Rabaul in present-day East New Britain) and Australia (Brisbane and Sydney) (Péter Maitz via Craig Volker, p.c.). All fluent speakers are over 60 years of age (Craig Volker, p.c.).

Germany established control over the Bismarck Archipelago and Kaiser-Wilhelms-Land in 1884 and set up a plantation economy. As mentioned above (Section 1.4.3), the labour force on the German plantations initially spoke Malay, then the newly imported pidgin English that became Tok Pisin (see 1.4.3). The German New Guinea Company administration did not take steps to introduce German as a mode of communication (Mühlhäusler 1984).

Rabaul, on the Gazelle Peninsula, was made the capital of the German colony around the turn of the century. The town was ethno-linguistically highly diverse, with the white population consisting of settlers, traders, plantation owners and missionaries from Germany, other European countries and Australia, and the non-white population consisting of Micronesian overseers and policemen, Filipino sailors, Ambonese clerks, Chinese and Melanesian labourers and skilled workers (Volker 1991). Most of these immigrants were men without their families, many of whom formed relationships with local women. In 1897 a school was established by German Catholic missionaries at Vunapope near Rabaul for the children of these immigrant colonists, labourers and visitors born to the local women. From early on, by 1903 at the latest, the school was a boarding school that only allowed visits home to the mothers' villages during holidays. The children were thus not regularly exposed to any of their parents' languages; typically the children of those families where the non-indigenous father was present had at most picked up a few phrases or

67. I am very grateful to Craig Volker for his helpful comments on this snapshot.

words from the father's language, but tended to know the mother's language to varying degrees as well as Tok Pisin (which was often the household language). However, many children arrived at the school as toddlers and would have been too young to have much command of any language (Volker 1991:146).

The pupils were taught in German and were only allowed to use German in the classrooms. However, among themselves the children used their own variety:[68]

> The oldest speakers of Rabaul Creole German I was able to interview would not have been at the school when it was first started, but they said they had been told that the language began when students started 'putting German words into Pidgin [i.e. Tok Pisin – VV] sentences', and in the dormitories students would consciously make up new expressions and constructions using the words they were learning in class. (Volker 1991:146)

After the Australian invasion in 1914 the medium of instruction was changed from German to English; however, many of the teachers had a poor command of English. German was therefore still used as a fall back language. At the same time the school began taking in many more pupils from a very young age (some merely infants).

A settlement grew near the mission of former pupils, who, as adults, tended to marry among themselves. Many remained and worked at the mission. Typically, Unserdeutsch was spoken at home, Normaldeutsch ("Normal German" a local colloquial form of Standard German) was spoken with the missionaries and Tok Pisin was spoken with other New Guineans.

Most of the Rabaul Creole Germans moved to Australia when Papua New Guinea gained independence, settling primarily in the Brisbane and Sidney areas. Already in the early 1990s the language was in steep decline, with children learning the language only if they grew up in a family where both parents spoke Rabaul Creole German and "where a grandparent plays a constant role in child rearing" (Volker 1991:149).

4.3.3.2 *A short linguistic sketch of Rabaul Creole German*

Although there seems to have been a certain amount of variation between individual speakers with respect to the Rabaul Creole German phonological system, the following segments seem generally consistent: 16 consonants, /p, b, m, w, t, d, n, s, ʃ, l, r, ç, k, g, ŋ, h/, and 11 vowels, /i, y, ɪ, e, ɛ, ə, a, ɔ, o, ʊ, u/ (Volker 1982).[69] Most final consonants tend to be elided:

68. This is very similar to the situation that led to the emergence of the mixed language Bilingual Navajo (see 3.3.1), showing how fluid these language type categories are. In fact, Volker (1989b, 1991) postulates that the motivation for the emergence of Rabaul Creole German was as an identity marker and a secret language, rather than due to communicative needs. For an overview of the various proposed motivations for Rabaul Creole German, see Strommer (2013).

69. The velar fricative /χ/ was recorded but was uncommon. The front rounded /ø/ and mid high /ɨ/ were recorded but appeared very rarely.

(75)	/aŋs/	'afraid'	(cf. St. German /aŋst/	'fear')
	/gəsa/	'say.PTCP'	(cf. St. German /gəza:gt/	'said.PTCP')
	/bɛr/	'mountain'	(cf. St. German /bɛʁk/	'mountain')
	/bryda/	'brother'	(cf. St. German /bru:dɐ/	'brother')
	/gekɔmə/	'come.PTCP'	(cf. St. German /gekɔmən/	'come.PTCP')
	/dɔ/	'but yes'	(cf. St. German /dɔχ/	'but, even so, anyway')

(Volker 1982: 22ff)

Notice that the German[70] uvular fricative /ʁ/ has become the alveolar /r/. Likewise, the German velar fricative /χ/ became the palatal fricative /ç/, which in turn tends to become /h/ word-medially. The Standard German /v/ became /w/, as in /was/ 'what' (cf. St. German /vas/). The Standard German affricates became fricatives:

(76)	/dasu/	'to that'	(cf. St. German /dat͡su:/	'with/to it/that')	
	/flansuŋ/	'plantation'	(cf. St. German /pflant͡suŋ/	'planting')	(Volker 1982: 23)

Some German affixes have been kept, such as derivational prefixes and suffixes. Compounding is common. Lexical verbs derived from English or Tok Pisin get the verbal marker *-en* (< St. German *-en* 'INFinitive'), as in *watʃən* 'to watch' (Volker 1982: 30).

Number is indicated with the plural marker *alle* 'all':

(77) a. ʃtɔr wo alle boi kɔm
store where PL indigenous come
'(The) store where the indigenous (people) come.' (Volker 1989a: 155)

b. alle klane mɛnʃ, di hɔlən dise buç
PL small person 3PL get DEM book
'The boys, they are getting those books.' (Volker 1982: 30)

Notice that the plural marker is dropped after a demonstrative. Case is not relevant for Rabaul Creole German, although there is a first person singular object pronoun form contrasting with the subject form (see below). There is no grammatical gender.

The personal pronoun system makes an inclusive/exclusive distinction in the first person plural:

	PERSONAL	POSSESSIVE
1SG	*i(ç)*	*man*
2SG	*du*	*dan*
3SG	*er* (M)/*si* (F)	*san*
1PL INCL	*uns*	–
1PL EXCL	*wir*	–
2PL	*oi*	*oiə*
3PL	*di*	–

70. To speak of "German" phonemes and to make reference to Standard German is a simplification: exactly which varieties of German the missionaries spoke has not been established, but it is fair to assume that it was not exclusively Standard German. In fact, it may well be that the majority of the missionaries spoke non-standard versions of German.

There is an object form *mi* 'me' (< St. German *mich*), although not all speakers make the subject/object distinction. Notice that in the pronoun system above the Standard German politeness distinctions have been dropped. The male/female distinction is not universally made and only concern natural gender. Most typically *er* is used gender neutrally in all contexts. There is no neuter form for the third person singular. The subject pronoun is optional in the clause if the referent is clear from the context.

Although there are possessive pronouns (though none were recorded for the first and third persons plural), the typical way of expressing possession is with the possessive marker *fi*:

(78) a. ɛsɛn fi du is sys
food POSS 2SG COP.3SG sweet
'Your food is good.'
b. də stɔv fi wir is gɛl
ART stove POSS 1PL COP3.SG yellow
'Our stove is yellow.' (Volker 1982: 34)

Another way of expressing possession is through juxtaposition ((79a)) or, less commonly, with a genitive *-s* inflection ((79b)):

(79) a. disɛ kar di tire is heruntergegaŋe
DEM car ART tyre COP.3SG flat
'This car's tyre is flat.'
b. man fater-s hɔs
1SG.POSS father-GEN house
'My father's house.' (Volker 1982: 42)

There are two demonstratives, *das* 'that' and *disɛ* 'this/that', none of which inflects for number.

Adjectives obligatorily take the adjectival suffix *-e* in prenominal position, but do otherwise not inflect. In postnominal position the *-e* suffix is ungrammatical. Comparison is expressed analytically with *mer* 'more'.

(80) a. der klanə mɛdhə(n) sagə(n) / *der klan mɛdhən sagən
ART small girl say
'The small girl says…'
b. Gale is mer klan / *Gale is mer klane
PN COP.3SG more small
'Gale is smaller' (Volker 1982: 37)

There is an optional indefinite article *an(e)* 'a' (identical to the numeral 'one') and an optional definite article *de(r)* 'the'. Both are invariant. The definite article is dropped with the plural marker.

The verb does not inflect for person or number of the subject. The base form is typically identical to the Standard German infinitive form. There is optional tense inflection: the past tense may take the optional (invariant) past marker *hat* plus a verb form inflected for the past (< St. German participial):

(81) i (hat) gelesə(n) buç
1SG PST read.PST book
'I read the book.' (Volker 1982: 44)

However, with verbs of motion the invariant past tense form of the copula is used:

(82) wɛn de knabə hat de bal ferstek wir war gegaŋə(n) fi suç
when ART boy PST ART ball hide.PST 1PL.EXCL COP.PST go.PST for search
'When the boy hid the ball, we went to look for (it).' (Volker 1982: 44)

The future tense is optionally marked with *wir(d)*:

(83) i wird geht
1SG FUT go
'I will go.' (Volker 1982: 46)

Progressive is indicated with the copula + *am*:

(84) i bin/war am lesesə(n) de buç
1SG COP.1SG.PRES/COP.PST PROG read ART book
'I am/was reading the book.' (Volker 1982: 46)

There are three modal markers: *will* (denoting the desiderative), *kan* (denoting ability and permission) and *mus* (denoting obligation).

There is a passive form, expressed with the copula + participle + *ba*:

(85) san ʃtɔa war gefɛrb ba an ʃinesən
3SG.POSS store COP.PST colour.PTCP PASS ART Chinese
'His store was painted by a Chinese (person).' (Volker 1982: 46)

Rabaul Creole German has fixed subject-verb-object verb order. Content questions are formed with question words, which may be fronted or may remain *in situ* (i.e. at the same position as the item asked about would be in a declarative clause), as in (86):

(86) du meçtə(n) was?
2SG want what
'What do you want?' (Volker 1982: 60)

Polar questions are indicated with rising intonation only. There is an invariant preverbal negator *ni(ç)*.

Rabaul Creole German has an obligatory copula, which inflects for tense, and, in the present, even for person and number:

	PRESENT	PAST
1SG	*bi(n)*	*war*
2SG	*bis*	*war*
3SG	*is*	*war*
1PL	*bis*	*war*
2PL	*sa(d)*	*war*
3PL	*sin(d)*	*war*

Clauses may be coordinated through juxtaposition or with the optional conjunctions *un(d)* 'and' and *aber* 'but'. A number of other subordinators were recorded. There are serial verb constructions with the motion verbs *kɔm* 'come' and *get* 'go':

(87) a. du hole(n) disə amɛr kɔm
2SG fetch DEM bucket come
'Bring the bucket!'
b. du lɔfə(n) get wo?
2SG run go where
'Where are you running to?' (Volker 1982: 49)

Relative clauses are formed with the relativizers *wo* 'who' and *was* 'which'.

4.3.3.3 *Short text*

(From Volker 1989a: 164)

Naher de kenigi(n) war der ganse abɛn am denkə(n) fɔn alɛ namə, was si
afterwards DEF queen COP.PST DEF whole evening PROG think of PL name REL 3SG.F

hat friher geher un(d) ʃikə(n) an bɔi get durç de ganse lan su finə(n)
PST before hear.PST and send INDEF male.servant go through DEF whole land to find

alɛ namə das er kan finə(n).
PL name that 3SG.M can find

'Afterwards the queen thought all evening long of all the names she had previously heard and sent a male servant throughout the land to find all the names he could find.'

4.3.3.4 *Some sources of data*

There is very little material available for Rabaul Creole German. Volker (1982) and (1989a) give a number of translated examples. The site *Unserdeutsch (Rabaul Creole German)* (http://uni-koeln.de/gbs/unserdeutsch/index.html, accessed 8 February 2015), set up by Friedel Frowein and hosted by the German *Society for Endangered Languages* (*Gesellschaft für Bedrohte Sprachen*), gives a number of links and references, as well as some sound files. It should be noted, however, that in most of these sound files, the speaker is switching between what seems a very acrolectal creole and the colloquial Standard German.

4.4 Summary

The majority of languages that we today call pidgins, creoles or mixed languages arose as a consequence of the European expansion and exploitation of the world. European powers colonized territories in both the New and Old World with the primary aim of producing raw material for the benefit of the European economy. Early colonial settlements were typically homesteads, i.e. small farm holdings of smaller households. In these settings interaction between owners and labourers would have been close. In most colonies plantations were eventually set up, i.e.

large-scale agricultural units with a large labour force. In these settings interaction between owners and labourers would have been restricted.

Plantations constantly demanded a large labour force. High mortality and low birth rates in the plantation societies therefore led to extended periods of large-scale immigration. The early plantations in the Atlantic and Indian Ocean colonies relied on slave labour, while the later plantations in the Pacific, as well as the Atlantic and Indian Oceans relied on indentured labour.

Demographic factors such as age, gender and origin of the labourers, as well as the ratio of males to females, Europeans to non-Europeans and locally to foreign born population may all have influenced the outcome of the contact variety.

Various sociolinguistic factors may also have influenced the outcome of the contact language, such as levels of interaction with potential lectal variation and diglossia, levels of prestige and potential identity marking, as well as education and the effect of missionary activities.

The colonial societies were dynamic and in a constant state of flux. There was considerable contact between the colonies. Diffusion is thus likely to have been an important factor in the formation of the various contact languages.

4.5 Key points

- **The main purpose of the European colonial territories was to bring profit to the metropolitan by producing cheap raw materials, to act as a market for metropolitan goods, and to exert strategic control over trade routes.**
- **The Triangular Trade brought European goods to West Africa, which was traded for slaves, who were brought to the New World and were traded for raw material, which was taken to Europe.**
- **The European expansion and exploitation involved mass relocation of different peoples.**
- **Both the European and the non-European settlers in the colonies had diverse ethnic and linguistic origins.**
- **Colonial settlements often started as homestead societies before evolving into large-scale plantation societies.**
- **Plantations were extremely labour intensive and demanded mass import of workers.**
- **A multitude of demographic and sociolinguistic factors may have influenced the outcome of the language in the colonial setting.**
- **There was considerable contact between the different colonies, meaning that diffusion is likely to have played a role in the formation of the languages that emerged.**
- **All colonies were multilingual and multistratal societies where a number of language varieties and linguistic registers are likely to have been used.**

4.6 Exercises

1. What were the driving forces behind the European expansion? What were its consequences?
2. What was the difference between a colonial homestead and a colonial plantation society? In what way may this difference have influenced the linguistic situation of the society?
3. Which were the main parties that were involved in the transatlantic slave trade?
4. What are the main demographic factors that may have influenced the formation of a given creole? In what way are the different factors relevant?
5. What role might such sociolinguistic factors as prestige and levels of interaction may have played in the colonial societies? How might that have influenced the linguistic situation of the societies?

Languages cited in Chapter 5

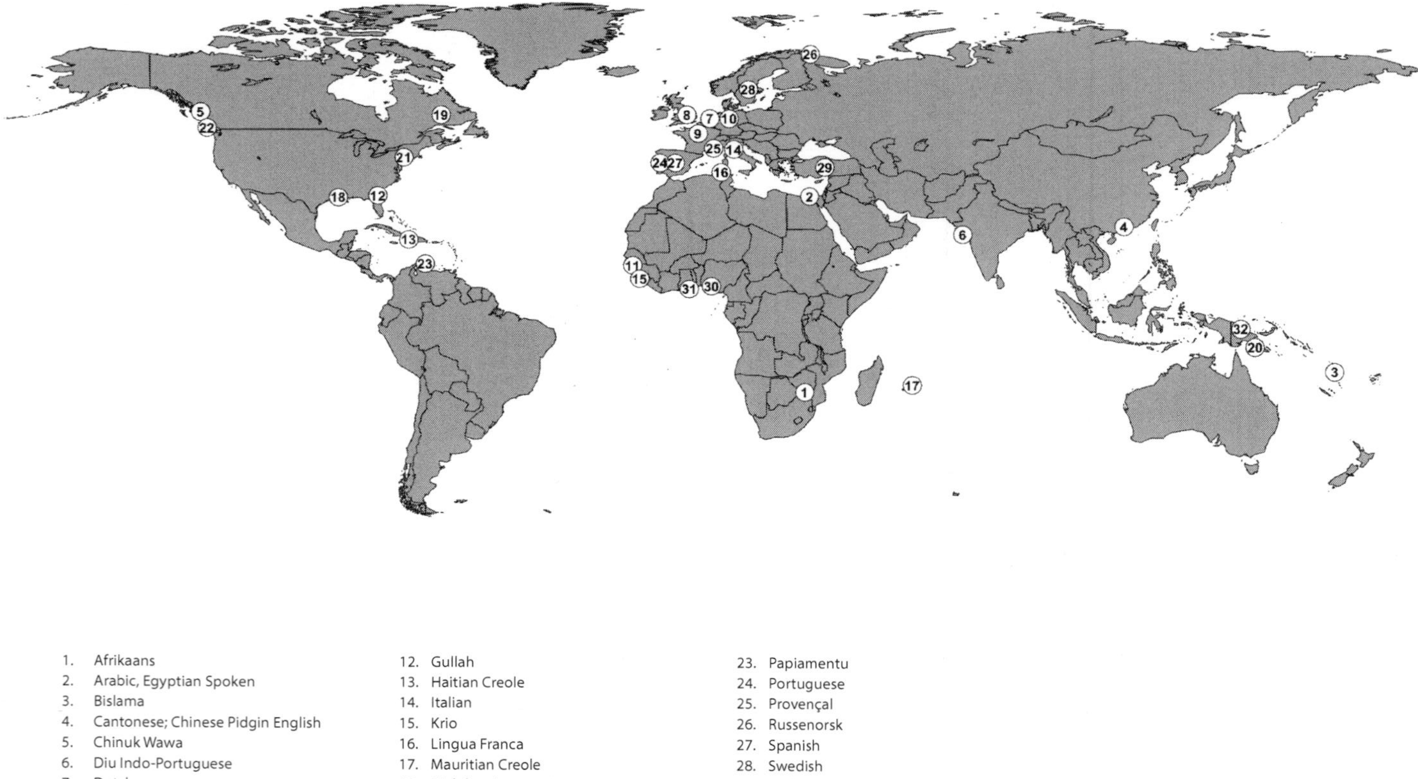

1. Afrikaans
2. Arabic, Egyptian Spoken
3. Bislama
4. Cantonese; Chinese Pidgin English
5. Chinuk Wawa
6. Diu Indo-Portuguese
7. Dutch
8. English
9. French
10. German, Standard
11. Guinea Bissau Kriyol
12. Gullah
13. Haitian Creole
14. Italian
15. Krio
16. Lingua Franca
17. Mauritian Creole
18. Mobilian Jargon
19. Montagnais
20. Motu; Tok Pisin
21. Munsee; Pidgin Delaware, Unami
22. Nuuchahnulth
23. Papiamentu
24. Portuguese
25. Provençal
26. Russenorsk
27. Spanish
28. Swedish
29. Turkish
30. West African Pidgin English
31. West African Pidgin Portuguese
32. Yimas-Arafundi-Pidgin

Chapter 5

Theories on the formation processes of pidgins

One of the major controversies in pidgin and creole studies is whether these languages share certain characteristics not found in other, non-pidgin and non-creole languages. A number of theories as to how this might have come about have been put forth. This chapter will briefly bring up some of the most commonly discussed theories, beginning with the Monogenesis and Relexification theory (5.1.1) and the Nautical Jargon theory (5.1.2), before moving on to some selected polygenesis theories (5.1.3). Section 5.2 gives a short definition of hybridization and its proposed role in pidginization. Section 5.3 presents short sketches of three extinct pidgins: Lingua Franca (proposed as a Proto-Pidgin), Chinese Pidgin English (a contact language not used by third parties) and Pidgin Delaware (a variety deliberately simplified by the lexifier speakers).

5.1 The development of pidgins

As mentioned above (Section 1.3), there has been a long tradition of viewing pidgins as simplified versions of their lexifier languages. Very often reference is made to the typical linguistic characteristics of pidgins that set them apart from non-pidgin languages.[71] Since the inception of the systematic study of pidgin languages, attempts have been made to account for where these characteristics may originate – that is, why pidgins share certain features that set them apart from other languages (if they do) – and which processes may be involved in the formation of a pidgin language.

Over the decades two main approaches to accounting for the presumed similarities between pidgins have been taken. The **monogenetic** approach postulates that all pidgins ultimately descend from one original pidgin. According to this theory there is thus ultimately a single (*mono*) origin (*genesis*) for all pidgin languages. The other

---

71. What exactly these characteristics are is often left vague "except perhaps when they refer to the absence of certain features commonly found in non-pidgins" (Parkvall & Bakker 2013:32). For a thorough empirical investigation on the possible characteristics of pidgin languages, see Parkvall & Bakker (2013). See also Part II in this book.

approach postulates that pidgins emerged independently of each other in different locations and at different times, but that the conditions and processes involved were similar. This could be called a **polygenetic** approach, as it assumes many (*poly*) different origins (*genesis*) for the known pidgin languages.

This section will first bring up the theory of monogenesis and relexification, as well as that of the nautical jargon theory, before moving on to some of the main polygenetic approaches to the emergence of pidgins. There are a number of theories on what exactly the various processes that lead to a pidgin language may have been; it is beyond the scope of this section to do justice to the lively discussion on the possible origins of pidgin languages, and this section should thus only be seen as an attempt to briefly introduce a few recurring concepts. For more detailed discussions on the origins of pidgins (as well as creoles), see, for example, Holm (1988: 13ff), Mühlhäusler (1997: 93ff) and Romaine (1988: 70ff), with further references.

5.1.1 Monogenesis and relexification

The **Monogenetic theory** argued that all pidgins and creoles with a European lexifier are descendants from one single Portuguese-lexified pidgin from the 15th century. This Proto-Pidgin was argued to itself be a descendent from Lingua Franca.[72]

The theory postulates that the Portuguese, when they started exploring the West African coast, would have brought this early maritime/trade pidgin along. This Portuguese version of Lingua Franca would therefore have been the first European contact language that would have been used in the interaction with West Africans. Similarly, because the Portuguese were the first European traders in South and Southeast Asia, this Portuguese version of Lingua Franca would also have been brought to the trading posts in the Indian and Pacific Oceans.

In subsequent centuries other European nations gained power over these areas for trade. The monogenetic theory puts forth that as new European powers took over from the Portuguese, the peoples they were in contact with already knew this Portuguese-based Proto-Pidgin and used it with the newcomers. However, as the Dutch, English, French or Spanish gained in power and came to dominate in the respective areas, the lexicon from these languages would come to replace the lexicon of the Proto-Pidgin, even though the actual structure of the pidgin remained the same. In other words, the Proto-Pidgin was **relexified** with a Dutch, English, French or Spanish lexicon, whereby most – but not all – of the vocabulary was replaced with words from the languages of the new dominating powers. It is important to notice here that the theory assumes that the major change occurred in the vocabulary only, while the grammar

72. Notice that this theory assumes *a priori* that all creoles emerged from pidgins, a point we will return to below (Section 6.2).

remained largely unaltered. This, the monogenesis theory argues, is why the structure of all pidgins is so similar, and why we find traces of Portuguese items, such as *pikin/picaninny* 'small; child' (Port. *pequenino* 'small') and *savvy* 'know' (Port./Span. *saber* 'know'), in such a high number of pidgins and creoles.[73]

The monogenesis theory thus postulates a family tree of pidgin languages, from which creole languages also descend, as illustrated in Figure 5.1.

An early version of this theory was brought up by Schuchardt (e.g. 1888a, 1890) but was most forcefully argued by Whinnom (e.g. 1956), Taylor (e.g. 1961, 1963, 1971) and Thompson (e.g. 1961). Notice, however, that the monogenetic theory does not take those pidgin languages into account that do not have a European lexifier. This theory, which was likely influenced by a historical approach to genetic lineages of languages, has by now largely been abandoned.

5.1.2 Nautical Jargon

The **Nautical Jargon theory** stresses the role of the jargons that were used on ships as a basis for pidgin formations. One of its first proponents was John E. Reinecke, who argued that the multinational nature of ships' crews was "[o]ne of the most favourable situations for the formation" of contact languages (1938: 107). According to this theory the various jargons that were used on English ships would have been the basis for what would become English-lexified pidgins, while the jargons used on French ships would have been the basis for what would become French-lexified pidgins, and so on. This essentially makes it a polygenetic theory in that several origins are proposed for the different lexifier languages, but it also has affinities with the monogenetic theory in that it postulates a common origin for each group of pidgins that have the same lexifier language.

There is, indeed, considerable anecdotal evidence for ship jargons. A vivid sample can be found in one of Edward Ward's writings, *The London Spy*, which appeared as monthly instalments in 1698–1703, and where he describes the lower strata of the London society. At one point he describes how he enters a tavern and sees "a knot of jolly, roughhewn [*sic*], rattling topers" sitting at a corner table:

> I soon found by their dialect they were masters of ships: 'Cheer up, my lads, pull away, save tide; come boys.' Then handling the quart, being empty, 'What, is she light? You, sir, that's next, haul the bar-line, and call the cooper's mate.' The drawer being come. 'Here, you fly-blown swab, take away this damned tankard, and ballast her well. Pox take her, there's no stowage in her hold. Have you ne'er a larger vessel?'
>
> (Ward 1927 [1698–1703]: 268)

73. As it turns out, however, *pikin/picaninny* and *savvy* are mainly found in Portuguese- and English-lexified pidgins and creoles (Huber 2013a, 2013b).

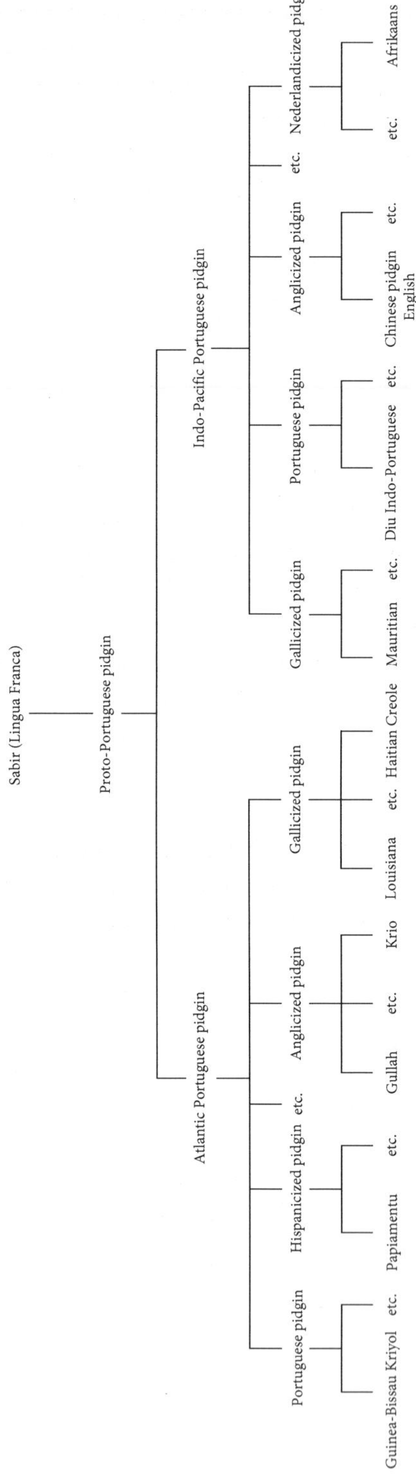

Figure 5.1 The monogenetic family tree for European-based pidgins and creoles (after Todd 1990:24 with slight modifications).

Ships' crews were typically composed of sailors from a number of different backgrounds, and they would by necessity have had to communicate with each other. The conditions were therefore favourable for some kind of contact variety to evolve (see also Matthews 1935 for a discussion on the speech on British ships in the second half of the 17th century as reflected in ship logs and journals).

It is likely that sailors had a role in spreading certain linguistic features to areas far removed from each other. Sailors would have changed ships and thus changed crew repeatedly; they would have travelled to various regions, all the time needing some kind of means of communication. They would have interacted with each other on board, as well as with other ships' crews and with people on land in the ports. This was, for example, suggested for English-lexified pidgins by Robert A. Hall, who proposed a Proto-Pidgin-English for the English-lexified pidgins and creoles, which, ultimately, goes back to "lower-class seventeenth-century English" speakers from "somewhere in the lower reaches of the Thames" (1966: 120). Similarly, a maritime Proto-Pidgin-French was proposed for the French-lexified pidgins and creoles by, for example, Faine (1939) and Hull (1968). However, the nautical jargon theory does not account for those pidgins that did not emerge through contact involving sailors. Also, it presupposes that the contact languages on board different ships were similar enough and, crucially, structured enough, to have a lasting effect on the non-sailing population using the pidgin. Without any real data of the kind of language spoken on various ships, we have no way of testing this assumption.

5.1.3 Polygenesis and proposed formation processes of pidgins

Regardless of whether the pidgins we know of today all stem from a common ancestor or from a limited number of jargons, or, in fact, were independent parallel developments, they did form somehow. There are a number of theories about the kinds of processes involved when contact between people speaking different languages leads to the formation of a pidgin. This section will very briefly bring up some of the most commonly mentioned theories. As pointed out above, it can by no means do justice to the full discussion that has been – and continues to be – held on the possible mechanisms involved in the emergence of pidgins.

It is worth keeping in mind that, for the most time, these proposed formation processes are meant to account for why pidgins with different input languages have similar structures. The theories therefore to a large extent rest on the assumption that pidgins in fact share affinities among each other as opposed to non-pidgin languages. Whether that is actually the case is, for the time being, left open and will only be addressed in Part II of this book.

5.1.3.1 *The Common Core theory*

The **Common Core theory**, put forth by Hall (1961), suggests that the structure of a given language derives from those parts of the input languages that overlap, that is, those core features of the grammars that are common to the languages in contact. In other words, when people of mutually unintelligible languages meet and have to interact, the structure of the resulting contact language will consist of those parts of the grammar that each contributing language has in common with the other language(s). This could be illustrated as in Figure 5.2.

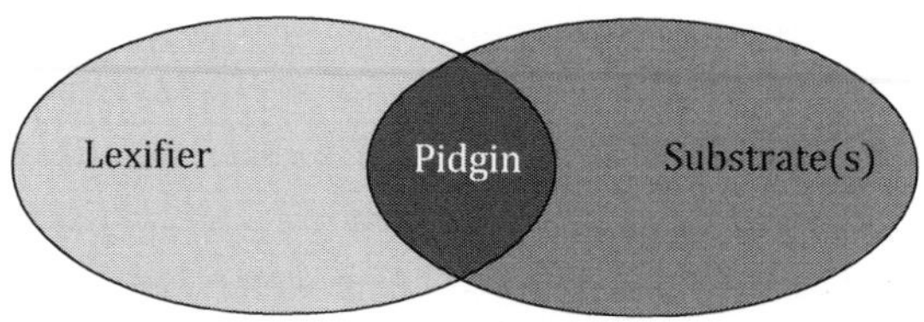

Figure 5.2 The Common Core theory. The darkest area represents the common core linguistic structure of both the lexifier and substrate languages, which form the basis of the new contact language. After Hall (1961) with slight modifications.

According to this theory, if a given linguistic feature is present in all input languages, it is likely to be present in the resulting contact language. For example, if both the lexifier and the substrate languages have obligatory plural marking for noun phrases, then the pidgin is likely to also have obligatory plural marking for noun phrases. A linguistic feature that is only present in some of the input languages, but not all of them, is consequently not likely to be present in the resulting contact language. For example, if the lexifier has obligatory plural marking for noun phrases (like English does) but the substrate does not (like Cantonese; Matthews & Yip 1994), then the pidgin is not likely to have it either (which was the case with Chinese Pidgin English; Matthews & Li 2013). Or, conversely, if, for example, the substrate has contrastive tone (like Cantonese does; Matthews & Yip 1994) but the lexifier does not (like English) then the pidgin is not likely to have it either (which seems to have been the case with Chinese Pidgin English; Matthews & Li 2013).

This theory could account for why pidgins may have similar structures. Not only because a number of pidgins may have had similar input languages (for example the same lexifier) but also because those linguistic structures that overlap may be typologically common features, found in many languages of the world. The theory could also account for why not all pidgins are exactly the same: because the exact combination of input languages would be unique for each contact language. Furthermore, the theory could account for why pidgins have 'reduced' linguistic systems compared to their input languages, in that those parts of the grammatical systems that do not overlap between the input languages would then not carry over into the resulting pidgin.

There are, however, a number of problems to the Common Core theory. For one, it does not explain why a given pidgin may end up not having a linguistic feature that can be found in all input languages. Chinuk Wawa, for example, has optional plural marking for noun phrases (Grant 2013a). However, the main input languages, namely English, French and Nuuchahnulth, all have obligatory plural marking for noun phrases. According to the Common Core theory that should have led to obligatory plural marking for noun phrases in the resulting pidgin, Chinuk Wawa. But it did not.

A more general problem is that the Common Core theory implicitly assumes that the language structures we see today in the input languages is what the speakers were using at the time in the contact situation too. In other words, we are comparing the resulting pidgin with present-day, usually standard, varieties of the input languages. However, it is likely that the people in the contact situation spoke a number of different varieties of the different languages. And it is certain that they did not speak the present-day varieties of the input languages. Furthermore, the Common Core theory ignores the fact that the contact situation was dynamic and on-going, that is, that the contact language did not emerge at one single point in time and then remain static.

Mühlhäusler (1997: 113) argues that yet another implicit assumption with the Common Core theory is that the speakers knew each others' languages well enough to be able to identify what was common to the various input languages (essentially that the creators of the pidgin were bilingual in the input languages). This contradicts what we know about the situations where pidgins arose, namely that speakers of mutually unintelligible languages, *who did not have any language in common*, ended up creating a bridge of communication which resulted in the pidgin. However, it could also be argued that the features that transferred into the contact languages were those that each party unconsciously recognized (because they were present in each party's mother tongue and way of expression).

5.1.3.2 *The Interlanguage theory*

The **Interlanguage theory** (also called the **Interlanguage Hypothesis**) proposes that pidgins emerged as incompletely learned versions of the model language, in this case the lexifier languages. This was proposed very early by, for example, Adoplho Coelho (e.g. 1881: 67) in his study of Portuguese-lexified creoles, and Dirk C. Hesseling (e.g. 1897 and 1933, reprinted and translated in 1979a and 1979b) in his study of Afrikaans and the contact languages of South Africa. The theory has seen a recent revival, e.g.

in the work of Plag (2008a, 2008b, 2009a and 2009b) and Siegel (2008a, 2008b). See also Winford (2003: 208ff).

The idea behind the Interlanguage theory is that there were two major groups of people involved in the formation of the resulting pidgin: those who spoke the target language natively, and those who did not. According to this theory the non-native speakers of the target language aimed to acquire the target language but, due to the conditions of the contact situation, were not able to fully master their model target and "[t]heir unsuccessful efforts result[ed] in the pidgin: a grammatically impoverished version of the lexifier with a very restricted vocabulary" (Sebba 1997: 79). The pidgin would thus represent a fossilized stage of the interlanguage (IL) process in L2 acquisition.

The Interlanguage theory would explain why the lexicon in pidgins are typically derived from one (or, occasionally, a few) languages. However, it does not explain why the non-native speakers of the target languages stop at a particular IL stage. One possible explanation might be that the learners had limited access to native speaker models. If a large community of non-native speakers of the target language only had access to a small number of language models, the various IL stages might have reinforced one another and thus slowed down the acquisition of the target language. Another factor may be social identity: the extent to which the individual or group may wish to integrate with the community of the language models may also affect the language learning (Saville-Troike 2012: 42). However, this does not explain how it can be that these non-native speakers stop at the same IL stage. Typically different individuals will progress with their second language acquisition at different rates (Gass & Selinker 2008, Saville-Troike 2012).

The Interlanguage theory furthermore implies that the speakers of the target language are entirely passive in the formation of the pidgin, acting only as language models, but are otherwise not involved in the communicative process that led to the contact language. In other words, that the speakers of the lexifier languages would not alter their language at all during the interaction with others, but that they would use their respective languages in the same way in the contact situation as they would in their home societies. However, we have seen that pidgins arose in situations where several parties interacted with each other due to some common interest, for example trade or the need to function in a workforce, etc. It thus seems unlikely that the speakers of the lexifier languages would not influence the outcome of the contact language in some way, for instance by themselves also speaking an altered variety of their language in the contact situation compared to the kind of variety they would speak in their respective home societies (cf., for example, the dialogue between an Englishman and two Chinese servants in 5.3.2.3 below).

In addition to the above, the Interlanguage theory implicitly assumes that the target model was the contemporary standard varieties of the European languages, which, as mentioned above, is not only anachronistic, but also regionally unrealistic.

To assume that pidgins are unsuccessful attempts at second language acquisition presupposes that the speakers of the contact language aimed to acquire native-like command of the target language.[74] However, in the contact situation it might have been much more relevant to acquire just enough needed to conduct whatever business was to be done, in which case pidgins could be seen as efficient and successful L2 learning (cf. Baker 1990, 1994). Furthermore, it could also be that the parties involved in the contact situation actually wished to communicate with each other in a reduced variety. Chinese Pidgin English, for example, was considered a useful bridge of communication by both the Chinese and the Europeans: the Chinese were not allowed to teach their language to foreigners, and the Europeans considered Chinese unlearnable (Matthews & Li 2013).[75] In other words, it would be simplistic to assume that the Chinese merchants, whom the European trading partners were dependent on, were trying but failing to acquire native-like competence of (modern) Standard English. See further 5.3.2.

5.1.3.3 *The Foreigner Talk theory*

The **Foreigner Talk theory** suggests that it was the conscious simplification of the lexifier speakers when interacting with speakers of other languages that formed the basis for the structure of the resulting pidgin. It is important to notice here that 'Foreigner Talk' (FT) refers to the way a native speaker simplifies his or her language when dealing with a non-native speaker. It is thus the kind of speech produced by the native speaker, not the kind of speech produced by the foreigner. It seems to be a near-universal phenomenon that speakers intuitively alter their speech when confronted with a person who is not fluent in their language. For example, if someone approaches

74. It is a matter of great contention how to define "successful" L2 acquisition and where exactly to draw the line between fluency or native-like competence and L2 fossilization, that is, when the L2 learning ceases to progress further (cf. Saville-Troike 2012: 42). The question is whether fossilization is in fact even an observable and quantifiable phenomenon, and what exactly interlanguage "successes" and "failures" are. For more on fossilization, see, for example, the chapters in Han & Odlin (2006).

75. A similar attitude was held by some German colonizers, who felt that while Pidgin English was a terrible gibberish (and it was a good thing that German did not get thus mangled), it nonetheless served as a useful means of communication, and it was also "pleasant that one can speak German in peace with one's equals, without a Boy [i.e. servant – VV] understanding [what one says]" ("*[a]ngenehm ist es auch, daß man sich mit seinesgleichen ruhig deutsch unterhalten kann, ohne daß ein Boy es versteht*"; Vollbehr 1912: 40, my translation).

you on the street and very haltingly asks you something like "*Please, where train?*", you are likely to answer in a different manner than if someone approaches you and asks "*Excuse me, do you know how to get to the train station from here?*". In the latter case you are likely to answer in your ordinary register, not paying much attention to your own language. In the former case you are likely to alter your language and pay attention to it, making it, in a sense, simpler. For instance, you might answer the latter question with something like "*Yes, you go down the hill and turn right at the traffic light; you'll see it on your left-hand side.*", whereas you are likely to answer the first question with something like "*Hill down. Traffic light, right.*", probably clarifying with gestures and pointing. FT denotes this kind of intuitive simplification of one's own native language.

The idea behind the Foreigner Talk theory is that the speakers of the lexifier languages simplified their speech into FT when they needed to communicate with speakers of other languages, thus providing these people with a simplified model of the lexifier language. The theory thus postulates that the reason that pidgins are simplified compared to their lexifiers is because that was the kind of input that was given. This idea was articulated as early as in the beginning of the 20th century (see, for example, Schuchardt 1909) and had currency especially in the first half of the 20th century.

Native speakers do tend to use a set of strategies to simplify their speech when addressing someone with low proficiency in their language. Typical strategies seem to be, for example, slower and louder speech, clearer articulation and longer pauses than normal speech, as well as a simple vocabulary (i.e. idioms and slang are avoided) with high-frequency words and fewer pronoun forms, shorter sentences and fronted topics (i.e. the main content item of the utterance appears first, as in *Traffic light, right* instead of *Turn right at the traffic light*); cf. Gor & Long (2004), Gass & Selinker (2008: 305ff) and Saville-Troike (2012: 112ff) with further references (see also Ferguson 1975, who was one of the first to systematically study FT features, as well as Hatch 1983).[76]

---

76. The term '**baby-talk**' is often and confusingly used in early writings, such as Bloomfield (1933). The author is here referring to a simplified register spoken by the socially powerful group, the "masters", i.e. the speakers of the lexifier languages. The assumption is that this 'baby-talk' is "the masters' imitation of the subjects incorrect speech" (Bloomfield 1933: 472) and this 'baby-talk' imitation then becomes a model for the "subject", who "can do no better now than to acquire the simplified 'baby-talk' of the upper language" (*ibid.*). But what is actually meant here is Foreigner Talk – the simplified register used with a speaker who is not fluent in the language – and not so-called 'baby-talk', more accurately termed **child-directed speech** (CDS), which is the kind of register used by caregivers when talking to small children (infants and toddlers). CDS is used by adults and even older children when addressing very young listeners. It typically involves a higher pitch and an exaggerated intonation pattern, with emphatic stress, a slower speech rate, more and longer pauses, in addition to various simplification methods, such less complex utterances (shorter sentences with fewer grammatical markers; cf. Field 2004: 54ff). The topics are typically local, i.e. involving things that are immediately

It does not seem unlikely that FT played a role between the respective parties engaged in trying to communicate with each other without having any language in common. However, it is important to keep in mind that FT is typically unsystematic, both across individuals and with the same individual (cf., for example, Ferguson 1975, Hinnenkamp 1982 and Mühlhäusler 1997). That is, different people will simplify their languages in different ways, and the same person is also likely to be inconsistent in whether, and if so how, s/he simplifies his/her language. FT can therefore not be considered a structured set of norms that could serve as a model for an emerging pidgin language.

The question is also in how far each party was aware of the fact that the language spoken to them was an FT variety. In many documented cases of FT the parties both seem aware that FT is being used; it is seen as a cooperation between the parties to create a communicative bridge among them and is as such not stigmatized (Mühlhäusler 1997: 101). In these cases it does not seem likely that FT would constitute an especially desirable target model. However, there are reports of so-called 'double illusions' (Silverstein 1972), where each party believes that they are speaking the others' language, when in fact both are speaking FT. In Papua New Guinea, for example,

> when Rev. W. G. Lawes of the London Missionary Society settled in Port Moresby in 1874 as the first European missionary amongst the Motu, he attempted to learn Motu. However it was not until some time later that his son, Frank, who played with the boys in the village and learned Motu from them, drew his father's attention to the fact that he did not speak "true" Motu but only a simplified version of it, which he also used in making his first [Bible – VV] translations into Motu. (…) This Simplified Motu was, moreover, used by the Motu "in speaking to foreigners", although they themselves would "never do so amongst themselves". (Dutton 1997: 16f, citing Taylor 1978)

Similarly, the French Jesuit Father Paul Le Jeune, who lived among the Montagnais in Quebec in 1633, reported about learning their language:

visible to both parties, and often involve alternative words for common items, such as *bow wow* for *dog* or *moo moo* for *cow*. While there are similarities between CDS and FT, such as a slower speech rate and less complex utterances, there are also notable differences in the manner and structure of the utterances, such as the high pitch of the voice and the word replacements; you are not likely to give an adult directions to the train station to the effect of "*choo choo place down hill, go spoon-hand side of blinky-light*" in a high pitched voice (at least not without causing offence). However, CDS is in any case irrelevant for the emergence of pidgin languages, since none of the parties involved in the contact situation were infants or toddlers (the implicit racist notions of certain ethnic groups having infant-like minds compared to others are, needless to say, no longer held by any serious scholar). For more on CDS, which will not be further discussed in this book, see, for example, Bryant & Barrett (2007), Ninio (2011) and Bryant et al. (2012), with further references.

> I have noticed in the study of their language that there is a particular jargon between the French and the Indians, which is neither French, nor Indian, and nevertheless when the French use it, they think they are speaking Indian, and the Indians in taking it up think they are speaking good French.
>
> (Romaine 1988:120, citing Silverstein 1972:14)

This kind of 'double illusion' may have played a role in the early stages of the development and formation of pidgins.

An interesting testimony of how a deliberately simplified version of the lexifier language was taught to others can be found in Naro (1978), who points to archival evidence of how, during the early phase of the Portuguese exploration of West Africa, in the 15th century, West Africans were captured and brought to Portugal, where they were taught a simplified version of Portuguese so that they could act as translators, as well as sources of information on the political and economical conditions of their regions of origin, for subsequent voyages: "[a]s early as 1435, when the Portuguese voyages had barely penetrated the Sahara coast, Prince Henry [the Navigator – VV] was quoted as giving his captains explicit orders to capture potential interpreters" (Naro 1978:318). What the early texts show is that a simplified form of Portuguese was used both by the Portuguese and by the captured West Africans. Notice that this took place in Portugal; the simplified Portuguese was subsequently brought to West African coast by way of translators, where it later spread with the increase of contact and intermediate interpreters.

Early reports of Pidgin Delaware also seem to indicate that the Unami speakers deliberately simplified their language when dealing with the European settlers (see further 5.3.3).

5.1.3.4 *Transfer and substrates in pidgin formation*

We have seen that the groups involved in the situations that gave rise to pidgin languages were typically adult and that pidgins typically are not anybody's first language. It therefore follows that pidgin language speakers have different L1s; even if the native language of the speaker happens to be the lexifier, that is still a different language variety from the pidgin.

All speakers who learn an L2 by definition already have at least one L1. L2 learners thus already have at least one other linguistic system to fall back on when they learn the second language. This knowledge is not infrequently **transferred** from the L1 to the L2 during the learning process; typically the transfer recedes as competence in the L2 increases (cf., for example, Gass & Selinker 2008). This transfer may occur for any part of the linguistic system, such as the phonology, morphology, grammar, pragmatics, and so on. For example, a German learner of English as a second language may transfer the German *Auslautverhärtung* of stops (where voiced stops are rendered voiceless in word-final position) into English and pronounce *bud* as /bʌt/ instead of /bʌd/ (which for an English speaker means two entirely different things). I have personally often heard Germans refer to *the hairs* (in the plural, as it should be in German) rather than the mass noun *hair* (not inflected for the plural), as in *I have washed my hairs* (rather than the English *I have washed my hair*). It is also common to hear announced on German trains that *Shortly we will arrive Frankfurt/München/ Berlin main station*, where the preposition *at* has been left out (mirroring the German *In kürze erreichen wir Frankfurt/München/Berlin Hauptbahnhof*, without any preposition). Word order may be influenced by the L1, as in *That's why I wouldn't recommend it to buy*, which I was advised by a German speaker and which mirrors the structure in Example (88):

German (Indo-European (Germanic): Germany)

(88)	deshalb	würde	ich	nicht	empfehlen	es	zu	kaufen
	therefore	would.SUBJ.1SG	1SG	NEG	recommend.INF	ART.N.ACC.SG	INF	buy.INF

'Therefore I wouldn't recommend buying it.' (source: personal experience)

Transfer may also involve the absence of features. My own two L1s (English and Swedish), for example, do not have case marking, which means that I routinely fail to inflect for the correct case in German. I also routinely fail to choose the correct gender, as Swedish only has two (neuter and common) and English none, compared to the three genders of German. Furthermore, the distinction in my L2 German between the familiar *you* and the polite *you* in both the singular and plural typically suffers noticeably from the absence of such distinctions in both my L1s.

Substrate theories focus on the potential L1 transfer by the speakers of other languages than the lexifier language as a source of the structure of the pidgins. In other words, according to substrate theories, while the lexifier provides the vocabulary to the contact language, the substrates provide the structure via substrate transfer. This may be determined by establishing which languages were in contact and what the structures of those languages were.

Substrate theories and L1 transfer would help account for the difference in structure between the resulting pidgin and its lexifier. They would also help account for the differences among the pidgins: different substrates would lead to different structures. To the extent that pidgins can be shown to have the same or similar languages as substrates, these theories may also help account for putative similarities between pidgin languages. However, this largely presupposes that speakers will consistently make the same kinds of L1 transfers, so much so that the L1 patterns will establish themselves as the pidgin structure. But just as various IL stages tend to be highly individual, transfer may also differ between speakers (Saville-Troike 2012). Furthermore, we again run the risk of simplifying matters if we compare structures in the pidgins with structures in the supposed substrate languages. First of all, we are not likely to be able to establish exactly which input languages were involved in the formation of a given pidgin – only very thorough archival research can help shed light on that and even then we are likely to have an incomplete picture. Secondly, we would need to compare the structure of the contact language with the language varieties spoken at the time of the formation of the pidgin, a near-impossible task. Third, we would need to establish that the given structure could not in fact have originated from the lexifier language. And fourth, we would need to have access to longitudinal data of both the contact language and the various input languages (to the extent that we can identify them), since, as has been mentioned repeatedly, any language is a dynamic system which will be in constant development.

5.1.4 The origin of pidgins: A summary

We have seen that pidgins arose in situations of intense contact where speakers of mutually unintelligible languages needed to communicate with each other. The agents involved in the formation of the pidgins were (or are) typically adults. Exactly which formation processes were involved in the emergence of pidgins is a matter of debate and each theory that has been brought up in this section has both merits and weaknesses. It is likely that a number of factors and mechanisms were involved in the formation of the contact language. It is not inconceivable that a given pidgin is the outcome of a combination of foreigner talk, interlanguage, substrate transfer and relexification, all of which may have been reinforced by a common core of features between the input languages. It may also be the case that certain pidgins were (or are) descendants of other, earlier pidgins. It is also not unlikely that various pidgins may have influenced each other through diffusion, due to the high mobility of the users. The merits and challenges of the various theories are summarized below.

Theory	Appeal factors	Challenge factors
Monogenesis/ relexification	– Explains structural similarities between many pidgins	– Ignores pidgins not lexified by European languages
Nautical Jargon	– Explains similarities between pidgins of the same lexifier spread over many locations	– Ignores pidgins that did not emerge through contact with sailors – Presupposes ship jargons were similar and structured enough to have a lasting effect on the non-sailing population

Theory	Appeal factors	Challenge factors
Common Core	– Explains why pidgins have similar structures – Explains why pidgins are not all exactly the same – Explains why pidgins have 'reduced' systems compared to the input languages	– Does not explain why features found in all input languages are not carried over to the pidgin – Assumes that the contemporary (standard) varieties represent the language structures of the input at the time – Ignores the fact that the pidgin did not emerge at one single point in time and remain static – Assumes that the speakers knew each others' languages well enough to be able to identify the common core of the input languages
Interlanguage	– Explains why the lexicon of a pidgin is derived from one or a few input languages;	– Does not explain why non-native speakers stop at the same IL stage – Assumes that the target language speakers are passive in the formation of the pidgin – Assumes that pidgin speakers aimed to acquire native-like command of the target language – Implicitly assumes that the contemporary (standard) varieties represent the language structures of the target language at the time
Foreigner Talk	– Explains why pidgins are 'simplified' compared to the lexifiers	– Ignores the fact that Foreigner Talk is not structured
Transfer/ substrates	– Explains the difference in structure between the pidgin and the lexifier – Explains why different pidgins have different structures – Explains why different pidgins are similar to each other	– Assumes consistency in L1 transfers; – Assumes we are able to establish exactly which input languages/varieties were involved in the formation of a given pidgin – Assumes we can establish whether a given structure originates with the lexifier or any of the other input languages

The only way to empirically test these hypotheses is to try and uncover as much data as possible about the respective situations. As pointed out by Anthony Naro:

> [r]ecently the general problem of pidginization has become a subject of much theoretical discussion; but this debate has, to date, been carried on in total isolation from empirically established fact. What we really need to know at this point is the answer to a WH-nightmare: who was saying what to whom, how and when – not to mention why – in some actual instance of pidginization. (Naro 1978: 314)

This highlights how fundamentally essential thorough archival research is for any discussion on the development of pidgin languages. While great advances have been made in uncovering historical data, we are nowhere near being able to confidently answer the *wh*-questions posed by Naro more than 35 years ago.

At this stage I repeat once again that any language is a dynamic system; the discussion on the emergence of pidgins should thus not be taken to imply that pidgins suddenly emerge at a certain point in time and then remain static, without any change to their linguistic systems during the time they are used.

5.2 Hybridization and the emergence of pidgins

A notion that has received much attention in the field of pidgin and creole studies is that of hybridization, especially something termed 'tertiary hybridization' which is widely considered a necessary step in the formation of a pidgin language.

The terms hybrid and hybridization are borrowed from biology. A **hybrid** is the offspring of genetically distinct parents. The parents may belong to the same species, in which case the hybrid is intraspecific, or to two different species, in which case the hybrid is interspecific (Rittner & McCabe 2004: 168). **Hybridization** is when a hybrid is produced by interbreeding two species (essentially an interspecific hybrid).

The term 'tertiary hybridization' was coined by Keith Whinnom (1971) and refers to a language specific phenomenon; he used it in analogy to the term 'primary' and 'secondary' hybridization. Whinnom defines 'primary hybridization' as the biological "smooth intergrading (…), due to the effect of waves of minimal mutations" (Whinnom 1971: 92) leading to new races and eventually new species, essentially what is termed **speciation** in biology; and he defines 'secondary hybridization' as the "interbreeding of distinct species" (*ibid.*), essentially what is termed *hybridization* in biology, as mentioned above.

Speciation (Whinnom's 'primary hybridization'), the gradual evolution into new species through various forms of mutation, would in linguistic terms be the equivalent of the family tree, where, over time, various languages have developed ("speciated") from a common ancestor.[77]

77. There are various forms of speciation: **allopatric speciation** occurs "when the ancestral population becomes segregated by a geographical barrier" (Rittner & McCabe 2004: 11). That is, the original population is split up by some kind of geographical barrier, and due to this reproductive isolation two new species evolve. A subform of allopatric speciation is **peripatric speciation**, where speciation occurs because a small part of the original population gets isolated from the main population, essentially forms a niche of its own, and evolves into a new species. **Parapatric speciation** is when a small part of the population forms its own niche, but remains in limited contact with the original

Hybridization (Whinnom's 'secondary hybridization'), the interbreeding of distinct species to form a new species, would in linguistic terms be the equivalent of mixed languages, i.e. distinct languages with their own norms and systems, that emerged as a result of the "interbreeding" of two or a few languages.[78]

Tertiary hybridization, on the other hand, would be a purely linguistic concept. According to Whinnom – and this concept has been widely followed – this is a necessary stage for **pidginization**, i.e. when a contact variety becomes stable enough to have its own norms. According to Whinnom a pidgin system will not emerge until the contact language is used between speakers of mutually unintelligible languages, none of which are the lexifier language. The reasoning behind this is that as long as the lexifier language is available as a language model, it will be the target for L2 learning. However, once the lexifier is not available as a normative model, and the contact language is used as a *lingua franca* between people who have no other language in common, the contact language may stabilize into a system of norms and a pidgin will emerge. That is, only when a reduced version of language A is used as a *lingua franca* between groups B and C does a stable pidgin emerge. As an example, Whinnom proposes that a pidgin French would not arise if an English schoolboy tried to communicate in French with a French schoolboy, because the French of the French schoolboy would be normative and the French of the English schoolboy would steadily improve during the interaction to become more like that of the French schoolboy. However, if an English and a German schoolboy were to communicate with each other in French, a pidgin might arise, since there is no native speaker of the target language (French) to act as a model. Thus "[n]either speaker has any model on which to improve his performance in French, nor any motive to improve it" (Whinnom 1971:105f) since the main motive would be communication with each other rather than achieving a native-like command of French. The imperfect French of the English and German schoolboys,

population. Finally, **sympatric speciation** is when a new species evolves within the original population, that is, there is no geographical separation between the two. Parallels in the evolution of languages can probably be found for all of these forms of speciation. For more on speciation, see, for example, *The Boundless Biology Open Textbook* (https://www.boundless.com/biology/), Chapter 18, accessed 9 February 2015.

78. Notice that this likeness differs from that done by Whinnom (1971). According to Whinnom the linguistic equivalent of what he terms 'secondary hybridization' (i.e. hybridization proper) would, for example, be immigrant communities within a larger host community who, as an interlanguage stage, produce a linguistic 'mixture'. However, Whinnom proposes that this 'mixture' would be unstable, as the immigrant community would be trying to learn the host community language. This linguistic 'secondary hybridization', then, would be the equivalent of a series of ILs, without any internal stable norms.

with their accented pronunciation, limited vocabulary and simplified grammar might then become its own normative system, unintelligible to French speakers.

There are examples of situations where pidgin languages have come to be used as *lingua francas* between people of different linguistic backgrounds even though the lexifier has been removed. To mention only a couple of examples, Tok Pisin is widely used in Papua New Guinea among Papuans of different linguistic backgrounds, and in Vanuatu, another area of great linguistic diversity, Bislama functions as a *lingua franca*. However, to propose that pidgins can only become stable systems through tertiary hybridization, that is, once a reduced version of the lexifier language is taken up and used by speakers of the substrate languages, implies that pidginization essentially boils down to imperfect L2 learning (the Interlanguage theory), since the assumption is that if the substrate speakers would have had access to native speakers of the lexifier language as language models, they would have acquired improved versions of the lexifier language (further implying that the aim of the substrate speakers was to acquire fluency in the lexifier language). This in turn implies that the speakers of the lexifier languages did not alter their language during the contact situation, but used the same versions in those situations as in their home societies – a rather unlikely scenario, as mentioned above.

The tertiary hybridization concept has been criticized by some, who have pointed out the existence of pidgins that clearly did not go through any tertiary hybridization stage, such as Russenorsk (used mainly between Russians and Norwegians), Chinese Pidgin English (used mainly between Chinese traders and Europeans), or Yimas-Arafundi Pidgin (used by Yimas and Arafundi traders), to mention only a few (see, for example, Thomason & Kaufman 1988:196ff and Bakker 1994:29). Furthermore, as mentioned above, Naro (1978) has shown that a simplified Portuguese was actually created and taught by the Portuguese and then brought to West Africa, where it subsequently spread with the increased frequency of European voyages and their interpreters. West African Pidgin Portuguese could therefore also be argued to have arisen without any tertiary hybridization.

5.3 Snapshots

The Monogenesis theory puts forth that all pidgins and creoles are descendants of a Portuguese-lexified Proto-Pidgin, which in turn is a descendant of the Romance-lexified Lingua Franca that was used in the Mediterranean area until the 19th century.

Chinese Pidgin English has been argued to exhibit some traces of an early South Seas Jargon, thus lending support to the Nautical Jargon theory. Chinese Pidgin English has further been argued to be a counter-example to the necessity for tertiary hybridization for the formation of a pidgin, since it emerged and stabilized when used between the speakers of the actual input languages, including the speakers of the lexifier. It has also been used to lend support to the Common Core theory.

The Foreigner Talk theory puts forth that the speakers of the lexifier languages deliberately simplified their languages when communicating with speakers of other languages. Pidgin Delaware is an example of a language where such claims were made in the early sources.

5.3.1 Lingua Franca: An extinct Romance-lexified pidgin in the Mediterranean Basin[79]

5.3.1.1 *A brief background sketch of Lingua Franca*

Lingua Franca, often referred to as *Sabir*,[80] was used between Italian, French, Spanish and Portuguese speaking people among each other and in contact with Turkish, Berber and Arab speaking people around the Mediterranean and even beyond. Lingua Franca (*lûghat al-Ifranj* in Arabic; Dakhlia 2008: 42) literally means 'language of the Franks', where 'Franks' was the general reference for 'European' in the Arab-speaking world of the late Middle Ages (Arends 2005). It arose no later than in the 14th century, possibly even earlier, and was used up until the end of the 19th century, making it an exceptionally long-lived pidgin.[81]

The language seems to have initially emerged in the eastern part of the Mediterranean, with the intense trade and crusading contacts between the Italian merchant city states, especially Genoa and Venice, and the Levant.[82] During this earlier phase the vocabulary seems to have been predominantly derived from northern Italian varieties as well as varieties from the Provençal. Eventually the Genoese commerce also moved to the western part of the Mediterranean, bringing Lingua Franca to the Iberian Peninsula as well as the Maghreb (the 'Barbary Coast' of North Africa). This brought a large component of Spanish and some Portuguese vocabulary to the language.

---

79. I am very grateful to Rachel Selbach for her helpful comments on this snapshot.

80. Notice that Sabir is sometimes used to designate a different language, namely a French-lexified pidgin that emerged in North Africa in the late 19th century (cf. Arends 2005, Reinecke 1937: 716f, Cifoletti 2004: 26ff; for a longer discussion on the path of development from Lingua Franca to Sabir as a different variety, see Dakhlia 2008: 409ff, esp. 424ff). Note that for Schuchardt (1909: 459f) Sabir may signify the French variety spoken by the Jews in Algeria.

81. Theories have been put forth that Lingua Franca derives from a kind of Jewish trading Latin ('Commercial Latin' in Hancock 1977) going back to the late classical and early medieval period (cf. Whinnom 1965, 1977). It certainly belongs to one of the most long-lived pidgins we know of: not only did it not become extinct until the end of the 19th century, but it lived on into modern times in the form of Polari (from Italian *parlare* 'speak'), which was predominantly used in the UK and was recorded as appearing sporadically as late as well into the 1980s (cf. Hancock 1984a: 394).

82. But see do Couto (2002: 187ff) for a discussion why this early Eastern Mediterranean contact language should not be equated with Lingua Franca but rather be seen as a separate language variety that would end up being the precursor of Lingua Franca proper.

The data for Lingua Franca is very scanty and consists of snippets found in literary sources, such as poems and plays (some of the most famous being passages in Molière's Le Bourgeois Gentilhomme and Le Sicilien), as well as in documentary sources, such as various accounts (of travel, of captivity, of diplomacy, etc.), descriptions and dictionaries. While all sources provide valuable information on the language, the fact that Lingua Franca was typically used in literary sources of comic effect, to give a burlesque tone, means that the data in those kinds of sources has to be used with some care: it is not unlikely that authors may have exaggerated their representation of the language. Nevertheless, they may still serve to give an idea of the language, and, also of great value, how the language was perceived. Many of the documentary sources "attest to both the use and function of L[ingua] F[ranca], not just providing text samples, but perhaps more importantly, careful descriptions as well as random anecdotes of the language situation" (Selbach 2008:36).

Most of the documents available to us about Lingua Franca are from the Ottoman trade and slave centres on the North African coast – with Algiers, Tunis and Tripoli being the largest centres – where European Christians were held as slaves in so-called *bagnos* (slave centres or prison complexes).[83] At the same time these urban centres, especially Algiers, saw a great influx of European Jewish and Moslem religious refugees, further adding to the multicultural nature of the city: Lingua Franca "is cited in both documentary and literary sources as spoken not only by Christian slaves, but across the population from private estate owners to prison guards, and by people in the streets" (Selbach 2008:34). For a thorough discussion on the sociolinguistic situation in Algiers in the 16th to 19th centuries, see Selbach (2008).

The earliest known record of what is clearly Lingua Franca dates from 1353, where a theatre piece, *Contrasto della Zerbitana*, from the island of Jerba gives the exchange in a quarrel between husband and wife in Lingua Franca. Between that source and the description provided by Hugo Schuchardt (1909) five and a half centuries later, at which point Lingua Franca was already extinct, the snippets we have of the language are widely spread in both time and place. It is likely that there were different varieties of the language in different parts of the Mediterranean and that people of different social strata and/or origins spoke different varieties of Lingua Franca. It is also likely that the language changed through time. We are thus not dealing with a static and monolithic language, but rather a dynamic language code that was identified as Lingua Franca for several centuries.

83. The term 'slave' was in the Ottoman North African dependencies used to denote both slaves and hostages (for whom ransom was demanded). These people were typically captured both on the seas in piracy raids as well as in land raids in mutual hostility between Christians and Muslims. The fact that there were about 25,000 Christian 'slaves' in Algiers around 1600 (Schuchardt 1909:451) gives a rough indication of the population figures.

5.3.1.2 *A short linguistic sketch of Lingua Franca*

It should be noted that the vast majority of the data for Lingua Franca is from the Barbary Coast (i.e. Maghreb) area. To what extent it is representative of the Lingua Franca of other areas is not known. It should also be noted that the variety described here primarily represents the language at its later stage, as described in *Dictionnaire de la langue franque ou petit mauresque* (Anonymous 1830).

Given that Lingua Franca was extinct already by the time Hugo Schuchardt wrote his sketch of it in 1909, and all data we have of the language is from written sources of different ages, where orthography varied greatly, we can only make some very tentative guesses about the phonological system.[84] It is also likely that pronunciation varied according to region and the background of the speakers. Furthermore, pronunciation is likely to have changed with time. With the caveat that we cannot be sure exactly which sounds the writers were referring to with their orthography, the following consonants seem attested: /p, b, m, f, v, t, d, n, s, z, l, r, ʦ, ʣ, k, g, h/ and the following vowels: /i, e, a, o, u/. It is possible that <gn> indicated /ɲ/ (as in *Signor* 'Sir', sometimes also spelled *senior*), that <ch> indicated /ʧ/ (as in *mouchou* 'much'), that <qu> or <qou> indicated /k^{w}/ (as in *questo* 'this'), that <gu> or <gou> indicated /g^{w}/ (as in *guanti* 'glove'), that <j> indicated /ʒ/ (as in *Jean* 'John') or /ʃ/ (as in *jonior* 'sir'), that <sch> indicated /ʃ/ (as in *conoschir* 'know'), that <gli> indicated /ʎ/ and that <gi> indicated /ʤ/ (as in *mangiaria* 'food'). There is no information on possible lengthening of vowels, nor on stress patterns.

The morphology seems to have been predominantly analytic, with only one inflectional affix for the past tense (see below),[85] although there are indications of gender agreement in the NP (Example (89); see also further below), as well as reduplication (Examples (90), (99)):

(89)	barbero	bono	bona	bastonada	
	doctor.M	good.M	good.F	beating.F	
	'(a) good doctor'		'(a) severe beating'		(Haedo 1612: fols. 120v, 201v)

(90)	mucho mucho	'very much'	
	siéme siéme	'together'	(Arends 2005: 626)

Nouns seem to have been invariant and not inflected for number, though plurality could be indicated through the plural form of the demonstrative:

(91)	questi	signor	estar	amigo	di	mi	
	DEM.PL	sir	COP	friend	of	1SG	
	'These gentlemen are my friends.'						(Anonymous 1830: 7)

84. As Schuchardt lamented, "*[a]lles Lautliche ist nämlich mit der größten Nachlässigkeit behandelt; es wimmelt von Druck- und Schreibfehlern*" ('everything concerning the sound is treated with the greatest carelessness; printing and spelling errors abound'; 1909: 457, my translation).

85. However, earlier sources portray a more synthetic language; whether the analytic nature is a later phenomenon or an effect of the French description of it in the *Dictionnaire de la langue franque ou petit mauresque* is a matter of debate (Rachel Selbach, p.c.).

Typically nouns were derived from the singular form, except in some cases of naturally occurring pairs or groups, where the plural form was adopted, such as *guanti* 'glove' (< Ital. plural form), *piedi* 'foot' (< Ital. plural form), *datoli* 'date (the fruit)' (< Ital. plural form), *tapetos* 'carpet' (< Span. plural form), and so on (Schuchardt 1909:444f). Case does not seem to have been relevant.

According to the *Dictionnaire de la langue franque ou petit mauresque* (1830), the pronominal system distinguished between three persons and two numbers, and, in the third person singular, two genders:

	PERSONAL	POSSESSIVE
1SG	*mi*	*di mi*
2SG	*ti*	*di ti*
3SG	*ell(u)o* (M)/*ella* (F)	*di ellu/ella*
1PL	*voi*	*di voi*
2PL	*noi*	*notro/a*
3PL	*elli*	*loro/di loro*

Notice that, as in the Romance languages, there is no third person singular neutral. There was no distinction between subject and object personal pronouns. There are some indications of possessive pronoun forms (*mia* 'my', as in *casa mia* 'my house'; *notre* 'our'; *votre* 'your'; *tuya*, as in *andar a casa tuya* 'go to your house'; Schuchardt 1909:449, 452). However, possession seems more typically to have been expressed through the preposition *di* 'of' (cf. also (91) above):

(92) a. la baréta di mi
DEF.F hat of 1SG
'my hat'

b. commé star il fratello di ti?
how COP DEF.M brother of 2SG
'How is your brother?'

c. sé mi star al logo di ti, mi counchar/fazir
if 1SG COP in.DEF.M place of 2SG 1SG do
'If I were in your place, I would do (it).' (Anonymous 1830:50, 94f)

There seems to have been a definite article (as in (93a, b)) and a demonstrative (as in (93c, d)), as well as an optional indefinite article (as in (93e–g)). All seem to have agreed with the noun in gender (see also (92)):

(93) a. aprir la bentana
open DEF.F window
'Open the window.' (Anonymous 1830:95)

b. massar il fouogo
light DEF.M fire
'Light the fire.' (Anonymous 1830:32)

c. qouesto libro star di mi
DEM.M book COP of 1SG
'This book is mine.' (Anonymous 1830:49)

d. anchora no estar tempo de parlar questa cosa
now NEG COP time COMP talk DEM.F thing
'Now is not (the) time to talk (about) this thing.' (Haedo 1612: fol. 129v)

e. ti dar una cadiéra al Signor
2SG give INDEF.F chair to.DEM.M sir
'Give a chair to the gentleman.' (Anonymous 1830: 94)

f. mi andar mirar oun amigo
1SG go see INDEF.M friend
'I'm going to see a friend.' (Anonymous 1830: 95)

g. star buona genti
COP good man
'(He) is (a) good man.' (Anonymous 1830: 94)

Notice that Example (93d) might indicate that the definite article was also optional. There seems to have been a remoteness distinction for the demonstrative. Compare (93c, d) with (94):

(94) quoello qué ti quérir
DEM.M REL 2SG want
'That which you (would) like.' (Anonymous 1830: 97)

The verb typically appeared in an unmarked form, etymologically derived from the Romance infinitive form, although the Lingua Franca verbs tended to only end in *-ir* or *-ar*, irrespective of the original Romance infinitival ending, as in *andar* 'go', *parlar/ablar* 'talk, speak', *portar* 'bring', *sentir* 'hear', *ténir* 'have', *quérir* 'want, like', and so on. The unmarked form seems to have been used for any temporal reference (as in *mi andar* 'I go/went/will go', *mi sentir* 'I hear/heard/will hear', etc., cf. also Example (99) below), although there was also an overt past tense form, denoted by the suffix *-ato* (< Ital. past participle suffix), and a future tense form, denoted by the marker *bisogno* (< Ital. 'need'):

(95) a. mi mir-ato in casa di ti
1SG see-PST in house of 2SG
'I saw (him/her/it) in your house.'

b. bisgogno andar domani
FUT go tomorrow
'(We) will go tomorrow.' (Anonymous 1830: 96)

In some texts something which looks like the present perfect seems to occur, as in *ha portato* 'has brought' (cf. the sample text below). The imperative was expressed with the unmarked form (see also (93a, b)):

(96) mirar qué ora star al orlogio di ti
see what time COP in.DEM.M watch of 2SG
'See what time it is on your watch.' (Anonymous 1830: 97)

The word order seems to have predominantly been subject-verb-object. The object (direct or indirect) was very often marked with *per* (but see (93d) above and the short sample text below):

(97) a. qouesto offendir per mi
DEM.M offend OBJ 1SG
'This offends me.'

b. mi poudir servir per ti per qoualké cosa?
1SG can serve OBJ 2SG OBJ some thing
'Can I serve you anything?' (Anonymous 1830: 54, 94)

The third person singular pronoun, whether clause subject or object, was often not overtly expressed (see Examples (92c), (93g) and (98a, c)). The copula *(e)star* seems to have been obligatory (see also (91)–(93), (96)); it was also used as a locative:

(98) a. no parlar que estar malato
NEG say that COP ill
'Don't say that (he) is ill.' (Haedo 1612: fol. 120)

b. mi star bonou
1SG COP good
'I am well.' (Anonymous 1830: 93)

c. star in casa? no star foura
COP in house NEG COP out
'Is (he) at home? No, (he) is (/has gone) out' (Anonymous 1830: 93)

Negation was expressed with preverbal *no(n)*, as shown in Examples (93d) and (98). Polar questions were marked through intonation only (Anonymous 1830: 9), while content questions seem to have been formed with clause initial content words:

(99) qui star qouesto Signor qué poco poco ablar per ti?
who COP DEM.M sir REL little~RED talk OBJ 2SG
'Who is the man who just spoke to you?' (Anonymous 1830: 97)

Subordination seems to have been expressed either through juxtaposition, or overt subordinators (conjunctions, complementizers or relativizers), as in Examples (93d), (94) and (99).

5.3.1.3 *Short text*

(From Haedo 1612: fol. 201v. I have kept the capitalizations and interpunctuation as they appear in the original. Glossing and translation were done by myself.)

Veccio, veccio, niçarante Christiano, ven aca, porque tener aqui tortuga? qui port-ato
old old Christian Christian come here why have here turtle who bring-PST

de campaña? gran vellaco estar, qui ha port-ato. Anda presto, puglia, porta fora,
from field big villain COP who have bring-PST go quickly take bring outside

guarda diablo, portar a la campaña, questo si tener en casa estar grande pecato. Mira
keep devil bring to DEF.F field DEM.M if have in house COP big sin see

no trouar mi altra volta, sino a fee de Dio, mi parlar patron donar bona
NEG find 1SG other.F time if.not to faith of God 1SG speak master give good.F

bastonada, mumucho [*sic*], mucho.
beating much~RED

'Old Christian, come here, why (do you) have a turtle here? Who brought (it) indoors? (He) who brought (it) is a great villain. Go quickly, take (it) and bring (it) outside,[86] (may the) Devil take (you), take (it) outside, (it) is a great sin if (you) have this in (the) house. See that I do not find (it) again, or else by God, I (will) speak (to the) master (and he will) give (you a) very severe beating.'

86. Note that *puglia, porta fora* 'take bring outside' might be an instance of a serial verb construction despite the interpunctuation.

5.3.1.4 *Some sources of data*

A valuable source of Lingua Franca is the anonymously published *Dictionnaire de la langue franque ou petit mauresque* from 1830, which contains a few grammatical notes, a dictionary from French to Lingua Franca, and some pages of phrases and dialogues. It has been made available for online viewing by *e-corpus* at http://www.e-corpus.org/notices/9183/gallery/90575, accessed 9 February 2015. Haedo's *Topographia e historia general de Argel* from (1612), which contains a number of examples of Lingua Franca, is available on Google Books. A number of texts and a glossary, as well as various articles on Lingua Franca, can be found at the site *A Glossary of Lingua Franca* (https://pantherfile.uwm.edu/corre/www/franca/go.html, accessed 9 February 2015). do Cuoto (2002) has collected a great number of texts containing Lingua Franca samples, from the 12th to the late 19th century and Cifoletti (2004) has collected those texts containing Lingua Franca from the Barbary Coast, as well as texts containing Sabir.

5.3.2 Chinese Pidgin English: An extinct English-lexified pidgin on the Chinese coast[87]

5.3.2.1 *A brief background sketch of Chinese Pidgin English*

Chinese Pidgin English, also known as *Chinese Coast Pidgin* or, in Cantonese, *Gwóngdūng fāanwáa*, and called *Pidgin* or *Pidgin English* by the users themselves, was once spoken by thousands of people in interior and coastal China as well as in South and North East Asia outside China (cf. Baker & Mühlhäusler 1990:109). The language is no longer used today, though there are those that remember it. Together with Lingua Franca, it was one of the most important trade languages the world has ever known (Philip Baker, p.c.).[88]

The British began to trade in the Chinese ports in the late 17th century and were initially confined to Guangzhou (Bolton 2003). At first European traders had to communicate through interpreters (typically from Macau, where a Portuguese-lexified creole would develop due to the Portuguese trading rights in Macau); the Chinese did not speak the European languages and they were forbidden to teach Chinese to foreigners:

> The Chinese government has endeavoured … to restrict the intercommunication of natives and foreigners as much as is consistent with its existence; and as one means of achieving this object, it has prevented foreigners from learning the Chinese language … denouncing as traitors all those natives who dare to teach the language of the 'central flowery nation' to outside barbarians. (Williams 1836:429f)[89]

87. This section relies heavily on Baker & Mühlhäusler (1990), Ansaldo et al. (2012) and Matthews & Li (2013). I am very grateful to Philip Baker for his helpful comments on this snapshot.

88. Though there were many other long-lived and widespread pidgins, such as West African Pidgin English, Mobilian Jargon (see 14.4.1) and Russenorsk (see 12.4.1), to mention only a few.

89. Williams (1836:431) goes on to comment on the mutual benefit for each partner to be able to speak a language that the other doesn't understand, in this case Cantonese and what he calls "good English", which, according to Williams, "is nearly as unintelligible to them as Chinese is to the foreigner".

Communication was thus done by means of a European language variety. After the end of the Opium War in 1842, five new treaty ports were opened up and Hong Kong was conceded to the British. Later even more treaty ports were opened up. With this the English contact language, formerly typical of the Guangzhou area, spread to other ports and areas (Ansaldo et al. 2012).

Chinese Pidgin English may have started as early as 1715. The language was used in all interactions between Chinese and Europeans, both in trade and in domestic contexts such as between foreign residents and their domestic staff (Bolton 2003: 159). It gradually started to decline from the second half of the 19th century, as a result of English language schools, which meant that an increasing number of people were able to negotiate with foreigners without using Chinese Pidgin English (Philip Baker, p.c.). With the Japanese occupation of Hong Kong in World War II, foreigners either left or were held in detention camps (and later left once the occupation was over), meaning that the contexts in which Chinese Pidgin English had been used disappeared (Ansaldo 2009: 197). However, there are reports of Chinese Pidgin English being used between Europeans and their Chinese servants through the 1960s (Matthews & Li 2013: 207).

It does not seem to have been a particularly stigmatized variety while it was used between trading partners (Ansaldo et al. 2012). However, when a class of Chinese educated in English began to emerge, Chinese Pidgin English became more and more associated with servants and service jobs, and thus lost in prestige (Holm 1988: 515, Bolton 2003: 159f).

There are three types of sources of Chinese Pidgin English. One kind is Chinese phrase books or glossaries meant for Chinese learners. They were written in Chinese characters that seem to constitute the closest phonetic approximations to the Chinese Pidgin English words. These glossaries seem to actually have "played a major role in both the propagation and stabilisation of C[hinese] P[idgin] E[nglish], as unprecedented event for any pidgin or creole language" (Baker & Mühlhäusler 1990: 112). Another source type is words and phrases found in European memoirs, travel accounts, and so on. These are meant for a European audience. A third kind of source is humorous verses and stories that are supposedly in Chinese Pidgin English, a famous example being Charles Leland's *Pidgin-English Sing-song* (1876). However, these third kinds of sources are generally considered unreliable and should be used with care, if at all, as the data there seems artificially constructed for the amusement of the (European) readers.

It should be noted that there is likely to have been considerable variation in Chinese Pidgin English, depending on the region it was used in and on the L1 of the individual user. It is also likely that Chinese Pidgin English, like any other language, changed over time (see Baker & Mühlhäusler 1990 for further details).

5.3.2.2 *A short linguistic sketch of Chinese Pidgin English*

Most of the Chinese Pidgin English data in this section is from the 19th century.

Any information on the phonological system of Chinese Pidgin English has to come trough inference, since the only sources left to us are in written form. Exactly which sounds the author of a particular passage meant to capture is thus to a great extent a matter of guesswork. Nevertheless, when comparing sources, it seems as if the following 17 consonants are attested:

/p, b, m, f, w, t, d, n, s, l, ʦ, ʤ, y, k, g, ŋ, h/. It may also be that European speakers of Chinese Pidgin English also used /θ, ð, z, š/ (Bakker 2009: 14). Sources seem to indicate that etymological /v/ > /b/ or /p/ (as in *hab* or *hap* 'have'), /θ/ > /t/ (as in *ting* 'thing'), /ð/ > /d/ (as in *dat* 'that'); /z/ > /ʤ/ (as in *squigi* 'extort' < Eng. *squeeze*). The English /ɹ/ seems to have either been rendered as /l/ (as in *chenawile* 'January'; Williams 1836: 432) or dropped (as in *etoo* 'earth'; *ibid.*). There may have been as many as 11 vowels /i, ɪ, e, ɛ, æ, a, ə, ɨ, ɔ, o, u/ (Matthews & Li 2013: 207), although that too is likely to have varied between speakers.

There is no evidence of tone in Chinese Pidgin English (notice that Cantonese, one of the main input languages, is a tone language). It may be that the tone associated with the Chinese characters in the glossaries represent stress patterns, with, for example, low tone representing unstressed syllables (Matthews & Li 2013: 207). The syllable structure seems to have been restricted to CV and CVC syllables and consonant clusters seem to have been avoided (cf. *chiloh* 'child', *sitop* 'stop' and *sileek* 'silk'; Baker & Mühlhäusler 1990: 96).

The morphology was predominantly analytic, although there was often a word-final *-um* added to verbs ending in *l*, as in *callum* 'call', *killum* 'kill', *sellum* 'sell', and so on.

Nouns were typically invariant and did not inflect for number (or case or gender), although there were some sporadic instances of plural *-s* in English sources (see also (101a)):

(100) a. he hap five piece chiloh – three piece bull chiloh, and two
3SG.M have five CL child three CL male child and two
piece cow chiloh
CL female child
'He has three children – two sons and two daughters.'
(Baker & Mühlhäusler 1990: 99, citing Holman 1834: 110)

b. I catchee flowero, all same put round head cow chilo
1SG catch flower like put around head female child
'I (will) get flowers, (to) put around (your) daughter's head.' (Downing 1838: 94)

The demonstratives *thisee* 'this' and *that* 'that' seem to have had a distance contrast. The definite article *the* occasionally appears in English sources (as in (101a)), but not in Chinese, where *that* sometimes functioned as a definite article (as in (101b)). The indefinite article was expressed by *one* (as in (101c), but cf. (107b) below):

(101) a. they wantshee too-muchee dollar for the fishee
3PL want too.much dollar for DEF fish
'They asked for too high a price for the fish.' (Downing 1838: 21)

b. that clock hap stop
that clock PFV stop
'The clock has stopped.' (Matthews & Li 2013: 208, citing Tong 1862: IV.51)

c. you wantchee catchee one piecee lawyer
you want catch INDEF CL capon
'You'll have to engage a lawyer.' (Ansaldo et al. 2012: 77, citing Tong 1862: IV.32)

Sometimes *alla* (sometimes rendered as *all a* or *allo*) appears as a marker for quantification:

(102) all right I come chop chop; show he allo man no makee wait
all.right 1SG come quickly show 3SG all man NEG make wait
'All right, I'll come directly; show them all (what I want so as) not to make (me) wait.'
(Anonymous 1860: 44)

The classifier *piece* commonly followed numerals (as in Example (100a) above) and sometimes also demonstratives (as in Example (104d) below).

Pronouns seem to have varied considerably (Matthews & Li 2013: 208):

	PERSONAL			POSSESSIVE
	DEPENDENT		INDEPENDENT	
	SUBJECT	OBJECT		
1SG	*my, I, me*	*my, me*	*my*	*my*
2SG	*you*	*you*	*you*	*you/your*
3SG	*he, she, it*	*he/him, she/her, it*	*he/him, she/her*	*he/his, she/her*
1PL	*we*	*us*	–	–
2PL	*you*	*you*	*you*	*you/your*
3PL	*he, they*	*he, them*	*he*	*he*

Notice that the third person was not always differentiated with respect to number. Possession was expressed by juxtaposition, as in Example (100b) above.

Comparison was indicated by *more* preceding the adjective:

(103) more better you go Macao
more better 2SG go Macau
'(It's) better (if) you go to Macau.' (Downing 1838: 299)

There was only one tense/aspect marker, *hap/hab* (sometimes as *have*), denoting perfective or the perfect ((104a, b), see also (101b) above). Unmarked verbs were used in any kind of time reference (cf. Examples (100b), (101a) and (102) above), which could optionally be specified through adverbials such as *by'm by/by and by* 'later' (as in (104c)) or *justee now* 'now' (as in (104b, d)):

(104) a. my hap go court one time
1SG PFV go court one time
'I have been to court once.' (Matthews & Li 2013: 209, citing Tong 1862: IV.32)

b. have makee too much lain, and just now my umbleller have bloke
PFV make too much rain and now 1SG umbrella COP broke
'It's been raining too much and now my umbrella is broken.' (Anonymous 1860: 47)

c. by-and-by can do, next year he go, my makee stop, so fashion
later can do next year 3SG go 1SG make stop so fashion
'Later he can do (it), next year he (will) go, I (will) stay, in that manner.'
(Anonymous 1860: 100)

d. you talkee my show that piece cookman makee eat –
2SG say 1SG tell DEM CL cook make eat
just now my suppose he makee finish chow chow
now 1SG think 3SG make finish eat
'You told me to tell the cook to eat (it) – now I think he finished eating (it).'
(Anonymous 1860: 46)

It seems as if preverbal *makee* 'make' was used as a kind of action marker, as in Examples (101c), (102) and (104c, d) above.

The word order was generally subject-verb-object, although topics could be fronted. Both subjects and objects could be dropped from the clause, as in Example (104c, d) and (105).

Negation was indicated with the invariant preverbal *no*:

(105) no have eye, no can see; no can see, no can savez
NEG have eye NEG can see NEG can see NEG can know
'If (you) don't have (the) eye, (you) can't see, if (you) can't see, you can't know'
(referring to painted eye on vessels; Downing 1838: 108)

In English sources the interrogative phrase tended to be fronted in content questions (as in (106a)), while in Chinese sources it could be either fronted or remain *in situ* (as in (106b)):

(106) a. what thing you wantshee?
what 2SG want
'What do you want?' (Downing 1838: 279)
b. you wantschee how much?
2SG want how much
'How much do you want?' (Matthews & Li 2013: 211 citing Tong 1862: IV.54)

Polar questions seem to have been marked through intonation only.

The use of the copula changed a great deal in the sources over time (Baker & Mühlhäusler 1990: 103). In general the copula would be lacking with adjectives (as in (107a); but cf. (104b) above), while with predicative nouns it could be lacking (as in (107b)) or could be expressed with *belong* (as in (107c)).

(107) a. thisee mutton too much hard
DEM mutton too much hard
'This mutton (is) too hard.' (Matthews & Li 2013: 210, citing Tong 1862: VI.25)
b. he honest man
3SG honest man
'He (is an) honest man.' (Matthews & Li 2013: 210 citing Tong 1862: IV.50)
c. my belong tailorman
1SG COP tailor
'I am a tailor.' (Anonymous 1860: 44)

Coordination and complementation generally seem to have been indicated through juxtaposition only. Conditional clauses seem to have been marked with *suppose* 'suppose, if' or remained unmarked and indicated through juxtaposition only. Relative clauses seem to have been very rare. There seem to have been a number of serial verb constructions, typically involving the verbs *come*, *go*, *take* and *give*.

5.3.2.3 *Short text*

(From Anonymous 1860:43ff. B = servant boy; M = English master; T = tailor.)

B: You makee ling?
2SG make ring
'Did you ring (sir)?'

M: Yes, sendee catchee one piece tailorman
yes send get INDEF CL tailor
'Yes, send for a tailor.'

B: Just now have got bottom side
now LOC below
'(He) is below at present.'

M: Show he come top side
tell 3SG come up
'Tell him to come up.'

(*Enter the tailor*)

M: You belong tailorman?
2SG COP tailor
'Are you the tailor?'

T: Yes, sar, my belong tailorman
yes sir 2SG COP tailor
'Yes, sir, I am a tailor'

M: My boy makee show you what thing my makee wantchee, more better you go
1SG boy make tell 2SG what 1SG make want more better 2SG go
bottom side askee he. He makee show you what thing.
below ask 3SG 3SG make tell 2SG what
'My boy (will) tell you what I want (done), (it is) better (if) you go down (and) ask him. He (will) tell you what (I want).'

B: What thing you wantchee?
what 2SG want
'What (do) you want?'

M: Show he makee mend that more olo piece coat, and suppose he can makee clean
tell 3SG make mend DEM more old CL coat and if 3SG can make clean
my thinkee more better
1SG think more better
'Tell him (to) mend that very old coat, and if he can clean (it), so much the better.'

5.3.2.4 *Some sources of data*

Snippets of Chinese Pidgin English can be found in various memoirs and travel accounts. A fair few examples can be found in *The Englishman in China* (Anonymous 1860), which is available on Google Books. Li et al. (2005) have translated Tong (1862) to English.[90] Baker (2003a, 2003b)

90. It should be noted that it is unclear from whom the Chinese Pidgin English found in Tong (1862) is: the data actually consists of notes in the margins of the book, where somebody has written

are collected data from English language sources; unfortunately these valuable corpora remain unpublished.

5.3.3 Pidgin Delaware: An extinct Unami-lexified pidgin on the Middle Atlantic coast of North America[91]

5.3.3.1 *A brief background sketch of Pidgin Delaware*

Pidgin Delaware (also called *Delaware Jargon* or *Trader's Jargon*) was a pidgin used between the Delaware Indians and the Europeans who settled around the area of the Delaware River in the early 17th century, especially because of the fur trade. The Delaware languages were spoken by the Lenape people and comprise two closely related East Algonquian languages, Munsee and Unami. The Europeans who settled in the area were Dutch (New Netherland), Swedish (New Sweden) and British (Pennsylvania and New Jersey). Pidgin Delaware was probably never used by more than a few thousand people. It seems to have gone in decline during the 18th century, possibly because English or some English contact variety gained stronger currency, although "[a]s late as 1785 … the Delaware learned by Whites on the frontier contained Pidgin Delaware features" (Goddard 1997: 43).

The first European settlers arrived in the Unami-speaking territory on the Delaware River in 1624. Very shortly after that, in 1628, possibly the first reference to Pidgin Delaware can be found in a letter by Reverend Michaëlius, where he states that the Unami use a simplified variety of their language with the Europeans:

> It also seems to us that they rather design to conceal their language from us than to properly communicate it, except in things which happen in daily trade; saying that it is sufficient for us to understand them in that; and then they speak only in half sentences, shortened words, and frequently call out a dozen things and even more; and all things which have only a rude resemblance to each other, they frequently call by the same name. In truth it is a made-up, childish language; so that even those who can best of all speak with the savages, and get along well in trade, are nevertheless wholly in the dark and bewildered when they hear the savages talking among themselves. (Michaëlius 1909: 128)

The Swedish settlers who later established the colony New Sweden along the Delaware River initially traded with the help of Dutch interpreters. Subsequently the British settlers of the Pennsylvania and New Jersey colonies initially used Swedish interpreters. Pidgin Delaware was thus spread from the Dutch to the Swedes, and from the Swedes to the British (Goddard 1997: 82).[92]

Chinese Pidgin English equivalents of the Standard English sentences in Chinese characters which approximate Cantonese pronunciations of Chinese Pidgin English (Philip Baker, p.c.).

91. This section relies almost exclusively on Goddard (1997).

92. See Thomason (1980) for a discussion on the possibility that Pidgin Delaware was a pre-European contact language already in use when the Europeans began to settle the area.

The two major sources of Pidgin Delaware are (i) a translation into Pidgin Delaware of Martin Luther's Small Catechism by the Swedish minister Johannes Campanius (1696), which also contains a vocabulary of words and phrases;[93] and (ii) the vocabulary *The Indian Interpreter* apparently compiled in West New Jersey in the late 17th century (1684). Other, minor sources, typically include scattered words and phrases. The earliest source of Pidgin Delaware data seems to be a vocabulary from 1633 from below the Falls of the Delaware at Trenton, compiled by Johannes de Laet (1633: 75). The last known source seems to be a vocabulary recorded among Delaware emigrants in western Pennsylvania, compiled by Major Ebenezer Denny in 1785 (Denny 1860: 478ff). For further details, see Goddard (1997).

The vocabulary of Pidgin Delaware is almost exclusively derived from Unami. There is material derived from both the Northern and the Southern dialects.

5.3.3.2 *A short linguistic sketch of Pidgin Delaware*

It should be noted that the original spelling from the sources has been retained.

Since all the information we have on Pidgin Delaware is via European written sources from the 17th to the 19th centuries, any description of the Pidgin Delaware phonological system is highly tentative at best. It is likely that there was regional variation as well as individual variation between speakers. Furthermore, the way sounds were written down seems to have varied between different authors; these spellings may then have been altered in the process of copying and printing (Goddard 1997). There seems to have been 13 consonants, /p, m, w, t, n, l, s, c, ʃ, j, k, x, h/, of which all of the voiceless consonants except /h/ seem to have had contrastive length (/p:, t:, s:, c:, ʃ:, k:, x:/), and six vowels /i, e, a, ə, ɔ, o, u/ that all seemed to have contrastive length (Bakker 2009: 12). Not infrequently /l/ was rendered as <r>.

In contrast to its lexifier Unami, which makes use of both affixation and non-linear markers (such as ablaut) and is highly synthetic morphologically, Pidgin Delaware was predominantly analytic in its morphological structure. While there are traces of Unami inflectional forms in Pidgin Delaware, these seem more likely to have been frozen into invariant "descriptively unanalyzable units" (Goddard 1997: 57).

Nouns seem to have been invariant and not inflected for number:

(108) ne olocko toon
1 hole go
'We run into holes.' (Goddard 1997: 58)

The Unami gender and case systems, as well as the possessive inflection, had been dropped; possession seems to typically have been indicated by juxtaposition only:

93. Although it was published considerably later, Campanius states in his prologue that the vocabulary was compiled during his stay in New Sweden 1642–1649, while the translation of the Small Catechism was completed in Sweden in 1656 (Campanius 1696: 3, 5).

(109) Renáppi Rω̃énse
person name
'(a) person's name' (Goddard 1997: 63)

There were three free pronominal forms, differentiated for person only, but not number or gender:[94]

	PERSONAL		POSSESSIVE	
1	*ni(r)*	I, we	*nirona*	my, our
2	*ki(r)*	you	*kirona*	your
3	*jon(i)*	s/he, it, they	*nekama*	his/her/their

The same forms were used in subject or object position, as well as for possession, though there seems to have been a pronominal set used exclusively for possession (derived from the Unami plural forms). There do not seem to have been any articles ((110a, b); cf. also (109) above), though the third person form (*joni*) could be used as a demonstrative (as in (110c)), which may occasionally have been interpreted as a definite article.

(110) a. Matcha pauluppa shuta
already buck successfully.shot
'(I) have caught (a) buck.'

b. chijr paétton mítzi suvvijvan mvvs
2 give eat all animal
'You give food (to) all (the) animals.'

c. jω̃ni Aana
3 road
'this/that road' (Goddard 1997: 59, 61)

A general indefinite, *chéko/kéko*, was used not only as an indefinite pronoun (as in (111a)), but also as an interrogative (as in (111b)) and a relative particle (as in (111c)):

(111) a. bakanta chéko
hit INDEF
'to hit someone'

b. Kec-loe Keckoe kee Wingenum
2-say INDEF 2 want
'Say what you want.'

c. thaan jω̃ni chéko tahóttamen nijr
PREP 3 INDEF love 1
'to those +who love me' (Goddard 1997: 61)

94. This contrasts with the complex pronominal system of Unami, which has several bound pronominal sets, as well as a free, emphatic, one, all of which differentiated between number (singular/plural), gender (animate/inanimate), inclusive/exclusive, and syntactic function.

The verb was invariant and neither marked for the subject and object in the clause (as in Unami), nor marked for tense, mood or aspect:

(112) a. ock paétton jω̃ni, mochijrick Nitáppi
and give 3 great friend
'and gave it (to) his disciples.' (Goddard 1997:59)

b. kacko pata
what bring
'What have you brought?' (Thomason 1980:171)

c. matta nijr tappin
NEG 1 sit
'I am not going to sit.' (Goddard 1997:62)

d. chijr mátta sijs cavínn cattúnga
2 NEG more lie sleep
'Do not lie sleeping any longer.' (Goddard 1997:59)

e. kako meele
what give
'What will you give for this?' (Thomason 1980:171)

f. Chingo kee peto nee chase
when 2 bring 1 skin
'When will you bring me skins?' (Goddard 1997:58)

Specific time reference seems to have been done with adverbials (cf. Example (110a) above):

(113) match poh
already come
'(He) has come.' (Goddard 1997:61)

The form of the verb reflects various fossilized inflectional forms in Unami.

While Unami does not have a fixed word order (although topics tend to be fronted), Pidgin Delaware seems to predominantly have had either a subject-verb-object or a subject-object-verb word order. Both the subject and the object were frequently dropped (as in Examples (110a), (112a, e) and (113)).

Negation was indicated by the invariant particle *matta*, which most often, though not always, appeared clause initially (as in Examples (112c, d)). Polar questions were not overtly marked for Pidgin Delaware in the sources, even though the translations indicated them through interpunctuation, which may have signified that they had a distinctive intonation:

(114) a. Pomuttamen cijr?
shoot 2
'Will you shoot?' (Thomason 1980:173)

There does not seem to have been any overt copula:

(115) a. nirj rω̃e, jω̃ni matta manúnckus
1 say 3 NEG bad
'We should say, he (is) not bad.' (Goddard 1997:59)

b. nittappe kire
friend 2
'You (are) (my) friend.' (Goddard 1997:63)

c. tana ke wigwham?
where 2 house
'Where (is) your house?' (Thomason 1980:174)

There were the conjunctions *og/ock* 'and' (see also (112a)) and *suck* 'but', and a subordinator *kónna* 'that':

(116) a. kee squa og enychan hatah?
2 wife and child have
'Do you have (a) wife and children?' (Thomason 1980:173)

b. Kónna nijr nirω̄na Nitáppi Zaéband, ock chéko pijri hátte mátta kommvvta
that 1 1.POSS friend money and what other have NEG steal
'...that we do not steal our neighbour's money or whatever else he has.' (Goddard 1997:61)

As mentioned above, the indefinite pronoun also functioned as a relativizer.

5.3.3.3 *Short text*

(The Lord's Prayer, from Campanius 1696:41ff. Glossing and translation done by myself.)

Nω̄r nirω̄na, chij jω̄ni hω̄rítt mochyrick Hocquaéssung táppin // Cíntikat chijre Rwǽnse //
father 1.POSS 2 3 good big heaven sit holy 2 name

Phaa chirje Tutæænungh // Hátte chéko chijr tahottamen, renáckot thaani
come 2 kingdom/property have INDEF 2 love like? PREP

Hocquaéssung renáckot ock taani Hácking // Nirω̄na shéu póón pææta chijr jocke //
heaven like? and PREP earth 1.POSS always bread give 2 day

Ock chijr sinkáttan chéko nijr mattarútti hátte maranijto renackot ock nijr sinkáttan chéko
and 2 do INDEF 1 useless have make like? and 1 do INDEF

manúnckus Rénappi maranijto nijre // Ock chijr, mátta bakíttan nijr taan manúckus Manétto //
evil name make 1 and 2 NEG bring? 1 PREP evil God

Suck bakittan nirω̄na suhwijvan manúckus // Kitzi
but bring? 1.POSS all evil true

'Our Father in heaven // hallowed be your name // Your kingdom come // your will be done, on earth as it is in heaven // Give us today our daily bread // Forgive us our sins, as we forgive those who sin against us // Lead us not into temptation // but deliver us from evil // Amen.'

5.3.3.4 *Some sources of data*

There is not much data available for Pidgin Delaware. Campanius translation of Martin Luther's Small Catechism (1696), with a vocabulary as an appendix, is available on Internet Archive (unfortunately only accessible to those who read Swedish and the Fraktur typeface). Prince (1912) provides a glossary based on *The Indian Interpreter* (Anonymous 1684). Goddard (1997) provides numerous glossed and translated examples.

5.4 Summary

There are numerous theories about the origins of pidgin languages and the mechanisms involved in their formation.

The Monogenesis theory assumes that all pidgins descended from one Proto-Pidgin. The Nautical Jargon theory assumes that the jargon of seamen formed the ancestors for various groups of pidgins: English-lexified pidgins would thus all descend from a common English Proto-Pidgin, French-lexified pidgins from a common French Proto-Pidgin, and so on.

Polygenesis theories assume that different pidgin languages emerged independently, but under similar conditions. The Common Core theory assumes that those features that were common to all the languages in the contact situation would enter the pidgin structural system. The Interlanguage theory puts forth that pidgins are fossilized stages of second language learning, where the lexifier would have been the target language. The Foreigner Talk theory puts forth that the speakers of the lexifier languages deliberately simplified their language when interacting with speakers of other languages, and this simplified version of the lexifier language would then constitute the target model.

Transfer refers to the influence of a person's first language(s) when acquiring a second language. Substrate theories put forth that the first languages, the substrate languages, of those speakers who were not native to the lexifier would have influenced the structure of the pidgin through transfer.

Tertiary Hybridization refers to the linguistic hybridization that is assumed to take place when one language is used as a *lingua franca* between speakers of other, mutually unintelligible languages.

5.5 Key points

- **Most theories on the genesis of pidgin languages assume that pidgins share structural affinities that differ from non-pidgin languages.**
- **Monogenetic theories propose that pidgins share structural affinities because different pidgins originate in one single parent language.**
- **Polygenetic theories propose that pidgins share structural affinities because individual pidgin languages evolved individually but under similar conditions.**
- **The theory of tertiary hybridization proposes that a pidgin does not arise unless it is systematically used as a lingua franca by third parties.**
- **It is likely that a combination of processes was involved in the formation of any given pidgin language.**
- **Diffusion and inheritance may also have affected the outcome of any given pidgin language.**
- **Like any other natural language, pidgins are dynamic systems that continually evolve.**

5.6 Exercises

1. Why has the monogenesis theory on the genesis of pidgins been abandoned?
2. In what way does the Nautical Jargon theory have affinities with both monogenetic and polygenetic theories?
3. What is 'tertiary hybridization' and how is that proposed to relate to the genesis of pidgins?
4. What is the difference between the Interlanguage theory and the Foreigner Talk theory?
5. What role are substrates and L1 transfer proposed to have in the emergence of pidgins?

Languages cited in Chapter 6

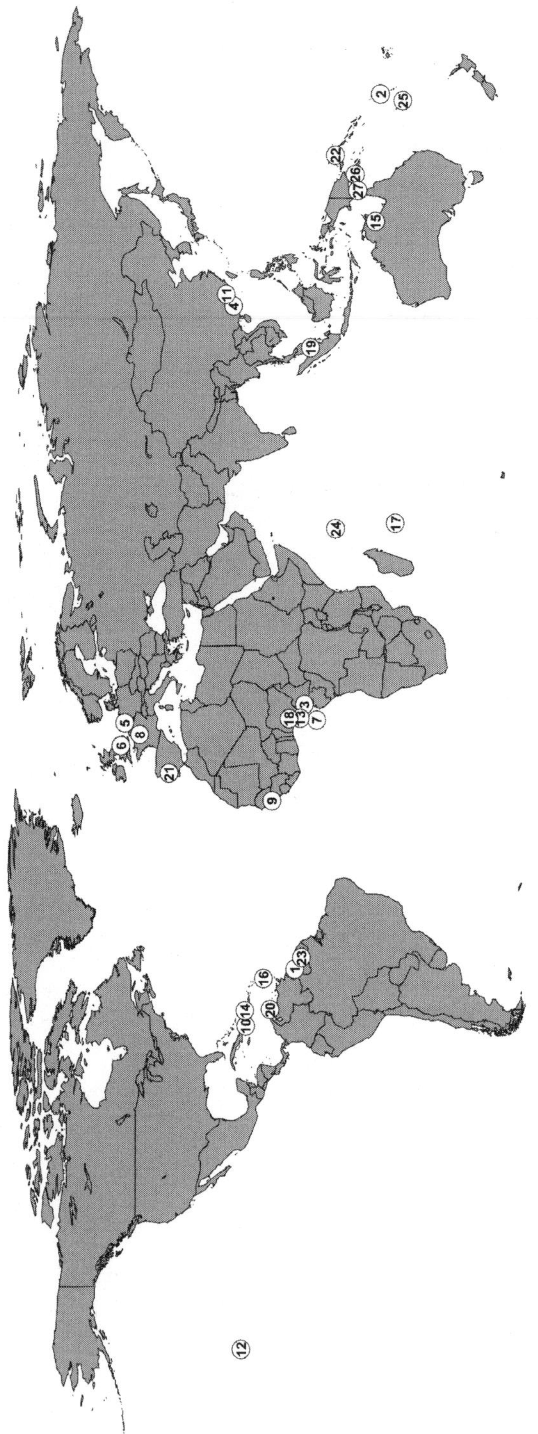

1. Arawak; Berbice Creole; Creolese
2. Bislama
3. Cameroon Pidgin English
4. Cantonese; Chinese Pidgin English
5. Dutch
6. English
7. Fa d'Ambô; Santome
8. French
9. Guinea Bissau Kriyol
10. Haitian Creole; Taíno
11. Hakka Chinese
12. Hawai'i Creole English; Hawai'i Pidgin English; Hawaiian; Pidgin Hawaiian
13. Ijo, Southeast
14. Jamaican
15. Kriol
16. Lesser Antillean Creole
17. Mauritian Creole; Reunion Creole
18. Nigerian Pidgin
19. Papiá Kristang
20. Papiamentu
21. Portuguese
22. Rabaul Creole German
23. Saramaccan; Sranan
24. Seychelles Creole
25. Tayo
26. Tok Pisin
27. Torres Strait Creole

Chapter 6

Theories on the formation processes of creoles

As with pidgins, it is a matter of great debate what kinds of formation processes might have been involved in the emergence of creole languages. The discussion hinges on whether creole languages share structural properties that set them apart from non-creoles and whether their developmental paths and processes differ from non-creole languages. One controversy is whether children or adults were the creators of the languages, another whether or not creoles per definition descend from pidgins. This chapter will very briefly bring up a few of the most commonly discussed theories on the development of creoles (6.1) before touching on the issues of the pidgin-to-creole life cycle (6.2) and the role of multilingualism in creole formation (6.3). Section 6.4 gives short sketches of three creoles that have been brought up in the creole genesis debate: Hawai'i Creole English (prominent in the Language Bioprogram Hypothesis debate), Haitian Creole (prominent in the Relexification Hypothesis debate) and Berbice Dutch (a language which seems to have an unusually uniform substratal input).

6.1 The development of creoles

We have seen that creole languages arose in societies that emerged when people of different linguistic backgrounds, many of whom had (or had been) resettled to new locations, were brought together. The new circumstances that this resettlement and interaction brought with it led to distinct new societies; hand in hand with the emergence of a distinct new culture would be the emergence of a distinct new language variety – we should never forget that language and cultural identity are two intimately interrelated concepts.

Perhaps the most central, and most contentious, debate in creolistics relates to the notion of **creolization**, that is, the possible mechanisms that lead to the emergence of creole languages. The debate hinges on two fundamental issues: (i) whether creoles per definition are descendants of pidgins, i.e. are pidgins that have nativized, and (ii) whether creoles in fact constitute a structurally identifiable class of languages, i.e.

form a separate language type. If we presume that creoles are descendants of pidgins, then the formation processes discussed for pidgins in Chapter 5 are equally relevant for creole languages: the difference found between pidgin and creole languages would then lie in the **nativization** process, i.e. in the process whereby the pidgin language becomes the mother tongue of an entire community. Creoles would thus be a separate language type, which came about not by the transmission of the fully-fledged mother tongue spoken by the parents and acquired by the children, but by children acquiring a restricted L2 language (the pidgin) as their L1, which they then functionally and structurally extended to suit any and all of their communicative needs. However, if we assume that the emergence of creoles is not necessarily dependent on a pidgin precursor, then the formation processes of creole languages may differ from those of pidgin languages. Depending on which formation processes are assumed for creoles, they may still be viewed as a separate language type, even if they are not per definition considered nativized pidgin languages.

This section will briefly present some of the most commonly discussed hypotheses on creole genesis. It is not possible to do full justice here to the ongoing discussion and the following sections should be seen as merely an introductory sketch of some of the most recurring terms and theories. It should be noted that a number of aspects in the different approaches are not mutually exclusive and that ultimately the theoretical stance and choice of linguistic method determines which factors are placed in the foreground. For more detailed summaries of theories on the genesis of creole languages, see, for example, Arends et al. (1994b), Mühlhäusler (1997) and Romaine (1988).

6.1.1 The Language Bioprogram Hypothesis and the Creole Prototype

Perhaps the most well-known and controversial theory on creolization is the **Language Bioprogram Hypothesis** (LBH) put forth by Derek Bickerton. The LBH was initially presented as a possible explanation for the origin of human language, but then successively developed into a theory specifically concerned with creolization. The reader interested in following the main developmental path of the LBH is referred to Bickerton (1974, 1977, 1980a, 1981, 1984, 1988) in chronological order.[95]

Because Bickerton argues that creoles "offer a special window on the human language faculty" (Veenstra 2008: 220), the LBH has attracted wide interest outside the field of creolistics, although few, if any, creolists were actually ever convinced by it. In

95. This is not an exhaustive list of the prolific writings by Derek Bickerton, but merely intended as a handful of starting points. The reader *very* interested in investigating the LBH further will find many useful references in, for example, Veenstra (2008).

fact, the LBH was so controversial that it "provoked an avalanche of research and publications throughout the 1980s and 1990s with the sole aim of disproving it" (Veenstra 2008: 219). The LBH remains controversial; as pointed out by Tonjes Veenstra in his very accessible overview of the development of the LBH and the influence it has had, the impact of the LBH on the field of creolistics cannot be overestimated (Veenstra 2008: 219).

Very simplified, the LBH argues that the adult workers (whether slaves or indentured labourers) who had been relocated to the colonial plantation societies produced simplified and unstable contact varieties of the lexifier. The children of these labourers thus received inadequate linguistic input when growing up; while the parents would have had other languages as their mother tongues, this would not be the case for the children in the new society, who would only have been exposed to this unstable and reduced contact variety spoken by the parents. Because the rudimentary contact variety spoken by the parents was not referentially adequate for the basic human linguistic needs of the children, the children would resort to the basic, innate (i.e. genetically encoded), human language faculty and would create a new, fully equipped and functional, language. According to the LBH creolization is thus an abrupt process that takes place over one single generation through nativization, i.e. through a language acquiring native speakers.

The LBH rests primarily on the contact situation in Hawai'i and the language varities that arose as a consequence of that. Bickerton argues that the Hawai'i Pidgin English of the elderly Japanese and Filipino plantation workers that he recorded differs so drastically from Hawai'i Creole English that the structural innovations in the latter can only be explained in one of two ways: (i) that they were produced by some kind of general problem-solving device, or (ii) that they were produced "by the operation of innate faculties genetically programmed to provide at least the basis for an adequate human language" (Bickerton 1981: 41).[96] In order to test which of these explanations is the most likely one, Bickerton compared twelve structural features in Hawai'i Creole English with several other creoles with different lexifiers, most of them (but not all) from the Caribbean. The comparison is summarized in Table 6.1. For a full discussion see Bickerton (1981: 51ff).

96. For more on Hawai'i Creole English, which in fact emerged before the plantation pidgin studied by Bickerton (Roberts 2013c), see Section 6.4.1 below.

Table 6.1 The prototypical features in Bickerton's (1981) cross-creole comparison, their predicted behaviour and the languages claimed to illustrate them.

Feature	Predicted behaviour	Exemplified languages[a]
(i) *word order and movement rules*	focussed elements move sentence-initially	HCE, GC
(ii) *articles*	definite for presupposed-specific NPs, indefinite for asserted-specific NPs, zero for nonspecific NPs	HCE, GC, PP, SC
(iii) *tense-mood-aspect systems*	one preverbal tense marker (anterior), one preverbal mood marker (irrealis), one preverbal aspect marker (non-punctual) placed in that order (T-M-A)	HCE, GC, SR, SA, HC, LAC
(iv) *complementation*	complementizers are selected by the semantics of the embedded clause	HCE, JC, SR, MC
(v) *relativization and subject copying*	no relative pronoun	HCE, GC, SC, AN, CR, HC
(vi) *negation*	negative concord	HCE, GC, PK
(vii) *existential and possessive*	the same item expresses both existential and possession	HCE, GC, HC, PP, ST
(viii) *copula*	zero copula for adjectival predication, varied for NP predication, special locative copula	HCE, SC, CR, GC
(ix) *adjectives as verbs*	adjectives behave as stative verbs	HCE, GC, MC
(x) *polar questions*	no change in word order; yes/no questions are indicated through intonation and optional particles	HCE, GC, HC
(xi) *question words*	bimorphemic question words occur sentence initially	HCE, GC, HC, ST, CC, RC, SC
(xii) *passivization*	no (or very rarely) passive	HCE, MC, SC, PP, GC, JC

[a] AN: Annobones (i.e. Fa d'Ambô), CC: Cameroons Creole (i.e. Cameroon Pidgin English), CR: Crioulo (i.e. Guinea-Bissau Kriyol), GC: Guyanese Creole (i.e. Creolese), HC: Haitian Creole, HCE: Hawai'i Creole English, JC: Jamaican, LAC: Lesser Antillean Creole, MC: Mauritian Creole, PK: Papiá Kristang, PP: Papiamentu, RC: Reunion Creole, SA: Saramaccan, SC: Seychelles Creole, SR: Sranan, ST: São Tomense (i.e. Santome)

Bickerton found that Hawai'i Creole English displays substantial similarity with the other creoles in all features except (v) and (viii), where Hawai'i Creole English only displays similarities with some of the other creoles, and (vi) and (xi), where Hawai'i Creole English displays little similarity with the other creoles.[97] Bickerton concludes

97. Notice, however, that the comparison is not presented as a systematic quantification and that the only creole that is consistently exemplified for each feature (except feature *iv*) alongside Hawai'i Creole English is Creolese (abbreviated GC).

that these twelve features are prototypical creole features derived directly from the innate Language Bioprogram, which, he argues, is why creoles are internally similar, despite their different locations and histories. Therefore, Bickerton argues, creoles can serve as a window on the human language faculty (and thus contribute to the question of the origin of human language) – since the creators of creole languages had to fall back on their innate language bioprogram in order to provide themselves with a fully functioning language, it follows that the structure of a creole language mirrors the most basic human Universal Grammar.

The extent to which the bioprogram would surface in any given creole language would, Bickerton argues, depend on the demographical history of the given creole (Bickerton 1984). This he quantifies with the **Pidginization Index** (*PI*), which he formulates as

$$PI = Y \times \frac{P}{R}$$

where Y is the number of years between colonization and the point at which the substrate and superstrate populations receive numerical parity (Event 1, see 4.2.1.3 above), P is the total number of substrate speaking population at Event 1, and R is the yearly average of immigration after Event 1 (Bickerton 1984: 178). The lower the *PI*, the more impoverished the input will be to the pidgin, and so the more the eventual creole will have to rely on the bioprogram (i.e. the creole will be more "radical"). Additional factors for the linguistic outcome of the contact situation, according to Bickerton (1988), is whether the situation involved permanent population displacement (as was the case with plantation societies), and whether the contact situation involved nativization (as he argued was the case with both plantation and trading fort societies). Due to the population displacement, plantation creoles would differ more from their lexifiers than fort creoles. So-called 'maritime creoles', however, would have been more influenced by the substrate languages than both plantation and fort creoles, due to the fact that 'maritime creoles' involved neither population displacement nor nativization.

The notion of a **Creole Prototype** (sometimes also called **Creole exceptionalism**) can essentially be seen as a modified continuation of the LBH (cf. McWhorter 2002). The aim of the Creole Prototype theory is to identify a limited set of traits that are unique to creole languages. This idea has been argued most forcefully by John McWhorter (a convenient collected overview of his work can be found in McWhorter 2005), but also by, for example, Bakker et al. (e.g. 2011) and Bakker & Daval-Markussen (in press), with further references). The purpose of identifying a Creole Prototype would be that it would allow us to identify languages as creoles without having access to their developmental history.

The Creole Prototype theory proposes that all creoles, and only creoles as opposed to non-creoles, have a combination of three features that essentially flag that they "were born recently of pidgins" (McWhorter 2011: 5):

> **phonological:** little or no use of tone to distinguish monosyllables or grammatical categories
> **morphosyntactic:** little or no inflectional morphology
> **semantic:** little or no noncompositional combinations of derivational markers and roots (McWhorter 2011: 6)

Both the LBH and the Creole Prototype theory presuppose the existence of a pidgin language as a necessary stage for a creole to emerge. The LBH hinges on the fact that the pidgin input to the children of the immigrants was linguistically so inadequate that the children had to create new languages. The Creole Prototype theory postulates that creole languages are essentially pidgin languages that have nativized – and argues that because the pidgins were by definition reduced languages, the creoles are thus also reduced. Once a creole has emerged it will behave as any other language and change in various ways just like any other language, evolving away from the initial prototype structure.

There has been, and continues to be, criticism against both the LBH and the notion of a Creole Prototype. For very accessible overviews on the criticisms of the LBH, see, for example, Sebba (1997: 178ff) and Veenstra (2008: 228ff), with further references.

One major criticism against the LBH is that it does not accommodate for diffusion between contact varieties, but assumes only that creoles arose independently of each other, each one as a local restricted contact variety. However, we saw in Chapter 4 that there was often intense contact between different colonial settlements; it seems likely that the varieties spoken in different colonial settlements would have influenced each other.

One major criticism against the Creole Prototype is that the features postulated as particular for creoles can be found in a number of other, non-creole, languages in the world. Riau Indonesian, for example, displays all three characteristics, but is not considered a creole (Gil 2001). The argument put forth by McWhorter (e.g. 2011: 207ff), namely that the reason Riau Indonesian conforms so well to the Creole Prototype is that the language probably emerged as a creole sociohistorically, is at risk of being circular. Furthermore, it has been shown in a number of studies that many creoles do not conform to the Creole Prototype (for an accessible overview, see, for example Ansaldo & Matthews 2007 with further refereneces, as well as the other chapters in Ansaldo et al. 2007 for language specific counter-examples). Extensive commentary to McWhorter's proposal was given by a number of authors in the journal *Linguistic Typology* (volume 5, 2001, pages 167–387).

Another major criticism against both the LBH and the Creole Prototype theory is that they do not take bi- and multilingualism into account. To assume that the pidgin was the only input that the children of the immigrants had when growing up is a very monolingual take on the situation and completely disregards the possibility that the child carers may have spoken their mother tongues, and not the contact variety, with the children. It seems likely that children born into multilingual societies would have grown up multilingual, as evidenced in the majority of the multilingual societies we have in the world today. This is, in fact, what happened in Hawaiʻi, where the locally born children tended to be bilingual in the languages of their parents and the creole, as shown by Roberts (2000).

Yet another major criticism is the notion of the nativization of the population. We have seen that in most of the societies where creoles emerged there could be a great flux in demographics and the composition of the population. In many cases there would be waves of immigration. This means that large numbers of adult immigrants would continue to arrive in societies where previous immigrants had already settled and produced a locally born generation. It seems likely that the new immigrants influenced the contact variety somehow.

Furthermore, both the LBH and the Creole Prototype theory risk circularity of argument:

> in order to be defined as a creole, a language must have as its primary historical source a language which has a sufficiently simplified grammatical structure. No grammatical property of a language can therefore be a counterexample to the theory that creoles have the world's simplest grammars, because in order to be a creole, the language has to originate from an earlier language which did not have that property (a pidgin), and if it has there are only two logical possibilities: either that the stage did not exist, in which case it is not a creole, or the property has been acquired later, in which case it is not a counterexample either, since it just means that the language is on its way to losing its creole character. (Dahl 2004: 111)

6.1.2 The Relexification Hypothesis

The **Relexification Hypothesis** was proposed by Claire Lefebvre concerning the language contact situation in Haiti especially (see, for example, Lefebvre 1998 and 2004 for detailed discussions and further references) and was an elaboration of Muysken's (1981, 1988) proposal for the formation process involved in the emergence of the mixed language Media Lengua (see Section 3.2.1.3 above; see also 10.4.3 for more on Media Lengua). Muysken's notion of relexification essentially entails the systematic substitution of phonetic shapes of lexical items, that is, that the phonetic shape of a root in one language is replaced with a root with the same meaning from some other language (cf. Muysken 2008: 292ff). Extremely simplified, relexification denotes an abrupt, mental process whereby speakers of language A replace the lexicon with that of language B but not the structure. In other words, while the speakers adopt the lexicon of language B, they do not adopt its grammar, but retain the grammar of language A. The result is a new language, C, which has its grammar from one source and its lexicon from another.[98]

The Relexification Hypothesis as suggested by Lefebvre with respect to Haiti postulates that it was immigrant adults, rather than locally born children, who acted as the creators of creole languages. The idea is that the adult workers who arrived in the colonial plantation societies, whether slaves or indentured labourers, used the process of **relexification** to acquire the language of the colonial society they arrived in, i.e. the lexifier (or superstrate) language.

The theory is that when the slaves, speakers of different languages, were brought together, they needed to be able to communicate with each other as well as with the colonizers. Since they were all exposed to the language of the colonizers, they used that as their *lingua franca*. However, they did not have enough access to the language of the colonizers to acquire it fully. Instead, they used the structures of their own native languages while importing the vocabulary of the colonizers' language. In other words, they relexified their own languages with the lexicon of the colonizers' language.[99] The slaves, who all had different linguistic backgrounds, would now have a common vocabulary, even if the way they structured their languages would have been different (because they would use the structure of their ancestor languages). There would thus have been a great deal of variation in this early *lingua franca*.

---

98. This is a highly simplified explanation of the process. For a more detailed overview of the various definitions of relexification and to what extent they differ from each other, see Lefebvre (2004: 38ff). The relexification theory was actually proposed as early as 1887 by Max Buchner in his description of Pidgin English in Cameroon: "As with most, if not all mixed languages, so it is with Negro-English. The grammatical skeleton, which expresses the way of thinking, belongs to the indigenous idiom and is clung to. Only the flesh, the vocabulary, is taken from the foreign, higher language and fitted to the shape of the skeleton." ["*Wie mit den meisten, wenn nicht allen Mischsprachen, verhält es sich auch mit dem Neger-Englisch. Das grammatische Skelett, welches die Art des Denkens ausdrückt, gehört der einheimischen Redeweise an und wird starr fest gehalten. Nur die Fleischteile, das Vokabular, werden dem fremden, höheren Idiom entnommen und den Formen des Skeletts angefügt.*" (Buchner 1887: 43), my translation.]

99. It is important to keep in mind that Lefebvre works within a generative framework, which means that it is not surface structures, but rather structures at a deep syntactic level that are compared. What may look like differences between the creole and its substrate(s) may thus turn out to be similarities at a deeper syntactic level. The generative framework of linguistics works on the assumption that all human languages share a fundamental structure at a deep level. For a very accessible introduction to Generative Syntax, see for example, Carnie (2002).

When the *lingua franca* used among the slaves, this highly variable relexified version of the colonizers' language, itself becomes a target for acquisition, a new language, a creole, is born. Once the incipient creole has become an L2 target, it starts to stabilize and to get more uniform through the process of dialect levelling, i.e. each party makes their language more similar to that of the other party. The process of dialect levelling would therefore account for how a given creole, with a structure as stable as any other natural language, may derive its features from several different substrate languages.

The idea that adults created the creole by retaining the structures of their native languages when trying to acquire the language of the colonizers essentially makes the Relexification Hypothesis a continuation of the Interlanguage Hypothesis (see Section 5.1.3.2), since both theories rest on the assumption that the structure of the creoles emerged due to imperfect learning of the target language (the lexifier); the Interlanguage Hypothesis essentially assumes that a pidgin arose by way of imperfect acquisition of the target language, and out of that pidgin a creole developed. The creole thus has its structure as a consequence of a crystallized stage of incomplete L2 acquisition. The Relexification Hypothesis seeks to explain why the creole languages crystallized the way they did, and how it can be that they reflect properties of both the lexifier and the substrate languages. Furthermore, the Relexification Hypothesis is not dependent on the existence of a pidgin language as a necessary stage for a creole language to develop.

One major criticism against the Relexification Hypothesis is that it assumes that adults were the principal agents of the creation of the creole. This would completely disregard the role of the locally born children in the formation of the language. These locally born children would not have been acquiring the creole as an L2, but as an L1: even if they – as seems likely – would have had access to some form of the ancestor languages, i.e. the substrates, (for instance acquiring one or more of the caretakers' native languages) they would have been born into a society where the creole was forming or had already formed. They would therefore have been exposed to the creole from early on. It seems likely that this locally born population contributed to the formation and development of the creole language.

Another major criticism is that the Relexification Hypothesis severely minimizes the role of the colonizers in the contact situation and the contribution of the lexifier to the structure of the resulting creole. It implies that the speakers of the lexifier language (the presupposed target) played no role whatsoever in the formation of the creole; in other words, it assumes that the contact variety took the form it took due to the fact that the workers did not have enough access to native speakers of the target language to be able to acquire it fully. The lexifier is assumed to have contributed only the phonological forms of the language, but that nothing from the structural or semantic system of the lexifier language has entered the system of the creole. This also disregards the fact that speakers of the lexifier languages spoke different varieties and may have consciously spoken an altered register with the workers.

Furthermore, the Relexification Hypothesis also does not accommodate for diffusion between contact varieties, but assumes only two major contributions to a given creole, namely the lexifier and the substrate language(s).

6.1.3 The Founder Principle

The diametric opposite of the Relexification Hypothesis is the position that it was not the substrate languages that contributed the most to the structure of the resulting creole, but that the creole is in fact a continuation of the colonial variety of the lexifier. This position was articulated most forcefully by Robert Chaudenson (e.g. 1992 and 2001), whose focus was on the settlement histories of the French colonial plantation societies especially.

Chaudenson points to the fact that the colonial plantation societies started out as small colonies where a small group of settlers established themselves as farmers – the homestead phase of the colony. During this phase the colony would be settled by people from various regions of the colonial power, speaking various non-standard varieties of the metropolitan language. The farmers would have a number of European indentured labourers, many of them disadvantaged people from the colonial power or other European countries. These indentured labourers worked and lived in close proximity with their masters. At this stage any non-European slaves would form a small proportion of the population and they, too, would live and work in close proximity with the farm owners. Therefore, with both farmers and labourers (whether free or slave, whether European or not) living on such intimate terms, access to native speakers of the language of the colonizers would be unimpeded. The non-native speakers among the labourers would thus have been likely to have acquired the colonizers' language fully. However, as the ratio of slaves increased, they would have had less access to native speakers of the colonizers' language and instead would have acquired it from other slaves. In other words, they would have had non-native speakers of the lexifier languages as their models and would therefore have acquired only an approximation of the target language. As the ratio of slaves kept increasing, the models got further removed and the new arrivals would have acquired approximations of approximations of approximations of the European target language, resulting in the creole, through what may be termed 'gradual basilectalization' (cf. Baker 2000 and Mufwene 2001).[100]

100. A **basilect** is the variety of a creole that is structurally furthest removed from its lexifier. Other kinds of 'lects' typically distinguished are **acrolects** (closest to the lexifier) and **mesolects** (falling somewhere between basilects and acrolects). For more on various 'lects', see Chapter 7.

This theory was further developed by Salikoko Mufwene and adapted for other contact situations (see, for example, Mufwene 1996 and 2001). Mufwene raised the concept of the **Founder Principle**. The term is borrowed from population genetics (where it is most commonly referred to as the **founder effect**) and refers to the phenomenon where the genetic variability typical of large population groups is lost when a new population is established by a small number of individuals of the original population, essentially a type of genetic drift. In other words, we have a large population, let's call it *X*, where much genetic variability exists (we might have the different allele types, i.e. gene alternatives, *A*, *B*, *C*, *D*, *E* and *F*). A small number of individuals break away from the ancestral population *X* and establishes a new population. This **founder event** "can lead to chance changes in genetic variation so that allele frequencies are different from those in the ancestral population" (Hedrick 2011: 342): because this new population is settled by only a small number of individuals from the ancestral population, only some of the alleles, or gene alternatives, are carried over to the new population. We might, for example, only have the types *A*, *C* and *E* represented in the new population. These features now have the advantage in the new population. A founder event may thus also quickly lead to genetic distance between the ancestral population and the new population (Hedrick 2011: 343). For accessible introductions to population genetics, see, for example, Hamilton (2009) and Relethford (2012).

Mufwene relates this to linguistic features in a contact situation, where the non-standard vernaculars of the founder population may have an advantage that they do not have in the ancestral society, where they might be stigmatized in various ways. Because of the founder effect, the vernaculars spoken by the settlers of the new colony (the founder event) would establish themselves as the targeted norm. Due to the specific combination of vernaculars and their features (essentially the makeup of alleles), a given colonial variety may therefore become different from the metropolitan variety (the new variety has genetically drifted away from the ancestral variety). It was the colonial variety of the European settlers that became the L2 target for any imported labour. The resulting creole language of a given colonial settlement is thus a restructured form of its lexifier, which was itself a new, colonial, variety of the ancestral metropolitan language.

Mufwene thus uses the Founder Principle to account for "how structural features of creoles have been predetermined to a large extent (though not exclusively!) by characteristics of the vernaculars spoken by the populations that founded the colonies in which they developed" (Mufwene 2001: 28f). Substratal influence is, however, also taken into account through the phenomenon of feature pools and feature selection (see below), as well as through the role of transfer in L2 acquisition, since, Mufwene argues, with the ratio of slaves increasing, gradual basilectalization ensued, and the new arrivals acquired approximations (of approximations of approximations) of the colonial variety. The principal agents of the creole formation are thus hypothesized to be both children and adults. Notice that this approach therefore does not assume any prior pidgin stage for a creole to emerge.

One of the main criticisms against the Founder Principle theory is that it does not allow enough room for the influence of the substrate languages and for the highly multilingual nature of these societies. As mentioned in Chapter 4, it seems likely that any colonial society was multilingual from its inception. Furthermore, it is likely that a number of different varieties and registers would have been spoken in the different kinds of interactions that are likely to have taken place.

Another major criticism is that the theory presupposes that the target language was the language of the colonizers, which then essentially got more and more imperfectly learned. This first of all implies that the colonizers would have spoken a reasonably uniform language or language variety, though settlement histories show that colonies were often settled by farmers from diverse European countries. Secondly it imples that the aim of the labour forces was to acquire the language of the farm owners. However, we have seen that the emerging contact language could, in fact, have been a target in its own right.

6.1.4 Feature pools and an evolutionary account of creole formation

A framework that builds strongly on the notion of the Founder Principle and the work of Salikoko Mufwene is the **evolutionary account** of creole formation, where theories about **language competition** consider language change in general (cf. Section 3.2.2.2 above). This framework allows for strong substratal elements through the notions of linguistic ecology and the feature pool for a given situation (cf. e.g. Croft 2000, Aboh & Ansaldo 2007, Aboh 2009 and Ansaldo 2009 with further references).

According to the evolutionary approach of creole formation, the makeup of a given creole depends on the **linguistic ecology** of the particular situation: the specific linguistic composition of any given settlement with respect to the origin of the settlers and their ancestral languages will lead to a unique **feature pool** for each situation (cf. Croft 2000). A feature pool is a linguistic equivalent of a **gene pool**, i.e. the total set of all genes in a population. The feature pool in a given situation is thus the sum of every individual's linguistic system, the 'linguemes' or 'linguistic genotypes' (Croft 2000, Aboh 2009) produced by a given individual in a linguistic setting. Each utterance produced may either represent an identical replication of a lingueme (for example, I produce the sentence *warm the teapot* /ˈwɔːm ðə ˈtiːpɒt/ in exactly the same way as I did in the previous utterance), or may involve some alteration (mutation) of the lingueme (for example, I produce the sentence *warm the teapot* /ˈwɔːm ðə ˈtiːpɒt/ slightly differently each time, e.g. /ˈwɔːm ði ˈtiːpɒt/, /ˈwɔːm ðiː ˈtiːpɒt/, /ˈwɔm ðə ˈtiːpɒt/, and so on). Mutated linguemes or linguistic genotypes, i.e. new linguistic structures, may catch on and propagate in the given linguistic setting.

While largely identical replication may be expected in linguistic settings with a high degree of monolingualism and normative tendencies, highly multilingual environments with low normative tendencies may lead to altered (mutated) replications (Aboh & Ansaldo 2007). Since creoles emerged in highly multilingual settings, the rate of lingueme mutations would have been high. The makeup of the feature pool is determined by the features of the input (or donor) languages; the possible mutations are thus limited by the kind of features that are included in the feature pool. The competitiveness of any given feature would depend on how well represented it is in a feature pool – better represented features would have a better chance of being replicated. For example, if the majority of the input (donor) languages had phonemic tone, then that feature would have a better chance to be replicated in the ecology. In other words, features that are prominent, frequent and typologically common for a given linguistic setting will be replicated and propagated (Aboh & Ansaldo 2007). This means that the principles of selection, i.e. which features become part of the resulting language, are governed by a combination of structural and social factors (Ansaldo 2009).

With the evolutionary framework the structure of the substrate languages are thus given a more prominent role than with the Founder Principle, since the substrates would have accounted for a large proportion of the feature pool. This would also explain why structural similarities can be found across various creoles: because the input (donor) languages of the given linguistic ecology were the same or similar and the structural features (linguistic genotypes) involved in the replication process where thus similar. However, since each feature pool makeup is unique, this also explains why the various creoles are similar but not identical. The principal agents of the creole formation are hypothesized to be both children and adults, that is, that both L1 and L2 acquisition was involved. Notice that this approach also does not assume any prior pidgin stage for a creole to emerge.

One of the major criticisms against both the Founder Principle and feature pool approach to explaining the emergence and development of creole languages is that it does not adequately account for why, given the linguistic genotypes that each input language contributes to the feature pool, the resulting creole will not display the same level of structural complexity that the linguistic ancestors have. If all ancestors had similar structural solutions for a given linguistic feature, the expectation would be that this would carry over to the new language variety. In other words, the Founder Principle and the feature pool approach, it is argued, does not adequately account for why certain features of the feature pool were *not* carried over to the new variety.

6.1.5 The Gradualist Model of creolization

The **Gradualist Model** of creolization is primarily associated with the work of Jacques Arends (e.g. 1989, 1992, 2008, with further references), although it is maybe better described as "a cover term for ideas and proposals that were initially put forward independently by a number of different scholars" (Arends & Bruyn 1994: 111), for example Carden & Stewart (1988) and Singler (1990a, 1995, 2008), as well as Jacques Arends, among others.

The Gradualist Model puts forth that creole languages developed gradually rather than emerged abruptly over one or a couple of generations. What Jacques Arends, John Singler, and others strongly advocate for is to base any theory on the development of a given creole on solid historical data.[101] Based especially on the contact situation in Suriname, Arends shows that Sranan had a formative period of about 75 years due to the ratio of foreign-born to locally-born slaves (Arends 1989). Given the fact that locally-born slaves would have been a small minority for many generations in Suriname, the role of nativization for a creole to develop can only have been a slow process.

Arends proposes the concept of 'transcreolization', that is, a transgenerational process of creolization, whereby creolization is an incremental process "driven by L2 acquisition of the language (e.g. by incoming African-born slaves, both children and adults, in the case of Suriname; see Arends 1994a) as well as a community of locally-born L1 learners that was initially relatively marginal" (Cardoso 2009a: 18).

Arends proposes that in the earliest stages of the contact situation a pidgin variety would have emerged, which would gradually have developed into an extended pidgin (pidgincreole) as the colonial society stabilized and expanded. This extended pidgin (pidgincreole) would gradually develop into a creole as the society stabilized further and slowly gained a locally-born population. The development of the creole would have taken place progressively, over several generations, and would have been continuous rather than discrete, in the sense that there would be no clear-cut divide between the extended pidgin (pidgincreole) and the creole. This would have been a differential rather than a monolithic process, in that different domains of the language system would have developed at different speed. However, Arends also proposes an "initial, first-generation creolization" (Arends 1989: 90), which he defines as the very earliest stage of language formation. Here the Founder Principle would come into play: the language ecology of the earliest stage would shape the outcome and transmission of the emerging creole, even if the population of the contributing languages was small in numbers. This would, for example, explain why the Surinamese creoles

101. Jacques Arends sadly and prematurely passed away in 2005. His legacy in creolistics and his championing for empirical, data-driven research is, however, very much with us, which is why I choose to write this section in the present tense.

are English-lexified, despite the fact that Suriname was a Dutch colony for most of its non-independent history, after only a short initial English rule.

The emerging creole would have been subject both to language-internal change as well as substrate transfer as ratios of the locally-born population (for whom the creole would have been an L1) and the foreign-born population (for whom the creole would have been an L2) shifted. Arends thus sees creolization not only as a gradual, but also a dynamic process.

Arends stresses the importance of basing any theory on data and devoted enormous efforts to try and uncover as much actual historical data as possible by conducting painstaking archival research. He based his model on the development of Sranan on as many primary sources as possible, all the while mindful of the fact that "the earliest texts written in any of the Surinam creoles go back no further than a post-initial stage of the language formation process" (Arends & Bruyn 1994: 112), meaning that we have no data for the very earliest stages of the formation of the creole, and that most of the primary sources available to us were written by Europeans who did not speak the creole natively.

One major criticism against the Gradualist Model is that extralinguistic data can never be seen as a substitute for linguistic data. In other words, that it cannot be justified to use sociohistorical and demographic data as a basis for presuming who said what to whom and how in the absence of adequate linguistic evidence in early contact situations.

Another criticism is that the Gradualist Model *a priori* assumes a pidgin stage for the development of a creole language, irrespective of whether there is evidence for a pidgin stage or not.

6.1.6 Afrogenesis or the Domestic Origin Hypothesis

A theory of origin that specifically relates to the Atlantic creoles is the idea that a single contact language was brought from West Africa and subsequently diffused throughout the Caribbean. This harks back to the principle of monogenesis (see Section 5.1.1) in the sense that a single parent pidgin would have emerged in and around the slave forts and depots in West Africa, which the slaves who were held there would have acquired and brought with them to the New World. This would then have formed the basis for the creoles that emerged there.

The possibility of **Afrogenesis** of the Atlantic creoles, i.e. that a pidgin which originated in West Africa was the parent language of the various Caribbean creoles was first proposed by Morris Goodman (1964) for French-lexified creoles and subsequently also by Ian Hancock with his **Domestic Origin Hypothesis** for the English-lexified Atlantic creoles (e.g. 1969, 1986b). Thus an English-lexified West African pidgin developed into a creole (Upper Guinea Coast Creole), which in turn would be the ultimate origin for the English-lexified Caribbean creoles, while a French-lexified West

African pidgin would be the ultimate origin for French-lexified Caribbean creoles, and so on.

The theory of Afrogenesis subsequently found supporters in, for example, Cassidy (1980), McWhorter (1995, 2000) and Parkvall (1999). McWhorter (1997), for example, argued that the trade post in Kormantin in present-day Ghana was the point of origin for the English-lexified Proto-Creole that would be transported to the New World. There would then essentially have been a founder principle phenomenon, where the initial small number of castle slaves from Kormantin transported to the New World would have had a disproportionately high influence on the linguistic outcome of the resulting community.

One of the main criticisms against the Domestic Origin or Afrogenesis Hypothesis is that it is debatable whether the historical data supports the theory that there were indeed European-lexified contact languages in the early 1600s that were stable enough to act as established varieties for the slaves who were to be transported to the New World, or whether the evidence at hand in fact rather points to jargons of limited use.[102]

It is doubtful whether the communities around the trade forts were numerous or strong enough to exert much influence in the area, since, as we have seen, the European trading posts were typically small and highly dependent on the goodwill of their African partners (cf. Section 4.1.2.1).

6.1.7 The origin of creoles: A summary

Exactly which formation processes were involved in the development of creole languages is a matter of debate. Each theory has its attractive aspects and it is fair to assume that a combination of factors were at work. There are a number of controversies involved: whether creoles are structurally different from non-creole languages,

102. An example of the importance of archival as well as archaeological data is the discussion of the proposed point of origin for the English-lexified Caribbean creoles in the West African trading post of Kormantin (as put forth by McWhorter 1997). The problem is that archival documents show the Kormantin post to be such a modest lodge that "the bulk of the trade had to be carried on from a ship until the mid-1630s" (Huber 1999b: 32). It is thus doubtful whether English would have been more than a jargon in the area. Furthermore, the English trade was in severe competition with the Dutch until 1645 and the fort itself was not completed until 1647 (Huber 1999a: 90). By then St Kitts and Barbados had already been settled for 23 years (Holm 1988: 446, 450), meaning that the Kormantin castle slaves would have arrived to an already existing plantation setting and would not have been part of the founder population. Moreover, Kormantin was never a large fort – as can be seen not only in early plans but also the existing archaeological remains – and likely did not have much more than 50 castle slaves simultaneously (Huber 1999a: 89), a very small number indeed to exert such an enormous influence on the already existing Caribbean slave settlements: in 1645, for example, Holm (1988: 447) counts some 6,000 slaves in Barbados and Batie's (1991: 49) figures point to a minimum of 1,000 slaves in St. Kitts. In this case the archival and archaeological evidence thus contradicts the theory.

whether creoles per definition descend from pidgins, whether they developed abruptly or gradually, whether the principle agents were adults or children, and what role demographic proportions play. The WH-nightmare highlighted by Naro (1978: 314; see Section 5.1.4) is as relevant for creolization as it is for pidginization: empirical data and thorough archival research is essential in order to try and uncover who said what to whom, how and why. The main points of the theories concerned with creole genesis as a phenomenon, as well as their main appeals and challenges, are summarized below. This leaves out the Domestic Origin Hypothesis, since that is only concerned with the Atlantic creoles specifically. Notice how a number of the approaches listed below essentially boil down to favouring one or the other linguistic method, such as universalist or substratist.

Some main points across theories on the emergence of creoles.

Theory	Pidgin descendants?	Speed of formation?	Main agents?
LBH	Yes	Abrupt	Children
Creole Prototype	Yes	Abrupt	Children
Relexification Hypothesis	No	Abrupt	Adults
Founder Principle	No	Gradual	Both children and adults
Evolutionary account	No	Gradual and dynamic	Both children and adults
Gradualist Model	Yes	Gradual and dynamic	Both children and adults

Appeals and challenges of the some of the main theories on the emergence of creoles.

Theory	Appeal factors	Challenge factors
LBH	– Explains structural similarities between many creoles – Explains how creoles could emerge so quickly	– Downplays the role of diffusion – Downplays the role of bi- and multilingualism – Downplays the role of several (large) waves of new arrivals to contact situation – *A priori* presupposes a pidgin stage – Accusations of circularity of argument
Creole Prototype	– Explains structural similarities between many creoles – Allows languages to be identified as creoles without access to its sociohistory	– Features listed as 'creole' can be found in a number of non-creole languages – Downplays the role of bi- and multilingualism – Downplays the role of several (large) waves of new arrivals to contact situation – *A priori* presupposes a pidgin stage – Accusations of circularity of argument

Theory	Appeal factors	Challenge factors
Relexification Hypothesis	– Explains how creoles could emerge so quickly – Explains why creoles crystallized structurally the way they did	– Downplays the role of the locally born population – Downplays the role of the colonizers – Downplays the role of diffusion
Founder Principle	– Explains why creoles have such affinities with lexifier vernaculars – Explains why creoles were not radically affected by colonies changing powers	– Does not give enough weight to the role of the substrates – Presupposes the target was the colonizers' language
Evolutionary account	– Explains structural similarity between many creoles – Explains why creoles are not identical to each other – Takes sociohistorical data as base for development of creoles	– Cannot account for why features of structural complexity found in the input languages do not get carried over to the creoles
Gradualist Model	– Explains why creoles were not radically affected by colonies changing powers – Takes sociohistorical data as base for development of creoles	– Assumes extralinguistic data can substitute linguistic data – *A priori* presupposes a pidgin stage

One point to take note of is that all the theories discussed above essentially assume that "the linguistic consequences of introducing Africans as slave labour in plantation societies were not those which anyone wanted, due to the failure of the Africans either to maintain their languages or to acquire fully the language of their owners" (Baker 2002: 33).[103] However, it could also be argued that the contact varieties that originally emerged in the respective situations were, in fact, successful results of what people needed and wanted in the situation. This would have been achieved by everyone involved, both Europeans and non-Europeans, collaborating in making use of whatever prior experience they might have had of communicating with people speaking different languages. Perhaps this contact variety was the initial target for the different parties (cf. Baker 1990, Baker & Huber 2001).

Michel DeGraff (2009) also highlights the necessity of differentiating between the **I(nternal)-languages**, i.e. the system of linguistic knowledge in any individual's brain,

103. While this specifically refers to Caribbean colonies which imported slaves from (West) Africa on a large scale, it is equally relevant for any other colony with a high level of labour immigration.

and the **E(xternal)-languages** of the societies in question, i.e. the communal norm. In other words, DeGraff stresses the fact that the I-languages that were represented by both those locally-born who acquired the new language as an L1 and by those who learnt it as an L2 influenced each other in the creation of what would become the E-language of the community.

Whether or not creoles form a specific typological class – i.e. whether or not the notion of creole exceptionalism is justified – continues to be an intense ideological debate. The issue is left open in this book, though I emphasize that it is only possible to address on the basis of actual data; the question whether creoles differ structurally from non-creoles can only be answered by actually comparing linguistic structures in creole languages with non-creole languages, as is done in Part II of this book.

6.2 The notion of the pidgin-to-creole life cycle

We have seen that it is a matter of debate whether or not creoles descend from pidgins. Very simplified, the idea behind the '**pidgin-to-creole life cycle**' is as follows: a contact situation leads to a makeshift jargon. This jargon stabilizes into a pidgin, thereby acquiring norms (the jargon pidginizes). This pidgin then comes to be used in a wider context than the initial contact situation, thereby expanding its domain as well as its structure: it becomes an extended pidgin (pidgincreole). At this stage the language may start to become the mother tongue for a minority of the users of the contact variety. Gradually more and more people grow up acquiring the contact variety as their mother tongue and eventually it has become the native language of an entire community; the language has nativized and creolized. This notion of the pidgin-to-creole life cycle is usually attributed to Hall (1962), who argued that a pidgin could achieve the status of a "normal" language when it creolized, "i.e. becomes the first language of a speech-community" (*ibid*: 155). However, the notion of a creole as a pidgin that has become the mother tongue of an entire community goes back at least to Hugo Schuchardt, who proposed that the contact languages used by the slaves in European colonies, the "slave languages … developed into mother tongues, due to the fact that the slaves, because of the great difference between their inherited languages, needed a common mode of communication among themselves" (1909: 442, my translation)[104] and that similar paths of development could be assumed for other creole languages. This idea was later echoed by, for example, Bloomfield (1933: 473f).

104. *"die Sklavensprachen … haben sich aus Vermittlungssprachen … selbst zu Muttersprachen fortentwickelt, indem die Sklaven auch unter sich, wegen der großen Verschiedenheit der ererbten Sprachen, eines allgemeines Verständigungsmittels bedurften."*

The notion of the 'life cycle' was then further refined to the 'developmental continuum' by Mühlhäusler (e.g. 1997) to three types of developmental paths: (i) the jargon-to-creole type (without any pidgin or extended pidgin stage), (ii) the jargon-to-pidgin-to-creole type (without the extended pidgin stage) and (iii) the jargon-to-pidgin-to-extended pidgin-to-creole type described above (considered the most common type), as summarized in Figure 6.1.[105]

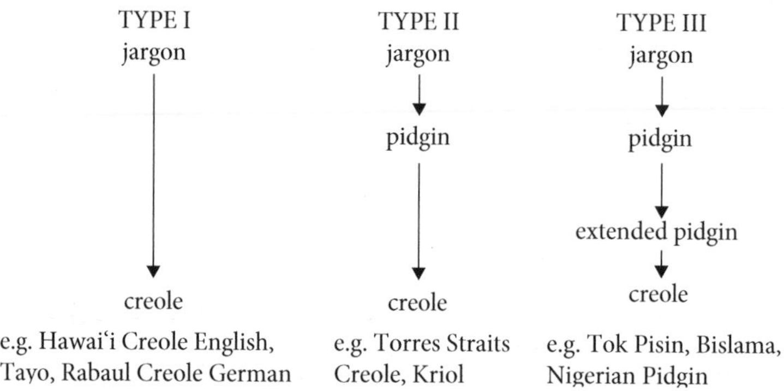

Figure 6.1 The three types of 'life cycles' proposed in Mühlhäusler (1997: 9).

It is important to keep in mind that the 'life cycle' theory does not propose that all jargons, pidgins and extended pidgins develop into creole languages. In fact it is known that most pidgins did not. In other words, while the 'life cycle' theory *a priori* assumes that creoles develop from a previous pidgin (or, occasionally, even a jargon) stage, it does not follow that the theory assumes all known pidgins to generate creoles.

The notion of the pidgin-to-creole life cycle is highly debated. The Language Bioprogram and the Creole Prototype theory, for example, assume that creoles are structured the way they are because they are descendants of a highly restricted language variety, i.e. a pidgin. The Gradualist Model assumes an initial pidgin stage which gradually evolves into a creole through the combination of L1 and L2 acquisition. The Relexification Hypothesis, on the other hand, does not allow for a prior pidgin stage in the development of a creole, but envisages adult speakers, using the grammar of their ancestor languages but the lexicon of the colonizers' languages, as creators of the resulting creole. Nor does the Founder Principle and feature pool theory allow for a prior pidgin stage, as the development of a given creole is seen as a gradual basilectalization of the European vernaculars spoken in the colony.

105. Notice that the languages given as examples for the 'Type III creoles' are generally defined as extended pidgins (not creoles).

The main problem is that we in many cases do not have enough archival evidence to actually empirically establish what the developmental history of a given creole was. In a few cases there is, in fact, a considerable amount of historical data available. This is, for example, the case for Hawai'i Creole English, where the painstaking archival research by Sarah Roberts shows that the creole developed from the 1880s onwards from an earlier Hawai'i Pidgin English (e.g. Roberts 2000, 2005).[106] However, for many known creoles there are at best only scattered attestations of the earlier forms of the language in the contact situation and it is thus often difficult to establish what the contact language actually looked like at the earliest stage of its formation. The assumption of a prior pidgin stage is therefore in many cases not empirically established (cf. Mufwene 1997, Ansaldo & Matthews 2007).

6.3 Multilingualism and creolization

One thing we must not lose sight of is that creoles emerged in multilingual settings. We saw in Chapter 4 that many colonies were settled by speakers of different European languages, and that the colonial societies were dependent on large-scale import of labour, people who had different origins and spoke different languages. The vast majority of those languages we today call creole thus arose in societies where the imported labour had different mother tongues – one exception seems to be Berbice Dutch, where it seems as if Eastern Ijo had an unusually significant influence on the creole. Even so, the Eastern Ijo speakers who arrived in Dutch Guyana would have contributed to a linguistic ecology of several languages. It is also likely that a fair number of the labourers were multilingual before they arrived in the colonial society; West Africa, for example, is a linguistically highly diverse region, where it is extremely common for people to use two or more languages in their daily interactions. It does not seem unlikely that this was also the case some centuries ago. Furthermore, we also saw in Chapter 4 that the high mobility between colonial communities renders it likely that different contact languages influenced each other. This all adds up to the fact that colonial societies per definition were multilingual societies. Multilingualism

106. The picture is, in fact, a great deal more complicated than that. Roberts (2013c) demonstrates that textual evidence indicates that an early Hawai'i Pidgin English, which may have been influenced by South Seas Jargon and Chinese Pidgin English, developed in the latter half of the 19th century in urban areas. A creole emerged no later than 1880 out of this variety. Towards the mid-1890s, i.e. after the emergence of the creole, a rural variety of Hawai'i Pidgin English emerged. It is an offshoot of this rural Hawai'i Pidgin English which was assumed in the LBH to be the ancestor of the creole, something that the chronology of the textual evidence thus belies. For more on Hawai'i Creole English, see Section 6.4.1.

is thus a factor that should be considered in the development of creole languages (cf. Muysken 2008, but see also Schuchardt 1890, 1909). A frequent phenomenon with bilinguals and multilinguals is **code-switching** or **code-mixing**, that is, when the speaker mixes two or several languages in the same utterance. Being bilingual myself I have experienced it (although I personally tend to allow myself to code-switch only with people I am intimately familiar with or with other bilinguals) and have produced such utterances as in Example (117), with the code-switched element in italics:

Swedish/English code-switching

(117) a. jag väntar *usually* tills vattn-et *boil*-ar
1SG.S wait-PRES until water-DEF -PRES
'I usually wait until the water boils.'

b. I saw him in the *matsal-en*
canteen-DEF
'I saw him in the canteen' (source: personal experience)

Notice that the code-switched English verb (*boil*, which is *koka* in Swedish) in (117a) is inflected with a Swedish present tense ending (pronounced /bɔɪlaɹ/). The word order is neither English nor Swedish: the adverb follows the verb rather than precedes it (*väntar usually* instead of the English *usually wait* or the Swedish *brukar vänta*). Notice also that the Swedish noun (*matsalen* 'the canteen') in (117b) is marked for definiteness twice, once in English (prenominal *the*) and once in Swedish (*-en*). For more on code-switching, see, for example, Myers-Scotton (2002) with further references.

Given the multilingual setting of colonial societies, "it is possible to imagine that frequent code-mixing was prevalent in the early plantation contact setting leading to creole genesis" (Muysken 2008: 298). The question is how long this multilingualism lasted in the creole communities. It seems reasonable to assume that as long as labour was imported on a fairly large scale, there would be a sizeable proportion of the population who was multilingual. Roberts (2000, 2005), for example, has shown that the first generation of locally-born children to immigrants in Hawai'i tended to be bi- or multilingual in the ancestor language(s) of the parents and the creole, and that different immigrant communities would shift away from the ancestor language at different rates. For settings such as that in Suriname, where life expectancy for slaves after arrival to the colony was very low (as were local birth-rates), import of slaves was consequently very high. During the early decades of the colony the majority of the population is thus likely to have been multilingual. Code-switching and code-mixing are therefore likely to have been prominent phenomena during the formation of what would become the creole language, something that should be taken into account in any theory of creole genesis.

6.4 Snapshots

One of the most well-known and controversial theories on the genesis of creole languages is the Language Bioprogram Hypothesis, which puts forth that creole languages were created by children who received inadequate linguistic input from their pidgin-speaking parents. The hypothesis is to a great extent based on the contact situation in Hawai'i.

Another well-known and controversial theory is the Relexification Hypothesis, which puts forth that creole languages were created by adults who, when forced to function in the new contact situation, replaced the vocabulary but retained the grammars of their ancestor languages. The hypothesis rests mainly on the history and development of Haitian Creole.

Most known creoles have several substrate languages, making it difficult to identify the exact origin of various structures. The extinct Berbice Dutch, however, seems to have an unusually uniform substratal input from Eastern Ijo. The long coexistence with the indigenous Arawak Amerindians also influenced the language noticeably.

6.4.1 Hawai'i Creole English: An English-lexified creole in Hawai'i[107]

6.4.1.1 *A brief background sketch of Hawai'i Creole English*

Hawai'i Creole English (also called *Hawai'i Creole* and *Hawaiian Creole* by scholars) is spoken natively by about half of the population of the Hawaiian Islands, located in the North Pacific Ocean, as well as some 100,000 people on the US mainland, bringing the figure to about 700,000 speakers (Lewis et al. 2014: *sv*). The language is called *Pidgin* by the speakers themselves.

The Hawaiian Islands were "discovered" by James Cook in 1778, at which time they had already been inhabited for many centuries. Their location became a convenient middle stop for the so-called "Alaska-Hawaii-Canton run" (Carr 1972) of fur and sandalwood trade between the northwestern American coast and China. With ships constantly returning to the islands, initially to the same few locations, the need for a *lingua franca* arose and very soon a pidgin with Hawaiian as its lexifier, Pidgin Hawaiian, developed (Roberts 2013a; for more on Pidgin Hawaiian, see 11.4.1).

From 1820 and the arrival of New England Christian missionaries, the English language gained in prestige. The missionaries initiated a drive for spreading religion, literacy and general education and set up schools. English schools were at first restricted to the royal family, but by 1850 English was used and had gained prestige to such an extent that public schools teaching in English were set up (Kuykendall 1968). This coincided with the whaling period (ca 1820–1860), which led to an increase of naval traffic to and from the islands, as well as to an increased mobility of Hawaiians, many of whom enrolled on the whaling ships. Supply enterprises on the islands grew and demanded more labour.

---

107. I am very grateful to Sarah Roberts for her helpful comments on this snapshot. The reasons for using the fuller name Hawai'i Creole English rather than Hawai'i Creole are given in footnote 24.

The first sugar plantation was founded in 1835; initially labour was indigenous while the owners and foremen were *haoles* ('white persons'). However, due to overwork and introduced diseases the indigenous population declined radically (by 1854 "by at least 75%"; Linnekin 1991: 95). By 1875 labour had to be imported and was supplied mainly from the Portuguese islands of Madeira and the Azores and from East Asia, particularly southern China. The plantations thus saw a reorganization, with Portuguese foremen and Chinese labour.

The first major input languages to the new contact variety, apart from English and the indigenous Hawaiian, were thus Portuguese and southern Chinese languages, particularly Cantonese and Hakka (Roberts 1999, 2005: 253ff, Siegel 2000). The English-lexified pidgin initially emerged in the urban areas in the latter half of the 19th century. There is textual evidence that a creole variety arose among the Hawaiians and part-Hawaiians in the urban areas as early as the 1880s (Roberts 2013c). Sociolinguistic evidence also indicates that the Hawaiians, part-Hawaiians, Portuguese, and Chinese were the earliest groups to shift to a form of English as a native language (Roberts 2000). In other words, when the large number of Japanese, Korean and Filipino immigrants, who would eventually form major ethnic groups on the islands, arrived in the first few decades of the 20th century, there was already an English-lexified contact language that had evolved into a creole.[108] Schools and playgrounds, as well as the plantation setting, then contributed to the spread of the language in the early 1900s (cf. Sato 1985).

Hawai'i Creole English has no official recognition and is still highly stigmatized, although attitudes are slowly changing thanks to, for example, targeted awareness programs at the University of Hawai'i at Mānoa (cf. Sakoda & Siegel 2003), as well as speakers starting to assert the validity of the language. It is mainly used as an informal spoken language, although literature partly or fully in Hawai'i Creole English has been published for many decades.

6.4.1.2 *A short linguistic sketch of Hawai'i Creole English*

Unless otherwise specified the examples in this section are based on my own fieldwork recordings, and represent naturalistic (non-elicited) spoken data.

Hawai'i Creole English has 25 consonants, /p, b, m, f, v, w, ð, l, t, d, n, ɾ, s, z, ɹ, ʃ, ʒ, ʧ, ʤ, j, k, g, ŋ, h, ʔ/, where /ð/ is allophonic with /d/ and /ɾ/ is allophonic with /t, d/; and ten vowels, /i, ɪ, e, ɛ, æ, a, ɔ, o, u, ʊ/, although /ɪ, e, ʊ/ mainly occur in diphthongs.

There is no standard orthography for Hawai'i Creole English, although one was suggested by Odo (1975).

The morphology is predominantly analytic, although there are some inflectional affixes and forms, such as the optional nominal plural marker *-s*, the associative marker, adjective comparison and past tense inflection.

There is no gender system for nouns; however, gendered pronouns may occur for the third person singular:

108. It was, as mentioned above, the later plantation pidgin variety of the predominantly Japanese and Filipino workers in comparison with the creole that formed the basis for Bickerton's LBH. However, as mentioned above, the demographic and textual evidence shows that this later plantation pidgin variety in fact developed after the creole had emerged (Roberts 2013c).

(118) ɾa lɔd fogiv ju no mæɾa wɛɛver ju kam fram waɾɛva
DEF Lord forgives 2SG NEG matter wherever you come from whatever
ju eɪʔ bra no wɚi hi wɛn in hi gon kam aʊʔ
2SG ate my.friend NEG worry it went in it FUT come out
'The Lord forgives you, no matter where you come from or what you ate. It went in, it will come out.' (29-year old male Hawaiian from Mau'i)

Generic nouns may optionally be in the singular (with or without an article), as in (119a), or in the plural with the definite article, as in (119b):

(119) a. dawg loyal, not laik kæt[109]
dog loyal NEG like cat
'Dogs are loyal, not like cats.' (Sakoda & Siegel 2003:35)
b. da menehunis kam out naitaim
DEF menehune.PL come out at.night
'Menehunes ("little people") come out at night.'
(50-year old male Japanese from Kaua'i)

There is a definite article *da* and an indefinite article *wan*, which is homophonous with *wan* 'one' (the numeral). There are two demonstratives, *dis* 'this' and *dæt/dæd* 'that'.

The pronominal system distinguishes between three persons and two numbers (though the second person plural form is only optionally distinguished), as well as subject and object in all forms except the second persons (but note one of the first person plural forms). There is a set of possessive pronouns.

	PERSONAL		POSSESSIVE
	SUBJECT	OBJECT	
1SG	*a(i)*	*mi*	*ma(i)*
2SG	*ju*	*ju*	*jɔ*
3SG	*hi, ʃi, id*	*him, hæ(˞), om, um*	*his, hæ(˞)*
1PL	*wi, as (gaiz)*	*as (gaiz)*	*aʊ(a)*
2PL	*ju (gaiz)*	*ju (gaiz)*	*jɔ*
3PL	*dɛ(i), dei, ðɛ(i), ðei*	*dɛm, ðɛm*	*dɛ(˞), ðɛ(˞)*

There is an associative plural form *-dɛm*:

(120) maɪ faɾɛ-ɾɛm justu go ahm sɛʔ ahm tɚɹonɛʔ ja
my father-ASS PST:HAB ACT set turtle.net
'My father and them used to, ahm, set, ahm, turtle nets, yeah.'
(50-year old female Hawaiian from Mau'i)

The comparative may either be an inflected form of the adjective or may be formed with a degree word ('more'):

(121) a. luk beɾa dæn ju
look better than 2SG
'...look better than you.' (24-year old male Hawaiian from Moloka'i)

109. Examples from written language sources and from Sakoda & Siegel (2003) are given in the original orthography. Sakoda & Siegel make use of the Odo transcription system.

b. da gaiz mo big
DEF guys more big
'The guys are bigger.' (50-year old male Japanese from Kaua'i)

The superlative tends to be the inflected form.

The bare form of the verb relates the event to a given reference point (not necessarily the moment of speech) and can thus denote either present or past tense, depending on the given context. Although the bare form of the verb is the most commonly used one for present tense contexts, the present may also be marked by *-s* in the third person singular, possibly indicating that the inflected form is an absolute present tense (cf. Velupillai 2003a: 139). The (absolute) past tense is indicated by verbal inflection, as in (122a, b), while the (absolute) future tense is indicated with *go(i)ŋ/gonna*, as in (122c) (cf. also Example (118)):

(122) a. so a tol ma frɛn ji no wə˞i bu
so 1SG told 1SG.POSS friend 2SG NEG worry mate
'So I told my friend, "Don't you worry, my friend".'
(29-year old male Hawaiian from Mau'i)

b. wɛn aɪ fə˞s stared tu wə˞k eɪtin jɛas agɔ æd da laɪbɛɹi […]
when 1SG first start.PST to work 18 years ago at DEF library
'When I first started to work at the library, eighteen years ago […]'
(61-year old female Hawaiian from the island of Hawai'i)

c. as da pat ji gonna paʊn on dɛ bɔd
DEM DEF part 2SG FUT pound on DEF board
'That's the part you will pound on the board.'
(75-year old male Japanese from Moloka'i)

It might be that *bumbye* is acquiring a remote future tense meaning (see further Velupillai 2003a: 62ff).

There are four aspect markers: *wen* (past perfective), *pau* (completive), *ste(i) (ing)* (progressive)[110] and *justu* (past habitual):

(123) a. a kud fɛo sambari waz aɹaʊn wɛn jɛo ma neɪm
1SG could feel INDEF was around PST.PFV yell 1SG.POSS name
'(Background:) I could feel somebody was around. (New event:) [(Then) someone] called my name.' (29-year old male Hawaiian from Mau'i)

b. æn dɛn ji no fo ɾa ɾa wahine jɛa ji no ɾa wan
and then 2SG know for DEF DEF woman yeah 2SG know DEF one
dæd ʤɛs paʊ hanaʊ
that just COMPL give.birth
'And then you know, for the, the woman, yeah, you know, he one who just finished giving birth.' (50-year old female Hawaiian from Mau'i)

c. wɛl a gɛd wan fɹɛn a justu wə˞k wiʔ
well 1SG POSS INDEF friend 1SG PST.HAB work with
'Well, I have a friend I used to work with.' (29-year old male Hawaiian from Mau'i)

110. For a discussion on the difference between VERB-*ing*, *ste* VERB and *ste* VERB-*ing*, see Velupillai (2003a: 81ff).

d. da mɛnehunɛs stɛ matʃin ju no kæn stɛ in ɾa wɛ
DEF menehunes march.PROG 2SG PROHIB LOC in DEF way
'The menehunes are marching, you can't be in the way.'
(50-year old male Japanese from Kaua'i)

There are several modality markers. Negation is expressed by the preverbal negative marker *no* (cf. Examples (118), (122), (123)), except in the past, which takes *nɛva*:

(124) deɪ nɛva pik ap dɛ tiŋ jɛt?
3PL NEG.PST pick up DEF thing yet
'Haven't they picked up the thing yet?'
(77-year old female Hawaiian from Moloka'i)

The word order is typically subject-verb-object. Existentials and possessives are expressed with *gɛt* in the present and *hæd* in the past, in both cases without any expletive subject. The copula is typically, but not always, absent in the present tense, but very commonly expressed with an inflected form of *be* in the past and future tenses. There is a locative copula *stɛ* (cf. also Example (123d)).

Polar questions are marked through intonation only (cf. Example (124)), which, unusually, is falling and not rising. Content questions also have falling intonation. The interrogative phrase is fronted:

(125) waɪ ʃi go?
why 3SG go
'Why did she go?' (85-year old male Portuguese from Kaua'i)

There are the coordinating conjunctions *æn* 'and', *ɔ* 'or' and *ba(ʔ)* 'but'. The latter may optionally appear sentence-finally. There are several kinds of subordinated clauses, including relative clauses.

6.4.1.3 *Short text*

(A 95-year old female Hawaiian from the island of Hawai'i tells about the shark man.)

Da ʃakmæn lio ba ɾa pɔn wɛ ða mɛn wɛ swimin. Hi tʃeindʒ himseol tu
DEF shark.man live by DEF pond where DEF man.PL were swim.PROG 3SG change himself to

ʃak bat his puka ɔn da maʊt hɛa. Dɛn wɛn da pipo go get opihi æs
shark but 3SG.POSS hole on DEF mouth here then when DEF people ACT get limpet that's

wɛn hi ɡɹæb om. Hi ɡɹæb da wan hi laɪɡ den hi it om yɛ? Æn dɛn hi
when 3SG grab 3SG.OBJ 3SG grab DEF one 3SG like then 3SG eat 3SG.OBJ yeah and then 3SG

go bæk æn dɛn naʊ ju luk araʊn eh? Wɛ aua patna?
go back and then now 2SG look around eh where 1PL.POSS partner

'The shark man lives by the pond, where the men used to swim. He changes himself to a shark, but his hole is here on the mouth. Then when the people go to gather limpets, that's when he grabs them. He grabs the one he likes then he eats him, yeah? And then he goes back. And then, now, you look around (and ask yourself), eh? Where is our partner?'

6.4.1.4 *Some sources of data*

There is a fair amount of data available for Hawai'i Creole English, especially in written form. Darrel H. Lum and Lois-Ann Yamanaka, for example, have published numerous short stories, novels and poems wholly or partly in Hawai'i Creole English (such as Lum 1990 and Yamanaka 1993, 1996, to mention only a couple). An extensive source of written data is the Bible translation (*Da Jesus Book* 2000), much of which is available online (http://www.pidginbible.org/Concindex.html, accessed 9 February 2015).

6.4.2 Haitian Creole: A French-lexified creole in Haiti[111]

6.4.2.1 *A brief background sketch of Haitian Creole*

Haitian Creole, called *créole haïtien* in French and *kreyòl* by the speakers themselves, is spoken by about 9.5 million people in Haiti and another 1.5 million or more of the Haitian diaspora (mainly in the USA, Canada, the Dominican Republic and Overseas France), making it the largest known creole language.

The island of Hispaniola, comprising the present-day nations of Haiti and the Dominican Republic, was conquered by the Spanish in 1492 with the arrival of Christopher Columbus. The indigenous Taíno population rapidly diminished due to introduced diseases, enslavement, outmarriages and social disruption and were virtually extinct by the mid-1520s (Rouse 1992). During the 16th century the Spanish engaged in sugar production on the island. However, further Spanish conquests on the American mainland saw the depopulation of Hispaniola. In the latter half of the 17th century immigrants from the western part of France and their indentured servants settled in the north-western part of the island.

The western part of the island came under French control in 1697, after which it became known as Saint-Domingue. With the development and increase of the sugar production, slave labour became necessary for the subsequent sugar plantations and was imported from West Africa. The numbers of West African slaves were initially fairly low, but grew exponentially as the sugar industry grew. In 1789, for example, Saint-Domingue had a population of about 556,000, of which 500,000 were West African slaves, and only 32,000 European colonists. The remaining 24,000 were *affranchis* or freedmen (Ferguson 2011). In total some 800,000 West African slaves were shipped to Saint-Domingue in the 18th century (d'Ans 1987: 1753). The origins of these slaves cover a vast area, "a hinterland that stretched out from the Atlantic Coast to Lake Chad and to the regions of the Gulf of Guinea located between modern-day Senegal and Cameroon" (Fattier 2013: 195). The slaves are thus likely to have spoken a number of different languages, making it difficult to pinpoint exactly where various substratal features may have originated.[112]

---

111. This section relies primarily on DeGraff (2007) and Fattier (2013). I am very grateful to Michel DeGraff for his helpful comments on this snapshot.

112. According to Eltis et al. (1999) the dominating regions of embarkation for the slaves that ended up in Saint-Domingue (i.e. Haiti) were West-Central Africa (42.10%) and the Bight of Benin (23.80%), which also comprises a huge and linguistically highly diverse area.

What became the Haitian society after independence in 1804 was stratified by skin colour, class and gender. The European population consisted of *grands blancs*, who were the landowners and merchants, *petits blancs*, who were craftsmen and overseers, and *blancs menants*, who were labourers and peasants. The *affranchis*, some of whom were slave owners themselves, were typically descendants of mixed European-African heritage, but also freed black slaves. Most slaves were African-born *bozals* (Ferguson 2011).

The Haitian Revolution led to a declaration of independence in 1804 of the western part of the island under the name Haiti, taken from the Taíno word *hayiti* or *ayiti* ('rugged, mountainous'; cf. Geggus 1997).

Haitian Creole has been an official language in Haiti since 1987, alongside French (which has been an official language since 1918), but most of the official administrative texts and documents are in French. Since 1979 Haitian Creole has been part of the education. However, the language is still in many ways stigmatized and viewed as an obstacle to advancement, although awareness programs, dictionaries and the advanced stage of the standardization process, which includes an official orthography, all contribute to moving away from this historical stigma.

6.4.2.2 *A short linguistic sketch of Haitian Creole*

Unless otherwise specified, the examples in this section are given in the official orthography. Note that vowel+*n* denotes a nasalized vowel (e.g. <an> for /ã/).

Haitian Creole has 16 consonants, /p, b, m, f, v, t, d, n, s, z, l, ʃ, ʒ, k, g, ɣ/, and three glides, /w, j, ɥ/. There are 7 vowels, /i, e, ɛ, a, ɔ, o, u/ of which three may be nasalized to /ã, ẽ, õ/. The official orthography differs from the IPA as follows:

OFFICIAL ORTHOGRAPHY	IPA
è	ɛ
en	ẽ
an	ã
ò	ɔ
on	õ
ou	u
y	j
u	w / ɥ
ch	ʃ
j	ʒ
r	ɣ

Haitian Creole has fixed word-final stress. Syllables may be simple (V, CV or VC) or moderately complex (CVC, VCC, CCV, CCVC, or CVCC) although there seems to be a preference for CV syllables (Fattier 2013:197).

The morphology is predominantly analytic, although some nouns referring to human beings show variation with respect to gender, such as *milat* 'mulatto.M' versus *milatrès* 'mulatto.F' (Fattier 2013:197) or *wangatè* versus *wangatèz* '(man/woman) who believes in and/or makes magical fetishes' (DeGraff 2001:73). There is also cliticization and reduplication.

Nouns are typically invariant with respect to number, case and gender (except for the kinds of cases mentioned above). There is a prenominal indefinite article *yon* 'a'. The postnominal portmanteau definite singular article *la* 'the.SG' (with the allomorphs *a*, *an*, *nan*, and *lan* depending on the phonological environment; DeGraff 2007:117) contrasts with the postnominal definite plural article *yo* 'the.PL':

(126) a.

Boukinèt	te	pran	yon	flè	bay	Bouki
PN	ANT	take	INDEF	flower	give	PN

'Boukinèt gave a flower to Bouki.'

b.

mwen	fè	kabann	lan	rapid-rapid	maten	an
1SG	make	bed	DEF.SG	quickly~RED	morning	DEF.SG

'I made the bed very quickly this morning.'

c.

mennen	timoun	yo	vini
lead	child	DEF.PL	come

'Bring the children.' (DeGraff 2007:112, 116)

The demonstrative is number specific, with *sa a* 'this/that' for the singular and *sa yo* 'these/those' for the plural.

The personal pronouns distinguish between three persons and two numbers, but not case or gender. There is a long and a short form, where the short form may cliticize on the preceding or following word.[113]

	SINGULAR	PLURAL
1	*mwen, m*	*nou, n*
2	*ou, w*	*nou, n*
3	*li, l*	*yo, y*

The possessive pronouns are identical to the personal pronouns.

Adjectives typically follow the noun, although some evaluative adjectives precede the noun:

(127) a.

yon	kaj	wouj
INDEF	house	red

'a red house'

b.

yon	gwo	kay
INDEF	big	house

'a big house' (Fattier 2013:197)

The lexical aspect of the verb is relevant for the tense/aspect interpretation of verbs. The bare verb may indicate past or nonpast time reference, depending on the context and the lexical aspect, and in some cases on the nature of the object. The anterior marker *te(t)* indicates past for stative verbs and past-before-past for non-stative verbs (but cf. Example (126a)). The markers *sot* or *fèk* indicate recent past. The marker *ap* indicates future tense for stative verbs and the progressive for non-stative verbs, while *(a)pral(e)* denotes immediate future for both statives and non-statives. The completive aspect is denoted by *fin*, while the inchoative aspect is denoted by *ap* for stative and

113. Fattier (2013) distinguishes between a dependent and an independent set, where the dependent pronouns are unstressed and have a short form that may cliticize on the preceding or following word, while the independent pronouns are stressed and have no short form.

pran for non-stative verbs. The markers *konn* and *a/ava* respectively denote habitual aspect and uncertain future for stative verbs. There are several modal markers. All tense, mood and aspect markers are preverbal and may also precede nouns and adjectives in predicative clauses:

(128) a. Elifèt te malad
PN ANT sick
'Elifèt was sick.'
b. Elifèt te (yon) doktè
PN ANT INDEF doctor
'Elifèt was a doctor.' (DeGraff 2007:104)

The word order is typically subject-verb-object. The preverbal *pa* marks negation:

(129) Toussaint pa te konnen si tout patriyòt t ap leve goumen
PN NEG ANT know if every patriot ANT FUT rise fight
'Touissant did not know if every patriot would rise and fight.' (DeGraff 2007:110)

There is negative concord:

(130) nan katye sa a pèsonn pa di pèsonn anyen
in neighbourhood DEM.SG nobody NEG say nobody nothing
'In this neighbourhood, nobody says anything to anybody' (DeGraff 2007:111)

Polar questions are formed either through rising intonation only, or through rising intonation plus the clause-initial question marker *èske* (< Fr. *est-ce que*). In content questions the interrogative phrase is typically fronted and is typically bimorphemic:

(131) a. (èske) ou manje diri a?
Q 2SG eat rice DEF
'Did you eat the rice?'
b. ki moun ou kwè ki renmen ki moun?
which person 2SG think COMP love which person
'Who do you think loves whom?' (DeGraff 2007:122)

There is no copula (cf. Example (128)). The existential and possessive is expressed with *gen*, which has a longer form *genyen* (< Fr. *gagner*) in certain syntactic contexts, for example when it appears clause-finally in questions:

(132) a. gen manje sou tab la
EXIST food on table DEF
'There is food on the table.'
b. Mari gen kouraj
PN POSS courage
'Mary has courage.'
c. ki sa ou ganyen?
which that 2SG POSS
'What do you have?' (DeGraff 2007:115)

With clause coordination the verb is obligatorily repeated:

(133)

m	ta	renmen	manje	mango	e	m	ta	renmen	bwè	dlo	kokoye
1SG	COND	love	eat	mango	and	1SG	COND	love	drink	water	coconut.palm

'I would love to eat a mango and drink coconut water.' (Fattier 2013: 202)

There are serial verb constructions, mainly directionals with 'go' and 'come' and beneficials with 'give' (cf. Example (126)). There are relative clause constructions with the relativizer *k(i)*, which is obligatory for subject noun phrase reference:

(134) a.

m	tande	on	avyon	k	ap	vole
1SG	hear	INDEF	plane	REL	PROG	fly

'I hear a plane that flies.'

b.

kay	kote	m	rive	a	bèl
house	place	1SG	arrive	DEF	beautiful

'The house where I arrived is beautiful.' (Fattier 2013: 202)

6.4.2.3 *Short text*

(From Fattier 2013: 203)

M	panse	m	di	mezanmi	genlè	e	lannuit	pou	tanpèt	van	sa	a	e	si	kay	la
1SG	think	1SG	say	friends	seem	HL	night	for	storm	wind	DEM	DEF	and	if	house	DEF

kraze	mezanmi!	E	si	kay	la	tonbe	sou	moun	nan	nan	nwa!	Radyo	te	bay
destroyed	friends	and	if	house	DEF	fall	on	people	DEF	in	black	radio	ANT	give

pou	tout	moun	pa	dòmi	san	alimèt,	san	gaz,	fò	ou	gen	ba(g)ay	la
for	all	people	NEG	sleep	without	matches	without	petrol	must	2SG	POSS	thing	DEF

met	nan	kay	la	pou	si	gen	on	move	kout-tan	pou	pase	alimèt	nan	lan	lannuit
put	in	house	DEF	for	if	EXIST	INDEF	bad	hurricane	for	light	match	DEF	in	night

lan	toujou.	Tout	bannann,	tout	te	tonbe	pye	zaboka	kraze,	pye	mango	kraze,
DEF	always	all	banana.tree,	all	ANT	fall	tree	avocado	destroy	tree	mango	destroy

tout	kay	dekouvri	nèt nèt
all	house	discover	completely~RED

'I thought, I said to myself: "Oh là là, it seems that the night is going to be stormy and what if the house gets destroyed, oh là là! And what if the house falls on the people in the dark!" On the radio they had announced that no one should go to bed without matches or petrol. You had to put these things in the house for the case that there would be a bad hurricane so that you always have a match to strike at night. All banana trees had fallen down, the avocado trees were destroyed, the mango trees were destroyed, all houses had completely lost their roofs.'

6.4.2.4 *Some sources of data*

Haitian Creole spoken data can accessed through radio (such as *Radio Haiti Creole*, http://rdiamfm.tripod.com, accessed 9 February 2015 or *Radio kreyol FM*, http://www.infokreyol.com/, accessed 9 February 2015, among many others) and TV broadcasts (such as Tele Image, http://teleimagetvshow.com/, accessed 9 February 2015, a web-TV, although some programs or speakers may also use French and/or English). Although French is more commonly used as a written language, there is literature in Haitian Creole, such as the works of Félix Morisseau-Leroy (or Feliks Moriso-Lewa), for instance the highly influential *Wa Kreyon* (1953).

6.4.3 Berbice Dutch: An extinct Dutch-lexified creole in Guyana[114]

6.4.3.1 *A brief background sketch of Berbice Dutch*

Berbice Dutch, by scholars also called *Berbice Dutch Creole*, was called *di lanʃi* ('the language') by the speakers themselves. It was officially declared extinct in 2010, a few years after the death of the last known speaker, Albertha Bell. It used to be spoken along the Berbice River in present-day Guyana.

Berbice was founded in 1627 when Abraham van Pere was given permission by the Dutch West India Company to establish a plantation colony (Postma 1990:13). The initial settlement consisted of "40 [white] men and 20 [white] youths" (Smith 2000 [1962]: Chapter 2) as well as six slaves (Postma 1990:13). About a century later, in 1732, the colony consisted of 113 plantations on the Berbice River and the neighbouring Canje Creek and by 1762 the Berbice colony had a population of 346 whites, 3,833 African slaves and 244 Amerindian slaves (Smith 2000 [1962]: Chapter 2). Tax records, which may well have underestimated figures for reasons of profit (see Kramer 1991 and Kouwenberg 2009b for a discussion), indicate that enslavement of Amerindians was abandoned in the latter half of the 18th century as part of Dutch efforts to "maintain good relations with the indigenous population" due to the planters' "need for Amerindian allies in tracking runaway slaves and preventing slave uprisings" (Kouwenberg 2009b:119) as well as for food supplies (Kouwenberg 2011). The indigenous Arawak Amerindians were thus part of the linguistic ecology in Berbice, both as slaves in the earlier years, and as a neighbour population for the whole duration of the colony.

There do not seem to be any historical records available for the origin of the African slaves in Berbice for the 17th century (Eltis et al. 1999), the crucial period for the formation of the creole, although linguistic evidence points to a high substratal influence of Eastern Ijo (Smith et al. 1987, Kouwenberg 2009b) which might indicate that the number of slaves from the Bight of Biafra (present-day Nigeria) to Berbice were proportionally higher than in the 18th century (cf. Postma 1990, Eltis et al. 1999).

During the 18th century plantations moved downriver and, during the 19th century, to the coastal areas. This locational shift, together with a shift to British ownership – the colony became part of British Guiana in 1814 – which led to new slaves being brought from Barbados, contributed to the emergence of an English-lexified creole (Creolese). The new creole rapidly gained ground, aided by the presence of missionaries and their English-language education efforts from the mid-19th century on, and caused a shift from Berbice Dutch.

The "Bovianders" (those of mixed heritage), a term that might derive from Dutch *bovenlanders* ('upriver dwellers'), remained in the original upriver plantation areas and continued to use Berbice Dutch for another century. This population was typically bilingual in Arawak, the language of the indigenous neighbours who had also remained in the area, and/or Creolese.

The dominance and prestige of English meant that Berbice Dutch was so stigmatized that some speakers refused to be interviewed by linguists (Kouwenberg 2013a:276). What is

114. This section relies heavily on Kouwenberg (1994) and (2013a).

presumably the last interview with the last known speaker of Berbice Dutch, Albertha Bell, who was 103 years old at the time, was conducted in 2004 (published by The Jamaican Language Unit at http://www.youtube.com/watch?v=5PH1TvEE8Vw, accessed 9 February 2015).

6.4.3.2 *A short linguistic sketch of Berbice Dutch*

Berbice Dutch had 16 consonants, /p, b, m, f, w, t, d, n, s, l, r, ʃ, j, k, g, h/, and six vowels, /i, e, ɛ, a, o, u/. The typologically rare front rounded vowels in Dutch were lost:

(135)	ʃiri	'sour'	(< Du. *zuur* /zy:r/)
	spuku	'vomit'	(< Du. *spugen* /spyxe/)
	loi	'lazy'	(< Du. *lui* /løy/)
	kuiti	'calf of leg'	(< Du. *kuit* /køyt/)

Syllables could be simple or moderately complex with consonant clusters of up to three consonants in the onset. Words could have up to three syllables. Stress was typically on the penultimate.

The morphology was predominantly analytic, though there was both derivational (nominalization) and inflectional (plural and tense/aspect marking) suffixation,[115] as well as reduplication (iteration and intensification):

(136) a. en gu fɛtɛ-jɛ jɛn=da kwakwani (cf. *en fɛtɛ)
one big fat-NMLZ COP=there Kwakwani
'A big fat one lives at Kwakwani'

b. did-ap da di kali tok-ap skɛpr-ap
DEM-PL COP DEF small child-PL paddle-PL
'Those are the small children's paddles.'

c. en sukw-a fu di kɛn-ap wat jɛn=da far-farə boʃ-ap=ang
3PL search-IPFV for DEF person-PL REL COP=there far~RED bush-PL=LOC
'They were searching for the people that were living far away (hidden) in the bush.'
(Kouwenberg 1994: 233, 237, 245)

Various unstressed elements, such as the negator and vowel-initial pronouns, could cliticize to a leftward host (see also (136a, c)):

(137) a. afta o dot-tɛ lahan=or biʃ ababa=kanɛ
after 3SG die-PFV leave=3SG speak anymore=NEG
'After he died (and) left (him) he doesn't speak (this language) anymore.'

b. o wa bangi mɛt=ɛkɛ
3SG PST fear with=1SG
'He feared for me.' (Kouwenberg 1994: 300f)

Nouns were inflected for plural with the suffix *-ap(u)*. Case and gender were not relevant. Possession was indicated either through juxtaposition or with the only existing possessive pronoun, *ʃi* (third person singular).

115. It should be noted that all productive bound morphology in Berbice Dutch derives from Ijo (Anthony Grant, p.c.).

There was a prenominal indefinite article *en* 'a', which was identical with the numeral 'one' and only occurred with count nouns, and a prenominal definite article *di* 'the'. Bare nouns could also have definite reference when "unique reference can be established outside the discourse through knowledge of the world, knowledge of the community or immediate situation which establishes pragmatic uniqueness" (Kouwenberg 2013a: 278):

(138) bi mama pi ɛkɛ bili gau
say mother give 1SG axe quick
'(He) says,: Mother, give me the axe quickly.' (Kouwenberg 2013a: 278)

The demonstrative was postnominal and required the definite article. The pronoun system distinguished between three persons and two numbers, but not for case or gender:

	SINGULAR		PLURAL
1	*ɛkɛ*	1	*enʃi, iʃi*
2	*ju*	2	*jɛndɛ*
3	*o, ori*	3	*eni, ini*

There were two tense markers, preverbal *wa* (past) and preverbal *wa* + the suffix *-tɛ* (anterior). In discourse the background was tense marked, whereas the bare verb was used for the foreground. There were four preverbal mood markers, *ma* (irrealis), *wa ma* (future-in-the-past/counterfactual), *sa* (improbable) and *wa sa* (past improbable/counterfactual). And there were five aspect markers, the suffixes *-tɛ* (perfective) and *-a(rɛ)* (imperfective); the preverbal *wa* + the suffix *-a(rɛ)* (past imperfective); and the preverbal *das* (habitual) and *justu* (past habitual).

The word order was typically subject-verb-object, although Berbice Dutch has some postpositions (e.g. *mu mɛr bof* 'further upriver', lit. 'go more top'; Kouwenberg 1994: 204). Negation was marked with the clause final *ka(nɛ)*, which could cliticize to the preceding word (cf. above). There was a preverbal negative resultative *noko*:

(139) a. en kɛnɛ mɛrɛ furi-da ka
INDEF person more NEG.EXIST-there NEG
'Nobody else is there.'
b. ɛkɛ horo-tɛ ori, bat ɛkɛ no-ko kiki en ka
1SG hear-PFV 3SG but 1SG NEG-RES see one NEG
'I heard it, but I haven't seen any.' (Kouwenberg 2007: 38)

Polar questions were formed through rising intonation only and content questions with a clause-initial interrogative phrase:

(140) a. ju waʃ-tɛ ju bara?
2SG wash-PFV 2SG hand
'Did you wash your hands?'
b. wanɛr ɛk ma jefi nau?
when 1SG IRR eat now
'When am I going to eat?' (Kouwenberg 1994: 34, 41)

Nominal predicates took the copula *da* and adverbial predicates the copula *jɛn(da)* 'exist, be (there)' or the negative *furi/furda* 'not.exist'. There was no copula with adjectival predicates (cf. also Example (136a–c), (139a)):

(141) a. di jɛrma wati o trou-tɛ, eni da Arwak kɛnɛ-apu
DEF woman REL 3SG marry-PFV 3PL COP Arawak person-PL
'The woman that he married, they (her people) are Arawak people.'

b. eni das habu eni plɛkɛ wanga eni jɛn-da, bat nau eni
3PL HAB have 3PL place where 3PL COP-there but now 3PL
fur-da ababa ka
NEG.EXIST-there anymore NEG
'They used to have their place where they stayed, but now they are no longer there.'

c. o bjɛbjɛ an nagwa
3SG yellow and long
'It (a mermaid's hair) is blond and long.' (Kouwenberg 2007: 36, 41, 49)

Complement clauses could optionally be headed by the complementizer *dati*:

(142) eni pama-tɛ ɛkɛ biʃi dati ɛkɛ ma mu danga ka
3PL tell-PFV 1SG say COMP 1SG IRR go there NEG
'They told me that I should not go there.' (Kouwenberg 2013a: 281)

There were various forms of directional, beneficial, instrumental and locative serial verb constructions:

(143) a. wɛl hiri wɛrɛ ju das deki gutu pi ju mati
well here again 2SG HAB take thing give 2SG friend
'Well over here, you give something to your friends.'

b. o grui-tɛ drai-tɛ gu bom
3SG grow-PFV turn-PFV big tree
'It grew into a big tree.' (Kouwenberg 2013a: 281)

Relative clauses were typically headed by *wati* (cf. Example (136c), (141a)).

6.4.3.3 *Short text*

(From Kouwenberg 1994: 508ff with minimal changes. Note that *manggiapu* is literally a nominalized plural of *manggi* 'run' but became a fossilized form that denoted the descendants of runaway slaves who settled in the bush.)

Di manggiapu wa musu.… So eni eni deki-tɛ eni kali-kali jat mu-tɛ birbiʃi bofu,
DEF runaway PST many so 3PL 3PL take-PFV 3PL small~RED boat go-PFV river top

andri kom-tɛ hiir an eni mu-tɛ hau faru eni kan mu=an=eni lasan-tɛ=eni jat
other come-PFV here and 3PL go-PFV how far 3PL can go=and=3PL leave-PFV=3PL boat

an dɛn eni mu-tɛ buʃ=ben. Eni wa habu couple of 100 fan eni di weldri man jɛs
and then 3PL go-PFV bush-inside 3PL PST have couple of 100 from 3PL DEF wild man yes

eni kriki-tɛ weldri ju nimi-tɛ bai di di wan di andri-apu wati wati nimi-tɛ kɛnɛ
3PL get-PFV wild 2SG know-PFV by DEF DEF one DEF other-PL REL REL know-PFV person

di gu-gu man-apu gu jɛrma eni-jɛ eni-jɛ doto-tɛ an di junggu generation-apu
DEF big~RED man-PL big woman 3PL-NMLZ 3PL-NMLZ get-PFV and DEF young generation-PL

nau ɛni-jɛ kriki-tɛ weldri
now 3PL-NMLZ get-PFV wild

'The runaway slaves were many. ... So they, they went upriver in their small boats. Some of them came here, and they went as far as they could go and they left their boats and then they went into the bush. There were several hundreds of them, the wild men. Yes, they got wild. You know, the, the ones, the others that, that knew people, adult men and women, they died, and the young generation, they got wild.'

6.4.3.4 *Some sources of data*

There is not much collected data available for Berbice Dutch. The interview with Albertha Bell can be viewed on YouTube (see above). Kouwenberg (1994) is a very comprehensive grammar which contains numerous examples and 47 pages of texts, all of them glossed and translated, as well as extensive vocabulary lists. Kouwenberg (2013b) provides numerous glossed and translated examples online.

6.5 Summary

It is highly debated what the formation processes involved in the development of creole languages may have been. Central to the debate is whether creoles per definition descend from pidgins, whether the emergence of creoles was an abrupt or gradual process and whether creoles constitute a structurally specific type of language.

The Language Bioprogram Hypothesis puts forth that creoles emerged abruptly in one single generation. The creators of the creole languages were the children of the immigrants, who, due to the restricted input of the contact variety (jargons or pidgins) used by the parents, resorted to a basic human blueprint for language to provide themselves with a linguistically adequate language. Creoles therefore display prototypical features of human language.

The Creole Prototype theory maintains that creole languages constitute a structurally specific and identifiable type of language due to the fact that they emerged abruptly out of prior severely restricted language varieties (pidgins). The creators of the creole languages were the children who nativized the pidgin of the community they were born into. Once a creole language emerged, it continued to develop and change like any other language, thus losing its prototypical character.

The Relexification Hypothesis proposes that creoles emerged abruptly when labourers (slaves or indentured labour) arrived in the colonial societies and had to function in the colonizers' language, at which point they resorted to the structures of their mother tongues but replaced the vocabulary. The creators of creole languages were therefore adults who had restricted access to the colonizers' target language. There was no prior pidgin stage.

The Founder Principle theory argues that any founder population in a settlement has a disproportionally high influence on the outcome of the resulting population. Given that the colonies were initially homestead economies, with small farms and intimate interactions between farmers and labourers, everybody would have had sufficient access to the colonizers' vernaculars to acquire them fully. The creole thus emerged gradually through basilectalization, when the ratio of immigrants increased and the newcomers got more restricted access to the target language models. The makeup of any given creole is dependent on the particular linguistic feature pool for that contact situation. There was no prior pidgin stage.

The Gradualist Model of creolization argues that historical data shows that the ratio of locally-born children was too low for any creole to nativize abruptly from a pidgin. Instead the envisioned scenario is that an early pidgin developed, which gradually and incrementally creolized as the ratio of a locally-born population increased. The emergence of the creole thus involved both adults and children, and was a dynamic and diffuse process which does not allow for any clear-cut divide between a pidgin and a creole stage in the given society.

The Afrogenesis or Domestic Origin Hypothesis takes a monogenetic approach to the development of the Atlantic creoles and argues that West African Portuguese, English, and French-lexified pidgins were spoken by the slaves who were transported to the New World. These pidgins then formed the parent languages for what would become respectively the Portuguese, English and French-lexified Caribbean creoles.

The notion of the pidgin-to-creole life cycle is highly debated and rests on the assumption that creoles are nativized languages of prior restricted varieties. In principle a creole may be a nativized jargon, though it is more often predicted to be a nativized pidgin or extended pidgin (pidgincreole). Due to the absence of historical data, it is often not possible to empirically test this assumption for a given creole.

Irrespective of whether creoles emerged abruptly or developed gradually, whether they had prior pidgin stages or not, or whether they constitute a structurally identifiably type of language, it is certain that they developed in multilingual societies. The role of multilingualism and code-switching is therefore also likely to be a relevant factor in the development of creole languages.

6.6 Key points

- **It is a matter of debate whether creoles form a special class of language, whether their developmental processes differ from that of non-creole languages, whether they per definition originate from pidgins, whether they emerged abruptly or gradually, and whether the children or adults were the principle agents of their formation.**
- **Most approaches to theories of the genesis of creole languages ultimately rest on the choice of linguistic method and whether universal or substratal factors are placed in the foreground.**
- **Since creoles emerged in multilingual settings, phenomena of multilingualism (e.g. code-switching) should be taken into account in any theory of creole genesis.**

- **The notion of the pidgin-to-creole life cycle presumes that any given creole originates in a previous contact variety (either a jargon, a pidgin or an extended pidgin).**
- **The developmental history of any given creole can only be traced by means of archival research.**
- **The question of whether creoles form a unique typological class can only be answered by empirically comparing creoles with non-creoles.**

6.7 Exercises

1. What does 'creole exceptionalism' mean?
2. What does the 'pidgin-to-creole life cycle' imply?
3. Which theories on creole formation emphasize the role of children and which the role of adults? Are there any that include both children and adults as agents in the formation of creole languages?
4. Which theories on creole formation assume an abrupt emergence of creoles and which assume a gradual emergence?
5. Are there any theories that accommodate for multilingualism in the formation of creole languages?

Languages cited in Chapter 7

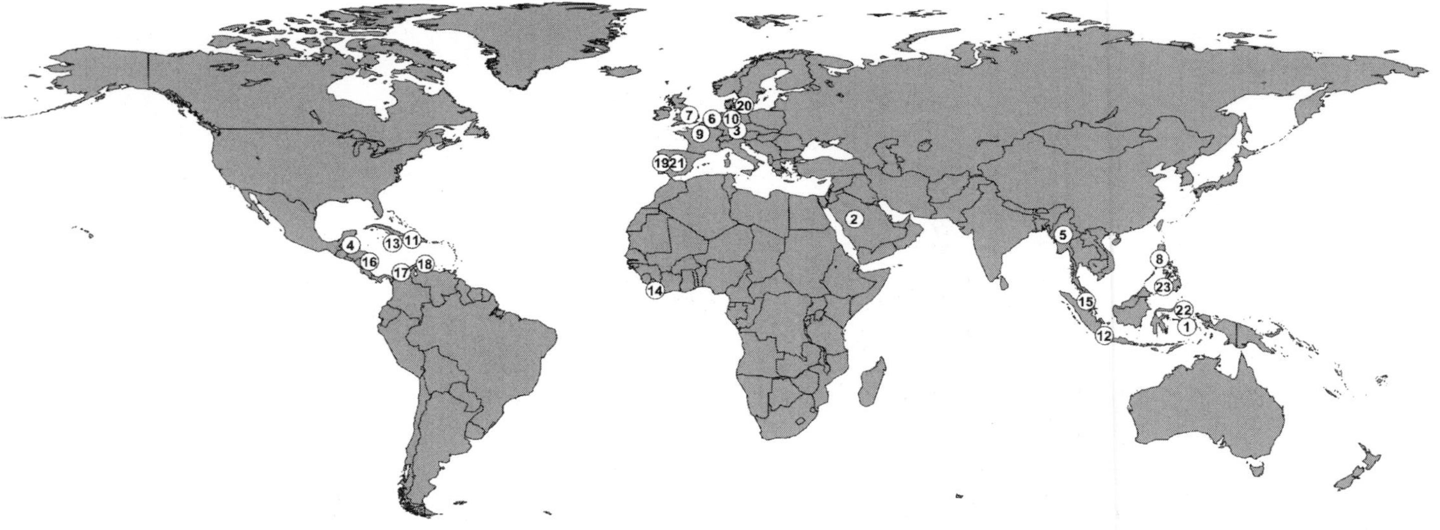

1. Ambon Malay
2. Arabic, Standard
3. Bavarian
4. Belizean Creole; Garifuna
5. Burmese
6. Dutch
7. English; British Jamaican
8. Cavite Chabacano; Filipino; Tagalog; Ternate Chabacano
9. French
10. German, Standard
11. Haitian Creole
12. Indonesian
13. Jamaican
14. Liberian Settler English
15. Malay
16. Nicaraguan Creole English; Rama Cay Creole
17. Palenquero
18. Papiamentu
19. Portuguese
20. Scanian (Southern Swedish)
21. Spanish
22. Ternate
23. Zamboanga Chabacano

Chapter 7

Variation and change

No linguistic system is monolithic, but will show variation to different degrees depending on such extralinguistic factors as region, social identity and domain of use. This variation may show continuous degrees of resemblance to a given standard language where speakers may use one of a range of 'lects' depending on the situation. Or the variation may be one of a more stable dichotomous relationship where speakers reserve one variety for some functions and another variety for other functions. This chapter will very briefly bring up the notion of lectal continua and implicational scales (Section 7.1.1), as well as that of diglossia (Section 7.1.2) before briefly discussing how these concepts have been related to ongoing language change in creole speaking societies (Section 7.2). Section 7.3 gives short sketches of three creole languages where lectal variation, diglossia and identity are closely connected: Belizean Creole (an English-lexified creole with a wide lectal continuum), Ambon Malay (a Malay-lexified creole which functions both as an H and an L variety) and Ternate Chabacano (a Spanish-lexified creole which coexists with a different standard language).

7.1 Variation

We must always keep in mind that languages are dynamic systems that will vary across time, place and situation, as well as between individuals. Furthermore, language forms an intimate part of our identity: the way we express ourselves and interact with others is not only an indication of our origins and what may have formed us, but also an indication of how we perceive ourselves and how we wish to be perceived by others. Thus the language of individual speakers may show **variation** according to, for example, the region they are from, their age, their gender, the amount of education they have had, their social class, whether they live in an urban or a rural area, and so on. Furthermore, the same speaker may vary his or her linguistic **register** according to the particular situation, in that s/he may speak in one way in a formal setting, while speaking in another way in an informal setting.

When the linguistic variation between individual speakers shows a certain degree of systematicity according to different extralinguistic factors we tend to classify the varieties as different kinds of **'lects'** (cf., for example, Ferguson 1972: 30ff and Hudson 1996: 22ff). That is, 'lects' are "varieties of a language that differ from each other in a minimal way" (de Rooij 1994b: 57). Regional variation, for example, is described as different **dialects** (sometimes also called **regional dialects**).[116] Variation according to social factors, such as age, gender, level of education, social class, and so on, is usually referred to as **sociolects** (sometimes also called **social dialects**). Language variation is the focus of the overlapping fields of dialectology and sociolinguistics. For an accessible introduction to dialectology, see, for example, Chambers & Trudgill (1998); for accessible introductions to sociolinguistics, see, for example, Meyerhoff (2006) and Wardhaugh (2006).

7.1.1 Continua and implicational scales

7.1.1.1 *Continuum of 'lects'*

Just like any other natural language, contact languages also show variation according to different factors. Just as with any other natural language, any given contact language may show regional variation (for example, people from upcountry areas might speak a different variety from lowcountry area speakers, or people from different islands in an archipelago community may speak different varieties, and so on) and/or social variation (for example, men and women may show systematic variation in their speech, educated people may speak differently from non-educated people, people from rural areas may speak differently from people from urban areas, younger people may speak differently from older people, and so on).

One measure of similarity that has been identified as definitional of pidgin and creole languages is the language's degree of similarity with the lexifier. This was originally brought up by Schuchardt (1884: 113f), who observed the fact that the Spanish-lexified creole of the Philippines showed different degrees of similarity with Spanish.

In actual fact this kind of variation is not particular to pidgin and creole languages, but can be thought of as a continuum of 'lects' that are more or less similar to a given standard language (as also pointed out in, for example, Bailey 1966: 1). It is important to note that we are dealing with a **continuum**, i.e. a non-discrete, continuous range of variation where there are no sharp borders. At the one end of the continuum we have the 'lect' least similar to the standard language, while at the other end of the continuum we have the 'lect' most similar to the standard language. To capture this kind of variation William Stewart (1965: 15) coined the terms **basilect** (from *basi* 'bottom') for the 'lect' least similar to the standard and **acrolect** (from *acro* 'apex') for the 'lect' most similar to the standard language. The stages between these two poles were subsequently coined **mesolects** (Bailey 1971). With pidgin and creole languages the standard language is most commonly the lexifier; the acrolect would thus be the variety that is very close to the lexifier in terms of its linguistic system, while the

116. But see Ferguson (1972: 34) who defines dialect as "something between a variety and a language".

basilect would be the variety that is very removed from the lexifier in terms of its linguistic system. For more on variation in pidgins and creoles, see, for example, de Rooij (1994b) and Patrick (2008) with further references.

Very simplified we can think of this continuum as a "ladder of lects" (Sebba 1997:210), which would mirror the terminology of basi (base) to meso (middle) to acro (top). An example of such a lectal continuum can, for instance, be found in Jamaican. Consider the sentence 'I am eating' in Figure 7.1, given in IPA.

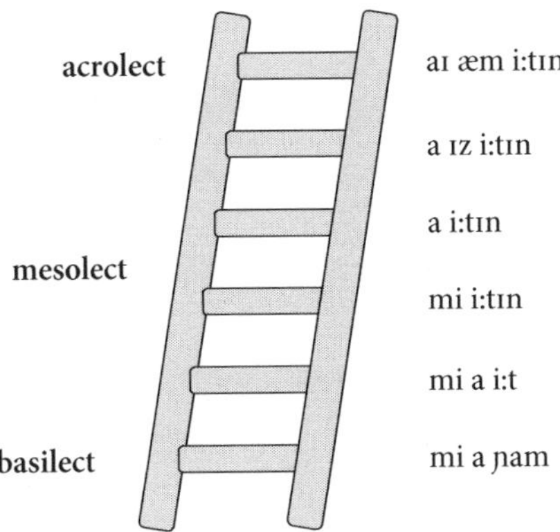

Figure 7.1 'I am eating' in various Jamaican 'lects' (from Sebba 1997:211, with minimal changes).

In Figure 7.1 various translations of the Standard English sentence *I am eating* are given. In the acrolect this sentence differs minimally from that in Standard English (the only difference lies in the pronunciation of the final *ng*). As we move down the ladder, each "rung" becomes successively different. For instance, on the second rung from the top there is an added change in that the auxiliary verb is no longer inflected (invariant *is* instead of an inflected form of *be*). The variety of the next rung has dropped the auxiliary verb. The fourth rung shows a change in pronoun. The fifth rung shows the invariant progressive marker *a* and an uninflected form of the verb. Finally, at the last rung, representing the basilect, which is most different from Standard English, the verb has been replaced with a completely different lexical item (*nyam* 'eat'). Notice how, while the two ends of the continuum are quite different, the difference between each rung is minimal.

This continuum of 'lects' is, as mentioned above, a "fluid linguistic situation" (Bailey 1966:1) with "a spectrum of variation linking the more standard end of the range (the acrolect) with the conservative creole extreme (the basilect)" (Winford 1993:7). In other words, there are no sharp boundaries between the varieties. As stated by Bailey with reference to the linguistic situation in Jamaica:

> Most observers of language in Jamaica have encountered extreme difficulty in distinguishing between the various layers of the language structure, and indeed the demarcation is very hard to draw. … it is perhaps more accurate to think not of layers, but of interwoven co-structures… (Bailey 1966:1)

It is not uncommon that speakers make use of several 'lects', depending on the situation. That is, a given individual may be **polylectal** in that s/he is competent in more than one 'lect' in a continuum. Polylectal speakers are likely to adjust the 'lect' according to the situation. For instance, an individual may use a more acrolectal variety in a formal setting in the city (during a job interview at a bank, for example), and then the same individual may use a more basilectal variety in an informal setting in the village (sitting on the veranda with the grandparents, for example). Polylectal competence is not uncommon in creole speaking societies; in Belize, for example, people are able to switch between varieties depending on the situation and who they are interacting with (cf. Escure 1982b). There are thus several factors that may determine which 'lect' will be used by whom in what situation.

I stress once again that this kind lectal continuum is not confined to only pidgin and creole languages, but can be found in any situation where a non-standard language is used along a standard one. In Germany, for example, there is a Standard German (High German), used in public and formal functions. However, each region has its own non-standard German variety which may exhibit a continuum of 'lects'. For instance, in Bavaria, in the south-east of Germany, regional TV programs and news items, or regional political debates and in generally urban settings, we are likely to find rather acrolectal varieties of Bavarian, whereas in rural or intimate, private settings, we are likely to find more basilectal varieties of Bavarian. Between these two poles of variation we are likely to find a spectrum of intermediate varieties (mesolects). Likewise, while my own southern Swedish is of an acrolectal nature, the speech of the older generation in the little fisherman's village where I grew up was basilectal enough to not be immediately intelligible to other Swedes, certainly not to those from, for example, the Stockholm area. Between these extremes there were various mesolects and people would adjust their 'lect' according to the situation (the fishermen would, for example, speak a more mesolectal variety when speaking with non-locals).

It is also important to keep in mind that, despite the terminology and the image of a ladder of 'lects', these are not simply situations of speakers collectively aiming for a certain target (the standard language) where some have come further than others in the upwards climb. The fact that standard varieties tend to carry a higher level of social prestige is rooted in the implied association with education and social status (while non-standard varieties carry the implied association of the opposite); in pidgin and creole speaking societies such social prestige was (and in very many societies still is) typically reserved for the lexifiers. However, non-standard varieties may carry their own prestige; depending on which group an individual wishes to identify with, the use of a non-standard variety may be much more acceptable than a standard one. Belize, for example, has four major ethnic groups (Amerindians, Mestizos, Creoles and Garifuna) who have their own languages. English is the only official language and education is done in English. However, the English-lexified Belizean Creole is "a thriving *lingua franca*, constantly gaining speakers thanks to its popularity and identity value even in the non-Creole population" (Escure 2013a: 93). Here the non-standard variety, the creole, carries its own prestige as an identity and solidarity marker. The choice of 'lect' may thus be conscious acts of identity. For a very detailed investigation on variation as acts of identity, see LePage & Tabouret-Keller (1985a), a classic by now. For more on Belizean Creole, see 7.3.1.

7.1.1.2 *Implicational patterns*

In identifying the variation of Jamaican, David DeCamp (1971) argued that this variation was systematic and predictable. In one of his examples he lists six features found in the speech of seven speakers. Each feature has two variants: that marked with [+] is acrolectal and that marked with [–] is basilectal, as shown in Table 7.1.

Table 7.1 DeCamp's (1971: 355) six 'mini-continuum' features in Jamaican.

	ACROLECT		BASILECT
+A	child	–A	pikni
+B	eat	–B	nyam
+C	/θ~t/	–C	/t/
+D	/ð~d/	–D	/d/
+E	granny	–E	nana
+F	didn't	–F	no ben

Each of the features in Table 7.1 has two alternatives; there are three lexical features (*child* contrasting with *pikni*; *eat* contrasting with *nyam*; *granny* contrasting with *nana*), two phonological features (in the acrolect *thick* and *tick* are pronounced differently, in the basilect they are both pronounced the same; in the acrolect *then* and *den* are pronounced differently, in the basilect they are not) and one grammatical feature (whether a speaker uses *didn't* or *no ben* for negated past actions). For each speaker DeCamp marked which of the two alternatives the speaker used, as shown in Table 7.2.

Table 7.2 shows us that most of the speakers have some [+] forms and some [–] forms, but speaker 4 only uses the basilectal alternatives and speaker 5 only the acrolectal. These two speakers could be argued to form each of the two extremes in this 'mini-continuum', while all other speakers make up the mesolectal intermediate spectrum. DeCamp then ordered the speakers according to what alternatives they used, as in Table 7.3.

Table 7.2 The features in the speech of DeCamp's (1971:355) seven Jamaican speakers.

SPEAKERS	FEATURES					
1.	+A	+B	+C	−D	+E	+F
2.	−A	+B	−C	−D	+E	+F
3.	−A	+B	−C	−D	−E	−F
4.	−A	−B	−C	−D	−E	−F
5.	+A	+B	+C	+D	+E	+F
6.	+A	+B	−C	−D	+E	+F
7.	−A	+B	−C	−D	+E	−F

Table 7.3 The features in the speech of DeCamp's (1971:355) seven Jamaican speakers by order of feature use.

SPEAKERS	FEATURES					
5.	+A	+B	+C	+D	+E	+F
1.	+A	+B	+C	−D	+E	+F
6.	+A	+B	−C	−D	+E	+F
2.	−A	+B	−C	−D	+E	+F
7.	−A	+B	−C	−D	+E	−F
3.	−A	+B	−C	−D	−E	−F
4.	−A	−B	−C	−D	−E	−F

The crucial thing to notice is that the use of features is systematic in that it is possible to predict which features a speaker will use. For example, if a speaker uses the [−C] form s/he can be expected to also use the [−D] form. If a speaker uses the [+F] form, s/he can be expected to also use the [+E] and [+B] forms. This **implicational pattern** is illustrated in Table 7.4.

Table 7.4 The implicational pattern of the features in the speech of DeCamp's (1971:356) seven Jamaican speakers.

SPEAKERS	FEATURES					
	B	E	F	A	C	D
5.	+	+	+	+	+	+
1.	+	+	+	+	+	−
6.	+	+	+	+	−	−
2.	+	+	+	−	−	−
7.	+	+	−	−	−	−
3.	+	−	−	−	−	−
4.	−	−	−	−	−	−

The method of arranging data according to an implicational scale was developed by Guttman (1944), who showed that arranging data according to implicational scales allows us to make predictions about different variables. What we see in Table 7.4 is that if a speaker uses a [−] alternative, all the features to the right will also be [−] alternatives, and conversely, if a speaker uses a [+] alternative, all features to the left will also be [+] alternatives. In other words, the features in the different 'lects' do not occur haphazardly. Thus the features in sentence *I am eating* in Figure 7.1 above are likely to combine in a certain way. For example, while we get /aɪ æm i:tɪn/ and /a ɪz i:tɪn/, we are not likely to get something like */mi æm ɲamɪn/.[117] This could thus be arranged according to the implicational pattern in Table 7.5.

Table 7.5 Implicational scale of *I am eating* in Jamaican (cf. Figure 7.1).

	ACROLECT		BASILECT	LECT	C	A	E	B	D
+A	1SG.S *I*	−A	1SG.S *mi*	1. acro	++	++	+	+	+
+B	∅	−B	PROG *a*	2. meso	+	+	+	+	+
+C	AUX	−C	∅	3. meso	−	+	+	+	+
+D	*eat*	−D	*nyam*	4. meso	−	−	−	+	+
+E	*-ing*	−E	∅	5. meso	−	−	−	−	+
				6. basi	−	−	−	−	−

The implication illustrated in Table 7.5 is that if an individual, for example, uses the inflected auxiliary (marked ++ in the table), then s/he will also pronounce *I* as /aɪ/ (also marked ++ in the table) as well as use the acrolectal alternatives of features E, B and D. If an individual uses *I* as the subject pronoun, the implication is that s/he will use the acrolectal alternatives of E, B and D, but not necessarily that of C. Conversely, if an individual uses *nyam* as the lexical verb, s/he is likely to use the basilectal alternatives of all other features. These continua have been proposed to be evidence of ongoing change (e.g. Bickerton 1973, 1975, 1980b), whereby the creole is gradually merging with the lexifier (see further Section 7.2.1 below).

The scale in Table 7.5 is not as neat as that in Table 7.4, with, for example, three alternatives for features C (either the auxiliary is present and inflected, or it is present and uninflected, or it is absent) and A (either the subject is /aɪ/, /a/ or /mi/). For a discussion on Guttman's scaling in general, see, for example Denzin (2009) with further references. Romaine (1988: 161ff) discusses various methodological problems with implicational scales. Rickford (1991) discusses scaling and other methods for investigating linguistic variation.

117. The use of the asterisk is here somewhat metaphorical, since it in this case doesn't mean impossible or ungrammatical, but merely unlikely.

7.1.2 Diglossia

The continuum of 'lects' presupposes that there is at least a certain amount of social continuity between the different 'lects', where we have, as mentioned above, a fluid linguistic situation without any sharp boundaries between the varieties. However, when we have a higher level of stratification, where there is either little contact between the groups who speak different varieties, or if the varieties have very distinct, separate functions for the speakers, we will not have a continuum, but rather a diglossic situation.

Diglossia (from Greek *di* 'two, double' + *glossa* 'language') refers to a situation where a speech community "has two distinct codes which show clear functional separation; that is, one code is employed in one set of circumstances and the other in an entirely different set" (Wardhaugh 2006: 89). Charles Ferguson, who introduced the term in English, defines diglossia as

> a relatively stable language situation in which, in addition to the primary dialects of the language (which may include a standard or regional standards), there is a very divergent, highly codified (often grammatically more complex) superposed variety, the vehicle of a large and respected body of written literature, either of an earlier period or in another speech community, which is learned largely by formal education and is used for most written and formal spoken purposes but is not used by any sector of the community for ordinary conversation. (Ferguson 1959: 338)

What we have is a situation where we have two quite different varieties, a **'high' variety (H)** and a **'low' variety (L)**, that have quite different functions. There is thus very little overlap between the varieties and their functions, meaning that there is, in fact, a definable boundary between the two codes.

A well-known example of diglossia is the Arabic language situation, where Classical Arabic is the H variety and the regional colloquial Arabic varieties are the L varieties of the different communities. The H and L varieties are only appropriate in their own specialized functions. The H variety is typically used for formal functions, such as giving sermons or formal speeches, for news broadcasts, and for formal writing (poetry, literature, editorials, and so on), while the L variety is typically used for informal functions, such as when talking to friends and family, or even when giving instructions to workers, especially domestic staff, or in less formal culture, such as soap operas, other popular programs, cartoons and so on. Similarly, Burmese is diglossic, with a literary High Burmese, which is also used in spoken form in formal contexts (e.g. radio/TV news), and a colloquial Low Burmese, which is used in informal contexts (Bradley 1996). The two varieties differ considerably in structure and lexicon (for example, the name of the country is *myanma* in the H variety and *bama* in the L variety, the latter is the origin of the English term Burma; Bradley 2008: 2012).

It is worth noting that, even though the H varieties tend to carry noticeably higher prestige with it (sometimes to the degree that speakers will deny the existence of L varieties), both varieties have their appropriateness: just as it would not be appropriate to use an L variety in a situation that would call for an H variety, it is also not appropriate to use an H variety in a situation that would call for an L variety. Even so, social power and prestige is typically attached to H varieties, while L varieties may be highly stigmatized and may be viewed as entirely inadequate for any kind of formal function, such as education. Efforts of translating certain bodies of work, such as religious texts, into L varieties may thus meet with vehement resistance.

An example of a creole in a diglossic situation can be found in Nicaragua, where Nicaraguan Creole English is spoken as a mother tongue by some 35–50,000 people on the Nicaraguan Caribbean coast, primarily by the Creoles and the Rama ethnic groups, but also by some Garifuna and Miskito. Although there has been bilingual schooling in (Standard) English and Spanish in the creole speaking areas since the 1980s (this is now slowly being changed to programmes with Nicaraguan Creole English), schooling has traditionally been done monolingually in Spanish, meaning that most people do their reading in Spanish. Newspapers, for example, are in Spanish. Most creole speakers are therefore bilingual in Nicaraguan Creole English, which functions as the L variety, and Spanish, which functions as the H variety. See further Bartens (2013b).

There is some debate as to whether the linguistic situation in a given pidgin or creole speaking society may be one of diglossia rather than a continuum of 'lects', and the same language situation may be classified by different researchers as one of diglossic variation or as one with a continuum of 'lects'. Haiti is typically given as an example of a diglossic situation, where Haitian Creole functions as the L variety and French as the H and where the functions of the two languages are clearly delimited, but this is refuted by, for example, Dejean (1993). Some have argued that the situations of various speech communities of English-lexified creoles are better described as diglossic (for example Lawton 1980, Winford 1985, Gibson 1992, Devonish & Harry 2004, with reference to English-lexified Caribbean creoles specifically). The debate hinges on whether or not the language situation is essentially one of stable bilingualism between the lexifier and the creole. However, these two kinds of variations do not necessarily have to be mutually exclusive: it may well be that a given standard language, for example French, functions as an H variety in a society, while the creole functions as the L variety and that a sizeable proportion of the speech community is bilingual in the two codes. However, *within* the L variety there might be a continuum of 'lects' ranging from more to less basilectal variation.

7.2 Change

The lectal continuum of basi-, meso- and acrolects discussed above is commonly referred to as the **creole continuum**, although, as mentioned above, this gradation of closeness with a standard language is not unique to creole languages. It is a matter of debate whether or not this lectal continuum is evidence of a predictable developmental stage in the life cycle of pidgin and creole languages. It is also a matter of debate whether or not the lectal continuum is evidence of a unidirectional process whereby contact languages merge with their lexifiers. It is furthermore a matter of debate whether speech communities may (more or less consciously) make their language variety more basilectal, essentially reversing a postulated unidirectional developmental path.

This section will very briefly bring up the notions of depidginization and decreolization and the issue of continua as recent phenomena with contact languages. It will also very briefly bring up the notion of repidginization or recreolization and the issue of contact languages moving away from their lexifier. It is beyond the scope of the section to adequately discuss the full debate on the potential developmental paths of contact languages. For more detailed discussions, see, for example, de Rooij (1994b), Mühlhäusler (1997: 211ff), Sebba (1997: 203ff) and Siegel (2008b: 250) with further references. For a very detailed discussion on the creole continuum, see Rickford (1987).

7.2.1 The notion of depidginization and decreolization

The continuum of 'lects' exhibited in Jamaican was argued by DeCamp (1971) to reflect a so-called **post-creole continuum**, namely the ongoing process of the final stage in the creole life-cycle. DeCamp gives two conditions for a creole to have a post-creole stage in its life-cycle:

> First, the dominant official language of the community must be the standard language corresponding to the creole. Thus Sranan or the French of St Lucia and Grenada have not developed a post-creole continuum, because there is no continuing corrective pressure from standard English in Surinam or from standard French in St Lucia and Grenada. Second, the formerly rigid social stratification must have *partially* (not completely) broken down. That is, there must be sufficient social mobility to motivate large numbers of creole speakers to modify their speech in the direction of the standard, and there must be a program of education and other acculturative activities to exert effective pressures from the standard language on the creole. (DeCamp 1971: 351)

In other words, the post-creole continuum will emerge only in those societies where the lexifier has continuously functioned as a prestigious variety *and* where the emancipation of slaves has changed the social conditions to allow increased access to education as well as desire for general upward social mobility, which is then also plausibly attainable (cf. also the discussion in Le Page & Tabouret-Keller 1985b). The post-creole continuum therefore reflects a gradual merging or reunion with the lexifier.

This notion was, in fact, already brought up by Hugo Schuchardt, who proposed that, for example, when "in a given area creolized English coexists with standard English, a number of stages emerge in-between, until finally the creole speakers do not speak creole anymore, but rather a modified form of standard English" (Meijer & Muysken 1977: 31). Schuchardt goes on to suggest that in those cases where the lexifier has been replaced by other European languages, as, for example, happened in Suriname (where the Dutch took over from the British and Dutch replaced English as the new standard), this gradual merging with the lexifier will either be slowed down or even cease altogether. Instead the creole will move towards the new standard, i.e. the language of the new European powers.[118]

This post-creole continuum was then interpreted as essentially "a mirror of the history of the linguistic community" (Sebba 1997: 217). As mentioned above, the continuum has been seen as evidence of ongoing change: Bickerton (e.g. 1973, 1975, 1980b) proposed that what the continuum actually shows is a "snapshot" of how the creole speech community is gradually assimilating their creole to the lexifier: the language is **decreolizing**, i.e. moving away from its original, basilectal, creole nature. The continuum can therefore be seen as evidence of ongoing, "non-spontaneous change … which owes its existence to the influence of another language" (Bickerton 1980b: 112f). That is, "non-spontaneous change" comes about due to the influence of another language, which has remained in proximity and which carries a higher prestige; in this case the change is towards the lexifier under the influence of that (more prestigious) language. Decreolization is thus proposed to be a unidirectional process leading to the final stage in the creole life-cycle, namely the disappearance of the creole language.

Notice that the notion of a post-creole continuum and decreolization requires the continued proximity of the lexifier as a standard. If a new standard is introduced, such as when a colony changes hands from one power to another, then the post-creole continuum is assumed to be interrupted and the decreolization process is assumed to either be slowed down or to stop altogether; alternatively, the creole will start to

---

118. "*Wo das N[eger]E[nglisch] im Schatten des europäischen Englisch fortlebt, bilden sich zwischen beiden eine Menge von Zwischenstufen; es wird aus dem NE. schliesslich ein Englisch der Neger, das sich von dem der Weissen nur in Aussprache, Tonfall, Redewendung unterscheidet… Wo es, wie in Surinam, von einer andern europäischen Sprache überschichtet ist, wird es sich vom Englischen abwenden und auf diese zu entwickeln.*" ('Where the N[egro] E[nglish] lives on in the shadow of the European English, a large amount of intermediate stages emerge between the two; the NE finally becomes an English of the Negro, which differs from that of the White only in pronunciation, intonation, idiom … Where, as in Suriname, it is superimposed by another European language, it will turn away from English and move towards this [i.e. the new European language – VV]'; Schuchardt 1914: viii–ix, my translation).

move towards the new standard. This was, for example, argued by Schuchardt for the creoles in Suriname (see above). Another example of a creole spoken in an area where the standard was replaced is, for example, the Chabacano varieties in the Philippines. These Spanish-lexified creoles might have their origin in a variety that emerged on the island of Ternate (present-day Indonesia), which was then relocated to the Philippines when the Spanish evacuated their Ternate garrison. The standard languages of the Philippines are now Filipino and English. However, unlike Suriname, where the Dutch took over after only a comparatively short period of English rule (a total of 30 years, not consecutive; Britannica 2011c), the Philippines remained in Spanish rule for 333 years (Britannica 2011b), which means that there was proximity with the lexifier for the major part of the history of the language. For more on the Ternate variety of Chabacano, see 7.3.3.

It should be noted that the exact nature of the lexifier language is not always uncontroversial, which might further blur the picture of post-creole continua and decreolization. Papiamentu, for example, clearly has Spanish and/or Portuguese as its lexifier(s), but the question of who used the lexifier(s) is not historically clear. Papiamentu emerged around the second half of the 17th century, by which time the colony was already Dutch. It is therefore not clear whether the Ibero-Romance lexifier(s) was or were spoken by the European settlers or if it was imported by the African slaves themselves. If the slaves played a key role, the input would have been influenced by various Portuguese-lexified creoles in West Africa (Maurer 2013c). For a very detailed discussion on the origins of Papiamentu, see Jacobs (2012). For more on Papiamentu, see 8.3.2.

It should also be noted that it is not a given that every creole speaking society that has remained in proximity with the lexifier has a continuum of lects. Palenquero, for example, has been in continued coexistence with its lexifier, Spanish, with a bilingual creole speaking community where code-switching is the norm. However, the creole has remained stable and shows very little, if any, lectal variation (Schwegler 2000).

The notions of a post-creole continuum and decreolization hinge on the debated assumption of a pidgin-to-creole life-cycle (see Section 6.2). Basically, and very simplified, the scenario would be one of a unidirectional sequence of stages, whereby a pidgin first evolves out of a lexifier, this pidgin then develops into a creole (it creolizes), which may then further evolve and redevelop back to the lexifier (it decreolizes). Because of the debated nature of the pidgin-to-creole life-cycle, the lectal continuum is nowadays more commonly referred to as simply the **creole continuum** (without the *post*). However, this latter term also disregards the fact that lectal continua are not unique to creole languages.

The notions of the post-creole continuum and decreolization further hinge on the assumption that these are recent phenomena, since these final stages of the life-cycle arise only after the societies have become more liberal in the social stratification, i.e. only after the emancipation of slaves and the subsequent opportunities for social mobility. This essentially presupposes that the mesolectal varieties developed after the basilectal and acrolectal ones, as a linguistic consequence of the socially disadvantaged communities' gradual climb up the social ladder. However, as discussed in Section 4.2.2 above, the plantation societies were in fact multilayered, with different levels of interaction. Different sections of the labour community would have had different levels of interaction with the speakers of the lexifier language. Therefore it does not seem implausible that a continuum of 'lects' existed from the very beginning, reflecting various sociolinguistic factors, such as levels of interaction between different social groups.

Alleyne (1971) argued that a continuum of 'lects' was part of the formation process of creole languages, in that different levels of interaction

> resulted in linguistic variation and instability which is characteristic of any dynamic acculturative process. Because field slaves constituted the greatest numbers and were in effective contact only with themselves, a linguistic medium, commonly referred to as 'creole', appears to have become crystallized within that group. At the beginning of the process, this creole was in fact everywhere only a major segment of a continuum of variation and marked the first stage in the process of adaption to a cultural model. … Where continua still exist, there will be a tendency for the segment called 'creole' to become more modified in the direction of the model language and to disappear as the acculturation process continues. (Alleyne 1971:182f)

In this view we have, right from the start, a unidirectional process moving towards the lexifier from more to less basilectal varieties, reflecting the relative access to the target language (the lexifier). This, however, presupposes that the lexifier was and has remained the target model language, which in turn disregards such sociolinguistic factors as identity and solidarity (cf. the discussion in Sections 4.2.2.2 and 7.1.1 above).

The principles of a post-creole continuum and decreolization could also be applied to pidgins, in which case we would have **post-pidgin continua** and **depidginization**. The assumption would then be that a jargon stabilizes into a pidgin, but before that pidgin has time to stabilize further into an extended pidgin (pidgincreole) the continued contact with the lexifier leads to post-pidgin 'lects' which in turn reflect a process of depidginization and gradual reunion with the lexifier (see, for example, Mühlhäusler 1997:211ff). Many of the assumptions and related caveats with respect to the notion of post-creoles and decreolization are also relevant for the notion of post-pidgins and depidginization, such as the assumption of a life-cycle and of a linear developmental process towards the lexifier. Various sociolinguistic factors such as levels of interaction and issues of prestige, identity and solidarity are also likely to have been, and still be, relevant for pidgin languages.

7.2.2 The notion of repidginization and recreolization

The notion of **repidginization** commonly refers to the phenomenon of a creole language being used as a *lingua franca* and thus in the process undergoing various changes (cf., for example, Romaine 1988: 156f). This is, for example, suggested to have happened with Nicaraguan Creole English when the Rama of Rama Cay off the Nicaraguan coast shifted to the creole English they encountered in their contacts with the local Afro-Europeans. The isolation of the Rama led to noticeable differences between the two creoles. This has been argued to constitute an instance of repidginization and subsequent creolization (Holm & Kepiou 1992: 341f). Notice, however, that this presupposes a pidgin-to-creole life cycle and the *a priori* assumption that the new creole first went through a pidgin stage. Other examples cited include, for example, Liberian Settler English, whose ancestor is the English spoken by those former US slaves who settled in Liberia. The English that was brought to Liberia by the slaves then came to be used as a *lingua franca* by various indigenous African people, who were not former US slaves or descendants of former US slaves, in the interior of the region (Singler 1984).

The notion of **recreolization** essentially refers to a speech community shifting to a more basilectal form of a creole. The most commonly cited example for this is British Jamaican, a variety spoken by descendants of Caribbean immigrants to the UK. This has been observed and studied in, for example, London (e.g. Sebba 1993), Birmingham (Wright 1984) and Bradford (Tate 1984). The common pattern seems to be that descendants of Caribbean immigrants make use of a basilectal form of Jamaican, irrespective of the origins of their parents (or grandparents). That is, irrespective of whether the immigrants came from Jamaica, Dominica, or any other Caribbean location, the speakers are using the same variety, which is based on Jamaican. It should be noted that the speakers of British Jamaican are fluent in the local British English variety. The use of British Jamaican is thus an act of solidarity; the language has covert prestige in being maximally different from Standard English and the acquisition of an as basilectal variety as possible is a conscious act of identity. For an accessible discussion on British Jamaican as a phenomenon of recreolization, see Sebba (1997: 225 ff). For discussions on recreolization and the covert prestige of more basilectal varieties in Belize and St. Lucia, see, for example, LePage (1977).

7.3 Snapshots

Lectal continua are often discussed in connection with social mobility and issues of prestige and identity. Very often the presumed target is the standard language of the society. However, non-standard varieties may have their own prestige. Belizean Creole is a language with a complex spectrum of lects, where the language functions as a *lingua franca* and enjoys high prestige as an identity marker.

Ambon Malay is in a diglossic relationship on two ends. On the one hand it functions as the L variety in relation to the H variety Indonesian. Constant pressure from Indonesian has led to a lectal continuum between the two languages. On the other hand Ambon Malay functions as a regional and ethnic identity marker and as such is the H variety in relation to the local vernaculars, which function as the regional L varieties.

If the standard language in a given creole speaking society changes from the lexifier to some other language, the creole language may be affected in various ways. Ternate Chabacano is a Spanish-lexified creole in the Philippines, which for the last 100+ years has had English, and later also Filipino, as the administrative languages. There is now widespread multilingualism and signs of a language shift away from the creole.

7.3.1 Belizean Creole: An English-lexified Caribbean creole with a wide lectal continuum and high prestige[119]

7.3.1.1 *A brief background sketch of Belizean Creole*

Belizean Creole, called *Kriol* or *Broken English* by the speakers themselves, is spoken by about 150,000 people, of which only about 70,000 are in Belize itself, located in Central America on the Caribbean coast of the Yucatan peninsula. The remaining 80,000 are diaspora communities, most of which are in the USA, Mexico and Honduras. Belizean Creole is also used as a *lingua franca* by several of the ethnic groups in the country.

Spain and Britain were in constant conflict over the Bay of Honduras area, which provided convenient shelters for British privateers (i.e. officially sanctioned pirates) and pirates in their attacks against Spanish wood transports from the region (Escure 2011:183). The settlement British Honduras was established in the early 1600s by the roughly eighty shipwrecked pirates who were led by the Scotsman Peter Wallace (or Wallis), whose name (possibly with a Spanish pronunciation /βalis/) might be the origin of the name Belize, although this could also be an instance of folk etymology (Escure 1997:26).

Belize was at first a logwood trade settlement and not a plantation settlement, due to its valuable woods, such as mahogany, logwood, rosewood and sapodilla (Escure 2011:183). It seems as if the first woodcutter slaves were imported from Jamaica (the closest British colony), possibly in the 1620s, although there are no records of when the first slaves arrived and what their origins were. Large-scale slave labour seems to have started from about the mid-1700s, parallel to that in Jamaica. There are records of Spain undermining the British by offering freedom to their slaves, leading to slave insurrections in the latter half of the 18th century (Escure 2011:183 citing Burdon 1935). The early import of slaves from Jamaica might mean that the basis for Belizean Creole was an early version of Jamaican. The isolated nature of the logwood camps might have had an effect on the outcome of the language, for instance the preservation of features of early Jamaican or of substratal features.

---

119. This section is primarily based on Escure (2013a). I am very grateful to Geneviève Escure for her helpful comments on this snapshot.

British logwood settlements expanded to other areas, such as the Honduran islands and the Nicaraguan Caribbean coast (The Miskito Coast), which led to conflicts with Spain. This in turn led to widespread population movements in the area. African slaves who had escaped from Spanish mines and British plantations settled on the Nicaraguan coast and a mixed ethnic group, the Miskito-Zambo, emerged and established trade with the British in the early 1700s, for instance engaging in slave raids and selling slaves to the Jamaican market. The British and their Miskito allies were forced by the Spaniards to evacuate the Nicaraguan coast in 1787 and settled in British Honduras, adding to the ethnic and linguistic ecology of that settlement. Yet another ethnic group that added to the ecology were the Garinagu (also called Garifuna or "Black Caribs"), a mixed Amerindian-Black (Maroons) population from the Eastern Caribbean (St Vincent and St Lucia).[120]

By 1830 British Honduras (Belize) had 4,200 inhabitants, ca 300 of which were white. Of the non-white population, 2,000 were free and 1,900 were slaves (Escure 2011:184). In 1862 it became a British colony and in 1967 an autonomous self-governed territory.

Belize gained independence in 1981. There are four major ethnic groups: Mestizos (with Spanish as L1), Creoles (with Belizean creole as L1), Garinagu (with Garifuna as L1) and Amerindians (with Amerindian L1s), as well as a number of smaller ethnic groups (Escure 1997:28). English is the only official language and "the required educational medium" (Escure 2013a: 93), and, as such, functions as the overt standard. However, Belizean Creole is widely used as a *lingua franca* and steadily growing due to its popularity and high identity value despite its "overtly assigned low value" (Escure 1997:36). This has led to a wide range of lects, from basilectal varieties that are typically unintelligible to Standard English speakers, to acrolectal varieties, which are close and similar to, but not identical with, the British or American Standard Englishes. Between these two extremes there is a spectrum of mesolects, which differ to varying degrees from both the basi- and the acrolects. The speech of any given individual will differ according to such factors as exposure to the basilect and acrolect, level of education and various language attitudes and identity projections (Escure 1997:28).

120. The history of the Garinagu is much more complicated than that. Very simplified, the *Yellow* or *Red Caribs* were the descendants of Arawak and Carib intermarriages on the Lesser Antilles in the Eastern Caribbean. Once the Europeans started colonizing the area and bringing slaves from West Africa, these Caribs welcomed among them African Maroons, such as shipwreck survivors or British and French runaway slaves. The descendants of this interethnic mix were called *Black Caribs*, *Charaibes Noirs*, *Karaib Negros*, *Garifs* or *Morenos*. These "Black Caribs" engaged in hostilities with both the British and the French, and, after a failed rebellion, were in 1797 deported by the British to Honduras. Most of the "Black Caribs" migrated either north, to Belize, or south, to Nicaragua. Once Belize gained independence in 1981 the "Black Caribs" were recognized as an ethnic group and the term *Garifuna* or *Garinagu* (the plural form of *Garifuna*) is, since then, used as a sign of respect. For more on the Garifuna, see, for example, Escure (2004) and Ravindranath (2009) with further references.

7.3.1.2 *A short linguistic sketch of Belizean Creole*

Belizean Creole has 21 consonants (including two glides), /p, b, m, w, f, v, t, d, n, r, s, z, ʃ, ʧ, ʤ, l, j, k, g, ŋ, h/ and seven vowels, /i, e, ɛ, a(:), (ɔ), o, u/, all of which may nasalize before a preceding nasal consonant (but notice that /ɔ/ is rare) and one of which (/a/) may be lengthened. It is a non-rhotic language. The velar nasal /ŋ/ is often rendered as /n/. Consonant clusters (of two or even three) may occur word-initially (as in /ska:pian/ 'scorpion' and /straŋ/ 'strong'; Decker 2006:12,22), but are rare word-finally.

Stress is evenly distributed over the sentence but is reserved for content words (nouns, verbs, adjectives, adverbs) and sometimes pronouns (Decker 2006:26). There seems to be a two-tone system (High/Low), but it is not well understood as yet.

The morphology is predominantly analytic, although there is adjectival suffixation and occasional plural marking with the suffix -/z/ (as in *ajstaz* 'oysters'; Escure 2013a:97). Reduplication may be used for intensification:

(144)

di	ha:s	big~big
DEF	horse	big~RED

'The horse is/was very big.' (Decker 2006:87)

Gender and case are not relevant categories for Belizean Creole. Number is typically indicated with adnominal pronouns, as in *dɛm pap* 'puppies' or *pilz dɛm* 'pills' (notice that the latter has a double plural marking; Escure 2013a:93). There is a definite article *di* 'the' and an indefinite article, which is identical to the numeral one, *wan* 'a; one'. Generic noun phrases remain unmarked:

(145) a.

wɛn	a	de	wok	laŋ	di	ki	ju	hia	wan	li	'kiliŋkiliŋ'
when	1SG.S	IPFV	work	along	DEF	quay	2SG	hear	INDEF	little	IDEO

'When I work on the quay, you can hear a noise.'

b.

krab	wa:k	onda	wata
crab	walk	under	water

'Crabs walk under water.' (Escure 2013a:93, 95)

There is the single demonstrative *dat* 'that'. For plural demonstratives adnominal pronouns may be used.

Personal pronouns differentiate between person and number, sometimes also between syntactic role in the clause (subject or object). There are possessive pronouns:

	PERSONAL		POSSESSIVE
	SUBJECT	OBJECT	
1SG	*a, aj, mi*	*mi*	*ma, maj*
2SG	*ju*	*ju*	*jo*
3SG	*i, in, mi*	*im, an*	*iz, fu im*
1PL	*wi*	*wi*	*awa, fi wi*
2PL	*unu*	*unu*	*jo, fu unu*
3PL	*dej, de*	*dɛm*	*dɛm, dɛa*

Notice that there is no gender distinction in the third person singular, and that the second person is differentiated by number. The subject and object forms are identical for the second persons and first person plural (optionally also for the first person singular).

Possession can be indicated either through juxtaposition or a possessive construction with *fi/fu*:

(146) a. di man kowt
DEF man coat
'the man's coat' (Decker 2006:75)
b. dog pa fi dɛm pap da wan big dog
dog father for 3PL puppy TOP INDEF big dog
'The puppies' father is a big dog.' (Escure 2013a:94)

Adjectives are invariant. Comparison is indicated through suffixation for both the comparative (*a*) and superlative (*ɛs*):

(147) a. wan najs-a wan dɛ ja
INDEF nice-COMPAR one LOC here
'There is a nicer one here.'
b. dis badl a me wana di big-es badl
DEM bottle TOP ANT one.of DEF big-SUPER bottle
'This bottle was one of the biggest (ever found).' (Escure 2013a:94)

When used predicatively, adjectives take the verbal tense, mood and/or aspect markers.

There are two tense markers (*wan* for future tense, *me/mi* for anterior tense) plus the bare form, which indicates simple past. There is the portmanteau *neva*, which indicates negated anterior events:

(148) a. im tɛl mi
3SG tell 1SG.O
'He told me.' (Escure 2013a:94)
b. dɛm njam op di kajk
2PL eat up DEF cake
'They ate (ravenously) the cake.' (Decker 2006:86)
c. da moni wan plit ina tri
DEM money FUT split in three
'That money will be split into three.' (Escure 2013a:96)
d. dɛm mi briŋ op da bwai
3PL ANT bring up DEM boy
'They raised that boy.' (Decker 2006:86)
e. a neva no a me de kum ja
1SG NEG.ANT know 1SG ANT IPFV come here
'I didn't know I was coming here.' (Escure 2013a:96)

Imperfective aspect is indicated with *de* (see Examples (150), (151a)) and past progressive is indicated with *me de* (i.e. the anterior marker combined with the imperfective marker; see (148e) above). There are a number of modal constructions.

Word order is typically subject-object-verb. Apart from the portmanteau *neva*, which specifically negates anterior events, there is the invariant negator *no*.

(149) no bred no dɛ
no bread NEG LOC
'There isn't any bread.' (Decker 2006: 91)

Polar questions are formed with rising intonation only. In content questions the interrogative phrase typically occurs clause-initially, but may also remain *in situ*:

(150) a. dɛm de bada ju?
3PL IPFV bother 2SG
'Are they bothering you?'
b. wɛ mek i se dat?
what make 3SG say that
'Why did s/he say that?'
c. i sista da hu?
3SG sister TOP who
'Who is her sister?' (Decker 2006: 95, 106)

Adjectives do not take a copula (cf. Examples (144), (146b), (147)). There is a locative *dɛ* (cf. Examples (147a), (149)).

There are the coordinating conjunctions *en* 'and', *bat* 'but' and *o* 'or'. Subordination is typically indicated with *dat* 'that', *fu* 'to' or juxtaposition. Serial verb constructions are not very common, but do occur. Relative clauses are typically indicated with the relativizer *we*, although *hu* may also occur with human subject noun phrases:

(151) a. ju had dis laja we dej de t:ak bot
2SG had DEM lawyer REL 3PL IPFV talk about
'There was this lawyer that they were talking about.' (Escure 2013a: 97)
b. a ga:n si di man hu fu dog bait ju
1SG went see DEF man REL POSS dog bite 2SG
'I went to see the man whose dog bit you.' (Decker 2006: 99)

The relativizer may be omitted with object noun phrases. Resumptive pronouns may occur.

7.3.1.3 *Short text*

(This is a shortened version of the story given in Decker 2006: 110ff.)

I me ga dɛm fo ko we dɛ ina dis pastʧa … en dɛm de fid. En wan lajan
3SG ANT go 3PL four cow REL LOC in DEM pasture and 3PL IPFV feed and INDEF lion

ʤomp ova di fens. En hi wan it wan a dɛm. Bat wen i ga:n a:ta dɛm di
jump over DEF fence and 3SG want eat one of 3PL but when 3SG went after 3PL DEF

fo ko dɛm ton roŋ en dɛm tai op dɛm tel tugeda so afta wan wail lajan …
four cow PL turn round and 3PL tie up 3PL tail together so after INDEF while lion

ga:n i wispa ina wan a dɛm ye-z. So afta wail i wispa tu al a dɛm tel
went 3SG whisper in one of 3PL ear-PL so after while 3SG whisper to all of 3PL tell

dɛm somtiŋ. En den di fo ko dɛm stat tu fait monks wan ada. En di
3PL something and then DEF four cow 3PL start to fight amongst one other and DEF

lajan ga:n rait dɛ en nakaf wana dɛm.
lion went right LOC and knock.off one.of 3PL

'Once there were four cows in a pasture and they were eating. A lion jumped over the fence and he wanted to eat one of them. But when he went after them, the four cows would turn around and they would tie their tails together. So, after a while, the lion went and whispered into one of their ears. So after a while, he had whispered to all of them, telling them something. Then the four cows started to fight amongst one another. Then the lion went right among them and killed one of them.'

7.3.1.4 *Some sources of data*

Escure (1982a) gives six longer translated and analyzed texts. The National Kriol Council (http://www.nationalcouncil.org/, accessed 10 February 2015) gives general information on Belizean Creole, as well as on cultural and language related topics. There are links to stories and the Bible translation project, including analyzed and translated examples. Decker (2006) is a grammar of Belizean Creole which provides a number of translated examples, some of them also glossed.

7.3.2 Ambon Malay: A Malay-lexified Pacific creole which functions as both an L and an H variety[121]

7.3.2.1 *A brief background sketch of Ambon Malay*

Ambon Malay, also called *Ambonese Malay* by scholars or, in Indonesian, *Bahasa Melayu Ambon*, is called *Malayu Ambong* by the speakers themselves. It is spoken by about 200,000 people natively on the island of Ambon and its neighbouring Maluku islands in the eastern Indonesian archipelago, as well as in regional urban centres, in Jakarta and in the Netherlands. In the rest of the Moluccas region it is used as a *lingua franca* by up to a million speakers.

Malay has functioned as a *lingua franca* in South-East Asia, stretching from the mainland to the present-day Philippines and Papua New Guinea "at least since the time of the Sri Wijaya empire (7–9th c. CE)" (Paauw 2008: 7), if not longer. This Vehicular Malay (often referred to as *Bazaar Malay*, *Pasar Malay* or *Bahasa Melayu Pasar*),[122] which was also used for spreading Islam, had already arrived in the Moluccas by the time the first Europeans found their way there and seems "to have its origin in pre-European contacts between Moluccans on the one hand, and on the other hand Malays and Javanese who used *lingua franca* Malay when establishing a spice trade monopoly in East Indonesia" (Adelaar & Prentice 1996: 675). Apart from the various forms of Vehicular Malay in South-East Asia, there was also a literary Malay (also called *Classical Malay* or *High Malay*), used in courts and aristocratic circles.

The first Europeans to be known to arrive in Ambon were the Portuguese, who set out from Malacca (present-day Malaysia) in search of the East Indonesian 'Spice Islands' and arrived in 1512 (Ricklefs 2001: 27). The island turned out to have a protected harbour where traders could wait out the monsoons and was subsequently used as a stop-over in the spice trade. That which is now the city of Ambon started with the Portuguese trading centre that was established in 1524. This centre was fortified some decades later and became the centre of Portuguese activities in the region after they had been expelled from the island of Ternate in 1575 (Ricklefs 2001).

121. This section relies primarily on van Minde (1997) and Paauw (2008, 2013a).

122. Notice that Bazaar Malay may also refer to a pidgin language spoken on the Malay Peninsula, cf. Smith & Paauw (2006).

With the arrival of the Portuguese, (Vehicular) Malay started to be used in the area as a medium for the spread of Roman Catholicism. In 1605 the Portuguese surrendered Ambon to the Dutch, who made it the centre for the Dutch East India Company 1610–1619, after which the headquarters were moved to Batavia (present-day Jakarta). In 1655 the Dutch made Ambon the centre for clove-production, drawing on the local population for plantation labour. The attempt to introduce Dutch as an administrative language failed and instead literary Malay was used for administrative affairs, education and (Calvinistic) missionary activities, the latter of which also included translations and dissemination of a large amount of religious texts. This caused "a serious gap in communication initially, and eventually led to the diglossia still found in the region" (Paauw 2013a: 95).

The region saw frequent skirmishes between the Dutch and the British in the quest for control over the spice trade, although it essentially remained Dutch until 1942, when Indonesia was invaded by the Japanese forces. The Revolution 1945–50 resulted in Indonesian independence.

Ambon Malay is typically viewed, even by the speakers themselves, as inferior to the national standard language, Indonesian.[123] As such it functions as the L variety in a diglossic relationship with Indonesian, which functions as the H variety and which most speakers are able to use. Indonesian is the sole official language of the country and is used in education, media administration and other official domains. There is a lectal continuum between Ambon Malay and Indonesian, influenced by such factors as domain of use and the speaker's level of education. However, while Ambon Malay is primarily used for daily interactions in the home and community, it is also a marker of regional and ethnic Maluku identity and is viewed as superior to the local vernacular languages; as such it constitutes the H variety in a diglossic relationship with the vernacular L varieties.

There is evidence of regional variation, with "distinct dialects developing, chiefly in the urban centres, of other regions of the province" (Paauw 2013a: 95).

7.3.2.2 *A short linguistic sketch of Ambon Malay*

There are 19 consonants, /p, b, m, f, w, t, d, n, r, s, l, c, ɟ, ɲ, j, k, g, ŋ, h/, although /f/ only occurs in loans, and five vowels, /i, e, a, o, u/. The phonemes /ɟ, ɲ, j, ŋ/ are rendered orthographically as <j, ny, y, ng> respectively. There is contrastive stress.

The morphology is predominantly analytic, although there is reduplication (denoting diversity, totality or plurality with nouns or iteration with verbs). There are some verbal prefixes.

Plurality may optionally be indicated with reduplication (cf. also Examples (153a), (155c), (160)):

(152) a. ...baru dong ketauan itu daun...
just 3PL find.out DEM leaf
'...only then did they realize it was leaves...'

123. Notice that Indonesian essentially is that form of Standard Malay (which is based on literary Malay rather than Vehicular Malay) that is used in Indonesia (cf., for example Grimes 1996 with further references).

b. ana-ana bisa dapa uang sadiki-sadiki karena sakarang ni
child~RED can get money little~RED because now DEM
cengke-cengke su abis
clove~RED PFV finish
'The children can have a (very) little money because now the clove trees are all destroyed.' (Paauw 2008: 413, 421)

There are no articles. There are two demonstratives, *(i)ni* 'this' and *(i)tu* 'that', which are used with generic nouns and may be used for previously mentioned elements. The third person singular neuter pronoun may also function as a demonstrative.

Possession is formed with the possessive marker *pung* (with the allomorphs *pong, ng, punya*), which may also serve as an intensifier, or through juxtaposition (cf. also Examples (156), (158a), (159), (161)):

(153) a. dolo orang ta-tua dong itu mau bikin bodo ana-ana itu
before people TA-old 3PL DEM want make stupid child~RED DEM
'In the old days, parents liked to fool their children...'

b. ...Nene Luhu punya kuda itu mati...
PN PN POSS horse DEM die
'...Nene Luhu's horse died...' (Paauw 2008: 397, 406)

The personal pronouns have a short and a long form; the latter may function either as subject or as object and may stand alone as the only word in the clause, while the shorter are restricted in their distribution. The pronouns are not obligatory to the clause if the context makes clear who the referents are.

	SUBJECT	OBJECT
1SG	*beta, bet, be*	*beta*
2SG.FAM	*ose, os, se; ale, al*	*ose, os, se; ale, al*
3SG	*dia, di, de*	*dia*
3SG.POL	*antua, ontua, ...*	*antua, ontua, ...*
3SG.N	*akang*	*akang, kang, ang*
1PL	*katong, tong*	*katong*
2PL	*dorang, dong*	*dorang, dong*
3PL	*dorang, dong*	*dorang, dong*

The second person singular forms are impolite, except for the short form *se*. However, in formal contexts pronoun use is avoided; instead a title or a title and name is used.

Numerals may optionally be followed by a classifier. Adjectives are a subclass of verbs; comparison is formed with the optional construction *lebe ... dari* 'more ... from':

(154) beta (lebe) bai (dari) dia
1SG more good from 3SG
'I am better than him' (Paauw 2013a: 97)

There is no tense, although the modal *mau* 'want' may be used to mark futurity. There are the aspect markers *su* (perfective, cf. Example (152b)) and *ada* (progressive) as well as the adverbials *masi* 'still' and *balong* 'not yet' which also carry aspectual connotations:

(155) a. de blong ada makang
3SG not.yet PROG eat
'He's not eating yet.' (van Minde 1997: 231)

b. tapi masi antua hidop seperti manusia biasa itu di-panggel Kristina
but still 3SG.POL live like human usual DEM PASS-call PN
'However, while she lived as a human, she was usually called Kristina…' (Paauw 2008: 416)

c. …waktu dulu kan seng ada di Ambong ini bolong ada oto
time before Q NEG EXIST LOC Ambon DEM not.yet EXIST car
bolong ada apa~apa
not.yet EXIST what~RED
'…at that time, there were no cars yet in Ambon or anything else…' (Paauw 2008: 402)

There are a number of modals. There are three verbal prefixes: *ba* (denoting intransitivization, deliberate or habitual actions or the sense 'to have/to use'), *ta* (denoting involuntary actions), and *baku* (denoting reciprocity).

The word order is typically subject-verb-object, though pragmatic topics may be fronted. Negation is expressed with the invariant *seng* (most common), *tar/tra* (especially for emphatic negation) or *tida*:

(156) dia seng percaya par dia pung mama pi di tampa itu
3SG NEG believe for 3SG POSS mother go LOC place DEM
'He didn't believe his mother would go to that place.' (Paauw 2008: 401)

There is a prohibitive marker *jang*:

(157) jang pi di tana Cina
PROHIB go to land China
'Don't go to China.' (van Minde 1997: 279)

Existential constructions are formed with *ada* and without any overt subject (cf. Example (155c)). Polar questions are typically indicated through rising intonation only, although there is an optional clause-final question particle *ka*. Content questions are formed with question words that remain *in situ*:

(158) a. se taro de pung pakiang for ganti (ka)?
2SG put.down 3SG POSS clothes for change Q
'Have you laid out her new clothes?' (van Minde 1997: 260)

b. mau bikin bagaimana?
want make how
'What (how) can we do?' (Paauw 2008: 404)

Passives are formed with *dapa* 'get' (but cf. Example (155b)):

(159) dia pung swara dapa dengar
3SG POSS voice get hear
'Her voice was heard.' (van Minde 1997: 325)

There is no copula (cf. Example (154)). There are serial verb constructions, typically with motion verbs:

(160) kalo memang jaring pigi dapa ikang, ya?
if truly net go find fish yes
'If we can truly go catch fish with nets, right?' (Paauw 2008: 418)

There are a number of coordinating conjunctions and some subordinating conjunctions. Complementation may be expressed with the complementizer *kata* 'word, say':

(161) bar beta tao (kata) Opi pung laki par dia
new 1SG know COMP PN POSS husband for 3SG
'I just found out that he is Opi's husband.' (van Minde 1997: 306)

Relativization is in basilectal speech expressed through juxtaposition and in more acrolectal speech with the relativizer *yang*.

(162) a. orang dud di pingger jalang tu mabo
person sit LOC side road DEM drunk
'That man (who is) sitting at the side of the road is drunk.' (van Minde 1997: 308)

b. ya, jadi pake kaki kuda yang di sa-bala
yes so use foot horse REL LOC one-side
'Yes, so she had a horse's hoof (which was) on one side.' (Paauw 2008: 412)

7.3.2.3 *Short text*

(This is a shortened version of the story in Paauw 2008: 624ff.)

Jadi yang beta mau cerita itu tentang Nene Luhu.... biasanya itu antua
so REL 1SG FUT tell.story DEM about grandmother PN usual DEM 3SG.POL

punya kehidupan ada di punca Sirimau. ... Antua punya perkerjaan itu cuma tiap
POSS life EXIST LOC peak S 3SG.POL POSS work DEM only every

hari suka menjai pake tangan, aa, menjai pake tangan. ... Aa, waktu antua menjai,
day like sew use hand INTERJ sew use hand INTERJ time 3SG.POL sew

antua punya benang itu benang di dalam akang punya, katakana-la, di dalam
3SG.POL POSS thread DEM thread LOC in 3SG.N POSS say-EMPH LOC in

gulungan itu, dia jato terguling, dia jato terguling di atas tana. Lalu antua Nene Luhu
roll DEM 3SG fall rolling 3SG fall rolling LOC on ground then 3SG.POL PN PN

itu iku, iku benang itu, iku iku dia, sampe ahirnya tida dapa, antua hilang.
DEM follow follow thread DEM follow follow 3SG until last NEG find 3SG.POL lost

'So, I will tell a story about Nene Luhu. Her usual life was led atop the peak of Sirimau Hill. (After she had lost her fiancée) her work every day was simply to sew by hand, sewing by hand. (One time while) she was sewing, her thread, the thread in its, we can say, in the roll, it fell, rolling, it fell rolling on the ground. Then Nene Luhu followed, followed the thread, followed it, until at last she couldn't find it, and she disappeared.'

7.3.2.4 *Some sources of data*

van Minde (1997) is a full grammatical description of Ambon Malay, and contains numerous glossed and translated examples as well as four long texts. Paauw (2008) also contains numerous glossed and translated examples, as well as three long texts. Paauw (2013b) provides numerous glossed and translated examples online.

7.3.3 Ternate Chabacano: A Spanish-lexified creole coexisting with non-Spanish standard languages[124]

7.3.3.1 *A brief background sketch of Ternate Chabacano*

Ternate Chabacano, called *ternateño, chabacano* or *chavacano* in Spanish and *bahra* by the speakers themselves, is spoken by some 3,000 people in the town of Ternate in the Manila Bay on Luzon in the Philippines. It is closely related to Cavite Chabacano, spoken by 3–7,000 people in the nearby Cavite City, and the southern Philippine Chabacano varieties, spoken in and around Zamboanga, Cotabato and Davao by more than 300,000 people (Lesho & Sippola 2013, Steinkrüger 2013). While the Chabacano varieties are all mutually intelligible they "should not be considered dialects of a uniform language" (Lesho & Sippola 2013: 2), as there are in fact considerable differences between them.

When the Philippines (named after the Spanish king Philip II) were "discovered" by the Spanish in 1521 there had as yet not developed any centralized government or dominating culture of any large area (Woods 2006) on the islands. The first Spanish settlement was established in 1565 and the Philippines would remain Spanish for the next 333 years, until 1898. The Philippine Revolution for an Independent Republic began in 1896 and was helped by the Spanish-American war in 1898, which ended Spanish colonial rule in the Americas and led to Spain ceding the Philippines (among other territories) to the United States (Britannica 2011b).[125] After World War II and the Japanese occupation, the Philippines was proclaimed an independent republic on 4 July 1946.

The origin of Ternate Chabacano is debated. It has been proposed that Ternate Chabacano has its beginnings not in the Philippines, but on the island of Ternate in the Moluccas (Whinnom 1956). The island was a highly strategic territory for the spice trade and was at the centre of constant clashes between Portuguese, Dutch and Spanish interests. In 1606 the Spanish acquired the Maluku spice islands from the Portuguese (Sippola 2011: 16). At the time there is likely to have been some kind of Portuguese-Malay contact variety on the island (Lipski 1996: 277). Spanish Jesuit missionary activity on the island led to a group of local Christians called the *mardikas* (approx. 'the free ones'). In 1663, after the Dutch had destroyed the clove plantations on the island in 1655, the Spanish evacuated their forces from Ternate to Manila, taking with them the *mardikas*, who were subsequently allowed to resettle in the Bay of Manila (Lipski 1996: 272, Sippola

124. This section is primarily based on Sippola (2011) and (2013b). I am very grateful to Eeva Sippola for her helpful comments on this snapshot.

125. An alternative view is that the USA annexed the Philippines (and other territories).

2011:16).[126] This hypothesis has, however, been challenged in recent years; on the basis of linguistic and demographic evidence, it has instead been proposed that Ternate Chabacano in fact emerged on the Philippines (cf., for example, Fernández 2012)

What exactly the *mardikas* spoke when they were resettled is not possible to establish. However, there is mention in the mid-1700s of how they "use three languages, Spanish, which they speak with the Father and the Spaniards, Tagalog, which they use with the Indians [i.e. local population – VV], and their own [language], which they speak among themselves and teach their children" (Murillo Velarde 1749: §668, cited in Sippola 2011:21).[127] Whether this 'language of their own' was the creole or Moluccan Malay (Bahasa Ternate) is disputed. Even though they are few, there are some possible traces of Portuguese, Moluccan Malay (e.g. *kuning* 'yellow', *bangkarung* 'reptile') and Ternate (the indigenous language of the island; e.g. *bay* 'uncle', *yay* 'aunt') (Molony 1973, Tirona 1924). These would then be the substrate languages of Ternate Chabacano, which is considered the oldest of the Chabacano varieties.

The official languages of the Philippines today are Filipino (which is based on Tagalog) and English, with English being the main language "of higher education, business, and media, while Filipino is generally employed for local communication, certain school subjects, and entertainment" (Lesho & Sippola 2013:2, cf. also Gonzalez 1998, 2003). Local languages are used for everyday communication and in the home. This diglossic relationship is a recent phenomenon, since the Spanish priests interacted with people in the local languages for most of the Spanish rule. With the change to American administration in 1898 there was a shift from Spanish to English as a prestige language. School instruction was done in English until 1933 when a small number of local languages were also recognized for education (though in practice English schools are most highly valued; Eeva Sippola, p.c.). This was later limited to lower level education (where English is still used for half of the curricula), while only English and Tagalog were reserved for higher level education.

All speakers of Ternate Chabacano are bilingual in Chabacano and Tagalog, and some are also proficient in English and/or other Filipino languages. While Ternate Chabacano is still being transmitted intergenerationally, the younger generation seems to be gradually shifting to English and Tagalog (Lesho & Sippola 2013). The local administration is supportive to the promotion and maintenance of the language, although very few concrete results, apart from some public signs, have been produced so far (Lesho & Sippola 2013) – even if primary schools of the town also recently started giving Chabacano classes (Eeva Sippola, p.c.). The language enjoys high status as an identity marker of a community proud of their history and ancestors, as well

---

126. It should be noted that the *mardikas* that were evacuated from the island of Ternate were not the same as the *mardikas* that founded the city of Ternate; the name Ternate for the town, which was previously known as Barra de Maragondon, was only given at the turn of the 20th century (Eeva Sippola, p.c.).

127. "*… vsan tres lenguas, la Española, en que hablan con el Padre, y los Españoles, la Tagala, en que se entienden con los Indios, y la suya propia, que hablan entre si, y la communican, y enseñan à sus hijos.*"

as the perceived connection of the language with Spanish. However, it at the same time carries the stigma as a language of the poor, which has no function outside the community (Lesho & Sippola 2013).

7.3.3.2 *A short linguistic sketch of Ternate Chabacano*

Ternate Chabacano has 17 consonants, /p, b, m, w, t, d, n, r, s, l, ʧ, j, k, g, ŋ, ʔ, h/, and five vowels, /i, e, a, o, u/. The consonants / ʧ, j, ŋ/ are conventionally rendered as <ch>, <y> and <ng> respectively. There is no official orthography. Syllables may be complex, with up to three consonants in the onset and two in the coda, as in *prjetu* 'black' or *sejs* 'six' (Sippola 2011: 54). Words may have up to four syllables. There is contrastive stress, as in /'kasa/ 'house' versus /ka'sa/ 'to marry' (Sippola 2013b: 144); I here follow Eeva Sippola's convention in rendering stress as <´>.

The morphology is predominantly analytic, although there is some verbal affixation. There is reduplication, which typically denotes plurality, diminutive or intensification:

(163) a. ta-yubá mihótru manga peskáw grándi~grándi
IPFV-lift 1PL PL fish big~RED
'We were carrying very big fish.'
b. únti~únti tasé kel di-mótru kása
little~RED IPFV.do DEM POSS-1PL house
'Little by little we made our house.' (Sippola 2011: 98)

Nouns are invariable, although natural gender may be distinguished by the final vowel (*-o*/*-a* for M/F respectively) in a small group of nouns or through compounding with *ómbri* 'man' or *muhér* 'woman'. With some nouns the Spanish definite article *la* fused with the stem to a fossilized whole, as in *lamár* 'sea' and *laberdád* 'truth' (Sippola 2011: 76).

Plural is typically indicated with the particle *mánga* but there are some nouns that have retained the Spanish plural -*s*, though this is no longer productive.

(164) tyéni manga híkaw na oréhas
have PL hoop LOC ear.PL
'They have earrings in their ears.' (Sippola 2011: 64)

There is an indefinite article *un* and the demonstrative *éste* 'this' and *kel* 'that', the latter of which may also function as a definite article:

(165) tyéni ya rin mótru manga pasilidád kel pang-emerdzénsi
have now too 2PL PL facility DEM INSTR-emergency
'We have facilities for the emergencies now too.' (Sippola 2011: 92)

Nominal possession is indicated with the possessor *di*:

(166) kel el gritu di kel muhér byéha kel
DEM DEF shout POSS DEM woman old DEM
'That was this old woman's shout.' (Sippola 2011: 125)

The personal pronouns have subject, object and possessive forms, distinguished by three persons and two numbers.

	PERSONAL		POSSESSIVE
	SUBJECT	OBJECT	
1SG	*yo*	*konmígo*	*mi/dimi*
2SG	*bo/(us)tédi*	*konbó/kontédi*	*bos/dibo*
3SG	*éle*	*konéle*	*su/diéle*
1PL	*mihótro/mótro/mótru*	*konmihótro/konmótro*	*dimótro/dimihótro*
2PL	*(us)tédi*	*kon(us)tédi*	*di(s)tédi*
3PL	*lohótro/lótro*	*konlohótro/konlótro*	*dilótro*

Notice that there is no gender distinction in the third person. The second person singular has a polite form, *(us)tédi*, identical with the second person plural form. It is possible to derive dual forms with the numeral two, *dos*, as in *mordós* (<*mótru dos* 'we two'), though this has not (yet) been fully grammaticalized. The subject pronouns may be left out of the clause if the subject is known.

Adjectives are typically invariant and most commonly precede the noun, though they may also follow. Comparison is done with *mas … kon/kóntra* 'more … than' for the comparative and *pínaka/kel más* for the superlative:

(167) a. no masyádu gránde kel a-pagá na hospitál
NEG too.much big REL PFV-pay LOC hospital
'(The bill) that I paid at the hospital wasn't too much.'

b. (mas) gwápa Imélda kon(tra) Kóri
more pretty PN COMP PN
'Imelda is prettier than Cory.'

c. ya-muri kel pinaka-salbáhi péhru kalyá
PFV-die DEF SUPERL-wild dog DEM
'This dog, the wildest one, died.' (Sippola 2011: 173, 176f)

There are three tense/aspect/mood markers: *ya/a* for perfective, *ta* for imperfective, *di* for irrealis/ future ('contemplated') (see also Examples (163), (167), (169), (170)):

(168) a. ya-kasá mihótro
PFV-marry 1PL
'We got married.'

b. ta-platiká lohótru na lengwáhe kómo espanyól
IPFV-speak 3PL in language like Spanish
'They spoke in a language like Spanish.'

c. di-kedá ya yo kwarénta-i-nwébe na agústu
CTPL-become now 1SG 49 LOC August
'I'll make 49 in August.' (Sippola 2011: 130, 148)

The markers do not combine and usually occur with those verbs which derive from the Spanish infinitive form. That limited group of verbs that derive from an inflected Spanish form, most of which function as modal verbs, do not take any tense, mood or aspect markers. Verbs in the base form may have present or past time reference.

The word order is typically verb-subject-object. The invariant negator *no* precedes all verbal particles (cf. also Example (167a)). There is a negative existential/possessive *nuwáy*.

(169) a. no éli di-pwédi sentá ayí sino por el manga hénti
NEG 3SG CTPL-can stay here if.not for DEF PL people
'S/he couldn't have been sitting here (i.e. had this position) if it hadn't been for the people.'
b. kel kályi kel kabá yubé nuwáy ma rin
DEM street DEM finish to.rain NEG.EXIST more too
'That very street, after it rained, doesn't exist anymore too.' (Sippola 2011:159, 161)

Adjectives do not take a copula (cf. above), but there is a locative copula *na/ta/taki* (<*ta akí* 'LOC here'; Examples (164), (167a), (168c)).

Polar questions are either marked by rising intonation only, or with rising intonation and the question particle *ba*. In content questions the interrogative phrase is fronted. The question particle may optionally be used.

(170) a. konosé kun Lébi?
know OBJ PN
'Does s/he know Levi?'
b. dóndi (ba) tédi dindá?
where Q 2PL CTPL.go
'Where are you going?' (Sippola 2011:67, 202)

There are the coordinating conjunctions *i/pati* 'and', *péro* 'but' and *o* 'or'. Juxtaposition is common. The complementizer *ki* is optional. There are a number of subordinators. The relativizer *ki/kel* (cf. Example (167a)) is typically not used in spoken language.

7.3.3.3 *Short text*

(This is a shortened and translated version of the story in Sippola 2011:300ff.)

mi táta Hep … tasé éli kel iglésya aglípay, ya, bebíw mi táta Hep
my father PN IPFV-do 3SG DEF church Philipine.independence now tipsy my father PN

ya-kayí na bintána, beng klárung~kláru éli a-mirá ay a-sanggá kon-éli mucháchu kolót,
PFV-fall LOC window INTENS clear~RED 3SG PFV-see FOC PFV-catch OBJ-3SG boy curly

ta-bisá mi táta Hep, ay a-kargá komíngu mucháchu, ta-bisá raw mi chung Nárdo
IPFV-say my father PN FOC PFV-carry 1SG.OBJ boy IPFV-say QUOT my uncle PN

ninó, yo a-kargá kon-bo, táta Hep, ninó, bágu bo mínggu resibí na kayí yo,
NEG.EMPH 1SG PFV-carry OBJ-2SG father PN NEG.EMPH before 2SG 1SG.OBJ receive LOC fall 1SG

ay a-kargá komíngu muchachu, kwándu ya-pensá mi táta Hep, nakú, Sánto Nínyo
FOC PFV-carry 1SG.OBJ boy when PFV-think my father PN EXCL holy child

di aglípay komíngu a-yud…
POSS Aglipay 1SG.OBJ PFV-help

'My uncle Hep … was making the Aglipaya church, now, my uncle Hep was tipsy, and fell out of the window. He saw very clearly that a curly (haired) boy caught him. My uncle Hep said: "He who caught me was a boy". My uncle Nardo said: "No, I caught you, uncle Hep". "No, before you caught me of my fall, a boy was carrying me". When my uncle Hep thought about it: "Oh, the Holy Child of Aglipay helped me…"'

7.3.3.4 *Some sources of data*

Sippola (2011) is a comprehensive grammar of the language, with a large number of glossed and translated examples, as well as four longer glossed and translated texts, unfortunately only accessible to those who read Spanish. Sippola (2013c) provides numerous glossed and translated examples online. Nigoza (2007) is a bilingual English-Ternate Chabacano collection of stories, proverbs, songs, and so on. The Ternate Cavite Website (http://ternate-cavite.tripod.com/, accessed 10 February 2015) contains local news items and reports, as well as some information on the language.

7.4 Summary

Languages are dynamic systems that vary across time and place, as well as between individuals and even within the language use of the same individual. Different 'lects' are language varieties that differ between each other according to various extralinguistic factors.

A continuum of 'lects' is a scale of language varieties that differ from each other minimally. At each end of the continuum the varieties will differ maximally, while the space between the two extremes is filled with a spectrum of intermediate varieties. Most commonly the continuum refers to relative closeness to a standard variety, which in pidgin and creole speaking societies tends to mean relative closeness to the lexifier. A basilect is furthest removed from the standard language in its structure, while the acrolect is closest (almost identical with) the standard language in its structure. The intermediate varieties, the mesolects, form a fluid gradation between two ends of the continuum.

Lectal continua may show implicational patterns in that the forms chosen vary systematically and predictably. A given form typically combines with some of the alternatives while being incompatible with other alternatives. This systematic patterning can be arranged in an implicational scale whereby the appearance of one form implies the appearance of certain other forms. Implicational scales have been used as evidence of ongoing change.

Highly stratified uses of different language varieties may lead to diglossia, where a High variety is used in formal contexts and a Low variety in informal contexts. The speech community is essentially bilingual in the two varieties.

The continuum of 'lects' has been termed a post-creole continuum to reflect the idea that it represents the final stage in the creole life-cycle, namely that of decreolization, where the creole reunites with the lexifier. This is assumed to be relevant only if the creole is in continued contact with its lexifier. It is a matter of debate whether this constitutes a recent phenomenon or whether lectal variation was present from the start in the contact situation. A more neutral term is the creole continuum. The notion of depidginization likewise assumes a gradual reunification with the lexifier due to continued contact with it.

Repidginization tends to refer to a creole language becoming the lexifier of a new creole language (thus assuming a necessary prior pidgin stage). Recreolization refers to the phenomenon whereby a language variety becomes more basilectal, typically due to covert prestige and acts of identity.

7.5 Key points

- **Lectal continua are fluid gradations of variation ranging from basilectal over mesolectal to acrolectal varieties depending on how far removed they are from the standard language.**
- **Lectal continua presuppose a social continuum between the different lects.**
- **Situations of lectal continua are not unique to pidgin and creole languages.**
- **Diglossia is when distinct linguistic codes are used in distinct situations.**
- **Situations of diglossia are not unique to pidgin and creole languages.**
- **Implicational patterns are patterns that show that a given variation is systematic and predictable.**
- **The notion of a (post-) creole continuum carries the unwarranted implication that lectal continua are unique for creole languages.**

7.6 Exercises

1. What is the difference between situations of a lectal continuum and diglossia? Are the two mutually exclusive? Are they unique for pidgins and/or creoles? Motivate your answer.
2. In what way have lectal continua been interpreted as evidence of ongoing change in pidgin and creole languages?
3. What does 'recreolization' mean?
4. What are implicational patterns and how do they relate to situations of lectal continua?
5. What are the three main levels of a lectal continuum scale? What do they relate to?

Languages cited in Chapter 8

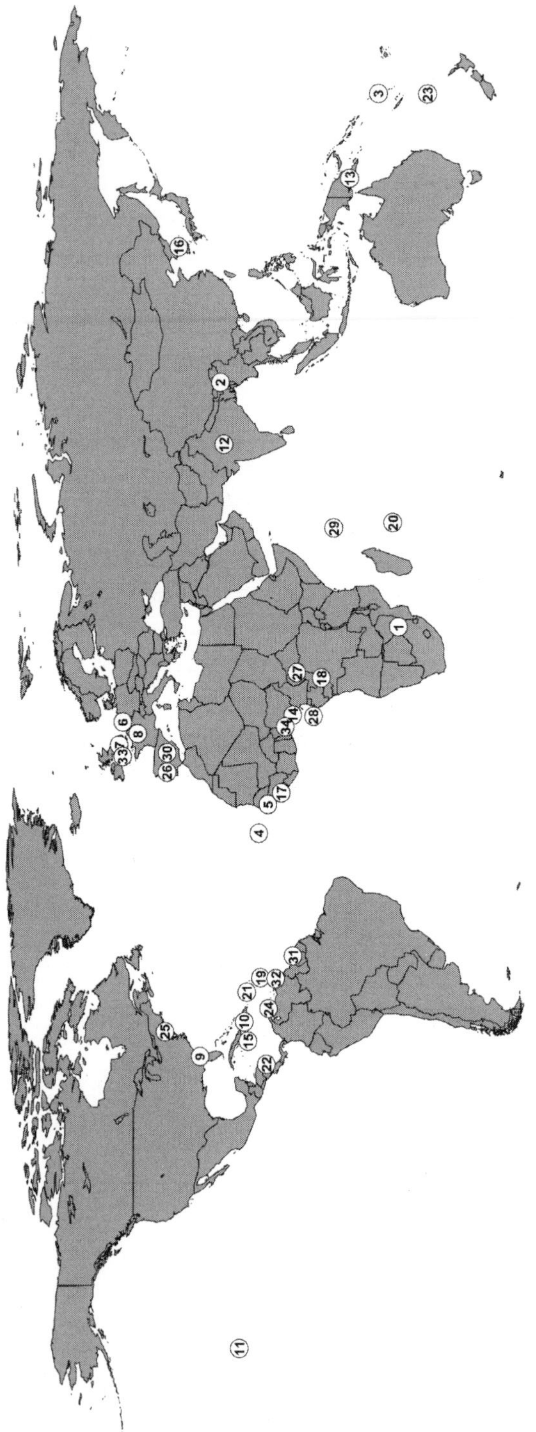

1. Afrikaans
2. Assamese; Nagamese
3. Bislama
4. Cape Verdean Creole
5. Casamancese; Guinea Bissau Kriyol
6. Dutch
7. English
8. French
9. Gullah
10. Haitian Creole
11. Hawai'i Creole English
12. Hindi
13. Hiri Motu; Tok Pisin
14. Igbo; Nigerian Pidgin
15. Jamaican
16. Korean
17. Guinea Coast Creole English; Krio; Limba; Mende; Temne
18. Lingala
19. Martinican Creole
20. Mauritian Creole; Reunion Creole
21. Negerhollands
22. Nicaraguan Creole English
23. Norf'k
24. Papiamentu
25. Pidgin Delaware
26. Portuguese
27. Sango
28. Santome
29. Seychelles Creole
30. Spanish
31. Sranan
32. Trinidad English Creole
33. Welsh
34. Yoruba

Chapter 8

Language in society

Language and culture is a fundamental part of any human society and is intimately linked with issues of identity, prestige and sense of solidarity, with some languages receiving official recognition and support and others not. This chapter will very briefly bring up some fundamental issues related to language attitudes (Section 8.1.1), language planning (Section 8.1.2) and language policies (Section 8.1.3), before giving a very short overview of the linguistic expression of culture in the form of oral and written literature as well as mass media (Section 8.2) in pidgin and creole speaking societies. Section 8.3 gives short sketches of three languages at varying stages of standardization and levels of recognition and acceptance: Nagamese (an Assamese-lexified extended pidgin/pidgincreole in South Asia), Papiamentu (an Iberian-lexified creole in the Caribbean) and Krio (an English-lexified creole in West Africa).

8.1 Sociology of language

Language is an integral part of any society. Organized communities that have shared laws or traditions or values are dependent on language to maintain these laws, traditions or values. Likewise, societies in the form of political units, such as countries, are dependent on language for the administration of these units. Exactly which language(s) will be used in a society is, however, not necessarily straightforward. Typically one or a few language(s) are used and are thus to varying degrees officially promoted and supported, often at the expense of other languages used in the same society. For instance, countries or other political units (such as more or less autonomous regions within a country) will have one or a few official language(s), either constitutionally specified (*de jure*) or simply in practice though not set down in law (*de facto*). Governmental business will then be conducted in this or these official language(s), for instance, official documents, legal proceedings and constitutional matters will be in these languages. Citizens are expected to be able to function in at least one of the official languages. This or these languages are promoted and supported in that they are, for example, used in media and any other public domain, and that they are the languages specified for use in education. They are typically further supported in the form of educational materials. This in turn means that the language(s) in question are standardized to a common norm in which materials can be produced.

Language policies are typically linked with issues of prestige: official support is typically only given to those languages considered viable or good enough to serve the functions of the society. Standard languages typically carry high overt prestige, as they are associated with upward social mobility and high education. However, prestige and standard languages is in many ways a two-way relationship: the reason these particular language varieties became standard languages is often due to the fact that they were already associated with high prestige and the fact that they are standard languages lends them high overt prestige and official support. One of the ways for low-prestige language varieties to gain recognition is thus through standardization. A crucial step in the standardization of a language is to codify it, that is, to find a uniform way of representing it, especially orthographically. Choosing which variety should be promoted and codified as a standard norm is, however, intimately linked with issues of attitude, identity and sense of solidarity.

This section will very briefly bring up some core issues of the interrelated fields of language attitudes, language planning (the conscious act of trying to influence which languages will be used in various domains of a society) and language policy (what a society effectively does to promote certain languages). It is quite beyond the scope of the section to do anything more than merely scratch the surface of the subject matter. For a very accessible introduction to language attitudes, see Garrett (2010). For accessible introductions to language planning, see, for example Kaplan & Baldauf (1997) and Ferguson (2006). For an accessible discussion on language policies, see, for example, Shohamy (2006). The chapters in Spolsky (2012) offer discussions on a very wide range of subjects indeed, such as, apart from general definitions, language policies related to national and international issues, non-governmental spheres, globalization and modernization, as well as regional issues. Wright (2003) is a detailed discussion on the interplay between language planning, policies and issues of social identity and mobility.

8.1.1 Language attitudes

We all have feelings, beliefs and attitudes about language one way or another, more or less consciously and more or less pronounced. We tend to draw a host of inferences about a person based on the way they speak. We also tend to, more or less consciously, try to influence the way we are perceived through the way we talk. Some of these attitudes are overt and others are covert. The study of **language attitudes** works to identify the kinds of attitudes that are held about different language varieties, how that affects the view of people who use those language varieties and what kinds of associations are formed about different language varieties.

8.1.1.1 *Attitudes and perception*

Language attitudes may have effects on a number of factors. For example, those languages or varieties spoken by people we think positively about are typically perceived as easier to understand and to learn than languages or varieties spoken by people we think negatively about. People using an overtly high status language variety are typically viewed as more educated, more intelligent, more confident and more suitable for leadership positions than people using an overtly low status variety. People using a low status variety are, on the other hand, typically viewed as friendlier and kinder, more sincere and more reliable than speakers of a high status variety. For example, in a seminal study on language attitudes towards French and English in Montreal (which has a history of tensions between the French-speaking and English-speaking communities) Lambert et al. (1960) developed what is called a **matched guise** technique, where four bilingual speakers were recorded reading a short paragraph in each language. The content of the paragraph was the same for both the French and the English version, which means that the only thing that differed was the language used. These four bilingual speakers thus produced two recordings each, and the resulting eight recordings were presented as if they were from eight different persons. A group of respondents were then asked to listen to the recordings and assess each 'speaker' (guise) for the following: height, good looks, intelligence, dependability, leadership, sense of humour, religiousness, self-confidence, entertainingness, kindness, ambition, character and likeability. The 'speakers' (guises) of the English passages were consistently ranked higher than those of the French passages, by both the English-speaking and the French-speaking respondents, except that the French-speaking respondents ranked the 'speakers' (guises) of the French passages higher for those traits concerned with various levels of solidarity, such as religiousness and kindness. In other words, the same people were rated differently depending on the language in which they read the passage. Here the majority language of the country, English, which historically has been the language of power, is given a higher status than French, and that difference in status is reflected in the perception of the speakers of the different varieties.

The way we perceive language may also differ according to more or less consciously held attitudes. For example, standard language varieties are typically held to be more formal and the speaker using it is typically perceived as more intelligent and successful, while non-standard language varieties are typically held to be more informal and the speaker using it is typically perceived as more friendly and trustworthy. In a mixed guise study, Levin et al. (1994) had a person bidialectal in British RP and a mild southeast Welsh English accent read a text describing a house. The text was done in two versions, one in a more formal style, with more Latinate words (such as *facade* or *interior*), and the other in a more informal style, with more Germanic words (such as *front* or *inside*). The speaker thus produced four passages, one in RP and a formal (Latinate) style, one in RP and an informal (Germanic) style, one in southeast Welsh English and a formal style, and one in southeast Welsh English and an informal style. Respondents were then divided up in four groups, each of which only heard one of these four guises, and were asked to rate the speaker according to a number of personality traits (e.g. whether the speaker seems intelligent, friendly, sincere, dominant, relaxed, ambitious, etc.) and a number of features concerned with his language (e.g. whether the speaker used simple grammar, formal speech, fancy words, long words, etc.). The 'speakers' (guises) of the RP passages were judged as being socioeconomically more successful (a better source of advice and more intelligent, dominant, ambitious, etc.) while the 'speakers' (guises) of the south-eastern Welsh English passages were judged as being socially more attractive (more sincere, flexible, relaxed, etc.). In other words, the same speaker was judged differently depending on the accent he was using. This matches the attitudes found in the Canadian bilingual mixed guise study mentioned above. However, it also turned out that the language of the 'speakers' (guises) was perceived differently depending on the accent used: both RP 'speakers' were perceived to be using longer and fancier words, more formal and less colloquial speech, and to be easier to listen to than the 'speakers' of the southeast Welsh English accent, despite the fact that the two texts were, in fact, identical. In other words, the language of this person was perceived differently depending on the accent he was using: the informal (Germanic) version of the text in the standard (RP) accent was judged as containing longer and fancier words and as being more formal than the formal (Latinate) version of the text in the non-standard accent.

It should be noted that extralinguistic factors, such as appearances and stereotypes may also influence the perception of a language variety. In a study conducted in the USA by Williams et al. (1971) videotapes of six different children were played to 15 teachers and prospective teachers. The children represented two social classes (working vs. middle class) and three ethnic groups (White American, African American and Mexican American). The respondents were asked to rank the children on the tapes according to different personality traits (essentially having to do with how confident the child seemed) and linguistic traits (essentially having to do with whether the child spoke a standard or nonstandard variety). Overall, the White American children were ranked higher on both the confidence and standard language scales. The same research team then prepared videos edited for the same children representing the same six groups (African American working/middle class, White American working/middle class and Mexican American working/middle class) but dubbed with the same audio track of Standard American English speech. The children were filmed from a side angle so that the lips could not be read, an important point since it was the same audio track for all six children. The same respondents were asked to judge the speakers for the same personality and linguistic traits as previously. It turned out that the White American were still perceived to be much more confident than the others and were much more likely to be perceived as speaking the standard language. In other words, the physical appearance of the children and the host of stereotypes associated with that appearance affected how their language was perceived: even when the African and Mexican American children were speaking the exact same language as the White American ones (it was the same audio track for all six children), the language was perceived as being different from the language of the White American children.

8.1.1.2 *Identity and accommodation*

Speakers may also more or less consciously **accommodate** their language or accent towards or away from that of their interlocutors, both in terms of language choice and/or in terms of various language variety characteristics, as well as in terms of such things as gestures, postures, facial expressions, and so on.

If we want to emphasize similarities with our interlocutors we **converge** our speech and behaviour towards theirs, essentially accentuating group belonging, association and solidarity. We might, for example, start to use similar mannerisms as the interlocutor (such accommodating to his or her speech rate or gestures) or we might make our accent more similar to the person(s) we are talking to, or choose a certain language over others in a multilingual context.[128]

If we want to emphasize differences between us and our interlocutors we **diverge** our speech and behaviour from theirs, essentially accentuating social distance. An example of divergence as a way of asserting social identity can be found in the study by Bourhis & Giles (1977) involving people learning Welsh. One group of the Welsh learners was taking the course for career purposes, while the other group was taking the course out of interest and because they valued their Welsh identity. In a language laboratory the learners listened to recorded questions posed by someone speaking in a British RP accent and in turn answered in English into a microphone, with their answers being recorded. After a few questions the recorded speaker started questioning why they were learning a dying language and talking in terms of 'Us' and 'Them'. The group of learners who were learning the language out of a sense of identity now began to diverge in their speech, giving their answers in a stronger Welsh English, or even mixing in Welsh (one of them simply conjugated an obscene Welsh verb as an

128. Notice, however, that linguistic convergence as an attempt to indicate solidarity is not always appreciated or accepted. To use a non-standard or low status variety in inappropriate contexts may come across as patronizing and cause alienation, even if the intentions were well meant.

answer). Here the offensive behaviour of the person asking questions led to a stronger need to disassociate the social identity from that of the interlocutor. See also, for example, the discussion in Giles and Powesland (1975).

8.1.2 Language planning

Language planning essentially refers to conscious efforts to influence or change the language use in a given community. Traditionally two types of language planning have been distinguished, originally set out by Kloss (1969): **status planning**, which essentially refers to determining which languages should be used in which societal domains (such as the official sphere, education, media, etc.) and **corpus planning**, which essentially involves language cultivation and the implementation of language policies (such as establishing a norm and producing materials in that language or variety). The two types reinforce each other: status planning involves language policies and decision makings, which are unlikely to make much progress without the implementation (corpus planning) of these policies. However, corpus planning is often shaped by official decision making, since the implementation of language cultivation is difficult to accomplish without supportive policies (cf. Bamgbose 1991).

Corpus planning essentially involves the cultivation of a certain language or language variety by means of setting up a linguistic norm in which materials will be produced. In order for languages or language varieties to be recognized as viable for official support, such as, for example, mediums of instructions in schools, there needs to be a certain body of material in that language or language variety. For instance, there needs to be primers, readers and other teaching materials to use in teaching. Literacy in the language is strengthened by the production of various texts in the language, such as fiction and poetry, as well as other, general texts. This would include translations of various works into the language or language variety, for example religious texts. In order to achieve this, the language or language variety needs to be codified and standardized. **Codification** of a language or language variety involves setting up a linguistic norm (code) through the production of dictionaries, grammars, pronunciation guides, as well as choosing a script and setting up spelling and punctuation guides. This leads to the **standardization** of the language or language variety, in that there now is a standardized norm to follow.

It should be noted that the principal aims of corpus planning is to provide a language variety that is maximally adequate for the needs of its users, that is maximally systematic in its rules and that is maximally acceptable for the community. While the standardization process by definition is normative – it leads to a variety that is seen as the targeted norm – and as such prescriptive, it should be noted that the concept of 'correctness' is based on pragmatic factors of communication efficiency. As stated by Kaplan & Baldauf:

> Standardisation, in language planning terms, is not about correctness for its own sake, but about achieving a basis for effective communication. Since language is a dynamic process, correctness is only a momentary (in historical terms) event. Self-appointed critics, language teachers, and sometimes language academics, who carry the concern for standardisation into hyper-correctness, defeat the basic purpose of standardisation and therefore communication. (Kaplan & Baldauf 1997: 67)

8.1.2.1 *Selecting the norm*

Before codification can start, a language variety has to be selected as a basis for the norm. Historically the linguistic norm has been the variety spoken in and around the centres of power, which in pidgin, creole and mixed language societies has typically been the colonizer's language. Efforts to standardize pidgin, creole or mixed languages thus give rise to a number of questions. For the standardization to work it has to gain acceptance. The question then is which variety of a pidgin, creole or mixed language would gain the widest acceptance. On the one hand it needs to have a certain distance from the competing standard (in this case the lexifier), enough to be seen as a different language rather than merely an inferior version of the existing standard (cf. Kloss 1967). On the other hand it needs to be representative of as many of the speakers in the community as possible. This may cause controversies both geographically and socially: if there are different regional varieties, which one should be chosen? And in case of a lectal continuum, which lect should be chosen? Choosing, for example, a basilectal variety might solve the problem of distance – it would be a maximally different variety from the competing standard – but might not satisfy the criterion of maximal representation in terms of number of speakers. Choosing a variety based on the number of speakers might satisfy the criterion of representability but might not solve the problem of distance. Papiamentu, for example, is spoken on the Netherlands Antilles islands Aruba, Bonaire and Curaçao. There is both regional and social variation of the language, with Aruban Papiamentu differing from that of the other islands and rural varieties differing from urban varieties, as well as a variety spoken specifically by the Sephardic Jews (Maurer 2013c), which raises a number of issues concerning the choice of a norm for standardization (Eckkrammer 1999). Krio, spoken in Sierra Leone, is both an L1 creole and an L2 *lingua franca* with varying degrees of fluency and L1 transfer. The language varies according to region, in that almost all of the L1 speakers are concentrated in one area, in the west, mainly in and around Freetown. Within the L1 speaking community there is variation according to the lectal continuum, age (with older speakers typically using a more basilectal variety) and religion (with the Moslem Aku Krio being a distinct variety). The L1 community is a clear minority, yet a norm is unlikely to be accepted unless it is based on the L1 variety. The L1 language of the younger generation tends to be more acrolectal than that of the older generation;

however, it is the basilectal variety that L2 users tend to target (Johnson 1992) – which, then, is the most 'representative' variety?

8.1.2.2 *Codifying the norm*

Once a language variety has been selected as the norm it needs to be codified in order to become standardized. Codification essentially means extracting and formulating the rules for pronunciation, grammar and the lexicon. Most typically **graphization**, the selection of a script and orthographic convention, is seen as an essential first step of codification.

There are different approaches to developing a written form of a language. The **morphemic principle** essentially means that the spelling has a fixed form for each morpheme, irrespective of its pronunciation alternatives. For example, the past tense suffix *-ed* in English is always spelled *-ed* irrespective of its pronunciation (cf. *walked* /wɔːkt/, *grabbed* /gɹæbd/, *lifted* /lɪftəd/). This may be confusing when there are homophones (same-sounding words with different meanings), since they would then be spelled differently despite the fact that they are pronounced similarly (cf., for example, the English might /maɪt/ versus mite /maɪt/).

A **phonemic orthography** (or **phonological orthography**) essentially works under the principle that each phoneme of the language has its own symbol. By this principle the English words *night* and *know*, for example, would be spelled 'nait' and 'no'. It could be argued that a phonemic spelling system would be easier to learn, as the writing would then match the pronunciation. Using the phonemic principle for pidgin, creole or mixed languages would stress the distance from the lexifier language. It should be noted that the symbols of a phonemic system may reflect the societal context of the language. For instance, a proposed orthography for Hawai'i Creole English, the Odo system (cf. Odo 1975, 1977), works on the phonological principle. Thus the words 'feet', 'you' and 'cow', for example, would be spelled *fit*, *yu* and *kau*. However, some of the symbols only make sense according to an English pronunciation and spelling conception, such as *baej* for 'badge' (where <j> represents /ʤ/, as is the case in many English words, but not, for example, in French, German or Spanish words), or even specifically Standard American English (the current normative standard in Hawai'i), such as *dawg* for 'dog' (where *aw* for speakers of American English tends to refer to /a:/ or /ɔ:/ while in, for example British English, it would refer to /ɒ:/ or /ɔ:/). Here we have a system that is coloured by the conventions of the lexifier, which on the one hand could be argued to lessen the distance between the creole and the lexifier, and on the other hand could be argued to make the creole more accessible to a community that is already used to a certain set of conventions.

An **etymological orthography** is a historically conservative solution, where earlier spellings are retained despite changes in pronunciation. These kinds of spellings typically reflect earlier pronunciations (that is, the original spellings were phonemic) that have since become obsolete. In English there is extensive etymological spelling, due to the conservative orthography, which is why we have such opaque forms as *knight* (/naɪt/), *enough* (/ɪnʌf/), or, impossibly, *Worcestershire* (/ˈwʊstərʃə/).[129] An etymological spelling for pidgin, creole or mixed languages would stress the historical connection with the lexifier. In those societies where the lexifier is the prestigious variety and the recognized standard "reading and writing abilities can be transferred more easily from the creole to the lexifier language when an etymological orthography is employed" (Appel & Verhoeven 1994: 67). Furthermore, with an etymological spelling it would be possible to avoid favouring the pronunciation of some particular dialect over other dialects (cf. Winer 1993: 66ff). Etymological spelling can also be important for identity building; Faroese, for example, favours Icelandic spelling over Danish, even though the actual pronunciation has become more similar to mainland Scandinavian norms (Miriam Meyerhoff, p.c.).

The choice of an orthographical principle can be ideologically charged and can lead to longstanding controversies. For some languages two different spelling systems have evolved, such as for Papiamentu, where the Aruba dialect is spelled according to an etymological principle, while the others have a phonemic system, reflecting the "cultural and political differences between the islands: Aruba is closest to the Spanish-speaking South American mainland and is generally more 'hispanized' than the other islands" (Sebba 1998: 226). For example, the word 'five' is spelled *cinco* in the Aruban system (reflecting the Spanish spelling) and *sinku* in the Curaçaoan spelling (Maurer 2013c: 166). Haiti has seen a long drawn debate about the relative merits of the two principles. Those arguing for a phonemic system stress the importance of a coherent and logical system that is easy to learn for monolingual creole speakers. This position essentially reflects a wish to distance Haitian Creole from French. Those arguing for an etymological system stress the connection between the creole and French and that an etymological system would ultimately make Standard French easier to acquire. This position essentially reflects a wish to link Haitian Creole with French. An intermediate camp proposes "a phonemic orthography but with some concessions to

---

129. The opacity of etymological spelling is captured very nicely in a famous limerick (note that 'Erse' means 'Irish'):

> There was a young man from Dun Laoghaire
> Who propounded an interesting thaoghaire:
> That the language of Erse
> Has a shortage of verse
> 'Cos the spelling makes poets so waoghaire.

French spelling" (Schieffelin & Doucet 1994:184).[130] For a recent discussion on the standardization and codification of Haitian Creole, see Dejean (2012).

8.1.3 Language policy

Language policy, also called status planning, essentially refers to the functional status of languages, whereby languages or language varieties are allocated to different societal domains, such as governmental bodies and institutions, education or media. Language policies are officially set by governments or government-related bodies and typically reflect extralinguistic social issues and concerns. Those languages or language varieties that are officially selected for various societal functions automatically function as a norm and gain a higher status. There are essentially three levels of language policies (Noss 1971): (i) the official level (stating which language(s) should be used in the governmental administrations), (ii) educational policies (stating which language(s) should be used in the education system), and (iii) general policies (stating which language(s) should be used in the media and business communications, etc.).

Pidgin, creole and mixed languages are almost invariably found in former (or, in some cases, present) colonial societies, where there is a history of an established political elite whose language or language variety has had official recognition and has been established as the norm on the various policy levels, namely the language of the colonizers. This is intimately connected with attitudes and issues of identity, where the politically powerful (minority) group commands the prestigious language. There is again mutual reinforcement at play: a language variety that is spoken by a political elite will automatically receive the status of a prestigious (standard) variety and thus official support. However, the fact that a variety has official support automatically lends it prestige and makes it a targeted norm (cf. also the discussion in Section 7.1). In other words, because pidgin, creole and mixed languages have traditionally been viewed as inferior non-standard language varieties, they are typically excluded from official recognition. For more on pidgins and creoles as official languages, see, for example, Devonish (2008). For more on pidgins and creoles in education, see, for example, Craig (2008) and the chapters in Migge et al. (2010b).

130. In fact the look of written Haitian Creole has become a charged issue. The International Phonetic Alphabet characters *w*, *y* and *k* have been taken by those arguing for an etymological orthography to represent an "Anglo-Saxon look", which by some has been taken as an expression of American imperialism with the purpose of replacing French with English. (In actual fact the IPA was originally founded by the French linguist Paul Passy in collaboration with a group of French and British language teachers; they together devised a script meant to be possible to use for any language. Cf. International Phonetic Association 1999.) Interestingly, the letter *k* has also been "claimed to represent the threat of communism" (Schieffelin & Doucet 1994:191) with literacy activists accused of being under cover communist agents (*ibid*).

8.1.3.1 *Official recognition*

Due to the long history of stigmatization of pidgin, creole and mixed languages, the majority of them remain unrecognized officially, irrespective of the proportion of the speech community or of the communicative importance of the language. In the vast majority of cases the language of the former (or, in some cases, present) colonizers have the role of official language (Devonish 2008). For example, the sole official language of Jamaica is English, despite the fact that Jamaican is the mother tongue of the majority population (most of them bilingual; Farquharson 2013a), and English is also the sole official language of Mauritius, despite the fact that Mauritian Creole is the dominant language of Mauritius and its dependencies (Baker & Kriegel 2013). Portuguese is the sole official language of DR São Tomé and Principe, despite the fact that Santome is spoken by the majority of the population (Hagemeijer 2013a).

There are notable exceptions to this pattern in that pidgin, creole and mixed languages are gradually being recognized alongside the colonial official languages (we have yet to see a case where a pidgin, creole or mixed language is the sole official language of a country). Papua New Guinea has three official languages, English, and the two extended pidgins (pidgincreoles) Tok Pisin and Hiri Motu (Smith & Siegel 2013a). In Vanuatu, the extended pidgin (pidgincreole) Bislama is one of the three official languages, together with English and French (Meyerhoff 2013a). The extended pidgin (pidgincreole) Sango is one of the two official languages of the Central African Republic (French is the other one; Samarin 2013a). Afrikaans, the third largest language of South Africa, is one of eleven official languages of the country, and has, due to its connection with the politically powerful population, consistently enjoyed a high status (van Sluijs 2013a). Seychelles Creole has been the official language of the Republic of the Seychelles together with English and French since 1978, two years after independence (Michaelis & Rosalie 2013). Haitian Creole has been an official language of Haiti since 1987 (together with French, which has been the official language since 1918; Fattier 2013). Norf'k, is, since 2004, the official language of Norfolk Island, together with English. Since 2007 Papiamentu is, together with Dutch, an official language of the Netherlands Antilles (Maurer 2013c).

It is not essential for a language to be standardized in order to be recognized as an official language – Bislama, for example, has no standard form (Meyerhoff 2013a) – but the absence of a standard typically constitutes one of the many hurdles for official recognition. In Jamaica, for example, the Joint Select Committee of the Houses of Parliament, when drafting a bill of rights to be taken up by the constitution, were presented with the issue of language discrimination and language rights (Joint Select Committee 2001). While the Committee did recognize the fact that language discrimination exists, "it expressed concern about the ability of the agencies of the state to provide services in Jamaican given the absence of a standard writing system" (Devonish 2008: 631). This illustrates the importance of careful corpus planning and language standardization efforts. The combined effects of linguistic research and language activism have, for example, now led to the *Charter on Language Policy and Language Rights in the Creole-speaking Caribbean*, which was signed by representatives (linguists, language activists and elected officials) from twelve Caribbean countries in 2011. The Charter outlines the language rights recommended for citizens of the creole-speaking Caribbean and "is now being circulated to governments and civil society groups as well as individuals for ratification, support and implementation" (ICCLR 2011). See further Brown-Blake & Devonish (2012).

8.1.3.2 *Language in education*

It may seem as a given, especially since the UN universal declaration of human rights includes the freedom of discrimination on the basis of language, that everybody should have access to education in their mother tongue. It has, in fact, been recognized since no later than the 1950s, that people should receive education in their mother tongue "to as late a stage in education as possible" (UNESCO 1953:48). Studies have repeatedly shown that educational success benefits from instruction in the first language of the students (cf. Cummins 2001, 2009 with further references), which may seem like stating the obvious: after all, how is a child supposed to learn about, for example, trigonometry, chemical processes or world history if s/he is told about it in a language that s/he is not fluent in? The child would quite obviously be put at a disadvantage in that s/he not only has to process the new information (trigonometry, chemical processes or world history), but receives that information through the filter of a foreign language. The idea that a German child would be instructed in, say, Dutch, or that a Japanese child would be instructed in, say, Korean, would presumably not meet with much acceptance. Yet astonishingly, a great many people in the world do *not* receive even primary education in their mother tongue. One of the main reasons for this is that education is almost invariably done in recognized (standard) languages, meaning that stigmatized non-standard languages tend to be excluded as mediums of instruction. Another reason for this state of affairs is that – and this is especially true of former colonies – it is assumed that socioeconomic success hinges on the ability to be able to function in and access tertiary education in standard European languages. For this reason the vast majority of pidgin, creole and mixed languages are excluded as recognized languages for education.

There are two main types of situations for pidgin, creole and mixed languages. One is that the lexifier language is the societal standard norm, such as in Hawai'i (with Standard (American) English being the targeted norm) or in Cape Verde (where Portuguese is the targeted norm). The other is that the societal standard norm is not the lexifier, such as in the Netherlands Antilles (where Dutch is the standard, but the creole is Iberian-lexified) or in Suriname (where again Dutch is the standard, but the creoles are English-lexified). In those situations where the lexifier is the societal standard norm, the prevailing attitude is that the pidgin or creole is simply an inferior variety of the standard language and as thus does not deserve recognition. The pidgin or creole is typically blamed for poor educational results (cf. Eades 1999) and is generally viewed as an obstacle to advancement. In those situations where the societal norm is not the lexifier, there tends to be less resistance to the idea that people are essentially bilingual, which indirectly gives the pidgin or creole a slight recognition. Nevertheless, the general attitude is that a child will profit from early exposure to the officially recognized language of the country (i.e. the former colonizer's language), in order to make higher level and international education available to him or her. This again illustrates how prevailing language attitudes may form language policies, which ultimately has the effect of perpetuating those same attitudes.

In some areas of high linguistic diversity, such as Papua New Guinea, where more than 800 languages are spoken, or in Vanuatu, with its more than 130 languages, it is not practically feasible to produce qualified teachers and material in every single language. In these kinds of societies it may be more beneficial if education is done in one or a few languages, preferably in a language that as many as possible are familiar with – i.e. the *lingua franca*, which would mean the (extended) pidgin rather than the language of the former colonizers.

Again there are some notable exceptions to this pattern, of which only a few are mentioned here. With the slow recognition that creoles are languages in their own right, which in turn is gradually leading to programs of corpus planning, more and more countries are working towards integrating creoles as a medium of education, although we have yet to see a case where the stated language for all levels of education, including the tertiary, is a pidgin or creole.[131] In Papua New Guinea Tok Pisin is used in elementary school in some areas (Smith & Siegel 2013a). In Haiti education was opened up for Haitian Creole in 1979, but various controversies have led to an unsystematic practice (Fattier 2013). Seychelles Creole is the medium of instruction in primary schools in the Republic of the Seychelles (Michaelis & Rosalie 2013). In the Netherlands Antilles, Papiamentu is used in the preschool and primary school on Curaçao and Bonaire (Migge et al. 2010a). In the Nicaraguan Creole English speaking area of Nicaragua (on the Caribbean Coast) a program has now introduced the creole as the medium of education in primary schools; evaluations showed, unsurprisingly, that the children of these schools "develop their reading and writing skills much faster and more easily than an approach that uses English as the language of instruction" and that they also learn to read and write Spanish faster and more easily (Koskinen 2010: 164). For an overview of various projects and pilot studies involving pidgins and creoles in education, see Migge et al. (2010b) with further references.

131. Bislama is, in fact, sometimes used at university in Vanuatu, however, it is not the language of education for primary or secondary levels of education (for which English or French is used).

A crucial step in achieving recognition for a language as a medium of instruction in education is that there are materials in and about the language, not only directed towards linguist specialists, but also for the wider audience, and especially for the teachers and pupils themselves. This once again illustrates the interdependence between language policy and language planning: without materials in a standardized variety, the language cannot be used or taught in schools (and will not be seen as meaningful enough to be used or taught in schools), but without recognition of the value of the language, standardization and materials are less likely to be produced.

8.2 Language and culture

Culture is an essential part of any human society. It is the sum of everything that defines a given community. The pidginization or creolization of culture is as an important field as any other in the study of pidgins, creoles and mixed languages. It is a vast topic in its own right and, unfortunately, beyond the scope of this book to adequately address. This section will thus only briefly look at the linguistic expression of culture, namely literature, fundamental to any human society. For a brief, but very informative, overview on the study of cultural creolization, see Bartens (2013a: 80ff) packed with useful further references. For a discussion on the role of culture and identity in the development of pidgin and creole languages, see Jourdan (2008).

Literature is and always has been an essential part of any human culture. We tell stories, sing songs, think up riddles and lean on proverbs, all of which is part of our accumulated understanding of the world we live in. In pidgin, creole and mixed language societies, the speakers of the various input languages would all have been imbued in the literary traditions of their ancestor cultures. For each society that emerged as a consequence of intense linguistic contact, a unique blend of literary traditions is likely to also have emerged.

Literature can be both oral, that is, delivered and handed down through the spoken (or, in deaf cultures, signed) word, and it can be written. Each of these types will be briefly discussed below. For a very accessible overview of creole literature, see Adamson & van Rossem (1994), which this section relies heavily on. For a discussion on literature in the creole-speaking Caribbean, see, for example, Buzelin & Winer (2008).

8.2.1 Oral literature

Oral literature (sometimes also called **orature**) is any body of literature, such as poetry, songs, tales, plays, narratives and so on, that is preserved and transmitted orally (or through signs in deaf cultures). This is the kind of literature that would, for example, have flourished on the plantations, as is indicated in post-slavery sources as well as present-day cultural inheritance in Suriname (Adamson & van Rossem 1994:76). For a thorough discussion on the possible origins of the oral literature of various creole-speaking societies, with emphasis on the French-lexified area, see Chaudenson (2001).

8.2.1.1 *Songs and drama*

Song, dance and music are a vital component in any culture. It seems as if they played an essential role in the lives of the slaves, starting with the time on the slave ships. Music and dancing

> were considered an effective way to keep up the morale of slaves, as well as providing salutary daily exercise outside the holds. Groups of slaves were taken up on deck by turns, where a cask or a trunk served as a drum, and they could make music and dance in the open air before returning to the hold. (Chaudenson 2001:198)

In Suriname, for example, the **banya** song and dance was performed, in particular on special occasions, such as New Year's Day or other celebrations (Voorhoeve & Lichtveld 1975:16). These songs could be dramatized in the **du** form, where set characters would act out different roles in a kind of musical comedy:

> The dramatized *banya* is based on a simple story with fixed characters: Afrankeri, who defends high morals; Asringri, singing in honor of the band; Abenitanta or Momoi, criticising persons or events; Temeku, explaining the hidden allusions in the song; Aflaw, so shocked by the revelations that she faints; and Datra, the doctor who treats the fainting woman. The last two characters are the main actors, to whom a nurse is sometimes added. The former are primarily singers.
> (Voorhoeve & Lichtveld 1975:17)

There was also the **lobisingi** ('love songs'), which originated after the emancipation, typically dealing with female (homo- or heterosexual) jealousy, and which was performed to the rival or in front of her house. The Du companies were organized into societies where slaves and freedmen came together, which may have been perceived as a threat to the government and might be the reason why, in these societies, songs and performances were repeatedly forbidden (Voorhoeve & Lichtveld 1975). Plays and dances would start with one or several songs in honour of the earth mother, *Aysa* (also called *Maysa*, *Wanaysa*, *Gronmama*, *Tobosi*), where the participants would ask Aysa permission to perform. Then the songs inviting the drums were performed, before the performance culminated in the *krioro dron* 'Creole drum', where people had the opportunity to voice, in the form of songs, issues they were frustrated with. The following are examples of banyas; the first one is a complaint about a *basya* (black overseer) who sends a man to town so that he can court the man's wife, the second one is a more general lament of conditions.

Sranan (Creole (English-lexified): Suriname) banya songs

(171) a.[132]

Sani ben abi dyendyen, a ben sa loy.	Were it a bell, it would have rung out loud.
Sani ben abi dyendyen, a ben sa loy.	Were it a bell, it would have rung out loud.
Basya seni mi na pondo,	The overseer sent me to the pontoon,
trawan de a mi oso.	the other one (is in) my house.
Sani ben abi dyendyen, a ben sa loy.	Were it a bell, it would have rung out loud.

(Voorhoeve & Lichtveld 1975: 23f, with slight changes)

b.[133]

Te mi masra dede, nowan yobo wani bay mi.	When my master passed away, no white man wanted me.
Te mi masra dede, nowan yobo wani bay mi.	When my master passed away, no white man wanted me.
Na bakabaka, tanbun masra kon bay mi.	A bad one later did.
Now dede wanwan kan bay mi.	Now death alone wants me.

(Voorhoeve & Lichtveld 1975: 29)

New banya songs are no longer composed, but many of the songs are still sung today (Adamson & van Rossem 1994). The above songs were recorded between 1957 and 1961 (Voorhoeve & Lichtveld 1975: 20).

Narrative songs were not only found in the Caribbean, but also in the creole-speaking societies in the Indian Ocean (Chaudenson 2001, Jackson 1990). Pidgin and creole songs are still widely composed, irrespective of whether the language in question enjoys high prestige or is stigmatized in the respective societies. In Nigeria, for example, where Nigerian Pidgin is widely used as a *lingua franca*, but is still highly stigmatized, Nigerian Pidgin songs have been performed and recorded at least since

132. The glossing is as follows:

sani ben abi dyendyen, a ben sa loy
thing PST have bell, 3SG PST FUT ring
basya seni mi na pondo
overseer send 1SG LOC pontoon [a boat for taking goods from the plantation to town]
trawan de a mi osu
the.other.one IPFV 3SG 1SG house

133. The glossing is as follows:

te mi masra dede, nowan yobo wani bay mi
when 1SG master die, nobody white.man want buy 1SG
na bakabaka, tanbun masra kon bay mi
LOC afterwards good.thing master come buy 1SG
now dede wanwan kan bay mi
now death only can buy 1SG

1965 (Sebastian Schmidt, p.c.). And on Corn Island in Nicaragua, for example, Miskitu children's songs and games mirror the multilingual environment of the children's everyday communication: learning not only Miskitu, but also Spanish and Nicaraguan Creole English (see Minks 2013 for examples and further references).

8.2.1.2 *Folktales*

Storytelling is another essential component of human culture and folktales can be found in all corners of the world. Very often the stories are moral or educational. The slave societies saw storytelling on the plantations that traces its roots to the storytelling traditions in West Africa. In many former plantation societies very similar stories can be found. For instance, a very common story seems to be the various forms of the story of *The Hare and the King's Pond*, where a rabbit or hare (*Brer Rabbit*) drinks water from the King's well and then befriends the various guards posted by the King (Chaudenson 2001). An exceptionally common type of educational tale is the *Anansistory*, where the trickster Anansi (a spider), who is also the cunning protagonist in Akan stories in present-day Ghana, outwits various adversaries. Anansi can be found throughout the Caribbean (as *Anancy*, *Nanzi*, *Anansi*, *Hanansi*, and so on) as well as in the Unites States (as *An' Nancy*, *Aunt Nancy*, *Ann Nancy*, and so on) and remains a spider, as the Akan original – Aunt Nancy, for example, is half woman and half spider, with seven arms and no hands (Bascom 1992: 86). Stories featuring the shrewd hare/rabbit and spider can be found in a number of West African cultures; for a detailed comparison of African and Caribbean/US American folktales, see, for example, Bascom (1992). For an accessible collection of Anansi stories, see, for example, Ishmael (2010).

8.2.1.3 *Riddles and proverbs*

Yet another common type of oral narrative, which can also be found in all human cultures, is the riddle and the proverb.[134] The **riddle** is an amusing word game that displays conventional wisdom. Again there seem to be similarities between the plantation societies, both those in the Caribbean and those in the Indian Ocean, and West Africa (Adamson & van Rossem 1994: 78). One example is the riddle of water standing up:

134. Metaphorical and "hidden" meanings in language, such as idiomatic expressions, proverbs and riddles, are often seen as a late development of a mature and complex language (see, e.g. Hurford 2012a, 2012b). The existence of such linguistic devices in creoles is thus a reason for not *a priori* treating creole languages as 'simpler' than non-creoles.

(172) **Jamaica**

a. *My father have a well; it have neither top nor bottom, yet it hold water.*
Water grow.
Water stan' up. (Answer: *Sugar cane*; Beckwith 1924: 190, 200)

Martinique

b. *De l'eau douboutde? Canne à sucre.* (Chaudenson 2001: 280)
('Upright water? Sugar cane.')

Mauritius

c. *Dileau diboute? Canne.* (Baissac 1887: 392)
('Upright water? Sugar cane.')

Réunion

d. *Delo debout? Canne à sucre.* (Chaudenson 2001: 280)
('Upright water? Sugar cane.')

The **proverb** is essentially a saying that expresses common sense world wisdom. Notice the similarity between the Negerhollands and Martinican Creole proverbs:

(173) **Negerhollands**

a. Makakku weet wa fo een boom fo klemm, am no
Makakku know what for ART tree COMP climb 3SG NEG
klemm stakkelboom.
climb thorn.tree
'Makakku (Monkey) knows what kind of tree to climb, he does not climb a thorn tree.' (Adamson & van Rossem 1994: 79 citing Pontoppidan 1881)

Martinican Creole

b. Macaque save qui bots il monté; il pas monté zaurangé.
Macaque know REL tree 3SG climb 3SG NEG climb orange.tree
'Monkey knows which tree he climbs, he does not climb the orange tree.'[135]
(Hearn 1885: 24)

In Jamaica proverbs are usually spoken by Anansi (Adamson & van Rossem 1994: 79).

8.2.2 Written literature

Written literature is obviously only produced once a society has a script and acquires a tradition of writing. For societies where pidgins, creoles and mixed languages are spoken, the written tradition has, for the vast majority, been that of the colonizers. In other words, while we are now slowly seeing a change in attitudes towards languages of education, until now schooling has been done in some other language than the

135. The orange tree has thorns.

respective pidgin, creole or mixed language of the community. This also means that people have been schooled in the literary traditions of the former colonizers, which means that their literary vocabulary is rooted in the language of the colonizers rather than in that of the community. This has in turn served to perpetuate the attitude of viewing pidgins, creoles and mixed languages as inferior and inadequate for higher level cultural expressions. Nevertheless, authors have used their pidgin, creole or mixed language in literature for decades, if not centuries. Novels, drama and poetry, wholly or partly in the language of the community, might not reach as wide an audience as they would in the language of the colonizers, but they not only speak to and for the community itself, they also help establish the unique voice that each language has and give that voice a place in the literary world. Translations into the pidgin, creole or mixed language of the society also not only brings classics to the community, but also helps establish the literary vocabulary of the community.

8.2.2.1 *Prose, plays and poetry*

While it is still most common, overall, that authors write in the language of education of the society, which in pidgin, creole and mixed language societies typically means the language of the former colonizer, novelists have been using pidgins, creoles and mixed languages for decades. Very typical is to have the narration in the standard language, but the dialogue in the pidgin, creole or mixed language. To use different language varieties to give voices to different characters is a well known literary device; the totality of the character's identity and position is conveyed through his or her voice.[136] However, works have also been published that are wholly in the pidgin, creole or mixed language. In Hawai'i, for example, the Bamboo Ridge Press has been publishing works wholly or partly in the creole, such as the work of Darrell H. Y. Lum. An example of a piece which combines the standard with the creole is *Victor* (Lum 1990: 19ff):

> It was almost ten o'clock before he woke. The morning sky through the sliding glass doors was cloudless. Pure, deep blue. Victor closed his eyes and remembered the noises of the night before. (…)
>
> After one wrong turn, he found the field. A cane company truck was pulled up beside the tractor. Two Filipino workers were pressing a wadded-up tee-shirt against the driver's right eye.
>
> "Hey, what happened?" Victor asked.
>
> "Cane stalk poke his eye," one of them said. "Danger, you know, work by da sugar cane. Da leaf tip sharp. Gotta wear goggles like us when you work by da cane."
>
> (Lum 1990: 22ff)

136. The way the pidgin, creole or mixed language is represented orthographically is, until the language has been standardized, left to the author. Representations may thus differ from author to author and even from piece to piece by the same author.

In this piece the narrative is in Standard English (as can be seen by, for instance, the consistent plural marking, verbal inflection and copula), but the language of the cane worker is the creole (as can be seen from the invariant form of both the verbs and nouns). Notice that the spelling is still Standard English (*stalk*, *sharp*), except for the article *da* 'the'. Another piece by the same author in the same anthology, *J'like Ten Thousand* (Lum 1990: 99ff), is wholly in the creole:

> My fahdah stay so tight, so pa-ke. He no like buy firecracker, man. He only buy one five hundred pack fo burn at New Year's time. Ho man, everybody get da thousands or da five thousand strings or even da ten thousand strings, but Daddy, he no like buy nutting fo me. He only say, "Jes throw away money dat. One boom and pau. All dat money go up in smoke. And da ting only make rubbish." He so tight.
>
> (Lum 1990: 99)

In Hawai'i, where the creole is still highly stigmatized, authors such as Edward Sakamoto, Lois-Ann Yamanaka, Joe Balaz and many others have been undeterred in using the creole for their prose, poetry or plays. In the Cape Verde Islands, writers started using the creole for their work as early as in the 1930s. By now there is a large body of work in Cape Verdean Creole, not the least the work produced by the authors of the Association of Cape Verdean Writers (Baptista 2010: 285). In the Caribbean authors have been using the creole languages for decades (cf. Buzelin & Winer 2008, Dance 1986).[137] In Nigeria the pidgin is used both in oral and written literature. Famously, the Onitsha Market Literature of the 1950s and 1960s comprised all sorts of written literature produced in the market town of Onitsha. The books and pamphlets include stories, plays, moral guidance and advice, and so on. The Onitsha Market Literature is a unique source in many ways, as it was written by and for the local community. Most of the literature is written in Nigerian English, but there are also instances of pidgin.[138]

137. For a very detailed overview of the history of literature in the Caribbean, see the chapters in Arnold et al. (1994, 2001) and Arnold (1997), discussing literature in the entire Caribbean region and the cross-cultural connections to Europe, Africa and the Americas.

138. The Spencer Research Library at the University of Kansas holds a large collection of Onitsha Market Literature, much of which has been digitized and made available online on their site *Onitsha Market Literature* (http://onitsha.diglib.ku.edu/index.htm, accessed 10 February 2015), which also contains general information and a number of helpful links for further research. See also the collection by Thometz (2001).

8.2.2.2 *Translations*

Translations of works in other languages also help enrich a society's literary landscape in various ways. By now a number of literary classics have been translated into different creole languages. Furthermore, religious literature, usually one of the first genres to be translated into a nonstandard language variety, has been translated into pidgin and creole languages for many centuries, especially the Bible.

Almost from the very beginning of contact, missionary activity accompanied the European expansion, and missionaries of various denominations engaged in producing Christian texts into the vernaculars they encountered, including pidgin and creole languages. With the settlement by Europeans on the east Coast of present-day USA, for example, Martin Luther's Small Catechism was translated into Pidgin Delaware (Campanius 1696). The Moravian missionaries translated Christian texts into the vernaculars they encountered in, for example, Suriname and the (at the time) Danish Antilles, i.e. Sranan (by Christian L. Schumann in 1778) and Negerhollands (by Jochum Magens in 1770) respectively, and at the same time also provided descriptions of the languages. An important aspect of these early bible translations and descriptions is that they were done by speakers of the colonial language, not speakers of the pidgin or creole language. Bible translations are still intensively produced, but nowadays they are usually done in teams which include native speakers and experts of the language in question.[139]

There is also a large body of translations of other literary works into pidgin and creole languages. Literature in the language of the colonizer is not seldom translated into the pidgins or creoles of the former colonies, for instance French classics into various French-lexified creoles and English classics into various English-lexified creoles. Works by Shakespeare have, for example, been translated into Krio (such as *Julius Ceasar* into *Juliohs Siza* and *As You Like It* into *Udat Di Kiap Fit*). Typically these kinds of translations are done by authors who are themselves native or at least very proficient speakers of the pidgin or creole languages.

8.2.3 Mass media

The more stigmatized a language or language variety is, the less it will be used in mass media, except for humorous purposes. This is very often the case with pidgins and creoles, where the pidgin or creole is often used only for cartoons and in caricatures, for advertisements, or for other kinds of less serious and jocular kinds of content.

139. For those readers interested in Bible translations into different languages, WorldBibles has provided digitized versions of some 4000 languages, including pidgins and creoles, available at http://worldbibles.org/search_languages/eng (accessed 10 February 2015).

Daytime drama on radio and TV may be in the pidgin or creole language of the society, but such items as news broadcasts, political debates, investigative reporting, and so on, are typically reserved for the standard language of the society. In those societies where the pidgin or creole does have official recognition, the language will also be widely found in the media, such as Tok Pisin in Papua New Guinea. This does not mean that only official languages are recognized enough to be used in media (and in schools). Nagamese, for example, spoken in the far north-eastern Indian state of Nagaland, where English is the state official language, is widely used in both media and as a language of instruction in schools.

However, with the attitudes slowly changing towards pidgin and creole languages, gradually leading to the recognition that these are languages in their own right, more and more countries are using the pidgin or creole of their society in media. Papiamentu, for example, enjoys high prestige nowadays and is widely found in all kind of public discourse, including mass media (Maurer 2013c). Krio is steadily gaining recognition and is widely used in media and "is one of the languages in which the national news is read" (Finney 2013a: 158). Sranan is nowadays common in the media in Suriname (Winford & Plag 2013), as is Seychelles Creole in the Republic of the Seychelles (Michaelis & Rosalie 2013) and Lingala in DR Congo (Meeuwis 2013a). There are bilingual web and media productions in Gullah and English in the USA (Klein 2013a). Trinidad English Creole is gaining acceptance in the media (Mühleisen 2013a), as is Cape Verdean Creole (Lang 2013a).

8.3 Snapshots

A language does not need be listed as a *de jure* official language of a society to enjoy widespread use and acceptance. Nagamese is not the official language of Nagaland, yet is used as a *lingua franca* by almost the entire population, including in official domains such as political discourse, news broadcasts and education.

Papiamentu is an example of a creole that enjoys high acceptance, has recently been made an official language and is increasingly taught in schools. It has a long history of literature, both oral and written. It is also an example of the complexities involved in the standardization process, which has led to two orthographic systems, one etymologically based and one phonologically based.

Krio is an example of a majority language that does not enjoy official recognition and is still stigmatized as an inferior variety of the lexifier language, despite widespread use, also in official discourse and broadcasting, and even inclusion as a subject in education. However, attitudes are changing and standardization efforts are underway.

8.3.1 Nagamese: An Assamese-lexified extended pidgin (pidgincreole) in South Asia[140]

8.3.1.1 *A brief background sketch of Nagamese*

Nagamese (also called *Pidgin Naga, Naga Pidgin, Naga-Assamese, Naga Creole Assamese, Bodo* and *Kachari Bengali* by scholars) is spoken as a *lingua franca* by most of the nearly 2 million inhabitants in the far north-eastern Indian state of Nagaland (formerly known as the Naga Hill District), on the border to Myanmar. It is called *Nagamese* by the speakers themselves. In and around the commercial centre of Dimapur the language has a growing population of Nagamese native speakers, especially among the ethnic Bodo Kacharis (Bhattacharjya 2001).

The present-day Nagaland, a mountainous and largely inaccessible area, is home to 23 different Naga ethno-linguistic groups, whose languages, which are part of the Tibeto-Burman sub-family, are all mutually unintelligible. Several non-Naga groups also inhabit the area, whose languages (also mutually unintelligible) belong to a different branch of the Tibeto-Burman languages. These are the indigenous groups that the Ahom rulers, belonging to the ethno-linguistic Tai group, encountered when they invaded and set up their Ahom Kingdom; specifically the Bodo Kacharis, a non-Naga indigenous group, seem to have been prominent and "are believed to have had a kingdom in the Assam valley for about 600 years prior to the advent of the Ahoms in 1228" (Bhattacharjya 2001: 47) and who had developed their own irrigation methods for rice cultivation (Guha 1983).

The Ahom kingdom gradually expanded through warfare or negotiations with the indigenous groups of the area. From the late 14th century on, Hindu Brahminic influence on the Ahom rulers increased (Guha 1983), coinciding with territorial expansion into Hinduized areas. By the mid-16th century the "Assamese-speaking Hindu subjects were now more numerous than the Ahoms themselves" (Guha 1983: 19) and the rulers started assuming Assamese titles and customs. The Assamese language gradually gained in usage, both at the court and outside, and came to be used alongside Tai before a complete shift to Assamese occurred after a period of Tai-Assamese bilingualism.[141] The Indo-European Assamese thus became the main vehicle of communication of the kingdom.

The area has seen rife ethnic conflict throughout its history, both among the different Naga tribes and among Naga and non-Naga ethnic groups. While there is hardly any information about the dealings of the various ethnic groups prior to the Ahom kingdom, it seems likely that there had been early contact of different kinds (both hostile and friendly) between Naga and non-Naga people, possibly including Assamese-speaking groups. During the Ahom kingdom there was both hostile contact and trade between the kingdom and the surrounding peoples

140. This section relies predominantly on Bhattacharjya (2001).

141. Literate Ahoms "retained the Tai language and script well until the end of the 17th century" (Guha 1983: 9) and some 30 years ago there were still a few priests who retained knowledge of the language (*ibid*).

(Bhattacharjya 2001, Sreedhar 1985). Continued conflict with the Bodo Kacharis eventually led to the invasion of Burmese rulers in the early 1800s, and in 1826 the British East India troops occupied the area, which essentially marked the end of the Ahom kingdom.

The British occupation was administered by Assam military and police forces. Civil servants were typically recruited from the valley areas, i.e. the Assamese speaking areas (Boruah 1993: 7). Furthermore, during the British occupation, Assamese was introduced as the medium of instruction in schools (*ibid*). This administrative use of Assamese, coupled with the constant trade and other dealings between the hill peoples and those from the valleys, and the fact of the high linguistic diversity, furthered the propagation of Assamese as a *lingua franca*. The first known potential reference to Nagamese is in the diary of Lt. Bigges from 1841, who mentions meeting Naga people coming down from the hills, many of which knew Assamese (Sreedhar 1985: 12). The earliest known record of the language can be found in Hutton (1921), who mentions "the 'pigeon' Assamese, which forms the lingua franca of the Naga Hills, and through the medium of which most of the information necessary for this monograph has been collected" (Hutton 1921: 327).

Although the policy in India is to have education in the mother tongue of the pupils and to introduce Hindi and English as second languages, this is not a pragmatic solution in Nagaland. The official language, English, chosen as a unifying measure due to the continued ethnic strife, is spoken only by a very small percentage of the population. The result is that both teachers and pupils have to function in an unfamiliar language, which has led to a *de facto* use of Nagamese in schools, as that is a language widely used by the absolute majority of the population (if not the whole population). Efforts of standardization with the aim of producing educational material was initiated by M.V. Sreedhar (e.g. 1976, 1985). As part of the standardization process, Sreedhar consulted with Naga leaders on the script to use for the codification. The Roman script was favoured over Devanagari, Assam or Bengali scripts (Bhattacharjya 2001: 13), as that was already widely familiar through various Christian texts – the vast majority of the population was Christianized during British rule – and was felt to be the most neutral option (Bhattacharjya 2001).

At present Nagamese is extensively used throughout the state in both official discourse, schools and mass media. The All India Radio Station broadcasts in Nagamese, and government affairs are widely communicated in Nagamese (Bhattacharjya 2001, Boruah 1993). The descendants of those Bodo Kacharis who did not flee up in the hills during the conflicts with the Ahom kingdom, but who stayed in the valley, speak Nagamese as their mother tongue. For this community the language has thus become a creole.

8.3.1.2 *A short linguistic sketch of Nagamese*

The orthography in this section follows that suggested by M.V. Sreedhar, which follows a phonological principle. There is considerable variation in Nagamese, depending on the regional and ethno-linguistic origin of the speakers; this section relies mainly on the data presented in Bhattacharjya (2001), which is primarily based on the language variety around the more urban areas in the south and could be argued to represent a more acrolectal variety than what is found in the central and northern regions of Nagaland.

There are 26 consonants, /p, b, p^h, b^h, m, w, t, d, t^h, d^h, n, s, z, l, r, ʧ, ʧ^h, ʤ, ʤ^h, j, k, g, ŋ, k^h, g^h, h/. The voiced stops and affricates are not relevant phonemes in mesolectal and basilectal speech. There are six vowels, /i, e, ɑ, o, ɔ, u/.[142] There are no nasal vowels. Both /o/ and /ɔ/ are represented by the grapheme <o>. The graphemes <c, ch, j, jh, y, ng> represent /ʧ, ʧ^h, ʤ, ʤ^h, j, ŋ/ respectively. Tone is not a relevant feature (though all Naga languages have 3–5 contrastive tones). Syllables may be complex with clusters of up to two consonants both in the onset and coda. Words can have up to four syllables, though tetrasyllabic words are few and tend to be either loans or compounds.

There is extensive affixation, with both nominal and verbal grammatical markers expressed syntactically.

Generic noun phrases remain unmarked:

(174) kuta to kotha-man-ia jontu ekta ase
dog FOC order-obey-NMLZ animal one be
'The dog is an obedient animal.'/'Dogs are obedient animals.' (Bhattacharjya 2001: 221)

Plurality is indicated with *-khan* (predominantly used with pronouns, but also with nouns) or *-bilak* (predominantly used with nouns), although plural marking is optional if the clause contains a quantifier:

(175) a. moy to modu bal-pa-y
1SG FOC wine like-get-PRES
'I like wine.'

b. moy-khan to dud no-kha-y
1-PL FOC milk NEG-drink-PRES
'We don't drink milk.'

c. bosa-bilak ketia ahi-se?
child-PL when come-PST
'When did the children arrive?'

d. Kohima-te Dilli pora sipai(-bilak) kisuman ahi-se
Kohima-LOC Delhi SRC soldier-PL some come-PST
'Some soldiers from Delhi arrived in Kohima.' (Bhattacharjya 2001: 227f)

Natural gender is indicated analytically with the words *mota* 'male' and *maiki* 'female' as in *mota kukura* 'cock' (male chicken) and *maiki kukura* 'hen' (female chicken) (Boruah 1993: 54). Under influence from Hindi, grammatical gender is gradually appearing, especially with Hindi words and expressions (Bhattacharjya 2001: 232).

There is an elaborate case system, with seven cases, where the case markers are either suffixed or postposed to the noun. The nominative and accusative may remain unmarked.[143]

142. Sreedhar (1985) lists 21 consonants, /p, b, p^h, m, w, t, d, n, s, t^h, l, c, j, c^h, ʃ, k, g, ŋ, k^h, h, j/, and six vowels, /i, e, ɑ, ə, o, u/.

143. Boruah (1993) differentiates between an ACC *-ke* and a DAT *-loi/le* while Sreedhar (1985) differentiates between an ACC *-k* and a DAT *-ke*. However, the speakers in Bhattacharjya's (2001) corpus consistently used *-ke* with DAT while ACC remained unmarked.

NOMinative	∅, *-(h)e*, *-ne*
ACCusative	∅
DATive	*-ke*
GENitive	*(-r)*, *laga*
LOCative	*-te*
SOURCe	*(-t)*, *(-r)*, *pora*
INSTRumental	*logote*

There is also a postposed 'SOCiative' marker, *logot* which indicates accompaniment and might originate from the instrumental marker:

(176) moy suali logot ja-yse
1SG girl SOC go-PST
'I went with the girl.' (Sreedhar 1985:104)

The indefinite article is identical with the numeral 'one'. There is a definite article suffix *-tu*.

(177) a. moi tai nimite kitab ekta kini di-se
1SG 3SG for book one buy give-PST
'I have bought a book for him/her.'
b. bosa-tu gos pora gir-ise
child-DEF tree from fall-PST
'The child fell off the tree.' (Bhattacharjya 2007:239, 248)

There are two demonstratives, *itu* 'this' and *otu* 'that'. The pronominal system has three persons and two numbers. The third person is differentiated by animacy but not gender. The plural is formed by adding the *-khan* to the singular forms.

	SINGULAR	PLURAL
1	*moy*	*moykhan*
2	*apuni*	*apunikhan*
3 ANIM	*tai*	*taikhan*
3 INANIM	*itu*	*itukhan*

Note that the third person singular inanimate is identical with the proximate demonstrative. Adjectives remain invariant and are typically postposed to the noun. There is an equative *nisina* 'like', a comparative *kori/koi* 'than' and a superlative *sob* 'all' + *koi/se* 'than':

(178) a. tai to Moa nisina mosto ase de
3SG FOC PN like stout be PCL
'S/he is as stout as Moa.'
b. Numingla Senti koi lomba ase
PN PN than tall be
'Numingla is taller than Senti.'
c. Krishna klas-te sob koi lamba chukri ase
PN class-LOC all than tall girl be
'Krishna is the tallest girl in class.' (Bhattacharjya 2001:226f)

Verbs are obligatorily inflected for tense, mood and aspect which may combine freely. There is no person marking on the verb. There are two tense markers, *-y* for present (cf. Example (175a, b)) and *-(i/y)se* for past (cf. Examples (175c, d), (176), (177)). There is a perfective marker *-i* (Example (184)), a present progressive marker *-iase/-yase* and a past progressive *-iasile*.

(179) a. Moa cha kha-iase
PN tea eat-PRES.PROG
'Moa is having tea'
b. moy to hu-iasile
1SG FOC sleep-PST.PROG
'I was sleeping.' (Bhattacharjya 2001: 206f)

There is an irrealis marker *-(i)bo*.

(180) a. bat bisi no-kha-bi nohoyle apuni bisi mosto ho-bo
rice much NEG-eat-IMP otherwise 2SG much fat be-IRR
'Don't eat too much rice, or you will become too fat.'
b. pani giri-bo hobola
water fall-IRR seems
'It might rain.' (Bhattacharjya 2001: 207, 212)

There is a conditional *–le*, a potential *pare* 'can' and an obligation/necessity marker *lage* 'need'.

The word order is typically subject-object-verb. There are two negators, the prefix *no-*, which occurs with all nonpast verb phrases, and *nai*, which functions as a negative past or as a negative existential:

(181) a. judi moi no-ja-yle tai n-ahi-bo
if 1SG NEG-go-COND 3SG NEG-come-IRR
'If I don't go, he won't come.' (Bhattacharjya 2007: 244)
b. moy ja nai
1SG go NEG.PST
'I did not go.' (Sreedhar 1985: 151)
c. tai to gor-te nai
3SG FOC house-LOC NEG
'S/he is not home.' (Bhattacharjya 2001: 188)

Polar questions are formed with the tag *niki* (essentially negative+'what') and content questions with a question word *in situ*. There is no change in word order:

(182) a. tai chuti time-te kam kor-i thak-e
3SG holiday time-LOC work do-PTCP remain-PRES
'S/he usually works during the holidays.'
b. tai chuti time-te ki kor-i thak-e?
3SG holiday time-LOC what do-PTCP remain-PRES
'What does s/he usually do during the holidays?'
c. tai chuti time-te kam kor-i niki?
3SG holiday time-LOC work do-PTCP Q
'Does s/he usually work during the holidays?' (Bhattacharjya 2001: 190)

There is an obligatory copula *ase* (cf. Examples (174), (178)) which also denotes the existential, as well as possession:

(183) a. Darjiling-te bisi cha-bagisa ase
D-LOC much tea-garden EXIST
'There are many tea gardens in Darjeeling.' (Bhattacharjya 2007: 247)

b. Dimapur-te to moy laga gor ekta ase
Dimapur-LOC FOC 1SG GEN house one EXIST
'I have a house in Dimapur.' (Bhattacharjya 2001: 214)

Serial verb constructions are most commonly used with motion verbs or the verb 'give' (Example (177a)). Constructions with two verbs are very common, though there are also constructions involving more:

(184) tai to tai laga maiki dusra manu logote sadi hui jai-se dekh-i kena
3SG FOC 3SG GEN girl another man with marriage be go-PST see-PFV CONJ
mori-ja-bole sesta-kori-se
die-go-COMP try-do-PST
'Having discovered that his girlfriend had been married off to another man, he tried to commit suicide.' (Bhattacharjya 2001: 215)

Complementation may be overtly marked or indicated through intonation (with a pause in the speech). Relative clauses are typically avoided, though there are the relativizers *jo/ji/kun*. Coordination is overtly marked with such conjunctions as *aru* 'and', *kintu* 'but', and *nahole* 'or'. There are several postpositions.

8.3.1.3 *Short text*

(From Bhattacharjya 2001: 230f, an excerpt from the All India Radio Kohima News on 6 December 1994.)

BJP-he jana-yse ah-ia esembly elekshon-bilak nimite itu laga asol bichar-bilak
BJP-NOM inform-PST come-PTCP assembly election-PL for this GEN main concern-PL

ho-yse: desh laga sikiurity, hadaron manu-khan jibon-te integriti-ke an-i di-a
be-PST country GEN security common man-PL life-LOC integrity-DAT bring-PFV give-COMP

aru sob-dike unoti kor-i lu-a. Bomby-te khobor manu logote kotha ko-a
and all-sides progress do-PFV take-COMP Bombay-LOC news man with talk say-NMLZ

taim-te parti laga chif Sri L.K. Advani-he jana-yse, ikonomik polisi khetro-te BJP-he
time-LOC party GEN chief Mr. PN-NOM inform-PST economic policy ground-LOC BJP-NOM

diregulason aru dilaisensing-ke mani-thak-e; hoylebi globaization-ke itu-he kara
deregulation and delicensing-DAT obey-remain-PRES however globalization-DAT this-NOM straight

pora birodh kor-e
SRC oppose do-PRES

'The BJP (Bharatiya Janata Party) has declared that their main issues in the upcoming elections will be the security of the country, integration, and development in all aspects of people's lives. While talking to the reporters in Bombay, the party chief, Mr. L. K. Advani, said that as far as the economic policy is concerned, while BJP accept deregulation and delicensing, it is strongly opposed to globalization.'

8.3.1.4 *Some sources of data*

Bhattacharjya (2001) gives numerous glossed and translated examples, long glossed and translated transcriptions of All India Radio Kohima News items and excerpts from films, as well as naturalistic and elicited speech. Sreedhar (1985) gives a number of examples as well as several pages of transcribed folktales, including the Assamese versions of the tales. There are also examples and some pages of text in Boruah (1993). Radio882 (Trans World Radio – India) is a Christian radio station, where a large number of broadcasts in Nagamese are available for download (http://radio882.com/download_nagamese.htm, accessed 10 February 2015).

8.3.2 Papiamentu: An Iberian-lexified creole in the Caribbean[144]

8.3.2.1 *A brief background sketch of Papiamentu*

Papiamentu is spoken by about 270,000 people in the former Netherlands Leeward Antilles consisting of the islands of Aruba, Bonaire and Curaçao (the so-called ABC islands). Of these the majority, some 120,000, live on Curaçao, while about 60,000 live on Aruba and about 10,000 on Bonaire. There is a large diaspora community, mainly in the Netherlands, but also in the USA, Belgium and other Caribbean states. The language is called *Papiamentu* by the Bonaire and Curaçao speakers and *Papiamento* by the Aruba speakers.

The Caribbean ABC islands were discovered and occupied by the Spanish in 1499, but were considered useless due to the lack of precious metals. When the Dutch West Indian Company took Curaçao in 1634 and Aruba and Bonaire in 1636, the remaining Spanish and most of the Amerindian population left for Venezuela, although some Amerindians would later return to Aruba and Bonaire "where they constituted the majority (or at least an important part) of the island's population until the end of the eighteenth century" (Maurer 2013c: 163). Shortly thereafter, in 1637, the Dutch West Indian Company captured the Portuguese trading centre of Elmina in present-day Ghana, which would mark the launch of the large-scale Dutch slave trade (Postma 1990: 13).

Curaçao was initially only a naval base used for its strategic location in the Dutch-Spanish conflicts. However, with the rise of plantation economies, especially sugar plantations, the need for slave labour increased and Curaçao became the main slave trading centre in the Americas. Most of the slaves that arrived in Curaçao were thus resold and transported to other locations in the Caribbean or the American mainland. However, with the population on Curaçao growing, the number of slaves who stayed on the island also grew (Jacobs 2012).

When the Dutch lost their Brazilian holdings to the Portuguese in 1654, the Portuguese and Spanish speaking Sephardic Jews who had been farming (sugar, among other things) in Dutch Brazil, had to leave. Many were offered attractive contracts for Curaçao as an effort to make use of their farming experiences.

It seems that Papiamentu emerged on Curaçao between 1650 and 1700, i.e. during the first period of the large-scale slave trade. Early records indicate that it may already have been

144. This section is based primarily on Kouwenberg & Ramos-Michel (2007) and Maurer (2013c). I am very grateful to Bart Jacobs for his helpful comments on this snapshot.

established as one of the main languages on the island by the turn of the 18th century (Jacobs 2012:15). It subsequently spread to the other two islands.

The origin of the slaves, and thus the possible substrate languages or other influences, is a matter of debate. Due to the bankruptcy of the first Dutch West Indian Company in 1674 most of the archives and records were lost or destroyed (Jacobs 2012:280). It is important, however, to notice that the particular section ('Chamber') of the Dutch West India Company that was in charge of the Caribbean ABC Islands, was also in charge of the trading centres of the Petit Côte in the Upper Guinea until the Dutch were driven out of the Senegambia region by the French in 1677.[145] Furthermore, the Dutch also had trading posts in Cacheu (in northern Guinea-Bissau). A Portuguese-lexified contact language was already established in these regions at the time. This coincides with the peak of the slave trade on Curaçao. There was a considerable collaboration between the Dutch West India Company and Sephardic Jews in the Senegambia region (Jacobs 2012). It may thus be that the slaves brought to Curaçao during the early, peak, trade phase spoke the languages of the Senegambia region, including the wide-spread Portuguese-lexified contact language which would later evolve into the Cape Verdean Creole varieties as well as Guinea Bissau Kriyol and Casamancese. This in turn may explain the similarities between Papiamentu and those languages (as shown by, for example, Jacobs 2012).

For the second Dutch West India Company the records survive and show that by then, i.e. from 1674 on, most of the slaves were shipped from the Congo-Angola and Benin-Togo areas (Postma 1990). The slave trade ended towards the end of the 18th century with the last slave ship arriving in 1778.

Papiamentu has been an official language of the Netherlands Antilles since 2007 and enjoys high prestige. It is used extensively in media and in political discourse, and is taught as a subject in schools. In some private schools in Curaçao it is the medium of instruction. It has been used in print media since the first half of the 19th century (Maurer 2013c:166), initially mainly for religious texts but subsequently also in newspapers as well as for prose and poetry.

While there are phonological and lexical differences between the varieties of the different islands, the dialects are mutually intelligible. There is also a certain amount of variety between urban and rural areas, especially on Curaçao. Various efforts to standardize Papiamentu have led to two orthographic systems: a phonologically based one in Curaçao and Bonaire and an etymologically based (Spanish derived) one in Aruba.

8.3.2.2 *A short linguistic sketch of Papiamentu*

Unless otherwise specified, the examples in this section are given in the Curaçaoan orthography.

There are 25 consonants, /p, b, m, w, f, v, t, d, n, r, s, z, ɲ, ʃ, ʒ, ʧ, ʤ, l, j, j̃, k, g, ŋ, x, h/, and ten vowels, /i, y, e, ø, ɛ, ə, a, ɔ, o, u/, which tend to be nasalized before nasal consonants. Notice that /j̃/ represents a nasal glide which occasionally has /ɲ/ as an allophone word-initially; /ŋ/

145. The Petit Côte covers an area in present-day Senegal stretching roughly from Dakar in the north to the Saloum Delta in the south.

occurs as an allophone to /n/ before velar consonants. The official orthography differs from the IPA as follows:

OFFICIAL ORTHOGRAPHY	IPA
è	ɛ
ò	ɔ
ü	y
ù	ø
sh	ʃ
zj	ʒ
ch	ʧ
dj	ʤ
y, i	j
ñ	j̃
g	x

Stress and tone are phonemic; there are two tones, high (´) and low (`), which can be combined with stress as follows: ˈHL, ˈLH and LˈH (cf. /ˈármà/ 'weapon' vs. /ˈàrmá/ 'to arm' vs. /àrˈmá/ 'armed'; Maurer 2013c: 167). Most nouns have a HL tone while most verbs an LH, which means that tone is grammatical in that it may distinguish word class (cf. /ˈbjáhà/ 'trip' vs. /ˈbjàhá/ 'to travel'; Maurer 2013c: 167).

The morphology is almost exclusively analytic, though the plural marker may be considered a suffix on the noun (the exact morphological status of the plural marker is debated) and nominalization can be formed with *-mentu* and *-dó* (Bart Jacobs, p.c.). There is reduplication, which typically indicates distribution or iteration (Kouwenberg & Murray 1994).

Nouns are invariable. Gender is not relevant, though natural gender may be distinguished with *muhé* 'woman' / *hòmber* 'man' for humans (as in *yu muhé* 'daughter' (lit. 'child female') / *yu hòmber* 'son' (lit. 'child male')) and *machu* 'male' / *muhé* for non-humans (as in *un buriku machu* 'a male donkey' / *un buriku muhé* 'a female donkey') (Maurer 2013c: 167f). Case is not relevant.

Bare nouns typically indicate generic reference, though may also refer to a singular entity in a generic type of chore:

(185) a. kachó tin kuater pia
dog have four leg
'Dogs have four legs.' (Maurer 2013c: 168)

b. ainda mi mester kumpra frishidèr
still 1SG must buy fridge
'I still need to buy a fridge.' (Kouwenberg & Ramos-Michel 2007: 323)

The plural is formed by postposing the third person plural pronoun *nan* 'they', as in *mesa* 'table' / *mesanan* 'tables' (cf. also Examples (190), (191a)), and may also function as an associative plural (*Marianan* 'Maria and those associated with her') (Maurer 2013c: 168).

There is an indefinite article *un* 'a', which is identical to the numeral 'one', and a definite article *e*:

(186) a. mi omo J tawa-tin un outo ku e mester a drecha promé
1SG uncle J PST-tin INDEF car REL 3SG must PFV repair before
ku Pasko
with Christmas
'My uncle J had a car which he should have repaired before Christmas.'
b. dia 24 di desèmber ainda e outo no tawa-ta klá
day 24 of December still DEF car NEG PST-COP ready
'On December 24th the car still wasn't ready.' (Kouwenberg & Ramos-Michel 2007:309)

The demonstrative is formed with the definite article + NP + the adverbs *aki* 'here' / *ei* 'there' / *aya* 'yonder', giving three distal distinctions, as in *e kas aki* 'this house' / *e kas ei* 'that house' / *e kas aya* 'yonder house' (Kouwenberg & Ramos-Michel 2007:324).

Possession is either expressed with the preposition *di* 'of' or with the third person singular possessive pronoun *su*:

(187) a. e kas di Wan / Wan su kas
DEF house of John John POSS house
'John's house' (Maurer 2013c:168)
b. boso tur su trabou
2PL all POSS work
'the work of you all' (Kouwenberg & Ramos-Michel 2007:326)

Pronouns are distinguished by two numbers and three persons. There are dependent and independent pronoun forms:

	DEPENDENT	INDEPENDENT
1SG	*mi*	*ami*
2SG	*bo/bu*	*abo*
3SG	*e/el(e)*	*e*
1PL	*nos*	*nos/anos*
2PL	*boso/bos(o)nan*	*boso/bos(o)nan/aboso*
3PL	*nan*	*nan/anan*

The distinct plural independent forms (i.e. those forms beginning with *a-)* are only found in Aruban Papiamentu. There are no gender or politeness distinctions. The possessive pronouns are identical to the dependent personal pronouns in all forms except the third singular, *su*.

Adjectives typically follow the noun, though in rare occasions it may precede (in which case the adjective is emphasized). The comparative is formed with *mas … ku* 'more than' and the superlative with *esun di mas* 'most':

(188) a. e ta mas grandi ku mi
3SG COP more big than 1SG
'S/he is bigger than I am.'
b. e ta esun di mas grandi
3SG COP the.one of more big
'S/he is the biggest.' (Maurer 2013c:169)

The base form of the verb indicates simple present tense or the present habitual. There are four tense/aspect markers: *ta* (present tense), *tabata* (past tense), *lo* (future tense)[146] and *a* (perfective aspect). The lexical aspect of the verb may affect the temporal reading of the clause. There are a number of modal verbs.

The word order is typically subject-verb-object. There is an invariant preverbal negator *no*.

(189)

awe	Wan	no	a	kumpra	Maria	un	bistí	na	pakus
today	John	NEG	PFV	buy	Maria	INDEF	dress	in	store

'Today John didn't buy Mary a dress in the store.' (Maurer 2013c: 179)

There is optional negative concord.

Polar questions are formed with rising intonation only, with an optional tag:

(190)

e	ta	bisti	e	sapatu	nan,	(no)?
3SG	PRES	wear	DEF	shoe	PL	NEG

'Is s/he putting on the shoes?' (Kouwenberg & Ramos-Michel 2007: 329)

In content questions the interrogative pronoun appears clause-initially.

Passive constructions may be formed with the auxiliary *wòrdu/ser/keda* or by simply omitting the subject. The agent is not obligatory.

(191) a.

e	outo-nan	a	wòrdu/ser/keda	pará	(dor di/pa	polis)
DEF	car-PL	PFV	PASS.AUX	stop.PTCP	by	police

'The cars have been stopped (by the police).'

b.

no	ta	duna	Papiamentu	na	skul
NEG	PRES	give	Papiamentu	LOC	school

'Papiamentu is not taught in school.' (Maurer 2013c: 176)

There is a copula, which inflects for tense: *ta* (present, cf. Example (188)), *tabata* (past, cf. Example (186b)) and *lo ta* (future). There is a locative copula *na* (cf. Example (191b)).

Sentences may be coordinated with the conjunctions *i* 'and', *ma/pero* 'but' and *òf* 'or'. Subordination may be indicated with the complementizers *ku/pa* or, in indirect questions, with *si* 'whether'. There are directional and qualifying serial verb constructions. Relative clauses are headed by the relativizer *ku* (cf. Example (186a)) or *kaminda* 'way'.

8.3.2.3 *Short text*

(Excerpt from Kouwenberg & Murray 1994: 54 with minimal changes; spoken by a native speaker of the Aruban dialect.)

Ora	mi	a	yega	kas,	banda	di	un	or	awe	mainta,	mi	a	bai	drumi	den
hour	1SG	PFV	reach	house,	around	of	one	o'clock	today	morning,	1SG	PFV	go	sleep	in

e	baki	di	e	pick-up	di	mi	padraso.	Paden	ta	mucho	kalor	pa	mi	drumi,
DEF	open.back	of	DEF	pick-up	of	1SG	stepfather	inside	COP	too.much	heat	for	1SG	sleep

146. Notice that *lo* is analyzed as a marker of irrealis in Kouwenberg & Murray (1994) and Kouwenberg & Ramos-Michel (2007).

p'esei	mi	a	disidí	di	drumi	pafó	bou	di	e	palo	di	koko	nan.	Awe	nochi	mi
thus	1SG	PFV	decide	of	sleep	outside	under	of	DEF	tree	of	coconut	PL	today	night	1SG

lo	drumi	ku	e	shelo	homo	mi	plafon.	Mi	a	pone	un	kama	den	kurá	pa	mi
FUT	sleep	with	DEF	sky	like	1SG	ceiling	1SG	PFV	put	INDEF	bed	in	yard	for	1SG

bolbe	drumi	pafó
return	sleep	outside

'When I reached home, around one o'clock this morning, I went to sleep in the back of my stepfather's pick-up. Inside (it) is too hot for me to sleep, that's why I decided to sleep outside under the coconut trees. Tonight I will sleep with the sky for my ceiling. I put a bed in the yard for me to sleep outside again.'

8.3.2.4 *Some sources of data*

There is a wealth of primary data available for Papiamentu. Berry-Haseth et al. (1988) is an anthology of Papiamentu literature and Juliana (1970) a collection of Papiamentu folktales. *Extra* (http://extra.cw/, accessed 10 February 2015) and *Bon Dia Aruba* (http://www.bondia.com/, accessed 10 February 2015), for example, are online newspapers in Papiamentu. TeleCuraçao (http://www.telecuracao.com/web/HomePage.aspx, accessed 10 February 2015) provides online videos from their program. For an extensive list of grammars, dictionaries and text corpora, see Maurer (2013c).

8.3.3 Krio: An English-lexified creole in West Africa[147]

8.3.3.1 *A brief background sketch of Krio*

Krio is spoken as a mother tongue by about 350,000 of the ca. 5,5 million inhabitants of Sierra Leone and is used by the vast majority of the population, over 4 million, as a *lingua franca*. It is the default language of communication in the country. The native speaker population is concentrated on the Western Area peninsula, which includes the capital, Freetown. There is a little studied 19th century offshoot, *Aku*, in the Gambia, with some 4–6,000 speakers (Yillah & Corcoran 2007).

The origin of Krio is a matter of debate. There are essentially two main positions, one that sees Krio as an offshoot of the Atlantic creoles, and one that sees Krio as an offshoot of a very early West African protocreole, Guinea Coast Creole English (the so-called Domestic Origin hypothesis, see 6.1.6). The latter theory is primarily put forth by Ian Hancock (e.g. 1986b, 1987) who suggests that Krio emerged "on the north bank of the River Gambia, the Sierra Leone River estuary, and the Sherbo Coast" (Hancock 1987:275). This very early creole would have emerged in the early decades of the 1600s in the interactions between English-speaking Europeans and the coastal West Africans, including intermarriages, the descendants of which would have been the first speakers of this proto-creole. This early creole would have pre-dated the slave trade and would therefore essentially have been one of the ancestors for the later English-lexified creoles in the New World, brought there by the slaves, who would already have been familiar with this early creole. This would account for the similarities between Krio and the New World English creoles. It

147. This section is primarily based on Yillah & Corcoran (2007) and Finney (2013a). I am very grateful to Magnus Huber for his helpful comments on this snapshot.

is debated, however, whether at that early date there was any English-lexified contact language in West Africa that was stable enough to act as a proto-creole (cf. Section 6.1.6 above).

More commonly, Krio is seen as a descendant of the New World creoles, transported to Sierra Leone by freed slaves. This was proposed as early as 1893 by Hugo Schuchardt, who suggests that Krio "was transplanted from America by the liberated slaves, who since the end of the previous century settled in Sierra Leone and Liberia" (1987: 20).[148] According to this theory, the ancestors of the Krio community are essentially four groups of settlers who colonized the Sierra Leone peninsula between 1787 and 1850 (for details, see, for example Huber 1999b, 2000 and 2004). The first, and smallest group, arrived from England in 1787 and consisted mainly of Black Poor (ex-slaves and sailors or ship staff), but also a sizeable group of whites. The second, and much larger, settlement in 1792 consisted of a large group of freedmen, the Nova Scotians, i.e. those ex-slaves who had been relocated to Nova Scotia after fighting for the British in the American War of Independence. Many of these Nova Scotians had been born in Virginia or the Carolinas. The third settlement arrived in 1800, a large group of Jamaican Maroons who were deported after an unsuccessful revolt. The largest group of settlers, however, were the 'recaptives', that is, West Africans who had been liberated from illegal slave ships after slavery was abolished by the British in 1808. Between 1808 and 1840 about 60,000 'recaptives' or 'Liberated Africans' were settled in Sierra Leone by the British Royal Navy (Huber 1999b: 63). These liberated Africans were either "enlisted in the army or 'apprenticed', i.e. given as servants to Nova Scotians, Maroons, or Europeans in Freetown" (Huber 1999b: 64), which means that they were placed in environments where they had to function in the language of their masters. The 'recaptives' had a wide variety of origins, but the main groups were Yorubas (who were called 'Akus', cf. above), Igbos and Gbe-speaking people (Huber 1999b: 64), possibly also Mende, Temne and Limba speaking people (Wyse 1989: 2).

Despite the wide use of Krio in Sierra Leone, it is not officially recognized. English is the sole official language of the country and the medium of instruction in schools. Krio is seen as an inferior form of English and is "believed to have a negative influence on the development of English" (Finney 2013a: 158), the language of prestige being British English. This in turn has led to a lectal divide between an acrolectal 'Anglicized Krio' as a symbol of education and high social status, contrasting with "Broad Krio" (a derogatory term). Yet another variety is that of the non-native speakers who migrated to Freetown.

However, attitudes are changing and Krio is gaining in acceptance. It is used in broadcast media, being one of the languages in which the national news is read, and is widely used in official and political discourse, though it is less used in print media. It has been incorporated in school curricula and is "one of the most popular languages taught in educational institutions" (Finney 2013a: 158). There are ongoing attempts to establish a standard orthography for the language, which might help in elevating its status.

---

148. "*…ist aus Amerika vepflanzt worden, und zwar durch die freigelassenen Sklaven, welche seit dem Ende des vorigen Jahrhunderts sich in Sierra Leone und in Liberia angesiedelt haben*" (Schuchardt 1987: 20, my translation). Note that this manuscript was published posthumously in 1987.

8.3.3.2 *A short linguistic sketch of Krio*

Krio has 24 consonants, /p, b, m, f, v, k͡p, g͡b, w, t, d, n, s, z, l, ɲ, ʃ, ʒ, ʧ, ʤ, j, k, g, ŋ, ʁ/ and seven vowels, /i, e, ɛ, a, ɔ, o, u/. All vowels may be allophonically nasalized. Vowel length is not contrastive (Fyle & Jones 1980). Notice that /j, ʁ/ are represented by <y, r> respectively. Krio is a tone language, with two tones, high (´) and low (`), as in *àlè* 'skin-irritating herb' vs. *àlé* 'go away' or *bàbá* 'a young boy' vs. *bábà* 'a barber' vs. *bábá* 'a type of drum' (Finney 2013a:160). Tone is both grammatically and lexically contrastive, for instance in marking the distinction between independent personal and possessive pronouns, in marking emphatic auxiliaries, and in forming distributives from reduplicated verbs (Fyle & Jones 1980:xx f). Tone is typically not indicated orthographically.

The morphology is predominantly analytic.

Case and gender are not relevant. Plurality is optionally marked with the third person plural pronoun *dɛm* 'they' before and/or after the noun phrase. Generic nouns are invariant and do not take any article:

(192) banana fayn fɔ it
banana fine COMP eat
'Bananas are good to eat.' (Yillah & Corcoran 2007:189)

There is an optional indefinite article, *wan*, which is homophonous with the numeral 'one' (cf. also Example (202), without any overt indefinite article) and a definite article *di*:

(193) a. a sabi wan bobo we bin kiss Baby K bifo i bin sik
1SG.S know INDEF boy REL ANT kiss Baby K before 3SG.S ANT sick
wit dis AIDS
with DEM AIDS
'I know a boy who kissed Baby K before she got sick with AIDS.'

b. di arata bin yala
DEF rat ANT yellow
'The rat was yellow.' (Yillah & Corcoran 2007:178f)

There are the demonstratives *dis* 'this' (cf. Examples (193a), (199a, c)) and *da(t)* 'that' (cf. Example (199b)) which both have the same plural form *dɛn* 'these/those'.

Pronouns are distinguished for three persons and two numbers. There is an independent and a dependent set. The object forms of the dependent set are identical to the independent set except for the third person singular.

	DEPENDENT		INDEPENDENT
	SUBJECT	OBJECT	
1SG	*a*	*mi*	*mi*
2SG	*yu*	*yu*	*yu*
3SG	*i*	*am*	*in*
1PL	*wi*	*wi*	*wi*
2PL	*una*	*una*	*una*
3PL	*dɛm*	*dɛm*	*dɛm*

The possessive pronouns are segmentically identical to the independent personal pronouns except in the tonal pattern (with the possessive pronouns consistently in a low tone and the personal pronouns consistently in a high tone; Fyle & Jones 1980:xxi). Adnominal possession may be formed through juxtaposition or with the third person pronoun (which agrees in number with the possessor):

(194) a. lɔya wok
lawyer work
'lawyer's work'

b. mi mama in lɔya
1SG.POSS mother 3SG.POSS lawyer
'my mother's lawyer'

c. di man dɛm os
DEF man 3PL.POSS house
'the men's house' (Yillah & Corcoran 2007:191)

Adjectives precede the noun they modify when used attributively, but follow the noun when used predicatively. Comparison is formed with *pas* 'surpass'. There is no specific superlative form.

(195) a. di pikin fain pas in mama
DEF child good.looking surpass 3SG.POSS mother
'The child is better-looking than his/her mother.'

b. di pikin fain pas dɛm ɔl na di os
DEF child good.looking surpass 3PL all LOC DEF house
'The child is the most beautiful of them all in the house.' (Finney 2013a:161)

The base form of the verb typically has a present tense reading with stative verbs and a past tense meaning with non-stative verbs:

(196) a. i lɛk di os wo Olu mek fɔ am
3SG.S like DEF house REL PN make for 3SG.O
'S/he likes the house which Olu built for her/him.'

b. Olu it in pɛtɛtɛ
PN eat 3SG.POSS potato
'Olu ate his potato.' (Yillah & Corcoran 2007:177)

There are six tense/aspect markers, which all appear preverbally and which may combine in different ways: *bìn* (anterior tense), *gò* (future tense),[149] *dè/dì* (progressive aspect), *kìn* (habitual aspect), *dɔ̀n* (perfective aspect) and *bà/blànt* (past habitual). There are several modal markers.

The word order is typically subject-verb-object. There is an invariant preverbal negator *nɔ*:

(197) ren nɔ de kam
rain NEG PROG come
'It is not raining.' (Yillah & Corcoran 2007:185)

There is negative concord:

149. The grammatical marker *gò* 'future' is distinguished from the lexical verb 'gó' through tone.

(198) natin nɔ de du yu
nothing NEG PROG do 2SG
'No ill will befall you.' (Lit. 'Nothing won't happen to you.') (Yillah & Corcoran 2007:186)

There is no copula with predicative adjectives, but with predicative nouns the affirmative copula is *na* and the negative is *noto*. The locative copula is *de*.

(199) a. dis wan ya na mi sista
DEM one here COP 1SG.POSS sister
'This is my sister.' (Finney 2013a:162)

b. da wan de noto mi brɔda
DEM one there NEG.COP 1SG.POSS brother
'That is not my brother.' (Finney 2013a:162)

c. di bɔta de biyɛn di milk
DEF butter COP behind DEF milk
'The butter is behind the milk.' (Yillah & Corcoran 2007:188)

Polar questions are formed through rising intonation only. The interrogative phrase in content questions is fronted:

(200) a. yu nɔ bin fɔ dɔn du am yɛstade?
2SG NEG ANT should PFV do 3SG.O yesterday
'Shouldn't you have done it yesterday?'

b. wetin di man de it?
what DEF man PROG eat
'What is the man eating?' (Finney 2013a:162f)

There is no specific passive construction. There is a focus marker *na* (homophonous with the copula) which highlights nominals, interrogative phrases and predicates:

(201) na tumara Olu go was di kalabas
FOC tomorrow PN FUT wash DEF calabash
'It is tomorrow that Olu will wash the calabash' (Yillah & Corcoran 2007:188)

There are several kinds of serial verb constructions, including directionals and benefactives. Serial verb constructions with three verbs are common and there are even some with four or more verbs.

(202) a. a kin bai ɔrintʃ gi am
1SG.S HAB buy orange give 3SG.O
'I usually buy him an orange.' (Finney 2013a:162)

b. Agnɛs rɔn kɔmɔt go lɛf in mama na makit
PN run leave go leave 3SG.POSS mother LOC market
'Agnes rushed out to drop her mother off at the market.' (Yillah & Corcoran 2007:189)

The coordinating conjunction *ɛn* 'and' may also function as a comitative 'with'. There are the complementizers *se* (homophonous with the verb 'say') and *fɔ*. There is a relativizer *we/wo*, which is obligatory for subject nouns phrases (cf. Example (193a)) and optional for object noun phrases.

8.3.3.3 *Short text*

(Excerpt from *Aw fɔ arenj yu biznɛs mek i fayn ɛn bɛtɛ* 'How to arrange your business so that it gets orderly and better'; Parkinson 1995. Glossed and translated by myself.)

Plɛnti uman dɛm na Salon de du smɔl smɔl biznɛs. (…) Bɔt, ɛniaw dɛm
many woman 3PL LOC Sierra Leone PROG do small.RED business but anyhow 3PL

uman ya arenj fɔ sɛl dɛm makit, na wan tin nɔmɔ de na dɛm ed –
woman here arrange COMP sell 3PL.POSS goods FOC one thing only COP LOC 3PL.POSS head

fɔ mek mɔni ɛn gɛt gud gud prɔfit we go ɛp mɛk dɛm layf bɛtɛ, so dat
COMP make money and get good.RED profit REL FUT help make 3PL.POSS life better so that

dɛm go ebul go bifɔ.
3PL FUT able go front

'Many women in Sierra Leone do small business. (…) But whatever way these women arrange to sell their merchandise, it is only one thing that is on their mind – to make money and get a very good profit which will help them make their lives better, so that they will be able to move on.'

8.3.3.4 *Some sources of data*

There is some primary data available for Krio, such as the volumes published by the *Krio Publications Series* (Umeå University), which include such things as practical advice on running a business or how to compose different kinds of texts (e.g. Jones & Shrimpton 1995; Fyle 2010) as well as plays and novels, including translations (e.g. Decker 1988, 2010; Taylor-Pearce 1984).

8.4 Summary

The attitudes towards a language or language variety colour the way we perceive the person using it. People using a language or variety with high prestige will be viewed as more successful than those using a language or variety with low prestige. The attitude towards languages is intimately connected with identity and sense of group solidarity. Speakers may therefore accommodate the language or variety they are using to indicate association or dissociation with the people they are addressing.

Language planning involves codifying and standardizing a nonstandard language or variety. This in turn involves careful considerations of which variety to choose as a normative standard and according to which principles to codify it. A phonetic written representation of the language emphasizes the unique identity of the language or variety, while an etymological orthography emphasizes the historical roots of the language.

Language policy involves the official allocation of languages in certain functional domains, such as for official discourse and the medium of education in schools. Official recognition of a language automatically elevates its status in the society in question. Typically a standardized norm is seen as an essential prerequisite for such recognition. Pidgins and creoles are gradually being recognized as languages in their own right, and are gradually being included as in educational programs.

Literature is a fundamental part of any human culture. Pidgins and creoles have typically been oral languages, with a rich oral literature in the form of songs, plays, folktales, riddles and proverbs. However, written literature in creole languages has existed for many centuries, initially as translations of religious texts, but original literature in the form of prose, poetry and drama has also been produced for many decades, if not longer.

With the increasing recognition and acceptance of pidgin and creole languages in their societies, they are also increasingly being used in mass media, which in turn helps further their status even more.

8.5 Key points

- **Attitudes towards different language varieties affect the perception of an individual's person and/or an individual's language depending on the language variety an individual uses.**
- **Issues of identity and solidarity may cause individuals to accommodate their language variety to become more similar or more different to that of their interlocutors.**
- **Selecting a norm for codification involves solving a host of issues of identity and solidarity to achieve maximal acceptance.**
- **Codification may be done according to a number of different principles.**
- **Standardization is often seen as necessary for a language to gain official recognition.**
- **Official recognition of a language is often closely related to status.**
- **Children do better in school and learn any subject faster if they are taught in their mother tongues.**
- **Literature is an essential component of any human culture, including creole speaking communities.**
- **Written literature and translations in pidgin, creole and mixed languages help give those languages a place in the literary world, as well as show that these languages are as adequate as any other for higher culture.**
- **The use of a language in media is closely related to recognition of that language.**

8.6 Exercises

1. What is a 'matched guise' experiment? What may such experiments tell us about the role of attitudes towards language varieties?
2. What is the difference between language planning and language policy?
3. What are some of the main difficulties involved in selecting and codifying a linguistic norm?
4. What are some of the main obstacles in introducing extended pidgins, creoles or mixed languages as media of education in schools?
5. What does such literature as folktales, riddles and proverbs imply about creoles as presupposed simple languages?

Part II

Linguistic features

Introduction to Part II

The following chapters will empirically test whether the features commonly assumed to be typical for pidgins and creoles, outlined in Sections 1.3 and 2.3 in Part I, in fact are representative of these languages. The chapters will also compare whether pidgin and creole languages differ from non-pidgins and non-creoles with respect to these features. For reasons of space each chapter has been limited to two or three of the linguistic features outlined in Sections 1.3 and 2.3. The chapters all follow the same general structure, and can, as in Part I, be used in isolation or in combination with each other (or with any or all of the chapters in Part I): I first give a general introduction to the chapter where the basic terminology is defined. Each linguistic feature is then discussed in turn for pidgins, extended pidgins (pidgincreoles), creoles and mixed languages. I then give short sketches of three languages that were mentioned in the chapter in connection with the features discussed; each chapter has a sketch of one pidgin, one creole, and one extended pidgin or mixed language. As with the chapters in Part I, the snapshots are independent and may be used as a complement to the chapter text, or can be used selectively or can be skipped in entirety without any loss of general context. Furthermore, also as in the chapters in Part I, the snapshots may be used in isolation without reference to the chapter text. Last in each chapter I give a summary of the findings.

It is beyond the scope of this book to discuss in detail how the respective findings relate to the many various theories about pidgin and creole languages. In order to remain theory neutral, I will in these chapters therefore limit myself to presenting the actual empirical data for the linguistically relevant features. The reader is then encouraged to apply these figures to various theories on the possible typological uniqueness of pidgin and creole languages.

Genetic affiliation

Languages are often grouped together according to their origins. Languages that descend from a common ancestor are grouped together into one language **family**. The family is the highest level of the affiliated languages. Examples of language families are Indo-European and Sino-Tibetan. Language families may be of radically different sizes, ranging from more than a thousand languages to only a handful of languages or even only one language, and may be estimated at radically different ages, ranging from many thousands of years to little more than 1,000 years (cf. for example Holman et al. 2011). A lower level of affiliation is the **genus** of a language, "a level of classification which is comparable across the world, so that a genus in one family is intended to be comparable in time depth to genera in other parts of the world" (Dryer 2013c). In other words, all genera across the world are hypothesized to be of roughly the same age. The term language genus was originally suggested by William Croft to mirror the classification level of 'genus' in biology, which is used for an obviously closely related set of species (Dryer 1989: 267). Examples of language genera are Germanic (to which, for example, English, Dutch and German belong), Romance (to which, for example, French, Spanish and Portuguese belong) and Celtic (to which, for example, Welsh and Irish Gaelic belong).

When it comes to pidgins, extended pidgins (pidgincreoles), creoles and mixed languages, the genetic affiliation is a matter of controversy, which ultimately boils down to the position taken regarding the emergence of these languages (see the chapters in Part I). Since the purpose of the following chapters is to test various assumptions that are made about these languages, especially pidgins and creoles, as well as to test whether they differ from non-pidgins and non-creoles, these languages have been classified and grouped as either 'Pidgin', 'Extended pidgin', 'Creole' or 'Mixed language' as their highest taxonomical level (essentially the equivalent of the 'family' level). The equivalent of a 'genus' level has here been indicated with the main lexifier language (or, in the case of mixed languages, of the major input languages).

Comparing languages, creating samples and the problem of bias

When making typological surveys, that is, when making cross-linguistic surveys that are intended to represent as best possible the various linguistic structures that can be found in the world, we are forced to rely on **samples**. This is because it is not humanly possible to include all human languages in a survey. First of all, we do not have descriptions of all known languages in the world. Furthermore, we do not have descriptions of those languages that remain undiscovered. But we also do not have access to all those languages that have already gone extinct, or to those languages that are yet to emerge. We therefore have to create samples of languages and attempt to make them as representative as possible. Because of this, it is important to keep in mind that all statements given here about the various patterns found are based on samples of languages and not of all known languages in the various groups that are being compared. There are a number of considerations to take into account when creating and using samples. For more on the methodological considerations involved in creating and using samples, see, for example, Song (2001: 17ff), Bakker (2010) and Velupillai (2012: 39ff).

In typological research one of the most important factors is to aim for **genetic** (or **genealogical**) **balance**. This is because a given feature may be genealogically inherited. In order to try to control for **genetic** (or genealogical) **bias**, typological surveys usually only allow one language per language genus. A typological sample should therefore only include, for example, one Romance language, one Germanic language, one Celtic language, and so on. When it comes to creating samples of pidgin and creole languages, however, this becomes problematic, because how to classify these languages is still a matter of debate. It remains problematic even if we take the lexifier as the equivalent of a language genus, since for most of these languages, especially creole languages, there is such a small group of lexifier languages. Most of those languages we today call creole languages have either English or Dutch (both Germanic), or French, Spanish or Portuguese (all Romance) as their lexifier languages. To choose only one Germanic- and one Romance-lexified creole for a typological survey and a comparison with non-creole languages would, however, yield much too small a sample to give any meaningful figures. In these kinds of cases it seems preferable to include as many languages as possible in the pidgin and creole samples respectively, in order to be able to empirically test sweeping claims about the nature of these languages, even though that leads to imbalance: the vast majority of these languages, especially creoles, have European languages as their lexifiers, and most of these European-lexified languages have English as their lexifier. Furthermore, most of the creoles are spoken in the Caribbean, which means that any sample of this kind will have an **areal imbalance** (i.e. that some areas are proportionally underrepresented while others are proportionally overrepresented). Despite this it is necessary to somehow empirically test the various claims made about the linguistic structure and possible uniqueness of pidgin and creole languages. For the chapters in Part II I have therefore, for each linguistic feature discussed, included as many pidgin and creole languages as I was able to get datapoints for. In the case of the creole samples this means almost all the creole languages that are available in APiCS, except for Early Sranan,[150] plus a couple of other

150. Sranan is the only language in APiCS to be represented by two varieties that differ diachronically. Since the chapters in Part II will focus on the synchronic data that is now available, Early Sranan has been excluded, to avoid a double data point for the language Sranan. Other, regional, varieties have been included, such as all three of the Chabacano Creoles in the Philippines, the different Cape Verde Creole varieties, as well as both Martinican and Guadeloupean, since they are treated as distinct in APiCS.

creoles not included in APiCS that I was able to get data for. The pidgin samples are based on the pidgin languages available in APiCS as well as any other pidgin language I was able to get data for.

Another problematic factor in any creole sample is the role of diffusion. We have seen in Part I that many creole languages are interrelated in various ways (cf. also the various snapshots in the book): settlement histories of individual languages indicate that a number of creoles, especially, but not exclusively, in the Caribbean may have common ancestors. The various settlement histories also point to the possibility of features spreading from one variety to another. In other words, to the genetic imbalance of any creole sample due to the common lexifier languages (and possibly also common substrate languages) is added a possible genetic imbalance due to creoles in the same sample being descendants of each other. On top of this many creoles have been in intense contact with each other, and may have affected the linguistic makeup of each other. This is thus another factor that may make creole languages internally similar.

It is important to keep the above considerations in mind when interpreting the results of the comparisons in the following chapters. Put simply, the samples used for the comparisons in these chapters are far from ideal, but are at this stage the best we can get hold of in order to empirically test the various assumptions made about pidgin and creole languages. To the greatest possible extent I have also compared pidgin and creole languages with non-pidgins and non-creoles. For this comparison I have predominantly made use of the databases available in WALS. In order to avoid language overlaps between the two samples, I have consistently taken out those languages in the WALS samples that can also be found in the pidgin or creole samples created here for the purpose of comparison.

It is very important to note here that these comparisons should not be seen as comparisons between 'contact languages' versus 'non-contact languages' since it would be a definitional nightmare to establish exactly which languages in WALS would qualify as 'contact languages'. For example, both English and Persian are languages that have seen intense contact with other languages during their history, but they are generally not called 'contact languages'. These comparisons should therefore be seen as comparisons between pidgins on the one hand and *all others* on the other, meaning that the non-pidgin samples may include any language that has not been classified as a pidgin (including 'contact languages'). Likewise, the comparisons are between creoles on the one hand and *all others* on the other, meaning that the non-creole samples may include any language that has not been labelled a creole (including 'contact languages').

Extended pidgins (pidgincreoles) as a separate group

In the following chapters all extended pidgins (pidgincreoles) are discussed in a separate section for each linguistic feature. This is because of the ongoing discussion on whether, when comparing pidgins and creoles with non-pidgins and non-creoles, extended pidgins (pidgincreoles) should be excluded when investigating structural features of pidgin languages, because the domains of use for extended pidgins (pidgincreoles) have led them to become structurally different from pidgins and show more similarities with creole languages (Bakker 2008). These sections may thus serve to answer the question of whether there in fact are differences between these groups of languages, whether they are internally similar, and whether extended pidgins (pidgincreoles) tend to align more closely to pidgins or to creoles.

It should be noted that the sample of languages that are classified as extended pidgins (pidgincreoles) is very small, consisting of only ten languages, which means that for these languages I am not able to give meaningful statistics. The languages are Bislama, Cameroon Pidgin English, Ghanaian Pidgin English, Hiri Motu, Juba Arabic, Nagamese, Nigerian Pidgin, Sango, Solomons Pijin and Tok Pisin. It should be noted that six of these are English-lexified.

A brief note on statistics

Once we have collected data for a given feature we need to know how to interpret it. The mere fact that, to take a fictive example, 15 pidgin languages have tone while 178 non-pidgins have tone does not tell us much about the proportions and distributions of tone in the two groups. Absolute figures on their own tell us nothing about the proportions that the tone languages make up in the respective groups. If, for example, we knew that 15 out of 28 (53.6%) pidgin languages have tone, while 178 of 423 (42.1%) non-pidgins have tone, we would have the proportions and it would seem that tone would be more common for pidgins than for non-pidgins. However, since we are dealing with samples, how do we know that these figures simply didn't come about by chance? If the risk is high that we got these results by chance, then they may or may not be representative for the total population, that is, for the two groups which we are trying to compare (pidgin languages and non-pidgin languages). In order to try to assess how high the risk is that a given distribution of features came about by chance, we apply various statistical tests. This section will only make the briefest of mentions of the tests that have been used for the figures in the chapters. It is beyond the scope of this section (and this book) to give an adequate introduction to statistics; for a very accessible introduction to statistics in general (as well as the programming language *R*), see Field et al. (2012). For introductions to statistics for linguistics especially, see Gries (2013), Baayen (2008) and Larson-Hall (2010a, 2010b), the latter of which is a supplementary volume, specifically using R, that has been made available online (http://cw.routledge.com/textbooks/9780805861853/guide-to-R.asp, accessed 11 February 2015). There is also a host of general statistics textbooks available online, such as *Electronic statistics textbook* (2013, at http://www.statsoft.com/Textbooks, accessed 11 February 2015), *Online statistics education* (2014, at http://onlinestatbook.com/2/index.html, accessed 11 February 2015) or *Concepts and applications of inferential statistics* (2013, at http://vassarstats.net/textbook/, accessed 11 February 2015), to mention only a few.

There are different kinds of data. For the chapters in Part II we will only be dealing with so-called **categorical data**, i.e. data that can be counted in discrete and mutually exclusive units. Examples of categorical data is whether individuals or units in a group are classified as male or female, dogs or cats, pencils or pens. For example, we could simply count how many in a given group (e.g. mountain climbers) are male or female and get the result that 24 are male and 18 are female. We may want to compare two groups of individuals or units for some feature, for example if more male mountain climbers slip while climbing than female mountain climbers. We could do that by setting up the mutually exclusive categories or **factors** (also called **variables**) 'slipped while climbing' versus 'did not slip while climbing'. This would still be categorical data, since we are assigning things to discrete groups. We might end up finding that 20 male climbers slipped at least once while only 7 female climbers slipped at least once. The question is now how high the risk is that these results came about by chance – if the risk is very low, then we are likely to get similar kinds of proportions in our results if we take entirely different groups of mountain climbers. If it seems that the risk is very low that the result came about by chance, then we consider the results **statistically significant**. And if that is the case then we might have a pattern worth trying to explain.

There are various ways to test whether distributions in categorical data are statistically significant. One very well-known and widely applied test is the **chi-square test** (or, more accurately, the **Pearson Chi-Square Test**), which may either be applied to only one group with several categories (e.g. the number of people in a group that have green, blue or brown eyes), a so-called **chi-square goodness-of-fit test** (sometimes also called a **one-dimensional chi-square test**), or it may be applied to a **contingency table**, that is two or more groups that are all subdivided into several categories (e.g. the number or males in a given group who have green, blue or brown eyes and the number of females in that same group who have green, blue or brown eyes), sometimes also called a **chi-squared contingency table test**. Extremely simplified, the chi-square test compares the **observed results** (i.e. the results you get in your particular survey) with the **expected results**. For example, all things being equal, you can expect a coin to land on the head side roughly half of the times you flip it. Or, all things being equal, you might expect half of the group of mountain climbers to be male and the other half to be female. Or, all things being equal, you might expect a third or the males in a given group to have green eyes, a third to have blue eyes and another third or have brown eyes, and then the same for the females in the same group. Or, again all things being equal, you might expect the same proportion of pidgin languages as non-pidgin languages to have tone. Extremely simplified, the more the observed result deviates from the expected result, the higher the **chi-square value** (usually expressed '$\chi = \ldots$') will be, and the more unlikely it is that the result came about by chance.

To know whether a result is statistically significant or not we need the ***p*-value** (i.e. the *probability* that we will get the same or a very similar test statistic result if we did the same kind of survey in a different group of units or individuals).[151] By convention a result is counted as 'statistically significant' if the p-value is 5% or less (expressed as 0.05); if it is 1% or less (expressed as 0.01) the result is counted as statistically 'very significant'; and if it is 0.1% or less (expressed as 0.001) the result is counted as statistically 'highly significant'. A common way of indicating the three significance levels is through asterisks: * means that the result is statistically significant ($p \leq 0.05$), ** means that the result is very significant ($p \leq 0.01$) and *** means that the result is highly significant ($p \leq 0.001$). Sometimes a p-value that lies between 5% and 10% is counted as 'marginally significant' ($p \leq 0.1$). Anything above $p = 0.1$ is counted as not statistically significant, meaning that the risk that the results came about by chance is too high for us to assume that they indicate an actual pattern. For our fictive example of tone in pidgin and non-pidgin languages the results would be as follows:

151. Due to the nature of the chi-square test equation, in general the resulting chi-square value will get higher the larger a contingency table is (i.e. the more different groups and categories there are). To control for this the p-value is arrived at by taking both the chi-square value and the so-called **degrees of freedom** (*df*) into account. It is quite beyond the scope of this note to explain what exactly the degrees of freedom is, but extremely simplified it indicates how many free choices there are available in a table for the given row and column sums. For example, if we have a one-dimensional table with one column and three rows, i.e. a total of three cells, and we know that the column sum is 10, then we can put whatever value we like in two of the cells, but in the third cell we have to put that value which will bring the total sum to 10. A possible way of thinking of it is that if a box of chocolate is passed around, each person except the last one has a choice between different chocolates; only the last person is stuck with whatever is left. Or it can be thought of as seats in a bus: every passenger has a choice of seats except the last one, who has to take whatever seat is left.

Fictive survey of tone in two language samples.

	Pidgin sample	Non-pidgin sample
has tone	15 (53.6%)	178 (42.1%)
lacks tone	13 (46.4%)	245 (57.9%)
Total	28	423

$\chi = 1.42$, $df = 1$, $p = 0.23$

In the case of our fictive example we would not be justified in assuming that there is a pattern that distinguishes pidgins (as having tone) from non-pidgins (as lacking tone), because the test statistics shows us that the result is not statistically significant (the *p*-value is above the statistically significant cut-off point of 0.05 and even the marginally significant cut-off point of 0.1). In other words, for these results the risk is too high that they could have come about due to random chance for us to accept them as showing any specific pattern.

The chi-square test can only give reliable results if the sample is not too small and if the expected values in each cell are not too low (the received wisdom is that no cell should have an expected value of less than 5, though this is debated). This can be a problem in linguistic studies, especially in typological studies, where very low frequencies of a feature usually are of interest: if a certain word order is extremely rare, this might tell us something about the nature of human language. One way of getting around this problem is to simulate a test very many times, each time with a randomly different combination of the results and calculate a chi-square value each time (cf. Janssen et al. 2006).[152] The resulting **simulated *p*-value** then essentially, and very simplified, tells us how many times the same or a higher chi-square value came about. The cut-off points for significance are the same for the simulated *p*-value. In the following chapters I will consistently give simulated *p*-values (expressed '$p_{sim} = \ldots$') based on 10,000 replicas (expressed 'B = 10,000'). In those cases where a table has very many empty cells, making the non-simulated *p*-value highly unreliable, I give only the simulated *p*-value.

Due to the nature of the equation applied in the chi-square test, it is actually an approximation of the distribution that is being calculated. A more exact test, which is becoming more common, is the **G-test** (or **likelihood ratio test**). Contrary to the chi-square test, the G-test is based on the specific distribution and not an approximation, but it is in all other respects very similar to the chi-square test and can be used in the same contexts. If the samples used are of a reasonable size, the resulting

152. I am grateful to Christoph Wolk for bringing this solution to my attention.

p-values are often very similar between the two tests. Nevertheless, now that computational power is not an issue, the G-test is increasingly being recommended for testing categorical data. Because the chi-square is so well-known, I have opted to give both the chi-square test and **G-test values** (expressed as '$G=\dots$') throughout the chapters in Part II.

Because statistics in a number of linguistic subdisciplines is (unfortunately) still not a self-evident component of data analysis, I have refrained from discussing in detail the values obtained for the respective features. However, because statistics are, in fact, of fundamental importance for anyone who wishes to analyze or use data, I have given the values for each feature in the respective tables (except in a few cases where the proportions are very extreme and would obviously yield a statistically significant test result), to make them available for those who do wish to know them.

Languages cited in Chapter 9

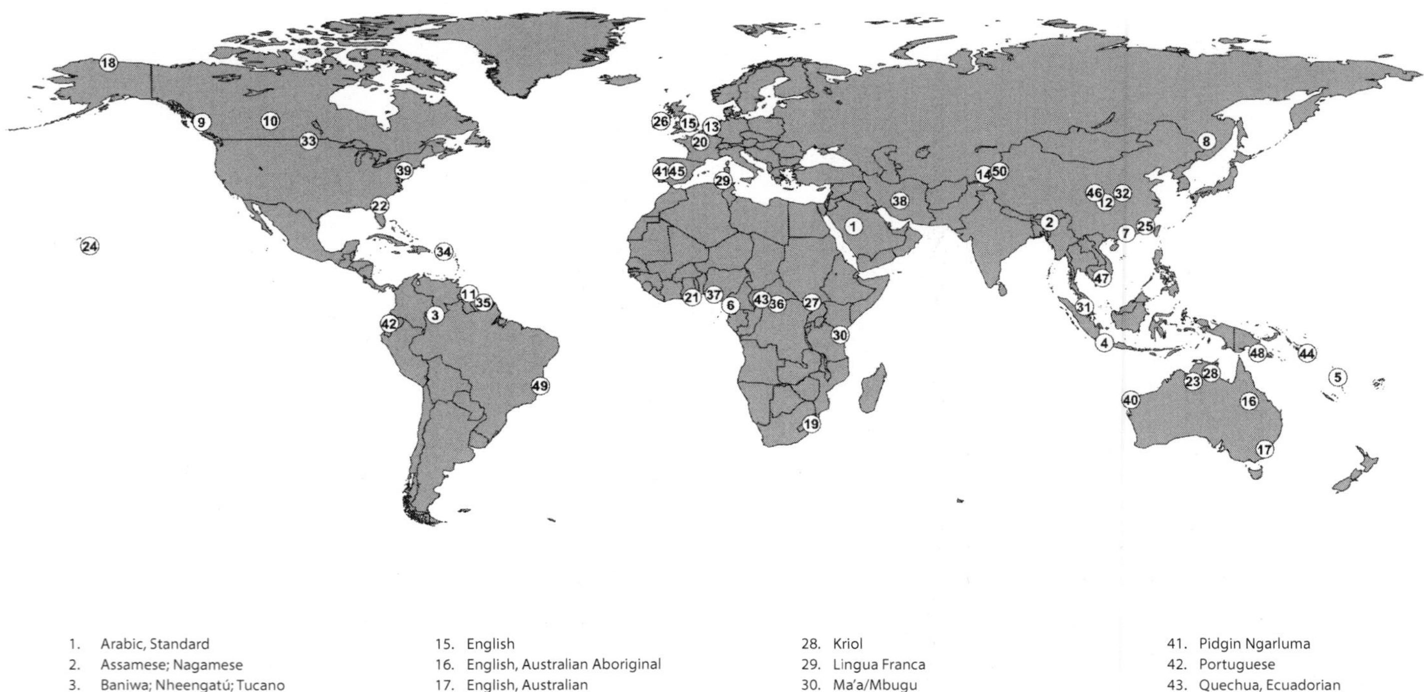

1. Arabic, Standard
2. Assamese; Nagamese
3. Baniwa; Nheengatú; Tucano
4. Batavia Creole; Petjo
5. Bislama
6. Cameroon Pidgin English; Pichi
7. Cantonese; Chinese Pidgin English
8. Chinese Pidgin Russian
9. Chinuk Wawa
10. Cree, Plains
11. Creolese
12. Dongxiang
13. Dutch
14. Ejnu
15. English
16. English, Australian Aboriginal
17. English, Australian
18. Eskimo Pidgin
19. Fanakalo
20. French
21. Ghanaian Pidgin English
22. Gullah
23. Gurindji; Gurindji Kriol; Mudburra
24. Hawai'i Creole English; Hawaiian; Pidgin Hawaiian
25. Hokkien
26. Irish; Shelta
27. Juba Arabic
28. Kriol
29. Lingua Franca
30. Ma'a/Mbugu
31. Malay; Papiá Kristang; Singapore Bazaar Malay
32. Mandarin Chinese
33. Michif
34. Negerhollands
35. Nengee; Saramaccan
36. Ngbandi
37. Nhengatu; Tucano
38. Nigerian Pidgin
39. Persian
40. Pidgin Delaware
41. Pidgin Ngarluma
42. Portuguese
43. Quechua, Ecuadorian
44. Sango
45. Solomon Islands Pijin
46. Spanish
47. Tangwang
48. Tây Bòi
49. Tok Pisin
50. Tupinambá
51. Unami
52. Uyghur

Chapter 9

Phonology

Both pidgins and creoles are assumed to have small phoneme inventories, to allow only simple syllable structures and to lack tone, while mixed languages are assumed to either reflect the system of one of the input languages or to reflect a blend of the two input systems. This chapter will empirically test whether pidgins and creoles differ from non-pidgins and non-creoles with respect to phoneme inventories (Sections 9.2.1 and 9.2.3), syllable structures (Sections 9.3.1 and 9.3.3) and tone (Sections 9.4.1 and 9.4.3). It will also briefly bring up phoneme inventories, syllable structures and tone in various extended pidgins (Sections 9.2.2, 9.3.2 and 9.4.2) and mixed languages (Sections 9.2.4, 9.3.4 and 9.4.4). Section 9.5 gives short sketches of three languages mentioned in the chapter: Tây Bồi (an extinct French-lexified pidgin in Vietnam), Nheengatú (a Tupinambá-lexified creole in Brazil) and Gurindji Kriol (a Gurindji/Kriol mixed language in Australia).

9.1 Introduction

A **phoneme** is the smallest meaning distinguishing unit of a language, i.e. a **contrastive segment**. There are two types of phonemes in spoken languages, **vowels**, which are formed when air passes freely from the lungs through the mouth, and **consonants**, which are formed by creating some kind of an obstruction for the airflow. These units are contrastive in that changing only one of them alters the meaning of the word, as in, for example, *bat* versus *hat* (where the initial consonants differ) or *hat* versus *hit* (where the vowels differ) or *hit* versus *hip* (where the final consonants differ). Consonants and vowels may be arranged into **syllables**, which are essentially larger units that can be produced in isolation. A syllable consists of an obligatory **nucleus** (usually a vowel), the core of the syllable, and optional consonantal **onsets** (the part appearing before the nucleus) and **codas** (the part appearing after the nucleus). A word consists minimally of one syllable (such as *a, go, as, sit, drink*) but syllables may also combine to form longer words (such as *wa.ter* or *tri.go.no.me.try*).[153] **Tone** is a phonemic feature that may carry over segments, a so-called **prosodic** or **suprasegmental** feature, where changes in pitch alter the meaning of the word. For

153. Syllable boundaries are usually indicated with a dot (.).

accessible introductions to phonetics and phonology, see, for example, Spencer (1996), Ladefoged (2005) and Ladefoged & Johnson (2010).

This chapter will test the assumption that pidgin and creole languages have smaller segment inventories than other languages, that they prefer simple syllable structures and that they lack tone.

9.2 Phoneme inventories

When measuring phoneme inventories it is the number of distinctive segments that is considered. That is, for consonants it is the number of contrastive consonantal segments and not the total number of possible consonants (including allophones). For vowels it is typically the number of vowel qualities that is measured, ignoring such features as length, nasalization or diphthongation. In this section the consonant and vowel quality inventories in a sample of pidgin and creole languages will be compared to those of the languages in WALS (Maddieson 2013a, Maddieson 2013e). Phonological inventories of extended pidgins (pidgincreoles) and mixed languages will also briefly be mentioned. It is beyond the scope of the section to discuss in detail the kinds of consonant and vowel quality inventories that languages tend to have. For more on the typology of phoneme inventories, see, for example, Velupillai (2012: 69ff) with further references.

9.2.1 Pidgin phoneme inventories

Pidgins are widely described as having a reduced inventory of phonemes compared to their major lexifier languages (cf. Mühlhäusler 1997: 139). They are typically described as having retained the common core inventories and have dropped those sounds that are not shared by the languages in contact (cf. Winford 2003: 277). Eskimo Pidgin, for example, had only 14 consonants (/p, m, v, t, n, r, s, l, ʧ, ʃ, k, g, ŋ, h/) and five vowels (/i, e, a, o, u/), giving total of 18 phonemes (van der Voort 2013: 167f). Tây Bồi, an extinct French-lexified pidgin in Vietnam, is an example of a pidgin with an average sized inventory, with 25 phonemes (cf. Reinecke 1971), but with both fewer consonants (15, /b, m, f, w, t, d, n, s, l, r, ɲ, ʃ, j, k, ɣ/) and fewer vowels (10, /i, e, ɛ, ə, ɜ, a, ʌ, ɔ, o, u/) than the lexifier French (21 consonants, /p, b, m, w, f, v, t, d, n, s, z, l, ʃ, ʒ, ɲ, j, ɥ, k, g, ŋ, ʁ/ and 11 vowels, /i, y, e, ø, ɛ, œ, ə, a, ɔ, o, u/), even though the number of vowel qualities is typologically high.[154]

154. See Bakker (2009) on how the number of segments for pidgins was counted.

In order to establish if pidgins tend to have smaller segment inventories than non-pidgins, the current sample was compared with that in WALS (Maddieson 2013a, 2013e),[155] which does not contain pidgins. The figures are summarized in Table 9.1:

Table 9.1 Size of consonant inventories in the current pidgin sample (based on Bakker 2009 with some additions) and in WALS (Maddieson 2013a). For a full legend of the languages in the pidgin sample, see http://dx.doi.org/10.1075/cll.48.additional.

	Pidgin sample		WALS	
	N	%	N	%
small (6–14)	4	16	89	15.1
moderately small (15–18)	14	56	122	21.7
average (19–25)	6	24	201	35.7
moderately large (26–33)	1	4	94	16.7
large (34+)	0	–	57	10.1
Total	25		563	

($\chi^2 = 18.04$; $df = 4$; $p_{\text{two-tailed}} = 0.0012^{**}$, $p_{\text{sim}} = 0.0013^{**}$ (B = 10,000))
($G = 17.40$; $df = 4$; $p_{\text{two-tailed}} = 0.0016^{**}$)

Table 9.1 shows the difference between the consonant inventories in the current pidgin sample and in Maddieson's (2013a) sample. Specifically it shows that the languages in the current pidgin sample are more likely to have moderately small consonant inventories than in Maddieson's (2013a) sample.

Table 9.2 Vowel quality inventories in the current pidgin sample (based on Bakker 2009 with some additions) and in WALS (Maddieson 2013e). For a full legend of the languages in the pidgin sample, see http://dx.doi.org/10.1075/cll.48.additional.

	Pidgin sample		WALS	
	N	%	N	%
small (2–4)	3	12	93	16.5
average (5–6)	18	72	287	50.9
large (7–14)	4	16	184	32.6
Total	25		564	

($\chi^2 = 4.43$; $df = 2$; $p_{\text{two-tailed}} = 0.109$, $p_{\text{sim}} = 0.109$ (B = 10,000))
($G = 4.54$; $df = 2$; $p_{\text{two-tailed}} = 0.103$)

155. See Maddieson (2013a, 2013e) on how the cut-off points for the individual categories were determined.

Table 9.2 shows the difference between the vowel inventories in the current pidgin sample and in Maddieson's (2013e) sample. Although there is a higher proportion of languages with an average vowel quality inventory in the pidgin sample, the difference between the samples is not statistically significant. Based on these samples it thus seems as if pidgins do not differ notably from non-pidgins with respect to number of vowel qualities.

The next question we have to consider is whether the difference in consonant inventories may be due to the size of the inventories in the main lexifiers of the languages. For example, Hawaiian, which is the main lexifier for Pidgin Hawaiian, only has 8 consonants (Roberts 2013a), and Unami, the main lexifier for Pidgin Delaware, only had 13 consonants (Goddard 1997). In these cases the small inventories in the pidgin languages are not due to any kind of reduction in the pidgin. It might therefore be worthwhile to compare the inventories of the pidgins and their main lexifiers, in order to check whether pidgins actually have reduced the number of segments. Following Bakker (2009), this is done in Table 9.3 for those pidgins which only have one major lexifier.

Table 9.3 Comparison of consonant and vowel quality inventories in the current pidgin sample (based on Bakker 2009 with some modifications) and their main lexifier languages. For a full legend of the languages in the pidgin sample, see http://dx.doi.org/10.1075/cll.48.additional.

Pidgin			Lexifier			Difference	
	N Cs	N Vs		N Cs	N Vs	Cs	Vs
Pidgin Ngarluma	15	5	Ngarluma	18	3	−3	+2
Pidgin Delaware	13	6	Unami	13	6	=	=
Pidgin Hawaiian	8	5	Hawaiian	8	5	=	=
Mobilian Jargon	15	3	Choctaw	15	3	=	=
Yokohama Pidgin Japanese	19	5	Japanese	19	5	=	=
WWII Bazaar Malay	17	5	Malay	19	6	−2	−1
Pidgin Fijian	14	6	Fijian	17	6	−4	=
New Caledonia Pidgin French	16	7	French	21	11	−5	−4
Pidgin Swahili	21	5	Swahili	26	6	−5	−1
Tây Bồi	15	10	French	21	11	−6	−1
Chinese Pidgin English	17	11	English	24	13	−7	−2
Pidgin Madame	18	3	Lebanese Arabic	25	3	−7	=
Taimyr Pidgin Russian	27	5	Russian	34	5	−7	=
Turku Pidgin Arabic	20	5	Chad Arabic	33	7	−13	−2
Fanakalo	21	5	Nguni	39	7	−18	−2

Table 9.3 shows that four of the 15 pidgins have the same number of consonants as their main lexifier language, while seven of 15 have the same number of vowel qualities as their main lexifier. In all of the cases where the number of vowel qualities has remained the same the lexifier had a small or average sized inventory (notice that Pidgin Ngarluma in fact has increased the number of vowel qualities). Though this sample is too small for statistical analyses, the pattern in Table 9.3 could indicate that pidgins might reduce the number of segments compared to their lexifiers if the inventories in the latter tend towards the higher numbers, but that smaller and average size inventories tend to remain intact.

9.2.2 Phoneme inventories of extended pidgins (pidgincreoles)

The sample of extended pidgins is too small for any kind of statistical analysis, but it is interesting to note that only one of the languages (Hiri Motu) has a small consonant inventory and three (Tok Pisin, Solomon Islands Pijin and Juba Arabic) have moderately small consonant inventories. Four of the languages, Cameroon Pidgin English, Ghanaian Pidgin English, Bislama and Sango, have average sized consonant inventories, while Nagamese has a moderately large and Nigerian Pidgin a large consonant inventory. In fact, both Nagamese and Nigerian Pidgin have larger consonant inventories than their main lexifier (Assamese and English respectively). All but three of the languages have average sized vowel quality inventories. Although Nigerian Pidgin, Ghanaian Pidgin English and Sango all have large vowel quality inventories (with 7 vowels each), their inventories are smaller than that of their main lexifier (English and Ngbandi).

9.2.3 Creole phoneme inventories

Creole languages are also widely described as having a reduced inventory of phonemes compared to their major lexifier languages, and to have retained the common core inventories of the languages in contact (cf. Winford 2003: 319). Pichi, for example, has only 16 consonants (/p, b, m, f, t, d, n, s, l, ʧ, ʤ, j, k, ŋ, w, ʁ/) and six vowels (/i, e, a, ɔ, o, u/; cf. Yakpo 2013), both a fair bit fewer than the lexifier English (24 consonants, /p, b, m, w, f, v, θ, ð, t, d, n, s, z, ɹ, l, ʃ, ʒ, ʧ, ʤ, j, k, g, ŋ, h/ and 13 vowels, /i, ɪ, e, ɛ, æ, ə, ɜ, ɒ, ɑ, ɔ, ʌ, ʊ, u/ in RP). For thorough discussions on creole segment inventories, see, for example, Smith (2008), Uffmann (2009), Webb (2009) and Klein (2011, 2013c).

In order to test whether creole languages tend to have smaller segment inventories than non-creoles, I compared the current creole sample with the languages in Maddieson's databases (Maddieson 2013a, 2013e). The figures are summarized in Tables 9.4 and 9.5:

Table 9.4 Size of consonant inventories in the current creole sample and in WALS (Maddieson 2013a)*. For a full legend of the languages in the creole sample, see http://dx.doi.org/10.1075/cll.48.additional.

	Creole sample		WALS*	
	N	%	N	%
small (6–14)	1	2.2	89	15.8
moderately small (15–18)	11	23.9	121	21.5
average (19–25)	28	60.9	201	35.8
moderately large (26–33)	6	13	94	16.7
large (34+)	0	–	57	10.1
Total	46		562	

($\chi^2 = 17.60$; $df = 4$; $p_{\text{two-tailed}} = 0.0015^{**}$, $p_{\text{sim}} = 0.0011^{**}$ (B = 10,000))
($G = 23.08$; $df = 4$; $p_{\text{two-tailed}} < 0.001^{***}$)
* Ndyuka (Nengee) has been removed from the WALS sample to avoid overlap with the creole sample.

The distribution in Table 9.4 is very significant; there is only one creole language (Nheengatú) with a small consonant inventory, while most of the other languages occupy the middle range (moderately small to moderately large). If we compare the figures of the three middle range groups between the samples, it turns out that there is no significant difference between the proportions.[156]

Table 9.5 Vowel quality inventories in the current creole sample and in WALS (Maddieson 2013e). For a full legend of the languages in the current creole sample, see http://dx.doi.org/10.1075/cll.48.additional.

	Creole sample		WALS	
	N	%	N	%
small (2–4)	1	2.2	93	16.5
average (5–6)	18	39.1	286	50.8
large (7–14)	27	58.7	184	32.7
Total	46		563	

($\chi^2 = 15.14$; $df = 2$; $p_{\text{two-tailed}} < 0.001^{***}$, $p_{\text{sim}} < 0.001^{***}$ (B = 10,000))
($G = 16.61$; $df = 2$; $p_{\text{two-tailed}} < 0.001^{***}$)

156. The distribution is then not significant according to a chi-square goodness-of-fit test ($\chi^2 = 3.49$; $df = 2$; $p_{\text{two-tailed}} = 0.174$).

Based on the distribution in Table 9.5 it seems as if creoles are likely to have average or large vowel quality inventories.[157] It may be the case that the figures for both the consonant and vowel quality inventories reflect the patterns of the major lexifier language. In fact, almost all of the lexifier languages in the current consonant sample have moderately small (Dutch), average (English, French, Spanish, Portuguese, Malay) or moderately large (Arabic) consonant inventories, and all have large vowel inventories except for Arabic (small), Malay (average), Tupinamba (average) and Spanish (average). When comparing the actual number of segments, most creoles differ from their main lexifier:

Table 9.6 Comparison of consonant and vowel quality inventories between the current creole sample and their lexifiers. For a full legend of the languages in the creole sample, see http://dx.doi.org/10.1075/cll.48.additional.

	C inventory		V inventory	
	N	%	N	%
smaller	26	56.5	41	89.1
same	2	4.3	1	2.2
larger	18	39.1	4	8.7
Total	46		46	

The figures in Table 9.6 indicate that the creoles in the current sample tend to differ from their lexifier with respect to segment inventories. A little over half of the languages have fewer consonants than their main lexifier, but almost two fifths have a larger consonant inventory than their main lexifier.[158] Almost all of the creoles in the sample have fewer vowels than their lexifier. For a discussion on the type of segments that tend to be replaced, see Smith (2008).

9.2.4 Phoneme inventories of mixed languages

Mixed languages are still not well studied, but are typically described to have phoneme inventories of roughly the same size as one of the contributing languages (cf. Bakker 2009 with further references), typically with some influence from the other contributing language.

157. Specifically, small inventories for creoles was significantly underrepresented ($p = 0.032^*$) and large inventories was significantly overrepresented ($p = 0.039^*$). These figures were generated with the HCFA 3.2 script provided by Stefan Th. Gries, the use of which is here gratefully acknowledged. See further http://www.linguistics.ucsb.edu/faculty/stgries/, accessed 11 February 2015.

158. It is interesting to note that all but two of the 12 Portuguese-lexified creoles have a larger consonant inventory than their lexifier language. Batavia Creole has the same amount of consonants and Papiá Kristang has two fewer. All but three of the 16 English-lexified creoles have fewer consonants than their lexifier. Gullah has the same amount, while Creolese and Saramaccan both have two more.

An example of a mixed language which has taken over the phoneme inventories of one of the contributing languages is Ejnu, a Uyghur/Persian mixed language spoken in the Xinjiang Uyghur Autonomous Region in western China, which has taken over the Uyghur phonological system wholesale (Lee-Smith 1996a: 851).[159] Similarly in Tangwang (Mandarin/Dongxiang, spoken in the Gansu province in north-central China) the phonological system is largely Mandarin (Lee-Smith 1996c: 875). Yet another example is Media Lengua (Spanish/Quechua), spoken in Ecuador, where the phonological system is essentially Quechua (Muysken 2013a: 145). For more on Media Lengua, see 10.4.3.

An example of a mixed language where the phoneme inventory can be seen as a compromise between the two contributing languages is the Tanzanian language Ma'á/Mbugu (Bantu/Cushitic), which has taken over the phonemic inventory of the contributing Bantu languages, but has added three consonants (/ɬ/, /χ/ and /ŋ̊χ/) from the Cushitic contributing languages (Mous 2003b: 95ff). Similarly, Michif (Cree/French), spoken in the Canada/USA border region, has 25 consonants, which is more than either of the contributing languages have (Cree has 13 and the relevant French variety has 21) and includes segments from both contributing systems. For more on Michif, see Section 3.3.2.

9.3 Syllable structures

Almost all languages in the world allow CV syllables, where C stands for any consonant and V for any vowel (long or short, monophthong or diphthong). This section will compare the kind of syllable structure allowed in a selection of pidgin and creole languages with the languages in WALS (Maddieson 2013c), as well as briefly bring up some syllable structures of extended pidgins (pidgincreoles) and mixed languages. The values for the pidgin and creole samples are based on those in Maddieson (2013c): a 'simple' structure means that the language maximally allows a CV syllable, a 'moderately complex' structure means that the language maximally allows a CCVC syllable and a 'complex' structure means that the language minimally allows a CCCVCC syllable.[160] It is beyond the scope of this section to discuss in detail the kinds of syllable structures that languages may allow and how syllables may pattern in individual languages. For a detailed study on the typology of syllables, see, for example, Levelt & van de Vijver (2004). For a detailed study on calculating syllable complexity, see, for example, Shosted (2006).

---

159. But see Johanson (2001: 21f), who considers the language an Uyghur variety with heavy Persian borrowing and who states that it is a secret language used by males only.

160. This conflates features 118 and 119 in Michaelis et al. (2013a).

9.3.1 Pidgin syllable structures

Pidgin languages are often described as preferring CV syllable structures (cf. Mühlhäusler 1997: 140f). The syllable structure in Chinese Pidgin Russian, for example, is essentially either V or CV (Perekhvalskaya 2013a: 71). However, there are also pidgin languages that allow more complex syllables, such as Chinuk Wawa – as in, for example, *makʷst* 'two', which exhibits a CVCCC structure (Grant 2013a: 152).

In order to test whether pidgin languages tend to have less complex syllable structures than non-pidgin languages, I compared the current pidgin sample with Maddieson's (2013c) sample. The figures are summarized in Table 9.7:

Table 9.7 Syllable structure in the current pidgin sample and in WALS (Maddieson 2013c). For a full legend of the languages in the pidgin sample, see http://dx.doi.org/10.1075/cll.48.additional.

	Pidgin sample		WALS	
	N	%	N	%
simple	5	25	61	12.6
moderately complex	12	60	274	56.4
complex	3	15	151	31.2
Total	20		486	

($\chi^2 = 3.96$; $df = 2$; $p_{\text{two-tailed}} = 0.14$, $p_{\text{sim}} = 0.14$ (B = 10,000))
($G = 3.67$; $df = 2$; $p_{\text{two-tailed}} = 0.16$)

Table 9.7 shows that pidgins are about as likely to allow moderately complex syllable structures as non-pidgins. While the current sample of pidgin languages is small, these figures might still very tentatively serve as an indication that pidgins in fact do not differ from non-pidgins with respect to syllable structure (cf. also the discussion in Bakker 2009).

9.3.2 Syllable structures in extended pidgins (pidgincreoles)

In the small sample of extended pidgins all but three languages allow complex syllables. Ghanaian Pidgin English, for example, allows up to three consonants in the onset, as in *strit* 'street' and up to two consonants in the coda, as in *plant* 'plant' (Huber 2013b). Solomon Islands Pijin, however, only allows maximally moderately complex syllables, such as *su.kul* 'school', with a single consonant coda, or *klos* 'closed', with a consonant cluster onset and a single consonant coda (Jourdan & Selbach 2004: 699, 702). Hiri Motu only allows simple CV syllables (Wurm & Harris 1963), as does spoken Sango (Samarin 2013b), while written Sango allows at most moderately complex syllables, such as *kir* 'to return', with a single consonant coda (Samarin 2013b).

9.3.3 Creole syllable structures

Creole languages have also been described as preferring CV syllable structures. In fact it has even been claimed that CV syllables are the only type of syllables allowed in creoles (cf. Romaine 1988: 63). This may be due to the occurrence of vowel insertion in various creole languages, for example the Negerhollands *miløk* 'milk' (van Sluijs 2013b: 267), where the consonant cluster *lk* has been broken up. However, there are a number of examples of creoles, including Negerhollands, that allow more complex syllables than CV, such as *ven.stər* 'window', with a CVC.CCVC structure or *skrẽw* 'scream', with a CCCVC structure (van Sluijs 2013b: 272f). For a thorough discussion on creole syllable structures, see, for example, Klein (2011, 2013c).

In order to test whether creole languages tend to allow less complex syllable structures than non-creole languages, I compared the current creole sample with the languages in Maddieson's (2013c) sample. The figures are summarized in Table 9.8:

Table 9.8 Syllable structure in the current creole sample and in WALS (Maddieson 2013c). For a full legend of the languages in the creole sample, see http://dx.doi.org/10.1075/cll.48.additional.

	Creole sample		WALS*	
	N	%	N	%
simple	4	7.8	61	12.6
moderately complex	12	23.5	273	56.3
complex	35	68.6	151	31.1
Total	51		485	

($\chi^2 = 28.86$; $df = 2$; $p_{\text{two-tailed}} < 0.001$***, $p_{\text{sim}} < 0.001$*** (B = 10,000))
($G = 26.94$; $df = 2$; $p_{\text{two-tailed}} < 0.001$***)
* Ndyuka (Nengee) has been removed from the WALS sample to avoid overlap with the creole sample.

What the figures in Table 9.8 indicate is that creoles actually seem significantly more likely to allow complex syllables than non-creoles. This could possibly be due to the fact that the absolute majority of the creoles in the sample have lexifiers which allow complex syllable structures (i.e. Dutch, English and French).

9.3.4 Syllable structures in mixed languages

The syllable structures of mixed languages are still not well studied, but many seem either to be a compromise between the two contributing languages or to essentially represent the system of one of the contributing languages. Petjo, a Malay/Dutch language spoken in Indonesia, is an example of a language whose syllable structure is in a sense a compromise between the two contributing languages. In general words have been adapted to the CVCV structure of Malay, but the language also does allow more complex syllables:

Petjo (Malay/Dutch: Indonesia)

(203)	/kerek/	<	Du. *kerk* 'church'	
	/seterop/	<	Du. *stroop* 'syrup'	
	/aseret/	<	Du. *arresteren* 'to arrest'	
	/duisent/	<	Du. *duizend* 'thousand'	
	/bors/	<	Du. *borst* 'chest'	(van Rheeden 1994: 228f)

In (203) most of the consonant clusters in the Dutch etyma have been broken up through vowel insertion, adapting the words to the Malay syllable structure, but the last two words show that coda consonant clusters are allowed (*nt* and *rs*).

Another example of a compromise system is that in Gurindji Kriol, a Gurindji/Kriol language spoken in Australia: while complex syllables are allowed (with up to three consonants in the onset and two in the coda), VC syllables are only allowed in words of Kriol origin (Meakins 2013a: 132). For more on Gurindji Kriol, see 9.5.3.

Shelta (Irish/English) is an example of a language where the syllable structure has essentially been taken over from one of the contributing languages, namely Irish. For instance, certain consonant clusters that are allowed in Irish but not in English also appear in Shelta, such as *sr-* in *srigo* 'king' (Grant 1994: 129). For more on Shelta, see 11.4.3.

9.4 Tone

It is quite common in the world to have contrastive tone. This section will compare the kinds of tone systems found in a selection of creole languages with the languages in WALS (Maddieson 2013d), as well as briefly mention some tone systems in pidgins, extended pidgins (pidgincreoles) and mixed languages. The values for the creole sample are based on those in Maddieson (2013d): a 'simple' tone system means that the language only has a two-way tonal contrast (typically H versus L);[161] a 'complex' tone system means that the language has more than two contrasting tones. It is beyond the scope of this section to discuss in detail the kinds of tone systems found in the world. For a thorough discussion on tone, see, for example, Yip (2002).

9.4.1 Tone in pidgin languages

Very little information is available on tone in pidgin languages. In many cases this is because the languages are already extinct (such as Lingua Franca or Pidgin Delaware) and the sources available do not mention tone. In a few cases we know that at least one of the input languages makes use of contrastive tone, but the pidgin is described as non-tonal, such as Chinese Pidgin Russian, where Mandarin was one of the major

161. This conflates the values 'Reduced tone system', 'Simple system, for lexical distinctions only' and 'Simple system, for lexical and grammatical distinctions' in Maurer & the APiCS Consortium (2013).

input languages (Shapiro 2012, Perekhvalskaya 2013b), Singapore Bazaar Malay, where Hokkien was one of the major input languages (Aye 2013) and Chinese Pidgin English, where Cantonese was one of the major input languages (Li & Matthews 2013). Mandarin, Hokkien and Cantonese are all tone languages (Yip 2002). In Fanakalo there is a very limited use of tone: the difference between *ló* 'that; relative particle' and *lò* 'the; this' is one of tone, but that is the only instance of contrastive tone in the language (Mesthrie 2013), though the lexifier Zulu has a two-way tone contrast (Maddieson 2013d).

9.4.2 Tone in extended pidgins (pidgincreoles)

All of the African extended pidgins have tone: Ghanaian Pidgin English, Cameroon Pidgin English and Nigerian Pidgin all have simple tone systems, in all cases used both for lexical and for grammatical distinctions. In both Ghanaian Pidgin English and Cameroon Pidgin English, the lexical verb *gó* 'to go' and the grammatical tense marker *gò* 'FUTURE' are distinguished through tone only (Huber 1999b: 221, Menang 2004: 915). In Ghanaian Pidgin English the free pronouns carry a high tone, while the bound pronouns carry a low tone (Huber 1999b: 200). In Nigerian Pidgin the copula *de* is distinguished from the incompletive aspect marker *dè* through tone only (Faraclas 1996: 170). Sango has a complex tone system, with three different tones (low, mid, high); they are mainly used to differentiate lexemes, as in *kwa* 'work' (low tone) versus *kwä* 'hair, feather' (mid tone) versus *kwâ* 'death, corpse' (high tone) (Samarin 2013b citing Samarin 1967).

9.4.3 Tone in creole languages

Tone is generally assumed to be of marginal relevance to creole languages, and, if present at all, to have only two contrasts restricted to the lexicon only (cf. McWhorter 2005: 13f). Hawai'i Creole English, for example, lacks tone, even though southern Chinese languages belong to the major substrates. However, there are creole languages with contrastive tone, such as Krio:

Krio (Creole (English-lexified): Sierra Leone)

(204) a. a wan fɔ gó na os
1SG want COMP go LOC house
'I want to go home.'

b. wi gò ebul am
1PL FUT able it
'We will overcome (the difficulties).' (Finney 2013a: 164f)

In (204a) we have the lexical verb *gó* 'to go' while in (204b) we have the future marker *gò*; the only difference between the two is the tone (for more on Krio, see Section 8.3.3).

In order to test whether creole languages are less likely to have tone than non-creole languages, I compared the creole sample with the languages in Maddieson's (2013d) sample. The figures are summarized in Table 9.9:

Table 9.9 Tone in the current creole sample and in WALS (Maddieson 2013d). For a full legend of the languages in the creole sample, see http://dx.doi.org/10.1075/cll.48.additional.

	Creole sample		WALS*	
	N	%	N	%
No tone	34	68	307	58.4
Simple tone system	16	32	131	24.9
Complex tone system	–	–	88	16.7
Total	50		526	

($\chi^2=9.98$; $df=2$; $p_{two\text{-}tailed}=0.0068$**, $p_{sim}=0.0069$** (B = 10,000))
($G=17.19$; $df=2$; $p_{two\text{-}tailed}<0.001$***)
*Ndyuka (Nengee) has been removed from the WALS sample to avoid overlap with the creole sample.

Table 9.9 shows that there is a difference in the distribution between the creole and WALS sample in that complex tone systems are very significantly underrepresented in the creole sample. It should also be noted that Maddieson (2013d) states that tone languages are likely to be underrepresented in his sample, in which case the difference between the two samples would be even more pronounced. A further point to note is that the absolute majority of the creoles in the current sample have nontonal lexifier languages.[162]

The assumption that creoles would only have lexical tone, however, is not borne out by the current sample, where seven of the 16 tonal languages have both lexical and grammatical tone. All but one (Saramaccan) are creole languages spoken in Africa.

9.4.4 Tone in mixed languages

The tone systems of mixed languages are not well studied, but it seems as if those languages where at least one of the contributing languages is tonal will have a tone system. This may either have carried over from the input language(s) wholesale or may be a compromise.

Ma'á/Mbugu (Bantu/Cushitic: Tanzania) is an example of a mixed language where the tone system seems to have been adopted wholesale from the Bantu input, including the tone sequence restrictions for verbs (Mous 2003b: 104).

Tangwang (Mandarin/Dongxiang: China) is an example of a mixed language which seems to show a compromise between the input languages in its tonal system. While Dongxiang (an Altaic Mongolic language) is nontonal, Mandarin has four contrastive tones. Tangwang also has four tones, but they have different values than the Mandarin ones and two of them seem to be merging (Lee-Smith 1996c: 876).

162. But notice that 13 of the 16 tonal creole languages have nontonal lexifiers (English and Portuguese).

9.5 Snapshots

Pidgins are assumed to have small phoneme inventories, simple syllable structures and no tone. Tây Bòi is an example of a pidgin language with a small consonant inventory but large vowel inventory, moderately complex syllables and five tones (which, however, were not phonemic).

Creoles are also assumed to have small phoneme inventories, simple syllable structures and no tone. Nheengatú is an example of a creole which, in fact, does have both a small consonant and a small vowel inventory, but which allows moderately complex syllables. There is no tone.

Mixed languages are assumed to have phonemic inventories, syllable structures and tone systems that are either adopted from one of the input languages or constitute a blend of the systems of the two input languages. Gurindji Kriol essentially shows a blend of the two input languages with respect to the phoneme inventory and syllable structure, but there is also stratification depending on the origins of the stems. There is no tone.

9.5.1 Tây Bòi: An extinct French-lexified pidgin in Vietnam[163]

9.5.1.1 *A brief background sketch of Tây Bòi*

Tây Bòi, also called *Vietnamese Pidgin French* or *Annamite French*, was spoken in and around Saigon and other urban centres of French Indochina from about the 1860s until about 1960. By 1971 there were only rememberers left (Reinecke 1971).

The area which is now Vietnam had been part of Imperial China until 939, when a succession of revolts resulted in independence. After that a series of royal dynasties expanded in various areas, leading to clashes with neighbours to the east and south. In 1772 a revolution directed against the northern and southern ruling houses, led by the Tay Son brothers, brought a 30-year period of political chaos and civil war. When the southern royal Nguyen family was massacred in 1777, one member, Nguyen Anh (later Gia Long) survived and went on to fight a series of battles against the Tay Sons (Lâm 2010).

While the Portuguese had already arrived in 1515 and had established a trading port in Faifo (modern Hoi An) by 1523, after which both Dominican and Jesuit missionaries arrived, the two ruling houses of the area "had lost interest in maintaining relations with European countries" by the end of the 17th century (Britannica 2011d). France tried unsuccessfully to gain access to the region for several decades, and it was not until the French support of Nguyen Anh's campaigns against the Tay Sons that France was able to secure a presence in the area, not the least through missionary work which led to a high number of converts to Catholicism. Nguyen Anh managed to gain control over the kingdom in 1802 and declared himself emperor, took the name Gia Long and named his empire Vietnam.

The empire grew increasingly anti-Western and anti-Catholic and started to dismiss French advisors as well as persecute missionaries and Vietnamese Christians. This, coupled with the wish to add Asian territories to the French domain, eventually resulted in a French military

163. This section is almost exclusively based on Reinecke (1971).

intervention in 1858. By 1867 the French had conquered the territory and named the colony Cochinchina (Lâm 2010).

Tây Bòi developed between the Vietnamese and the French, initially in the French colonial garrisons (Reinecke 1971). The name essentially means something like 'Westerner's houseboy' from the Vietnamese *tây* 'west(ern)' and *bòi* 'houseboy, waiter', the latter via French (Nguyễn 1995) but ultimately possibly from Chinese Pidgin English *boy* 'servant'. It was predominantly used "in the armed services, the police, the lower ranks of government service, and between masters and servants in French households" (Reinecke 1971: 47). It seems to have been quite stigmatized, with French being the normative H variety and the "language of command" (*ibid.*), which was taught only to a small minority of Vietnamese. While there was a great deal of variation, the pidgin was stable enough to be used for such things as comic strips in print media where the Tây Bòi speaker "might typically be a Vietnamese soldier addressing his French officer" (Reinecke 1971: 48).

Anti-colonial sentiment started from the very beginning of the French colonial rule, expressed in various forms, including guerrilla group attacks and revolutions. During the Japanese occupation in World War II the Indochinese Communist Party, under Nguyen Ai Quoc (known as Ho Chi Minh) formed the League for the Independence of Vietnam (later Viet Minh), which briefly seized power after the Japanese surrender. France sought to re-establish its colonial rule, causing the First Indochina War in 1946 which ended in 1954 with the Geneva Accords, where France renounced their claims to any territory in Indochina. With the withdrawal of French rule and the departure of almost all the French, the contexts in which Tây Bòi had been used in effect disappeared, leading to the rapid decline of the language.

9.5.1.2 *A short linguistic sketch of Tây Bòi*

It should be noted that there was a great deal of variation in Tây Bòi, depending on the nature and intensity of the dealings with the French that the speakers had, as well as depending on the ethno-linguistic backgrounds of the speakers. The variety described here represents that of servants in Ho Chi Minh City (Saigon).

Tây Bòi had 15 consonants, /p, m, f, w, t, d, n, s, l, r, ɲ, ʃ, j, k, ɣ/ and 10 vowels, /i, e, ɛ, a, ɘ, ɐ, ɔ, ɤ, o, u/. There were no nasalized vowels. There were five tones, "though without phonemic function" (Reinecke 1971: 48). Syllables could be moderately complex with up to one consonant onset and one consonant coda.

The morphology was overwhelmingly analytic. There was no reduplication.

Nouns were invariant, with no plural marking (as in (205a, b)), though some plural forms had fossilized (as in (205c)).

(205) a. demain moi bouver thé avec ami
tomorrow 1SG drink tea with friend
'Tomorrow I will drink tea with my friend(s).'

b. couper deux ce gâteau
divide two DEF cake
'Divide these two cakes equally.'

c. haut les mains
up the hands
'Hands up!' (Reinecke 1971: 51, 53)

Gender and case were not relevant. Definiteness was typically not indicated, except in a few set expressions such as *larobe, leriz*, etc. (and see (205c) above), although the fusion of the article with the noun, which is otherwise common in French-lexified varieties, is generally not found. There were five classifiers:

CLASSIFIER	MEANING	EXAMPLE	TRANSLATION
cái	general classifier	*cái trois tasse*	'the three cups'
bộ	set	*bộ pyjama*	'the suit of pyjamas'
chiếc	item (especially in sets of two)	*chiếc sabot*	'the wooden slipper(s)'
con	living non-human being	*con cochon*	'the pig(s)'
trái	fruit	*trái coco*	'the coconut(s)'

(Reinecke 1971:50)

When pointing out objects, however, the French demonstratives were used, as in *Ce robe ci sale* 'This dirty dress here' (cf. also Example (205b)). In acrolectal speech there were postposed demonstratives *içi* 'this, these' and *làbas* 'that, those', as in *livre içi* 'this/these book(s)' and *madame làbas* 'that/those woman/women' (Stageberg 1956:169).

Adjectives were invariant, typically in the masculine form; the comparative was expressed with *beaucoup* 'much' and the superlative with *plus* 'more'. For equatives *que* was used.

(206) a. cái robe blanc
CL.GEN dress white
'The white dress.' or 'The dress is white.'

b. moi beaucoup vieux
1SG much old
'I am older than you.'

c. Paul plus paresseux dans classe
PN more lazy in class
'Paul is the laziest of his class.'

d. mon garçon grand que mon fille
1SG.POSS boy big as 1SG.POSS girl
'My son is as big as my daughter.' (Reinecke 1971:51f, 54)

The personal pronouns were differentiated by three persons and two numbers. Politeness was distinguished in the second person singular (with the second person plural form). The possessive pronouns were identical to the personal except for the singular forms.

	PERSONAL	POSSESSIVE
1SG	*moi*	*mon*
2SG.FAM	*toi*	*ton*
2SG.POL	*vous*	*son*
3SG	*lui*	*lui*
1PL	*nous*	*nous*
2PL	*vous*	*vous*
3PL	*eux, lui*	*eux, lui*

The pronominal subject and/or object could be omitted:

(207) combien jour finir travail?
how.many day finish work
'How long will it take you/him/… to finish the job?' (Reinecke 1971: 51)

The verb was invariant. There was no tense, mood or aspect marking; temporal, modal and aspectual connotations had to be inferred from context (cf. (208a)) or were indicated adverbially (cf. (208b), cf. also (205a)), although acrolectal Tây Bòi might have had a completive aspect indicated by *ila/ija* or *dèja* (cf. (208c)):

(208) a. moi voir rien
1SG see nothing
'I saw/have seen/see/am seeing/will see nothing.' (Reinecke 1971: 54)

b. moi bouver thé jour avant
1SG drink tea day before
'I drank/was drinking tea yesterday.' (Reinecke 1971: 53)

c. lui ija finir travail
3SG COMPL finish work
'He has finished his work' (Stageberg 1956: 167)

The word order seems to have been subject-verb-object. Negation was indicated by the invariant *pas*:

(209) lui pas dire autres monsieurs
3SG NEG say other men
'He didn't/doesn't/won't tell other men.' (Stageberg 1956: 168)

There was no passive:

(210) lui là frapper
3SG there beat
'He was/is/will beating (somebody)' Or:
'He was/has been/is being/will be beaten (by somebody)' (Reinecke 1971: 53)

There was no copula (cf. Example (206)).

Polar questions were either indicated through intonation only (as in (211a)), or, in acrolectal varieties, could be indicated with a clause-final question particle *moyen* (as in (211b)) or through an A-not-A question (as in (211c)):

(211) a. vous ijena livre?
1PL EXIST book
'Do you have a book?'

b. toi dire encore moyen?
2SG say again Q
'Will you please repeat?'

c. toi venir pas venir?
2SG come NEG come
'Will you come?' (Stageberg 1956: 168)

Complex sentences, e.g. relative clauses, were indicated through juxtaposition only:

(212) la fille moi voir
DEF girl 1SG see
'The girl whom I saw.' (Stageberg 1956: 169)

9.5.1.3 *Short text*

(From Reinecke 1971: 54f: a policeman, who has arrested a man not carrying any identification, is reporting to his superior.)

La quanh Sa-đec vener la quanh Tân-an, trois jour déjà, pas travail; moi
there province S come there province T three day already NEG work 1SG

demander sa carte; lui dire nà pas; moi signer M. le Commissaire.
ask 3SG.POSS.F card 3SG say have NEG 1SG report Mr. the C

'He came from Sa-đec province to Tân-an province, has been here three days, has no job. I asked for his card; he said he did not have one; so I am reporting to M. le Commissaire.'

9.5.1.4 *Some sources of data*

There is very little data available for Tây Bòi. Reinecke (1971) and Stageberg (1956) provide a number of translated examples; the latter represents a more acrolectal variety. There are some sentences in Schuchardt (1888c), for which an English translation by Nguyen Dang Liem is given in Holm (1988: 360).

9.5.2 Nheengatú: A Tupinambá-lexified creole in Brazil[164]

9.5.2.1 *A brief background sketch of Nheengatú*

Nheengatú, also called *Ñeegatú, Nheengatu, Nyengato, Nyengatú, Waengatu, Yeral, Geral, Língua Geral, Coastal Tupian, Modern Tupí* by scholars, is called *Nheengatú* ('good talk') by the speakers themselves.[165] In 2010 it had about 4,500 mother tongue speakers in north-western Brazil, about 1,000 of them monolingual (Ethnolingüistica 2014). It is used as a *lingua franca* by another 14,000 (approximately) speakers in north-western Brazil and the bordering Colombian and Venezuelan areas (Lewis et al. 2014). There are several varieties, of which the best documented is the Upper Rio Negro dialect.

When the Portuguese settled on the north-eastern coast of what became Brazil, the entire coastal area from the mouth of the Amazon river down to what is now São Paolo was populated by people speaking Tupinambá, one of the many Tupian Tupi-Guaraní languages. Intermarriages between Portuguese colonists and Tupinambá women were common; Tupinambá was the language of the homes and was acquired by the mixed heritage (mestizo) children.

The Portuguese colonists, being under the impression that all indigenous people spoke Tupinambá, aimed to learn it in order to facilitate colonization and conversion. Jesuit missionaries

164. This section relies almost exclusively on da Cruz (2011).

165. The autoglossonym Nheengatú was initially suggested by José Couto do Magalhães and is a compound of the Nheengatú words *nheen* 'language' and *katu* 'be.good' (Couto de Magalhães 1876: xxxviii f).

produced descriptions of the language as early as 1595 (de Anchieta 1595) and initially referred to it as *Lingua Brasilica*, later as *Língua Geral*.

Portuguese colonization of the Amazonian region began with the establishment of Forte do Presépio on the mouth of the Amazon River in 1616. As the colonization pushed further inland in search for heavy metals, slaves and other sources of wealth, the colonizers were met with great linguistic diversity.

The Jesuits played a significant role in the spread of Língua Geral. In 1686 the Jesuit established control over a large portion of Amazonia and in 1689 the Portuguese government recognized Língua Geral as the official language of Amazônia and sanctioned its spread. The Jesuits increased efforts to relocate indigenous peoples to resettlement villages and established education in Língua Geral. These (forced) population movements were on a massive scale while the European population remained very small:

> in the four years 1687–1690, just from the areas reached by the Tocantins, Amazon and Negro Rivers, 184,000 Indians were seized and relocated for King and Church. By comparison, the European population was tiny. The 150 Europeans who arrived in 1616 had only grown to 1,000 by 1720, whereas only in Pará, excluding Maranhão, there were 63 resettlement villages with 54,264 Indians, as well as more than 20,000 Indian slaves and a number of mestizos. (Moore et al. 1993: 95)

Língua Geral became a means of communication between the resettled slaves as well as between the slaves and their European masters. The Europeans also used Língua Geral in their dealings with indigenous allied peoples, as well as in their everyday life among each other – both the Brazil born Europeans and the mestizos used Língua Geral. By the mid-1700s Língua Geral was "nearly universal in colonized Amazônia" (Moore et al. 1993: 95), which in turn meant that the Jesuits and their strong control over the indigenous population became a political threat against the Portuguese state. During the second half of the 18th century the Portuguese state thus sought to regain control over the area and, as part of that effort, persecuted Língua Geral and tried to establish Portuguese as the main means of education and communication. However, by now the indigenous population was in severe decline, due to slavery and introduced diseases, which did not favour the spread of Portuguese.

The 19th century saw a decline of Língua Geral: violent repressions of rebellions and uprisings cost tens of thousands of lives of Língua Geral speaking people. At the same time Portuguese settlers and their West African slaves were introduced into the areas, and, later, the rubber boom saw further introduction of Portuguese speaking people in the area.

It is not possible to pinpoint when the Língua Geral of the Jesuits (which was initially essentially late 16th-century Tupinambá) became the modern Língua Geral, i.e. Nheengatú. It was noted already in 1858 by Correa de Faria that modern Nheengatú differed considerably from the Língua Geral described in Figueira (1621); the multilingual backgrounds of the users, the geographic relocation to the Amazonian inland, which hosted a different linguistic environment than the coastal areas, as well as internal language change, are all likely to have led to the restructuring of what was once a variety of Tupinambá but what by the mid-19th century had become a different language.

While the shift to Portuguese continues, Nheengatú still survives in the far north-western area of Brazil, especially on the Rio Negro, not only as a mother tongue, but also as a *lingua franca* in a linguistically highly diverse area. In fact, its status is improving and its usage spreading. In 2003 Nheengatú was recognized as one of the official languages in the municipality of São Gabriel da Cachoeira (together with Portuguese, Baniwa and Tucano), which means that it may be taught in schools, is accepted for court dealings, and should be used in official government documents. Its use is also spreading to media, with local radio stations having begun to broadcast in Nheengatú.

9.5.2.2 *A short linguistic sketch of Nheengatú*

The orthography in this section follows that proposed in da Cruz (2011).

Nheengatú has 14 consonants, /p, b, m, w, t, d, s, n, ɾ, ʃ, ɲ, j, k, g/ and four vowels /i, e, a, u/. All vowels may be contrastively nasalized, as in *kawera* 'drunk' versus *kãwera* 'bone' or *ti* 'NEGator' versus *tĩ* 'nose' (da Cruz 2011: 58f). Notice that /ɾ, ʃ, ɲ, j/ are represented by <r, x, nh, y> respectively. Syllables may be moderately complex with maximally one consonant onset and one consonant coda, where the coda may only be either a glide (/w, j/) or a nasal (/m, n, ɲ/). Stress is contrastive, and is indicated with an accent (´) unless it falls on the first syllable of the stem (excluding affixes):

(213)	pirá	/pi'ɾa/	'fish'
	pira	/'piɾa/	'body'
	mirá	/mi'ɾa/	'tree'
	mira	/'miɾa/	'people'
	ayuká	/a-ju'ka/	'I kill' (lit. '1SG-kill')
	ayuka	/a-'juka/	'I pull' (lit. '1SG-pull') (da Cruz 2011: 75)

There is extensive affixation, both inflectional and derivational. Reduplication is used with verbs to indicate repetition.

Count nouns are inflected for plural with the particle *ita*, which may be omitted with quantifiers.

(214) a. taina ita kuera ta-yenù balaiu upe
child PL EGN 3PL-lie basket LOC
'Those who were children were lying in the basket.'

b. aitekua ita se-anama ita puru Warekena
DEM.PROX PL 1SG-family PL purely Warekena
'These, my family (members), are purely Warekena.' (da Cruz 2011: 149, 170)

Case is not relevant. There are two series of person prefixes, 'stative' and 'dynamic', which distinguish between three persons and two numbers:

	STATIVE	DYNAMIC
1SG	*se-*	*a-*
2SG	*ne-*	*re-*
3SG	*i-, s-*	*u-*
1PL	*yane-*	*ya-*
2PL	*pe-*	*pe-*
3PL	*ta-*	*tau-, ta-, tu-*

The stative prefixes appear on nouns (as possessive or definite markers) and stative verbs (as subject person markers), while the dynamic prefixes appear on dynamic verbs (as subject person markers). Nominal possession is indicated through juxtaposition, while pronominal possession is indicated with the stative person markers.

(215) ne-mena nheenga
2SG-husband language
'the language of your husband' (da Cruz 2011: 258)

The stative prefixes may also appear on postpositions (as person references):

(216) a. ti=ya-putai awa u-ri u-tumari yane-sui kua yane-iwi
NEG=1PL-want GHN 3SG-come 3SG-take 1PL-from DEM.PROX 1PL-land
'We don't want anyone to come and take our land from us.'
b. ixe a-uri pe-piri
1SG 1SG-live 2PL-with
'I live near you.' (da Cruz 2011: 202, 207)

There is a set of independent personal pronouns, with three persons and two numbers:

	SINGULAR	PLURAL
1	*ixe*	*yande*
2	*inde*	*penhe*
3	*ae*	*ai(n)ta*

The same pronominal forms function both as subjects and objects in the clause. There is an indefinite article *yepe* 'a' (cf. (222)) and two demonstratives, *aitekua/kua* 'this' and *aitenkaã/nhaã* 'that'.

Verbs are obligatorily inflected for person (as in (217a, b)). There is a perfective enclitic =*wã* (cf. (218a)), an imperfective proclitic *re*= (as in (217c)), and a proximate future particle *kuri* ((217d)). Iteration is expressed through reduplication (as in (217e)).

(217) a. nhaã kunhã u-u paa nhaã kumã
DEM.DIST woman 3SG-ingest REP DEM.DIST cuma.fruit
'(S/He said that) that woman ate that cuma (fruit).'
b. pai ita te ta-mbue yande
father PL FOC 3PL-teach 1PL
'The fathers did teach us.'
c. ti=re=re-pudei re-yawika
NEG=IPFV=2SG-can 2SG-lower
'You still can't bend (down).'
d. u-yupiru-sa kua Namuĩ pe-kua kuri
3SG-begin-NMLZ DEM.PROX Anamoim 2PL-know FUT
'You will (soon) know the beginning of this Annamoim.'
e. u-tuka~tuka ukena
3SG-knock~RED door
'They knocked (on the) door (repeatedly).' (da Cruz 2011: 181, 184, 251, 311, 405)

There is an evidential marker *paa* 'REPortative' (cf. (217a)), as well as several other modal and aspectual particles.

Stative verbs are essentially the equivalent of adjectives in other languages. There are two types of stative verbs, a small, closed set that take the stative person markers (cf. (218a)), and an open set that do not take person markers (as in (218b)). Comparison is done with the postposition *sui* 'from' (as in (218c)).

(218) a. kurumĩ i-kuere=wã
boy 3SG-be.tired=PFV
'The boy was tired.'
b. kirimba ainta
be.strong 3PL
'They are strong.'
c. ixe waimĩ pi(ri) ne-sui
1SG old.woman be.more 2SG-from
'I am older than you.' (da Cruz 2011:190, 192, 203)

The word order is typically subject-verb-object. Even so, the adpositions are typically postnominal. There is a causative prefix *mu-*:

(219) nhaã kurumĩ u-mu-pinima itá
DEM.DIST boy 3SG-CAUS-be.colourful stone
'The boy painted the stone.' (Lit. 'The boy made the stone colourful') (da Cruz 2011:288)

Negation is expressed with proclitic *ti=* (cf. (216a), (217c)). There are the interrogative particles *taa* 'general interrogative', *maã* 'what' and *awa* 'who(m)'. Polar questions are formed with the question particle *será*, which appears after the verb:

(220) re-pudei será re-mẽ tata?
2SG-poder Q 2SG-dar fire
'Can you give me fire?' (da Cruz 2011:343)

The copula is optional:

(221) a. yande mira
1PL person
'We are persons.'
b. penhe ike
2PL here
'You are here'
c. ixe a-iku=wã ike
1SG 1SG-be=PFV here
'I was here.' (da Cruz 2011:143, 475)

There are a number of coordinators and subordinators. Relative clauses are indicated with the postposed relativizer *waa*:

(222) aitenhã u-riku mukũi tayera ita aikue yepe puranga
DEM.DIST 3SG-have two daughter PL EXIST INDEF be.beautiful
waa aikue amu puxuera waa
REL EXIST other be.ugly REL
'That (one) had two daughters. (He) had one who was beautiful (and he) had one who was ugly.'
(da Cruz 2011:267)

9.5.2.3 *Short text*

(From Moore et al. 1993: 111f; the speaker is a woman in her thirties from the Upper Rio Negro region. The original orthography and glossing has been modified to match that in da Cruz 2011.)

Ixe	akayu	novi	akayu-ana	a-yuiri	se-retãma	sui.	Ixe	a-yupukua	ike.	Ixe
1SG	year	nine	year-already	1SG-return	1SG-region	from	1SG	1SG-accustom	here	1SG

ti=a-manduari	a-yuiri	se-familia	ita	ruka	kiti.	A-kwakatu	ixe	ti=a-yupukua	a-kiti.
NEG=1SG-think	1SG-return	1SG-family	PL	house	to	1SG-believe	1SG	NEG=1SG-accustom	DEM-to

A-pita	kuri	ike	ate	mairamẽ	Tupana	ita	kuri	u-kua.	Maye	taa	a-su	anhu
1SG-stay	FUT	here	until	when	God	PL	FUT	3SG-know	be.how	INTERROG	1SG-go	only

a-wata	se-retãma	kiti	a-maã	arã	se-anama	ita?	Ixe	ti=a-manduari	a-yuiri
1SG-walk	1SG-region	to	1SG-see	DAT.PROSP	1SG-family	PL	1SG	NEG=1SG-think	1SG-return

a-kiti.	A-yuiri	kuri	anhu	a-maã	arã	se-anama	ita
DEM-to	1SG-return	FUT	only	1SG-see	DAT.PROSP	1SG-family	PL

'It has been nine years that I live in this city. I got used to this place. I don't think of returning to my family's house. I think I cannot accustom myself to that place anymore. Only God knows how long I'm going to stay here. How can I go back to that place only to see my family? I don't think of going back there. I will go back there just to visit my family.'

9.5.2.4 *Some sources of data*

There is a lot of data available on Nheengatú. da Cruz (2011) provides a large number of glossed and translated examples, as well as longer texts. *Ethnolingüistica* has made available a large number of publications about the language under the entry 'Nheengatú' (http://www.etnolinguistica.org/lingua:nheengatu, accessed 11 February 2015), including some very early grammatical descriptions. Unfortunately most of these sources are only accessible to those who read Portuguese. Moore et al. (1993) provide a number of examples and two texts, glossed and translated into English.

9.5.3 Gurindji Kriol: A Gurindji/Kriol mixed language in Australia[166]

9.5.3.1 *A brief background sketch of Gurindji Kriol*

Gurindji Kriol is spoken by about 1,000 people in and around Kalkaringi in the Victoria River District of northern Australia. It is called *Gurindji* or *miksimap* by the speakers themselves.

Before the European colonization of their lands, the Gurindji were a semi-nomadic people surviving on seasonal hunting and gathering on their traditional lands. Their land was created during a period called the Dreaming, when creatures in various forms sang the land into being and crossed it in tracks or lines, which shaped its features. The physical and spiritual well-being of the Gurindji hinges on the proper care of these lines and their places. The songs which tell about the Dreaming and how to maintain the land are passed down through family lines. Thus the land and the language are intimately connected and provide the basis for the Gurindji identity.

166. This section relies primarily on Meakins (2013a).

Europeans began settling the Victoria River District starting with the Gregory brothers' explorations in 1855, who found the land suitable for cattle stations. The Europeans brought with them diseases that the Aboriginal people were not able to cope with, causing severe depopulation. Added to that, the European settlers engaged in a series of massacres, which in some cases led to the virtual extinction of entire ethnic groups (such as the Karrangpurru). The survivors were taken as labour for the cattle stations. This was effectively slave labour: at Jinparrak (Old Wave Hill Station), where most of the Gurindji were forced to live and work, they were not paid any salaries and the living conditions were horrendous:

> They worked as station hands and stockmen in exchange for goods such as tobacco, salted meat, flour, sugar and tea, and occasionally clothes and blankets. Gurindji women were often forced into sexual liaisons with *kartiya* [white people – VV] stockmen. The Gurindji lived in humpies (shelters) which were constructed from discarded material from the station. Fresh water had to be drawn and carried some distance from a well. (Meakins 2008: 78)

The general health was consequently low and mortality high. A report on the conditions in 1948 (Berndt & Berndt 1948) did not lead to any noticeable change.

On 23 August 1966 Vincent Lingiari, a Gurindji stockman, announced a worker's strike and gathered his people for what became known as the Gurindji Walk-Off, when the group walked to what would eventually become a Gurindji settlement in Daguragu (one of the Dreaming points). Efforts to convince them to return to the station failed, including an offer of salaries equal to the white stockmen. The Gurindji held out for a return of their traditional land which had been colonized by Lord Vestey (owner of the Old Wave Hill Station, among a large number of other cattle stations). The struggle lasted nine years; in 1975 the Gurindji were granted a lease of land around Daguragu. In 1986, two decades after the Walk-Off, the Gurindji were granted inalienable freehold title of the land under the Northern Territory Land Rights Act.

The cattle station seems to have been multilingual, where Gurindji and Mudburra seem to have dominated and even acted as *lingua francas* among the Aborigines, while an Aboriginal English was used in dealings with white people (Berndt & Berndt 1987). By the mid-1970s Kriol (an English-lexified creole) was becoming the main language of many Aboriginal ethnic groups and the shift is still ongoing. Studies conducted in the mid-1970s by Patrick McConvell (cf. e.g. 1985, 1988) show that it was becoming common among the Gurindji people to code-switch between Kriol and different varieties of Gurindji. However, rather than being a stage in language shift from Gurindji to Kriol, the code-switching systematized into a new, mixed language. This makes Gurindji a very young language indeed; the fact that it has been documented since its inception in the 1970s is also highly unusual.

The crystallization of the code-switching into Gurindji Kriol is in many ways likely to be part of the identity of the Gurindji people, whose determined struggle for land recognition won them respect for their strength. The language is seen as a maintenance of Gurindji identity and a resistance to cultural invasion:

> the land claim and mixed language can both be viewed in terms of the persistence of the Gurindji identity under pressure from some of the follow-on effects of colonization such as the subsumption of Gurindji land for cattle and the spread of Kriol. (Meakins 2008: 86)

Today Gurindji Kriol is the first language of the younger generation (people under 35) in Kalkaringi and is also spreading to other areas. While it serves as an identity marker for Gurindji-ness, it is viewed by the older generation as a diluted and incorrect version of Gurindji (which is in such contexts usually referred to as "hard Gurindji", "rough Gurindji" or "proper Gurindji", Meakins 2013a:132). The community is multilingual, with Gurindji, Kriol, Gurindji Kriol as well as Aboriginal English and Standard Australian English being part of the linguistic environment.

9.5.3.2 *A short linguistic sketch of Gurindji Kriol*

Gurindji Kriol has 20 consonants, /p, b, m, t, s, n, l, ɾ, ɽ, ɳ, ɭ, r, ɟ, ʃ, ɲ, ʎ, j, k, ŋ, w/, and five vowels, /i, e, a, o, u/. The phonemic system is stratified in that some phonemes are only used in Kriol words (/f, s, ʃ, e, o/). Notice that /ɾ, ɽ, ɳ, ɭ, ɟ, ʃ, ɲ, ʎ, j, ŋ/ are represented by <rr, rt, rn, rl, j, sh, ny, ly, y, ng> respectively. The stratification is also visible in the syllable structures: VC syllables are only allowed in Kriol-derived words, while only Gurindji-derived words allow coda consonant clusters.

There is extensive suffixation, both inflectional and derivational. Reduplication may be used to express plurality or iteration.

Gurindji Kriol is essentially an N-V mixed language in that the grammatical structure for the noun phrase reflects the Gurindji structure while the grammatical structure for the verb phrase reflects the Kriol structure. While the language derives both nouns and verbs from both source languages, the grammatical markers and morphological structure are stratified according to the N/V divide. Consider the following:

(223)	an	skul-ta=ma	jei	bin	hab-im	sport	karu-walija-ngku
	and	school-LOC=TOP	3PL.S	PST	have-TR	sport	child-PAUC-ERG

'And the kids had sport at school.' (Meakins 2011:138)

In (223) two nouns (*skul* 'school' and *karu* 'child') are inflected with Gurindji bound grammatical markers (the suffixes *-ta* 'LOCative', *-walija* 'PAUCal' and *-ngku* 'ERGative', and the clitic *=ma* 'TOPic'), even though they have different source languages (*skul* < Kriol but *karu* < Gurindji). Similarly, the verb phrase takes Kriol verbal markers, even if the origin of the lexical verb is Gurindji (cf. Examples (224), (225c), (227b, c)).

Nouns may be optionally marked for plural with a Gurindji number suffix (*-kujarra* 'DUal', *-walija* 'PAUCal' or *-rrat* 'PLural') or with a co-indexed pronoun. There are six cases:

ERGative	*-ngku, -tu*
LOCative	*-ngka, -ta*
DATive	*-yu, -wu, -ku*
ALLative	*-ngkirri, -jirri*
ABLative	*-nginyi*
COMitative	*-yawung, -jawung*

There are a number of other nominal suffixes, such as agentive (*-kaji, -waji*), focus (*-na*) and topic (*-ma*) markers.

The pronominal system distinguishes between subject and object personal pronouns, a set of emphatic pronouns – which may take case marking – and a set of possessive pronouns. All sets have three persons; the personal pronoun set has three numbers; the personal pronoun object and possessive pronoun sets have an inclusive/exclusive distinction:

	PERSONAL		EMPHATIC	POSSESSIVE
	SUBJECT	OBJECT		
1SG	*ai*	*ngayu*	*ngayu*	*ngayini*
2SG	*yu*	*yu*	*nyuntu*	*nyununy*
3SG	*i*	*im*	*nyantu*	*nyanuny*
1DU	*wi*	*ngali*	–	–
2DU	*yutu(bala)*	*yutu(bala)*	–	–
3DU	*tu(bala)*	*tu(bala)*	–	–
1PL.INCL	–	*ngantipa*		*ngantipany*
1PL.EXCL	*wi*	*ngaliwa*	*ngaliwa*	*ngaliwany*
2PL	*yumob*	*yumob*	*nyurru(lu)*	*nyurruluny*
3PL	*dei*	*dem*	*nyarru(lu)*	*nyarruluny*

Possession is marked with the dative suffix:

(224) wartarra yu bin kirt det ngakparn-ku hawuj
goodness 2SG PST break DEF frog-DAT home
'Goodness me you broke the frog's home (the bottle).' (Meakins 2013a: 133)

There are eight tense/aspect markers: *bin* for past (cf. (223), (224)), *-l* for future (cf. (225a)), *garra* for future or potential (cf. (225b)), *-m* for present progressive (cf. (225c)), *olweis* for present habitual, *yusta* for past habitual (cf. (225d)), *til* for progressive, *stat* for inceptive, *-karra* for continuative (cf. (227c)), and a number of modal markers. The present is zero-marked (cf. (225e)). Many of the tense, mood or aspect markers may cliticize to subject pronouns (cf. also (228)).

(225) a. partaj motika-ngka wi-l teik-im-bek yu hospel
climb car-LOC 3PL.S-FUT take-TR-back 2SG hospital
'Climb into the car and we'll take you to the hospital.' (Meakins 2011: 200)

b. trajij ai garra put-im-an bo ngayini bebi Nikita karu
trousers 1SG.S POT put-TR-on DAT 1SG.DAT baby PN child
'I've got to put the trousers on my baby, Nikita's child' (Meakins 2011: 166)

c. warlaku i=m makin atsaid shop-ta
dog 2SG.S=PRES.PROG sleep outside shop-LOC
'The dog, it is sleeping outside the shop.' (Meakins 2013a: 134)

d. wi yusta gu kanyjurna la riba inti?
1PL.S PST.HAB go down LOC river Q
'We used to go down to the river, didn't we?' (Meakins 2011: 268)

e. an jinek-tu bait-im jat karu-yu dedi
and snake-ERG bite-TR DEF child-DAT father
'And the snake bites the child's father.' (Meakins 2011: 166)

There are also a large number of verbal suffixes (such as the transitive suffix *-im* or the many adverbial suffixes, which may denote space, lexical aspect, etc.).

The word order is predominantly subject-verb-object. There is a passive construction with *git* 'get':

(226) man i bin git bait warlaku-nginyi wartan-ta
man 3SG.S PST get bite dog-ABL hand-LOC
'The man got bitten by a dog on the hand.' (Meakins 2013a: 135)

Negation is formed with *kaan* for nonpast clauses (as in (227a)) and *neba* for past tense clauses (as in (227b)). There is a separate negator *don* for negative imperative (i.e. prohibitive) clauses (as in (227c)).

(227) a. yu put-im nyawa kuya so yu kaan nurt laiya-ngku nyanta
2SG put-TR this thus so 2SG NEG press liar-ERG DUB
'You put this one like that so you won't tread on it, you little liar' (Meakins 2013b)

b. i neba bin paraj nyila wartiya kanyjurra-k najing
3SG.S NEG.PST PST find that tree down-ALL nothing
'He didn't find the tree on the ground at all.' (Meakins 2013b: feature 50)

c. don pirr-karra la=im
PROHIB snatch-CONT OBL=3SG
'Don't snatch it from him!' (Meakins 2013b: feature 56)

There is no copula. Polar questions are either indicated by intonation only, or formed with a question particle *inti/init* (cf. (225d)) or *wayi*:

(228) an ngayu-ngku ai=rra luk-abta im wayi?
and 1SG-ERG 1SG.S=POT look-after 3SG.O Q
'And me, do I have to look after him?' (Meakins 2013b: feature 154)

There are a number of conjunctions, such as *an* 'and', *o* 'or', *dumaji/bikos* 'because', *bat* 'but', *ib* 'if', *den* 'then', etc. Coordinated clauses may also simply be juxtaposed. Subordinated clauses are indicated with a case marker on the verb of the subordinate clause.

(229) karu teik-im kajirri-yu makin-ta keik
child take-TR old.woman-DAT sleep-LOC cake
'The child takes the cake to the old woman who is sleeping.' (Meakins 2011: 199)

Relative clauses are formed with the relativizer *wen* or *weya* and an optional resumptive pronoun. There are serial verb constructions:

(230) i garra put-im makin yard-ta
3SG.S POT put-TR lie.down yard-LOC
'He will lay him down in the yard.' (Meakins 2013a: 136)

9.5.3.3 *Short text*

(From Meakins 2011:273f. Excerpt of a story about a boy who fell off his bicycle, narrated by a 25 year old woman to her 3 year-old child.)

I	bin	baldan	wartiti.	I	bin	lungkarra	na.	Nyanuny	kapuku	bin	kam	la=im
3SG.S	PST	fall	poor.thing	3SG.S	PST	cry	SEQ	3SG.DAT	sister	PST	come	OBL=3SG.O

"Yu	rait	papa	wat	rong,"	im=in	tok	la=im	"ai	bin	baldan	kapuku"	i
2SG	alright	brother	what	wrong	3SG.S=PST	talk	OBL=3SG.O	1SG.S	PST	fall	sister	3SG.S

bin	tok	det	karu.	I	bin	teik-im	jarrpip	najan	kapuku-ngku=ma	nganta	ankaj
PST	talk	DEF	child	3SG.S	PST	take-TR	carry	another	sister-ERG=TOP	DUB	poor.thing

an	i	bin	tok	la=im	kuya.	"Yu	liwart	hiya	baba	yarti-ngka	yu	liwart
and	3SG.S	PST	talk	OBL=3SG.O	thus	2SG	wait	here	brother	shade-LOC	2SG	wait

yarti-ngka	ai-l	kambek	igin	ai-l	gu	get-im	help."	I	bin	gon
shade-LOC	2SG.S-FUT	come.back	again	2SG.S-FUT	go	get-tr	help	3SG.S	PST	go

'He fell off his bike, poor thing. And then he cried. His sister came along to him. "Are you OK brother? What's wrong," she said to him. "I fell off (my bike) sister," the kid said. Another of his sisters tried to carry him away, poor thing. And she said to him like this: "You wait here in the shade, brother, you wait in the shade. I'll return. I've got to get some help." She went.'

9.5.3.4 *Some sources of data*

Meakins (2011, 2013a) contain numerous glossed and translated examples, as well as texts of Gurindji Kriol. The vast amount of data collected by Felicity Meakins has been collected in various databases (The ACLA database 2003–2006, the Gurindji Kriol database 2003–2006 and the DOBES database 2007–2008); unfortunately these are (as yet) not publicly available.

9.6 Summary

Pidgins tend to have moderately small consonant inventories and average sized vowel quality inventories; the segment inventories tend to be smaller than that of their main lexifiers. Pidgin languages do not seem to differ from non-pidgins in terms of syllable structures allowed. They do not seem to have contrastive tone.

Extended pidgins (pidgincreoles) seem to have average sized consonant inventories and large vowel quality inventories; most of the segment inventories in the sample are smaller than that of their main lexifiers. Most of the languages in the sample allow complex syllables and all of the African languages have contrastive tone.

Creole languages tend to have average sized consonant inventories and large vowel quality inventories; the segment inventories tend to be smaller than that of their main lexifiers. Creoles seem significantly more likely to have complex syllable structures than non-creoles. Creoles seem less likely than non-creoles to have complex tone systems, though simple tone systems are not uncommon.

Mixed languages seem to have segment inventories which are either taken over from one of the input languages or which represent a compromise or combination of the segment inventories in the input languages. The same seems to be the case with respect to syllable structure. Tone seems to be present in those mixed languages where at least one of the input languages is tonal.

9.7 Key points

- **The assumption that pidgins have smaller phoneme inventories than their lexifiers and that they lack tone is supported by the sample studied here.**
- **The assumption that pidgins prefer CV syllables is not supported by the sample studied here.**
- **The assumption that creoles have smaller phoneme inventories than their lexifiers is supported by the sample studied here.**
- **The assumption that creoles prefer CV syllables and either lack or have limited use of tone is not supported by the sample studied here.**
- **Extended pidgins (pidgincreoles) align with creoles rather than pidgins with respect to phoneme inventory size, syllable structure and tone.**
- **Mixed languages either adopt their phoneme inventories and syllable structure from one of the input languages or represent a blend of the input languages.**
- **Mixed languages are tonal if at least one of the input languages is tonal.**

9.8 Exercises

1. Give examples of mixed languages that represent a blend or compromise of their input languages with respect to phoneme inventory size, syllable structure and tone. What are the outcomes of these compromises?
2. How do the findings on creole phoneme inventories, syllable structures and tone relate to the notion of creoles as structurally simple languages?
3. How do the findings on creole phoneme inventories, syllable structures and tone relate to the notion of creoles as typologically unique languages?
4. How do the findings on pidgin phoneme inventories and syllable structure relate to the notion of pidgins as reduced linguistic systems?
5. What are the implications of the findings on the phoneme inventories, syllable structures and tone in extended pidgins (pidgincreoles)?

Languages cited in Chapter 10

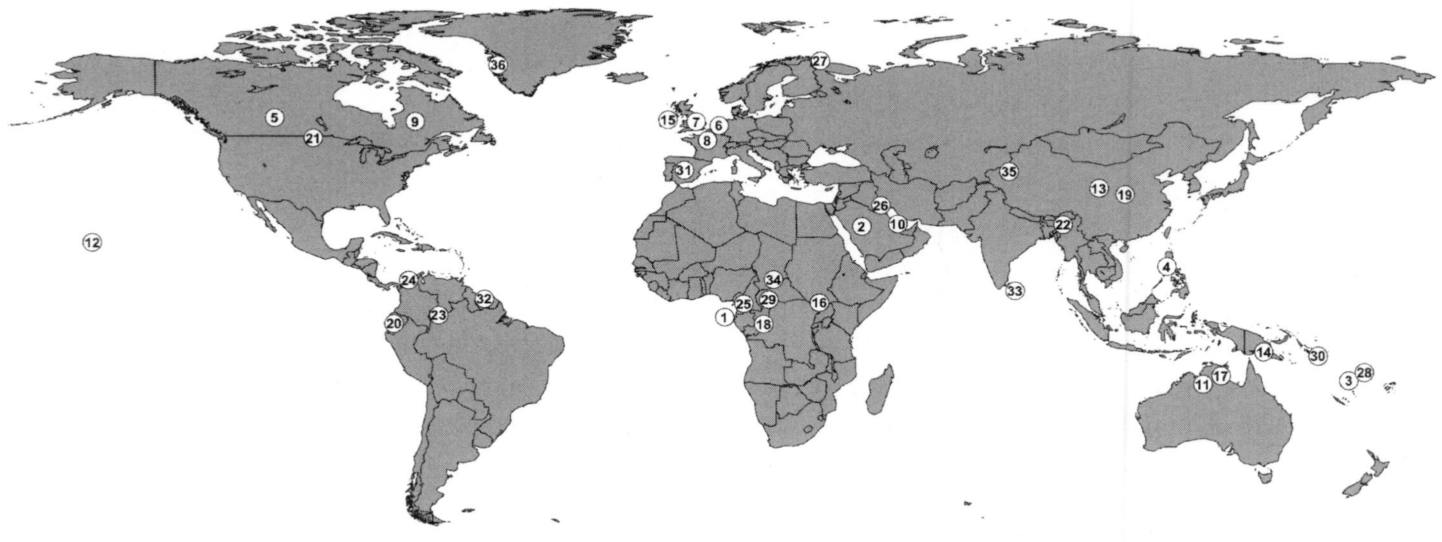

1. Angolar
2. Arabic, Standard
3. Bislama
4. Cavite Chabacano
5. Cree, Plains
6. Dutch
7. English
8. French
9. French, Canadian
10. Gulf Pidgin Arabic
11. Gurindji; Gurindji Kriol
12. Hawai'i Creole English
13. Hezhou
14. Hiri Trading Language, Eleman; Hiri Trading Language, Koriki; Tok Pisin
15. Irish; Shelta
16. Juba Arabic
17. Kriol
18. Lingala
19. Mandarin Chinese
20. Media Lengua; Quechua, Ecuadorian
21. Michif
22. Nagamese
23. Nhengatu
24. Palenquero
25. Pidgin A70
26. Romanian Pidgin Arabic
27. Russenorsk
28. Samoan Plantation Pidgin
29. Sango
30. Solomon Islands Pijin
31. Spanish
32. Guyanais; Nengee; Sranan; Tiriyó
33. Sri Lanka Portuguese
34. Turku
35. Uyghur
36. West Greenland Eskimo pidgin

Chapter 10

Morphology

Both pidgins and creoles are described as highly analytic morphologically, with little or no affixation. Reduplication is described as lacking in pidgins, while it is believed to be particularly common for creoles. Mixed languages are assumed to either have adopted one of the input systems, or to represent a blend of the two ancestral systems. This chapter will briefly discuss synthesis in pidgin, extended pidgin, creole and mixed languages (Section 10.2). Section 10.3 will empirically test whether pidgins and creoles differ from non-pidgins and non-creoles with respect to reduplication, and will provide some examples of reduplication in extended pidgins as well as mixed languages. Section 10.4 gives short sketches of three languages mentioned in the chapter: Turku (an extinct Arabic-lexified pidgin in Chad), Sranan (an English-lexified creole in Suriname) and Media Lengua (a Spanish/Quechua mixed language in Ecuador).

10.1 Introduction

A **morpheme** is the smallest meaning carrying unit in a language. Morphemes can be either free or bound: **free** morphemes can stand alone as their own words while **bound** morphemes need a host to attach to. In *I will go to work tomorrow* there are only free morphemes, while in *The children started school yesterday* there are two bound morphemes (*-en* and *-ed*). **Affixes** are obligatorily bound morphemes that carry grammatically inflectional or lexically derivational information. There are different kinds of affixes; **prefixes** attach at the beginning of a word (such as *un-* in *un-happy*), **suffixes** attach at the end of a word (such as *-ed* in *walk-ed* or *-less* in *luck-less*), **infixes** attach inside a host and **circumfixes** attach at both the beginning and the end of a host. **Clitics** are also bound morphemes, often (though not always) reduced forms of a free allomorph, but unlike affixes are not syntactically dependent on their host. For example, while a tense suffix like *-ed* can only attach to verbs (compare *walk-ed* with **dog-ed* or **small-ed*), a clitic may attach to words that belong to a different syntactic category than what the clitic is a marker of. For instance, the future marker *will* can reduce to *=ll*, and when it does so, it attaches to the previous word, irrespective of word class (as in *He'll be back tomorrow*, where *=ll* attaches to the subject pronoun and not the verb).[167]

---

167. Affix boundaries are indicated with '–' while clitic boundaries are indicated with '='.

Grammatical markers can be either **isolating**, in which case they are free morphemes (as in *will* for 'FUTURE' above), **concatenative**, in which case they are attached to a host (as in *-en* 'PLURAL' and *-ed* 'PAST' above), or **non-linear**, in which case they modify the host in some way (as in *sing* vs. *sang*, where tense is marked through vowel change). Morphological processes may differ in terms of **synthesis**, which, very simplified, is the level of accumulated information a word can hold. In **analytic** constructions there is no affixation while in **synthetic** constructions there is. For example, in *Lisa is **more beautiful** than Jane* we have an analytic comparative construction (indicated with the free morpheme *more* plus the adjective *beautiful*), whereas in *Lisa is **small-er** than Jane* we have a synthetic comparative construction (indicated with the affix *-er* on the adjective *small*). **Reduplication** is a morphological process which involves copying part or all of a base form and fusing it to that base form. In **full** reduplication the whole base is copied while in **partial** reduplication only some elements of the base are copied. Standard English does not have reduplication, but something like *happyhappy* (as in *I made a happyhappy dance*) would be an example of full reduplication, while something like *hahappy* (as in *I made a hahappy dance*) would be an example of partial reduplication. It is important not to confuse full reduplication with repetition: extremely simplified, a reduplicated form is one phonological word, with one primary stress, while repetitions are simply the phonological word repeated two or more times. In an expression like *Many, many thanks* (pronounced /ˈmenɪˈmenɪˈθæŋks/) the phonological word *many* is merely repeated, with each of the repeated instances carrying their own primary stress. The reduplicated equivalent would be something like /ˈmenɪ(ˌ)menɪ/, with only one primary stress and possibly one secondary (weaker) stress.

For accessible introductions to morphology, see, for example, Haspelmath (2002) and Bauer (2003). For more in-depth discussions of various morphological concepts, see, for example, the chapters in Spencer & Zwicky (1998).

This chapter will test the assumption that pidgin and creole languages lack inflectional and derivational affixes, and thus do not have synthetic constructions. It will also test the assumptions that pidgins do not tend to have reduplication and that reduplication is more common in creoles than in non-creoles.

10.2 Synthesis

Quantifying how analytic or synthetic languages are is not straightforward – does one count every single bound morpheme that the language has or only the number of grammatical categories where inflectional morphemes occur? Does one include derivational morphology or not? Should one count allomorphs separately or not? And what about non-linear inflections such as stem changes and grammatical tone? Most languages make use of more than one morphological strategy, and may, for example, express tense and aspect synthetically but nominal possession or negation analytically. This section will bring up some examples of inflectional morphology in pidgins, extended pidgins (pidgincreoles), creoles and mixed languages, but will not attempt to quantify synthesis in them. It is beyond the scope of the section to discuss in detail the kinds of strategies that languages may employ. For more on morphological typology, see, for example Bickel & Nichols (2007) and Velupillai (2012: 95ff), with further references. For a proposal on how to measure analyticity and syntheticity in a selection of creoles and extended pidgins, see Siegel et al. (2014).

10.2.1 Synthesis in pidgin languages

Pidgins are widely described as lacking inflectional and derivational affixes, and thus to use analytic rather than synthetic morphological strategies (cf. e.g. Kaye & Tosco 2003). The Eskimo pidgin in West Greenland, for example, hardly had any of the inflectional and synthetic morphological processes of the contributing languages (van der Voort 1996). However, there are a number of pidgins which actually did make use of inflectional affixation, even if it in most cases was to a lesser extent than in the contributing languages. For thorough discussions on inflectional morphology in pidgin languages, see, for example, Bakker (2003b) and Roberts & Bresnan (2008).

An example of a pidgin with verbal affixation is the Koriki variety of Hiri Trading Language in Papua New Guinea, where the suffix *-varia* indicates future tense (Dutton 1983: 94). In the Eleman variety of Hiri Trading Language there is a derivational suffix *-naia* which forms transitive verbs (Dutton 1983: 92). In Pidgin A70 (Bantu-lexified: Cameroon) there is subject agreement on the verb (*a-/be-* for sinGular/pLural animates and *e-/bi-* for sinGular/pLural inanimates) as well as the past tense and negative prefixes *nga-* and *(te)ke-* respectively (Alexandre 1963).

There are also examples of affixation on nominals. Gulf Pidgin Arabic, for example, has plural suffixes *-āt* and *-īn* (Smart 1990: 93). The Koriki variety of Hiri Trading Language has a possessive suffix *-nu*:

Koriki Hiri Trading Language (Pidgin (Motu-lexified): Papua New Guinea)

(231) ni vake-nu noe koana
your friend-POSS name who
'What is your friend's name?' (Dutton 1983: 84)

In Example (231) *vake* 'friend' is marked with the possessor *-nu*.

There are a number of examples of word class markers in pidgin languages. Russenorsk, for example, typically (though not always) marked verbs with *-om* and nominals with *-a*:

Russenorsk (Pidgin (Russian/Norwegian-lexified): Norway)

(232)	mokk-a	'flour'	moj-a	'I, me, my'	
	silk-a	'herring'	tvoj-a	'you, your'	
	fisk-a	'fish'	skaff-om	'eat'	
	star-a	'old'	drikk-om	'drink'	
	bols-a	'big'	robot-om	'work'	(Broch & Jahr 1984a: 43ff)

In Example (232) the nouns, adjectives and pronouns take the nominal marker *-a* while the verbs show the verbal marker *-om*. In Turku (Arabic-lexified: Chad) verbs tend to end in *-u* and nouns in *-a* (Tosco & Owens 1993: 212).

10.2.2 Synthesis in extended pidgins (pidgincreoles)

There are several examples of languages with affixation in the small sample of extended pidgins. Solomon Islands Pijin, for instance, is to a large extent analytic, but has the derivational suffixes *-fala* (which creates adjectives), *-wan* (which creates nouns) and *-em/-im/-um* (which creates transitive verbs; the choice of the form varies according to the verb stem vowel and is as such a case of vowel harmony) (Jourdan 2004). A similar derivational adjective suffix can be found in the closely related Tok Pisin (*pela*), as can a transitivizer (*-im*) (Smith & Siegel 2013a, see further Section 1.4.3). Likewise, *-fala* (adjectivizer), *-wan* (nominalizer) and *-im* (transitivizer) can be found in Bislama, which is also closely related to Solomon Islands Pijin and Tok Pisin (Meyerhoff 2013a).

In Sango there is not only the nominalizer *-ngo*, but also the obligatory predicate marker *-a*, which prefixes to verbs after a nominal subject, as well as the plural marker *-a* (Samarin 2013a). Juba Arabic has the plural suffix *-át/-ín* and the proclitics *ge=* 'PROGressive' and *bi=* 'FUTure, IRRealis' (Manfredi & Petrollino 2013a). Nagamese makes extensive use of affixation: plurality, case and definiteness is marked syntactically, as is tense, mood and aspect (see further Section 8.3.1).

10.2.3 Synthesis in creole languages

Creoles are also typically described as having little or no inflectional or derivational affixation (cf. e.g. Kaye & Tosco 2003). For example, case, gender, possession, and TMA is typically described as being expressed though analytic means rather than with affixes. However, there are a number of creole languages that do, in fact, have both derivational and inflectional synthetic morphology, of which only a few will be mentioned here. For an accessible discussion on creole morphology, see, for example Crowley (2008).

An example of a creole with a number of both derivational and inflectional affixes is Kriol. There is, for example, the collective/associative plural *-mob*, the progressive *-bat*, the adjective marker *-wan*, the transitive marker *-im* and a large number of adverbial suffixes:

Kriol (Creole (English-lexified): Australia)

(233) a. len-kanjil-mob thei jabi
land-council-ASS 3PL know
'The land council people know (about this)'

b. hi weik-im-ap-bat
3SG wake-TR-up-PROG
'She is waking her up.'

c. bat that nyu-wan Wulis im gud-wan du, ngabi
but DEM new-ADJ Woolworths 3SG good-ADJ too Q
'But the new Woollies is good too, isn't it?' (Schultze-Berndt et al. 2013: 244f, 247)

In Example (233a) the collective marker *-mob* is suffixed to the noun, while in (233b) three suffixes are concatenated to the verb (the transitive marker *-im*, an adverbial suffix and the progressive marker *-bat*) and in (233c) the adjective marker *-wan* appears twice.

Nheengatú has two series of person prefixes, one for verbs and one for nouns, each with three persons (first, second, third) and two numbers (singular and plural); there are a number of derivational affixes as well as clitics (da Cruz 2011; see also Section 9.5.2). Sri Lanka Portuguese is another example of a creole with extensive affixation: there is an optional plural suffix, three obligatory case suffixes (plus one zero form), three tense prefixes, one or two (depending on the dialect) aspect prefixes, two portmanteau negative prefixes[168] and a number of dependent verb affixes (Smith 2013a). In Lingala "nouns are organized into classes, each marked by a distinguishing prefix and forming pairs of singular-plural formation" (Meeuwis 2013a: 28). There are also eight verbal subject markers (distinguishing three persons, two numbers and, in the third persons, animate/inanimate gender), a reflexive affix *-mí-*, a number of TMA affixes (two of which, *-ko-* 'FUTure tense' and *-zô-* 'PRESent PROGRessive' are infixes) as well as a number of verb derivational infixes (Meeuwis 2013a). A very common strategy in English-lexified creoles is to form reflexive pronouns with a form of the suffix *-self* (cf. Prescod 2009 for a discussion).

10.2.4 Synthesis in mixed languages

Mixed languages are typically described as either having inherited the structure of one of the input languages, or to be a structural blend of the two input languages.

An example of a language which has inherited the structure of one of the input languages is Media Lengua, where the lexicon derives from Spanish but the structure and grammatical markers from Quechua:

168. There are three more free form negative markers. It should be noted that all negative markers, whether free or bound, are portmanteau aspect/mood+negation markers (Smith 2013a).

Media Lengua (Mixed language (Spanish/Quechua): Ecuador)

(234) ML: no sabi-ni-chu
NEG know-1-NEG
Q: mana yacha-ni-chu
NEG know-1-NEG
S: no sé
NEG know.1SG.PRES
'I don't know.' (Muysken 1997b: 383)

In (234) we see that Media Lengua has inherited the inflectional morphemes and the largely concatenative structure of Quechua. Hezhou is another example of a mixed language where the morphological structure essentially reflects that of one of the input languages:

Hezhou (Mixed Language (Mandarin/Uyghur): China)

(235) H: bɛɕĩŋ-ta xui lɛ-liɔ
B-from return come-PST
M: cong Beijing huilai
from B return
U: bejʤiŋ-din qɑjt-ip kɛl-d-i
B-from return-PROG come-PST-3SG.S
'(He) returned from Beijing.' (Lee-Smith 1996b: 866)

In Example (235) we see that the synthetic morphological structure of Uyghur is reflected in Hezhou (notice also the verb serialization in both Hezhou and Uyghur), rather than the analytic structure of Mandarin.

An example of a mixed language that essentially shows a blend of the morphological structure of the two input languages is Michif, where the largely synthetic structure of Cree appears in the VP while the analytic structure of French appears in the NP:

Michif (Mixed language (French/Cree): Canada)

(236) ki:-mɪčɪmɪn-am a:tɪht la pɛj
pst-hold-TI.3→4 some DEF.F payment
'He kept part of the payment.' (Bakker 1997b: 316)

In (236) the verb phrase shows a synthetic structure with two inflectional markers attached to the verb (the tense marker *ki:-* and the person marker *-am*), while the noun phrase shows an analytic structure, with the definite marker *la* appearing as a free form.

10.3 Reduplication

Reduplication is a very common morphological process among the languages of the world. This section will compare the occurrence of reduplication in a selection of pidgin and creole languages with the languages in Rubino (2013), as well as mention reduplication in extended pidgins (pidgincreoles) and mixed languages. It is important to notice that only productive reduplication is considered here, that is, a process that can be "systematically generalized to a set of open class words" (Rubino 2013). In other words, fossilized forms that historically derive from a reduplicated form are not counted. The values for the pidgin and creole samples are 'Reduplication does not exist' and 'Reduplication exists'. The latter conflates the values 'Full reduplication' and 'Partial reduplication' in Rubino (2013). The value 'Reduplication exists' also conflates the values 'Only iconic functions', 'Attenuating function', 'Word-class-changing function' and 'Attenuating and word-class-changing function' in Haspelmath & the APiCS Consortium (2013a). It is beyond the scope of this section to give a detailed discussion on the different kinds of reduplication processes that can be found. For a classic discussion on reduplication, see Marantz (1982).

10.3.1 Reduplication in pidgin languages

Pidgins are typically described as lacking reduplication (cf. Parkvall & Bakker 2013: 45), although a number of sources might indicate repetition (not to be confused with the morphological process of reduplication). In Samoan Plantation Pidgin English, for example, there are indications of repetition, but not of reduplication (Mühlhäusler 1983). However, there are in fact quite a few examples of reduplication in pidgin languages. In Romanian Pidgin Arabic, for example, reduplication denotes intensification, as in *kulu* 'each' versus *kulukulu* 'all, completely' (Avram 2010: 28). For a detailed discussion on reduplication in pidgins, see, for example, Bakker (2003c).

In a sample of 34 pidgin languages, it turned out that some two fifths of the languages actually do have reduplication. The assumption that pidgins lack that morphological process therefore does not hold. However, when comparing the current pidgin sample Rubino's (2013) sample, we see that pidgins differ considerably from non-pidgins. The figures are summarized in Table 10.1:

In Table 10.1 we see that about two fifths of the pidgin languages in the current sample actually do have reduplication.[169] However, the proportions differ significantly from those in WALS. Specifically the group of languages in the pidgin sample that

169. According to a chi-square goodness of fit test the distribution of languages that have and lack reduplication in the pidgin sample is not statistically significant ($\chi^2 = 0.74$; $df = 1$; $p_{\text{two-tailed}} = 0.390$).

Table 10.1 Reduplication in the current pidgin sample and in WALS (Rubino 2013). For a full legend of the languages in the pidgin sample, see http://dx.doi.org/10.1075/cll.48.additional.

	Pidgin sample		WALS	
	N	%	N	%
reduplication exists	14	41.2	313	85.1
reduplication does not exist	20	58.8	55	14.9
Total	34		368	

($\chi^2 = 36.65$; $df = 1$; $p_{\text{two-tailed}} < 0.001$***, Yates' Correction, $p_{\text{sim}} < 0.001$*** ($B = 10{,}000$))
($G = 29.58$; $df = 1$; $p_{\text{two-tailed}} < 0.001$***)

have reduplication is very underrepresented, while the group of languages in the pidgin sample that lack reduplication is highly overrepresented. In other words, pidgin languages seem considerably less likely to have reduplication than non-pidgins.

10.3.2 Reduplication in extended pidgins (pidgincreoles)

All but one (Nagamese) in the small sample of extended pidgins have reduplication. In Bislama, for example, reduplication indicates augmentation of various kinds. Consider the following:

Bislama (Extended pidgin (English-lexified): Vanuatu)

(237) a. i stap pul~pulum ol feta blong hem
3SG CONT RED~pull PL feather PREP 3SG
'He was pulling out its feathers.'

b. bihaen long han blong hem olsem ol smol~smol hil
behind PREP hand PREP 3SG like PL RED~small hill
'On the back of her hand, it's like little wee hills.' (Meyerhoff 2003: 236f)

In (237a) the reduplication of the verb indicates the repeated act of pulling out feathers, while in (237b) the reduplication of the adjective indicates an intensification of the property (in this case 'very small').

10.3.3 Reduplication in creole languages

Reduplication is typically described as particularly common for creole languages. In fact, reduplication is "said to be present in Creoles to a greater extent than in other languages" (Mühlhäusler 1997: 196f). In Angolar, for example, reduplication changes the word class of a word, such as turning the verb *foga* 'suffocate' into the noun *fofoga/fogafoga* 'asthma' (Maurer 2013b). In Sranan, for example, reduplication may be used to indicate attenuation (the diminishing of something), augmentation, distribution and iteration as well as to change the word-class of a root; the difference in interpretation lies in the stress pattern. Consider the following reduplicated forms of the verb *férfi* 'to paint'.

Sranan (Creole (English-lexified): Suriname)

(238) a. Norfu e férfi~férfi
PN PROG paint~RED
'Norval is painting a bit.' (attenuation)

b. Norfu e ferfi~férfi
PN PROG paint~RED
'Norval is painting too much.' (augmentation)

c. Norfu e férfi~ferfi
PN PROG paint~RED
'Norval is painting and painting.' (iteration)

d. Norfu de férfi~férfi
PN COP paint~RED
'Norval is painted.' (word-class change verb > adjective)
(Adamson & Smith 2003: 89f)

In (238a) both parts of the reduplicated form are stressed, while in (238b) only the second part is stressed and in (238c) only the first part is stressed. In (238d) both parts are again stressed; the use of a copula indicates the adjectival function of the form.

There are, however, also examples of creole languages that lack productive reduplication, such as Hawai'i Creole English (cf. Velupillai 2003b), Palenquero (cf. Schwegler 2013b) or Guyanais (cf. Pfänder 2013b). For more on reduplication in creole languages, see, for example, the chapters in Kouwenberg (2003).

In order to test whether creole languages might be more likely to have reduplication than non-creole languages, I compared a creole sample with the languages in Rubino's (2013) sample. The figures are summarized in Table 10.2:

Table 10.2 Reduplication in the current creole sample and in WALS (Rubino 2013). For a full legend of the languages in the creole sample, see http://dx.doi.org/10.1075/cll.48.additional.

	Creole sample		WALS*	
	N	%	N	%
reduplication exists	45	86.5	311	85
reduplication does not exist	7	13.5	55	15
Total	52		366	

($\chi^2 = 0.008$; $df = 1$; $p_{two\text{-}tailed} = 0.93$, Yate's Correction, $p_{sim} = 0.83$ (B = 10,000))
($G = 0.09$; $df = 1$; $p_{two\text{-}tailed} = 0.77$)
* Chavacano and Ndyuka (Nengee) have been removed from the WALS sample to avoid overlap with the creole sample.

As can be seen in Table 10.2 there is no difference in proportions between the creole sample and Rubino's (2013) sample in terms of reduplication. The assumption that creoles are more likely than non-creoles to have reduplication is thus not supported by these figures.

10.3.4 Reduplication in mixed languages

Reduplication seems as common in mixed languages as in other languages. In a number of cases the strategy is found in at least one of the input languages, such as in Gurindji Kriol (where both input languages have reduplication) or Michif (where both input languages have reduplication; intensification may be expressed through reduplication in Canadian French varieties, cf. Bakker 1997b: 331). In Gurindji Kriol, for example, the pattern of reduplication is dependent on the source language of the stem: words of Kriol origin (typically verbs) are fully reduplicated while words of Gurindji origin (typically nominals) are partially reduplicated:

Gurindji Kriol (Gurindji/Kriol: Australia)

(239) a. jatlot kid ran streitap langa jat modika dumaji im reinrein.
DET.PL child run straight.up LOC DEF car because 3SG rain.RED
'The kids ran straight to the car because it was raining.' (Meakins 2011: 196)

b. Kajijirri-ma dei yusta jing-im-bat darrei yawulyu.
old.woman.RED-TOP 3PL.S used.to sing-TR-CONT that.way sacred.song
'The old women used to sing sacred songs over there.' (Meakins 2013b: feature 26)

In (239a) the Kriol origin verb *rein* 'rain' is fully reduplicated to *reinrein*, indicating continuous or iterative aspect. In (239b) the Gurindji origin noun *kajirri* 'old woman' is partially reduplicated to *kajijirri*, indicating plurality. For more on Gurindji Kriol, see Section 9.5.3.

Shelta is an example of a mixed language that lacks reduplication (Grant 1994), possibly because both of the input languages (Irish and English) lack that morphological process. However, Media Lengua shows instances of reduplication which would not appear in either of the input languages:

Media Lengua (Spanish/Quechua: Ecuador)

(240) yo-ga bin~bin tixi-ya-da pudi-ni
1SG-TOP well~RED weave-INF-ACC can-1SG
'I can weave very well.' (Muysken 2013b: feature 26)

The intensification indicated in (240) by *binbin* 'very well' would have been indicated analytically in both input languages (cf. *muy bien* in Spanish and *sumaq allapa* in Quechua).

10.4 Snapshots

Pidgins are assumed to lack affixation and reduplication. Turku is an example of a pidgin language that in fact has some affixation, and possibly also reduplication.

Creoles are also assumed to lack affixation, but to have prolific reduplication. Sranan is an example of a creole language which has derivational affixation and reduplication.

Mixed languages are assumed to have adopted the morphological strategies of one of the input languages, or to represent a blend of the two ancestral systems. Media Lengua is an example of a mixed language that has adopted the concatenative structure of Quechua, but where reduplication may be an innovation.

10.4.1 Turku: An extinct Arabic-lexified pidgin in Chad[170]

10.4.1.1 *A brief background sketch of Turku*

Turku, called *Tourkou* in French, was an Arabic-lexified military pidgin spoken in present-day Chad and probably also in the present-day Central African Republic.

As ivory and slave traders began moving southwards from the north into present-day southern Sudan in the early 19th century, camps were set up in an area comprising roughly present-day southern Sudan, north-eastern DR Congo and western Central African Republic. These camps became the base for a heterogeneous population speaking various southern Sudanese languages and Arabic dialects, in which an Arabic-lexified pidgin emerged.

In 1875 the Egyptian government installed Lieutenant Rabeh in one of the main camps in south-western Sudan. When Rabeh sought to establish himself independently, he was challenged by Egyptian armies and withdrew with his army in 1879 into present-day south-eastern Chad. The precise demographics of Rabeh's army and followers is not known, though it seems to have consisted of a sizeable number of soldiers, women and slaves from southern Sudan, as well as Arab traders. One source, Gessi (1892), who was himself in Sudan at the time and part of the campaign that forced Rabeh westwards, quotes the captured lieutenant Lemin (who had been part of Rabeh's army):

> We were a company of at least five or six thousand persons, men, women, children, slaves and Jelabbas [traders – VV]. … The native population of all the villages we passed were carried away with us, and the Arabs and Jelabbas followed voluntarily. … The number of Jelabbas who had joined us was not more than three thousand, but they were accompanied by more than five thousand woman and slaves. Adding to this number about two thousand five hundred Besingers [south Sudanese troops – VV], their wives, servants and slaves, I do not think it an exaggeration to say that the whole number of fugitives was twenty thousand … (Gessi 1892: 326ff)

What this quote indicates is that there was not only a sizeable proportion of southern Sudanese people, but also a sizeable proportion of traders and Arab-speaking people, and that new ethnic

170. This section is based almost exclusively on Tosco & Owens (1993).

groups were added along the way. This heterogeneous group would eventually settle in eastern Chad and form the basis of the pidgin that would become known as Turku.

As late as 1931 there were reports which stated that Turku was one of the three trade languages in French Equatorial Africa (Tosco & Owens 1993:183), into which Chad had been incorporated by the French colonial army.

The origin of the name Turku is a matter of controversy. The term 'turk' was typically used to refer to "virtually any outsider in the southern Sudan in the 19th century" (Tosco & Owens 1993:181). However, the suggestion that Turku derives from the name for African troops in the French army, 'Turko', assembled in 1842, has also been put forth (cf. Prokosch 1986).

All of the data known to us is based on the description by the French colonial medical commander Gaston Muraz (1931), which provides a grammatical sketch, an extended lexicon and some texts. The description is aimed at Frenchmen needing to be able to communicate with their colonial subjects. The material indicates a certain amount of lectal variation.

10.4.1.2 *A short linguistic sketch of Turku*

The orthography in this section follows the transliteration proposed by Tosco & Owens (1993).

Turku had 22 consonants, /p, b, m, f, v, w, t, d, n, s, z, l, r, ʃ, ʧ, ʤ, ɲ, j, k, g, ŋ, h/ and five vowels, /i, e, a, o, u/. Notice that /ʧ, ʤ, ʃ, ɲ, ŋ/ are represented by <c, j, sh, ny, ng> respectively. Syllables seem to have been complex, with clusters of up to two consonants in both the onset and the coda. There might have been contrastive stress, as in *saba* 'seven' versus *sabah* 'east', where the *-h* possibly indicates word-final stress (Tosco & Owens 1993:188). Stress is here marked with an accent (´).

The morphology seems to have been predominantly analytic, though there were examples of non-linear plural forms, as well as inflectional affixation, such as the word-class suffixes *-u* (verb stems) and *-a* (noun stems) pronoun cliticization (cf. Example (242)) and some reduplication (though the latter may have been fossilized forms). There are two instances where *-u* seems to indicate transitivization:

(241) déli 'put down, descend' → déllu 'take down' (tr.)
góbul 'go back' → góbulu 'return (something)' (Tosco & Owens 1993:215)

Gender seems not to have been relevant, though there are examples of natural gender compounding with *mára* 'female' / *rájel* 'male' as in *kanamáye mára/rájel* 'she/billy goat' (Tosco & Owens 1993:213).

Number was optionally indicated with the suffix *-in/-en* or (possibly fossilized) non-linear forms:

(242) a. kam inte fákar pfil(in) fi gidam=na?
how.many 2SG think elephant(-PL) EXIST in.front=1PL
'How many elephants do you think there are ahead of us?'

b. batán jijere ma béji fi híle íntekum kútulu yal wála
again smallpox NEG come to village 2PL kill child.PL or
besáo le=ku amyán
make to=2PL blind
'Never again will smallpox come to your village, kill your children or make you blind.'
(Tosco & Owens 1993:197, 200f)

There was a demonstrative *da* 'this' which could also serve as a definite article. Indefiniteness was not overtly marked, except indirectly in that indefinite nouns could not take the possessive marker. Possession was indicated with *ana*, which was prefixed to personal pronouns:

(243) a. shíli rangáye laam wadín ana poktər anína
take basket meat other POSS porter 1PL
'Take some of our porters' baskets of meat.'
b. kútu búnduk ana-hi fi kídif=ak
put rifle POSS-1SG on shoulder=2SG
'Put my rifle on your shoulder.' (Tosco & Owens 1993: 203, 210)

The pronominal system distinguished between three persons and two numbers. The same forms were used in subject and object position:

	SINGULAR	PLURAL
1	*ána*	*anína*
2	*ínte, tu*	*íntukum, íntekum, íntokum*
3	*(h)ú, hia*	*úmun, úman*

The second person singular *tu* might actually have been a second dual pronoun. Possessive pronouns were formed by prefixing the possessive marker *ana-* to the personal pronoun.

There was an adjective comparative construction with *fut* 'pass':

(244) ínte awán fut Kedabgel
2SG bad pass PN
'You are worse than Kedabgel.' (Tosco & Owens 1993: 211)

The bare form of the verb was used for all tenses, with context or adverbials indicating the temporal meanings, although there are some indications of a plural prefix *b(e)-*:

(245) a. doktór be-shúfu al-dóro
doctor FUT-see REL-want
'The doctor will see those who want (to be seen).'
b. kan ke mafi b-ámbti mardán ana-hu le awín ketír
if so NEG FUT-give sick POSS-3SG for woman.PL many
'If not, he will give his sickness to many women.' (Tosco & Owens 1993: 200, 217)

There were three aspect markers: *gaed/gahed* 'CONTinuous' (cf. Example (248b)), *kulyum* 'HABitual' and *yaoda* 'IMMinent'.

The word order was typically subject-verb-object, although it seems as if pragmatic topics might have been fronted. There was a clause-final negator *mafi* (possibly occasionally shortened to *ma*, cf. Example (242b)):

(246) úman kútulu bágar alyum máfi
3PL kill cattle today NEG
'They won't kill their cattle today.' (Tosco & Owens 1993: 202)

Polar questions were formed with the question particle *wala* and in content questions the interrogative phrase remained *in situ*:

(247) a. laam da shuf anína wála?
animal DEM see 1PL Q
'Did the animal see us?'
b. fi híle ana-ki ajusén ma nás mardan-ín kám bágdər kéfu
in village POSS-2PL old and people sick-PL how.many can pay
limpó máfi?
tax NEG
'How many old and sick people in your village are not able to pay the tax?'
(Tosco & Owens 1993: 202)

There was no copula (cf. Example (244)), though there was a locative *yaoda* and an existential *fi* (cf. Example (242), (248b)).

There were the coordinators *e* 'and', *ma* 'and' and *wala* 'or'. Coordination could also be done through juxtaposition. There were a number of adverbial subordinators. Headless relative clauses were indicated with the relativizer *al-* (cf. Example (245a)), while headed relative clauses were optionally indicated with *al-* or the demonstrative *da*:

(248) a. ágaba fádal da ana nas híle
rest remain DEM POSS people village
'The rest that remains belongs to the villagers.'
b. fí inák bojéni katír gahéd jíbu mardán num le nás
EXIST there tsetse many CONT bring sick sleep to people
'There there are many tsetse flies, which infect people with sleeping sickness.'
(Tosco & Owens 1993: 208)

There are indications of possible serial verb constructions:

(249) a. hu béji sálam ána
3SG come greet 1SG
'He is coming to greet me.'
b. doktór béji shuf íntukum fishan sáo dáwa
doctor come see 2PL so do medicine
'The doctor is coming to see you to make your medicine.'
c. káli tabel bára máfi jíbu kútu fi rakuba
let table outside NEG bring put on porch
'Don't leave the table outside, bring it and put it on the porch.'
(Tosco & Owens 1993: 195, 201)

10.4.1.3 *Short text*

(The following are sample sentences, rather than a continuous text, from Tosco & Owens 1993: 194, 198–200, 209.)

Inte shúfu sáme fi mande mardán num máfi ták.
2SG see well in Mande sick sleep NEG at.all
'You know perfectly well that there is no sleeping sickness in Mande.'

God fi lopitál wen ínta légi ákul ma num.
stay in hospital where 2PL get food and sleep
'Stay in the hospital, where you'll get food and rest.'

Góbulu mal ana ákit ana mára da le rájel jamán góbel te ákut ma hu.
return money POSS marriage POSS woman DEM to man previous before 2SG take with 3SG
'Return the dowry to the woman's former husband before you marry her.'

Rujál kúlu awín kúlu yal dugág kúlu ínte lúmu gidám ana-hu.
man.PL all woman.PL all child.PL young all 2SG gather front POSS-3SG
'You gather all the men, women and young children in front of it.'

Kan íntukum shíli álme ákər batán íntukum légu penshon kan sáne áshara kámza kalás.
if 2PL take water other again 2PL get pension if year ten five finished
'If you reenlist again you get a pension when 15 years are up.'

10.4.1.4 *Some sources of data*

The only data of Turku known to us is that which is presented in Muraz (1931), much of which has been glossed and translated in Tosco & Owens (1993).

10.4.2 Sranan: An English-lexified creole in Suriname[171]

10.4.2.1 *A brief background sketch of Sranan*

Sranan, also called *Taki-Taki, Surinaams, Suriname Creole English* and *Surinamese* by scholars, is spoken as a mother tongue by about 126,000 people in Suriname and French Guiana and is also widely used as a *lingua franca* in Suriname. It is called *Sranan tongo* by the speakers themselves.

In 1651 a hundred English colonizers arrived from Barbados and settled along the Suriname River, where they founded Willoughbyland. These early settlers, and those who subsequently arrived in 1652, also from Barbados, as well as from St. Kitts, Nevis and Montserrat (Adamson & Smith 1994), already had experience in sugar production. It is therefore generally supposed that this new colony developed into a plantation society comparatively quickly: in the early 1650s there were about 50 homestead farms, while only a decade later, in 1663, there were already 175 small plantations. Population figures also show a rather rapid growth: in 1652 there were 200 British, 200 African slaves (brought by the settlers from the previous colonies) and 90 Amerindians, while in 1665 there were 1,500 British, 3,000 African slaves and 400 Amerindians (Voorhoeve & Lichtveld 1975: 3). From 1666 on non-British Europeans also started settling in the colony. After various skirmishes between the British and the Dutch in 1667, the colony was handed over to the Dutch in 1668.

171. This section relies primarily on Winford & Migge (2004) and Winford & Plag (2013). It should be noted that Sranan is an exceptionally well-studied creole, and that these sources in turn build on their own as well as earlier work and insights of many other scholars, such as Jacques Arends (e.g. 1989), Adrienne Bruyn (e.g. 1995), Eithne B. Carlin (e.g. 2002), Eddy Charry, Geert Koefoed and Pieter Muysken (e.g. 1983), Antoon Donicie (e.g. 1954), Norval Smith (e.g. 1987), Margot van den Berg (e.g. 2007), Jan Voorhoeve and Ursy M. Lichtveld (e.g. 1980), among very many others. I stress that these are only a very few examples of scholars who have worked on Sranan (and only one example of the many published works per scholar), as space limitations do not allow for a proper listing of the depth and breadth of material available on Sranan. For helpful starting points for lists of references, see van den Berg & Smith (2013) and Winford & Plag (2013). I am very grateful to Margot van den Berg for her helpful comments on this snapshot.

While the colony seems to have developed into a plantation society very rapidly, there seems to have been reasonably intense interactions between the Europeans and the non-Europeans, especially the European indentured labour, who was English-speaking before 1668, and the slaves (Voorhoeve & Lichtveld 1975).

The period between 1667 and 1680 saw a decline of the colony, due to conflicts between colonial powers as well as with the indigenous population and the slaves and Maroons. A large number of English-speaking plantation owners left, taking their older slaves with them (the slaves acquired during Dutch rule had to remain). At the same time there were only few new arrivals.

The 1680s marked a turning point. Efforts were made to encourage settlement and planters of different European backgrounds arrived in large numbers (not only Dutch, but also Portuguese Jews and French Huguenots); by 1684 there were 80 plantations (Postma 1990:182). The slave trade grew exponentially, with the slave population (primarily from the area stretching from present-day Togo down to present-day Angola) having quintupled by the end of the 1680s (Arends 1995). By 1775 the number of slaves had grown to about 60,000, while the European population only numbered some 2,000 (Arends 1995). Due to the slow growth of the locally-born population, the majority of the slaves were African-born until the last quarter of the 18th century (Arends 1995; cf. also the discussion in Borges 2013 and van den Berg 2007).

The Suriname colonial society showed a complex social stratification with such factors as ethnicity, social status, place of birth, place and length of residence affecting the styles and registers of the language. Linguistic variation is evidenced already in early sources of Sranan (van den Berg 2007).

Emancipation was declared in 1863, leading to a large-scale import of indentured labour from China, India and Java to the plantations. The Chinese indentured labourers, who were almost exclusively Hakka men (Tjon Sie Fat 2009:68), were imported between the 1850s and 1870s. Most of these workers neither renewed their contracts, nor stayed on the plantations but remained in Suriname, and turned to trade and set up families with Creole wives (Tjon Sie Fat 2009, Borges 2013). These immigrants would form "the kernel of what would become Chinese identity and supported chain migrations from other Hakka in the Guangdong lasting until the 1930's" (Borges 2013:25). There was a second wave of immigration from China beginning in the 1960s and a third one beginning in the 1990s.

Because the Chinese tended to not renew their contracts or remain on the plantations, cheap labour was instead imported from India, especially the central and eastern parts of Northern India (Borges 2013:26), starting in the 1880s. Most of the workers chose to remain in Suriname and settle as small-scale farmers. However, since they originated from a British colonial territory, they remained British subjects. This subsequently led to the transition from a plantation economy to independent small scale farming in Suriname (van Lier 1971:220f). The years leading up to World War II saw rapid urbanization of the Indian community.

The fact that the Indian labour in Suriname remained British subjects was seen as potentially problematic by the Dutch government. Starting in the 1890s labour was therefore imported from Java, which belonged to the Dutch East-Indies colony. The majority of the Javanese also ended up remaining in Suriname, usually on government farm settlements, then later on independent small scale farms (van Lier 1971: 221, 235).

The indigenous Amerindian population was severely decimated as a consequence of the mass immigration. However, a number of groups have survived and many have clustered on the Sipaliwini River (Borges 2013: 13). They consist of several ethnic groups, but all speak Tiriyó and identify as Tiriyó to non-Amerindians (Carlin & Boven 2002: 37).

Suriname achieved independence from the Netherlands in 1975. The events leading up to and following independence, as well as the subsequent civil war, resulted in mass emigration from Suriname, predominantly to the Netherlands. However, the 1990s saw a wave of immigration to Suriname, especially of Chinese peoples (cf. above) and of Brazilians (Borges 2013: 29). The present population of about 540,000 is thus highly diverse, with about half of the population of African descent, some 10,000 Amerindians and the majority of the rest of Asian descent. For accessible overviews on the multilingual situation in Suriname, see, for example Borges (2013), Migge & Léglise (2012) and Kroon & Yağmur (2012, unfortunately only accessible to those who read Dutch).

Dutch is the sole official language of Suriname and is the medium of instruction in education (and has been since 1876). There is a growing body of modern literature in Sranan, including poetry, drama and prose. Sranan has become common in mass media and popular music, as well as "in communication between the government and the people, in areas such as health, taxes, and of course politics" (Winford & Plag 2013: 16), though it should be noted that the interaction between Sranan and Surinamese Dutch is complex – for example, there are no instruction leaflets on taxes written in Sranan and while people might mix between Surinamese Dutch and Sranan in political discourse, they are not likely to exclusively use Sranan (Margot van den Berg, p.c.). The national anthem contains two verses, the first in Dutch and the second in Sranan. In 1986 the government of Suriname announced an official orthography of Sranan (Margot van den Berg, p.c.).

There is considerable linguistic variation depending on such factors as ethnicity, social class and status. Of great importance to the study of Sranan are the chapters in Charry et al. (1983) as well as in Arends & Carlin (2002).

10.4.2.2 *A short linguistic sketch of Sranan*

Sranan has 18 consonants /p, b, m, w, f, t, d, n, s, ʧ, ʤ, l, ɲ, j, k, g, ŋ, h/ and five vowels, /i, e, a, o, u/. Contrastive vowel length is marginal, though there are a few minimal pairs (as in /blaka/ 'black' versus /bla:ka/ 'very black'; Adamson & Smith 1994: 224). Notice that /ʤ, ŋ, ɲ, ʧ, j, au, eu, ou/ are usually represented by <dy, ng, ny, ty, y, aw, ew, ow> respectively. Syllables can be moderately complex, with up to two consonants in the onset and one (nasal) consonant in the coda. Sranan may show traces of once having been a tonal language (Smith & Adamson 2006).

The morphology is predominantly analytic, though there is derivational suffixation (e.g. *wroko* 'work' → *wroko-man* 'worker' and *bere* 'belly' → *bere-man* 'pregnant woman'; Adamson & Smith 1994: 222) and compounding (*dungru* 'dark' + *oso* 'house' → *dungru-osu* 'prison' and *dray* 'turn' + *ay* 'eye' → *dray-ay* 'dizziness'; Adamson & Smith 1994: 224), as well as reduplication (which indicates attenuation, augmentation, iteration or intensification). See further Braun (2009).

Nouns are invariant in form and number distinctions are only indicated through the definite articles (*n*)*a* (singular) and *den* (plural) (cf. Bruyn 2007):

(250) a boi leisi den buku
DEF.SG boy read DEF.PL book
'The boy read the books.' (Winford & Plag 2013: 17)

Generic nouns remain unmarked. There is an indefinite article *wan*, which is identical with the numeral 'one'. There are two demonstratives, the proximate *disi* 'this' and the distal *dati* 'that', both of which are invariant for number (Bruyn 2007):

(251) a. den ten disi a son e faya
DEF.PL time DEM.PROX DEF.SG sun IPFV fire
'These days it is hot.' (Winford & Migge 2004: 507)

b. ma yu no musu du den sani dati
but 2SG NEG must do DEF.PL thing DEM.DIST
'But you mustn't do those things.' (Winford & Plag 2013: 17)

For a thorough discussion on the articles and demonstratives of Sranan, see Bruyn (2007).

Possession is formed either through juxtaposition only or with the preposition *fu*. Personal pronouns are differentiated by three persons and two numbers:

	SINGULAR	PLURAL
1	*mi*	*un(u), wi*
2	*yu, i*	*un(u)*
3	*a*	*den*

Notice that the third person forms are identical to the definite article. The third person singular has a distinct object/possessive form, *en*.

The unmarked form denotes present time reference with stative verbs (as in (252a)) and past time reference with dynamic verbs (as in (252b)). There is a past tense marker *ben* (as in (252c)) and a future tense marker *o* (as in (252d)).

(252) a. a pikin lobi nyam
DEF.SG child love eat
'The child loves to eat.' (Winford & Plag 2013: 18)

b. a kownu dede
DEF.SG king die
'The king has died.' (Winford & Plag 2013: 18)

c. den ben bigin ferteri yu wan sani, san yu musu ben sabi a fesi
3PL PST begin tell 2SG INDEF thing REL 2SG must PST know at first
'They started to tell you things that you had to know beforehand.' (Winford 2000: 74)

d. en mi hoop dati a kondre o kon bun yere
and 1SG hope DEM.PROX DEF.SG country FUT come good hear
'And I hope that the country will get better, right.' (Winford & Migge 2004: 499)

There are two aspect markers, *(d)e* 'IMPERFECTIVE' (cf. Example (251a)) and the postverbal *kaba* 'COMPLETIVE' (cf. Example (253)). There are a number of modal markers.

The word order is subject-verb-object. Negation is marked with an invariant preverbal negator *no* and there is negative concord:

(253) no wan suma no man verklaar yu wan oorlog tori, want den ala dede kaba
NEG one person NEG can explain 2SG one war story for 3PL all dead COMPL
'No one can tell you war stories, for they are all dead already.' (Winford 2000:77)

Polar questions are formed through rising intonation only; in content questions the interrogative phrase is fronted.

(254) a. yu sa kon sii mi tide neti?
2SG MOD come see 1SG today night
'Will you visit me tonight?' (Winford & Plag 2013:19)

b. san yu bo taki?
what 2SG PST.FUT talk
'What were you going to say?' (Winford & Migge 2004:495)

There are two copulas, the equative *(n)a*, used for nominal predication in the present (as in (255a)), and the locative/existential *de* (as in (255b)), which is also used for non-present nominal predication (as in (255b)):

(255) a. Sranan liba na wan bun bradi liba
Suriname river COP INDEF good broad river
'Suriname is a really broad river.' (Winford & Migge 2004:489)

b. a ben de n' a pernasi
3SG PST LOC at DEF.SG plantation
'She lived at the plantation.' (Bruyn 2007:370)

c. mi prakseri a boi disi nanga a man dati musu de brada
1SG think DEF.SG boy DEM.PROX with DEF.SG man DEM.DIST must COP brother
'I think this boy and that man must be brothers.' (Winford & Migge 2004:490)

In adjectival predication the copula is optional; the comparative is formed with *pasa* 'pass' or *moro* 'exceed':

(256) Amba tranga moro/pasa Kofi
PN strong exceed/pass PN
'Amba is stronger than Kofi.' (Winford & Migge 2004:497)

Property items behave like stative verbs and may be marked for tense, mood or aspect.

There are the coordinators *dan* 'then', *en* 'and', *ma* 'but' and *of* 'or'. Subordinated clauses may be introduced with the complements *taki* or *dati*, or may be simply juxtaposed. Relative clauses may be introduced with the relativizers *di* or *san* (cf. Example (252c)). There are a number of different serial verb constructions:

(257) a. mi seri a oso gi en
1SG sell DEF.SG house give 2SG
'I sold the house to her.'

b. Kofi teki a nefi koti a brede
PN take DEF.SG knife cut DEF.SG bread
'Kofi took the knife and cut the bread.' (Winford & Migge 2004: 497)

10.4.2.3 *Short text*

(From Nickel & Wilner 1984: Appendix 1.)

So, mi o ferteri wan pikin tori baka fu Anansi nange Ontiman. Anansi de wan
so 1SG FUT tell INDEF small story again about Anansi with hunter Anansi COP INDEF

man. Ala sma sabi taki Anansi abi tumsi furu triki. Anansi e sidon ai
man all person know COMPL Anansi have very many trick Anansi IPFV sit.down 3SG.IPFV

prakseri wan sani fosi a du en. Anansi no e go wroko leki fa ala sma.
think INDEF think before 3SG do 3SG Anansi NEG IPFV go work like how all person

Libisma e waka wroko, ma Anansi sabi fa ai psa en dei.
human.being IPFV walk work but Anansi know how 3SG.IPFV pass 3SG day

'So, I'm going to tell you a little story again about Anansi and Hunter. Anansi is really a person. Everybody knows that Anansi has many tricks. Anansi sits down and thinks about something before he does it. Anansi does not work like everyone else. People go to work, but Anansi knows how to spend his day.'

10.4.2.4 *Some sources of data*

There is a great deal of data available for Sranan, both early and contemporary. Voorhoeve & Lichveld (1975) is a large anthology of literature. van den Berg & Smith (2013) and Winford & Plag (2013) provide numerous references to sources of primary data. The *Sranan Tongo Interactive Library* (http://www-01.sil.org/americas/suriname/sranan/English/SrananEngLLIndex.html, accessed 11 February 2015) allows users to access stories in Sranan and get glossing and translations interactively. The journal *Osu* (http://www.osojournal.nl/oso/hello-world/, accessed 11 February 2015) gives much valuable information on the languages and cultures of Suriname. The forthcoming *Suriname Creole Archive* (SUCA, hosted by the MPI Language Archive at https://corpus1.mpi.nl/ds/asv/?0, accessed 11 February 2015) will provide an extensive corpus of digitized 18th century texts.

10.4.3 Media Lengua: A Spanish/Quechua mixed language in Ecuador[172]

10.4.3.1 *A brief background sketch of Media Lengua*

Media Lengua, also called *Chaupi Lengua*, *Chaupi Quichua*, *Chaupi Shimi* and *Quichañol* by scholars, is spoken throughout the Ecuadorian highlands. Estimates vary as to number of speakers; there are some 200 mother tongue speakers in the Cotopaxi province (Muysken 2013a: 143),

172. This section relies primarily on Muysken (1997b and 2013a). I am very grateful to Pieter Muysken for his helpful comments on this snapshot.

directly south of the capital Quito. There are also native speakers in the Loja and Imbabura provinces (Gómez Rendón 2008). The total number of speaker is estimated at about 1,000 in *Ethnologue* (Lewis et al. 2014) and 2,600 in *Wikipedia*.[173] The language is called *Chaupi Lengua*, *Catalangu*, *Utilla Ingiru* or *Quichañol* by the speakers themselves.

Quechua was introduced into present-day Ecuador by the Incas not long before the Spanish conquest around 1540. Its use was encouraged by the Spanish and it gradually became the native language across the various indigenous tribes, carrying prestige through "the growing identification of the Indian peasantry" and a (mythicized) Inca past (Muysken 1997b: 368). However, the Ecuadorian independence in 1830 brought with it urban migration by the indigenous population, which increased bilingualism and lessened the status of Quechua, which now became associated with backwardness and ignorance. This stigma persists among the European and mestizo (people of mixed heritage) population and Spanish has become the majority language of the country "spoken by everybody except some of the Indian peasants in the Highlands … and tribal groups in the Amazonian and Coastal Lowlands" (Muysken 1997b: 369).

Between 1905 and 1925 the railway linking Quito to the Pacific port of Guayaquil was built, drawing a high number of workers from the provinces south of Quito, especially Cotopaxi Province. The railway allowed large scale cyclical migration to the capital, and runs through many of the areas where Media Lengua speakers are found. Theories as to why Media Lengua evolved differ, though it seems as if pertinent factors were migration by the indigenous population to urban areas, especially Quito, coupled with increased commercial activities between the indigenous population and the mestizos, as well as increased contact with outsiders, such as official workers, all of which was made possible with the increased mobility that the railway allowed. Muysken postulates that

> [i]t is not at all unlikely that Media Lengua emerged as a result of the migration to the capital, among the young adult males who were suddenly much more affluent and independent than their peasant relatives, and suddenly confronted with Hispanic urban society. (Muysken 2013a: 144)

In fact, Gómez Rendón (2008) states that his informants from the Imbabura province (north of Quito) claimed that Media Lengua had been spoken since the 1960s and came about because it was usual for the fathers to learn Spanish in the city and then, when they came home, to speak Spanish with their children but Quechua with their spouse.

It should be noted that the different varieties may not have emerged at the same time. There are indications that, due to the railway, the Cotopaxi variety may be considerably older than the Imbabura variety as well as the varieties of Saraguro and Cañar. The different varieties of Media Lengua may thus have evolved more or less independently rather than as one single original system that then split into dialects (Pieter Muysken, p.c.).

173. http://en.wikipedia.org/wiki/Media_Lengua, accessed 11 February 2015.

Media Lengua thus did not emerge through any need for communication, as speakers knew both Spanish and Quechua, but rather through the expressive needs of a community that neither identified fully with the urban Hispanic culture, nor with the rural Quechua culture.

While Media Lengua is not a secret language, it is widely reported to be an in-group, private language: Spanish is used with the non-indigenous population and in official settings, such as the school environment, while Quechua is used with other indigenous people and Media Lengua is reserved for the family and the daily life within the community (Muysken 2013a: 145).

The shift to Spanish is continuing. For example, in the Imbabura province there seems to be a generational stratification in that only those who are above the age of 45 have Quechua as their mother tongue, while those younger than 45 speak Media Lengua (Gómez Rendón 2008: 54). Many speakers, who are now in their early middle age, are trilingual in Media Lengua, Spanish and Quechua, while younger speakers are less proficient in Quechua. Media Lengua thus also serves as a link to the Quechuan heritage for the younger generation.[174]

10.4.3.2 *A short linguistic sketch of Media Lengua*

Unless otherwise indicated, the variety described here represents that spoken in the Cotopaxi province.

Media Lengua has 23 consonants, /p, p^h, b, m, w, t, d, ʦ, s, z, n, r, l, c, ʃ, ɲ, ʎ, j, k, k^h, g, x, h/, and five vowels, /i, e, a, o, u/. The phoneme inventory essentially reflects a blend, with the Quechuan consonants and Spanish vowels. Notice that /p^h, c, ʃ, ɲ, ʎ, j, k^h/ are represented by <ph, ch, sh, ñ, ll, y, kh> respectively. Syllables may be moderately complex with up to two consonants in the onset and one consonant in the coda. There is no tone.

Media Lengua can be described as a G-L mixed language in that the structure matches that of Quechua while the lexicon derives from Spanish (although there are a few Spanish-derived affixes, such as the gerundive *-ndu*, the diminutive *-itu/ita* and the past participle *do*). The concatenative nature of Quechua is thus reflected in Media Lengua. There is reduplication, indicating augmentation (such as *bin* 'well' → *binbin* 'very well' or *brebe* 'quickly' → *brebebrebe* 'very quickly'; Muysken 1997b: 384).

Nouns are optionally marked for number with the plural suffix *-kuna/-guna*:

(258) a. kuyi-buk yirba nuwabi-shka
guinea.pig-BEN grass NEG.EXIST-EVID
'There turns out to be no grass for the guinea pigs.' (Muysken 1997b: 266)

b. isti trasti-guna-da aki-mu trayi-y
this dish-PL-ACC this-all bring-IMP
Bring these dishes over here. (Muysken 2013b: feature 22)

174. But see Stewart (2011), who claims that speakers younger than 25 have already shifted to Spanish in the Imbabura province, making Imbabura Media Lengua a moribund language.

Gender is not relevant. There are several optional case suffixes, the most common of which are the following:

-ta/-da	ACCusative	
-mu(n)	DATive/DIRectional	
-pi/-bi	LOCative	
-munda	ABLative	
-pu(k)/-bu(k)	GENitive/BENefactive	
-(u)n	INSTRumental/COMitative	
-kama/-gama	'until'	(Muysken 2013a: 145)

There is also a topic marker *=ka/=ga* (cf. Examples (261c), (263b), (264)). There is no definite article. The indefinite article *uno* is identical to the numeral 'one'. There are two demonstratives, the proximal *isti* 'this' (cf. (258b)) and the distal *isi* 'that' (cf. (263a)). Possession is marked synthetically with the genitive case:

(259) Xwana-mi Marko-bu platu-da kibra-shka
PN-AFF PN-GEN plate-ACC break-EVID
'Juana has broken Marco's plates.' (Muysken 2013b: feature 38)

The personal pronouns distinguish between three persons and two numbers:

	SINGULAR	PLURAL
1	*yo, miu*	*nustru(s), nosotros, ñukuchi*
2	*bos, tu*	*bos-kuna*
3	*el, ele*	*el-kuna*

The first person singular has a specific possessive form (*miu*) and oblique form (*ami*). There is no gender distinction.

Adjectives may either precede or follow the noun (though the former is preferred). Comparison is formed with an inflected form of *gana-* (< Sp. *ganar* 'win'):

(260) a. Xwan-mi Pedro-da gana-sha grande ga-n
PN-AFF PN-ACC win-SUB.SS tall COP-3SG
'Juan is taller than Pedro.'

b. Takunga-mi riko gan-n Salsedo-da gana-n
Latacunga-AFF rich COP-3SG Salcedo-ACC win-3SG
'Lacatunga is richer than Salcedo.' (Muysken 1997b: 397)

Verbs are obligatorily marked for person:

	SINGULAR	PLURAL
1	*-ni*	*-nchi*
2	*-ngi*	*-ngichi*
3	*-n*	*-nakun*

The obligatory tense, mood and aspect markers precede the person suffixes. The present tense is zero marked, while there is a past tense suffix *-(r)ka* (as in (261a)) and the future tense suffixes *-sha* (as in (261b)) and *-nga* (as in (261c)), for first and third person future respectively:

(261) a. inki kuchillu-n=di korta-ka-ngi pan-da
what knife-INSTR=EMPH cut-PST-2SG bread ACC
'With what knife did you cut the bread?' (Muysken 2013a: 146)

b. llubi-kpi mañana no i-sha-chu
rain-SUB.DS tomorrow NEG go-FUT. 1SG-NEG
'If it rains, I won't go tomorrow.' (Muysken 2013a: 146)

c. ahida=ga abin piru tarde-ya-ndo=ga gana-u-nga=y
there=TOP EXIST but late-become-SUB=TOP win-PROG-FUT.3SG=EMPH
'It is there, but when it becomes late he will be winning.' (Muysken 1997b: 386)

There is also a progressive marker *-(x)u* (as in (261c)), an evidential (mirative) *-shka* (cf. Examples (258a), (259)) and an imperative *-y* (cf. Example (258a)).

The word order is predominantly subject-object-verb (cf. Examples (259), (260a)), though subject-verb-object is not infrequent (cf. Example (260b)). Negation is formed with the negator *no* and an optional negative suffix *-chu* (cf. Example (261b)). Polar questions are formed with the question clitic *=chu* (identical to the negative suffix):

(262) bos=ka na plata-ta tini-ngui=chu?
2sg=TOP NEG money-ACC have-2SG=Q
'Don't you have money?' (Gómez Rendón 2008: 98)[175]

In content questions the interrogative phrase is fronted (cf. Example (261a)).

The copula *ga-* is optional (cf. also Example (260)):

(263) a. isi-guna mio muxer-pu hermana-guna
that-PL 1SG.POSS woman-GEN sister-PL
'Those are my wife's sisters.' (Muysken 2013a: 145)

b. alli-bi anda-xu-k runa=ga malu-mi
there-LOC walk-PROG-AG man=TOP bad-AFF
'The man who walks over there is bad.' (Muysken 1981: 69)

There are the coordinating conjunctions *i* 'and', *pero* 'but', *o* 'but' and *sino ke* 'but rather', as well as some subordinators, such as *ki* 'that', *porque* 'because' and *aunke* 'although'. However, subordination is more commonly formed with verbal suffixes, such as *-sh(p)a* (cf. Example (260a)) for same subject subordination, *-kpi* (cf. Example (261b)) for different subject subordination and *-ndu* as a general subordinator (as in (264)) or through nominalizations.

175. Notice that this represents the Imbabura variety of Media Lengua.

(264) alla-bu=ga entonces=ga artu terreno proprio tini-ndu=ga
there-LOC=TOP then=TOP much land own have-SUB=TOP
riku-ya-na no?
rich-become-NMLZ no
'There one could become rich then, having one's own land, no?' (Muysken 1997b: 385)

Relative clauses are formed through an agent marker on the verb (cf. Example (263b)).

10.4.3.3 *Short text*

(From Gómez Rendón 2008: 175f. Notice that this represents the Imbabura variety.)

Yo-mi naso-ri-rka-ni komunidad Casco Valenzuela-pi mil novesientos
1SG-AFF born-REFL-PST-1SG community C V-LOC thousand nine.hundred

sinkuenta y nuebe año-pi y yo=ka apenas tres mes-ta teni-kpi-lla mio
fifty nine year-LOC and 1SG=TOP as.soon.as three month-ACC have-SUB.DS-DIM 1SG.POSS

papito-kuna mio-ta encarga-shka kria-chi-chun mio tia abuela-man. Yo-mi
father-PL 1SG-ACC entrust-DEF.NMLZ raise-CAUS-HORT 1SG.POSS aunt grandparent-DAT 1SG-AFF

kria-rka-ni tia abuela casa-pi tia abuela mori-bgakaman. Diai-manta
raise-PST-1SG aunt grandparent house-LOC aunt grandparent die-TERM thence-ABL

tia abuela-kuna eskuela-man-pash poni-wa-rka. Eskuela-man dentra-rka-ni edad de
aunt grandparent-PL school-ADL-ADD place-1SG.OBL-PST school-ADL enter-PST-1SG age of

ocho año. Diai-manta ese tiempo no kompleto abi-k ka-rka Casco-pi. Ese eskuela-pa
eight year thence-ABL this time NEG complete EXIST-HAB COP-PST C-LOC this school-GEN

numbri ka-rka Galo Plaza Lasso.
name COP-PST G P L

'I was born in the community of Casco Valenzuela in 1959 and when I was just about three months old, my parents entrusted me to my great-aunt (so that she could) raise me. I grew up in my great-aunt's house until my great-aunt died. After that my relatives placed me in school. I started school when I was eight years old. In those days we didn't have the whole school in Casco. The name of this school was Galo Plaza Lasso.'

10.4.3.4 *Some sources of data*

There is very little primary data available for Media Lengua. Muysken (1997b) and (2013a) provide a number of glossed and translated examples, the latter also a longer text. Stewart (2011) gives a number of glossed and translated examples of the Imbabura variety. Gómez Rendón (2008) also provides a large number of glossed and translated examples, as well as a long text, accessible to those who read Spanish.

10.5 Summary

Most pidgins seem to predominantly make use of analytical morphological constructions; however, there are a number of examples of pidgins with inflectional and derivational affixation. Reduplication is not uncommon in pidgin languages, though considerably less common than in non-pidgins.

Most of the extended pidgins in the sample predominantly make use of analytic constructions, although there are several examples of languages with derivational affixation as well as some examples of languages with inflectional affixation. Reduplication seems very common.

While creoles seem to mainly make use of analytical morphological constructions, there are a number of examples of creoles with inflectional and derivational affixation. Reduplication is equally common in creoles as in non-creole languages.

The synthetic structure of mixed languages seems to either be inherited from one of the input languages or to be a blend of the two input languages. Reduplication seems to be as common in mixed languages as in other languages.

10.6 Key points

- **There are a number of examples of pidgins, extended pidgins (pidgincreoles) and creoles that use bound morphemes for inflectional and derivational purposes.**
- **Mixed languages tend to take over the morphological structure of one of their input languages, or represent a blend of the input languages.**
- **The assumption that pidgins lack reduplication is not supported by the samples studied here, but they do seem to be less likely than non-pidgins to make use of it.**
- **Extended pidgins (pidgincreoles) align with creoles rather than pidgins with respect to reduplication.**
- **Reduplication is as common in creoles as it is in non-creole languages.**
- **Reduplication seems to be as common in mixed languages as in any other language and may also represent an innovation in the mixed language compared to the input languages.**

10.7 Exercises

1. What are some of the main difficulties in trying to assess quantitatively whether pidgins and creoles differ from other languages with respect to synthesis?
2. Give examples of different ways in which the morphological structure of the input languages may be represented in mixed languages.
3. What are the implications of the findings on pidgin and extended pidgin reduplication respectively?
4. How do the findings on creole reduplication relate to the notion of creoles as typologically unique languages?
5. Give examples of how reduplication may represent a blend of the input languages in a mixed language.

Languages cited in Chapter 11

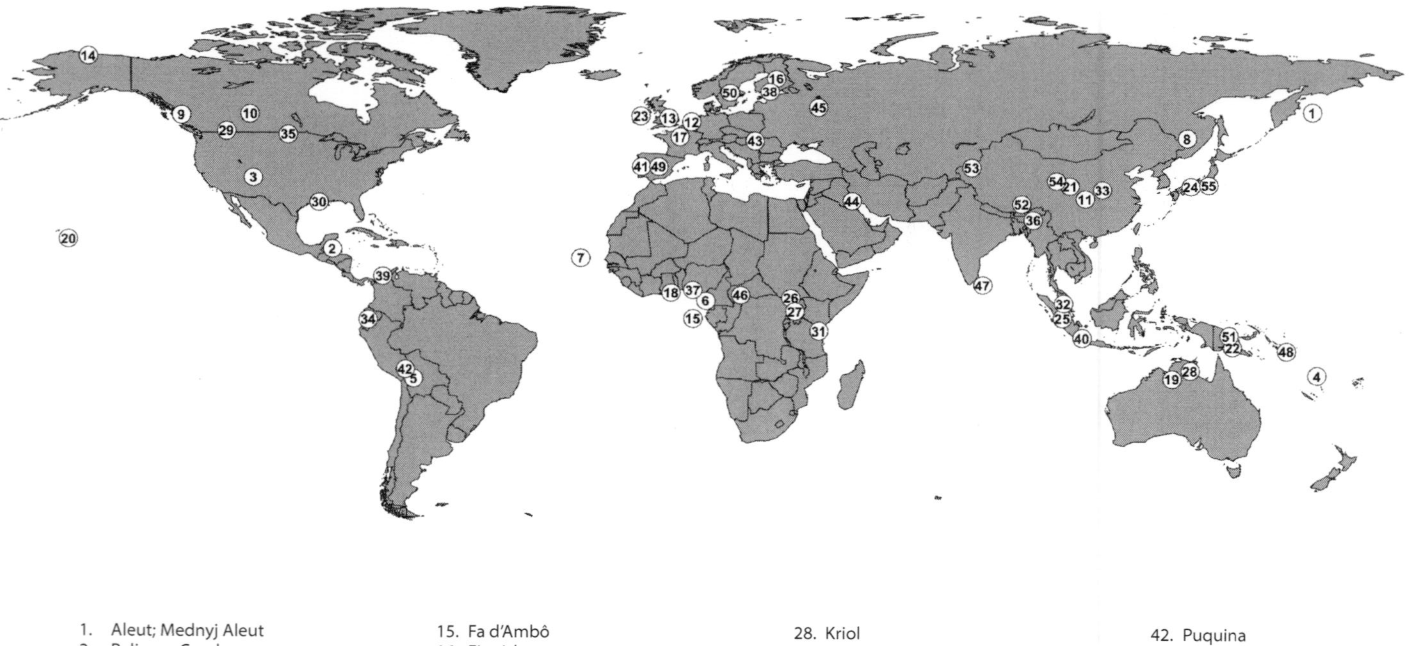

1. Aleut; Mednyj Aleut
2. Belizean Creole
3. Bilingual Navajo; Navajo
4. Bislama
5. Callahuaya
6. Cameroon Pidgin English; Pichi
7. Cape Verdean Creole
8. Chinese Pidgin Russian
9. Chinuk Wawa
10. Cree, Plains
11. Dongxiang
12. Dutch
13. English; Angloromani
14. Eskimo Pidgin
15. Fa d'Ambô
16. Finnish
17. French
18. Ghanaian Pidgin English
19. Gurindji; Gurindji Kriol
20. Hawaiian; Hawai'i Pidgin English; Pidgin Hawaiian
21. Hezhou; Tangwang
22. Hiri Motu; Tok Pisin
23. Irish; Shelta
24. Japanese
25. Javanese
26. Juba Arabic
27. Kinubi
28. Kriol
29. Kutenai
30. Louisiana Creole
31. Ma'a/Mbugu; Mbugu
32. Malay
33. Mandarin Chinese
34. Media Lengua; Quechua Imbabura
35. Michif
36. Nagamese
37. Nigerian Pidgin English
38. Old Helsinki Slang
39. Palenquero
40. Petjo
41. Portuguese
42. Puquina
43. Romani, Vlax
44. Romanian Pidgin Arabic
45. Russian
46. Sango
47. Sinhala; Sri Lankan Malay; Tamil
48. Solomon Islands Pijin
49. Spanish
50. Swedish
51. Tauya
52. Tibetan, Central
53. Uyghur
54. Wutun
55. Yokohama Pidgin Japanese

Chapter 11

The noun phrase

Pidgins are described as lacking nominal plurality and articles, while creoles are described as having optional plurality, which is indicated analytically, as well as having definite articles that are identical with the demonstrative, and indefinite articles that are identical to the numeral 'one'. Mixed languages are assumed to either have adopted the systems of one of the input languages, or to represent a blend of the two input languages. This chapter will empirically test whether pidgin and creole languages differ from non-pidgins and non-creoles with respect to nominal plurality, as well as briefly discuss nominal plurality in extended pidgins and mixed languages (Section 11.2). Section 11.3 empirically tests whether pidgin and creole languages differ from non-pidgins and non-creoles with respect to articles, and briefly brings up articles in extended pidgins and mixed languages. Section 11.4 gives short sketches of three languages mentioned in the chapter: Pidgin Hawaiian (an extinct Hawaiian-lexified pidgin on the Hawaiian Islands), Cape Verdean Creole (a Portuguese-lexified creole on the Cape Verde Islands) and Shelta (a secret English/Irish mixed language in Ireland).

11.1 Introduction

Nouns refer to concrete or abstract entities such as things, persons, places, feelings, ideas, and so on. A **noun phrase** (**NP**) is that unit of the clause which may function as a syntactic argument, such as a subject or an object. It is minimally made up of a noun (or a substitute for a noun, such as a pronoun), but may also consist of several words that belong together as a phrase, where the noun (or its substitute) is the central element (the **head**). For example, in the sentence *Puppies play* we have one noun phrase (*Puppies*) and one verb phrase (*play*). However, the sentence *The happy puppies with floppy ears are playing* also consists of only one noun phrase (*The happy puppies with floppy ears*) and one verb phrase (*are playing*).

Nouns may be marked for **number**, which indicates how many entities are referred to. Most commonly languages distinguish between two numbers, **singular** (referring to one entity exactly) and **plural** (referring to more than one entity), but there are also languages that indicate **dual** (referring to two entities exactly), **trial** (referring to three entities exactly) or **paucal** (referring to more than two or three entities but not many). Number may be indicated either synthetically (with bound morphemes) or analytically (with free morphemes).

Nouns may be divided into different categories. For example, **proper nouns** are those that refer to specific individuals or places (such as *Alice, Mr. Bean, Paris, Spain, Mount Everest*) as opposed to **common nouns** (all others). **Count nouns** refer to discrete entities that can be counted (such as *apple, planet, library*) as opposed to **mass nouns**, which refer to continuous entities that cannot be counted (such as *dust, air, greed*). Languages may also distinguish noun phrases for **animacy**, which essentially classifies entities according to how animate or inanimate they are. For example, a dog is more animate than a stone. Languages have various degrees of animacy, for instance distinguishing between human versus non-human animate versus inanimate nouns (such as *man* versus *dog* versus *stone*).

Nouns may be coded for **definiteness**, that is, coded for whether the entity is identifiable or not. The **definite** indicates that we are referring to a particular, identifiable noun (such as *the book*, which indicates that we are referring to a specific, identifiable book), while the **indefinite** indicates that we are referring to a general, non-specific entity (such as *a book*, which indicates that we are referring not to a particular book, but some book in general). Definiteness is indicated with either bound or free **articles**.

For more on the noun and noun phrase in general, see, for example, Lehmann & Moravcsik (2000) and Velupillai (2012:155ff). For detailed discussions on the noun phrase in a selection of creole languages, see the chapters in Baptista & Guéron (2007). For a very detailed discussion indeed on the noun phrase in creole languages, see Bobyleva (2013).

11.2 Nominal plurality

It is very common for languages to indicate nominal plurality. More often than not this is done with a plural marking affix, although it is not uncommon to have a free form plural marker. Most languages obligatorily mark all nouns for the plural if more than one entity is referred to, but a number of languages have optional plural marking. Some languages have different strategies for different kinds of nouns, for instance that only human nouns are marked for the plural, while all others remain invariant in form irrespective of number, or that plural marking is obligatory in animate but optional in inanimate nouns. This section will compare nominal plurality in a selection of pidgin and creole languages with the languages in Haspelmath's (2013) sample, as well as mention nominal plurality in extended pidgins (pidgincreoles) and mixed languages. Furthermore, the strategies used to indicate nominal plurality will be compared between the creole sample and Dryer's (2013a) sample. It is beyond the scope of this section to give a detailed discussion on the types of number marking that can be found in various languages. For more on number, see, for example, Corbett (2000).

11.2.1 Nominal plurality in pidgin languages

Pidgins are typically described as lacking number distinctions for noun phrases (cf. Sebba 1997: 39). In Chinuk Wawa, for example, there is no plural (Grant 2013b), which means that the reading of any given noun is context bound with respect to number. Likewise, Romanian Pidgin Arabic nouns are invariant with respect to number:

Romanian Pidgin Arabic (Pidgin (Arabic-lexified): Iraq)

(265) sadik la ani work la sonda
friend PREP 1SG work PREP rig
'My friend works on the rig.' / 'My friends work on the rig.' (Avram 2010: 22)

The reading of *sadiq* 'friend' in (265) can be either singular or plural, depending on the context.

In order to test whether pidgin languages tend to be less likely to indicate nominal plurality than non-pidgin languages, I compared the current pidgin sample with Haspelmath's (2013) sample. The figures are summarized in Table 11.1:

Table 11.1 Nominal plurality in the current pidgin sample and in WALS (Haspelmath 2013). For a full legend of the languages in the pidgin sample, see http://dx.doi.org/10.1075/cll.48.additional.

	Pidgin sample		WALS	
	N	%	N	%
No nominal plural	23	63.9	28	9.6
Only human nouns, optional	4	11.1	20	6.9
Only human nouns, obligatory	0	–	40	13.7
All nouns, always optional	7	19.4	55	18.9
All nouns, optional in inanimates	0	–	15	5.2
All nouns, always obligatory	2	5.6	133	45.7
Total	36		291	

($\chi^2 = 80.59$; $df = 5$; $p_{\text{two-tailed}} < 0.001$***, $p_{\text{sim}} < 0.001$*** (B = 10,000))
($G = 66.82$; $df = 5$; $p_{\text{two-tailed}} < 0.001$***)

Based on the figures in Table 11.1 it seems as if pidgins are indeed less likely than non-pidgins to make a singular/plural distinction for nouns: the absolute majority of the pidgin languages lack nominal plural, while most of the non-pidgins have obligatory plural for all nouns. In both samples those languages that make animacy distinctions with respect to plurality are in the minority.

11.2.2 Nominal plurality in extended pidgins (pidgincreoles)

In almost all of the extended pidgins nominal plural is optional for all nouns, except for Juba Arabic and Bislama, where plurality has become obligatory (Manfredi & Petrollino 2013a and Meyerhoff 2013b respectively). In Solomon Islands Pijin plurality is optional, but again this seems to be changing: "[u]nder pressure from English, the official language of the country and the language of education, an increasing number of common words seem to be marking plural both morphologically [i.e. synthetically – VV] and analytically" (Jourdan 2004: 708). In Tok Pisin plurality may optionally be indicated with the plural marker *ol*:

Tok Pisin (Extended pidgin (English-lexified): Papua New Guinea)

(266) em i stap nau ma(ma) bl' em wokim spia nao em i
3SG PM stay now mother POSS 3SG make spear now 3SG PM
kam nau ma bl' em wokim ol bet
come now mother POSS 3SG make PL bed
'He stayed and his mother made spears, he came and his mother made beds.'
(Smith 2002: 202)

In (266) the first noun, *spia* 'spear', remains unmarked, while the second noun, *bet* 'bed' is marked for plural with *ol*, even though the translation shows that both nouns refer to more than one entity. In Tok Pisin too it seems as if plural marking is becoming obligatory, especially in first language speech (Smith & Siegel 2013a: 216). For more on Tok Pisin, see Section 1.4.3.

11.2.3 Nominal plurality in creole languages

Creoles are usually described as having optional nominal plural marking expressed analytically with a free form plural marker (cf. Holm 2000: 215). In Palenquero, for example, plurality may optionally be marked with the free form *ma*:

Palenquero (Creole (Spanish-lexified): Colombia)

(267) (ma) ngombe asé nda leche rimá
PL cow HAB give milk a.lot
'Cows give a lot of milk.' (Schwegler 2013a: 185)

Example (267) shows that the Palenquero plural marker *ma* is not obligatory for clauses referring to more than one entity, even if it is quite a bit more common to mark plural than not (Schwegler 2007). For more on Palenquero, see 12.4.3.

In order to test whether creole languages tend to be less likely to indicate nominal plurality than non-creole languages, I compared the current creole sample with Haspelmath's (2013) sample. The figures are summarized in Table 11.2:

Table 11.2 Nominal plurality in the current creole sample and in WALS (Haspelmath 2013). For a full legend of the languages in the creole sample, see http://dx.doi.org/10.1075/cll.48.additional.

	Creole sample		WALS	
	N	%	N	%
No nominal plural	1	1.9	28	9.6
Only human nouns, optional	1	1.9	20	6.9
Only human nouns, obligatory	0	–	40	13.7
All nouns, always optional	41	77.4	55	18.9
All nouns, optional in inanimates	0	–	15	5.2
All nouns, always obligatory	10	18.9	133	45.7
Total	53		291	

($\chi^2=77.69$; $df=5$; $p_{\text{two-tailed}}<0.001$***, $p_{\text{sim}}<0.001$*** (B = 10,000))
($G=72.34$; $df=5$; $p_{\text{two-tailed}}<0.001$***)

The figures in Table 11.2 show that the absolute majority of the languages in the creole sample have optional plural marking while about a fifth of the languages have obligatory plural marking, as opposed to the WALS sample where obligatory plural marking represents the largest group of languages. Furthermore, Table 11.2 shows that animacy seems to be of very marginal relevance with respect to plural marking in the creole sample, while the picture is more mixed in the WALS sample.

Creoles are, as mentioned, also described as predominantly expressing plurality through analytic constructions. In order to test whether creole languages tend to be more likely than non-creole languages to indicate nominal plurality analytically, I compared the current creole sample with Dryer's (2013a) sample. It should be noted that it is the dominant strategy that has been coded here. For example, Belizean Creole makes use of a free form plural marker (*dem*), which may appear either before or after the noun, as well as a plural suffix *-s* to indicate plurality:

Belizean Creole (Creole (English-lexified): Belize)

(268) a. a de taak bawt siywid dem
1SG PROG talk about seaweed PL
'I am talking about seaweed.'

b. sam a dem bway wuda go awt
some of PL boy would go out
'Some of the boys want to go out.'

c. yu gat li aysta-z we grow pan de
2SG got little oyster-PL REL grow on them
'There are little oysters that grow on them.'

(Escure 2013b: feature 23 citing Escure 1982a: 35f)

Example (268) shows that Belizean Creole has two ways of marking plurality. However, the free form plural marker is used most of the time, while the other strategy is much rarer (Escure 2013b). Belizean Creole has therefore been coded with the value 'Plural word'. For more on Belizean Creole, see Section 7.3.1.

In those cases where none of the strategies is dominant, the language has been coded as having 'No dominant strategy' (the equivalent of 'Mixed morphological plural' in Dryer's survey). The figures are summarized in Table 11.3:

Table 11.3 Coding of nominal plurality in the current creole sample and in WALS (Dryer 2013a). For a full legend of the languages in the creole sample, see http://dx.doi.org/10.1075/cll.48.additional.

	Creole sample		WALS*	
	N	%	N	%
No nominal plural	1	1.9	98	9.2
Plural affix[176]	11	20.8	639	60.0
Non-linear plural marking[177]	1	1.9	10	0.9
Plural reduplication	3	5.7	8	0.8
Plural clitic	0	–	81	7.6
Plural word	31	58.5	169	15.9
No dominant strategy	6	11.3	60	5.6
Total	53		1065	

($\chi^2 = 87.32$; $df = 6$; $p_{\text{two-tailed}} < 0.001$***, $p_{\text{sim}} < 0.001$*** (B = 10,000))
($G = 63.23$; $df = 6$; $p_{\text{two-tailed}} < 0.001$***)
* Ndyuka (Nengee) has been removed from the WALS sample to avoid overlap with the creole sample.

Table 11.3 shows that the absolute majority of the languages in the creole sample express plurality with a free form, i.e. analytically, while the absolute majority of the languages in the WALS sample express plurality through affixation, i.e. synthetically.

176. This conflates the values 'Plural prefix' and 'Plural suffix' in Dryer's (2013a) sample.

177. This conflates the values 'Plural stem change' and 'Plural tone' in Dryer's (2013a) sample.

11.2.4 Nominal plurality in mixed languages

Mixed languages are usually described as having taken over the system of one of the input languages, or to represent a blend between the input languages. Bilingual Navajo, for example, an English/Navajo mixed language in the USA, does not mark nominal plural, following the system of Navajo (where nominal plurality is not marked); those forms that appear in the plural are typically fossilized forms and do not represent productive pluralization (Schaengold 2004; for more on Bilingual Navajo, see Section 3.3.1). In Ma'á/Mbugu the nominal plural is obligatorily indicated with a prefix, reflecting the Bantu system (Mous 2003b). Michif essentially shows a combination of the two input systems in that nouns are obligatorily inflected for plural; the few nouns that derive from Cree take the Cree plural suffixes, which differentiate between animate (*ak*) and inanimate (*a*) nouns, while the majority of nouns derive from French and take a free form plural marker *lii* (< French *les*), which is invariant for animacy as well as gender (Bakker 2013b). For more on Michif, see Section 3.3.2.

In Media Lengua, however, plurality is only optionally marked with the suffix *kuna/guna* which is identical to the Imbabura Quechua plural suffix (Cole 1982: 128). However, plurality is in Imbabura Quechua obligatory except if the noun is preceded by a numeral:

Imbabura Quechua (Quechuan (Quechuan): Ecuador)

(269) ishkay wasi(-kuna)-ta chari-ni
two house(-PL)-ACC have-1SG
'I have two houses.' (Cole 1982: 128)

Example (269) shows that the plural marker *-kuna* is optional in Imbabura Quechua if the noun is preceded by a numeral. Spanish, the other input language for Media Lengua, has obligatory plural marking, also if the noun is preceded by a numeral (as in *Tengo dos casa-s* 'I have two houses', where *casa* 'house' is marked with the plural *-s*). In this case the mixed language reflects an innovation, or possibly a compromise in that the semi-optionality of Quechua plural marking (where the plural suffix is not obligatory if the noun is preceded by a numeral) has in Media Lengua been generalized to all contexts. For more on Media Lengua, see Section 10.4.3.

11.3 Articles

Although it is more common than not for languages to have definite and indefinite articles, it is also rather common for languages to lack articles altogether. This section will compare a selection of pidgin and creole languages with the languages in Dryer's samples for definite and indefinite articles (2013b and 2013d respectively), as well as briefly discuss definite as well as indefinite articles in extended pidgins (pidgincreoles) and mixed languages. It should be noted that languages are coded as having articles irrespective of whether they are obligatory or not. In English, for example, articles (both definite and indefinite) are obligatory: a sentence like **I saw man*, where *man* appears without any article, is not acceptable. In some languages, however, the article may be optional. Kutenai (Isolate: Canada, USA), for example, is coded as having a definite article, even though it is optional (Dryer 2013b) and Tauya (Trans-New Guinea (Madang): Papua New Guinea) is coded as having an indefinite article, although it is optional (MacDonald 1990).

11.3.1 Articles in pidgin languages

Pidgins are usually described as lacking articles altogether, that is, to have neither definite nor indefinite articles (cf. Parkvall & Bakker 2013: 38). Definiteness is thus described as context bound in pidgin languages. Eskimo Pidgin, for example, lacked articles:

Eskimo Pidgin (Pidgin (Eskimo languages-lexified): North-eastern Siberia to West Greenland)

(270) a. wai'hinni artegi annahanna pûgmûmmi
woman coat sew now
'The woman is sewing a coat now.'

b. ak'lūña mē'k-fast kiñma
rope tie dog
'Tie the dog with a rope.' (Stefánsson 1909: 223f)

None of the nouns in Example (270) are marked for definiteness. Notice, however, that the lexifiers may also have lacked definite or indefinite markers. For example, Chinese Pidgin Russian lacked articles (Perekhvalskaya 2013b), but so does the lexifier Russian (Timberlake 2004). Likewise, Yokohama Pidgin Japanese lacked articles (Inoue 2007), as does the lexifier Japanese (Shibatani 1990).

11.3.1.1 *Definite articles*

It is not uncommon for languages to lack articles. Furthermore, there are a fair few pidgin languages that do (or did), in fact, have either a definite or an indefinite article, or both. Pidgin Hawaiian, for example, had a definite article *ke/ka* (as well as an indefinite article; see below):

Pidgin Hawaiian (Pidgin (Hawaiian-lexified): Hawaiian Islands)

(271) keia keiki liilii paa ka pakeke
this child little hold DEF package
'This little child was holding the package.' (Roberts 2013a: 123)

In order to test whether pidgin languages tend to be less likely to have definite articles than non-pidgin languages, I compared the current pidgin sample with Dryer's (2013b) sample. The figures are summarized in Table 11.4:

Table 11.4 Definite articles in the current pidgin sample and in WALS (Dryer 2013b). For a full legend of the languages in the pidgin sample, see http://dx.doi.org/10.1075/cll.48.additional.

	Pidgin sample		WALS	
	N	%	N	%
Definite article distinct from demonstrative	2	6.3	216	34.8
Definite article identical with demonstrative	7	21.9	69	11.1
Definite affix on noun	0	–	92	14.8
No definite, but indefinite article	0	–	45	7.3
Neither definite or indefinite article	23	71.9	198	31.9
Total	32		620	

($\chi^2 = 31.84$; $df = 4$; $p_{two\text{-}tailed} < 0.001$***, Fisher's exact test, $p_{sim} < 0.001$*** (B = 10,000))
(G = 36.57; $df = 4$; $p_{two\text{-}tailed} < 0.001$***)

Table 11.4 shows that it is indeed more common for the languages in the pidgin sample to lack definite articles than for the languages in the WALS sample.

11.3.1.2 *Indefinite articles*

It is slightly more common for the languages in Dryer's (2013d) WALS sample to lack indefinite articles than to lack definite articles. Again, there are examples of pidgin languages that have (or had) indefinite articles, such as Pidgin Hawaiian, where the indefinite article (*akahi*) was identical to the numeral 'one':

Pidgin Hawaiian (Pidgin (Hawaiian-lexified): Hawaiian Islands)

(272) a. Ahi kuai iaia $2.50 akahi omole alua omole $5.00
PN sell 3SG one bottle two bottle
'Ahi sold one bottle to him for $2.50 and two bottles for $5.00.'

b. kela lio oe inaha akahi eke palani
DEM horse 2SG.POSS tear one sack bran
'Your horse tore into a sack of bran.' (Roberts 2013b: feature 21)

Example (272) shows that the numeral 'one' (*akahi*) was also used as an indefinite article in Pidgin Hawaiian. In order to test whether pidgin languages tend to be less likely to have indefinite articles than non-pidgin languages, I compared the current pidgin sample with Dryer's (2013d) sample. The figures are summarized in Table 11.5:

Table 11.5 Indefinite articles in the current pidgin sample and in WALS (Dryer 2013d). For a full legend of the languages in the pidgin sample, see http://dx.doi.org/10.1075/cll.48.additional.

	Pidgin sample		WALS	
	N	%	N	%
Indefinite article distinct from numeral 'one'	0	–	102	19.1
Indefinite article identical with numeral 'one'	7	23.3	112	21
Indefinite affix on noun	0	–	24	4.5
No indefinite, but definite article	2	6.7	98	18.4
Neither definite or indefinite article	21	70	198	37.1
Total	30		534	

($\chi^2 = 17.27$; $df = 4$; $p_{\text{two-tailed}} = 0.00171$**, $p_{\text{sim}} = 0.0027$** (B = 10,000))
(G = 23.16; $df = 4$; $p_{\text{two-tailed}} < 0.001$***)

The figures in Table 11.5 show that the absolute majority of the languages in the pidgin sample lack articles altogether. While the languages in WALS which lack articles dominate, the proportion is not as high as in the pidgin sample.[178]

11.3.2 Articles in extended pidgins (pidgincreoles)

The majority of the languages in the small sample of extended pidgins do, in fact, have both definite and indefinite articles. Three out of ten languages, Solomon Islands Pijin, Juba Arabic and Hiri Motu, lack articles altogether.

11.3.2.1 *Definite articles*

In four of the six languages that have definite articles (Cameroon Pidgin English, Nigerian Pidgin, Ghanaian Pidgin English and Sango), the definite article is distinct from the demonstrative. Sango, for example, has a definite article *ni*:

178. Specifically, the lack of articles in the pidgin sample is marginally significant ($p = 0.071$), while the lack of indefinite articles that are distinct from the numeral 'one' in the pidgin sample is significant ($p = 0.043$*). These figures were generated with the HCFA 3.2 script provided by Stefan Th. Gries, the use of which is here gratefully acknowledged. See further http://www.linguistics.ucsb.edu/faculty/stgries/, accessed 11 February 2015.

Sango (Extended pidgin (Ngbandi-lexified): Central African Republic)

(273) a. lo leke a-kungba (ti) lo na a ti da ni kwe
3SG prepare PL-belonging of 3SG OBL interior of house DEF all
'She gathered up all her belongings in the house.'

b. a-melenge so ka a-ke na yoro a-lingbi ape
PL-child DEM there PM-COP OBL charm PM-be.possible NEG
'Those kids over there have an awful lot of charms.' (Samarin 2013a: 15f)

Example (273) shows that the Sango definite article (*ni*) differs from the demonstrative (*so*).

Bislama has an optional postposed particle *ia* which may function either as a definite article or a demonstrative:[179]

Bislama (Extended pidgin (English-lexified): Vanuatu)

(274) haos ia longwe i bigwan moa
house DEF there AGR big more
'This/The house over there is bigger.' (Meyerhoff 2013b: feature 28)

Example (274) shows that the particle *ia* may function either as a demonstrative or as a definite article.

Nagamese has the definite suffix *-tu* (see further Section 8.3.1). Tok Pisin lacks a definite but does have an indefinite article.

11.3.2.2 *Indefinite articles*

Of the seven languages that do have an indefinite article in the sample of extended pidgins (pidgincreoles), five of them (Cameroon Pidgin English, Nigerian Pidgin, Tok Pisin, Bislama and Nagamese), have an indefinite article which is identical to the numeral 'one'. In Sango and Ghanaian Pidgin English the indefinite article is distinct from the numeral 'one'. Compare the following:

Cameroon Pidgin English (Extended pidgin (English-lexified): Cameroon)

(275) a. wan boi an wan gel di plei fo rut
one boy and one girl IPFV play for road
'A boy and a girl are playing in the street.' (Schröder 2013b: feature 29)

b. i bin di kof fo wan awa
3SG.S PST IPFV cough for one hour
'S/he had been coughing for one hour.' (Schröder 2013a: 189)

179. Notice that Bislama is listed with the value 'No definite, but indefinite article' in APiCS Online.

Ghanaian Pidgin English (Extended pidgin (English-lexified): Ghana)

(276) a. à gɛt sɔm frɛn sɛf we ì kam frɔm Togo
1SG POSS INDEF friend TOP REL 3SG come from Togo
'I have a friend who comes from Togo.'

b. wɛn jù tek sɔmtin nak àm wan
when 2SG take something knock 3SG.O one
'...when you knock it once with something.' (Huber 1999b: 192, 203)

Example (275) shows that Cameroon Pidgin English uses the same form to indicate the numeral 'one' (cf. (275b)) as well as indefiniteness (cf. (275a)), while Example (276) shows that Ghanaian differentiates between the two (with the indefinite *sɔm* versus the numeral *wan*).

11.3.3 Articles in creole languages

Creoles are generally described as having "created [definite articles] anew from demonstratives and other particles" (Holm 2000: 213) and to have indefinite articles that are identical with the numeral 'one'. In Kinubi, for example, the demonstrative may also be used as a definite article and the numeral 'one' may be used as an indefinite article:

Kinubi (Creole (Arabic-lexified): Uganda, Kenya)

(277) a. úwo rúo áinu terebíya ta binia de
3SG go see education POSS girl DEM
'He will observe the education of the girl.' (Luffin 2013a: 52)

b. úmun kan kúlu anás wáy kabila de kúlu Núbi Uganda muzima
3PL were all people one tribe DEM all Nubi Uganda all
'They were forming one people, this whole tribe was Nubi all over Uganda.'
(Luffin 2013a: 53)

c. fi nyerekú wáy kamán rúo ma bába t-o
EXIST child one too go with father GEN-his
'There was also a child who went with his father.'
(Luffin 2013b: feature 29 citing Luffin 2005: 330)

Example (277) shows that the same word (*de*) may be used as a definite article (as in (277a)) or a demonstrative (as in (277b)). We also see that the numeral 'one' (as in (277b)) may be used as an indefinite article (as in (277c)).

11.3.3.1 *Definite articles*

Overall it seems more common for languages to have a definite article that is distinct from the demonstrative than to have one that is identical with it. This is also true for a number of creole languages. In Fa d'Ambô, for example, the two forms are distinct:

Fa d'Ambô (Creole (Portuguese-lexified): Equatorial Guinea)

(278) ngatu-syi namsedyi bé iai sa xa na dyividyil
cat-DEM 2PL see there COP thing DEF neighbour
'This cat you have seen belongs to the neighbours.' (Post 2013b: 83)

Example (278) shows that the Fa d'Ambô definite article (*na*) differs from the demonstratives (*-sai/-syi* for proximal and *-sala/-ski* for distal).

In order to test whether creole languages tend to behave differently from non-creoles with respect to the definite article, I compared the current creole sample with Dryer's (2013b) WALS sample. The figures are summarized in Table 11.6:

Table 11.6 Definite articles in the current creole sample and in WALS (Dryer 2013b). For a full legend of the languages in the creole sample, see http://dx.doi.org/10.1075/cll.48.additional.

	Creole sample		WALS*	
	N	%	N	%
Definite article distinct from demonstrative	30	56.6	215	34.7
Definite article identical with demonstrative	13	24.5	69	11.1
Definite affix on noun	0	–	92	14.9
No definite, but indefinite article	6	11.3	45	7.3
Neither definite or indefinite article	4	7.5	198	32
Total	53		619	

($\chi^2 = 32.20$; $df = 4$; $p_{\text{two-tailed}} < 0.001$***, $p_{\text{sim}} < 0.001$*** (B = 10,000))
(G = 39.76; $df = 4$; $p_{\text{two-tailed}} < 0.001$***)
* Ndyuka (Nengee) has been removed from the WALS sample to avoid overlap with the creole sample.

Table 11.6 shows that there does indeed seem to be a significant difference between the languages in the creole sample and those in the WALS sample. First of all it seems a fair bit more common for creoles to have a definite article than for non-creoles (92.5% in the creole sample as opposed to 68% in the WALS sample). Secondly, the absolute majority of the creole languages have a definite article that is distinct from a demonstrative, a fair few more than the languages in the WALS sample. The assumption that creoles tend to use demonstratives as a definite article is thus not supported by these figures.

11.3.3.2 *Indefinite articles*

It is not uncommon for languages to use the numeral 'one' as an indefinite article. This is also true for a number of creoles. In Cape Verdean Creole, for example, the numeral 'one' is used as an indefinite article:

Cape Verdean Creole (Creole (Portuguese-lexified): Cape Verde Islands)

(279) un bes un ómi di lonji bá kása di un mudjer
one time one man of far.away go house of one woman
'One time, a man from far away went to the house of a woman.' (Lang 2013a: 6)

Example (279) shows that the numeral 'one' (*un*) is also used to mark indefiniteness in Cape Verdean Creole. It should be noted, however, that many creole languages have lexifiers which also use the numeral 'one' as an indefinite article: Portuguese, Spanish and French, for example, fall into that category. Having said that, not all creoles with those lexifier languages have an indefinite article that is identical to the numeral 'one'. The Portuguese-lexified Fa d'Ambô, for example, differentiates between the two (*wa(n)* 'INDEFinite article' versus *úña* 'one'; (Post 2013a)), as does the French-lexified Louisiana Creole (*ẽ* 'INDEFinite article' versus *en* 'one'; Neumann-Holzschuh & Klingler 2013).

In order to test whether creole languages tend to behave differently from non-creoles with respect to the indefinite article, I compared the current creole sample with Dryer's (2013d) WALS sample. The figures are summarized in Table 11.7:

Table 11.7 Indefinite articles in the current creole sample and in WALS (Dryer 2013d). For a full legend of the languages in the creole sample, see http://dx.doi.org/10.1075/cll.48.additional.

	Creole sample		WALS*	
	N	%	N	%
Indefinite article distinct from numeral 'one'	15	28.3	102	19.1
Indefinite article identical with numeral 'one'	34	64.2	111	20.8
Indefinite affix on noun	0	–	24	4.5
No indefinite, but definite article	0	–	98	18.4
Neither definite or indefinite article	4	7.5	198	37.1
Total	53		533	

($\chi^2 = 62.98$; $df = 4$; $p_{two\text{-}tailed} < 0.001$***, $p_{sim} < 0.001$*** ($B = 10{,}000$))
($G = 66.73$; $df = 4$; $p_{two\text{-}tailed} < 0.001$***)

* Ndyuka (Nengee) has been removed from the WALS sample to avoid overlap with the creole sample.

Based on the figures in Table 11.7 is does, in fact, seem as if creole languages are significantly more likely than non-creoles to use the numeral 'one' as an indefinite article. Furthermore, it seems as if creoles are more likely than non-creoles to actually have articles at all.

11.3.4 Articles in mixed languages

Mixed languages are usually described as reflecting the grammatical system of one of the input languages, or a blend of the two input systems. If both systems have similar strategies, then that is typically expected to carry over into the mixed language. For example, neither of the input languages for Hezhou, Mandarin and Uyghur, have any articles (Li & Thompson 1981 and Hahn 1998 respectively), which is also reflected in Hezhou:

Hezhou (Mixed language (Mandarin/Uyghur): China)

(280) a. fatsi-xa kɛ vɛ̃li-mu?
house-OBJ build finished-Q
'Is the house built?'

b. mɛ ʂu tɕʰɪ-li ʂɪtʂə tʂʰutɕʰɪliɔ
buy book go-INTENT say go.out.3SG
'He went out to buy a book.' (Lee-Smith 1996b: 866, 870)

Example (280) shows that Hezhou lacks both definite and indefinite articles, which reflects the system of both input languages.

11.3.4.1 *Definite articles*

In a small sample of 15 mixed languages, 11 languages lack the definite article. In four cases this reflected the system of both input languages, in that both input languages lack definite articles: Mednyj Aleut (Russian/Aleut), Wutun (Mandarin/Amdo Tibetan), Hezhou (Mandarin/Uyghur) and Tangwang (Mandarin/Dongxiang) all lack definite articles, as do their input languages. Six languages that lack definite articles have adopted the system of one of the input languages: Ma'á/Mbugu (Bantu/Cushitic) reflects the Mbugu (Bantu) system, Old Helsinki Slang (Finnish/Swedish) reflects the Finnish system, Callahuaya (Puquina/Quechua) reflects the Quechua system, as does Media Lengua (Quechua/Spanish), Sri Lankan Malay (Malay/Tamil/Sinhala) reflects the Malay system and Petjo (Javanese/Dutch) reflects the Javanese system. In Old Helsinki Slang, for example, the Swedish definite suffix fused with the stem and lost the definiteness value:

Old Helsinki Slang (Mixed language (Finnish/Swedish): Finland)

(281) mä en muista niiden nime-t
1SG NEG remember 3PL.GEN name-PL
'I don't remember their names.' (Jarva 2008:74)

The noun *nime* 'name' in Example (281) is inflected for plural (*-t*) but not for definiteness, which reflects the Finnish system. However, the stem *nime* reflects the Swedish definite form (*namn-et*); the definite suffix *-et* has fused with the stem and lost its grammatical value. This also happened with, for example, such nouns as *blude* (< Sw. *blod-et* 'blood-DEFinite'), *hunde* (< Sw. *hund-en* 'dog-DEFinite') and *skuuge* (< Sw. *skog-en* 'forest-DEFinite') (Jarva 2008:70).[180]

Shelta (Irish/English) seems unusual in that while both input languages have an obligatory definite article, this has not carried over to the mixed language in that the definite article is optional and most frequently omitted (Macalister 1937).

Bilingual Navajo (English/Navajo) uses the Navajo demonstratives as definite articles (Schaengold 2004). Angloromani (English/Romani) uses the English articles (Matras 2010), while Michif (Cree/French) uses the French articles, which differ from the Cree-derived demonstratives (Bakker 2013b), and Gurindji Kriol (Gurindji/Kriol) uses a form derived from English 'that' (*dat*) as a definite article, which differs from the Gurindji-derived demonstratives (Meakins 2013b).

11.3.4.2 *Indefinite articles*

Eight of the 15 languages in the small sample of mixed languages lack articles altogether. In four of the cases (Mednyj Aleut, Wutun, Tangwang and Hezhou) that reflects the system of both input languages (see above). In the other four the lack of articles reflects the system of one of the input languages; these are the same languages as listed above (also lacking the definite article), except for Shelta, where the lack of an indefinite article reflects the system of Irish.

Two of the mixed languages, Michif and Angloromani, are similar in their systems to one of their input languages (French and English respectively). In Michif the indefinite article is *aen/enn* (MAsculine/FEminine), reflecting the French indefinite articles (*un/une*), while the numeral 'one' is *henn*, also derived from French (Bakker 2013b). In Angloromani the indefinite article is *a* (<English) while the numeral 'one' is *yak/yeg/yek*, derived from Romani (Matras 2010).

In four languages the indefinite article is identical with the numeral 'one'. For Bilingual Navajo this is the Navajo numeral *ła'* (Schaengold 2004), while in Gurindji

180. A similar process is very common for French-lexified contact languages, where the prenominal definite article fused with the stem and lost its definiteness value.

Kriol it is the Kriol article/numeral *wan* (Meakins 2013b). Media Lengua and Sri Lankan Malay reflect a blend of the two input systems: neither of the languages have any definite articles (which reflects the system of one of the input languages, namely Quechua and Malay respectively), but both of them have an indefinite article which is identical with the numeral 'one'. In Media Lengua something like *uno musica* may thus either translate to 'a tune' or 'one tune' depending on context (Muysken 2013b). This matches the system of the other input language, Spanish (cf. *un hombre* 'a/one man'). Sri Lankan Malay also has an indefinite article which is identical to the numeral 'one' (*(h)a(t)thu*):

Sri Lankan Malay (Mixed language (Malay/Tamil/Sinhala): Sri Lanka)

(282) hathu haari, hathu oorang thoppi mà-juval=nang kampong=dering
one day one man hat INF-sell=DAT village=ABL
kampong=nang su-jaalang pii
village=DAT PST-walk go
'One day, a man walked from village to village to sell his hats.' (Nordhoff 2009: 570)

Example (282) shows that the word for 'one' may also be used as an indefinite article in Sri Lankan Malay. This might be an innovation, as neither Malay nor Tamil has an indefinite article (Prentice 1990 and Lehmann 1993 respectively), while Sinhala has an indefinite suffix *-ak* and the numeral *eka* 'one' (Matzel 1966). For more on Sri Lankan Malay, see Section 3.3.3.

11.4 Snapshots

Pidgins are assumed to lack plural marking and articles. Pidgin Hawaiian is an example of a pidgin language which in fact has some optional plural marking, as well as definite and indefinite articles.

Creoles are assumed to have optional plural marking, expressed analytically, and to have a definite article identical with the demonstrative and an indefinite article identical with the numeral 'one'. Cape Verdean Creole is an example of a creole which has an optional plural suffix, and where plural marking is animacy dependent. It has no definite article, but an indefinite article identical with the numeral 'one'.

Mixed languages are assumed to have adopted the strategies of one of the input languages, or to represent a blend of the two ancestral systems. Shelta is an example of a mixed language which represents a blend of the two input systems in that the plural marking most commonly (though not always) derives from English, and where the optional articles derive from both input languages.

11.4.1 Pidgin Hawaiian: An extinct Hawaiian-lexified pidgin on the Hawaiian Islands[181]

11.4.1.1 *A brief background sketch of Pidgin Hawaiian*

Pidgin Hawaiian, which was called *'Ōlelo pa'i 'ai* by the users themselves, is a now extinct pidgin spoken on the Hawaiian Islands and beyond roughly between the 1790s and the 1940s.

The Hawaiian Islands had been inhabited for many centuries when they were "discovered" by James Cook in 1778. Some ten years later they became a convenient middle stop for the so-called "Alaska-Hawaii-Canton run" (Carr 1972) of fur and sandalwood trade between the north-western American coast and China. Ships kept returning to the same few locations on the islands and European and American visitors relied on native Hawaiians proficient enough in English, as well as non-native Hawaiian long-term residents proficient enough in Hawaiian, to act as interpreters (Schütz 1994: 44ff). These early non-native settlers were "likely crucial to the development of linguistic conventions" (Roberts 2013a: 119) which would soon become Pidgin Hawaiian; the first known attestations of Pidgin Hawaiian were recorded by Esteban Martínez as early as 1789, only 11 years after James Cook's arrival (*ibid*).

The use of Pidgin Hawaiian increased from the early decades of the 19th century on. With the growth of the sandalwood and whaling industries, contact with the Hawaiian Islands intensified and brought an increasing number of foreigners to the islands. Also, more and more Hawaiians signed up on the whaling ships, bringing them into contact with multilingual crews. Especially the whaling industry led to the spread of Pidgin Hawaiian westwards to Eastern Polynesia and eastwards to California, and, in fact, even left traces in the Eskimo pidgins spoken in Alaska and in Chukchi in eastern Siberia (Bickerton & Wilson 1987: 62 citing Clark 1977: 3), such as *wahine* 'woman' and *hanahana* 'work' (Sarah Roberts, p.c.). At the same time missionary activities increased on the islands and early records show that the missionaries used an early version of Pidgin Hawaiian in their interactions with the indigenous population.

Large-scale sugar cultivation began in 1835. Labour was initially Hawaiian, but with the steep decline of the indigenous population – which had decreased by at least 75% by 1854 (Linnekin 1991: 95) – due to overwork and introduced diseases, labour import became a necessity. An even more dominant reason for the labour import was economical: the foreign contract labours were more willing to work for cheaper wages and submit to indentured servitude (as aliens they lacked the rights of native citizens; Sarah Roberts, p.c.). The last quarter of the 19th century saw massive immigration, predominantly from southern China and the Portuguese Atlantic islands (Madeira and the Azores), later also from Japan. The primary means of communication on the plantations during the last couple of decades in the 19th century was Pidgin Hawaiian (cf. Glick 1938, Jones 1942).

Archival data show that Pidgin Hawaiian existed alongside an English-lexified pidgin (and even a mixture of the two) on the Hawaiian Islands, especially in the urban areas, from the first

181. This section is based almost exclusively on Roberts (2013a). I am very grateful to Sarah Roberts for her helpful comments on this snapshot.

half of the 19th century. Hawai'i Pidgin English steadily gained in prestige and had, by the 1910s, replaced Pidgin Hawaiian on the plantations.[182] By the 1940s Pidgin Hawaiian was all but gone, although it in fact only became extinct in the 1980s, when the last known speaker, Mr Thomas Quihano, passed away.

11.4.1.2 *A short linguistic sketch of Pidgin Hawaiian*

Pidgin Hawaiian, like its lexifier Hawaiian, had only eight consonants, /p, m, w, l, n, k, ʔ, h/, and five vowels, /i, e, a, o, u/. There seems to have been noticeable variation in pronunciation depending on the first language of the speaker. For example, /l/ was typically indicated as <r> for Japanese speakers in the sources. The glottal /ʔ/ seems often to have been dropped or, with Chinese speakers, to have been realized as /h/ word-initially. The syllable structure was simple (CV), with maximally one syllable onset consonant and no syllable codas. Tone does not seem to have been relevant. It should be noted that any kind of inference about the phonology of Pidgin Hawaiian is based on written sources (where such features as vowel length and the glottal were rarely indicated).

The morphology was predominantly analytic, though there was a transitivizing suffix *-hana* and a pronominal object/oblique prefix *ia-*. There are numerous examples of reduplication (which typically indicated intensification).

Case and gender were not relevant. Nouns could optionally be marked for plural with the invariant *mau*:

(283) wau aole nana kela (mau) poho kiwi
1SG NEG see that PL container horn
'I didn't see those bullhorn containers.' (Roberts 2013a: 121)

There was a definite article *ke/ka* (cf. Examples (284a), (285b), (288)) and an indefinite article *akahi*, which was identical with the numeral 'one' (cf. Examples (284b), (286a), (288)). There were two demonstratives, *keia* (proximal) and *kela* (distal), which were also commonly used to indicate definiteness:

(284) a. aole laua hakaka maloko o ka lumi
NEG 3DU fight inside POSS DEF room
'The two didn't fight inside the room.' (Roberts 2013b: feature 28)

b. wau ike kela Kipau ki kela pu kela Moaka, kela Moaka
1SG see DEM PN shoot DEM gun DEM PN DEM PN
akahi pahi
one knife
'I saw Kipau shoot his gun at Moaka, Moaka had a knife.' (Roberts 2013a: 121)

Possession was either indicated through juxtaposition only or with the possessive marker *o* (cf. also Example (284a)):

182. This early pidgin English would later develop into the creole which is still spoken on the islands today (see further Section 6.4.1).

(285) a. Akoi ma kela lumi Lam See
PN LOC DEM room PN
'Akoi was in Lam See's room.'
b. wau hele no ma ka hale o Joe
1SG go INTENS LOC DEF house POSS PN
'I went to Joe's house.' (Roberts 2013b: feature 38)

The personal pronoun set distinguished between three persons and three numbers.

	SINGULAR	DUAL	PLURAL
1	*wau*	*maua*	*makou*
2	*oe*	*olua*	*oukou*
3	*iaia*	*laua*	*lakou*

There was also a set inflected with the object/oblique marker *ia* (< Hawaiian *iā-)*, preposed to the personal pronoun form.

Verbs were invariant. Temporal and aspectual connotations were optionally indicated with adverbs, such as *kela manawa* 'then' (lit. 'that time') or *mamua* 'before' for events in the past (as in (286a)), *keia manawa* 'now' (lit. 'this time') for events in the present (as in (286b)), *mahope* 'later' for events in the future (as in (286c)), *pauloa manawa* 'always, often' (lit. 'all time') for recurring events (as in (286d)), *pau* 'finish' for completed events (as in (286e)), and so on.

(286) a. oe mamua aie akahi dala, aole hoihoi mai, wau aole
2SG before borrow one dollar NEG return DIR 1SG NEG
makana akahi dala iaoe
give one dollar 2SG.OBJ
'You previously borrowed a dollar that you never returned to me, so I'm not going to give you a dollar.' (Roberts 2013b: feature 49)
b. aole wau manao make ana wau, aka wau nui loa eha
NEG 1SG think die IPFV 1SG but 1SG much very hurt
keia manawa
this time
'I don't think I will die but I am in a lot of pain right now.' (Roberts 2013a: 123)
c. ina aole loaa kela kala mahope oe ike
if NEG get DEM money later 2SG see
'If you don't get the money, you will be sorry.' (Roberts 2013a: 123)
d. aole hiki wau malama kela ohana wau pauloa manawa
NEG able 1SG take.care DEM family 1SG all time
'I was usually unable to care for my family.' (Roberts 2013b: feature 48)
e. pau noho oe me Kalo
finish live 2SG with PN
'Have you stopped living with Kalo?' (Roberts 2013a: 123)

However, there was an imperfective marker *ana* (cf. also (286b)):

(287) olelo hou ana
speak again IPFV
'(He) was speaking again.' (Roberts 2013b: feature 46)

There were a number of modal expressions, such as *makemake* 'want' (expressing desire; cf. Example (289b)), *hiki* 'able' (expressing ability; cf. Example (286d)), and so on.

Property concepts (the equivalent of English adjectives) were expressed with stative verbs and could take mood markers. Comparison was indicated with a negation of *like pu* 'same as':

(288) a. oe ikaika no, ina oe ikaika oe pimai
2SG strong PROB if 2SG strong 2SG come
'Are you so strong? If you are strong, come (to me).'
b. kela pepa nuinui maikai aole like pu kela pepa ia Wainui
DEM paper very good NEG same as DEM paper DEF W
'That paper is much better than Wainui's newspaper.' (Roberts 2013a: 122)

The word order was typically subject-verb-object. There was an invariant preverbal negator *aole*. Polar questions seem to have mostly been indicated through intonation only (as in (289a)), though there was an optional clause-initial question particle *pehea* 'what, how, why' (as in (289b)):

(289) a. A: oe ike mamua Lauman puhi? B: ae wau ike
2SG see before PN smoke yes 1SG see
'A: Did you previously see Lauman smoke? B: Yes, I did.' (Roberts 2013a: 125)
b. A: pehea makemake oe hana? B: ae
Q want 2SG work yes
'A: Do you want (some) work? B: Yes.' (Roberts 2013b: feature 103)

Interrogative phrases in content questions typically appeared clause-initially. There was no passive construction and no copula (cf. Example (288)).

There were the coordinating conjunctions *a* 'and' and *aka* 'but'. Complement clauses were simply juxtaposed:

(290) pehea oe kamailio oe hele moemoe?
why 2SG talk 2SG go sleep
'Why did you say that you were going to sleep?' (Roberts 2013a: 125)

There seems to have been some serial verb constructions:

(291) wau nana Wong See ike no
1SG look PN see PROB
'I spotted Wong See.' (Roberts 2013a: 124)

Subject relative clauses were simply juxtaposed:

(292) mahope akahi pake holo mai, kela Makawela hanapaa wau kui wau ma ka
later one Chinese run DIR DEM PN hold 1SG hit 1SG LOC DEF
umauma wau, mahope kela pake holo mai hemo kela puka wau holo mawaho
chest 1SG later DEM Chinese run DIR open DEM door 1SG run outside
'Then a Chinese ran to me as Makawela held me down punching my chest, then the Chinese who ran to me opened the door and I ran outside.' (Roberts 2013a: 125)

Object relative clauses could be marked with *ke/kela mea* 'the/that thing'.

11.4.1.3 *Short text*

(A witness statement from Hanapepe, Kaua'i, 1891 (1CR-1615), transcribed and glossed by Sarah Roberts.)

Wau	mamua	moe	ma	kela	hale	maua	laiki,	mahope	kela	kaikamahine	pimai,	wau
1SG	before	sleep	LOC	DEM	house	plantation	rice	later	DEM	daughter	come	1SG

olelo,	"Oe	makemake	moe?"	Mahope	kela	kaikamahine	moe	maanei,	mahope	kela	bepe
speak	2SG	want	sleep	later	DEM	daughter	sleep	here	later	DEM	baby

uwe,	wau	makana	poi	kela	bepe	paina,	pau	paina	wau	hoihoi	kela	poi	ma	ka	hale,
cry	1SG	give	poi	DEM	baby	meal	finish	meal	1SG	return	DEM	poi	LOC	DEM	house

mahope	pepe	hele	maloko	hui	pu	mama,	mahope	wau	pii	hou	mai	ma	kela
later	baby	go	inside	together	with	mother	later	1SG	come	again	DIR	LOC	DEM

hale	wau	moe	maluna	ma	kela	papa
house	1SG	sleep	upon	LOC	DEM	bed

'I was sleeping in the rice plantation house when my daughter came. I said to her, "Do you want to sleep?" Then my daughter slept here. My baby started crying and so I fed her some poi. After she ate it, I took the poi back into the house and then the baby went inside with its mother. After that I returned to my house to sleep in my bed.'

11.4.1.4 *Some sources of data*

There is very little primary data available for Pidgin Hawaiian. Roberts (2013a) provides numerous glossed and translated examples and two shorter texts (also glossed and translated) and Roberts (2013b) provides a large number of glossed and translated examples online. Frazier (2001) gives Hawaiian text with an English translation; some of the witness statements given are in Pidgin Hawaiian.

11.4.2 Cape Verdean Creole: A Portuguese-lexified creole on the Cape Verde Islands[183]

11.4.2.1 *A brief background sketch of Cape Verdean Creole*

Cape Verdean Creole (also called *Kriolu*, *Kabuverdianu* or *Cape Verdean* by scholars), spoken by approximately one million people, is a cover term for three closely related varieties spoken on the Cape Verdean islands (located in the Atlantic some 500 km west of Senegal) and by the diaspora: the creole of Santiago, also called *Santiago Creole* in English or *crioulo da ilha de Santiago (Cabo Verde)* in Portuguese and called *badiu* or *kriolu* by the speakers themselves (ca. 450,000 speakers on Santiago); the creole of São Vicente, also called *São Vicente Creole* in English and *crioulo da ilha de São Vicente (Cabo Verde)* in Portuguese and called *kriol* or *kriol d'Sonsent* by the speakers themselves (ca. 76,000 speakers on São Vicente island); and the creole of Brava, also called *crioulo da ilha de Brava (Cabo Verde)* in Portuguese and called *Kriolu di Dja Brava*, *Crioulo*, *Kriolu* or *Bravense* by the speakers themselves (ca. 6,000 speakers on Brava island).

183. This section relies almost exclusively on Baptista (2013), Lang (2013a) and Swolkien (2013a). I am very grateful to Marlyse Baptista for her helpful comments on this snapshot.

The nine inhabited Cape Verde islands are usually grouped into the Sotavento or Leeward islands (Maio, Santiago, Fogo and Brava) and the Barlavento or Windward islands (Santo Antão, São Vicente, São Nicolau, Sal and Boa Vista). The settlement histories vary for the different islands.

The islands of the Cape Verde archipelago were discovered by the Portuguese in 1456. They were conveniently located and became a middle stop for ships on the West African trade routes, later also for the transatlantic slave trade. The first settlement was founded on the island of Santiago in 1462. In order to encourage settlements, Portugal soon set up favourable trading conditions for Cape Verdean colonists. Cotton and horse farms were founded on the islands of Santiago and Fogo and colonists traded horses and cloth for African goods and slaves. Most slaves were then resold to the European and American markets.

The settlers arrived without families or servants and found both partners and servants among the West African populations with which they traded. Usually children born out of mixed heritage unions were freed, leading to an early mixed descendant free population, which very soon outnumbered the white population. A report in 1582 shows that Santiago had a population of about 13,400 people, more than half of which lived in the urban areas in 708 households and had about 6,700 slaves among them, while the other half, both whites, free mixed descendants and free Africans, lived in the rural areas and had about 5,000 slaves among them. There are indications that Wolof was the majority language among the slaves during the first century of the colony (Lang 2006), which is likely to be the period when the creole emerged.

With the end of the Portuguese monopoly in trade with West African rulers at the end of the 16th century, an economic crisis followed on Santiago. Landowners left and freed their slaves, many of whom in turn resettled on other Cape Verdean islands in order to find arable land. Furthermore, "a system of slavery was replaced with a system of tenancy with small tenants working the lands of absentee landowners" (Lang 2013a: 4). All this led to a blurring of social boundaries, which is likely to also have affected the development of the creole.

The island of Brava was settled much later, in 1573, more than a century after it was discovered, originally by European settlers. While the slave population grew until the mid-19th century, the white population seems to have remained dominant on this island, which is likely to have affected the creole variety spoken there. There were different waves of settlement, one important one at the end of the 17th century when the volcano erupted on the nearby Fogo Island and caused a wave of refugees to Brava. The 19th century saw frequent visits by New England whaling ships, recruiting labour and sailors on Brava, an attractive opportunity for many due to the limited possibilities for agriculture, leading to a steady emigration to New England in particular. The intense connection with America, especially the American whaling ships, has left noticeable traces in the Brava variety of the creole.

The island of São Vicente was settled even later, in 1795, more than 300 years after it was discovered, when a group of settlers arrived from the island of Fogo (bringing with them the creole from the Leeward islands) as well as from Portugal (both continental and from Madeira and the Azores). Slavery did not play an important role in the demographics of the island; for example, in 1856, one year before abolition, the island had 1,100 inhabitants, of which only 32 were slaves (divided up by 14 different owners). Most of these slaves came from other Cape Verdean islands, meaning that it is likely that their primary language was the creole. The island rapidly became highly metropolitan from the second half of the 19th century onwards, particularly due to its role as a coal depot from British coal mining companies. This made the island an important transit point for ships and, as a result, a massive amount of passengers passed through the harbour centre Mindelo. This also led to a high level of immigration from other Cape Verdean islands and caused a demographic boom. The urbanization brought with it social stratification and increased the status of Portuguese.

The Cape Verde islands and Guinea-Bissau as a single state became independent from Portugal in 1975. This single state was split with the military coup in Guinea-Bissau in 1991 and the Republic of Cape Verde was formed.

The linguistic situation is highly complex. There is variation in the creole among the different islands and on each island there is also urban/rural, geographical, social and register variation. Furthermore, with Portuguese being the sole official language of the country, there is a diglossic relationship between Portuguese and the creole. While Portuguese enjoys a higher prestige than the creole, efforts are being made to also make Cape Verdean Creole an official language of the country. There is an official orthography, *ALUPEC* (*Alfabeto unificado para a escrita do Cabo-Verdiano*), though this orthography is not accepted on all islands: on São Vicente, for example the local elite is resisting it because "in the minds of the speakers, [the ALUPEC] reflects the Sotavento but not the São Vicente variety" (Swolkien 2013a: 22). The creole has been recognized as a language of administration and education. It is also increasingly being used in media, especially the Santiago variety.

11.4.2.2 *A short linguistic sketch of Cape Verdean Creole*

Unless otherwise indicated, the examples in this section are given in the ALUPEC orthography.

Cape Verdean Creole has 20 consonants, /p, b, m, f, v, t, d, n, r, s, z, l, ʃ, ʒ, c, ɟ, ɲ, ʎ, k, g/ (the São Vicente variety has an added /ɾ/), and eight vowels, /i, e, ɛ, a, ɐ, ɔ, o, u/ (the Brava variety has an added /ə/). All vowels may be nasalized (indicated orthographically by the vowel + <n>). The orthography differs from IPA as follows:

IPA	ALUPEC
ɛ	é
ɐ	a
a	á
ɔ	ó
ə	e
ɾ	r
ɲ	nh
ʃ	x
ʒ	j
ʧ	tx
ɟ	dj
ʎ	lh

Syllables may be moderately complex with up to three onset consonants (such as *splika* 'to explain') and up to one coda consonant (such as *irmon* 'brother'), though the São Vicente variety allows codas of up to two consonants (such as *ólt* 'tall'). Tone is not relevant.

The morphology is predominantly analytic, although there is some suffixation and cliticization. There is also reduplication (which indicates augmentation, intensification, iteration or lexical conversion) in the Santiago and Brava varieties (but not in the São Vicente variety; Swolkien 2013b).

Nouns may optionally be marked for plural with the plural suffix *-(i)s* (as in (293a), cf. the bare noun *kasa* in (293b)):

(293) a. amigu-s di=Lusiu purgunta-l si=e=kre-ba entrá-ba na=djogu
friend-PL of=PN ask-3SG.O if=3SG.S=want-ANT enter-ANT into=game
'Lusiu's friends asked him if he wanted to join the game.' (Brüser et al. 2002: 151)

b. kasa d=es rua ta parse bedju
house of=DEM street IPFV look old
'The houses in this street look old.' (Baptista 2002: 38)

Typically the plural suffix appears on human nouns and is less common with inanimate nouns. There is no specific definite article but there is an indefinite article *un* (identical with the numeral 'one'), which inflects for the plural (*uns*) and has an augmentative form (*uma*):

(294) a. mudjer resebe-l ben resebe-du
woman receive-3SG.O well receive-PASS
'The woman received him very well.' (Lang 2013a: 6)

b. un bes un ómi di Inji bá kása di un mudjer
one time one man of far.away go house of one woman
'One time, a man from far away went to the house of a woman.' (Lang 2013a: 6)

c. to ki N ta ten uns problema
when 1SG.S IPFV have INDEF.PL problem
'When I have some problems...' (Baptista 2002: 27)

d. na kel baskudja, N diskubri uma libron
in DEM rummage.about 1SG.S discover INDEF.AUGM book.AUGM
'In that rummaging through, I discovered a huge book.' (Lang 2013a: 6)

There are two demonstratives, the proximal *es* and the distance neutral *kel*, which inflects for plural (*kes*).[184] Both demonstratives may be used as definite articles.

Possession may be indicated with the possessive marker *di* (cf. Examples (293a), (294b)) or *-l*, or, in the Santiago and Brava varieties (but not the São Vicente variety; Swolkien 2013b), through juxtaposition only.

The pronominal system distinguishes between personal and possessive pronouns. There are two dependent sets (subject versus object) and one independent set of personal pronouns. There is an adnominal and an independent set of possessive pronouns. Where the São Vicente variety differs from the others, the São Vicente variety has been given after a slash (indicated with SV):

184. In the São Vicente variety the proximal *es* also inflects for plural (/es/ versus /eʃ/) and *kel*/*kes* represents a distal rather than a neutral demonstrative (Swolkien 2013a: 24).

	PERSONAL			POSSESSIVE	
	DEPENDENT		INDEPENDENT	ADNOMINAL	INDEPENDENT
	SUBJECT	OBJECT			
1SG	*N*	*-m*	*(a)mi*	*nha*	*di meu*
2SG.FAM	*bu*	*-(b)u* / SV:*-b*	*(a)bo*	*bu*	*di bo*
2SG.POL.F	*nha*		*(a)nha*		*di nha*
2SG.POL.M	*nhu*		*(a)nho*		*di nho*
3SG	*e(l)*	*-l*	*(a)el* / SV: *se*	*si/se*	*di sel*
1PL	*nu*	*-nu* / SV:*-nos*	*(a)nos*	*nos*	*di nos*
2PL	*nhos* / SV: *bzot*		*(a)nhos* / SV: *bzot*	*nhos* / SV: *bzot*	*di nhos*
3PL	*es*	*-s*	*(a)es*	*ses*	*di ses*

Notice that there is a polite form *nho/nha* (which distinguishes for gender) in the second singular subject dependent and independent personal set, as well as in the independent possessive set in the Santiago and Brava varieties. The *a-* in the independent set is optional and indicates topicalization in the Santiago and Brava varieties. The São Vicente variety lacks gender distinction in the second singular polite form (which is *bosê* in all sets) but, contrary to the other varieties, has a separate second plural polite form (*bosés* in all sets).

In all varieties adjectives agree in gender with human nouns (as in *un óm prigoz* 'a dangerous man' / *un amdjer prigóz**a*** 'a dangerous woman'; Swolkien 2013a:23) but most commonly remain invariant with inanimate nouns. Adjective comparison is in the Santiago and Brava varieties indicated with *más … (di) ki* 'more … (of) than' for the comparative and *más … di* 'more … than' for the superlative:

(295) a. Artur e mas bedju (di) ki Djon
PN COP more old of than PN
'Artur is older than John.' (Baptista 2002:71)

b. es kása li e más áltu di (es) tudu
DEM house here COP more high than DEM all
'This house is the highest of all (these).' (Lang 2013a:6)

In the São Vicente variety the comparative is indicated with *má(s) … diki/k/duki/d'k* 'more … than' and the superlative with *má(s) … k/de* 'more … of':

(296) a. kavála e má(s) kór diki/k/duki/d'k atun
mackerel COP more expensive than tuna
'Mackerel is more expensive than tuna.'

b. atun e má(s) kór k/d' tud pex
tuna COP more expensive of all fish
'Tuna is the most expensive of all fish.' (Swolkien 2013a:24)

The reading of unmarked verbs depends on the lexical aspect: unmarked stative verbs usually have a present time reading, while dynamic verbs usually have a past time reading:

(297) a. N ka sabe kuze ki tene-m duenti
1SG.S NEG know what COMP have-1SG.O sick
'I don't know what is making me sick.' (Baptista 2002:76)

b. el toká y el kantá
3SG.S play and 3SG.S sing
'He played and sang.' (Swolkien 2013b: feature 51)

In the Santiago and Brava varieties there are six verbal markers indicating tense, mood, aspect and voice: the preverbal *ál* 'DESIDerative', *sa* 'PROGressive' and *ta* 'IMPerFective' (cf. Example (293b), (294c)), and the suffixes *-ba* 'ANTerior' (cf. Example (293a)), *-du* 'PASSive' (cf. Example (294a)) and *-da* 'PASSive.ANTerior', while the São Vicente variety has *ta/te* 'IMPerFective', *tá(va)* 'PaST.IMPerFective', *tita* 'PRESent.PROGressive' and *tá(va)ta/te* 'PaST.PROGressive'. In the Santiago and Brava varieties there is also the completive marker *dja* (the equivalent of *ja* in the São Vicente variety). In the São Vicente variety the present tense marker *te* is becoming increasingly obligatory for a present tense reading of stative verbs:

(298) a. N te podê spendê sen kil
1SG.S PRES can lift hundred kilo
'I can lift a hundred kilograms.' (Swolkien 2013a: 25)

There are several modal verbs.

The word order is typically subject-verb-object. Negation is formed with the invariant negator *ka* (cf. Example (297a) and (299)). There is negative concord:

(299) N ka odja ningen
1SG.S NEG see nobody
'I didn't see anybody.' (Lang 2013a: 9)

Polar questions are formed through rising intonation only. In content questions the interrogative phrase is typically fronted (followed by the complementizer/relativizer *ki*), though it may also remain *in situ*.

(300) a. bu bai merkadu onti?
2SG.S go market yesterday
'Did you go to the market yesterday?' (Baptista 2013: 17)
b. pamódi ki bu sta tristi?
why COMP 2SG.S COP sad
'Why are you sad?' (Lang 2013a: 8)
c. bo e kenhê
2SG.S COP who
'Who are you?' (Swolkien 2013a: 26)

There are obligatory copulas: *e* typically indicates permanent properties (cf. Examples (295), (296), (300c)), while *sta* typically indicates temporary properties (cf. Example (300b)). There is a locative copula, which in the Santiago and Brava varieties appears as *sta* and in the São Vicente variety as *ta/te*.

(301) el ta lá na kaldera
3SG.S LOC there in pot
'It (the food) is there in the pot.' (Swolkien 2013a: 25)

There are the coordinating conjunctions *y* 'and', *má(s)* 'but', *o* 'or', *o* … *o* 'either … or' and *(nen)* … *nen* '(neither) … nor' as well as the complementizers *ki* 'that' (which also introduces relative clauses), *(ku)ma* 'that' and *si* 'if, whether'. The Brava variety also has the complementizer *pa* 'that/for'. The São Vicente variety complementizers are *k* 'that' (which also functions as a relativizer), *(k)ma* 'that' (for object clauses) and *pa* 'for'.

11.4.2.3 *Short text*

(From Baptista 2002: CD. The speaker is from Santiago and relates his experiences with the famine of 1947.)

Na kel fomi di korenti seti, ami N ta sta-ba na Praia, e fomi ki leba-ba
in DEM famine of forty seven 1SG 1SG.S IPFV COP-ANT in P COP hunger COMP take-ANT

mi. Kuando ki era fomi, ami N ta parti-ba kumida, pa N da-ba
1SG.O when COMP COP.ANT hunger 1SG 1SG.S IPFV distribute-ANT food for 1SG.S give-ANT

koitadu ta ba ku tripa di pexi, ta ba poi ku pratu, pa N po-l kumida
poor IPFV go with guts of fish IPFV go put with plate for 1SG.S put-3SG.O food

riba d=el.
on.top of=3SG

'During the 1947 famine, I was in Praia, it is the famine that took me there. In the times of hunger, I used to distribute the food, to give it to the poor; the poor would go with fish guts, they would put them in a plate, so that I put food on top.'

11.4.2.4 *Some sources of data*

There is a wealth of primary data available for Cape Verdean Creole. Baptista (2010: 284f) gives a long list of Cape Verdean linguists and writers who have produced materials in the creole. Lang (2013a), Baptista (2013) and Swolkien (2013a) give several text corpora for different varieties of Cape Verdean Creole, as well as dictionaries for and grammars in and on the creole.

11.4.3 Shelta: A secret English/Irish mixed language in Ireland[185]

11.4.3.1 *A brief background sketch of Shelta*

Shelta, also called *Sheldru*, *Cant*, *Irish Traveller Cant* and *Gammon* by scholars, and called *The Cant* or (less commonly) *Gammon* by the speakers themselves, is spoken by some 6,000 people in Ireland and another roughly 80,000 speakers in various English speaking countries (mostly the UK and the USA, but also Canada, South Africa and Australia). It is spoken by the Irish Travellers, an ethnic group formerly known as Tinkers (a pejorative term). This is

> a generally endogamous group of (traditionally) itinerant craftsmen, small traders, musicians and beggars, sharing a number of cultural traits, such as common patterns of livelihood, customs relating to birth, marriage and domestic affairs, and adherence to Roman Catholicism.
> (Grant 1994: 123)

185. This section relies almost exclusively on Macalister (1937) and Grant (1994). I am very grateful to Anthony Grant and Ian Hancock for their helpful comments on this snapshot.

The ethnonym Traveller stems from the Shelta word *minkʲe:ry* 'Traveller' (Arnold 1898) and Irish Travellers refer to themselves as *Minceirs* (Ian Hancock, p.c.).

The origin of the Irish Travellers is a matter of debate. In a DNA study it was found that the Travellers have shared heritage with the settled Irish community, but diverged as long as 1–2,000 years ago and now form a "distinct genetic group as different from the settled Irish as Icelanders are from Norwegians" (Hough 2011). The reason for this split is not known.

Travellers have traditionally suffered a high level of stigmatization and discrimination (Helleiner 2003). While the UK recognizes Travellers as a minority ethnic group, Ireland does not. Discrimination is both on a general level, such as lack of equal access to education, and on more personal levels, where individuals repeatedly experience discrimination on the basis of being Travellers, such as denial of service in pubs, shops and hotels, or even being asked to leave or cancel reservations (Irish Traveller Movement Survey, http://itmtrav.ie/keyissues/myview/7 accessed 12 February 2015).

The relative age of Shelta is also a matter of debate (cf. Hancock 1986a). It is essentially a G-L mixed language, with a predominantly Irish lexicon (much of which has undergone some or several forms of sound-substitution disguising) and a predominantly English structure. It is a secret language and is not meant to be revealed to *Buffers* (non-Travellers). In fact even the existence of the language remained a secret until 1876, when it was discovered by chance when Charles Godfrey Leland met an itinerant knife-grinder near Bath (Macalister 1937: 130). The knife-grinder complained that while he knew some Romani, it was getting to be too "blown" (English Cant for 'made the subject of general knowledge'; Grant 1994: 124), but that there existed another language that was not blown:

> "But we are givin' Romanes up very fast, – all of us is," he remarked. "It is a gettin' to be too blown. Everybody knows some Romanes now. But there *is* a jib [language – VV] that ain't blown," he remarked reflectively. … "I heard there's actilly a book about Romanes to learn it out of. But as for this other jib, its wery hard to talk. It is most all Old Irish, and they calls it Shelter." (Leland 1882: 354f)

Shelta thus serves the dual function of an in-group identity marker and of a secret language, i.e. a way of communicating that is not understandable to outsiders (cf. Hancock 1986a). There are several varieties of Shelta, such as Irish Gaelic Shelta, Scottish Gaelic Shelta, Manx Gaelic Shelta and English Shelta.

11.4.3.2 *A short linguistic sketch of Shelta*

Shelta has 27 consonants, /p, pʲ, b, bʲ, m, mʲ, w, t, tʲ, d, dʲ, n, nʲ, θ, ð, r, rʲ, l, ʎ, ʃ, tʃ, y, k, kʲ, g, gʲ, χ/, and six vowels, /i, e, a, ə, ɔ, u/. All vowels except /ə/ have a phonemic long form. Syllables may be complex with up to three consonants in both the onset and the coda, as in *skraχo* 'tree, bush' and *tarsp* 'die'. There is no tone. Most words have initial stress (i.e. on the first syllable). The lenition and nasalization processes (so-called 'mutations') common in Irish are very rare, if not absent, in Shelta.

The morphological system is essentially taken over from English and is thus predominantly analytic but with some suffixation.

Case and gender are not relevant. Plural is typically formed with the suffix *-s* (< Eng.), as in *kadʲo:g* 'stone' versus *kadʲo:g-s* 'stone-PLural' or, occasionally, *-i* (< Ir.), as in *nʲuk* 'head' versus *nʲuk-i* 'head-PLural' or *gloχ* 'man' versus *gloχ-i* 'men'. Nouns may also carry both markers (a double plural), as in *gloχ-i-s* 'men-PLural-PLural'.

There is an optional indefinite article *a* (< Eng.) and an optional definite article *the* (< Eng.), *a* or *in* (both < Ir. *an*), though most commonly articles are omitted:

(302) a. nʲurt ʎesk mwi:lʃa tul ta:ri-s bʲorʲ
now tell 1SG price speak-PRES.3SG woman
'Now tell me (the) price, says (the) woman.'

b. the ni:dʲa-s of the kʲena don't grani what we're a-ta:ri:-in
DEF person-PL of DEF house do.NEG know what we.COP at-speak-PROG
'The people of the house don't know what we're saying.'

c. su:ni in gloχ-swudal
look DEF man-above
'Look at the gentleman.' (Macalister 1937: 157f, 193)

There is considerable variation in pronominal forms. The forms are derived from English, except for the first and second singular, which are derived from Irish (*mo* and *do* respectively, though *I/me* and *you* are also used), with the form *dʲil* 'self' and the emphatic *-ʃa* appended:

	SINGULAR	PLURAL
1	*mwi:lʃa*	*our*
2	*tu:/hu:/di:lʃa*	*your*
3.M	*his dʲil*	*their dʲils*
3.F	*her dʲil*	

There are also examples of the neutral third person singular *it* (as in (303a)), though expletive ('dummy') *it* is generally not used (as in (303b)):

(303) a. goχʲ it to the Da:ʎon
leave it to DEF Lord
'Leave it to the Lord.'

b. gre:di-s ni:dʲa-s ri:lu:
make-3SG.PRES person-PL mad
'(It) makes people mad.' (Macalister 1937: 185, 188)

Possessive pronouns are formed with the possessive marker *-s* suffixed to the personal pronoun form.

Nominal possession is formed with the possessive suffix *-s* (< Eng.):

(304) a. nadʲramʲ-s mʲiskon
mother-POSS breast
'mother's breast'

b. gloχ-s nʲuk
man-POSS head
'(the) man's head' (Macalister 1937: 158, 163)

Adjectives may be used as verbs. Comparison is formed with the English suffixes *-er* (comparative) and *-(e)st* (superlative), as in *gʲami* 'bad' versus *gʲami-er* 'bad-COMPARative' versus *gʲami-est* 'bad-SUPERLative' (Macalister 1937: 159).

While most function words are derived from English, the numerals (which may also be used as ordinals) are not: *nʲuk*[186]*/wart/awárt/e:n/ein* 'one', *od/ad/dʲasag/do* 'two', *ʃi:ka/ʃi:kr* 'three', *ʃa:ka/ʃa:kr* 'four', *ʃu:ka/ʃu:kr* 'five', *ʃe:* 'six', *ʃeltu:* 'seven', *oχt* 'eight', *ni:* 'nine', *tʲal gʲetʲa* 'ten' (lit. 'half twenty), *gʲeta* 'twenty', *ad gʲeta* 'forty' (lit. 'two twenty'), *ʃu:ka gʲeta* 'one hundred' (lit. 'five twenty') (Macalister 1937: 159). Notice that the hybrid vigesimal system is similar (but not identical) to that in Irish (cf. e.g. Doyle 2001).

The verbal markers are mostly derived from English and are optional. There is a present tense marker *-s* (cf. Example (302a), (303b), (311), which is also used for other persons than the third singular, cf. the text below), a past tense marker *-d* (for all persons), a future tense marker *-a* (though the future tense is also commonly expressed with the English *will* VERB construction), a progressive aspect marker *-in(g)* (e.g. *to:r-in* 'come-PROGressive', *misli:-in* 'go.PROGressive', cf. also Example (317)).

(305) a. mwi:lʃa su:ni-d
1SG see-PST
'I saw.'

b. he gje:gj-d mwi:lʃa aχim
3SG.M ask-PST 1SG out
'He asked me out.'

c. lo:br-a me: dʲi:ʲl ar a pi:
hit-FUT 1SG self on DEF mouth
'(I'll) hit you on the mouth.'

d. ʎesk my dʲi:ʲl and my dʲi:ʲl will ʎesk your dʲi:ʲl ayi:rt
tell 1SG self and 1SG self FUT tell 2SG self again
'Tell me, and I will tell you in turn.'

e. I=ll ʃark your nʲuk when I misli aχim
1SG=FUT cut your head when 1SG go out
'I'll cut your head (off) when I go out.' (Macalister 1937: 160, 162, 176, 199, 218)

There is a *going-to* future construction, mirroring that in English:

(306) a. I=m mesli:-in to su:ni my ni:dʲa menthroh
1SG=be.1SG.PRES go-PROG to see 1SG person friend
'I am going to see my friend.'

b. misli-in to sahu his dʲi:l
go-PROG to drown 3SG self
'(He is) going to drown himself.' (Macalister 1937: 202f)

The verb may also remain unmarked.

(307) a. di:lʃa ta:ri gʲami laburt
2SG speak bad swear
'Did you say a bad curse?'

b. tom kamʲra ʃur-al gʲami gri:taθ
big dog run-NMLZ bad sickness
'The big racing dog has some bad sickness.' (Macalister 1937: 161f)

186. This actually means 'head' (Macalister 1937: 159).

The perfect is formed on the Hiberno-English model 'after VERB-PARTICIPLE' (as in *I am after going home* for 'I have gone home') (as in (308a)), although there are also examples of the English 'had VERB' construction (as in (308b)):

(308) a. ste:ʃ gloχ ar gwiʎ-o
AFF man after lie.down-PTCP
'The man has lain down.' (Macalister 1937: 162)
b. has that la:ki:n nop-ed her dʲi:l?
has DEM girl give-PST her self
'Has that girl wet herself?' (Cash 1977: 178)[187]

The pluperfect is formed with a *had VERB-PAST* construction:

(309) the swibli a kʲen-ga:ter had bog-d his gris ʎesk-d
DEF boy of house-drink had get-PST 3SG.POSS fortune tell-PST
'The boy of the public-house had got his fortune told.' (Macalister 1937: 189)

The modals derive from English:

(310) that the mi:dril may tarsp you, you glodaχ kriʃ bʲo:rʲ
that DEF devil may die 2SG 2SG dirty old woman
'That the devil may kill you, you dirty old woman.' (Macalister 1937: 184)

The word order is typically subject-verb-object:

(311) bʲorʲ a kʲena bwikad-s the ri:ʃpa
woman of house hold-3SG.PRES DEF pair
'The woman of the house wears the trousers.' (Macalister 1937: 178)

Subject pronouns are optional to the clause:

(312) a. nap-d a grifin
take.off-PST his coat
'(He) took off his coat.'
b. su:ni-d the gloχ spurku the bʲorʲ nup of the gre:d
see-PST DEF man flirt DEF woman back of DEF bridge
'(I) saw the man flirt (with) the woman behind the bridge.' (Macalister 1937: 206f)

Negation is expressed with the invariant *ni:dʲeʃ* (as in (313a, b)). There is no negative concord (as in (313c)).

(313) a. ni:dʲeʃ grani
NEG know
'(I) don't know.'
b. ni:dʲeʃ bug-a
NEG give-FUT
'(I) will not give.'
c. ni:dʲeʃ ni:dʲa
NEG person
'There is no one.' (Macalister 1937: 161, 186, 206)

187. Note that I have adjusted the orthography in this example to that suggested in (Macalister 1937).

Polar questions may be formed through intonation only (cf. Example (307a)) or with inverted word order. There is an optional question particle *a*.

(314) a. a tje:rp-a hu:
Q cook-FUT 2SG
'Will you cook?'
b. can I inoχ my stʲi:ma at the tʲera?
can 1SG thing 1SG.POSS pipe at DEF fire
'Can I light my pipe at the fire?'
c. do you grani gored?
do 2SG want money
'Do you want money?' (Macalister 1937: 174, 186, 193)

In content questions the interrogative phrase is fronted:

(315) a. What munika did you bog asturt
what name did 2SG get in
'What name did you assume?'
b. nulsk you su:ni mwi:lʃa?
when 2SG see 1SG
'When (will) you (come and) see me?' (Macalister 1937: 177, 207)

There is an obligatory copula derived from English *be*, which is always inflected for the third person:

(316) mwi:lʃa=s a munʲi mʲauso
1SG=COP INDEF good dance
'I'm a good dancer.' (Macalister 1937: 205)

There is no specific existential construction:

(317) od gloχ guʃ-in in the mamʲrum ga:ter
two man sit-PROG in DEF room drink
'There are two men sitting in the tap-room.' (Macalister 1937: 191)

The coordinating conjunctions derive from English. Complementation is not overtly indicated:

(318) a. ʎesk the bʲo:rʲ nʲok to su:ni her dʲi:l
tell DEF woman want to see her self
'Tell the woman (that I) want to see her.'
b. mwi:lʃa ʃang-s the gloχ ta:ri-in suba
1SG think-3SG.PRES DEF man speak-PROG nonsense
'I think (that) the man is speaking not much of account.' (Macalister 1937: 208, 218)

Relative clauses may be expressed through juxtaposition only:

(319) Da:ʎon awart ste:ʃ ʃi:kr ni:dʲa-s
God one AFF three person-PL
'One God who is three persons.' (Macalister 1937: 179)

11.4.3.3 *Short text*

(The Lord's Prayer, from Macalister 1937: 139f.)

Mwi:ʃa-s ga:ter swurt a munʲiaθ, // munʲi-gra a kradʲ-i di:lʃa-s munik. // Gra be
1SG-POSS father above in goodness good-luck at stand-PROG 2SG-POSS name love be

gre:di-d ʃedi ladu as aswurt in munʲiaθ. // Bug mwi:lʃs talosk-minʲurt goʃta dura. //
make-PST upon earth as above in goodness give 1SG day-now enough bread

Getʲal our ʃako are:k mwi:lʃa getʲa-s ni:dʲa-s gre:di gʲamiaθ mwi:lʃa. // ni:dʲeʃ
forgiveness our sin like 1SG forgive-PRES person-PL do badness 1SG NEG

salk mwi:l sturt gʲamiaθ but bog mwi:lʃa aχim gʲamiaθ. // Di:l the sri:dug ta:dʲiraθ
take 1SG into badness but take 1SG out.of badness 2SG DEF kingdom strength

and miúnʲiaθ gradum a gradum.
and goodness life and life

'Our Father in heaven // hallowed be your name // Your kingdom come // your will be done, on earth as it is in heaven // Give us today our daily bread // Forgive us our sins, as we forgive those who sin against us // Lead us not into temptation // but deliver us from evil // For the kingdom, the power, and the glory are yours now and forever. // (Amen.)'

11.4.3.4 *Some sources of data*

There is very little primary data available for Shelta. Macalister (1937) contains a large vocabulary, a number of example sentences and many translated (but not glossed) texts, as well as a grammatical description.

11.5 Summary

Pidgins seem less likely than non-pidgin languages to have nominal plural marking. If they have plural marking, it seems more often to be optional than obligatory. Pidgins also seem less likely than non-pidgins to have articles. With those pidgins that do have articles it is more common that the definite is identical with the demonstrative and that the indefinite is identical with the numeral 'one'.

Optional nominal plural marking seems very common for extended pidgins (pidgincreoles). It also seems common for these languages to have articles, both definite and indefinite.

Nominal plurality seems very common indeed for creole languages, the majority of which have optional plural marking. Creoles seem to differ from non-creoles in that plurality tends to be indicated analytically rather than synthetically. It seems more common for creoles to have articles than for non-creoles. The definite is typically distinct from the demonstrative, while the indefinite is typically identical with the numeral 'one'.

Mixed languages most commonly seem to adopt the system of one of the input languages, or to represent a blend of the two input languages, both with respect to nominal plurality as well as with respect to definite and indefinite articles.

11.6 Key points

- **The assumption that pidgins are less likely than non-pidgins to have plural marking, definite and indefinite articles is supported by the samples studied here.**
- **Extended pidgins (pidgincreoles) tend to have optional plural marking and both definite and indefinite articles.**
- **The assumption that creoles are more likely than non-creoles to have optional plurals marked analytically is supported by the samples studied here.**
- **Mixed languages tend to have plural marking if at least one of the input languages has it; the strategy may reflect a blend of the input languages.**
- **The samples studied here indicate that it is more common for creoles than non-creoles to have definite and indefinite articles.**
- **Creole definite articles tend to be distinct from the demonstrative, while indefinite articles tend to be identical with the numeral 'one'.**
- **Mixed languages tend to have definite and/or indefinite articles if at least one of the input languages has them.**

11.7 Exercises

1. What are the implications of the findings on plural marking and articles in pidgins and extended pidgins (pidgincreoles)?
2. What are the implications of the findings on plural marking in creoles?
3. In what way may plural marking in mixed languages reflect a blend of the input languages? Give examples.
4. How do the findings on creole definite and indefinite articles relate to the notion of creoles as simple languages?
5. Is the following statement true or false? Motivate your answer.
   Mixed languages are simplified versions of their input languages, which is reflected in the fact that they lack articles.

Languages cited in Chapter 12

1. Aleut; Mednyj Aleut
2. Arabic, Standard
3. Bislama
4. Broome Pearling Lugger Pidgin
5. Cameroon Pidgin English
6. Chinese Pidgin English
7. Chinese Pidgin Russian
8. Chinook
9. Chinuk Wawa
10. Cree, Plains
11. Creolese
12. Dongxiang
13. Dutch
14. Ejnu
15. Angloromani; English
16. French
17. Ghanaian Pidgin English
18. Guadeloupean Creole; Martinican Creole
19. Gullah
20. Gurindji; Gurindji Kriol
21. Guyanais
22. Haitian Creole
23. Hiri Motu; Tok Pisin
24. Jamaican
25. Javanese
26. Javindo; Petjo
27. Juba Arabic
28. Kikongo-Kimanyanga
29. Kikongo-Kituba
30. Krio
31. Kriol
32. Kvensk
33. Ma'a/Mbugu
34. Malay; Papiá Kristang; Singapore Bazaar Malay
35. Mandarin Chinese
36. Maridi Pidgin Arabic
37. Media Lengua; Quechua, Ecuadorian
38. Michif
39. Nagamese
40. Ngbandi
41. Nigerian Pidgin
42. Norwegian, Bokmål
43. Ojibwe
44. Palenquero
45. Persian
46. Pidgin Delaware
47. Pidgin Dutch
48. Pidgin Ojibwe
49. Romani, Vlax
50. Russenorsk
51. Russian
52. Saami, South
53. Sango
54. Berbice Dutch; Saramaccan; Sranan; Trio-Ndyuka
55. Seychelles Creole
56. Sinhala; Sri Lankan Malay; Tamil
57. Solomon Islands Pijin
58. Spanish
59. Tangwang
60. Taymir Pidgin Russian
61. Ternate Chabacano
62. Uighur
63. Hezhou; Tibetan, Amdo; Wutun
64. Yimas; Yimas-Alamblak Pidgin; Yimas-Arafundi Pidgin

Chapter 12

The verb phrase and predication

Pidgins are described as lacking tense, aspect and mood marking, as well as any overt copula with nominal and adjectival predication. Creoles are assumed to have one tense marker, one mood marker and one aspect marker which combine in that order. Furthermore, in creole languages the temporal reading of a clause is expected to be affected by the lexical aspect of the verb. Creoles are also assumed to lack the copula in nominal and adjectival predication, as well as to allow verbal encoding on adjectives. Mixed languages are assumed to either have adopted the systems of one of the input languages, or to represent a blend of the two input languages. This chapter will empirically test whether pidgins differ from non-pidgins with respect to tense, aspect and mood marking, whether creoles conform to the assumed prototypical creole tense/mood/aspect system, as well as briefly discuss tense, aspect and mood in extended pidgins and mixed languages (Section 12.2). Section 12.3 will empirically test whether pidgins and creoles differ from non-pidgins and non-creoles with respect to the presence or absence or the copula in nominal and adjectival predication, and whether adjectives are more likely to be encoded as verbs, as well as bring up nominal and adjectival predication in extended pidgins and mixed languages. Section 12.4 gives short sketches of three languages mentioned in the chapter: Russenorsk (an extinct Russian/Norwegian pidgin in the Barents Sea), Solomon Islands Pijin (an English-lexified extended pidgin in the Pacific) and Palenquero (a Spanish-lexified creole in South America).

12.1 Introduction

Verbs refer to actions (*run*, *bake*, etc.), processes (*grow*, *burn*, etc.) and states (*know*, *exist*, etc.). The **verb phrase** (**VP**) of the clause is minimally made up of only one verb, but may also consist of several elements that together form a unit. For example, in the sentence *Puppies play* we have one noun phrase (*Puppies*) and one verb phrase (*play*). However, the sentence *The puppies should have been playing* also consists of only one noun phrase (*The puppies*) and one verb phrase (*should have been playing*). Furthermore, in both sentences the verb phrases contain the same basic semantic content, that of the action PLAY, because both verb phrases contain the same **lexical verb**, or 'main' verb. It is the lexical verb that carries the semantic content of the verb phrase, the basic meaning of the event or action. The remaining elements in the verb phrase of the second sentence (*should have been*) are **auxiliary verbs**. These tend to be semantically empty and mainly convey grammatical or functional information, such as tense, aspect and mood.

Verbs may be marked for **tense**, which essentially places the event on a time line. Most commonly, though by no means always, events can be placed in the past (it happened before now), the present (it is happening at the same time as now) or in the future (it will happen after now). If the event is placed on a timeline in relation to the moment of speech (something happens before, at the same time as or after the moment of speech), then the tenses are **absolute**. If the event is placed on a timeline in relation to some given reference point – not necessarily the moment of speech – then the tenses are **relative**.

Verbs may also be marked for **aspect**, in which case it is the perspective taken on the event that is coded. A major aspectual divide is between **perfective** and **imperfective** events. Very simplified, perfective events are typically viewed from the outside as bounded wholes, while imperfective events are viewed from the inside, as ongoing. The English progressive could be argued to be a subtype of the imperfective, where an event like *The puppies are playing* is viewed from within, as ongoing.

Another common verbal category is **mood**, which, very simplified, essentially codes the attitude taken towards an event, such as the speaker's belief in the reality of the event, the likelihood that the event will occur, or the quality of information that the speaker has about the event. A major modal divide is between **realis** and **irrealis**, where realis events are those where the speaker is very sure that the event has happened or that the state of affairs holds true, and irrealis lacks that assertion. In other words, irrealis events are simply not (yet) real world facts. When the term 'mood' is distinguished from **modality**, mood tends to denote a higher level distinction for the whole clause of realis versus irrealis while modality denotes semantic labels of attitudes towards events.

Verbs may have different **lexical aspects** (also called ***Aktionsart***, **actionality** or **derivational aspect**), where the inherent semantics specify the inner structure of an event. It is important to notice that while aspect is a grammatical category, lexical aspect is a semantic specification. **Dynamic** verbs, for example, involve some kind of change (e.g. *boil, run, fall, sneeze*), while **stative** verbs do not (e.g. *know, dwell, contain*).

Assertions, or **predications**, made about the subject of the clause may be non-verbal, for instance if the subject is described in some way. In **equative clauses** the assertion is made that the subject is the same as the entity of the predication, as in *Mark is a teacher*. Here the noun phrase *a teacher* is the predication to *Mark* (i.e. asserts something about Mark) and as such functions as a **predicative noun phrase** (also called **nominal predication** or **predicate nominal**). In attributive clauses some attribute or quality about the subject is stated, as in *Mark is tall.* Here the adjective *tall* is the predication to *Mark* and as such functions as a **predicative adjective** (also called **adjectival predication** or **predicate adjective**). In some languages a connector, a **copula**, is used between the subject and the predication. Standard English, for example, demands a copula, namely some form of the verb *be*: something like **Mark a teacher* or **Mark tall* is not acceptable.

12.2 Tense, aspect and mood

It is not uncommon for languages to lack tense, aspect or modality distinctions. This section will discuss the occurrence of tense, aspect and modality in a selection of pidgins, extended pidgins and mixed languages. With respect to creoles, proposals have been made that the prototypical creole system would consist of only one tense, one mood and one aspect marker, that these would be invariant preverbal forms which would combine in a given order (tense-mood-aspect) and that the lexical aspect of the verb would affect the temporal reading of the clause. This section will check this proposed prototypical system against a sample of creole languages. It is beyond the scope of this section to properly discuss the kinds of tense, aspect and mood systems that can be found in the languages of the world. For a general overview, see Velupillai (2012: 193ff) with further references; for detailed discussions on tense and aspect, see the classics Comrie (1976 and 1985) and Dahl (1985); for a detailed discussion on mood, see Palmer (2001). Singler (1990b) is a volume dedicated to the tense, mood and aspect systems of pidgins and creoles.

12.2.1 Tense, aspect and mood in pidgin languages

Pidgins are typically described as lacking tense, aspect and mood, and are generally expected to rely on context or adverbials to convey such distinctions (cf. Parkvall & Bakker 2013: 41). In Pidgin Delaware, for example, the verb was invariant and not marked for tense, aspect or mood, though adverbials could optionally be used to indicate time (Goddard 1997; for more on Pidgin Delaware, see 5.3.3).

12.2.1.1 *Tense in pidgin languages*

Pidgin languages are usually described as lacking the grammatical category tense, and instead optionally indicating when an event occurred either through context or through adverbials (cf., for example, Parkvall & Bakker 2013: 41). Chinuk Wawa is an example of a pidgin that lacks tense altogether and only context or adverbials can determine the temporal reading of the verb:

Chinuk Wawa (Pidgin (Chinook-lexified): Canada, USA)

(320) náyka ískam kənim
1SG take canoe
'I took/am taking/will take the canoe.' (Grant 2013a: 153)

In Example (320) there is no way of knowing the temporal reading of the verb without access to the context of the utterance.

There are, however, a number of pidgin languages that do have tense. In Yimas-Arafundi Pidgin, for example, tense is obligatorily marked on the verb:

Yimas-Arafundi Pidgin (Pidgin (Yimas-lexified): Papua New Guinea)

(321) a. aykum mariak-nan
woman talk-NFUT
'The woman spoke/is speaking.'
b. mən naŋga kandək skul kandək taka-t anak?
3SG where OBL school OBL make-FUT FUT
'Where will he teach?' (Foley 2013a: 108f)

Example (321) shows that Yimas-Arafundi has the nonfuture marker *-nan* and the future marker *-t anak*. The verb must obligatorily carry one of these markers.

In order to test whether pidgin languages tend to be less likely to have tense than non-pidgin languages, I compared the current pidgin sample with the sample in Velupillai (2014). The figures are summarized in Table 12.1:

Table 12.1 Tense in the current pidgin sample and in Velupillai (2014). For a full legend of the languages in the pidgin sample, see http://dx.doi.org/10.1075/cll.48.additional.

	Pidgin sample		**Velupillai sample**	
	N	%	N	%
Tense exists	12	32.4	241	75.8
Tense does not exist	25	67.6	77	24.2
Total	37		318	

($\chi^2 = 28.34$; $df = 1$; $p_{two\text{-}tailed} < 0.001$***, Yates' Correction), $p_{sim} < 0.001$*** (B = 10,000))
($G = 26.67$; $df = 1$; $p_{two\text{-}tailed} = 2.42e\text{-}07$***)

Table 12.1 shows that the group of pidgin languages that have tense is underrepresented while the group of pidgin languages that lack tense is overrepresented, which might indicate that it is indeed more common for the languages in the pidgin sample to lack tense than for non-pidgin languages.

12.2.1.2 *Aspect in pidgin languages*

Pidgin languages are generally described as lacking aspect altogether (Parkvall & Bakker 2013: 41). There are, however, examples of pidgins with aspect markers. Chinese Pidgin Russian, for example, had a perfective marker *-la* and it seems as if Maridi Pidgin Arabic had an imperfective or continuous marker *dy*.

Chinese Pidgin Russian (Pidgin (Russian-lexified): Russia)

(322) Hedzu liba kupi-la
PN fish buy-PFV
'Hedzou bought fish.' (Perekhvalskaya 2013a: 74)

Maridi Pidgin Arabic (Pidgin (Arabic-lexified): Mauretania)

(323) ʔm-ny dy rwħ ʔʕd-ny by mħl
2-DU IPFV/CONT go sit/stay-DU LOC place
'They (two) were going to stay in a place.' (Thomason & Elgibali 1986: 324)

The Chinese Pidgin Russian perfective marker *-la* in Example (322) indicates that an action is viewed as a bounded whole. The Maridi Pidgin Arabic imperfective/continuous marker in Example (323) indicates that the event was ongoing.

In the current pidgin sample only 7 of 30 languages (23.3%) have some kind of aspect marking, which may indicate that it is indeed rather unlikely for pidgin languages to have aspect.[188]

12.2.1.3 *Mood in pidgin languages*

Modal distinctions are also expected to be rare or lacking for pidgin languages (Parkvall & Bakker 2013: 41). Pidgin Ojibwe is an example of a pidgin with modal markers:

Pidgin Ojibwe (Pidgin (Ojibwe-lexified): Canada, USA)

(324) ni-daa-nitoon giin
1SG-MOD-kill 2SG
'I should kill you.' (Nichols 1995: 12)

Example (324) shows the modal marker *daa* in Pidgin Ojibwe. In the current pidgin sample it is indeed very rare with modal markers, the only other language being Taymir Pidgin Russian. The remaining 24 languages (92.3%) lack modal marking altogether, which may indicate that pidgin languages are unlikely to have modal marking.[189]

---

188. This distribution is statistically very significant according to goodness-of-fit tests: $\chi^2 = 8.53$; $df = 1$; $p_{\text{two-tailed}} = 0.0035^{**}$; $p_{\text{sim}} = 0.0068^{**}$ and $G = 8.85$; $df = 1$; $p_{\text{two-tailed}} = 0.0029^{**}$.

189. This distribution is statistically highly significant according to goodness-of-fit tests: $\chi^2 = 18.62$; $df = 1$; $p_{\text{two-tailed}} < 0.001^{***}$; $p_{\text{sim}} < 0.001^{***}$ and $G = 21.53$; $df = 1$; $p_{\text{two-tailed}} < 0.001^{***}$.

12.2.2 Tense, aspect and mood in extended pidgins (pidgincreoles)

While the sample of extended pidgins is too small for any statistical analyses, it is worth noting that almost all of them have some kind of tense, aspect and mood marking. Tok Pisin, for example, has future and past tense markers (*bai* and *bin*), completive, habitual and progressive aspect markers (*pinis, save* and *wok lo(ng)/i stap*), and obligative, permissive and abilitive markers (*mas, ken* and *(i)nap*) (Smith & Siegel 2013a; for more on Tok Pisin, see 1.4.3).

12.2.2.1 *Tense in extended pidgins (pidgincreoles)*

Eight of the ten extended pidgins have tense marking. Nagamese, for example, has the present and past tense markers *-y* and *-(i/y)se* (for more on Nagamese, see 8.3.1), while Bislama has the anterior marker *bin*:

Bislama (Extended pidgin (English-lexified): Vanuatu)

(325) brata blong hem i bin wok long ples ia long Santo
brother of 3SG AGR ANT work at place DEF in S
'His brother had worked in the (same) place in Santo.' (Meyerhoff 2013a: 126)

The anterior marker *bin* in Example (325) places the event before some other given reference point. The only two languages that lack tense in the small sample are Sango (Samarin 2013a) and Solomon Islands Pidgin (Jourdan 2004). Instead temporal adverbs, or, in the case of Solomon Islands Pidgin, aspect, is used to place an event in time (see further 12.4.2).

12.2.2.2 *Aspect in extended pidgins (pidgincreoles)*

Sango is the only language in the extended pidgin sample that does not have aspect marking, although the copula when used with a verb in the bare form may function as a general auxiliary marking the event as continuative, habitual, imperfective, repetitive, unrealized, and so on:

Sango (Extended pidgin (Ngbandi-lexified): Central African Republic)

(326) a. nyen' a-ke so mo?
what PM-COP hurt 2SG
'What's hurting you?'

b. ala ma wango so a-médecin a-ke mu na ala so
2PL hear warning REL PL-doctor PM-COP give OBL 2PL REL
'Listen to the advice that the doctors will give you.' (Samarin 2013a: 18, 20)

Example (326) shows how in Sango the copula with a verb in the base form may function as a general auxiliary; in (326a) the construction *ake so* 'is hurting' indicates continuity, whereas in (326b) the construction *ake mu* 'will give' indicates futurity (an unrealized event).

All the other nine languages, however, have specific aspect markers. Ghanaian Pidgin English, for example, has the progressive/habitual *dè*, ingressive *bigin (dè)* and completive *finif*:

Ghanaian Pidgin English (Extended pidgin (English-lexified): Ghana)

(327) a. wan gò giv sain se sɔmbɔdi dè kam
one IRR give sign COMP somebody PROG come
'One will give a sign that somebody is coming.' (Huber 1999b: 225)

b. dè bigin dè fait~fait dɛ̀m
3PL INGR PROG fight~RED 3PL.O
'They started/are starting to fight them.' (Huber 2013a: 171)

c. laik ì ren finif bifɔ jù kam, jù no gò fit kam
like 3SG rain COMPL before 2SG come 2SG NEG IRR ABIL come
hiɛ sɛf
here FOC
'If it had rained before you came, you would not have been able to come here.' (Huber 1999b: 226)

12.2.2.3 *Mood in extended pidgins (pidgincreoles)*

Mood is also common in the small sample of extended pidgin languages, found in eight of nine languages (data is missing for Hiri Motu). Again, Sango is the only language that deviates, in that it lacks mood marking, although, as shown in Example (326b) above, the copula with a bare verb may indicate an unrealized event, effectively a future or irrealis (Samarin 2013a). The irrealis occurs in five of the languages in the sample. Juba Arabic, for example, has an irrealis marker *bi=* as well as a number of modal auxiliaries:

Juba Arabic (Extended pidgin (Arabic-lexified): Sudan)

(328) a. úmon bi=raja búkra
3PL IRR=come.back door
'They will come back tomorrow.'

b. múmkin ita bi=rákabu ákil íta bi=kútu fi=talája
MOD.AUX 2SG IRR=cook food 2SG IRR=put in=fridge
'You can cook the food and then put it in the fridge.'

c. Margaret bukún ja mbári de
PN MOD.AUX come yesterday DEM.PROX.SG
'Margaret might have come yesterday.'

d. ána bágder sádu ita
1SG MOD.AUX help 2SG
'I can help you.'

e. lázim úo bi=kun éndu íštira
MOD.AUX 3SG IRR=be have permission
'He must have a permission.' (Manfredi & Petrollino 2013a: 59f)

For more on Juba Arabic, see 15.4.1.

12.2.3 Tense, aspect and mood in creole languages

A controversial and widely discussed proposal made by Bickerton (e.g. 1981) suggested that prototypical creole languages would have only one tense marker (expressing the anterior), one mood marker (expressing the irrealis) and one aspect marker (expressing the progressive). These would be preverbal markers, which would combine in a fixed order (tense-mood-aspect). The reading of the base form of the verb would be affected by its lexical aspect: unmarked stative verbs would have a present tense reading, while unmarked dynamic verbs would have a past tense reading.

12.2.3.1 *Tense in creole languages*

Bickerton (1981 and subsequent) proposed that prototypical creole languages have only one tense marker, denoting the anterior. In Kikongo-Kituba, for example, there is only one overt tense marker, indicating the relative past (i.e. anterior):

Kikongo-Kituba (Creole (Kikongo-Kimanyanga-lexified): Congo, DR Congo, Angola)

(329) ngá mon-áka náni?
2SG see-ANT who
'Whom did you see?' (Mufwene 2013: 6)

Notice that the anterior marker in Example (329) is a suffix and not a preverbal invariant form.

There are, however, a number of creole languages that have more than one tense. Jamaican, for example, not only has an anterior, but also a future tense:

Jamaican (Creole (English-lexified): Jamaica)

(330) mi wi go de sonde
1SG FUT go there Sunday
'I will go there on Sunday.' (Patrick 2007: 133)

Example (330) shows the future marker *wi* in Jamaican; given that the anterior is not the only overt tense marker, Jamaican would thus not conform to the prototypical creole in its tense system (for more on Jamaican, see 14.4.2). A few languages lack tense markers altogether, such as, for example, Ambon Malay (Paauw 2008), meaning that these languages would also not conform to the proposed prototype (for more on Ambon Malay, see 7.3.2). In fact, most of the languages in the current creole database deviate from the assumed prototype with respect to their tense systems, as shown in Table 12.2:

Table 12.2 Number of languages in the creole sample with only one overt tense marker, specifically indicating the anterior or past tense. For a full legend of the languages in the creole sample, see http://dx.doi.org/10.1075/cll.48.additional.

	N	%
only one overt tense marker exists (denoting anterior or past)	11	21.2
other overt tense markers exist	37	71.2
tense markers do not exist	4	7.7
Total	52	

($\chi^2 = 34.88$; $df = 2$; $p_{two\text{-}tailed} < 0.001$***), $p_{sim} < 0.001$*** (B = 10,000))
($G = 33.94$; $df = 2$; $p_{two\text{-}tailed} < 0.001$***)

The figures in Table 12.2 show that only about one fifth of the languages in the sample conform to the assumed prototypical creole tense system.[190]

12.2.3.2 *Aspect in creole languages*

Bickerton's (1981 and subsequent) proposed prototypical creole languages also only have one aspect marker, denoting the progressive or similar (e.g. the continuous). Guyanais, for example, only has the progressive marker *ka*, which, if combined with a stative verb, denotes currently relevant situations:

Guyanais (Creole (French-lexified): French Guiana)

(331) a. i ka brè
3SG PROG drink
'He is drinking.' (Pfänder 2013b: feature 49)

b. mo ka krè an Bondyé
1SG PROG believe in God
'(These days) I am believing in God.' (Pfänder 2013a: 223)

It should be noted that there are regional variations for the use of *ka* in Guyanais: in coastal regions it is more often used to mark the habitual.

Most of the languages in the database, however, have other aspect markers. Creolese, for example, has a progressive marker *a* (which may also be used as a habitual marker) as well as the general habitual marker *doz/das*, the past habitual *yuustu* and the completive *don*:

---

190. According to both a chi-square and a log likelihood ratio goodness of fit test this distribution is highly significant, even when the figures have been collapsed into only two categories "conforms to the prototype" (11 languages) versus "does not conform to the prototype" (41 languages): $\chi^2 = 17.31$; $df = 1$; $p_{two\text{-}tailed} < 0.001$***; $p_{sim} < 0.001$*** / $G = 18.25$; $df = 1$; $p_{two\text{-}tailed} < 0.001$***. The former category is highly underrepresented while the latter is highly overrepresented, which may indicate that creole languages might not be likely to conform to the proposed prototype with respect to tense.

Creolese (Creole (English-lexified): Guyana)

(332) a. all o dem a jomp forom
all of 3PL PROG jump for.it
'All of them were jumping in to get it.'
(Devonish & Thompson 2013b: feature 47 citing Rickford 1987: 131, line 253f)

b. dem das plaent dem faam an ting an dem das yuustu
3PL HAB plant 3PL.POSS farm and thing and 3PL HAB PST.HAB
stan de
remain there
'They used to cultivate their farm and so on, and they used to stay there.'
(Devonish & Thompson 2013a: 55)

c. awii manggo don raip laang taim
1PL.POSS mango COMPL ripe long time
'Our mangoes have ripened some time ago.' (Devonish & Thompson 2013a: 55)

Example (332) shows that Guyanais has other aspectual markers apart from the progressive marker (which may also be used for the habitual). In other words, Guyanais would therefore not conform to the prototypical creole with respect to its aspect system.

Again, most of the languages in the current creole database deviate from the assumed prototype, as shown in Table 12.3:

Table 12.3 Number of languages in the creole sample with only one overt aspect marker, specifically indicating the progressive or imperfective aspect. For a full legend of the languages in the creole sample, see http://dx.doi.org/10.1075/cll.48.additional.

	N	%
only one overt aspect marker exists (denoting progressive or imperfective)	5	9.6
other overt aspect markers exist	47	90.4
Total	52	

($\chi^2 = 33.92$; $df = 1$; $p_{\text{two-tailed}} < 0.001$***, $p_{\text{sim}} < 0.001$*** (B = 10,000))
($G = 38.79$; $df = 1$; $p_{\text{two-tailed}} < 0.001$***)

The figures in Table 12.3 show that less than one tenth of the languages in the sample conform to the assumed prototypical creole aspect system.

12.2.3.3 *Mood in creole languages*

Bickerton (1981 and subsequent) further proposed that prototypical creole languages have only one mood marker, denoting the irrealis. Ternate Chabacano, for example, has only one modal marker *di*, which denotes irrealis and contemplated events (here glossed as 'conTempLative'):

Ternate Chabacano (Creole (Spanish-lexified): Philippines)

(333) si di yubá raw manyána na munisípyu, bo di indá húntu
if CTPL take ENCL tomorrow LOC town.hall 2SG CTPL go together
'If I am taken to the town hall tomorrow, you will come with me.'
(Sippola 2013b: 146)

The general contemplative marker *di* in (333) denotes unrealized and future events. For more on Ternate Chabacano, see 7.3.3.

Most of the languages in the database, however, have other kinds of modal markers than just a single irrealis marker. Berbice Dutch, for example had the irrealis *ma*, the improbable *sa*, and the two counterfactuals *wa ma* and *wa sa* (see further 6.4.3), and would thus not conform to the proposed creole prototype with respect to its modal system.

Here too, most of the languages in the current creole database deviate from the assumed prototype, as shown in Table 12.4:

Table 12.4 Number of languages in the creole sample with only one overt mood marker, specifically indicating the irrealis. For a full legend of the languages in the creole sample, see http://dx.doi.org/10.1075/cll.48.additional.

	N	%
only one overt mood marker exists (denoting irrealis)	3	5.8
other overt mood markers exist	47	90.4
mood markers do not exist[191]	2	3.8
Total	52	

The figures in Table 12.4 show that only three languages (5.8%) in the sample conform to the assumed prototypical creole tense system.[192] It should be noted that these three languages are the Chabacano creoles.

191. Guadeloupean Creole and Martinican Creole are here listed as lacking mood markers because while the marker *ké* is treated as a modal in Colot & Ludwig (2013b and 2013c), it is described and glossed as a future tense in Colot & Ludwig (2013a).

192. According to both a chi-square and a log likelihood ratio goodness of fit test this distribution is highly significant, even when the figures have been collapsed into only two categories "conforms to the prototype" (3 languages) versus "does not conform to the prototype" (49 languages): $\chi^2 = 40.69$; $df = 1$; $p_{\text{two-tailed}} < 0.001$***; $p_{\text{sim}} < 0.001$*** / $G = 48.68$; $df = 1$; $p_{\text{two-tailed}}0.001$***. The former category is highly underrepresented while the latter is highly overrepresented, which might indicate that creole languages are not likely to conform to the proposed prototype with respect to mood and modality.

12.2.3.4 *The internal order of tense, mood and aspect markers in creole languages*

The hypothesis of a creole prototype in Bickerton (1981 and subsequent) also proposed that the expected tense, mood and aspect markers would appear in that order if they co-occurred with a verb. In Saramaccan, for example, the tense, mood and aspect markers may combine in the order tense-mood-aspect:

Saramaccan (Creole (English-lexified): Suriname)

(334) a ɓi o sa ta wooko
3SG PST IRR POT ASP work
'He could have worked' (lit. 'He could have been able to work.')
(Aboh et al. 2013a: 32 citing Veenstra 1996: 20)

In Example (334) the tense, mood and aspect markers appear in a certain order, with the aspect marker closest to the verb, the tense marker furthest away from it and the mood marker in-between.

Theoretically there could be six different combinations for tense mood and aspect markers: T-M-A (as is the case in Saramaccan), T-A-M, A-T-M, A-M-T, M-T-A and M-A-T. Interestingly, the combinations which place the tense marker furthest away from the verb do not occur in the current database. Neither does the combination M-A-T. In other words, only the combinations T-M-A, T-A-M and M-T-A are attested in the database. However, even more interesting is that for the majority of languages the feature does not apply for various reasons. In Gullah, for example, three tense, mood and aspect markers rarely, if ever co-occur (cf. Klein 2013b; for more on Gullah, see 4.3.1). In the Cape Verdean Creoles the tense marker is a suffix while the mood and aspect markers are preverbal particles (cf. Lang 2013b; for more on the Cape Verdean Creoles, see 11.4.2). And Papiá Kristang, for example, lacks a tense marker altogether (cf. Baxter 2013b; for more on Papiá Kristang, see 15.4.2). These languages therefore all deviate from the prototypical creole with respect to their internal ordering of tense, mood and aspect markers. The figures are summarized in Table 12.5:

Table 12.5 The internal ordering of tense (T), mood (M) and aspect (A) markers in the current creole sample. For a full legend of the languages in the creole sample, see http://dx.doi.org/10.1075/cll.48.additional.

	N	%
T-M-A	12	24
T-A-M	2	4
M-T-A	3	6
the feature does not apply	33	66
Total	50	

($\chi^2 = 49.68$; $df = 3$; $p_{\text{two-tailed}} < 0.001$***, $p_{\text{sim}} < 0.001$*** (B = 10,000))
($G = 46.42$; $df = 3$; $p_{\text{two-tailed}} < 0.001$***)

As the figures in Table 12.5 indicate, for the absolute majority of the languages, the internal ordering of tense, mood and aspect marker is a feature that does not apply. In fact, that latter value is highly overrepresented, which might indicate that creole languages are not likely to conform to the proposed prototype with respect to the internal ordering of tense, mood and aspect markers.

12.2.3.5 *The reading of the base form of verbs in creole languages*

The hypothesis of a creole prototype in Bickerton (1981 and subsequent) further proposed that the reading of the base form of the verb would be affected by its lexical aspect in that unmarked stative verbs would have a present tense reading, while unmarked dynamic verbs would have a past tense reading. In Krio, for example, the lexical aspect of the verb affects the tense reading:

Krio (Creole (English-lexified): Sierra Leone)

(335) a. wi gɛt fo pikin
1PL have four child
'We have four children.'

b. wi win di gem
1PL win ART game
'We won the game.' (Finney 2013b: feature 51)

In (335a) the base form of the stative verb *gɛt* 'have' gets a present tense reading, while in (335b) the base form of the dynamic verb *win* 'win' gets a past tense reading. The lexical aspect of the verb thus affects the temporal reading of the clause (for more on Krio, see 8.3.3). This is true for two thirds of the languages in the current creole sample, as shown in Table 12.6:

Table 12.6 The reading of stative and dynamic verbs in the current creole sample. For a full legend of the languages in the creole sample, see http://dx.doi.org/10.1075/cll.48.additional.

	N	%
the lexical aspect affects the tense reading of the verb	33	67.3
the lexical aspect does not affect the tense reading of the verb	16	32.7
Total	49	

($\chi^2 = 5.898$; $df = 1$; $p_{\text{two-tailed}} = 0.015^*$, $p_{\text{sim}} = 0.021^*$ (B = 10,000))
($G = 5.96$; $df = 1$; $p_{\text{two-tailed}} = 0.015^*$)

The figures in Table 12.6 show that there is a significant preference for the languages in the database to have different readings of the same form (usually the base) of the verb depending on its lexical aspect. This may indicate that creole languages do conform to the proposed prototype with respect to whether the lexical aspect affects the reading of the clause. Whether this sets creoles apart from non-creoles can only be answered by comparing this distribution with one in a database consisting of non-creoles – a matter for future research.

12.2.4 Tense, aspect and mood in mixed languages

Mixed languages are typically described as reflecting the grammatical system of one of the input languages, or a blend of the two input systems. With G-L mixed languages the tense, mood and aspect system is likely to follow that of the input language which provides the bulk of the structure, while for N-V mixed languages the tense, mood and aspect system is likely to follow that input language which provides the bulk of the structure for the verb phrase. F-S languages are likely to represent a blend of both input languages, in that the tense, mood and aspect forms are likely to derive from one of the input languages, while the way they are employed is likely to mirror the system of the other input language(s).

Examples of G-L mixed languages are Angloromani (Romani/English), Media Lengua (Spanish/Quechua) and Ma'á/Mbugu (Cushitic/Bantu), where the tense, mood and aspect systems reflect those of the languages that provided the bulk of the grammatical structure, i.e. the English system for Angloromani, the Quechua system for Media Lengua and the Bantu system for Ma'á Mbugu (Matras 2010, Muysken 2013a and Mous 2003b respectively. For more on Angloromani, see 15.4.3; for more on Media Lengua, see 10.4.3). Ejnu, for example, reflects the Uighur system of tense marking:

Ejnu (Mixed language (Persian/Uighur): China)

(336)

PAST		NONPAST	
niga(r)li-dim	'I saw (it)'	*niga(r)jtmɛn*	'I see/will see (it)'
niga(r)li-duq	'we saw (it)'	*niga(r)jtmiz*	'we see/will see (it)'
niga(r)li-diŋ	'you saw (it)'	*niga(r)jsɛn*	'you see/will see (it)'
niga(r)li-di	'he/they saw (it)'	*niga(r)jdu*	'he/they see/will see (it)'

(Lee-Smith 1996a)

The stem of the verb in (336) reflects the Persian *nigah* 'to look' (Uighur *kør*), while the tense marking reflects the Uighur suffixes. Similar to the Uighur system, verbs may function as so-called converbs, where they appear in a fixed form and conveys the semantic content of the verb phrase, while an inflected auxiliary verb conveys the various aspectual and modal connotations. For instance, the converb form of *niga(r)* 'to look, see' together with *qal* 'to remain', which as an auxiliary denotes that an action has resulted in a new state, gives *nigalap qal* 'to meet' (Lee-Smith 1996a: 859). It should be noted that the absence of features may also carry over from the input language which provides the bulk of the grammar. Javindo, for example, reflects the absence of tense marking also found in Javanese:

Javindo (Mixed language (Dutch/Javanese): Indonesia)

(337) sing kom soëfen papa
DEM come just papa
'The one who just came is daddy.' (de Gruiter 1990: 65)

The verb *kom* 'come' remains in the base form, reflecting the Javanese system where temporal connotations are indicated through adverbials, as opposed to the Dutch system where tense is obligatorily indicated. The Dutch equivalent would here thus be *is gekomen* 'has come'. Similarly, Petjo (Dutch/Malay) lacks tense marking and instead relies on temporal adverbs, reflecting the system of Malay (van Rheeden 1995).

Examples of N-V mixed languages are Michif (French/Cree), Gurindji Kriol (Gurindji/Kriol) and Mednyj Aleut (Aleut/Russian). In these languages the tense, mood and aspect systems reflect the systems of the language from which the bulk of the verb phrase structure derives, namely Cree, Kriol and Russian respectively. For more on Michif, see 3.3.2; for more on Gurindji Kriol, see 9.5.3; for more on Mednyj Aleut, see 13.4.3.

Examples of F-S mixed languages are Sri Lankan Malay (Malay/Sinhala/Tamil), Wutun (Mandarin/Amdo Tibetan) and Hezhou (Mandarin/Uighur). In these languages the forms derive from one input language (Malay, Mandarin and Mandarin respectively) while the structure derives from the other(s). In Tangwang, for example, the forms derive from Mandarin, while the structure reflects that of Dongxian:

Tangwang (Mixed language (Mandarin/Dongxiang): China)

(338) a. uə^{224} k^{h}ɛ̃^{31}-liɔ
1SG look-PST.COMPL
'I have looked.'

b. uə^{224} k^{h}ɛ̃^{31}-tʂɛ
1SG look-CONT
'I am looking.' (Lee-Smith 1996c: 878f)

The structure of the sentences in (327) reflects that of Dongxiang, while the forms derive from Mandarin. For example, the Tangwang marker *-liɔ* in (338a) derives from the Mandarin perfective *le*, which may be used for present, past and future events, and may also be used for non-completed events (Li & Thompson 1981: 213ff), but which in Tangwang has been reanalyzed to reflect the past completive function of Dongxiang *-wo*. The Tangwang marker *-tʂɛ* in (338b) derives from the Mandarin durative marker *zhe* but reflects the continuous of Dongxiang.

12.3 Predication

Languages vary with respect to whether they demand a copula or not in clauses with non-verbal predication. Languages also vary with respect to adjectives: in some languages adjectives form a separate word class, while in others they are essentially stative verbs and behave like verbs. In the latter case an overt copula would be superfluous. Pidgin and creole languages are typically described as lacking overt copulas with both predicative noun phrases and predicative adjectives. Furthermore, creole languages are often described as having verb-like adjectives, i.e. that adjectives do not form a separate word class but are essentially stative verbs. This section will check whether pidgin and creole languages differ from non-pidgins and non-creoles with respect to so-called zero copulas in nominal predication,[193] as well as discuss nominal predication in extended pidgins (pidgincreoles) and mixed languages. The section will also check how pidgins and creoles pattern with respect to the copula in adjectival predication as well as compare the pattern of verbal/nonverbal encoding of adjectives with non-pidgins and non-creoles. Adjectival predication in extended pidgins (pidgincreoles) and mixed languages are also briefly discussed. It is beyond the scope of this section to adequately discuss predication in the languages of the world. For an accessible overview of non-verbal predication, see, for example Payne (1997: 111ff). For a very thorough discussion on adjectival predication, see Wetzer (1996). For a thorough discussion on predication in English-lexified Caribbean creole languages, see Winford (1993).

12.3.1 Predication in pidgin languages

Pidgins are usually described as lacking the copula altogether (cf. Sebba 1997: 39). In Russenorsk, for example, neither predicative noun phrases nor predicative adjectives take any overt copula:

Russenorsk (Pidgin (Russian/Norwegian-lexified): Barents Sea)

(339) a. kak pris på tvoja?
what price PREP 2SG
'What (is) your price?'

b. sijpper pjan
skipper drunk
'(The) skipper (is) drunk.' (Broch & Jahr 1984a: 51, 57)

193. Notice that I here follow Stassen in the definition of zero copula, namely that it is "used here as a strictly neutral technical label, in that it refers purely to a construction in which the relation between a subject and a nominal predicate is not marked by an overt item" (Stassen 2013b).

Example (339) shows how Russenorsk lacks an overt copula for both predicative noun phrases and predicative adjectives. It should be noted, however, that the lexifiers may also lack the copula for these kinds of phrases. While overt copulas are obligatory for Norwegian, Russian lacks them (Timberlake 2004). For more on Russenorsk, see 12.4.1.

12.3.1.1 *Predicative noun phrases in pidgin languages*

It is not uncommon for languages to lack an overt copula with predicative noun phrases. Some pidgins did, or do, have overt copulas with predicative noun phrases, such as Yimas-Arafundi Pidgin, where the copula is obligatory for both predicative noun phrases and predicative adjectives (see below):

Yimas-Arafundi Pidgin (Pidgin (Yimas-lexified): Papua New Guinea)

(340) andi anak
ground COP
'(That) is land.' (Foley 2013b: feature 73)

The copula *anak* in Example (340) is obligatory in Yimas-Arafundi Pidgin. Most pidgins of the current sample, however, lack an overt copula with predicative noun phrases, as shown in Table 12.7:

Table 12.7 The copula with predicative noun phrases in the current pidgin sample. For a full legend of the languages in the pidgin sample, see http://dx.doi.org/10.1075/cll.48.additional.

	N	%
No copula	18	66.7
Optional copula	6	22.2
Obligatory copula	3	11.1
Total	27	

($\chi^2 = 14$; $df = 2$; $p_{\text{two-tailed}} < 0.001$***, $p_{\text{sim}} = 0.0015$** (B = 10,000))
($G = 13.17$; $df = 2$; $p_{\text{two-tailed}} = 0.0014$**)

Table 12.7 shows that the languages in the current pidgin sample which lack an overt copula are overrepresented, while the languages with obligatory copula are underrepresented. In order to test whether pidgin languages pattern differently from non-pidgins, I compared the current pidgin sample with Stassen's (2013b) sample. The figures are summarized in Table 12.8.

The figures in Table 12.8 show that there is a difference in distribution between the languages in the pidgin sample and the languages in Stassen's (2013b) sample: in the pidgin sample the languages that allow a zero copula are highly overrepresented, while the languages that do not allow a zero copula are highly underrepresented. This might indicate that pidgin languages are more likely to allow a zero copula for predicative noun phrases than non-pidgins.

Table 12.8 Predicative noun phrases in the current pidgin sample and in WALS (Stassen 2013b). For a full legend of the languages in the pidgin sample, see http://dx.doi.org/10.1075/cll.48.additional.

	Pidgin sample		WALS	
	N	%	N	%
Zero copula is possible	24	88.9	175	45.3
Zero copula is not possible	3	11.1	211	54.7
Total	27		386	

($\chi^2 = 17.47$; $df = 1$; $p_{\text{two-tailed}} < 0.001$***, Yate's correction, $p_{\text{sim}} < 0.001$*** (B = 10,000))
($G^2 = 21.02$; $df = 1$; $p_{\text{two-tailed}} < 0.001$***)

12.3.1.2 *Predicative adjectives in pidgin languages*

To allow a zero copula with adjectives is also not uncommon. However, some pidgins do have a copula with predicative adjectives. In Yimas-Arafundi Pidgin the copula is obligatory:

Yimas-Arafundi Pidgin (Pidgin (Yimas-lexified): Papua New Guinea)

(341) mən panmas anak
3SG good COP
'It is good.' (Foley 2013b: feature 58)

It is important to notice that in a number of languages predicative adjectives actually take the same encoding as predicative verbs, thus rendering an overt copula superfluous (cf. Stassen 2013a). In Broome Pearling Lugger Pidgin, for example, the predicative adjectives take the 'predicate formation particle' *-ya*:

Broome Pearling Lugger Pidgin (Pidgin (Malay-lexified): Australia)

(342) a. po:rr kotor-ya
pearl dirty-PRED
'The pearl is clouded.'
b. po:rr kicchi:-ya
pearl small-PRED
'The pearl is small.' (Hosokawa 1987: 288, 291)

The predicate formation particle *-ya*, which may also attach to verb forms (Hosokawa 1987), would render an overt copula superfluous to the clause.

In the current pidgin sample the majority of languages lack an overt copula with predicative adjectives, as summarized in Table 12.9:

Table 12.9 The copula with predicative adjectives in the current pidgin sample. For a full legend of the languages in the pidgin sample, see http://dx.doi.org/10.1075/cll.48.additional.

	N	%
No copula	27	81.8
Optional copula	4	12.1
Obligatory copula	2	6.1
Total	33	

($\chi^2 = 35.09$; $df = 2$; $p_{\text{two-tailed}} < 0.001$***, $p_{\text{sim}} < 0.001$*** (B = 10,000))
($G = 32.91$; $df = 2$; $p_{\text{two-tailed}} < 0.001$***)

The figures in Table 12.9 show that languages which lack an overt copula with predicative adjectives are highly overrepresented, while languages that have an overt copula with predicative adjectives (whether optional or obligatory) are highly underrepresented. Of the languages that lack an overt copula, only four (Broome Pearling Lugger Pidgin, Mobilian Jargon, Pidgin Hawaiian and Pidgin Ojibwe) have adjectives that are encoded as verbs.[194] This may indicate that pidgin creoles tend to lack an overt copula with predicative adjectives, even if the adjective is not encoded as a verb.

12.3.2 Predication in extended pidgins (pidgincreoles)

The sample of extended pidgins is too small for any statistical analyses, but the picture seems rather more mixed than for pidgin languages.

12.3.2.1 *Predicative noun phrases in extended pidgins (pidgincreoles)*

In four of the ten languages, Ghanaian Pidgin English, Nigerian Pidgin, Cameroon Pidgin English and Nagamese, the copula is obligatory with nominative noun phrases:

Nigerian Pidgin (Extended pidgin (English-lexified): Nigeria)

(343) im bì man
3SG COP man
'He is a man.' (Faraclas 1996: 51)

A predicative noun phrase like *man* in (343) demands a copula in Nigerian Pidgin. The copula is optional in Bislama and Sango, while there is no overt copula with predicative noun phrases in Tok Pisin, Solomon Islands Pijin, Hiri Motu and Juba Arabic.

194. Data on whether predicative adjectives are encoded as verbs is missing for the following five languages: Maridi Pidgin Arabic, Pidgin Dutch, Singapore Bazaar Malay, Trio-Ndyuka and Yimas-Alamblak Pidgin.

Juba Arabic (Extended pidgin (Arabic-lexified): South Sudan)

(344) ána kátib
1SG salesclerk
'I am a salesclerk.' (Manfredi & Petrollino 2013b: feature 73 citing Manfredi 2005: 185)

Example (344) shows that there is no overt copula in Juba Arabic with a predicative noun phrase predication such as *kátib* 'salesclerk'.

12.3.2.2 *Predicative adjectives in extended pidgins (pidgincreoles)*

In Nagamese the copula is obligatory also for predicative adjectives (for more on Nagamese, see 8.3.1), while the copula is optional for predicative adjectives in Sango.

It is more common for extended pidgins to lack an overt copula with predicative adjectives. In Cameroon Pidgin English, Nigerian Pidgin, Ghanaian Pidgin English, Tok Pisin, Bislama and Solomon Islands Pijin this is because the adjective is encoded as a verb (i.e. effectively is a stative verb), and can take tense, mood or aspect markers just like any other verb:

Ghanaian Pidgin English (Extended pidgin (English-lexified): Ghana)

(345) jù gò sɔri
2SG IRR be.sorry
'You will be sorry.' (Huber 1999b: 231)

In (345) *sɔri* inflects like a verb and takes the irrealis marker *gò*, and is thus best viewed as a stative verb; a copula would thus be superfluous to the clause. Juba Arabic also lacks any overt copula with predicative adjectives, even though the adjective is not encoded as a verb:

Juba Arabic (Extended pidgin (Arabic-lexified): South Sudan)

(346) marísa tamám
PN good
'Merisa is good.'
(Manfredi & Petrollino 2013b: feature 74 citing Manfredi 2005: 185)

In (346) there is no overt copula with the predicative adjective *tamám* 'good'.

12.3.3 Predication in creole languages

Creoles are generally described as lacking an overt copula with predicative noun phrases as well as predicative adjectives (cf. Arends et al. 1994a: 323). Ternate Chabacano, for example, lacks an overt copula in both kinds of clauses:

Ternate Chabacano (Creole (Spanish-lexified): Philippines)

(347) a. méstra Lólling
teacher PN
'Lolling was a teacher.'
b. grándi éle
big 3SG
'He is big.' (Sippola 2013c: feature 74)

Example (347) shows that Ternate Chabacano does not take any overt copula with predicative noun phrases and adjectives (for more on Ternate Chabacano, see 7.3.3).

12.3.3.1 *Predicative noun phrases in creole languages*

As mentioned above, it is not uncommon for languages to lack on overt copula with predicative noun phrases. A number of creoles have an overt copula optionally or in certain contexts, while for a number of creoles a copula is obligatory with predicative noun phrases. In Palenquero, for example, an overt copula is obligatory with predicative noun phrases (as well as predicative adjectives, see below):

Palenquero (Creole (Spanish-lexified): Colombia)

(348) ele e músiko
3SG COP musician
'S/He is a musician.' (Schwegler 2013b: feature 73)

Example (348) shows one of the several copulas in Palenquero; while an overt copula is obligatory, the mechanisms for the choice of copula is still not properly understood (Schwegler 2013b; for more on Palenquero, see 12.4.3). To have an obligatory copula with predicative noun phrases is in fact the most common in the current creole sample, as shown in Table 12.10:

Table 12.10 The copula with predicative noun phrases in the current creole sample. For a full legend of the languages in the creole sample, see http://dx.doi.org/10.1075/cll.48.additional.

	N	%
No copula	13	25
Optional copula	13	25
Obligatory copula	26	50
Total	52	

($\chi^2 = 6.5$; $df = 2$; $p_{\text{two-tailed}} = 0.039^*$, $p_{\text{sim}} = 0.043^*$ (B = 10,000))
($G = 6.05$; $df = 2$; $p_{\text{two-tailed}} = 0.049^*$)

Table 12.10 shows that half of the languages in the creole sample have an obligatory copula with predicative noun phrases, making this group significantly overrepresented. In order to test whether creole languages pattern differently from non-creoles, I compared the current creole sample with Stassen's (2013b) sample. The figures are summarized in Table 12.11:

Table 12.11 Predicative noun phrases in the current creole sample and in WALS (Stassen 2013b). For a full legend of the languages in the creole sample, see http://dx.doi.org/10.1075/cll.48.additional.

	Creole sample		WALS*	
	N	%	N	%
Zero copula is possible	26	50	175	45.7
Zero copula is not possible	26	50	208	54.3
Total	52		383	

($\chi^2 = 0.19$; $df = 1$; $p_{\text{two-tailed}} = 0.66$, Yate's correction, $p_{\text{sim}} = 0.66$ (B = 10,000))
($G^2 = 0.34$; $df = 1$; $p_{\text{two-tailed}} = 0.56$)
* Haitian Creole, Seychelles Creole and Sranan have been removed from the WALS sample to avoid overlap with the creole sample.

The figures in Table 12.11 show that there is no significant difference in proportion between the current creole sample and Stassen's (2013b) sample, which in turn indicates that creoles do not pattern differently from non-creoles with respect to overt copulas with predicative noun phrases.

12.3.3.2 *Predicative adjectives in creole languages*

Again, as mentioned above, to allow zero copulas with predicative adjectives is also not uncommon. However, as with predicative noun phrases, many creole languages do have overt copulas with predicative adjectives, and in a number of them the copula is obligatory, as, for example, in Palenquero:

Palenquero (Creole (Spanish-lexified): Colombia)

(349) eso ta gueno
DEM COP good
'This is good!' (Schwegler 2013b: feature 74)

Example (349) shows a clause with a predicative adjective, which in Palenquero obligatorily takes a copula. However, with predicative adjectives, and as opposed to predicative noun phrases, most languages in the current creole sample actually do not have any overt copula, as shown in Table 12.12.

The figures in Table 12.12 show that the group of languages that do not take any overt copula with predicative adjectives is significantly overrepresented in the creole sample.

Table 12.12 The copula with predicative adjectives in the current creole sample. For a full legend of the languages in the creole sample, see http://dx.doi.org/10.1075/cll.48.additional.

	N	%
No copula	26	50
Optional copula	14	26.9
Obligatory copula	12	23.1
Total	52	

($\chi^2 = 6.62$; $df = 2$; $p_{two\text{-}tailed} = 0.037$*, $p_{sim} = 0.038$* (B = 10,000))
($G = 6.20$; $df = 2$; $p_{two\text{-}tailed} = 0.045$*)

The discrepancy between predicative noun phrases and predicative adjectives might be due to the fact that in a number of languages adjectives actually take the same encoding as verbs (i.e. that adjectives essentially are stative verbs). This is, for example, the case in Jamaican, where adjectives may take the same tense, mood or aspect markers as verbs:

Jamaican (Creole (English-lexified): Jamaica)

(350) mi ongl se im did shaat
1SG only say 3SG PST short
'I only said he was short.' (Patrick 2007: 130)

Example (350) shows how *shaat* 'short' may take the past tense marker *did*. In other words, in Jamaican adjectives are actually encoded as verbs, i.e. are effectively stative verbs, and may take tense, mood or aspect markers just like verbs. For such languages an overt copula would be superfluous. It is common for languages of the world to have verbal encoding on predicative adjectives. In order to test whether creole languages pattern differently from non-creoles, I compared the current creole sample with Stassen's (2013a) sample. The figures are summarized in Table 12.13:

Table 12.13 Encoding of predicative adjectives in the current creole sample and in WALS (Stassen 2013a). For a full legend of the languages in the creole sample, see http://dx.doi.org/10.1075/cll.48.additional.

	Creole sample		WALS*	
	N	%	N	%
Verbal encoding of predicative adjective	19	38.8	148	52.9
Nonverbal encoding of predicative adjective	30	61.2	132	47.1
Total	49		280	

($\chi^2 = 2.77$; $df = 1$; $p_{two\text{-}tailed} = 0.0961$, Yate's correction, $p_{sim} = 0.083$ (B = 10,000))
($G^2 = 0.3.29$; $df = 1$; $p_{two\text{-}tailed} = 0.070$)

* Haitian Creole, Seychelles Creole and Sranan have been removed from the WALS sample to avoid overlap with the creole sample. Notice that Stassen's value 'Mixed' is not included here.

The figures in Table 12.13 show that there is a marginally significant difference in proportion between the current creole sample and Stassen's (2013a) sample, although it should be noted that the category 'Mixed' has been removed from Stassen's sample. The figures in Table 12.13 thus possibly indicate that creoles might be slightly less likely to allow verbal encoding for predicative adjectives than non-creoles.

12.3.4 Predication in mixed languages

The sample of mixed languages is too small for statistical analyses, but in general mixed languages are expected to follow the structure of one of the input languages, or to exhibit a blend of the input languages. Ma'á/Mbugu, for example, follows the Cushitic system of obligatory copulas for both predicative noun phrases and predicative adjectives (Thomason 1997a: 475):

Ma'á/Mbugu (Mixed language (Cushitic/Bantu): Tanzania)

(351) a. kilúgwi ni kinyongôlé
chameleon COP insect.Q
'Is the chameleon an insect?'

b. mshwá ni m-kusá
ant COP 3-bad
'White ants are bad.' (Mous 2003b: 146)

In Ma'á/Mbugu the copula *ni* (or its negative equivalent *si* 'is.not') in Example (351) is obligatory in clauses with predicative noun phrases or predicative adjectives.

Mednyj Aleut follows the Russian system in a general absence of any overt copula for both predicative noun phrases and predicative adjectives, but follows Aleut in that adjectives take verbal encoding and are essentially stative verbs:

Mednyj Aleut (Mixed language (Russian/Aleut): Mednyj Island, Russia)

(352) a. eta moj asxinu-ŋ
DEM 1SG.POSS daughter-1SG.POSS
'This is my daughter.' (Thomason 1997b: 458)

b. yesli by oni ukaala-ag'aa-l-i huzu-um by txichi qala-chaa-l
if SUBJ 3PL here-move-PST-PL all-REFL SUBJ REFL.PL be.glad-CAUS-PST
'If they came, everybody would be glad.' (Golovko 1994: 115)

As shown in Example (352) Mednyj Aleut does not have any overt copula. Furthermore, Example (352b) shows that adjectives pattern like verbs, here taking the causative marker *-chaa* and the past tense marker *-l*. For more on Mednyj Aleut, see 13.4.3.

In Michif French-derived adjectives take a copula while Cree-derived descriptives, which pattern as verbs, do not take any copula but are instead inflected as verbs:

Michif (Mixed language (French/Cree): Canada)

(353) a. li veer li i kleer
DEF.M.SG glass ART COP transparent
'The glass is transparent.'

b. li zaabr miishiikiitii-w
DEF.M.SG tree be.big.AI-3
'The tree is big.' (Bakker 1997a: 90)

As shown in (353), Michif exhibits a mixed pattern with respect to overt copulas, derived from both input languages.

12.4 Snapshots

Pidgins are assumed to lack tense, aspect and mood marking as well as the copula. Russenorsk is an example of a pidgin language which in fact has an optional future tense, but which lacks the copula.

Extended pidgins are often assumed to be more similar to creoles than to pidgins. Solomon Islands Pijin is an example of an extended pidgin which does not have tense, but does have aspect and mood marking, and where there is no copula because the adjective patterns as a stative verb.

Proposals have been put forth of a prototypical creole system with only one tense marker, one aspect marker and one mood marker, which are all preverbal and combine in that given order. Furthermore, the lexical aspect of the verb has been assumed to affect the temporal reading of the clause. Creoles are assumed to lack the copula. Palenquero is an example of a creole language with several tense, aspect and mood markers, but where the lexical aspect of the verb affects the reading of the clause. There is an obligatory copula.

12.4.1 Russenorsk: An extinct Russian/Norwegian pidgin in the Barents Sea[195]

12.4.1.1 *A brief background sketch of Russenorsk*

Russenorsk is a now extinct pidgin which was used for about 150 years from the last quarter of the 18th century to the Russian Revolution in 1917. It was called *Moja på tvoja sproget* (lit. *Our language*) by the Norwegian fishermen. At its peak Russenorsk was used in an area stretching from Tromsø (northern Norway) in the west to Kola (north-western Russia) in the east.

Trade between the north-western Russian and northern Norwegian territories had been going on for many centuries and was formalized in treaties from the early 16th century onwards. This so-called Pomor trade (from Russian *pomorje* 'area by the ocean', which refers to the area of

195. This section relies almost exclusively on Broch & Jahr (1984a and 1984b).

the White Sea coast; the inhabitants of the area were called Pomors) was a barter trade between the north-western Russian area around the White Sea and the northern Norwegian areas of Troms and Finnmark, but occasionally went as far south as the Lofoten islands (Jahr 1996). Initially this Pomor trade was illegal, though vibrant, but by the end of the 18th century it had been legalized. The Norwegians traded fish, salt, hides, grindstones and so on for Russian flour, grain, hemp, rope, linen, birch bark, wood and so on. This took place during the summer months, when fish was abundant on the Norwegian coast and difficult to sell in Norway but difficult to come by on the Murmansk coast. It was a profitable trade for both parties and the Russian merchants would usually return to the same locations in northern Norway each summer. It should be noted, however, that it was not uncommon for Russians to stay in Norway during the winter, "partly to take odd jobs, partly to get a head start on the next year's trading" (Broch & Jahr 1984b: 57), since Russian boats could only set out for Norway after the ice had broken. It therefore does not seem farfetched to assume that Russenorsk was used outside the immediate trade situation.

The first known attestation of Russenorsk is from a lawsuit in 1785 where a Norwegian priest was sued by a Russian skipper for refusing to pay wages to a couple of sailors who, after having capsized, had become unable to carry out their tasks. A witness in the case was referred to as "Rusmand Gergorius Petterson Breche" where the Russenorsk *Rusmand* is used for 'Russian' (rather than the Norwegian *Rus(s)* or *Rys(s)*, which was commonly used in legal documents; Broch & Jahr 1984a: 65). Russenorsk was first referred to as a language by Baron Wedel Jarlsberg, who was Amtmann in Finnmark between 1812 and 1814. In his records he mentions a trade language used with Russian traders specifically:

> In addition a fourth language is spoken in the Finnmark, composed of Norwegian, Russian, Dutch, German, Finnish [i.e. Sami – VV] and maybe Kvænsk, one could call it the Trade Language; for the traders make use of it to understand each other; however it is only used when trade is to be made with Russians.[196]
>
> (Wedel Jarlsberg, Frederik Vilhelm 1887: 152, my translation)

The parties that used Russenorsk were of equal social status. Initially both fishermen and merchants used the language. The language enjoyed an accepted status, and was viewed as a language on par with any other, as for example indicated in the quote above. However, around 1850 this started to change in that Norwegian merchants increasingly sent their sons to Russia, especially Archangel, for longer stays, where they learned Russian. With this Russenorsk became the Russian of the fishermen and its status declined. By the end of the 19th century it was frequently referred to as a "crow-language" (*Kragemaal*) and 'hodgepodge' and so on.[197] At the same time the socioeconomic situation changed: the barter trade was gradually replaced with a cash-trade

196. *"Endnu tales i Finnmarken et fjerde Sprog, sammensat av Norsk, Russisk, Hollandsk, Tysk, Finsk og maaske Kvænsk, man kunde kalde det Handelssproget; thi heraf betjener de Handlende sig for indbyrdes at gjøre sig forstaaelige; dog benyttes det kun naar Handel skal sluttes med Russer."*

197. Although Reusch (1895: 47) refers to Russenorsk as a fixed idiom ("*en fæstnet taleform*") similar in function to Chinese Pidgin English.

and trading was increasingly being concentrated to big merchants. The Pomor trade ended with the First World War and the Russian Revolution. With this the context for Russenorsk also ended.

12.4.1.2 *A short linguistic sketch of Russenorsk*

The exact nature of the Russenorsk phonological system is not accessible to us, since all data available is in written form. The following should be seen as qualified guesses. Russenorsk had 17 or 18 consonants, /p, b, m, f, v, t, d, n, s, (z), r, l, ʧ, j, k, g, ŋ, h/ and six vowels, /i, e, a, o, ɔ, u/. Syllables could be complex, with examples of clusters with three consonants in the onset (e.g. *sprek* 'say, speak') and clusters of two consonants in the coda (e.g. *kuasalt* 'salted meat'). Tone does not seem to have been relevant. The Norwegian spelling convention of <aa>/<å> for /ɔ/ has here been streamlined to <å> only.

The morphology seems to have been predominantly analytic, although there was suffixation, such as the word class markers *-om* (for verbs) and *-a* (for nominals). There was the derivational suffix *-mann* denoting persons of different ethnic or social groups (e.g. *russman* 'Russian' or *kukmann* 'merchant'). There is evidence of compounding, such as *kuasalt* 'salted meat' (lit. cow. salt), *smalatreska* 'small cod' or *gammeldag* 'yesterday' (lit. old.day). There are a few examples of reduplicated forms, such as *morra-morradag* 'day after tomorrow' and *dobra-dobra* 'very good'.

Nouns tended to be marked with the nominal word class suffix *-(k)a*, as in *klæba* 'bread', *silka* 'herring' and *damosna* 'customs office'. Number, gender and case were not indicated.

(354) a. på moja kona, tri juŋka, to piga
PREP 1SG wife three boy two girl
'I have a wife, three boys and two girls.'
b. nogoli dag tvoja reisa på Arkangel otsuda?
some day 2SG travel PREP A here
'How many days did you travel from Archangel to here?' (Broch & Jahr 1984a: 112f)[198]

In Example (354) all nouns remain in invariant form, even if *juŋka* 'boy', *piga* 'girl' and *dag* 'day' clearly refer to plural entities.

There do not seem to have been any articles:

(355) a. davai påsmotrom på skip
please look PREP boat
'Let us have (a) look at (the) boat.'
b. på kajyt vaskom
PREP cabin paint
'(The) cabin is to be painted.'
c. kak pris?
what price
'What (is) (the) price?' (Broch & Jahr 1984a: 109f, 116)

There does, however, seem to have been the two demonstratives *etta* 'this' and *den* 'that':

198. Notice that all examples in this section are based on the text material in Broch (1930), cited in Broch & Jahr (1984a: 107ff).

(356) a. etta njet dobra
DEM.PROX NEG good
'That was not good.'
b. den junka njet dobra
DEM.DIST boy NEG good
'That boy is not good.' (Broch & Jahr 1984a: 115f)

Possession was indicated either through juxtaposition or with the general preposition *på* (cf. also (354a)):

(357) a. eta samme slag kak kua sjorta
DEM.PROX same type how cow shirt
'That's the same as the cow's shirt.'
b. mangeli klokka på ju?
many clock PREP 2SG
'How much is your watch?' (i.e. 'What time do you have?') (Broch & Jahr 1984a: 114, 117)

Little is known about whether there was a full pronominal system, but the personal pronouns *moja* 'I, me, my', *tvoja/ju* 'thou, thee, thine' and *han* 'he, him, his' are attested. It seems as if *moja på tvoja* served as the pronoun 'we, us, our'.

Adjectives preceded the noun and were invariant (cf. (358a)). The comparative was typically formed analytically with *mere* 'more' (as in (358b), notice that this is translated with a superlative), though there are attestations of comparative suppletive forms (as in (358c)).

(358) a. russmann bra mann
Russian good man
'The Russian is a good man.'
b. den gammel uri, den mere bra, den på moja
DEM.DIST old catfish DEM.DIST more good DEM.DIST PREP 1SG
'That old catfish, that's best, that (one) I want.'
c. mera better på moja
more better PREP 1SG
'It is better for me.' (Broch & Jahr 1984a: 110, 112, 114)

Verbs generally, though by no means always, took the verbal word class suffix *-om*, as in *kralom* 'steal', *slipom* 'sleep' or *robotom* 'work', but were otherwise invariant and did not inflect for person or number. Tense, aspect and mood were typically also not indicated:

(359) a. Gilbert, gammel go ven, sprek på moja: tvoja grot rik
PN old good friend say PREP 1SG 2SG much rich
'My good old friend Gilbert told me that you are very rich.'
b. han ikke sandfærdig sprek
3SG NEG truthful speak
'He is not telling the truth.'
c. moja tvoja på vater kastom
1SG 2SG PREP water throw
'I will throw you in the water.' (Broch & Jahr 1984a: 113)

However, there are examples of a future construction *ska(l)* VERB (as in (360a, b)) and a future+volition construction with *vil* VERB (as in (360c, d)):

(360) a. moja ska si på ju: kak ju vina trinke, Kristus grot vre
1SG FUT say PREP 2SG how 2SG wine drink Christ much angry
'I'll tell you: if you drink wine, Christ will be very angry.'
b. tvoja skal bli kammerat på moja på anner år
2SG FUT become friend PREP 1SG PREP other year
'You'll be my friend next year.'
c. vil ju på moja stova på morradag skaffom?
will 2SG PREP 1SG house PREP tomorrow eat
'Will you eat at my place tomorrow?'
d. moja vil spræk på principal
1SG will speak PREP skipper
'I want to speak to the skipper.' (Broch & Jahr 1984a: 107, 109, 112, 116)

The word order was typically subject-verb-object. Imperatives were formed with the base form, but there seems to have been a way of forming polite requests with either *værsågo* or *davaj* (cf. (355a)). Negation was formed with the invariant *njet/ikke* (cf. (356), (359b)). Polar questions seem typically to have been formed through intonation only (but cf. (360c)).

(361) a. tvoja kopom oreka?
2SG buy nut
'Will you buy nuts?'
b. tvoja har konna?
2SG have wife
'Are you married?' (Broch & Jahr 1984a: 108f)

In content questions the interrogative phrase was fronted (cf. (354c), (355b), (357b)). There was no copula (cf. (355b, c), (356), (357), (358)).

There were the coordinating conjunctions *og/i/ja/jes* 'and' (notice that the two latter conjunctions literally mean 'yes'), though coordination could be indicated with juxtaposition only (cf. (354a)). The interrogative *kak* 'how' also functioned as a subordination marker (cf. also (360a)):

(362) moja smotrom kak ju pisat
1SG see how 2SG write
'I saw/see that you wrote/are writing.' (Broch & Jahr 1984a: 48)

12.4.1.3 *Short text*

From (Broch 1930), cited in Broch & Jahr (1984a: 134). My glossing and translation. Capitalization of letters as in original.

På Burmain jes måja njet vil ha,
PREP fisherman yes 1SG NEG will have

Fiska skirom, Fiska skirom,
fish gut fish gut

Kak tvoia Rusmain, så mera bra,
how 2SG Russian so more good

Jes på Skip kom, Jes på Skip kom.
yes PREP ship come yes PREP ship come

Kak ju vil skaffom ja drikke The,
how 2SG will eat and drink tea

Davai på Skip tvoia ligge ne,
please PREP ship 2SG lie down

Grot på slipom, Grot på slipom.
much PREP sleep much PREP sleep

'Norwegian fisherman I verily do not want to be / Gut fish, gut fish // It would be better to be Russian / Come aboard, come aboard / If you want to eat and drink tea / Please (come) aboard and lie down / Sleep first, sleep first.'

12.4.1.4 *Some sources of data*

All known attestations of Russenorsk are collected in Broch & Jahr (1984a), unfortunately only accessible to those who read Norwegian. However, Broch & Jahr (1984b) is a condensed version of the former and gives a thorough discussion in English of the history, origins and structure of Russenorsk, including a high number of glossed and translated examples.

12.4.2 Solomon Islands Pijin: An English-lexified extended pidgin (pidgincreole) on the Solomon Islands[199]

12.4.2.1 *A brief background sketch of Solomon Islands Pijin*

Solomon Islands Pijin, also called *Neo-Solomonic* and *Solomons Pidgin* by scholars, and called *Pijin* by the speakers themselves, is spoken throughout the Solomons archipelago in the Pacific just east of Papua New Guinea. As of 1999 there were about 24,000 native speakers of Solomon Islands Pijin and another 307,000 people who use it as a second language (Lewis et al. 2014). It is one of the Melanesian pidgins, together with Tok Pisin (see 1.4.3) and Bislama.

The Solomon Islands had been inhabited for many millennia when first contact with Europeans came with the arrival of Alvaro de Mendaña de Neira in 1568. The Mendaña Expedition had set out from Peru in order to find Terra Australis, or the great Southern Continent, which was presumed to lie somewhere west of Peru and contained Ophir, the biblical region which had provided King Solomon with riches (Delaney 2010). Once word of Mendaña's discovery had been received, the islands were named the Solomon Islands.

The early 19th century saw regular contact with whaling ships, which called at various islands in order to trade for fresh food and other products (Holm 1988: 535) and missionaries started frequenting the islands from the mid-19th century. However, in many Melanesian coastal areas, including many of the Solomon Islands, unarmed or unprotected strangers were treated as enemies, which often included head-hunting and/or cannibalism (Knauft 1999: 103). Despite this,

199. This section is based primarily on Jourdan & Selbach (2004) and Jourdan (2004). I am very grateful to Christine Jourdan for her helpful comments on this snapshot.

plantation owners in Queensland and Fiji started recruiting labour from the Solomon Islands in the mid-1870s (often through 'blackbirding' or kidnapping of workers). On these plantations the Melanesian islanders, who came from a variety of linguistic backgrounds, encountered what was then called Kanaka Pidgin English. Once the Solomon Islanders returned home they brought this pidgin English with them.

In 1893 Great Britain established a protectorate over the southern islands, which was extended to most of the northern islands in 1899. This led to an increased use of the pidgin English, not only between the British and the Solomon Islanders, but also among islanders of various linguistic backgrounds. Furthermore, the early 1900s saw an expansion of the plantation economy and labour was recruited from different islands (mostly Malaita island), resulting in a migration within the archipelago. The first labourers to be employed were those with experience from Queensland and/or Fiji, which led to the establishment of Kanaka Pidgin English as a *lingua franca* on the local plantations as well, where it gradually acquired local characteristics.

The British laid heavy emphasis on English in teaching and in administrative use, which led to an early urban well-educated and English-speaking elite (Jourdan & Keesing 1997).

Long drawn and heavy battles in 1942–3 during World War II brought the American Army to the archipelago. A number of Solomon Islanders were enrolled in forces and corpses and used either Solomon Islands Pijin or English with American soldiers.

During the Maasina Rulu 'the rule of brotherhood' (from the 'Are'Are *maasina* 'brotherhood' and the English *rule*), the emancipation movement 1944–1952, Solomon Islands Pijin became a unifying tool and spread to large portions of the society. The Solomon Islands became independent in 1978.

By now Solomon Islands Pijin is spoken throughout the archipelago. It was initially used mainly by adult males, since women and children were typically not part of the plantation, mission station or schooling settings.[200] However, it is, since the 1960s, the main language of Honiara (the capital), and increased mobility as well as increased primary schooling and urbanization, has brought the language to women and children as well. The high level of language diversity on the islands (71 languages; Lewis et al. 2014) furthered the use of the *lingua franca*. This is especially true of Honiara, where most of the languages of the archipelago are represented (Jourdan & Keesing 1997). Solomon Islands Pijin is now used in all domains, including religious services, media, political discourse, the public service, and so on. A high number of interethnic marriages has led Solomon Islands Pijin to become the domestic language in many families, which in turn has led to a growing number of urban children and young adults to acquire the language as their mother tongue (Jourdan 2009:250). Influence from English, especially in the phonology and lexicon, has led to a certain friction between urban and rural Solomon Islands Pijin, with the speakers of the latter finding the urban variety (and its speakers) too anglicized.

Despite its wide use, Solomon Islands Pijin is not recognized as an official language, which instead is English. It remains a largely spoken language, due to lack of official support and due

200. There are still older women in remote areas who do not know Solomon Islands Pijin at all (Jourdan & Selbach 2004:692).

to higher level schooling in English. Multilingualism is the norm, and many will switch effortlessly between their ancestral languages, Solomon Islands Pijin and English, depending on social setting and context, although this is gradually changing among the younger generations, who have essentially shifted to Solomon Islands Pijin and by now have little or no knowledge of their parents' ancestor languages (Jourdan 2009; cf. also Jourdan & Angeli 2014).

12.4.2.2 *A short linguistic sketch of Solomon Islands Pijin*

There is a high degree of variability in Solomon Islands Pijin, depending on region, the respective vernaculars, degrees of influence from English and urbanization. The following description is a conservative basic description and it should be noted that it does not cover the full range of variability found in the language.

Solomon Islands Pijin has 18 consonants, /p, b, m, f, v, t, d, n, s, l, ɾ, ʧ, j, k, g, ŋ, w, h/, and five vowels, /i, e, a, o, u/. For many speakers /a/ and /u/ have contrastive length. Syllables are typically simple, with CV the preferred structure, though monosyllabic words are either CVC or CVV. However, more complex syllable structures occur, especially in the urban varieties, such as /dres/ 'dress' or /skwea/ 'square'. Stress essentially follows the pattern of the etymon, with Oceanic words typically having a penultimate stress, while English words have first or penultimate syllable stress.

The morphology is predominantly analytic, though there is derivational suffixation: the nominalizer *-wan*, the verbalizer or transitivizer *-em/-um/-im* and *-fala* for forming adjectives. Compounding is common, as in *lemantri* 'lemon tree', *masolman* 'strong man', *levolples* 'flat land' or *stilman* 'thief' (Jourdan 2004:708). There is both partial and full reduplication, which indicates intensification, continuation or iteration, such as in *save* 'know' → *sasave* 'to be very knowledgeable', *silip* 'sleep' → *sisilip* 'sleep a long time', *suim* 'swim' → *susuim* 'swimming', *siki* 'be.sick' → *sisiki* 'keep being sick', *wan* 'one' → *wanwan* 'one at a time' (Jourdan & Selbach 2004:707). It may also function as a nominalizer, as in *was* 'wash' → *waswas* 'laundry' (Jourdan 2004:711).

Nouns are invariant; case and gender are not relevant categories. There is optional plural marking with the third person plural *olketa*:

(363) mi havest-em olketa iam blong mi finis
1SG harvest-TR 3PL yam POSS 1SG COMPL
'I have harvested my yams.' (Jourdan 2002:155)

It seems as if the short form *ota* is grammaticalizing among young urban speakers as a plural marker while *olketa* is increasingly being reserved for the third person plural pronoun in object position (Jourdan & Selbach 2004:702).

There are no definite or indefinite articles:

(364) a. fis mi pe-em long maket stap long kol distaem
fish 1SG pay-TR PREP market CONT PREP fridge now
'The fish I bought in the market is now in the fridge.'
b. mi herem nius abaot plen hem foldaon
1SG listen news about plane 3SG fall
'I heard that a plane had crashed.' (Jourdan 2002:103, 106)

However, *wanfala* 'one' is increasingly being used as an indefinite article:

(365) hem stanap long saetrod olsem, batawea, wanfala trak bangam hem nao
3SG stand PREP road.side like but one truck collide 3SG PFV
'He was standing at the side of the road when unexpectedly a truck came and hit him.'
(Jourdan 2002: 225)

There is the preposed demonstrative *disfala* (cf. (373), (374b)) and the postposed demonstrative *ia* (as in (366a)), which is increasingly being used as a definite article (as in (366b)):

(366) a. man ia iumi luk-im astede hem dae finis
man DEM 2PL.INCL look-TR yesterday 3SG die COMPL
'That man whom we saw yesterday is dead.' (Jourdan 2002: 76)

b. olketa dadi long laen blong mi kam for mektambu long
3PL elder PREP lineage POSS 1SG come for consecrate PREP
ples ia
place DEM
'The male relatives of my lineage come to consecrate the area.' (Jourdan 2004: 712)

The pronominal system distinguishes between three persons and four numbers. Case and gender is not relevant.

	SINGULAR	DUAL	TRIAL	PLURAL
1.INCL	*mi*	*iumitufala*	*iumitrifala*	*iumi*
1.EXCL	–	*mitufala*	*mitrifala*	*mifala*
2	*iu*	*iutufala*	*iutrifala*	*iufala*
3	*hem*	*tufala*	*trifala*	*olketa*

Possession is indicated with the invariant possessive marker *blong*:

(367) haos blong sif hem kolsap long stoa ia
house POSS chief 3SG near PREP store DEM
'The chief's house is next to the store.' (Jourdan 2002: 107)

There is a small closed class of adjectives denoting colour terms, size and age, which are often (though this seems to be gradually disappearing) marked with *-fala* (which is also optionally used for numbers). The comparative is indicated with *winim* 'win' or *ovam* 'over':

(368) a. man ia hem iang(fala) iet, hem no marit iet
man DEM 3SG young still 3SG NEG be.married still
'This man is still young, he is not married.'

b. Dafua hem olo winim Tafui
PN 3SG old win PN
'Dafua is older than Tafui.'

c. pikpik ia hem big(fala) ovam narawan
pig DEM 3SG big over other
'This pig is bigger than the other one.' (Jourdan 2002: 77, 160, 262)

However, the majority of descriptives are functionally stative verbs.

Verbs are invariant. There is no tense system; temporal readings are either context bound or indicated with adverbials.[201]

(369) a. bikfala dogi ia fraet-em mi tumas
big dog DEM be.scared-TR 1SG very
'This big dog scares me a lot.'

b. staka long olketa kam long naet.
many PREP 3PL come PREP night
'Many of them came at night.'

c. tumoro nomoa iumi go
tomorrow only 1PL.INCL go
'It is tomorrow that we will go.' (Jourdan 2004: 705, 710, 714)

There are four aspect markers: *stap* indicates continuation (cf. (364a)), *finis* indicates completion (cf. (363), (366a)), *nao* is a telic perfective marker (cf. (365)) and *save* indicates the habitual (as in (370)).

(370) olketa Sevende no save kaekae pig
3PL Seventh.Day.Adventists NEG HAB eat pig
'The Seventh Day Adventists do not eat pork.' (Jourdan 2002: 199)

There are two modal markers: *bae* indicates irrealis and *save* indicates ability or permission (whether this is a separate but homophonous marker from the habitual marker is not clear):

(371) a. bae mifala go sevis
IRR 1PL.EXCL go service
'We will go to church.'

b. sapos iumi mit-im iumi moa, bae iumi stori
if 1PL.INCL meet-TR 1PL more IRR 1PL.INCL story
'If we meet each other again, we will chat.'

c. Pita no save draeva
PN NEG MOD drive
'Peter cannot drive.'

d. waswe, mi save kaekae kek tu?
why 1SG MOD eat cake too
'Tell me, may I also eat some cake?' (Jourdan 2004: 707, 710, 714)

---

201. Notice, however, that the past marker *bin* has been imported from Tok Pisin:

mi bin go long Ruasuara
1SG PST go PREP Ruasuara
'I went to Ruasuara.' (Jourdan 2004: 714)

The marker is mainly used by people from the western areas and by those who have been educated in Papua New Guinea (Jourdan 2002: 21).

The word order is typically subject-verb-object. Negation is indicated with the invariant *no* (cf. (368a), (370), (371c)). Polar questions are indicated with rising intonation only (cf. (371d)). In content questions the interrogative phrase may optionally be fronted, or, more commonly, appear clause-finally:

(372) wataem nao bae iu kam? / bae iu kam wataem?
when PFV IRR 2SG come
'When will you come?' (Jourdan 2004: 718)

There is no copula (cf. (367), (368)).

There are the coordinating conjunctions *an/na* 'and', *bat/ma* 'but' and *o* 'or'. There are serial verb constructions with *go* 'go' and *kam* 'come':

(373) tek-em kam disfala bik fis ia
take-TR come this big fish DEM
'Bring this big fish.' (Jourdan 2002: 19)

There are two main ways of forming relative clauses: either without any marker, i.e. through juxtaposition, but with an altered intonation pattern (with a rising intonation for the relative clause), which distinguishes the relative clause from a chained clause (Jourdan & Selbach 2004: 708). Alternatively the relative markers *hu/wea* may optionally be used, though this is more representative for young and urban speakers.

(374) a. pikpik ia hem kil-im mifala kaeka-em
pig DEM 3SG kil-TR 1PL.EXCL eat-TR
'We ate the pig that he killed.'
b. disfela gele (wea/hu) mi luk-im, hemi sick
this girl REL 1SG look-TR 3SG be.sick
'The girl (whom) I saw is sick.' (Jourdan 2004: 717f)

12.4.2.3 *Short text*

(From Jourdan 2002: xxiii. The speaker is a 40-year old man from the island of Choiseul but who has lived in Honiara all his adult life.)

Mi bon longo Soisol ia. Nao mi bon kam ngo ngo, nomoa tisa long vilij nao,
1SG born PREP Choisel DEM TOP PST born come go go no teacher PREP village STATM

so mi no sukul. Mi stapu nomoa. Ngo ngo ngo, wanfala tisa from nara vilij
so 1SG NEG school 1SG stay only go go go one teacher from other village

hemi kam tek-em mi. Mi stap wetem hem, olsem haos bo eia. Den prom dat taem
3SG come take-TR 1SG 1SG stay with 3SG like house boy DEM then from that time

nao, mi stati skul long 1958.
STATM 1SG start school PREP 1958

'I was born on Choisel. I was born, and the time passed, and because there was no teacher in the village, I did not go to school. I just hung around. Then, a teacher from another village came to get me. I stayed with him and worked as his house boy. It is from that moment, in 1958, that I started school.'

12.4.2.4 *Some sources of data*

There is a fair bit of primary data available for Solomon Islands Pijin. The entry in the OLAC Language Resource Catalogue (http://search.language-archives.org/search.html?q=Pijin, accessed 12 February 2015) gives a large number of texts and primers, as well as language descriptions. There are broadcasts both on radio and TV. *Klaemet Chens: Evriwan busnis* is a very accessible 10-minute animation available on YouTube (http://www.youtube.com/watch?v=uLIYx9uowY8, accessed 12 February 2015) about global warming.

12.4.3 Palenquero: A Spanish-lexified creole in Colombia[202]

12.4.3.1 *A brief background sketch of Palenquero*

Palenquero, often referred to as *Lengua* ('tongue') by the speakers themselves, is spoken by about 2,000–3,000 people in the village of El Palenque (also called San Brasilio de Palenque or El Palenque de San Brasilio) in northern Colombia. It is the only known Spanish-lexified creole on the South American mainland.

Cartagena de Indias, founded in 1533 and located some 60 km north-west of the village of El Palenque, was the major slave trade centre of Latin America between 1600 and 1640. At the height of its role as a trading centre Cartagena was teeming with newly imported slaves from West and Central-West Africa, making it ethnically and linguistically highly diverse, with over 70 African languages spoken locally (Schwegler 2013a). Marronage was common and by the end of the 17th century there were several maroon communities and *palenques* ('fortifications') in the marshlands and hilly areas to the north and south east of Cartagena (Navarrete 2001, Navarrete 2008).

It is not known exactly when El Palenque was founded, but it is likely to have been sometime between 1660 and 1713 (Schwegler 2011: 242); the first reliable evidence is the description of San Brasilio in the *Noticia Historial de la provincia de Cartagena de las Indias, año 1772* by Diego de Peredo (bishop of Cartagena) and Francisco Escuerdo (his secretary):

> Population of blacks in the interior of the mountain; it had its origin in many escaped slaves of various people in this town … [who] established their *palenque*. … they speak among themselves a peculiar idiom that they themselves teach their children, nevertheless they execute the Castilian [Spanish – VV] that they generally use with much proficiency. … Their priest administers 178 families with 396 converted souls and 90 slaves.[203]
>
> (Blanco Barros 1971–72: 140; my translation)

202. This section is primarily based on Schwegler (2013a). I am very grateful to Armin Schwegler for his helpful comments on this snapshot.

203. "*Población de negros en lo interior del monte; tuvo su origen de muchos esclavos fugitivos de varias personas de esta ciudad … establecieron su palenque. … hablan entre sí un particular idioma en que a sus solas instruyen a los muchachos, sin embargo de que cortan con mucha expedición el castellano de que generalmente usan. Administra su cura 178 familias con 396 almas de confesión y 90 esclavos.*"

The quote indicates that the early inhabitants of Palenque were already fully bilingual in Palenquero and Spanish.

The inhabitants of El Palenque did not mix much with other populations and the village has remained relatively homogenous culturally and linguistically.[204] Extra- as well as intra-linguistic factors indicate that the main (and perhaps only) African substrate language seems to have been Kikongo (Schwegler 2011, Schwegler 2015+).

Until the mid-1960s, the village remained bilingual and remote (the first dirt road to Palenque was constructed in the late 1950s). Palenquero language and culture was heavily stigmatized throughout most of the 20th century, which led to a generational shift to Spanish starting around the 1970s. This development was accompanied by the migration of Palenqueros to nearby cities, where rarely, if ever, the creole was used. However, as of this millennium, improved public transport and other amenities have made the village better connected to the outside world "thus strengthening its linguistic and sociocultural ties with the diaspora" (Schwegler 2013a: 183).

During the 20th century, the creole was often perceived as the ultimate source of the "backwardness" of Palenque. As a result, Palenquero became highly stigmatized. However, with the arrival of linguists in the 1970s (Derek Bickerton and Germán de Granda) and 1980s (Carlos Patiño Rosselli, Armin Schwegler and Thomas Morton), the attitude towards the creole started to change. At first a small group of young Palenqueros expressed interest in learning more about their language and history. This led to informal programs of language and culture education by Patiño Rosselli and Schwegler, which in turn prompted local educators, who had attended these programs, to incorporate Palenquero in their teaching (Schwegler 2013a: 184). At the same time the pan-Columbian Black Awareness movement (*negritud*) raised the status of African heritage.

Roughly from the year 2000 onward, Palenquero has experienced a revival in that it has become a positive identity marker. As a result, the young generation was generally keen to learn the creole. Whether this revival might reverse its status as an endangered language remains to be seen (but cf. Lipski 2012). However, both national and international fame is likely to further increase its status: in 2005 the UNESCO proclaimed El Palenque a "Masterpiece of the Oral and Intangible Heritage of Humanity" (cf. http://www.unesco.org/culture/intangible-heritage/11lac_uk.htm, accessed 12 February 2015) and the Colombian Ministry of Culture has declared it part of the "spiritual patrimony" of Colombia (Lipski 2012: 22). While Palenquero continues to be predominantly an oral language, and there is as yet no official orthography, the current fame of the language may lead to more institutional support and even its introduction in primary schools.

12.4.3.2 *A short linguistic sketch of Palenquero*

Palenquero has 23 consonants, /p, b, ᵐb, m, f, t, d, ⁿd, n, r, ɾ, s, l, ʧ, k, ɡ, ɲ, j, k, kʷ, ɡ, ᵑɡ, w/ and 6 vowels, /i, e, a, ɔ, o, u/. Nine of the consonants, /p, b, m, t, d, n, k, ɡ, l/, have contrastive length. Compare the following minimal pairs:

---

204. Genetic research on the Y-chromosome in the area showed that in Palenque the majority of the male lineages were African, though the European input actually accounted for 38% (Noguera et al. 2013).

(375) /'a.ma/ 'owner' vs /'a.m:a/ 'soul'
/'ka.la/ 'face' vs /'ka.l:a/ 'Carla'
/'mi.na/ '(a) mine' vs /'mi.n:a/ 'Mirna'
/'to.do/ 'all' vs /'to.d:o/ 'cloth' (Schwegler 2013a:184)

Syllables tend to be open; the most complex kind of syllable is either CVC or CCV(C), with up to two consonants in the onset and one in the coda (as in *flen.de* 'front, forehead'). Tone is not a relevant feature, despite its uniform Kikongo substrate (Hualde & Schwegler 2008).

The morphology is predominantly analytic, though there is some plural as well as aspect suffixation.

Nouns are typically invariable, though there is a small group of nouns that distinguish number through suffixation, as in *muhé* 'woman' (< Sp. *mujer*) / *muhe-re* 'woman-PL' (< Sp. *mujeres*) (Schwegler 2013a:185). There is an optional plural marker *ma*:[205]

(376) ma ombe bieho sibirí nu
PL man old serve NEG
'(The/these) Old men are useless.' (Schwegler 2013a:185)

Case and gender are not relevant categories, though natural gender is commonly expressed with *hembra* 'female' and *barón* 'male' (as in *moná hembra* 'girl', lit. 'child female' and *moná barón* 'boy', lit. 'child male'; Schwegler 2013a:185). There is no definite article but there is an optional indefinite article *un* 'a', which is identical to the numeral 'one':

(377) a. un muhé bonito ta aí loyo
one woman pretty be there creek
'A pretty woman is at the creek.' (Schwegler 2013a:185)
b. mahaná sí asé kombedsá de un fomma
children 2SG.OBL HAB converse of one way
'Your children converse in one way.' (Schwegler & Green 2007:280)

There are the demonstratives *e(se)* 'this/these' and *aké* 'that/those', which usually precede the noun, but which may follow the noun, indicating semantico-pragmatic nuances (e.g. the pejorative).

(378) a. ese ma ombre e k'era ombre kasao
DEM.PROX PL man COP man married
'These men were married men.'
b. aké lentó hué grande
DEM.DIST (fish) COP big
'That lentó (type of fish) is/was big.' (Schwegler & Green 2007:293)

Nominal possession may be indicated through juxtaposition only or with the possessive marker *(r)i/(d)i/(d)e*. Possessive pronouns follow the noun (cf. also (377b)).

205. For a thorough discussion on the use and context of *ma*, see Schwegler (2007).

(379) a. á pesé-a karabelo pelo
look.like-PST skull dog
'They looked like dog's skulls.' (Schwegler & Green 2007: 285)

b. moná lo ke sabé fecha e tat' ele ta aí
child REL know date POSS father 3SG.S COP there
'The child who knows the father's birthday over there.'
(Schwegler & Green 2007: 285)

c. i tan buká ma ngaína mi
1SG.S go look.for PL chicken 1SG.OBL
'I am going to look for my chickens.' (Schwegler 2013a: 185)

The pronominal system distinguishes between three persons and two numbers:

	PERSONAL		OBJECTIVE/POSSESSIVE
	INDEPENDENT	DEPENDENT	
1SG	*yo*	*i*	*mi*
2SG	*bo / (u)té*	*o*	*sí*
3SG	*ele*	*e*	*ele*
1PL	*(s)uto/(ma) hende*	–	*suto/hende*
2PL	*utere/enú*	–	*utere*
3PL	*ele/ané*	–	*ané*

There is no gender distinction in the third person. Notice that the second persons distinguish for number. The dependent personal pronouns may co-occur with the independent ones; they are not obligatory to the clause if context has disambiguated person and number. Independent pronominal possessors are identical to the objective/possessive pronouns preceded by the possessive marker *ri* (as in *ri mi* 'mine', *ri sí* 'yours', etc.).

Adjectives are most commonly invariant and typically follow the noun. Comparison is marked with *má … ke* 'more … than'.

(380) a. ele kelé komblá ese kasa blanko
3SG.S want buy DEM.PROX house white
'S/He wants to buy this white house.' (Schwegler 2013a: 185)

b. eso ndá-ba Palenge má fuedza ke Malagana
DEM.PROX give-PST Palenque more strong than Malagana
'This made Palenque stronger than Malagana.' (Schwegler & Green 2007: 288)

Palenquero has several overt tense, aspect and mood markers: *tan* (future), *tan-ba* (future of the past); *a* (past perfective), *-ba* (past imperfective),[206] *ta* (progressive), *-ndo* (progressive), *ta-ba/ ta …-ba* (past progressive), *asé/sabé* (habitual/iterative), *asé-ba/sabé-ba* or *asé …-ba/sabé …-ba* (past habitual/iterative); *aké* (hypothetical), *aké-ba* (counterfactual). Lexical aspect affects the reading of the clause in that zero marked dynamic verbs imply a habitual or iterative reading,

206. This collapses the functions past habitual, past iterative and past progressive, all of which are denoted by the suffix *-ba* (cf. Schwegler 2013a: 187).

which stative verbs do not. Imperatives are distinguished between singular and plural in that the bare form is used for the singular, while in the plural *-enu/-eno* (the second person plural pronoun) is suffixed to a truncated form of the verb. Negative commands take the same word order as positive commands.

(381) a. ¡bitto, kitá ri kaa mi, ombra!
PN leave from face 1SG.OBL man
'Victor, get out of my face, man!'
b. ¡kamin-enu!
walk.IMP-2PL.S
'Walk!'
c. ¡min-eno nu!
come.IMP-2PL.S NEG
'Don't come!' (Schwegler 2013a: 188)

The word order is typically subject-verb-object. There is an invariant negator *nu*, which may occur both pre- and post verbally, as well as doubled (which is the most frequent strategy):

(382) e nu fue bueno / e nu fue bueno nu / e fue bueno nu
it NEG COP good
'It was/is not good.' (Schwegler 2013a: 188)

Interrogatives have the same word order as declaratives. Polar questions are marked through intonation. In content questions the interrogative phrase tends to be fronted.

(383) a. ¿bo a kottá bo memo?
2SG.S PST cut 2SG.S self
'Did you cut yourself?'
b. ¿ke kusa bo a asé?
what 2SG.S PST do
'What did you do?' (Schwegler & Green 2007: 301)

There is no passive voice. There are several copulas, which are obligatory to the clause: *é*, *fue/fwé/hwé/we* and *era* are used for permanent conditions, while *ta* is used for temporary conditions and is commonly used as a locative copula:

(384) a. papa mi hwe pekaró
father 1SG.OBL COP fisherman
'My father is a fisherman.' (Schwegler & Green 2007: 289)
b. ¡eso ta gueno!
DEM.PROX COP good
'This is good!' (Schwegler 2013b: feature 74)
c. Rosalío ta lendro monte.
PN COP in field
'Rosalio is in the field.' (Schwegler 2013b: feature 75)

There are the coordinating conjunctions *i* 'and', *pero/pelo* 'but' and *o* 'or'. There are no serial verb constructions. Relative clauses are most commonly marked with the relativizer *lo ke* or (less commonly) *i*, though gapping is also possible:

(385) a. ma kusa lo ke ta aí
PL thing REL COP there
'The things that are over there.' (Schwegler 2013a: 189)

b. i a kohé kafé tinto i Lole a asé
1SG.S PST take coffee black REL PN PST make
'I took the coffee that Lole made.'
(Schwegler 2013b: feature 93 citing de Friedemann & Patiño Rosselli 1983: 177)

c. ¿planda hué uté ta yebá?
banana COP 2SG.S PROG bring
'Bananas is (what) you are bringing?' (Schwegler 2013a: 189)

12.4.3.3 *Short text*

(The Lord's Prayer, from Paulo 2000: 15, with slight modifications by Armin Schwegler)

Tatá sí lo ke ta riba sielo // santifikaro sendá nombre sí // miní a reino
father 2SG.S REL COP up heaven blessed COP name 2SG.OBL come there kingdom

sí // asé Ño bolunta sí // aí tiela kumo aí sielo. // Nda suto agüé
2SG.OBL make Lord will 2SG.OBL there earth how there heaven give 1PL today

pan ri tó ma ría // peddoná ma fatta suto // asina kumo suto asé peddoná //
bread from all PL day forgive PL fault 1PL this.way how 1PL HAB forgive

lo ke se fattá suto. // Nu rejá suto kaí andí tentasió nu // librá suto ri má. //
REL HAB fault 1PL NEG make 1PL fall where temptation NEG free 1PL from bad

Amén.

'Our Father in heaven // hallowed be your name // Your kingdom come // your will be done, on earth as it is in heaven // Give us today our daily bread // Forgive us our sins, as we forgive those who sin against us // Lead us not into temptation // but deliver us from evil. // Amen.'

12.4.3.4 *Some sources of data*

Primary data for Palenquero is rather scarce. Armin Schwegler's many publications include numerous examples, most of them glossed and translated (e.g. Schwegler & Green 2007, Schwegler 2013a, the latter of which also contains a longer dialogue; see also Schwegler 2013b for a number of glossed and translated examples online). A book of prayers was translated into Palenquero in 2000 by Father Pedro Antonio Paulo, which is available online at http://issuu.com/secretaria_cepac/docs/misa_andi_lengua_ri_palenque_katajena_21mayoo, accessed 12 February 2015.

12.5 Summary

Pidgins seem less likely than non-pidgins to have tense, mood and aspect marking. Pidgins also seem more likely than non-pidgins to allow a zero copula in predicative noun phrases as well as in predicative adjectives. Adjectives are not commonly encoded as verbs in pidgin languages.

It seems very common indeed for extended pidgins (pidgincreoles) to have tense, aspect and mood marking. A zero copula is possible for a number of extended pidgins, though it is not uncommon for copulas to be obligatory with predicative noun phrases. With predicative adjectives a zero copula is more common; in most cases this is because the adjective is encoded as a verb.

The absolute majority of creole languages have tense, aspect and mood marking. Furthermore, the absolute majority have more than one tense, aspect and mood marker, thus not conforming to the proposed prototypical creole tense/mood/aspect system. Moreover, the proposed internal ordering of the markers as tense-mood-aspect is a feature which does not apply for the absolute majority of creoles, again in contrast to the proposed creole prototype. However, in accordance with the proposed creole prototype, creoles tend to have different temporal readings of the same form of the verb depending on its lexical aspect. As for predication, creoles do not pattern differently from non-creoles with respect to zero copulas with noun phrase predication. Creoles do tend to have zero copulas with predicative adjectives; in many cases this is because the adjective is encoded as a verb, though creoles seem slightly less likely to allow verbal encoding on adjectives than non-creoles.

Mixed languages typically reflect the system of one of the input languages or a blend of the input systems, both with respect to the tense, aspect and mood marking, and with respect to predication.

12.6 Key points

- **The assumption that pidgins tend to lack tense, aspect and mood marking as well as the copula is supported by the samples studied here.**
- **Extended pidgins (pidgincreoles) tend to have tense, aspect and mood marking.**
- **Extended pidgins (pidgincreoles) do not exhibit any particular pattern with respect to noun phrase predication, but tend to lack adjective predication (in several cases because the adjective is a stative verb).**
- **Mixed languages tend to take over the tense, aspect and mood marking, as well as the predication, from one of the input languages or to represent a blend of the input languages.**
- **The assumption that creoles have one tense marker, one mood marker and one aspect marker that combine in that order is not supported by the samples studied here.**
- **The assumption that creoles lack the copula and that creole adjectives tend to be stative verbs is not supported by the samples studied here.**
- **The assumption that the lexical aspect affects the reading of the clause in creole languages is supported by the samples studied here.**

12.7 Exercises

1. Do extended pidgins (pidgincreoles) align more closely with pidgins or with creoles with respect to tense, mood and aspect and with respect to non-verbal predication?
2. What are the implications of the findings on creole tense, mood and aspect systems?
3. Is it possible to predict the source of the tense, mood and aspect system in a mixed language? Motivate your answer and give examples.
4. How do the findings on creole non-verbal predication relate to the notion of creoles as typologically unique languages?
5. Is it possible to predict the source of the structure of non-verbal predication in a mixed language? Motivate your answer and give examples.

Languages cited in Chapter 13

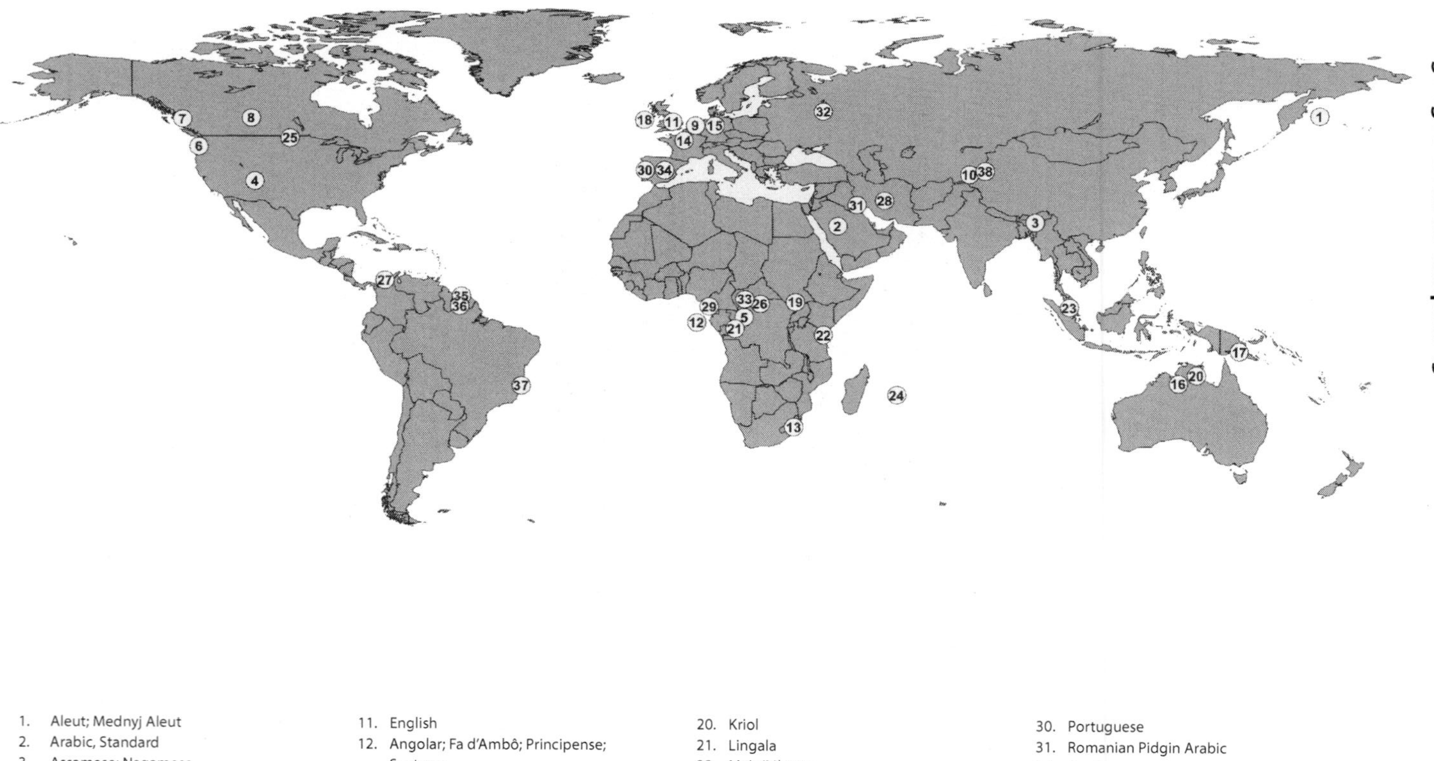

1. Aleut; Mednyj Aleut
2. Arabic, Standard
3. Assamese; Nagamese
4. Bilingual Navajo; Navajo
5. Bobangi
6. Chinook
7. Chinuk Wawa
8. Cree, Plains
9. Dutch
10. Ejnu
11. English
12. Angolar; Fa d'Ambô; Principense; Santome
13. Fanakalo; Zulu
14. French
15. German, Standard
16. Gurindji; Gurindji Kriol
17. Hiri Motu; Motu
18. Irish; Shelta
19. Juba Arabic
20. Kriol
21. Lingala
22. Ma'a/Mbugu
23. Malay
24. Mauritian Creole
25. Michif
26. Ngbandi
27. Palenquero
28. Persian
29. Pichi
30. Portuguese
31. Romanian Pidgin Arabic
32. Russian
33. Sango
34. Spanish
35. Ndyuka-Trio Pidgin; Nengee; Sranan
36. Trio
37. Tupinambá
38. Uyghur

Chapter 13

Simple sentences

Both pidgins and creoles are described as having fixed subject-verb-object word order and lacking passive constructions. Mixed languages are assumed to either have adopted the system of one of the input languages, or to represent a blend of the two input languages. This chapter will empirically test whether pidgin and creole languages differ from non-pidgins and non-creoles with respect to dominant word order, as well as briefly discuss word order in extended pidgins (pidgincreoles) and mixed languages (Section 13.2). Section 13.3 empirically tests whether pidgins and creoles differ from non-pidgins and non-creoles with respect to passive constructions, and gives a short discussion on passive constructions in extended pidgins (pidgincreoles) and mixed languages. Section 13.4 gives short sketches of three languages mentioned in the chapter: Ndyuka-Trio Pidgin (a Nengee/Tiriyó-lexified pidgin in Suriname), Fa d'Ambô (a Portuguese-lexified creole in Equatorial Guinea) and Mednyj Aleut (an Aleut/Russian mixed language on Bering Island).

13.1 Introduction

Clauses consist of a **predicate** and the **arguments** of that predicate. The predicate is usually a verb phrase, which establishes the structure of the clause, while the arguments are usually noun phrases, which fill the structural slots set by the verb. Different verbs demand a different amount of participants; arguments (also called **core participants**) are obligatory to make the clause grammatical, while **adjuncts** (also called **peripheral participants**) are optional. An **intransitive verb** demands one argument, as in *Mary walked*, where the subject (*Mary*) is the argument of the verb; leaving out the subject would not be grammatically acceptable in Standard English (cf. *___*walked*). A sentence like *Mary walked to the park* contains one argument (*Mary*) and one adjunct (*to the park*), where the non-obligatory constituent, the adjunct, may be left out without making the sentence ungrammatical (cf. *Mary walked*, where *to the park* has been left out). A **transitive verb** demands two arguments, a subject and an object, as in *Mary bought a book*; both arguments are necessary for the clause to be grammatical (cf. *___*bought a book* or **Mary bought*___). A **ditransitive verb** demands three arguments for the clause to be grammatical, as in *Mary gave Peter a book*; removing any of the arguments would normally not be acceptable (cf. *___*gave a book to Peter* / **Mary gave Peter* ___ /??*Mary gave* ___ *a book*).

Clauses may have different grammatical **voice** (also called **diathesis**), which, very simplified, states the semantic role of the subject in the clause. In the **active voice** the subject is the agent or actor of the event (as in *Mary opened the door*, where *Mary* is the active entity and *the door* is the passive entity to which something happens), while in the **passive voice** the subject is the patient, recipient or benefactive of the event (as in *The door was opened*, where *the door* is now the subject, but retains the semantic role of patient).

13.2 Word order

The way clause constituents are ordered may be relatively fixed or relatively free. English is an example with a fixed ordering of constituents, i.e. has a rigid word order, because the syntactic roles of the constituents in the clause are determined by the order in which they appear: the subject comes before the verb and the object comes after it. In a sentence like *The man phoned the woman*, we know that *the man* is the subject and *the woman* the object in the clause because of their relative positioning to the verb. If we swap the positions the clause gets a different meaning: *The woman phoned the man* automatically means that it was the woman who did something (i.e. *the woman* is the subject).

Theoretically there may be six types of word order involving the subject (S), object (O) and verb (V): SVO, SOV, VSO, VOS, OVS and OSV. It should be noted that not all languages have a rigid word order. Languages with case systems, for example, are able to indicate the syntactic roles of the constituents by other means than word order (for example, subjects are in the nominative and objects in the accusative). Other languages order their constituents according to other criteria, for example pragmatic roles (such as whether the information is new, i.e. is focussed, or is already known, i.e. is a topic), rather than the syntactic roles of subject and object. These are sometimes labelled languages with 'free' word order (or with no dominant word order).

This section will compare the word order in a selection of pidgin and creole languages with the languages in Dryer's (2013f) sample, as well as bring up word order in extended pidgins (pidgincreoles) and mixed languages. It should be noted that it is the dominant word order that is considered here; if a language has variable word order, but where, for example, SVO is stated as occurring in the majority of cases, the language will be listed as having SVO word order. It should also be noted that if a language differs with respect to the word order between clauses containing only full noun phrases (as in *The man phoned the woman*) as opposed to when one or both of the noun phrases are pronominal (as in *He phoned the woman*, *The man phoned her* or *He phoned her*), the language has been coded according to the word order of the clauses with full noun phrases.

It is beyond the scope of this section to give a detailed discussion on the full complexity of constituent order in the languages of the world. For more on word order typology, see, for example, Song (2009) and (2010).

13.2.1 Word order in pidgin languages

Pidgins are usually described as having a fixed word order, most commonly SVO (cf. Mühlhäusler 1997:145). Romanian Pidgin Arabic, for example, has this word order:

Romanian Pidgin Arabic (Pidgin (Arabic-lexified): Iraq)

(386)	pipol	rumani	drink	mai	tumatʃ
	people	Romanian	drink	water	much
	S		V	O	

'We, Romanians, drink much water.' (Avram 2010:24)

In (386) the subject (*pipol rumani*) comes before the verb (*drink*) and the object (*mai*) comes after the verb. A number of pidgins, however, have SOV word order, such as Ndyuka-Trio Pidgin:

Ndyuka-Trio Pidgin (Pidgin (Ndyuka/Tiriyó-lexified): Suriname)

(387)	Tano	mati	ondoo	kolu	so	teke
	PN	partner	100	guilder	?	take
	S		O			V

'Tano's partner took 100 guilders.' (Huttar & Velantie 1997:105)

In (387) the subject (*Tano mati*) precedes the object (*ondoo kolu*) and the verb (*teke*) is clause-final. It should be noted that the respective word orders may reflect the word orders in the lexifiers: Arabic, for example, has SVO word order, while Tiriyó has SOV (for more on Ndyuka-Trio, see 13.4.1). The two pidgins above do thus not deviate from their lexifiers in their constituent order.

In order to compare whether pidgin languages tend to have a different kind of word order than non-pidgins, I compared the current pidgin sample with Dryer's (2013f) sample. The figures are summarized in Table 13.1.

As can be seen in Table 13.1, there are no verb-initial languages at all in the pidgin sample and no languages with OVS order, categories that are uncommon also in the WALS sample. More than half of the pidgin languages have SVO word order, but a fair number have SOV; this differs somewhat from the WALS languages, where the SOV group is bigger than the SVO group.[207]

207. Due to the many empty cells in the pidgin sample in Table 13.1, the chi-square is not reliable. When conflating the categories to 'SVO', 'SOV', 'Other' and 'No dominant order' the result is only marginally statistically significant: $\chi^2 = 6.40$; $df = 3$; $p_{\text{two-tailed}} = 0.094$; $p_{\text{sim}} = 0.088$ and $G^2 = 6.51$; $df = 3$;

Table 13.1 Dominant word order in the current pidgin sample and in WALS (Dryer 2013f). For a full legend of the languages in the pidgin sample, see http://dx.doi.org/10.1075/cll.48.additional.

	Pidgin sample		WALS	
	N	%	N	%
SVO	19	54.3	488	35.4
SOV	10	28.6	565	41.0
VSO	–	–	95	6.9
VOS	–	–	25	1.8
OSV	1	2.9	4	0.3
OVS	–	–	11	0.8
ND	5	14.3	189	13.7
Total	35		1377	

As shown above, the constituent order of the pidgin may follow that of the lexifier, which means that the dominance of SVO could be because many of the lexifiers also have SVO order. I therefore compared the pidgins with their lexifiers with respect to dominant word order. Table 13.2 summarizes the figures:

Table 13.2 Comparison of dominant word order in the current pidgin sample with the lexifiers. For a full legend of the languages in the pidgin sample, see http://dx.doi.org/10.1075/cll.48.additional.

	N	%
Word order is the same as in the lexifier	21	60
Word order is not the same as in the lexifier	14	40
Total	35	

($\chi^2 = 1.4$; $df = 1$; $p_{\text{two-tailed}} = 0.24$, $p_{\text{sim}} = 0.32$ (B = 10,000))
($G = 1.3$; $df = 1$; $p_{\text{two-tailed}} = 0.24$)

As shown in Table 13.2 it is somewhat more common for the languages in the pidgin sample to have the same word order as their lexifier than not; however, it should be noted that this distribution is not statistically significant.

$p_{\text{two-tailed}} = 0.089$, with SVO being somewhat overrepresented in the pidgin sample. However, even the latter values should be taken with caution, as 2 out of 8 cells (25%) have an expected frequency of less than 5.

13.2.2 Word order in extended pidgins (pidgincreoles)

All ten extended pidgins in the sample have the same word order as their lexifiers. In eight cases that means SVO, while Nagamese and Hiri Motu have SOV word order, matching that of their lexifiers (Assamese and Motu respectively). Hiri Motu is an example of a language where the word order differs depending on the type of noun phrase: full noun phrases are SOV, but if one of the noun phrases is a pronoun, the order tends to be OSV. Compare the following:

Hiri Motu (Extended pidgin (Motu-lexified): Papua New Guinea)

(388) a. sisia ese boroma ia itaia
dog pig he it see
S O V
'The dog saw the pig.'

b. lau be sisia ia itaia
I FOC dog it see
O S V
'The dog saw me.'

c. sisia lau itaia
dog I see
O S V
'I saw the dog.'

d. oi lau itaia
you I see
O S V
'I saw you.' (Dutton 1997: 30)

Example (388) shows how the word order in Hiri Motu tends to be SOV with full noun phrases, while pronouns tend to trigger an OSV word order. This differs from the lexifier Motu, which has SOV word order for both types of noun phrases (Lawes 1888).

13.2.3 Word order in creole languages

Creoles are also often described as having SVO word order (cf. Bartens 2013a: 126). Fa d'Ambô is an example of such a language:

Fa d'Ambô (Creole (Portuguese-lexified): Equatorial Guinea)

(389) mai laba mina sunzu
mother wash child dirty
S V O
'The mother washed the dirty child.' (Post 2013a: feature 1)

It should be noted that the dominant word order of SVO in Fa d'Ambô as shown in Example (389) matches that of its lexifier (Portuguese; for more on Fa d'Ambô, see 13.4.2). In fact this is by far the most common word order in the current creole sample, as shown in Table 13.3:

Table 13.3 Dominant word order in the current creole sample and in WALS (Dryer 2013f). For a full legend of the languages in the creole sample, see http://dx.doi.org/10.1075/cll.48.additional.

	Creole sample		WALS*	
	N	%	N	%
SVO	49	92.5	487	35.4
SOV	1	1.9	565	41.1
VSO	3	5.7	95	6.9
VOS	–		25	1.8
OSV	–		4	0.3
OVS	–		11	0.8
ND	–		189	13.7
Total	53		1376	

* Ndyuka (Nengee) has been removed from the WALS sample to avoid overlap.

Table 13.3 summarizes the distribution of word order in the current creole sample and in Dryer's (2013f) sample. The distribution varies considerably: almost all of the creoles have SVO word order, while only about a third of the WALS languages have that order. This could possibly be due to the fact that all of the lexifiers have SVO word order, except Dutch, German, Malay and Tupinambá, which do not have any dominant word order. I therefore compared the creole languages with their lexifier with respect to dominant word order. Table 13.4 summarizes the figures:

Table 13.4 Comparison of dominant word order in the current creole sample with the lexifiers. For a full legend of the languages in the creole sample, see http://dx.doi.org/10.1075/cll.48.additional.

	N	%
Word order is the same as in the lexifier	44	83
Word order is not the same as in the lexifier	9	17
Total	53	

($\chi^2 = 23.1132$; $df = 1$; $p_{\text{two-tailed}} < 0.001$***, $p_{\text{sim}} < 0.001$*** (B = 10,000))
($G = 24.946$; $df = 1$; $p_{\text{two-tailed}} < 0.001$***)

As shown in Table 13.4, the absolute majority of the creole languages in the sample have the same word order as their lexifier languages; this distribution is highly significant statistically and may thus indicate that creole languages are likely to take over the constituent order of their lexifier languages.

13.2.4 Word order in mixed languages

Mixed languages typically inherit the word order of one of the input languages. If both input languages have the same word order, the mixed language is likely to have that order too, as is the case in Ejnu, which has an SOV word order just like both Uyghur and Persian.

Ejnu (Mixed language (Uyghur/Persian): China)

(390)	pedir-im	hatta-din	jɛk	saŋ	atɛʃ	yndi
	father-1SG	market-ABL	one	stone	fire	came
	S		O			V

'My father brought a flint-stone from the market.' (Lee-Smith 1996a: 860)

More commonly, however, the input languages have different word orders, one of which carries over to the mixed language, typically that order found in the language which has contributed most of the grammar and structure. Shelta is an example of such a language, which has the SVO order also found in English, as opposed to the VSO order of the other contributing language, Irish (for more on Shelta, see 11.4.3).

Shelta (Mixed language (English/Irish): Ireland)

(391)	tom	kamʲra	ʃur-al	gʲami	gri:taθ
	big	dog	run-NMLZ	bad	sickness
	S		V	O	

'The big racing dog has some bad sickness.' (Macalister 1937: 161f)

Example (391) shows the SVO word order of Shelta, a G-L mixed language which has most of its structure from English. Similarly, Bilingual Navajo has most of its structure from Navajo and has taken over the word order of Navajo, where pragmatic roles (topic and focus) determine the order and not syntactic roles (subject and object) (Schaengold 2004).

Mednyj Aleut is an example of a mixed language where the word order might represent an innovation: Aleut, one of the input languages, has a predominantly SOV word order, while Russian, the other input language, has a predominantly SVO word order, but Mednyj Aleut itself has a free word order (Thomason 1997b; for more on Mednyj Aleut, see 13.4.3).

13.3 Passive constructions

A passive construction reduces the number of obligatory participants in a clause by promoting the object of a transitive clause to subject status, while demoting the subject to an adjunct status. That is, in a transitive clause like *The dog bit the man*, we have the subject *the dog* and the object *the man*. A passive construction like *The man was bitten by the dog* promotes the object to subject status (*the man* is now the subject of the clause), and demotes the original subject (*the dog*) to a non-obligatory constituent, an adjunct, which may be left out without rendering the clause ungrammatical: a sentence like *The man was bitten*, without the adjunct *by the dog*, is also acceptable.

This section will check whether passive constructions can be found in pidgin and creole languages, as well as discuss passive constructions in extended pidgins (pidgin-creoles) and mixed languages. It will also check whether creoles differ from non-creoles with respect to the absence or presence of passive constructions. It is beyond the scope of the section to adequately discuss the types of passive constructions that can be found in the languages of the world. For a detailed discussion on grammatical voice, see Klaiman (1991). For detailed and accessible discussions on the passive voice, see, for example, Keenan & Dryer (2007) and Siewierska (1984), the latter a classic by now.

13.3.1 Passive constructions in pidgin languages

Pidgin languages are usually described as lacking any passive construction (cf. Sebba 1997:39). Chinuk Wawa is an example of a pidgin which does not have any passive construction:

Chinuk Wawa (Pidgin (Chinook-lexified): Canada, USA)

(392) kámuks mákmak sáplil
dog eat bread
'The dog eats bread.' OR 'The bread was eaten by the dog.' (Grant 2013b: feature 90)

The sentence in (392) can be translated either in the active or passive voice. However, there are pidgin languages that do have passive constructions. In Fanakalo, for example, the passive voice is indicated with the suffixes *-wa* (present tense) or *-iwe* (past tense):

Fanakalo (Pidgin (Zulu-lexified): South Africa)

(393) lo skafu yena phek-iwe (ga lo Jane)
DEF food it cook-PASS AG DEF PN
'The food was cooked (by Jane).' (Mesthrie 2013: feature 90)

In (393) the suffix *-iwe* indicates that the clause is in a passive voice.

While the current pidgin sample is too small for any statistical analyses, it should be noted that six of 13 languages do have some form of passive, while the remaining seven do not.

13.3.2 Passive constructions in extended pidgins (pidgincreoles)

Among the eight extended pidgins in the current sample, all the English-lexified ones lack passive constructions. Juba Arabic forms passive through word-final stress:

Juba Arabic (Extended pidgin (Arabic-lexified): Sudan)

(394) bi=dabaó gánam bad dabaó gánam kalás
IRR=slaughter.PASS goat after slaughter.PASS goat finished
'A goat is slaughtered, after it has been slaughtered, all is over.'
(Manfredi & Petrollino 2013b: feature 90)

The verb *dába* 'slaughter' is marked with the word-final stress in Example (394) (*dabaó*), rendering the clause passive. For more on Juba Arabic, see 15.4.1.

In Sango the passive is expressed by separating the subject marker from the verb:

Sango (Extended pidgin (Ngbandi-lexified): Central African Republic)

(395) lo sara ni na ngangu so a mu na lo
3SG do DET PREP strength REL PM.PASS give PREP 3SG
'She did it with the power that was given to her.' (Samarin 2013b: feature 90)

In (395) the subject marker *a-* has been separated from the verb *mu* 'give'; the free form marks the passive voice. In Nagamese the passive is formed by fronting the object:

Nagamese (Extended pidgin (Assamese-lexified): India)

(396) gos-tu maiki pora kat-ise
tree-DEF girl by cut-PST
'The tree was cut by the girl.' (Bhattacharjya 2007: 246)

While in Nagamese in an active declarative the subject would have appeared before the object, the passive is indicated by placing the object clause-initially, as shown in Example (396). For more on Nagamese, see 8.3.1.

13.3.3 Passive constructions in creole languages

Creole languages are also usually described as lacking the passive voice (cf. Bartens 2013a: 107). This is, for example, the case in Palenquero (see 12.4.3). However, there are a number of creoles that do have the passive voice in some form. In Lingala, for example, the passive is expressed with the suffix *-ám*:

Lingala (Creole (Bobangi-lexified): Congo, DR Congo)

(397) papá a-kund-ám-áki na bandeko
father 3SG-bury-PASS-PST by family.member
'The father was buried by the family members.' (Meeuwis 2013b: feature 90)

Example (397) shows a passive construction in Lingala with the suffix *-ám*. A number of creoles have passives without any verbal coding, such as in Angolar:

Angolar (Creole (Portuguese-lexified): São Tomé & Principe)

(398) umbatu m laba
clothes my wash
'My clothes were washed.' (Maurer 2013b: feature 90)

The passive construction in (398) lacks any kind of verbal marking and literally means 'My clothes washed', but functions as a passive construction. It is, in fact, more common for creoles to have passive constructions than to lack them, as shown in Table 13.5:

Table 13.5 Passive constructions in the current creole sample. For a full legend of the languages in the creole sample, see http://dx.doi.org/10.1075/cll.48.additional.

	N	%
Passive construction with zero coding	15	28.8
Typical passive construction	16	30.8
Atypical passive construction	1	1.9
Both typical and zero-coded passive construction	6	11.5
No passive construction	14	26.9
Total	52	

($\chi^2 = 16.65$; $df = 4$; $p_{\text{two-tailed}} = 0.0023^{**}$, $p_{\text{sim}} = 0.0022^{**}$ (B = 10,000))
($G = 21.40$; $df = 4$; $p_{\text{two-tailed}} < 0.001^{***}$)

The figures in Table 13.5 show that about a quarter of the creole languages lack a passive construction as defined in Haspelmath & the APiCS Consortium (2013b). In order to test whether creole languages differ from non-creoles with respect to the passive voice, I compared the current creole sample with that in Siewierska (2013). It should be noted that Siewierska's definition of a passive construction is, among other things, that it is marked on the verb somehow (by an affix or an auxiliary). This means that the languages in the creole sample with the value 'Zero coded passive constructions' and 'Atypical passive constructions' would not be categorized as having passive constructions in Siewierska (2013) and have here, for the purpose of comparison, been included in the group 'Passive construction does not exist'. The figures are summarized in Table 13.6:

Table 13.6 Passive constructions in the current creole sample and in WALS (Siewierska 2013). For a full legend of the languages in the creole sample, see http://dx.doi.org/10.1075/cll.48.additional.

	Creole sample		WALS*	
	N	%	N	%
Passive constructions exist	22	42.3	162	43.7
Passive constructions do not exist	30	57.7	209	56.3
Total	52		371	

($\chi^2 = 0.0013$; $df = 1$; $p_{two\text{-}tailed} = 0.97$, Yate's Correction, $p_{sim} = 0.89$ ($B = 10{,}000$))
($G = 0.034$; $df = 1$; $p_{two\text{-}tailed} = 0.85$)
* Mauritian Creole and Ndyuka (Nengee) have been removed from the WALS sample to avoid overlap.

As can be seen in Table 13.6, the proportions of languages that have passive constructions versus those that do not are almost identical in the two databases. This indicates that creoles do not seem to differ from non-creoles with respect to the absence or presence of passives.

13.3.4 Passive constructions in mixed languages

Mixed languages are expected to either adopt the system of one of their input languages or to represent a blend of the input languages. Ma'á/Mbugu is an example of a G-L mixed language that has adopted the passive from one of the input systems, the Bantu system, with the verbal suffix *-w*:

Ma'á/Mbugu (Mixed language (Cushitic/Bantu): Tanzania)

(399) u-ku-dárá-w-e ní luáhe
2SG-COND-catch-PASS-PRF by flu
'You are caught by a flu.' (Mous 2013: 46)

The Ma'á/Mbugu passive marker *-w* in (399) reflects that of the Bantu system, from which most of the grammar stems.

Gurindji Kriol is an example of an N-V mixed language, which has a passive construction derived from Kriol, the input language which has provided most of the verb phrase structure:

Gurindji Kriol (Mixed language (Gurindji/Kriol): Australia)

(400) man i bin ged bait warlaku-nginyi wartan-ta
man 3SG PST get bite dog-ABL hand-LOC
'The man got bitten on the hand by a dog.' (Meakins 2011: 44)

The *get* VERB construction in (400) represents the passive construction in Kriol, however, the agent of the clause (here *a dog*) is inflected with the Gurindji ablative case. For more on Gurindji Kriol, see 9.5.3.

An example of an N-V mixed language which represents a blend of the input systems is Michif, which has several passive constructions. Most of the structure of the verb system derives from Cree.

Michif (Mixed language (French/Cree): Canada, USA)

(401) a. kii-atim-iko-w lii polis
PST-overtake-INV-3 DEF.PL police
'The police overtook him.' OR 'He was overtaken by the police.'
(Bakker 2013b: feature 90, citing Laverdure et al. 1983: 211)

b. kii-atim-ikaashoo-w par lii polis
PST-overtake-PASS-3 by DEF.PL police
'He was overtaken by the police.'
(Bakker 2013b: feature 90, citing Laverdure et al. 1983: 211)

c. namo wihkom-ikaashoo-w
NEG invite-PASS-3
'She had not been invited.' OR 'She was not invited.' (Bakker 2013b: feature 90)

One of the ways to form a passive construction in Michif is with the Cree inverse marker *-iko*, as in (401a), while another way is with the passive marker *-ikaashoo*, as in (401b & c). Notice, however, that the reading is only unambiguously passive in the example with a *by*-construction (as in (401b)), with the French '*par* ...'. For more on Michif, see 3.3.2.

13.4 Snapshots

Pidgins are typically expected to have a fixed word order (specifically subject-verb-object) and to lack passive constructions. Ndyuka-Trio Pidgin is an example of a pidgin language with subject-object-verb word order. There do not seem to be passive constructions.

Creoles are also described as having fixed subject-verb-object word order and as lacking passive constructions. Fa d'Ambo is an example of a creole with that word order and which lacks "true" passive constructions, but where the passive voice is achieved by placing the indefinite pronoun in subject position.

Mixed languages are expected to represent the system of one of the input languages or to represent a blend of both input languages. Mednyj Aleut is an example of a mixed language where the word order is free, as opposed to Aleut, which has subject-object-verb word order and Russian, which has a predominantly subject-verb-object word order. Valency changing devices are derived from Aleut.

13.4.1 Ndyuka-Trio Pidgin: A Nengee/Tiriyó-lexified pidgin in Suriname[208]

13.4.1.1 *A brief background sketch of Ndyuka-Trio Pidgin*

Ndyuka-Trio Pidgin is or was a pidgin language used in southern Suriname between the speakers of the Ndyuka dialect of Nengee (see 2.4.2) and speakers of *Tiriyó* (also called *Trio*), one of the indigenous languages of Suriname. The language is or was called *Alukuyana* 'Wayana' or *Ingii* 'Indian' by the Ndyuka speakers, while it is or was called *Mekolo* 'Negro' by the Wayanas.

The Nengee maroon society, which consists of three separate ethno-linguistic varieties, the Ndyukas, the Alukus and the Pamakas, was formed in the early 1700s by escaped slaves along the Tapanahoni and Marowijne Rivers on the border to French Guiana (Migge 2013a). Here they came into contact with the indigenous Carib population, especially the Tiriyós and, later, the Wayanas. The maroon societies fought the colonial government through organized raids and attacks on plantations. In 1762, however, the Ndyukas signed a peace treaty with the colonial government (Migge 2013a). Based on both linguistic observations made by de Goeje (1908) and on oral history among the Ndyukas, it seems as if trade contact between the Ndyukas and the Tiriyós began shortly after this.

Although trade continued with the Tiriyós, they gradually moved upriver, away from both Nengee and European settlements. A second Carib group, the Wayanas, moved into the area, and is reported to, by the early 20th century, often have acted as middlemen between the Tiriyós and the Maroon societies. The pidgin was thus also used between the Ndyukas and the Wayanas.

Despite the respective names of the language by the various users (see above), all parties seem to recognize that they are using a separate language from those of the respective groups. It is a language that "must be specially learned, usually by observation" (Huttar & Velantie 1997:103), and seems to have been used as a secondary language by all parties. It should be noted that the language does not seem to have been confined to trade situations only; in 1883, for example, Crevaux reports an encounter with a Tiriyó woman who addresses him in the pidgin:

> Apalou went scouting with Yacouman to try to find some people in the area; they soon come back followed by an Indian couple. The woman refused my gifts, and showing me three freshly filled graves, uttered the following words with a solemn look:
>
> "Panakiri ouani oua… A la pikininialele… Nono poti… Echimeu ouaca… Cassava mia oua." ('Whites not wanted… all children dead… (they have been) put in (this) hole… quickly leave… (there is) no cassava to eat')[209] (Crevaux 1883:275f, my translation)

208. This section is based almost exclusively on Huttar & Velantie (1997).

209. "*Apalou est parti en éclaireur avec Yacouman pour tâcher de trouver quelques habitants dans les alentours; ils reviennent bientôt suivis d'un couple d'Indiens. La femme refuse mes presents, et, me montrant trois fosses fraichement comblées, prononce d'un air sombre les paroles suivantes. …*". Translation of Ndyuka-Trio Pidgin utterance from Huttar & Velantie (1997:120); the last part can be taken to mean 'leave right away, don't stay around to eat' (ibid).

Ndyuka trade with the Tiriyós and Wayanas continued to prosper into the 1960s and the pidgin was still in use in the 1970s (Huttar 1983); the Ndyukas especially valued the hunting dogs and game provided by the Tiriyós. Though not confined to men, as shown above, the trade was primarily between one Ndyuka male and one Tiriyó male, who would form a partnership and refer to each other as *mati* 'friend' (Huttar 1983).

The last half century has seen increased travel of the indigenous population to the coastal areas, which has led to a gradual reduction of the trade along the river as well as a gradual spread in use of Sranan. While reports from the end of the 20th century indicated that the pidgin was still used between the Ndyukas on the one hand and Tiriyós and Wayanas on the other, for both trade and general conversation, the language seems to be in decline, possibly even moribund: already in the late 1990s "many Ndyuka men in their 30s (perhaps even older) and younger do not know it" (Huttar & Velantie 1997:103).

13.4.1.2 *A short linguistic sketch of Ndyuka-Trio Pidgin*

Ndyuka-Trio Pidgin had 15 consonants, /p, b, m, w, t, d, n, s, l, ɲ, ʃ, j, k, g, ŋ/, and five vowels, /i, e, a, o, u/. Syllable structure could be moderately complex, with clusters of up to two consonants in the onset but none in the coda. There are possible indications of contrastive tone, such as the pairs *nóno* 'No!' versus *nonó* 'hole, ground', which differed in pitch only.

The morphology seems to have been predominantly analytic, though there seems to have been some reduplication.

The noun was invariant with no overt marking for number, gender or case:

(402) a. pinyeke fumi panali teki
peccary 1SG ear take
'I hear some peccaries.' (Huttar 1983:4)
b. mekolo mati fosi ye
negro friend first EXCLAM
'Long ago the blacks became our friends indeed!' (Huttar & Velantie 1997:106)

There do not seem to have been any articles:

(403) a. tide tuna munu
today water big
'The river is high now.'
b. pumi tata mati so apukuta teke
1SG father friend ? paddle take
'My father gave his friend a paddle.' (Huttar & Velantie 1997:105f)

There was no separate demonstrative (the third person singular was used for such functions):

(404) disi fumi kanawa
3SG 1SG boat
'This/It is my boat.' (Huttar 1983:5)

Invariant pronominal forms for the singular are known: *fumi/pumi* 'I, me, my', *fij(u)/pij(u)* 'you, your', *disi* 's/he, it'.

Possession was indicated through juxtaposition only:

(405) a. Tano mati baakoto so silon wa
PN friend house ? EXIST NEG
'Tano's partner has no dogs at his house.' (Huttar 1983: 6)
b. peade so piyu kalala silon
where ? 2SG bead EXIST
'Where are your beads?' (Huttar & Velantie 1997: 108)

Adjectives were invariant.

(406) disi dili mama
3SG expensive very
'It's too expensive.' (Huttar & Velantie 1997: 110)

The verb was invariant and not marked for any tense, mood or aspect, which was inferred through context or with adverbials.

(407) a. mékolo so grandwei tlio akoloni brudu miang
negro ? long.ago Tiriyó ACCOMP blood ingest
'Long ago the blacks drank blood with the Tiriyós [to take an oath].'
(Huttar & Velantie 1997: 106)
b. kaikushi mofu so taki
dog mouth ? talk
'The dog is barking.' (de Goeje 1908: 212)
c. tide pumi apataya piyu silipi ye
today 1SG village 2SG sleep EXCLAM
'Tonight you'll stay in my village!' (Huttar & Velantie 1997: 105)

The word order was typically subject-object-verb for clauses with full noun phrases. If, however, the subject was a pronoun, the object was fronted, giving an object-subject-verb order:

(408) a. kaikushi pumi wani wa
dog 1SG want NEG
'I don't want dogs.'
b. disi pumi luku
3SG 1SG see
'I see him.' (Huttar & Velantie 1997: 105)

There was an invariant negator *wa*:

(409) kaikushi silon wa
dog EXIST NEG
'There are no dogs here.' (Huttar & Velantie 1997: 110)

Polar questions were distinguished through rising intonation only:

(410) a. walapa sale
bow bring
'I brought bows.'
b. walapa sale?
bow bring
'Did you bring any bows?' (Huttar & Velantie 1997: 107)

In content questions the interrogative phrase could either be fronted or remain *in situ*:

(411) a. sama piyu akoloni kon?
INTERROG 2SG with come
'With whom did you come?' / 'Who came with you?'
b. piyu sama so sale?
2SG INTERROG ? bring
'What did you bring [to sell]?' (Huttar & Velantie 1997:107f)

There was no copula:

(412) a. panakiri granwee mati wa, tidei yenulu luku
white.man long.ago friend NEG now eye see
'Long ago the whites were not our friends, now [you] see [them before you as friends].'
b. piyu moime ye
2SG good EXCLAM
'You're great!' (Huttar & Velantie 1997:106, 108)

Coordination as well as subordination was indicated through juxtaposition only:

(413) a. tlio akoloni, mekolo akoloni kasaba miang
Tiriyó with negro with cassava ingest
'[They] eat cassava with the Tiriyós and the blacks.' (Huttar & Velantie 1997:111)
b. sonten pumi luku kulutu, nóno Agaasi pumi luku wa
maybe 1SG see converse no PN 1SG see NEG
'Maybe if I'd seen Agaasi, we would have talked, but I didn't see him.' (Huttar 1983:6)
c. weju pikinme, pumi kon
sun small 1SG come
'I came as the sun was low.' (de Goeje 1908:207)
d. peade pumi kaikushi piyu sale?
where 1SG dog 2SG bring
'Where is my dog that you brought/were to bring?' OR 'Where did you bring my dog?'
(Huttar & Velantie 1997:109)

13.4.1.3 *Short text*

(From de Goeje 1908:214f. The orthography has been altered to match that in Huttar & Velantie 1997.)

panakiri so kon, pai, moime kon, krashi wa, oli wani wa, pikinini wani wa;
white.man ? come friend good come fight NEG woman want NEG child want NEG

tingene pasi so waka, pampila meki; sabana so munu luku wani, Sipaliwini wani, hesime
only path ? go paper make savanna ? big see want Sipaliwini want quick

pampila poti, tlonbaka; akaba, tlawan kon wa, pasi so atapu. panakiri tinigenee so
paper place return finish other come NEG path ? closed white.man only ?

kon, nóno, moime wa, ala tlio pelele, hesime busi kibri, sontem alele, nono,
come no good NEG all Tiriyó fear quick jungle hide maybe die no

takrume pai!
bad friend

'When the whites came, friend, they came in peace, didn't fight, didn't want women, didn't want children (for slavery). They wanted the Sipaliwini, quickly they drew contracts, returned; that's finished (now), others will not come, the road is closed (it is prohibited to pass there). If only whites came, no, that would not be good, all the Tiriyós would be afraid, and would quickly hide in the jungle, where perhaps they would die – no, that would be bad, friend!'

13.4.1.4 *Some sources of data*

There is very little data available for Ndyuka-Trio Pidgin. Huttar & Velantie (1997) provide numerous glossed and translated examples, based on their own fieldwork as well as the data available in de Goeje (1908). The latter is, however, unfortunately only available to those who read Dutch.

13.4.2 Fa d'Ambô: A Portuguese-lexified creole in Equatorial Guinea[210]

13.4.2.1 *A brief background sketch of Fa d'Ambô*

Fa d'Ambô, by scholars also called *Fa d'Ambu* or *Annobonese*, and called *Annobonense* in Spanish, is spoken by some 5,000 people on the island of Annobón in the Gulf of Guinea, as well as in Malabo, the capital of Equatorial Guinea. The speakers themselves call their language *Fa d'Ambô*. The language belongs to a group of four closely related creoles, the other three being Santome, Angolar (both spoken on the island of São Tomé) and Principense (spoken on the island of Príncipe) (Christofoletti Silveira et al. 2013).

The Gulf of Guinea islands were uninhabited when they were discovered by the Portuguese in 1470. São Tomé was populated almost immediately and was permanently settled in 1493 (Hagemeijer 2013a: 50) by free Portuguese settlers as well as deported Portuguese prisoners, 2,000 deported Spanish Jewish children and free as well as enslaved Africans (Maurer 2013d: 72). During the homestead period, which seems to have lasted until about 1520, most slaves seem to have come from present-day Nigeria, especially the area where Ediod languages are spoken (Hagemeijer 2013a: 50). During this initial phase, each settler was by royal decree granted a female slave, with the purpose of colonizing the island; these women and their children were emancipated in 1515 and 1517 respectively (Hagemeijer 2013a: 50), thus increasing the non-white free population. One of the designations for Santome and its speakers is *forro*, which, in fact, means 'freed slave' (Hagemeijer 2013b: 190). When the island shifted to a plantation economy, the new slaves were mainly imported from the areas of present-day Congo and Angola, where Bantu languages are spoken, and São Tomé became an entrepôt for the transatlantic slave trade (Hagemeijer 2013a: 50). By the time the Bantu-speaking slaves came in large numbers, an early creole was already formed, meaning that the Bantu languages had more of an adstratal than a substratal influence on the language (Hagemeijer 2013b).

Annobón, the smallest of the three Gulf of Guinea islands, was probably settled by slaves from São Tomé, to work on the plantations there. It is therefore likely that Fa d'Ambô is an offshoot of early 16th-century Santome. Because the island is so small, it was never a commercial

210. This section is based primarily on Post (1994) and (2013b).

centre; plantation owners came only sporadically, and occasionally ships would stop over for a short while to restock on fresh water and fruit, and maybe to barter. The islanders thus remained cut off, since the other islands were too far away for them to reach with their canoes (Post 2013b: 81). Fa d'Ambô therefore developed with very little outside influence.

The Portuguese ceded the island to the Spanish in 1771, which does not seem to have affected the development of the language to any large degree. Since 1968 the island belongs to Equatorial Guinea, where the official language is Spanish. On the island of Annobón, Fa d'Ambô is used in almost all contexts, with Spanish only used in formal contexts and in the educational system. Most children are therefore monolingual in Fa d'Ambô until they start school.

The language enjoys a high status and is a source of pride among the speakers. It also enjoys a high status as an identity marker among the diaspora, who are mainly in the capital Malabo. Even so, Spanish influence is now starting to be noticeable, especially among the younger speakers, who tend to code-switch or shift between Fa d'Ambô and Spanish (Post 2013b: 82). This is especially true in the highly multilingual setting of Malabo, where not only Spanish is used as a general vernacular, but also Pichi (an English-lexified creole), and where the Bubi and Fang constitute two other major ethnic groups, which means that children growing up in Malabo are often bi-, tri- or quadrilingual (Post 1994: 192). Most Annobonese men are bilingual, since most of them go to Malabo to work. Bilingualism is not as high for women, many of whom have never left Annobón and have only used Spanish in school (Post 2013b: 81).

Fa d'Ambô is an oral language, and is not used in written form by the speakers, most of whom do know how to read and write in Spanish.

13.4.2.2 *A short linguistic sketch of Fa d'Ambô*

Fa d'Ambô has 24 consonants, /p, b, m, ^{m}b, f, v, t, d, n, ^{n}t, ^{n}d, s, z, l, ʃ, ʧ, ʤ, ɲ, j, k, g, ŋ, ^{n}g, x/ (where s/ʃ and z/ʤ are in complementary distribution), and five vowels, /i, e, a, o, u/. The vowels may be lengthened and nasalized, though vowel length is only rarely phonemic while nasalization is allophonic and occurs when followed by a nasal consonant. There is tone: syllables with long vowels are always pronounced with a rising tone and the following syllable with a high level tone, as in /ˈpa:tu/ (LH-H) 'plate' versus /ˈpatu/ (H-H) 'bird' or /ke:ˈse/ (LH-H) 'to grow up' versus /keˈse/ (H-H) 'to forget' (Post 2013b: 82). However, tone seems not to be relevant except for in the few examples of length differentiation. The syllable structure is typically CV, where in polysyllabic words the last vowel is often dropped. Orthographically /ɲ, ʃ, ʧ, ʤ, j/ are rendered <ñ, sy, tsy, dzy, y> respectively.

There is affixation, reduplication and compounding. Diminutive or argumentative prefixes may be added to the noun, and articles may be prefixed, while demonstratives may be suffixed. Verbs may take the participial suffix *-du*. Reduplication may be full or partial and is iconic in that it gives an intensive, iterative or distributive meaning, as in *gavu* 'good' → *gagavu* 'very good', *fa(la)* 'speak' → *fafal* 'chat' or *bodo* 'edge' → *bódobodo* 'coast' (Post 1994: 196).

Nouns are invariant and are typically not marked for the plural, though plurality may optionally be indicated with a demonstrative, through numerals or quantifiers, or with reduplication.

Natural gender may optionally be indicated with *miela* 'female' / *napay* 'male' (as in *mina miela* 'girl/daughter', lit. 'child female', and *mina napay* 'boy/son', lit. 'child male'; Post 2013b: 83).

There is the optional definite article *na(-)*, which is used both for the singular and the plural and the optional indefinite article *(w)an*:

(414) a. na-may banku
DEF-woman white
'the white woman' (apics83)

b. ba-tela-sai sa baya na-masyivín tisy
dance-land-DEM.PROX.PREST COP dance DEF-youngster three
'These traditional dances are danced by three youngsters.' (Post 1994: 199)

c. Mala xoze wa bluz ku guya
PN sew INDEF.SG shirt with needle
'Mary sews a shirt with a needle.' (Post 2013b: 86)

Demonstratives distinguish between singular and plural, proximal and distal, as well as presentative and absentative:

	PRESENTATIVE		ABSENTATIVE	
	SINGULAR	PLURAL	SINGULAR	PLURAL
PROXIMATE	*(i)sai*	*(i)nen-sai*	*(i)syi*	*(i)nen-syi*
DISTAL	*(i)sala*	*(i)nen-sala*	*(i)ski*	*(i)nen-sky*

The pronominal system distinguishes between dependent (with both subject and object forms, though they differ minimally) and independent pronouns. The possessive pronouns differ minimally from the dependent subject pronouns.

	PERSONAL			POSSESSIVE
	DEPENDENT		INDEPENDENT	
	SUBJECT	OBJECT		
1SG	*(a)m(u)*	*m(u)*	*amu*	*mu*
2SG	*bo*	*bo*	*bo*	*bo*
3SG	*eli/e/i*	*l(i)*	*eli*	*d'eli*
1PL	*no/nõ*	*no/nõ*	*no*	*no*
2PL	*namisedyi/namse*	*namisedyi/namse*	*namisedyi*	*namisedyi*
3PL	*ine(ni)/ineñ*	*ine(ni)/ineñ*	*ine(ni)/ineñ*	*ineni*
INDEF	*a/bo/nge/xa/kuzu*			

Adjectives are invariable and most commonly follow the noun (cf. (414a)). The comparative is formed with *masy(i) ku* 'more/most than' or *pasa* 'to pass', while the superlative is formed with *masyi* 'more/most':

(415) a. meza-i-sai sa ngandyi masy ku i-syki
table-3SG-DEM COP big more CONJ 3SG-DEM
'This table is bigger than that one.'

b. meza-i-sai sa ngandyi pasa i-syki
table-3SG-DEM COP big pass 3SG-DEM
'This table is bigger than that one'

c. iai no te pisyisi ngandyi masyi
here 2PL have fish big most
'We have the biggest fish here.' (Post 2013b: 84)

Verbs are invariant and may optionally combine with the following preverbal tense, mood and/or aspect markers (in the order tense-mood-aspect): *xa/ga* (for nonpunctual realis or evidential), *sa* (for realis), *s(a)xa* (for progressive), *(s)ke* (for irrealis) and *bi* (for anterior).

(416) a. bibi patu-syi na xa lega pa ten li-f
bibi bird-DEM NEG EVID let for have 3SG-NEG
'Bibi is a bird that does not let itself be caught.' (Post 2013b: 86)

b. am na sa mule-f
1SG NEG REAL die-NEG
'I haven't died yet.' / 'I did not die.' (Post 2013b: 85)

c. no sxa fe wan xadyi pa non-tudu
1PL PROG make INDEF house for 1PL-all
'We are making a house for us all (our family).' (Post 1994: 197)

d. bi ske sa gavu masyi mindya xadyi
ANT IRR be good more stay house
'It would have been better to stay at home.' (Post 2013b: 85)

e. bo bi sa na-mina
2SG ANT COP DEF-child
'You were a child.' (Post 2013a: feature 49)

The word order is typically subject-verb-object. Negation is formed with the construction *na … -(a)f(a)*, where *na* reflects the starting point of the negation and *-(a)f(a)* appears sentence-finally, even if the sentence contains a subordinate clause which is not part of the negative scope:

(417) a. amu na po fe-f
1SG NEG can make-NEG
'I am not able to make it.'

b. amu po na fe-f
1SG can NEG make-NEG
'I am able not to make it.'

c. se eli na ngo pa se fa eli sa nge d'Ambu-f
CONJ 3SG NEG want for know speak 3SG COP person of.Annobón-NEG
'And he did not want them to know that he was an Annobonese.' (Post 1994: 197f)

Polar questions are formed through intonation only. In content questions the interrogative phrase is fronted:

(418) a. bo tyana kuma za?
2SG finish eat already
'Have you finished eating?' (Post 2013a: feature 103)

b. xa bo fala?
thing 2SG speak
'What do you say?' (Post 1994: 199)

Passive constructions are rare; a passive voice reading is typically achieved by placing the indefinite pronoun *a* 'someone' in the subject position and placing the semantic subject sentence-finally:

(419) lala fumo~fumozu a xa be ngolo
beach pretty~RED GENER EVID see shell
'Shells can be seen on the gorgeous beach.' (Post 2013b: 87)

There is an optional copula *sa*, which is also used for locative phrases.

There are the coordinating conjunctions *ku* 'and', *mindyi/mandyi* 'but' and *o* 'or'. Relative clauses may be indicated by juxtaposition only, or by the demonstrative *-syi* on the head, or with the complement *ku*, or by both.

(420) a. xadyi no xata-e sa xa tudyia
house 1PL live-ADV COP thing old
'The house that we live in is very old.'

b. amu mata layan-syi bi sa xodyian-mu osasyi
1SG kill spider-DEM ANT COP room-1SG then
'I killed the spider that was in my room.'

c. amu saxa funda ku sa xa me-mu
1SG have packet CONJ COP thing mother-1SG
'I have a packet that is for my mother.'

d. poxodul-nen-syi ku fe vadyi-ai sa na-nge gavu
person-PL-DEM CONJ make trip-ADV COP ART-person good
'The people who travelled are good people.' (Post 1994: 197, 202)

Serial verb constructions are common and have several connotations: directional, locative, benefactive, purposive, resultative, excessive, complementation, iteration, ingressive, terminative and causative.

13.4.2.3 *Short text*

(From Post 1994: 203. The speaker is a 52 year old man who grew up in Annobón but moved to Malabo.)

se amu bila-oio tela-mu Ambu. amu na xonse pe-mu-syi pali mu-f se
CONJ 1SG open-eye land-1SG Annobón 1SG NEG know father-1SG-DEM give.birth 1SG-NEG CONJ

amu sxa ma mavida ku me-mu. se amu sxa ma xa mavida-syi… se… amu
1SG PROG take suffering with mother-1SG CONJ 1SG PROG take FOC suffering-DEM until 1SG

tyila poxodulu amu ga geza ku panu amu ga skuela ku panu na sa
turn adult 1SG EVID church with rag 1SG EVID school with rag NEG COP

mavida-syi-f. amu na suku nge-syi zuda me-mu pa da ma xa pa amu
suffering-DEM-NEG 1SG NEG have person-DEM help mother-1SG for give take thing for 1SG

bisyi-f.
dress-NEG

'I was born in my homeland Annobón. I did not know who my father was and I suffered with my mother. And I suffered so much. Until I grew up I went to church in rags, I went to school in rags. It was a real hard life. I had nobody to help my mother to offer me something to wear.'

13.4.2.4 *Some sources of data*

Primary data of Fa d'Ambô is scarce. Schuchardt (1888b) is an early description of the language available online (http://schuchardt.uni-graz.at/werk/jahr/1888, accessed 13 February 2015), containing a number of examples; unfortunately only accessible to those who read German. Marike Post has published a number of articles on the language, all containing glossed and translated examples, e.g. Post (1994) and (2013b), each of which also contains a short text. Post (2013a) provides numerous glossed and translated examples online. There are a couple of videos in Fa d'Ambô available on YouTube, e.g. a ca. 3 minute long monologue (http://www.youtube.com/watch?v=oeiyghRzcwo, accessed 13 February 2015) and a ca 2 hour long Christian feature film (*The Story of Jesus*, http://www.youtube.com/watch?v=2t_FB6putD4, accessed 13 February 2015).

13.4.3 Mednyj Aleut: A Russian/Aleut mixed language on the Commander Islands[211]

13.4.3.1 *A brief background sketch of Mednyj Aleut*

Mednyi Aleut, also called *Attuan*, *Copper*, *Copper Island Aleut*, *Copper Island Attuan*, *Copper Island Creole*, *Creolized Attuan* and *Medny* by scholars, is a nearly extinct N-V mixed language spoken in the village of Nikolskoye on Bering Island, one of the two Commander Islands in the Russian Bering Sea. Estimates places its emergence around the 1880s or 1890s (Golovko & Vakhtin 1990). In 1996 the number of speakers was estimated to 10–12, all of which had, in the 1960s, moved to Bering Island from the other Commander Island, Copper (Mednyj) Island, whence the language name (Golovko 1996). It is unintelligible to both Russian and Bering Aleut speakers (Golovko 1994).

The Aleutian Islands (including their western extension of the Commander Islands) were "discovered" in 1741 by Vitus Bering, sailing under the Russian flag. Survivors of the expedition brought back seal furs, which led to fur-hunting expeditions and early settlements of Russian fur trappers and traders ('promyshlenniki').[212] In 1797 the Russian-American Company, a state-sponsored chartered company, was granted exclusive rights to the Aleutian Islands, including the Commander Islands. The company established settlements on what was now referred to as the Company's colonies and which was administered by the Company until the 1867, when the USA bought Alaska and the Aleut Islands (excluding the Commander Islands) from Russia.

While the Commander Islands were uninhabited at the time of their "discovery", a number of other Aleutian Islands were not, but the population decreased sharply after the "discovery" of the islands, due to introduced diseases (especially smallpox and venereal diseases) and due to warfare.

Mixed marriages between Aleut women and Russian promyshlenniki followed soon after the expeditions started. In 1826 the Russian-American Company started to settle the Commander Islands with Russian promyshlenniki, Aleuts, and so-called Creoles, in order to set up outposts

211. This section is based primarily on Golovko & Vakhtin (1990), Golovko (1996) and Sekerina (1994). I am very grateful to Anthony Grant for his helpful comments on this snapshot.

212. It should be noted that these promyshlenniki included not only those who spoke Russian as their L1, but also, for example, Komis, Roma, Itelmen and others, who spoke Russian as their L2 (Anthony Grant, p.c.).

for seal breeding and slaughtering, as well as processing of their skins (Wurm 1992). It seems as if the initial indigenous settlers on Bering Island were predominantly from the Atka Island, while the initial indigenous settlers on Copper (Mednyj) Island were predominantly from the Attu Island (Thomason 1997b), while later indigenous settlers had a variety of origins, not only the Aleutian Islands, but also the Pribylof Islands, the Kuril Islands and Kamchatka (Wurm 1992). The so-called Creoles were the descendants of the Russian men and Aleut women; they were granted a privileged social status by the Russian-American Company (for example receiving the same wages as the Russian workers, some five times more than the Aleut workers, and exempting them from taxes), which placed them between the Aleuts and the Russian hierarchically (Wurm 1992, Golovko 1994). However, despite the fact that they were in an economic and politically better position than the Aleuts, they were stigmatized by both Russians and Aleuts as illegitimate.

After 1867 the Russian population declined sharply. Also, with the end of the Russian-American Company, the legal distinction between Creoles and Aleuts faded away, which may have caused the social distinction to fade away (Thomason 1997b). However, reports from the early decades of the 20th century indicate that the Creoles had formed their own identity in that they called themselves Creoles and got offended when called Aleut (Golovko & Vakhtin 1990: 116 citing Suvorov 1912: 98). It is possible that the language also played a role as an in-group marker of a new and unique ethnic identity (Golovko 1994).[213]

Soon after the colonization of the Aleutian Islands, the Russian Orthodox Church set up several schools on the islands, where Russian as well as a written form of Aleutian was taught. It is therefore likely that there was a high degree of bilingualism in Russian and Aleut among the indigenous settlers on the Commander Islands. Due to the settlement history of Copper (Mednyj) Island, it seems as if the Atta Aleut dialect constituted the major Aleut input to Mednyj Aleut. Once the seal fur trade decreased and the Aleutian Islands were sold to the USA in 1867, the Russian presence on the islands was negligible until the 1940s, when the Russian government started with educational programs again. With that, Russian was reintroduced and bilingualism again increased. Between the 1950s and 1980s children were sent to boarding schools by the state (Lewis et al. 2014). By now almost all inhabitants have shifted to Russian; those who speak Aleut or Mednyj Aleut are all bilingual in Russian, although Mednyj Aleut is taught in primary schools until the 4th grade (Lewis et al. 2014).

13.4.3.2 *A short linguistic sketch of Mednyj Aleut*

Mednyj Aleut has 30 consonants, /p, b, m, m^h, f, v, t, d, n, n^h, s, z, r, l, l^h, ʃ, ʒ, c, j, j^h, k, g, ŋ, w, x, ɣ, q, χ, ʁ, h/ and five vowels, /i, e, a, o, u/. All vowels have contrastive length, which are orthographically rendered as double vowels (<ii, ee, aa, oo, uu>). The phonemic system is thus a blend of both input languages, with some segments that are not found in Russian (/m^h, n^h, l^h, j^h, q, χ, ʁ/ and long vowels) and some segments that are not found in Aleut (/p, b, f, v, e, e:, o, o:/). The consonants /m^h, n^h, l^h, ʃ, ʒ, j, j^h, ŋ, ɣ, χ, ʁ/ are orthographically rendered as <hm, nh, nl, sh, zh, y, hy, ng, g, x̂, ĝ>

213. But see Vakhtin (1998) for a discussion that Mednyj Aleut is rather an outcome of efforts to retain a threatened ethnic identity.

respectively and an apostrophe (') indicates that the consonant is palatalized. The intonation contour resembles that of Russian. Tone is not relevant.

The morphology is predominantly concatenative, matching the concatenative nature of Aleut morphology.

Mednyj Aleut has taken over the number, case and possession system of Aleut. There are three numbers, singular (*-x̂*), dual (*-x*) and plural (*-n/-s*), and two cases, absolutive (*-ĝ*) and relative (*-m*). The subject of a transitive clause and the possessive in a possessive construction carry the relative case:

(421) a. ana-x̂ aniqyu-un saĝa-ni-it
mother-SG.ABS baby-SG.REFL sleep-CAUS-3SG.PRES
'Mother makes her child sleep.' (Golovko 1996: 67)

b. ula-mis yaga-m ilaagaa agugii-iit
house-1PL.POSS wood-REL from make-3SG.PRES
'Our house is wooden.' (Sekerina 1994: 22)

Animacy and gender are not relevant, though there is optional feminine marking in the past tense singular:

(422) roza rascve-l-a
rose bloom-PST-F
'The rose bloomed'. (Golovko 1996: 69)

There are no articles:

(423) boochki-ĝ ni-umnaa-l poetomu taanga-gan huzu-u hyuu-l
barrel-ABS.SG NEG-tight-PST so water-POSS all-POSS drip-PST
'(The) barrel had (a) hole in it, so all (the) water went away.' (Golovko 1994: 115)

There are the demonstratives *eta* 'this' (<Russian), as well as *híŋa* 'this' and *tamá* 'that' (<Aleut):

(424) a. eta moy asxinu-ng
this my daughter-1SG.POSS
'This is my daughter.'

b. hínga axsugyi-x̂ amgix̂sii-it cem tamá axsugyi-x̂
this girl-SG.ABS pretty-3SG.PRES than that girl-SG.ABS
'This girl is prettier than that girl.' (Sekerina 1994: 23, 25)

The pronominal system represents a blend of Russian and Aleut: Russian derived personal pronouns are used for the subject position, while the Aleut derived pronouns are used for the object position. It distinguishes between three persons and two numbers.

	SUBJECT	OBJECT
1SG	*ya*	*ting*
2SG	*ti*	*tin*
3SG	*on*	*tin*
1PL	*mi*	*timis*
2PL	*vi*	–
3PL	*ani*	–

Notice that the personal pronoun system does not have any dual forms, as opposed to the possessive suffixes (see below).

(425) a. patom ax̂salaa-l-i ani
then die-PST-3SG.PL 3PL.S
'Then they died.'
b. tin cignii-l
3SG.S get.wet-PST
'He got wet.'
c. ya ivo kataa-l a on icaa-l
1SG.S 3SG.O touch-PST and 3SG.S fall-PST
'I touched it and it fell.' (Sekerina 1994: 24)

There is also an indefinite pronoun *kiinax̂ta* 'somebody' from Aleut *kiin* 'who' and *-ax̂* 'AGent' plus Russian *-to* (< Russian *kto* 'who', *kto-to* 'somebody') (Golovko & Vakhtin 1990: 111).

There is a separate possessive pronoun system in the form of suffixes, which distinguishes between three persons and three numbers (i.e. this system does have dual forms).

	SINGULAR		DUAL		PLURAL	
1SG	*-ng*	'my one'	*-king*	'my two'	*-ning*	'my many'
2SG	*-n*	'your one'	*-kin*	'your two'	*-m*	'your many'
3SG	*-V:*[224]	'his/her/its one'	*-ki*	'his/her/its two'	*-ngi*	'his/her/its many'
1PL	*-mis*	'our one'	*-ki*	'our two'	*-mis*	'our many'
2PL	*-ci*	'your one'	*-ki*	'your two'	*-ci*	'your many'
3PL	*-V:*	'their one'	*-ki*	'their two'	*-ngi*	'their many'

(426) a. kayu-ngi huzu-ngi nana-it
muscle-3PL.POSS each-3PL.POSS ache-3SG.PRES
'All his muscles ache.'
b. tsvetki-ning hula-l-a
flower-1SG.POSS bloom-PST-3SG.F
'My flowers bloomed.' (Golovko 1996: 69)

However, possession may also be indicated with the Aleut marker *-gan*:

(427) ni-suu-y quicigá-gan haya-gaa
NEG-take-IMP edge-POSS sharp-POSS
'Do not take it by its sharp edge!' (Golovko & Vakhtin 1990: 102)

There is no adjectival word class; instead, qualitative attributes are expressed with the noun inflected for the possessive (as in (428a)) and qualitative predications are expressed by verbs (as in (428b)).

(428) a. ukuxta-l-ya ula-m uluyaa
see-PST-1SG house-REL red.POSS
'I saw a red house.' (Sekerina 1994: 24)
b. ulaa uluyaa-it
house.3SG.POSS be.red-3SG.PRES
'His house is red.' (Golovko & Vakhtin 1990: 106)

214. This means that the final vowel of the word is lengthened.

Comparison is expressed either with the Russian comparative marker *cem* (cf. Example (424d)) or with Aleut postpositions:

(429) atáqan gooda-x̂ luyaĝiisaa-it íglu-ng ilaagaa
one year-SG.ABS be.old-3SG.PRES grandchild-1SG.POSS from
'He is one year older than my granddaughter.' (Sekerina 1994:24)

Verbs are inflected for person, number and tense with Russian verbal suffixes, though the suffixes have been rearranged to a concatenation of tense-number-person to form the following paradigm:

	PRESENT	PAST
1SG	*-∅-∅-yu*	*-l-∅-ya*
2SG	*-∅-∅-ish*	*-l-∅-ti*
3SG	*-∅-∅-it*	*-l-∅-∅/a*
1PL	*-∅-i-m*	*-l-i-mi*
2PL	*-∅-i-ti*	*-l-i-vi*
3PL	*-∅-y-ut*	*-l-i-∅*

The present tense has no marker (∅), nor does the singular, but the past is indicated with *-l* and the plural with *-i*. The future tense is formed analytically with the auxiliary *bu(d)-* inflected for the correct person, number and tense, plus the infinitive marker *-t'* on the main verb:

(430) taana-x̂ ni-buud-ish ukuu-t'
land-SG.ABS NEG-will-2SG.PRES see-INF
'You won't see the land.' (Sekerina 1994:25)

The Russian aspect inflections are lacking and gender inflections are only optional. The only mood is the imperative, marked with the suffix *-y* (cf. Example (427)), though there are several Russian modal verbs as frozen forms (i.e. that do not take verbal inflection markers).

There are examples of verbal topic-number agreement, where the verb agrees with the subject in person but with the topic in number. In (426b) the flowers (plural) are the subject, but the topic is the first person singular ('my'), so the verb inflects for the singular (but the third person).

There are a number of valency-changing derivational suffixes, derived from Aleut.

The word order is relatively free. Negation is expressed with the Russian negative prefix *ni-* (cf. Examples (423), (430)). Content questions may contain question words from either Aleut or Russian. The interrogative phrase is fronted.

(431) qanaaga máĝi-x̂
where.from smoke-SG.ABS
'Where (is the) smoke (coming) from?' (Golovko & Vakhtin 1990:106)

The copula *u-* 'to be' is not used in the present tense, but is used for past tense nominal predications. Since the adjective is functionally a verb, adjectival predication does not take any copula in any tense, but instead itself inflects like a verb:

(432) a. tátka-ng u min'a aleuuta-x̂ uu-l
father-1SG.POSS at me Aleut-SG.ABS be-PST. 3SG
'My father was (an) Aleut.' (Sekerina 1994: 28)

b. ya cuquyaa-l-a
1SG.S be.small-PST-3SG.F
'I was small.' (Sekerina 1994: 28)

c. suupa-x̂ taĝayu-t
soup-SG.ABS be.salty-PRES.3SG
'The soup is salty.' (Golovko 1996: 66)

Complex clauses are formed with Russian conjunctions and complementizers.

(433) a. ona hix̂ta-it tsto ona ego ilax̂ta-it
3SG.S say-PRES.3SG that 3SG.S 3SG.O love-PRES.3SG
'She says that she loves him.' (Golovko 1996: 71)

b. kak tin ikucaa-l, tak saĝaaĝa tin hninii-l
as.soon 3SG.O return-PST.3SG as sleep.INTENT 3SG.S go-PST.3SG
'As soon as he returned, he went to bed to sleep.' (Sekerina 1994: 27)

Relative clauses are formed with interrogatives:

(434) agitaaya-ning u min'a katorəye agítaki abaa-l, pucti huzúngi ax̂salaa-l-i
friend-1SG.POSS.PL at me which with work-PST.3SG almost all die-PST-3PL
'Of my friends with whom I worked, almost all are dead.' (Sekerina 1994: 29)

13.4.3.3 *Short text*

(Excerpt from Golovko & Vakhtin 1990: 118f, with minimal adjustments to the orthography. Glossed and translated by Anthony Grant. Russian derived material appears in italics.)

Tis'aca div'atsoot dvatsat' cetv'oorti góda ya agaa-*l* *Midn*-am ila. *Ya*
thousand 900 twenty fourth year 1SG.S be.born-PST mednyj-LOC on 1SG.S

cuquyaa-*l-a*. *Mámka*-ng *u min'a toože kamcadaalka*-x̂ uu-*l-a,* *tatka*-ng
small-PST-F mother-1SG.POSS by me also itelmen.woman-NOM be-PST-F dad-1SG.POSS

aleuut-ax̂ uu-*l*. Uu-*l-í-mi* *diiv'at'* anĝaĝína-x̂ aníkyun, *patóm* ax̂salaa-*l-i-ani*. Aláx u-*l*
aleut-NOM be-PST be-PST-PL-1PL nine girl-NOM children then die-PST-PL-3PL two be-PST

timis agisaa-*l-i,* *siistra*-ng agiita-*l*. *Ish'o braat*-ang ilí-mis uu-*it*
1PL.O remain-PST-PL sister-1SG.POSS with still brother-1SG.POSS he-1PL.POSS be-3SG.PRES

Vladivastook-am ila. Sami cuqúya-x̂, *v tritsatəm godú on* agax̂taa-*it*.
vladivostok-LOC in most young-NOM in thirtieth year he be.born-3SG.PRES

'I was born in Copper Island in 1927. I was small. My mother was an Itelmen woman and my father was Aleut. There were nine of us, then they died. Two remain there, me and my sister. My brother is living in Vladivostok. He is the youngest and was born in 1930.'

13.4.3.4 *Some sources of data*

There is very little primary data available for Mednyj Aleut. Golovko (1996) and Sekerina (1994) provide numerous glossed and translated examples. Golovko and Vakhtin (1990) provide two longer texts, translated but not glossed.

13.5 Summary

Pidgins seem to tend to have SVO or SOV word order; a little more than half seem to have adopted the word order of the lexifier languages. It is not uncommon for pidgins to have passive constructions.

All extended pidgins (pidgincreoles) in the sample have the same word order as their lexifier languages. Some have passive constructions, though all English-lexified extended pidgins lack them.

The absolute majority of the creoles in the sample have SVO word order; creoles seem likely to adopt the word order of their lexifier languages. Passive constructions are as common in creole languages as in non-creoles.

Mixed languages typically adopt the word order of the input language(s) which has or have provided the bulk of the grammatical structure. When it comes to passive constructions the G-L mixed languages tend to adopt the system of the language(s) which provided the bulk of the structure, while N-V mixed languages tend to adopt the passive constructions from the language(s) which provided the bulk of the verb phrase structure.

13.6 Key points

- **Pidgins tend to have subject-initial word order; they do not necessarily have the same word order as their lexifiers.**
- **Extended pidgins (pidgincreoles) tend to have the same word order as their lexifiers.**
- **Creoles tend to have subject initial word order, most commonly the same word order as the lexifier.**
- **Mixed languages tend to adopt the word order of the language that has provided the bulk of the grammatical structure.**
- **Pidgins are not especially likely to lack the passive voice.**
- **English-lexified extended pidgins (pidgincreoles) tend to lack the passive.**
- **Creoles are not more likely than non-creoles to lack the passive voice.**
- **Mixed languages tend to adopt the passive voice strategies of the language that has provided the bulk of the grammatical or verb phrase structure.**

13.7 Exercises

1. Is the following statement true or false? Motivate your answer.
   It is not possible to predict with reasonable accuracy the source(s) of the word order in a given pidgin language.
2. Is the following statement true or false? Motivate your answer.
   It is not possible to predict with reasonable accuracy the source(s) of the word order in a given creole language.
3. Is the following statement true or false? Motivate your answer.
   It is not possible to predict with reasonable accuracy the source(s) of the word order and passive construction of a given mixed language.
4. Do extended pidgins (pidgincreoles) align more closely with pidgins or with creoles with respect to word order and the passive voice?
5. How do the findings on the passive voice in creole languages relate to the notion of creoles as typologically unique languages?

Languages cited in Chapter 14

1. Akan; Ghanaian Pidgin English
2. Arabic, Standard
3. Berbice Dutch
4. Caló
5. Chinese Pidgin English
6. Chinese Pidgin Russian
7. Chinuk Wawa
8. Chickasaw; Choctaw; Mobilian Jargon
9. Cree, Plains
10. Dutch
11. English
12. English, American
13. Eskimo Pidgin
14. Ethiopian Simplified Italian
15. Fanakalo
16. French
17. Gulf Pidgin Arabic
18. Gurindji; Gurindji Kriol
19. Igbo; Nigerian Pidgin
20. Italian
21. Jamaican
22. Juba Arabic
23. Kriol
24. Michif
25. Nagamese
26. Hawaiian; Pidgin Hawaiian
27. Pidgin Hindustani
28. Romani, Vlax
29. Sango
30. Shelta
31. Singapore Bazaar Malay
32. Spanish
33. Tãi Bòy
34. Trinidad English Creole
35. Turku
36. Yimas-Arafundi-Pidgin

Chapter 14

Complex sentences

Subordinate clauses, including relative clauses, are often described as infrequent in both pidgin and creole languages, while serial verb constructions (a form of cosubordination) are described as being particularly common for creole languages. Mixed languages are assumed to have adopted the system of one of the languages, or to represent a blend of the input languages. Section 14.2 in this chapter will test whether pidgins and creoles differ from non-pidgins and non-creoles with respect to the expression for the head in subject relative clauses, and discuss these strategies in extended pidgins and mixed languages. The same section will test in how far pidgins, extended pidgins, creoles and mixed languages make use of a relative particle to indicate a relative clause. Section 14.3 tests how common directional serial verb constructions are in pidgins, extended pidgins, creoles and mixed languages. Section 14.4 gives short sketches of three languages mentioned in the chapter: Mobilian Jargon (an extinct Muskogean-lexified pidgin in USA), Jamaican (an English-lexified creole in Jamaica) and Caló (a Spanish/Romani mixed language in Spain).

14.1 Introduction

Clauses may combine to jointly form a sentence or a **complex clause**. Combined clauses may be of the same or of different ranks. **Coordination** is when independent linguistic units of the same rank combine (are coordinated) to form a larger unit, but where none of the units is dependent on the other. Coordination can be of words, or phrases or entire clauses. For example, in the sentence *The man peeled and ate an orange* we have two verbs (*peeled and ate*) which jointly combine on the same syntactic level to carry out the function of the clause predicate, but none of the verbs are dependent on each other: it is not essential for the verb *peel* to combine with the verb *eat* to form a grammatical sentence. In the sentence *The man ate an apple and an orange* we have two noun phrases (*an apple* and *an orange*) which jointly combine on the same syntactic level (that of the object of the clause), where again none of the units are essential to the other in order to form a grammatical sentence. And in *The man peeled an orange and the woman ate an apple* we have two full clauses (*the man peeled an orange* and *the woman ate an apple*) that combine on the same level, again none of which is dependent on the other to form a grammatical sentence.

Subordination is when a **dependent clause** functions as a constituent within another clause; the dependent clause is **embedded** within a **main** (or **superordinate) clause**. A main clause is sometimes termed a **matrix clause**; when the terms are differentiated the term 'main clause' denotes a clause that is independent and fully functional on its own (as in *The man called a taxi*, *The man told the taxi driver where to pick him up*, *The man saw the taxi as it drove up to him*, *The man got into the taxi which had driven up to him*, etc.). The term 'matrix clause' on the other hand, is essentially a main clause minus its dependent (subordinate) clause, for example *The man told the taxi driver* and *The man saw the taxi* in the sentences above. The difference between a main clause and a matrix clause is thus that a matrix clause always has a dependent (subordinate) clause as one of its constituents, and might therefore not always be independent (**The man told the taxi driver*, for example, is not grammatical without the second object for the verb *told*). A dependent (subordinate) clause may function as a constituent to its matrix clause, as in *The man said that he would be taking a taxi home*, where the clause [*that he would be taking a taxi home*] serves as the object to the verb *said*. Or a dependent (subordinate) clause may function as an adjunct to its matrix clause, as in *The man took a taxi home after having had dinner with his friends*, where the clause [*after having had dinner with his friends*] functions as an adverbial. Or a dependent (subordinated) clause may function as a modifier to a noun phrase, as in *The man got into the taxi which he had ordered*, where the clause [*which he had ordered*] serves as a modifier to the noun phrase *the taxi*.

Cosubordination is when clauses are neither embedded in each other (making them similar to coordinated clauses), nor are able to function independently (making them similar to subordinated clauses). In other words, none of the clauses function as a constituent to the other clause, so none is embedded in the other. However, none of the clauses are independent units that can function on their own. A type of cosubordination are serial verb constructions (see below), which can be found in colloquial English in such expressions as *We had to come pick you up*, where *come pick* are two units that jointly function on the same syntactic level as one predicate denoting one single event.

14.2 Relative clauses

Relative clauses (sometimes also called **adjective clauses**) are clauses that narrow the reference of a noun phrase (the head). For example, in the sentence *I talked to the man who wore pink glasses*, the matrix clause has the noun phrase [*the man*] and the relative clause [*who wore pink glasses*] narrows the reference of the noun phrase to only those men for which the proposition in the relative clause holds true, that is, only that man who wore pink glasses.[215]

The matrix clause is the clause in which the relative clause is embedded (*I talked to the man* in the sentence above). The **head** is the noun phrase that the relative clause refers to (*the man* in the sentence above). The relative clause is the clause that narrows the reference to the head (*who wore pink glasses* in the sentence above). Relative clauses are often indicated with square brackets, as in *I talked to the man [who wore pink glasses]*.

A relative clause may be flagged by a **relative particle** (also called **relativizer**), such as *that* in English, as in *I talked to the man* ***that*** *[wore pink glasses]*, where *that* announces that what follows is a relative clause. The relative clause may also contain an overt element that is coreferential with the head in the matrix and which indicates the role of the head inside the relative clause, such as the **relative pronouns** in English, as in *I talked to the man [**who** wore pink glasses]*, where *who* is coreferential with *the man* in the matrix clause and indicates that the role of the head inside the relative clause is subject (as opposed to object, in which case the coreferential element would have been *whom*). Lack of any such overt elements is often referred to as a **gap**, as in *I talked to the man that [___ wore pink glasses]*, where there is a gap where the coreferential element would have been. There are other ways of indicating the role of the head, of which only two are relevant for this section. With a **resumptive pronoun** the relative clause is set off with a relative particle and contains a pronoun which is coreferential with the head (something like *I talked to the man* ***that*** *[**he** wore pink glasses]*). With a **correlative** the relative clause is set off by a relative particle and the head occurs inside the relative clause, but is also referred to in the matrix (either pronominally or with a repetition of the head noun, something like *I talked to him* ***that*** *[**the man** wore pink glasses]* or *I talked to* ***the man that*** *[**the man** wore pink glasses]*).

The role of the head may differ: in *I talked to the man [who wore pink glasses]* or *I talked to the man that [___ wore pink glasses]* the role of the head noun is subjectival (the man$_{\text{SUBJECT}}$ wears glasses), whereas in *I talked to the man [whom I told to wear glasses]* or *I talked to the man that [___ I told to wear glasses]*, the role of the head is objectival (I told the man$_{\text{OBJECT}}$ something). It should be noted that languages may have different strategies for relative clauses depending on the role of the head inside

215. This kind of relative clause is sometimes – and especially in studies of English – called a **restrictive relative clause**, because it restricts the potential referents of a referent, in contrast to **non-restrictive relative clauses**, which are purely descriptive and do not involve specifying one referent out of many. Compare *The man who wore pink glasses told me to sit down* (restrictive) with *The man, who wore pink glasses, told me to sit down* (non-restrictive). This section focuses on restrictive clauses only.

the relative clause. English, for example, allows relative clauses that lack any relative particle ('zero marking') and that have a gap for the role of the head inside the relative clause, but only if the role is an object: compare *I talked to the man [___ I told to wear glasses]*, where there is no relative particle to set off the relative clause, and where only a gap is coreferential with the head noun, with **I talked to the man [___ wore pink glasses]*.

This section will check whether pidgins, extended pidgins (pidgincreoles) and creoles tend to have relative particles or not. It will also compare whether pidgins and creoles tend to differ from non-pidgins and non-creoles with respect to the element inside the relative clause that is coreferential with the head, as well as discuss the coreferential element in extended pidgins (pidgincreoles). Relative clauses in mixed languages will also be discussed. Because of space limitations, only subject relative clauses will be discussed. For the comparisons, languages that have more than one strategy will be coded for their dominant strategy only.

It is beyond this section to adequately discuss relative clauses in the languages of the world. For very accessible overviews of the typology of relative clauses, see Comrie (1989: 138ff), Givón (2001b: 175ff) and Andrews (2007).

14.2.1 Relative clauses in pidgin languages

Pidgins are often described as lacking subordinate clauses and to express complex clauses by way of juxtaposition only (cf. Sebba 1997: 39). Tâi Bòi, for example, is a pidgin language where relative clauses are expressed by simply placing the clauses next to each other, without any overt marking at all:

Tâi Bòi (Pidgin (French-lexified): Vietnam)

(435) la fille moi voir
DEF girl 1SG see
'The girl whom I saw.' (Stageberg 1956: 169)

In (435) there is no overt marking to indicate that the subordinate clause (*moi voir*) modifies the head (*la fille*).

There are, however, a number of pidgin languages that do overtly indicate relative clauses, such as Ethiopian Simplified Italian, with the relative particles *ki/kwello*, or Mobilian Jargon, with the relative particle *nanta*:

Ethiopian Simplified Italian (Pidgin (Italian-lexified): Ethiopia)

(436) iyo bɛrduto soldi ki/kwello tu da-to bɛr me
1SG.S lost money REL 2SG.S give-PST for 1SG.O
'I lost the money that you gave me.' (Marcos 1976: 179)

Mobilian Jargon (Pidgin (Muskogean-lexified): USA)

(437) nanta ʃno banna, ʃno ʧõpa
REL 2SG want 2SG buy
'You buy what you want.' (Drechsel 1997: 127)

A third of the languages in the current pidgin sample have a relative particle to mark off a relative clause. The figures are summarized in Table 14.1:

Table 14.1 Presence or absence of relative particle in the current pidgin sample. For a full legend of the languages in the pidgin sample, see http://dx.doi.org/10.1075/cll.48.additional.

	N	%
Relative clause is marked with relative particle	6	33.3
Relative clause is not marked with relative particle	10	55.5
Relative clause is optionally marked with relative particle	2	11.1
Total	18	

($\chi^2 = 5.33$; $df = 2$; $p_{two\text{-}tailed} = 0.070$; $p_{sim} = 0.074$ (B = 10,000))
($G = 5.61$; $df = 2$; $p_{two\text{-}tailed} = 0.060$)

The figures in Table 14.1 show that in a little more than half of the languages a relative clause is not indicated with any kind of relative particle. The figures are, however, only marginally significant statistically.

The sentence in (435) also lacks any overt expression for the role of the head inside the relative clause, i.e. the relative clause has a gap for the role of the head. This is by far the most common strategy in the current pidgin sample, as shown in Table 14.2, which also compares the distribution in the pidgin sample with that in Comrie & Kuteva (2013):

Table 14.2 Relativization on subjects in the current pidgin sample and in WALS (Comrie & Kuteva 2013). For a full legend of the languages in the pidgin sample, see http://dx.doi.org/10.1075/cll.48.additional.

	Pidgin sample		WALS	
	N	%	N	%
Gap	14	77.8	125	75.3
Resumptive pronoun	2	11.1	5	3
Non-reduction	2	11.1	24	14.5
Relative pronoun	–	–	12	7.2
Total	18		166	

($\chi^2 = 4.24$; $df = 3$; $p_{two\text{-}tailed} = 0.24$; $p_{sim} = 0.21$ (B = 10,000))
($G = 3.97$; $df = 3$; $p_{two\text{-}tailed} = 0.27$)

As can be seen in Table 14.2, the absolute majority of the languages in WALS also have a gap for the head in subject relative clauses. In fact, the difference in proportions between the two samples is not statistically significant. Based on these figures it therefore does not seem as if pidgins are more likely than non-pidgins to lack an overt expression for the head in subject relative clauses.

14.2.2 Relative clauses in extended pidgins (pidgincreoles)

Seven of nine of the extended pidgins in the sample have a relative particle to mark off a relative clause as their dominant strategy, such as in, for example, Ghanaian Pidgin English:

Ghanaian Pidgin English (Extended Pidgin (English-lexified): Ghana)

(438) wí hav sɔm difrɛn taip ɔf ʧif-s wé dɛ̀m dé hiɛ
1PL have some different type of chief-PL REL 3PL COP here
'We have different kinds of chiefs who are here.' (Magnus Huber, fieldwork data)

In (438) the relative particle *wé* indicates that the following clause is a relative clause.

In Example (438) a pronoun (*dɛ̀m*) indicates the role of the head inside the relative clause (lit. '… chiefs, that they are here'). This strategy is the dominant one for four of the languages in the sample, while having a gap for the head is the dominant strategy for the remaining five, as in, for example, Juba Arabic:

Juba Arabic (Extended pidgin (Arabic-lexified): South Sudan)

(439) zol al kan éndu guruʃ de
individual REL ANT have money DEM.PROX
'the man who had money' (Manfredi & Petrollino 2013b: feature 92)

In (439) there is no overt expression inside the relative clause for the role of the head (lit. 'this man that ___ had money'). For more on Juba Arabic, see 15.4.1.

14.2.3 Relative clauses in creole languages

Most of the creole languages in the sample have a relative particle to mark off their relative clauses, such as, for example, in Jamaican:

Jamaican (Creole (English-lexified): Jamaica)

(440) di man huu mek di hat-dem gaan a Merica
DEF man REL make DEF hat-PL gone to America
'The man who makes the hats has gone to America.' (Farquharson 2013b: feature 92)

In Example (440) the relative particle *huu* indicates that what follows is a relative clause (for more on Jamaican, see 14.4.2). For most of the languages this is the dominant strategy, while in some languages the relative particle is optional, usually depending on what the coding for the role of head in the relative clause is. In some languages there is no overt marker for a relative clause. The figures are summarized in Table 14.3:

Table 14.3 Presence or absence of relative particle in the current creole sample. For a full legend of the languages in the creole sample, see http://dx.doi.org/10.1075/cll.48.additional.

	N	%
Relative clause is marked with relative particle	31	59.6
Relative clause is not marked with relative particle	9	17.3
Relative clause is optionally marked with relative particle	12	23.1
Total	52	

($\chi^2 = 16.42$; $df = 2$; $p_{\text{two-tailed}} < 0.001$***; $p_{\text{sim}} < 0.001$*** (B = 10,000))
($G = 15.23$; $df = 2$; $p_{\text{two-tailed}} < 0.001$***)

As shown in Table 14.3, only a minority of the languages lack any overt marker for a relative clause.[216] This distribution is statistically significant, possibly indicating that creole languages tend to have relative particles to flag a clause as a relative clause.

In Example (440) there is no overt expression indicating the role of the head in the relative clause (there is a gap in the relative clause). This is by far the most common strategy in the current creole sample. Some languages have mixed strategies for their relative clauses. Trinidad English Creole, for example, may either have a relative particle and a gap (as in (441a)) or no relative particle but a resumptive pronoun (as in (441b)) (lit. 'the girl she came yesterday'):

Trinidad English Creole (Creole (English-lexified): Trinidad)

(441) a. de gal weh reach Trinidad yesterday
DEF girl REL reach Trinidad yesterday
'The girl that came to Trinidad yesterday'

b. de gal she reach yesterday
DEF girl 3SG.F reach yesterday
'the girl that came yesterday' (Mühleisen 2013b: feature 92)

In fact, for six of the languages in the creole sample, the occurrence of the relative particle depends on how the role of the head is coded.

In order to compare whether creole languages behave differently from non-creoles with respect to the coding of the head in subject relative clauses, I compared the current creole sample with that in Comrie & Kuteva (2013). To make the two databases comparable, I excluded those languages with a mixed strategy (i.e. where there were

216. Specifically, the group of languages with a relative particle is significantly overrepresented, while the group of languages lacking any overt marker is significantly underrepresented in the sample.

several ways in equal proportion of coding the head in the relative clause). The figures are summarized in Table 14.4:

Table 14.4 Relativization on subjects in the current creole sample and in WALS (Comrie & Kuteva 2013). For a full legend of the languages in the creole sample, see http://dx.doi.org/10.1075/cll.48.additional.

	Creole sample		WALS*	
	N	%	N	%
Gap	37	80.4	123	75
Resumptive pronoun	3	6.5	5	3
Non-reduction	–	–	24	14.6
Relative pronoun	6	13	12	7.3
Total	46		164	

($\chi^2 = 9.38$; $df = 3$; $p_{\text{two-tailed}} = 0.025$*; $p_{\text{sim}} = 0.025$* (B = 10,000))
($G = 13.44$; $df = 3$; $p_{\text{two-tailed}} = 0.0038$**)
* Lingala and Ndyuka (Nengee) have been removed from the WALS sample to avoid overlap.

It should be noted that for both databases a gap is the dominant strategy for the absolute majority of the languages. However, the distributions differ between the two databases, possibly indicating that creoles might pattern differently from non-creoles with respect to how the head of subject relative clauses are coded. Specifically, it seems more common for the languages in the WALS sample to have the non-reduction strategy than for the languages in the creole sample.

14.2.4 Relative clauses in mixed languages

Mixed languages are usually described as having taken over the system of one of the input languages, or as representing a blend of the input languages. Caló, for example, a G-L Spanish/Romani mixed language, primarily has its grammatical system from Spanish. Relative clauses are introduced with the relative particle *sos* (< Romani *so* 'what'), which is similar in function to the Spanish *que*:

Caló (Mixed language (Spanish/Romani): Spain)

(442) o manu sos terela duis conel-es
DEF man REL have two shirt-PL
'the man who has two shirts' (*Embéo e Majaró Lucas* 1837: 3.11)

In (442) the relative particle *sos* functions in a similar way as the Spanish *que*. However, it should be noted that this is also very similar to the structure of relative clauses in Romani, where relative clauses are introduced with a relative particle *kaj* ('where') or *so/ho* ('what'), although unlike in Spanish, if the role of the head inside the relative clause is not that of the subject, a resumptive pronoun is used (Matras 2002). For more on Caló, see 14.4.3.

It seems as if N-V mixed languages might derive their relative clause strategies from the language which provided the bulk of the verb phrase structure. In Michif, for example, relative clauses are typically indicated with a verbal affix, as in Cree:

Michif (Mixed language (French/Cree): Canada, USA)

(443) bakwat-a:w-ak li: mũd ka:-kimuti-ʧik
1.hate-TA-3PL DEF.SG.M people COMP-steal-3PL
'I hate people who steal.' (Bakker 1997b: 329)

In (443) the complementizer prefix *ka:-* indicates that the clause is a conjunct and functions as a relative clause to the preceding noun. This matches the strategy found in Cree, whereas relative clauses in French are formed with a relative pronoun. For more on Michif, see 3.3.2.

Languages may have several strategies for forming relative clauses, as is, for example, the case in English as well as in Kriol. In Gurindji Kriol, which is, like Michif, an N-V mixed language, the relative clause strategy is again, like in Michif, inherited from the language which has provided most of the verb phrase structure, namely Kriol.

Gurindji Kriol (Mixed language (Gurindji/Kriol): Australia)

(444) dat karu wen i bin jayijayi jamut spiya-yawung
DEF kid REL 3SG.S PST chase turkey spear-COM
'the kid who chased the turkey with a spear' (Meakins 2013b: feature 92)

Example (444) shows how relative clauses in Gurindji Kriol are formed with a relative particle (*wen*) and a resumptive pronoun (lit. 'the kid that he chased (the) turkey with (a) spear'), which is one of the strategies for forming relative clauses in Kriol (the other strategies are to either lack the relative particle but have a resumptive pronoun, or to lack the relative particle and have a gap for the role of the head inside the relative clause). For more on Gurindji Kriol, see 9.5.3.

Shelta might exhibit a slight innovation. It has taken over one of the English strategies, namely to not have any overt marking for the relative clause and to have a gap for the role of the head noun inside the relative clause:

(445) Da:ʎon awart ste:ʃ ʃi:kr ni:dʲa-s
God one AFF three person-PL
'One God who is three persons.' (Macalister 1937: 179)

In (445) there is no overt expression indicating that the clause is a relative clause, and there is also no overt expression for the role of the head noun inside the relative clause. However, in Shelta the zero + gap strategy is used for a subject relative clause, which is not possible in (Standard) English. In (Standard) English a zero+gap strategy is only possible in object relative clauses (compare *The man* ∅ ___ *I saw*, where the gap refers to the man, who is the object in the relative clause, with **The man* ∅ ___ *saw me*, which would not be a grammatically acceptable way to express something like *The man who saw me*). For more on Shelta, see 11.4.3.

14.3 Serial verb constructions

Serial verb constructions (also called **serial verbs**) are constructions where several verbs act as one predicate – that is, a series of two or more verbs, which are not compounded and do not belong to separate clauses, are combined to describe one event. They typically form a single clause, i.e. there are no overt markers of syntactic dependency (such as coordination or subordination) and often grammatical categories, such as person agreement, negation, or tense, mood and aspect, are only indicated on one of the verbs in the construction. They also typically share at least one argument in the clause. They typically refer to one single event and typically form one intonation unit (i.e. there are no pauses between the individual verbs of the construction). English does not have grammaticalized serial verb constructions; the closest examples would be certain kinds of expressions in colloquial English (especially in American English) such as *Run go fetch the paper!*, where [*run go fetch*] jointly serve as the predicate of the clause.

There are many kinds of serial verb constructions in the languages of the world. One of the most common types involves motion verbs of some kind, such as 'come' and 'go', which often function as directionals. Other common kinds of semantic functions of serial verb constructions are to indicate orientation, aspectual and modal notions, complementation, change of valency, comparison, sequence and causation, manner, and so on.

This section will briefly discuss directional serial verb constructions with 'come' and 'go' in pidgins, extended pidgins (pidgincreoles), creoles and mixed languages. Due to space limitations other kinds of serial verb constructions will largely be ignored. I stress that this should not be taken to mean that other kinds of serial verb constructions are irrelevant for contact languages.

For an accessible introduction to the typology of serial verb constructions, see Aikhenvald (2006b), the introduction to Aikhenvald & Dixon (2006), which presents examples and discussions of serial verb constructions in a number of diverse languages. Bisang (2009) is a very accessible survey of serial verb constructions, including their developmental processes. A classic discussion on serial verb constructions from a creolistics perspective is Sebba (1987).

14.3.1 Serial verb constructions in pidgin languages

In a small sample of 11 pidgins, six of the languages have directional serial verb constructions with the verbs 'come' and 'go', such as Pidgin Hawaiian:

Pidgin Hawaiian (Pidgin (Hawaiian-lexified): Hawai'i Islands)

(446) a. mahope kela Kepani kii mai hopu iaia hele
later DET Japanese fetch DIR seize 3SG go
'Then the Japanese took him away'

b. pehea oe loihi hele pimai
why 2SG long go come
'Why did it take so long for you to come?' (Roberts 2013b: feature 84)

In (446a) the verb *hele* 'go' serves as a postposed directional rather than separate lexical verb, as does *pimai* 'come' in (446b). In both cases the directional verbs share the argument of the clause with the other verbs in the serial verb construction and the clauses relate a single event (for more on Pidgin Hawaiian, see 11.4.1). The other languages in the sample with such constructions are Chinese Pidgin English, Gulf Pidgin Arabic, Singapore Bazaar Malay, Turku and Yimas-Arafundi Pidgin.

In the remaining five languages (Chinese Pidgin Russian, Chinuk Wawa, Eskimo Pidgin, Fanakalo and Pidgin Hindustani), such directional serial verb constructions do not occur. It is impossible to make any generalizations about directional serial verb constructions in pidgin languages based on the distribution in this small sample.

14.3.2 Serial verb constructions in extended pidgins (pidgincreoles)

All the English-lexified extended pidgins have directional serial verbs constructions with 'come' and 'go', such as Nigerian Pidgin:

Nigerian Pidgin (Extended pidgin (English-lexified): Nigeria)

(447) a. im kari nayf ko̱m
3SG.S carry knife come
'S/He brought the knife.'

b. im kari nayf go
3SG.S carry knife go
'S/He took the knife away.' (Faraclas 2013b: feature 84)

In both (447a & b, the verbs *ko̱m* and *go* serve as postposed directionals rather than separate lexical verbs; in both cases the argument of the clause is shared with the other verbs in the construction and the clause relates one single event.

In Nagamese, there are 'go' directionals but no 'come' directionals (Bhattacharjya 2007; see further 8.3.1), while Sango and Juba Arabic lack these constructions altogether.

14.3.3 Serial verb constructions in creole languages

Serial verb constructions are described as being particularly common in creole languages (cf. Muysken & Veenstra 1994: 124). Berbice Dutch is an example of a language which had 'come' and 'go' directional serial verb constructions:

Berbice Dutch (Creole (Dutch-lexified): Guyana)

(448) a. alma kɛnɛ ʃima-tɛ fan danga mu-tɛ oflar
all person move-PFV from there go-PFV everywhere
'Everybody moved away from there to all sorts of places.'

b. afta iʃi skif-tɛ kum-tɛ dis-kani…
after 1PL move-PFV come-PFV this-side
'After we moved to this place…' (Kouwenberg 1994: 412)

The verbs *mu* 'go' and *kum* 'come' in (448) serve as directionals rather than full verbs, and are essentially best translated with an adverbial or a preposition (*away* and *to* respectively). In both cases the argument is shared with the other verb in the clause and in each case the clause relates one single event. For more on Berbice Dutch, see 6.4.3.

There are, however, a number of creole languages that do not have 'come' and 'go' directional serial verb constructions. The figures are summarized in Table 14.5:

Table 14.5 Presence or absence of 'come' and 'go' directional serial verb constructions (SVCs) in the current creole sample. For a full legend of the languages in the creole sample, see http://dx.doi.org/10.1075/cll.48.additional.

	N	%
Directional SVCs exist	29	58
Directional SVCs do not exist	21	42
Total	50	

($\chi^2 = 1.28$; $df = 1$; $p_{\text{two-tailed}} = 0.26$; $p_{\text{sim}} = 0.32$ (B = 10,000))
($G = 1.27$; $df = 2$; $p_{\text{two-tailed}} = 0.26$)

As can be seen from the figures in Table 14.5, it is somewhat more common for the languages in the current creole sample to have 'come' and 'go' directional serial verb constructions than to lack them. However, the distribution is not statistically significant, meaning that these figures do not allow us to assume that creoles are particularly prone to having directional serial verb constructions.[217] Whether this sets creoles apart from non-creoles is a matter for future research.

217. The assumption that these kinds of constructions are particularly common in creole languages may possibly lie in the fact that it seems quite common for the Caribbean creoles to have them: a full 18 of the 21 (i.e. 85.7%) Caribbean creoles in the sample have these constructions.

14.3.4 Serial verb constructions in mixed languages

Directional serial verb constructions with 'come' and 'go' do not seem to be attested for mixed languages (cf. also Maurer et al. 2013), although similar kinds of constructions can be found in Gurindji Kriol, where there is a closed class of 15 verbs which may combine with different kinds of verbs in serial verb constructions and which function to indicate a variety of properties, such as aspect, path and direction, change of valency or semantic modifications of the main verb. Compare the following:

Gurindji Kriol (Mixed language (Gurindji/Kriol): Australia)

(449) a. an warlaku bin top kutij nyantu-warinyj
and dog PST CONT stand 3SG-ALONE
'And the dog was standing by himself'
b. dat karu im gon partaj karnti-ngka
DEF kid 3SG go climb tree-LOC
'The kid climbs up the tree.'
c. binij i bin baldan pangkily
suddenly 3SG.S PST fall hit.head
'...suddenly he fell on his head'. (Meakins 2010: 15, 17)

In (449a) the verb *top* 'stop' is in a serial verb construction with the main verb *kutij* 'stand' and gives the event a continuous reading; in (449b) the verb *gon* 'go' is in a serial verb construction with the main verb *partaj* 'climb' and indicates motion along a path; and in (449c) the verb *baldan* 'fall' is in a serial verb construction with the transitive verb *pangkily* 'hit (on the head)' and detransitivizes the main verb. In all cases the combined verbs share arguments and denote one single event.

14.4 Snapshots

Pidgins are not expected to have overt markers for subordinate clauses, including relative clauses. Mobilian Jargon is an example of a pidgin that has a relative particle.

Subordination is often described as infrequent for creole languages, while serial verb constructions are described as prolific in creoles. Jamaican is an example of a creole that has both relative clauses and directional serial verb constructions.

Mixed languages are expected to represent the system of one of the input languages or to represent a blend of both input languages. Caló is an example of a mixed language which has taken over the structure of the relative clause from Spanish, but the etyma of the relative particles are Romani.

14.4.1 Mobilian Jargon: An extinct Muskogean-lexified pidgin in the USA[218]

14.4.1.1 *A brief background sketch of Mobilian Jargon*

Mobilian Jargon, also called *Mobilian Trade Language, Mobilian Trade Jargon, Chickasaw-Choctaw Trade Language* and *Yamá* by scholars was a mainly Choctaw and Chickasaw (both Western Muskogean languages) lexified pidgin spoken in south-eastern North America, mainly in the lower Mississippi River valley and along the Gulf of Mexico coast. Historical evidence suggests that it was used as far away as into the Missouri River valley (Drechsel 1996). The users themselves called the language *anõpa ēla* ('(the) different language'), *yoka anõpa* ('slave/servant language'), *ʧahta/ʃata* ('Chochtaw') or *yam(m)a/yamã/yamõ* ('yes, right, indeed; that') (Drechsel 1996). In the 20th century the users themselves called Mobilian Jargon *The broken/old/lost language* in English (Drechsel 1997). The language existed for at least 250 years, between 1700 and 1950, though as late as the 1980s there were still elderly rememberers left.

The Mississippi River valley and Gulf Coast area had long been a highly linguistically diverse region and it was common for people to be multilingual. It is not known when exactly Mobilian Jargon developed, though the fact that it seems to have been a well established intertribal means of communications by the time the European explorers encountered it implies that it had developed long enough before the European expansion in the area to have become a stable pidgin.[219] It was not readily intelligible to speakers of Muskogean languages, but had to be specifically learned (Drechsel 1996).

Mobilian Jargon takes its name from the Mobilian Indians: when the French set up an outpost on the Gulf Coast in the early 18th century, they named what would become the first capital of French colonial Louisiana after the Mobilian Indians. It seems conceivable that the French traders and explorers were the ones who named the main medium of communication that they encountered in the area 'Mobilian Jargon' (Drechsel 1997).

The first known attestation of the language is from 1700 by the French Jesuit priest Paul du Ru, who recounted his travels in the Mississippi delta area with the explorer brothers Pierre and Jean Baptiste Le Moyne, and gave a sample of what he and the brothers termed *Bayogoula*. Both Paul du Ru and the Le Moyne brothers mentioned how this language was used as an intertribal medium among a dozen tribes with highly diverse languages.

Mobilian Jargon was used not only in trade with other tribes, but also in other intertribal activities, such as hunting or such social functions as games and dances, seasonal gatherings or social visits. It was also used in diplomatic exchanges, such as negotiations of various kinds (whether peaceful or hostile) and as the *lingua franca* of various associations and alliances, such as the Creek Confederacy (cf. also Knight 1990). Furthermore, it was used between master and slave or servant, for instance if the masters were European and the slaves or servants indigenous, or if the masters were indigenous and the slaves or servants either indigenous (from other tribes)

---

218. This section is based almost exclusively on Crawford (1978) and Drechsel (1996, 1997).

219. But see Crawford (1978) for a discussion on the possibility that Mobilian Jargon originated after the French established their colony in Louisiana.

or African. There is also evidence that marooned African slaves who found refuge among the indigenous population acquired and used Mobilian Jargon. There is even evidence of Mobilian Jargon having been used as a home language in multiethnic marriages – although it did not creolize: "apparently children first acquired their parents' native language(s), French, and/or English" (Drechsel 1997:263).[220]

With the European expansion, Mobilian Jargon also became the means of communication between the indigenous population and the European explorers, traders and settlers, as well as, later, their slaves. In fact there are also attestations of Mobilian Jargon having been used in encounters between non-indigenous people, such as an encounter in 1741 between the Frenchman Antoine Bonnefoy and British traders. Bonnefoy had fled from Cherokee captivity and ended up in an Alabama village, where, at the time, there were also six Englishmen from Carolina:

> During the time that I was in the council-house, the English came and gave me their hands .... I told them in the Mobilian language, which they understood, that having been taken by the Cherakis [Cherokees – VV] in December, I had escaped their villages a month before .... (Bonnefoey 1916:254)

Until well into the 20th century, it was used between Acadians and African Americans (Drechsel 1997:256). The language additionally had the function of a "sociocultural buffer" against unwelcome intrusion from outsiders, which not only confirmed the speakers' native identity, but also helped preserve their heritage.

Mobilian Jargon survived the longest among the Alabama-Coushattas in Louisiana and was used as late as the 1950s in a number of contexts, such as intratribal gatherings and interethnic communication, both among various tribes and among indigenous and non-indigenous people (for example during trapping, share-cropping or employment of different kinds). As late as in the 1970s there were still a few elderly speakers of the language left (Crawford 1978). It does not seem to have been stigmatized among its users.

14.4.1.2 *A short linguistic sketch of Mobilian Jargon*

Much, though not all, of the information on Mobilian Jargon comes from written sources, which means that statements about the sound system should be seen as tentative.

The phonological system of Mobilian Jargon could vary according to the speakers' first language. Even so, there seems to have been a relatively uniform system, with 15 consonants, /p, b, m, w, f, t, ɬ, s, n, l, ʧ, ʃ, j, k, h/ and 3 vowels, /e, a, o/. The vowels could be allophonically nasalized (indicated orthographically with ˜). Syllables could be moderately complex, with clusters of up to two consonants in the onset (as in *pleʃa* 'to work'), but clusters in the coda were rare; CV syllables seem to have been preferred, and vowel epenthesis was not infrequent. Words could have up to four syllables. Stress predominantly occurred on the final syllable in disyllabic words and on the penultimate in polysyllabic words.

---

220. The wide use of Mobilian Jargon means that it could also be seen as an extended pidgin (pidgincreole), which shows how fluid these categories are.

Despite the largely polysynthetic structure of the main input languages, the morphology in Mobilian Jargon was predominantly analytic, though there was a negative suffix *-(e)kʃo* which derived the antonym of a word, as in *aʃa* 'to have' / *aʃakʃo* 'to not have', *tana* 'to know' / *tanakʃo* 'to not know', and so on.

Nouns were typically invariant. Case and gender was irrelevant, though natural gender could be indicated though compounding with *nakne/nagane* 'male' or *ta(j)ek* 'female', as in *hat(t)ak nakne* 'man' (lit. 'person male'), *hat(t)ak ta(j)ek* 'woman' (lit. person female), *wak nagane* 'bull' (lit. 'cattle male'), and so on. Number was not indicated:

(450) eno poʃkoʃ lawa
1SG child many
'I have many children.' (Drechsel 1997:118)

There were no articles:

(451) a. aʃobolle eno hopone
fireplace 1SG cook
'I cook (it) in (the) fireplace.'
b. baʃpo eno baʃle taha
knife 1SG cut PST
'I've cut (it) with (a) knife.' (Drechsel 1997:120)

There was the demonstrative *yako* 'this, that':

(452) a. yako hatak atʃokma fehna
DEM man be.good very
'This man is very good.' (Drechsel 1997:142)
b. nanta yako
Q DEM
'Who is that over there?' (Crawford 1978:93)

The pronominal system differentiated between three persons, and in the first person only, between two numbers. There was no distinction between subject and object.

	SINGULAR	PLURAL
1	*(e)no*	*poʃno*
2	*(e)ʃ(no)*	*(e)ʃ(no)*
3	*(e)lap*	*(e)lap*

There were no specific possessive pronouns, except that the second person only allowed the longer form of the pronoun (*(e)ʃno*) in possessive constructions.

(453) a. enu tʃokka
1SG house
'my house'

b. (e)ʃno ēke / nakfe / tajek
2SG father brother female
'your father/brother/wife' (Crawford 1978:86, 95)

In possessive constructions the possessor pronoun was not obligatory:

(454) a. anõpa eno tana-kʃo
talk 1SG know-NEG
'I don't know his talk/language.'
b. eno mokla fehna
1SG friend very
'I am your good friend.' (Crawford 1978: 87, 93)

Adjectives were postnominal and invariant, and patterned as verbs.

(455) lap ʧokma-kʃo
3SG be.good-NEG
'It is not good.' (Drechsel 1997: 118)

Comparison was done analytically with the adverbial *fehna* 'very', as in *ʧo(o)kma* 'good' / *ʧok(o) ma fehna* 'better'.

Verbs were invariant. There was a postverbal past tense marker *taha*.

(456) a. pel(la) eno nowa
away 1SG walk
'I walk away / am walking away.'
b. eno noʃe taha
1SG sleep PST
'I slept.' (Drechsel 1997: 119f)

The word order was predominantly subject-object-verb with full noun phrases and object-subject-verb if the subject was a pronoun:

(457) a. sapõta(k) bolokfa belesõ
mosquito nose(?) sting(?)
'A mosquito stung (his) nose.'
b. neta eno hojo
bear 1SG hunt
'I hunt bear.' (Drechsel 1997: 120, 130)

Negation was formed with the negative marker *(e)kʃo*, which suffixed onto verbs and adjectives (cf. Examples (454a), (455) and (458c)). Polar questions were formed with rising intonation only:

(458) a. kafe no banna
coffe 1SG want
'I want coffee.'
b. kafe ʃno banna?
coffe 2SG want
'Do you want coffee?'
c. eno topakʃo
1SG be.sick
'I am not sick.'
d. ʃno topa?
2SG be.sick
'Are you sick?' (Crawford 1978: 82, 92)

In content questions the interrogative phrase was fronted and occurred clause initially (cf. (459a–c)), unless a full noun phrase was involved, in which case the question word appeared post-nominally in second position (as in (459d)).

(459) a. katema ʃno eja?
where 2SG go
'Where do you go?' / 'Where are you going?'

b. nanta lap anõpa taha?
what 3SG say PST
'What did she say?'

c. katome ʃno albe?
how.much 2SG pay
'How much do you pay?'

d. poʃkoʃ katome eʃno aʃa?
child how.much 2SG have
'How many children do you have?' (Drechsel 1997: 123)

There was no copula (cf. also Examples (452a) (454b), (455), (458)):

(460) a. atak ʧokma-kʃo
man be.good-NEG
'(The) man (is) not good.' (Crawford 1978: 85)

b. eno palama
1SG strong
'I (am) strong.' (Crawford 1978: 86)

c. eno nagane hemeta
1SG man young
'I (am a) young man.' (Drechsel 1997: 118)

Complex clauses were usually formed through juxtaposition only, though there are examples of the interrogatives being used as relative particles.

(461) a. tamaha olʧefo eno hakalo banna
town name 1SG hear want
'I want to hear (the) name of (the) town.' (Crawford 1978: 85)

b. yako hatak pake lap mente, eno yokpa fena
DEM man afar 3SG come 1SG glad very
'I am very glad that this man (from) afar comes (here)' / '…that this man comes (here from) afar.' (Drechsel 1997: 127)

c. nanta ʃno banna, ʃno ʧõpa
what 2SG want 2SG buy
'You buy what you want.' (Drechsel 1997: 127)

14.4.1.3 *Short text*

(This is an excerpt of a monologue uttered by a Choctaw Coushatta medicine woman, "a very old lady" (Crawford 1978: 116), recorded by James M. Crawford (Drechsel 1997: 141ff).)

Yako	hatak	atʃokma	fehna.	Katema	oja	lap	nowa	banna,	lap	aja.	Ena	tʃokha	eno	aja
DEM	man	good	very	where	all.over	3SG	travel	want	3SG	go	1SG	house	1SG	go

banna.	eno	aja	bana	eno	nowa-kʃo…	eno	nowa-kʃo.	Eno	tʃokha	eno	eja-kʃo. …	Katema
want	1SG	go	want	1SG	travel-NEG	1SG	travel-NEG	1SG	house	1SG	go-NEG	anywhere

õja	eno	nowa	banna.	Eno	nowa	banna.	Eno	eje	tʃokma-kʃo.	Katema	eno	nowa-kʃo
all	1SG	walk	want	1SG	walk	want	1SG	foot	good-NEG	anywhere	1SG	travel-NEG

fena.	Ena	noʃkobo	õja	tʃokma-kʃo,	tʃokma-kʃo,	tʃokma-kʃo.	Yako	hatak	lap	kaneya
very	1SG	head	all.over	good-NEG	good-NEG	good-NEG	DEM	man	3SG	leave

falama	lap	mente?
back	3SG	come

'This man is very good. He goes wherever he wants to travel. I want to go (to) my home. I want to go. I don't travel… I don't travel. I don't go (to) my home… I want to walk all over. I want to walk. My foot/feet is/are bad. I do not really travel anywhere. My head all over is bad, bad, bad. Does this man, (once) gone, come back?'

14.4.1.4 *Some sources of data*

There is very little primary data available for Mobilian Jargon. Crawford (1978) has a short word list, which includes a number of phrases and sentences, translated but not glossed. Drechsel (1996) is a very extensive wordlist and Drechsel (1997) is an in-depth study of Mobilian Jargon, including numerous glossed and translated examples, as well as a monologue and a song. A recording of a short interview by James M. Crawford, as well as a word list recording, have been made available by the *American Philosophical Society* (http://www.amphilsoc.org/exhibit/natamaudio/mobilian, accessed 13 February 2015). The Mezcal Jazz Unit and GrayHawk Perkins collaborated in 2012 to make the musical recording *Thirteen Moons*, a collection of Mobilian Jargon traditional chants, songs and folk tales, as well as modern stories, arranged to jazz rhythms (for short samples, see http://elalliance.org/2014/01/unheard_of_5/ or http://www.mezcalproduction.com/13moons.html, accessed 13 February 2015).

14.4.2 Jamaican: An English-lexified creole in Jamaica[221]

14.4.2.1 *A brief background sketch of Jamaican*

Jamaican, also called *Jamaican Creole*, *Jamaican Dialect*, *Jamaican Patwa*, *Jamaican Patwa Creole English*, *Bongo Talk*, *Jamiekan*, *Patois* or *Quashie Talk* by scholars, and called *Patwa* or *Jamaican Patwa* by the speakers themselves, is the mother tongue of the majority of the almost 3,000,000

221. This section is based primarily on Patrick (2007) and Farquharson (2013a). I am very grateful to Peter L. Patrick for his helpful comments on this snapshot.

inhabitants of Jamaica, as well as the Jamaican diaspora (chiefly in the UK, USA and Canada). Daughter varieties of Jamaican are *British Jamaican* (including *London*, *Birmingham* and *Bradford Jamaican*) in the UK and *Limonense* or *Limon Creole English* in Costa Rica (which is called *Mekatelyu* by the speakers themselves).

The island that came to be known as Jamaica was inhabited by Taino Arawakans when Columbus reached it in 1494. Estimates vary with respect to the number of indigenous inhabitants, but they seem to have been at least in the several tens of thousands (Britannica 2011a, Lalla & D'Costa 1990). Spanish settlement started in 1509 and used the indigenous population as slaves for their mining, farming, building and stock breeding. Diseases and maltreatment caused a massive population decline, which in turn led to an increased import of African slaves to the island, as well as an import of slaves of indigenous origin from other Caribbean colonies (Lalla & D'Costa 1990). By 1611 only 74 Tainos remained, while there were some 700 Spaniards (including a high number of recent Spanish immigrants from Puerto Rico) and 670 slaves on the island (Lalla & D'Costa 1990: 11).

In 1655 the British attacked and took possession of Jamaica. The Spanish population fled or was expelled from the island. A number of slaves escaped to the mountains and set up Maroon communities, which would continue the struggle against the British army. In 1739 the first Maroon War was won by the Maroons and led to a treaty which granted the Maroon settlements in the interior of the island. The second Maroon War was won by the British and led to a massive destruction of Maroon settlements, as well as the deportation of some 600 Maroons to Nova Scotia.

Once the British had taken possession of Jamaica, the British Governor encouraged not only settlers from other British colonies with lack of available arable land (e.g. the Lesser Antilles), but also buccaneers and privateers to settle on the island, to help ward off possible attacks from the Spanish and French forces of the nearby colonies. The economy of the first couple of decades was thus mostly by privateering rather than by farming (Kouwenberg 2009a).

The first slaves of African descent to be imported to Jamaica during British rule came with settlers from other British Caribbean colonies, especially Barbados and Suriname (Farquharson 2013a, Patrick 2007). However, the large scale plantation industry did not take off until the last quarter, with sugar quickly becoming the most planted crop. This led to a rapidly increasing demand of labour, and slaves started to be imported in large numbers. While the white population never exceeded ca. 10,000 for the period up to the Maroon Wars, and by 1713 had decreased to 7,000, the black population increased dramatically, despite high mortality rates, from ca. 2,500 in 1670 to 50,000 in 1713 (Kouwenberg 2009a: 331f).[222] It seems likely that Jamaican emerged during the booming plantation stage in the last quarter of the 17th century (Patrick 2004, Kouwenberg 2009a). Archival evidence suggests that the majority of the slaves came from the Bight of Biafra,

222. However, the white population increased in the late 18th and early 19th century, with a peak of 28,000 in 1810, before then subsequently decreasing again (Peter L. Patrick, p.c.).

the Gold Coast and West Central Africa as well as the Bight of Benin, meaning that Bantu and Gbe languages, as well as Akan and Igbo (and possibly also Lower Cross and Ijoid languages) would have been likely substrate languages to the creole (Kouwenberg 2009a). The superstrate languages are likely to have been nonstandard varieties of English, such as south-western, Scots and Irish varieties, as well as varieties from the other Caribbean settlements (Lalla & D'Costa 1990, Patrick 2004, Farquharson 2013a). It does not seem farfetched to assume a high level of multilingualism and code-switching.

With Emancipation in 1838, many former slaves moved from the plantation into remote villages, which removed them from contact with the superstrate varieties and allowed for the maintenance of basilectal varieties of Jamaican (Patrick 2007). The economic and political dominance of the small minority of native speakers of Standard English has led to a continuum of lects ranging from basilectal to acrolectal varieties of Jamaican.[223] This socio-political dominance has remained even after Jamaica achieved full independence from the United Kingdom in 1962 and English is still the official language of the country, while Jamaican remains stigmatized (Patrick 2004). Most Jamaicans are bilingual in some form of Jamaican and in English, although there is a sizeable population (a little more than 1/3) that is monolingual in Jamaican (Farquharson 2013a). Mass urbanization and a rural to urban migration, especially since the period between the two World Wars, have led to dialect levelling (Patrick 2004).

Jamaican oral culture is vibrant and especially the vocal music is very well known worldwide. But Jamaican has also long been used in novels and short stories, mainly for dialogues, to mark character or to set the scene (Lalla & D'Costa 1990). By now there is also an established tradition of Jamaican poetry (Farquharson 2013a). However, such prose as narration, journalistic writing and op-eds are still written in English rather than Jamaican.

14.4.2.2 *A short linguistic sketch of Jamaican*

Unless otherwise specified, the following describes basilectal Jamaican. The orthography of the sources has been retained.

Jamaican has 20 consonants, /p, b, m, f, v, t, d, n, s, z, ɹ, l, ʧ, ʤ, ʃ, j, k, g, ŋ, w/, and five vowels, /i, e, a, o, u/ of which three (/i:, a:, u:/) may be phonemically lengthened (Harry 2006) and four (/ĩ, ɛ̃, ã, õ/) may be phonemically nasalized (Farquharson 2013a). The Western dialect of Jamaican has an additional contrastive consonant, /h/, which is lacking in the Eastern dialect, where /h/ is either dropped or may appear non-contrastively (also in hypercorrections) (Harry 2006). Jamaican is variably rhotic (Peter L. Patrick, p.c.). There is no tone (Gooden 2003, but see Harry 2006). Syllables may be complex, with up to two consonants in both the onset and the coda, as in /pla:nt/ 'plant' (Devonish & Harry 2004: 473).

223. The linguistic situation in Jamaica is one of those that have led to the various continuum models that have been proposed (for an accessible short overview, see Patrick 2004: 408ff with further references). See further Chapter 8.

The morphology is predominantly analytic, though reduplication is prolific and there is optional suffixation of the plural markers *-dem* and *-s/-z*, prefixing of possessive *fi-* to the pronoun, as well as examples of compounding.

Nouns are invariant. Natural gender is indicated through compounding with *man* 'man' and *uman* 'woman', as in *man-foul* 'rooster' and *uman-foul* 'hen' (Farquharson 2013a: 84). Case is not relevant. Number may be indicated with the postnominal plural marker *dem*,[224] though this is only used with definite noun phrases (compare (462a) with b), or variably with *-s/-z* (which may also co-occur with *-dem*). Generic nouns usually remain unmarked (cf. (462c)).

(462) a. di man-dem dig di hole and di woman-dem plant di corn
DEF man-PL dig DEF hole and DEF woman-PL plant DEF corn
'The men dug the holes and the women planted the corn.'

b. police shoot Starman … dem rain down gunshot pon him
police shoot PN 3PL rain down gunshot on 3SG
'The police shot Starman at a dance.'

c. papa have him knife weh him use to stick cow
papa have 3SG knife REL 3SG use to stick cow
'Papa had his knife that he used to stick cows.' (Patrick 2007: 142f)

There is a definite article *di* 'the' and an indefinite article *wahn* 'a', which is related to the numeral 'one' (though it is debated whether there is any difference in pronunciation). There are the prenominal demonstratives *dis* 'this' (which may combine with *ya* 'here', as in *dis-ya*), *dat* 'that' (which may combine with *de* 'there', as in *dat-de*) and *dem* 'these, those' (which may combine with both *ya* and *de*, as in *dem-ya/dem-de*). The demonstratives may be conjoint (as in *dis-ya bwai* 'this boy') or disjoint (as in *dis bwai ya* 'this boy').

The pronoun system distinguishes between three persons and two numbers. Mesolectal forms (shown in parenthesis) distinguish between subject and object pronouns, as well as gender in the third person singular.

	SUBJECT	OBJECT
1SG	*mi, (a)*	*mi*
2SG	*yu*	*yu*
3SG.M	*im/ihn*	*im*
3SG.F	*(shi)*	*(ar)*
1PL	*wi*	*wi*
2PL	*unu*	*unu*
3PL	*dem/dehn*	*dem*

Possessive pronouns are formed by prefixing *fi-* 'for' to the personal pronoun, though adnominal possessives are identical with the personal pronoun. Nominal possession is typically expressed through juxtaposition:

224. But see Stewart (2007) for a discussion on why *-dem* should be seen as an inclusiveness marker rather than a plural marker.

(463) di nieba-dem ous wash we ina di laas flod
DEF neighbour-PL house wash away in DEF last flood
'The neighbours' house got washed away in the last flood.' (Farquharson 2013a: 84)

Adjectives precede the noun. Predicative adjectives inflect like (stative) verbs and may take such verbal markers as the negator or tense, aspect or mood markers. Comparison is optionally indicated with *-a*.

(464) a. mi ongli se im did shaat!
1SG only say 3SG ANT short
'I only said he was short!' (Patrick 2007: 130)

b. Jan big-a dan im sister Mieri
PN big-COMPAR than 3SG sister PN
'John is older than his sister Mary.' (Farquharson 2013b: feature 42)

The temporal reading of a clause may depend on the lexical aspect of the verb: bare stative verbs may have a present tense reading (as in (465a)), while bare dynamic verbs may have a past or habitual reading (as in (465b)). The anterior marker *did* or *ben/wehn* may give a past reading with stative verbs (as in (464a)) and a past-before-past reading with dynamic verbs (as in (465c)). The past tense may also variably be indicated with the suffix *-(e)d/-t* (Patrick 1999). There is a future marker *wi* (as in (465d)).

(465) a. Jan sick an im daata nuo
PN sick and 3SG daughter know
'John is sick and his daughter knows.' (Farquharson 2013b: feature 51)

b. Mieri kuk di fuud
PN cook DEF food
'Mary cooked the food.' (Farquharson 2013b: feature 15)

c. Jan wehn daans
PN ANT dance
'John had danced.' (Farquharson 2013a: 85)

d. mi wi go de sonde
1SG FUT go there Sunday
'I will go there on Sunday.' (Patrick 2007: 133)

In addition to the tense markers, there are the aspect markers *de/d(a)/(a)go(o)* for progressive and *don* for completive, as well as several modal markers.

The word order is typically subject-verb-object. Negation is expressed with the preverbal *no*, though the tense-neutral *duon(t)* and *nat*, as well as the past negative *neva* are also common.

(466) a. Jiemz no riid di buk don yet
PN NEG read DEF book COMP yet
'James has not finished reading the book yet.'

b. im duon sari fi dem agen
3SG NEG sorry for 3PL again
'He is not sorry for them anymore.'

c. ef dem neva bring op dis piis man, plenti piipl wuda ded
if 3PL NEG.PST bring up DEM peace man many people MOD die
'If they hadn't started this peace (movement), lots of people would have died.'
(Patrick 2007: 130, 132)

Polar questions are indicated through rising intonation:

(467) a. Stiesi gaan a skuul
PN gone LOC school
'Stacy has gone to school.'
b. Stiesi gaan a school?
PN gone LOC school
'Has Stacy gone to school?' (Farquharson 2013a: 88)

In content questions the interrogative phrase is fronted. The focus particle *a* may appear clause initially in any kind of interrogative construction. In focus constructions the focus particle appears clause initially and the focussed constituent immediately after that. With focussed verb phrases the verb phrase is doubled, but inflection is marked only on the focussed copy.

(468) a. a di man Piita biit op kaaz im iizi a beks
FOC DEF man PN beat up because 3SG easy of vex
'Peter beat up *the man* because he (Peter) is irritable.'
b. a no rait dehn rait i
FOC NEG write 3PL write 3SG
'They didn't *write* it.' (Farquharson 2013a: 88)

Since predicative adjectives are functionally stative verbs, they do not take a copula. In nominal predication, however, the copula, which is identical to the focus marker, is obligatory:

(469) Jan a obya-man.
PN COP witchcraft-man
'John is a ritual specialist.' (Farquharson 2013b: feature 73)

There are various coordinating constructions. Subordination may be indicated with *dat* 'that' or the optional complementizer *se*, but juxtaposition is also common. Relative clauses are expressed with the particle *huu(fa)* for human referents and *we* for either human or non-human referents, plus a gap (cf. Example (462a)). There are a number of serial verb constructions, for example expressing direction or instrumentation, among many others.

(470) a. im kyar di yam go/kom
3SG carry DEF yam go/come
'He carried the yam(s) (away)/brought the yam(s).'
b. mi tek stik pick mango
1SG take stick pick mango
'I pick mangoes with a stick.' (Farquharson 2013a: 87)

14.4.2.3 *Short text*

(Excerpt from Farquharson 2013a: 89.)

I man gu back agen ahn lik i uman. So siem so ihn dash we i uman sipaz.
DEF man go back again and hit DEF woman so same so 3SG throw away DEF woman slippers

So aafta dat nou, dehn di de. Ier i uman nou "Bot yu no aadineri. Yu dash
so after that now 3PL LOC there hear DEF woman now but 2SG NEG ordinary 2SG throw

we mi gud bran nyuu sipaz we mi jos bai laas wiik? A lik im shuda lik yu
away 1SG good brand new slippers REL 1SG just buy last week FOC hit 3SG MOD hit 2SG

ina yu feis man."
in 2SG face man

'The man went and hit the woman again. And he threw away the woman's slippers, just so. So, after that, they were there, and the woman said: "You must be crazy. You threw away my perfectly new slippers that I just bought last week? Man, he should have *punched* you in the face."'

14.4.2.4 *Some sources of data*

There is a wealth of primary data available for Jamaican. Sistren (2005), for example, is a recent collection of life stories. Lalla & D'Costa (1990) provide a number of texts and excerpts of Jamaican, ranging from the late 17th to the late 19th century. Cassidy & LePage's (1980) *Dictionary of Jamaican English* is a classic. A number of authors use or used Jamaican for poetry, fiction and drama, such as Louise Simone Bennett-Coverley, Joan Andrea Hutchinson, Erna Brodber, John Figueroa, Esther Figueroa, Linton Kwesi Johnson, Trevor Rhone, among many others. There are a number of videos available on and in Jamaican on YouTube.

14.4.3 Caló: A Spanish/Romani mixed language in Spain[225]

14.4.3.1 *A brief background sketch of Caló*

Caló, by scholars also called *Spanish Romani* and *hispanorromani* (Adiego 2002), is spoken by a minority of the Kalé people, a total about 40,000 in Spain, 15,000 in France, 5,000 in Portugal and 10,000 in Brazil (Lewis et al. 2014).[226] The speakers usually refer to their language as *chipé* (Anthony Grant, p.c.).

While there is general consensus that the Roma originate in northern or north-western India and that Romani is an Indo-Aryan language, the exact origin of the Roma, when they emigrated from India and how their migration path evolved is debated. For a concise and accessible overview, with numerous further references, see Matras (2002: 14ff). A recent genomic study with data

225. This section is based predominantly on Mayo (1870) and Quindale (1867). I am very grateful to Vijay John for his helpful comments on this snapshot.

226. But cf. Boretzky & Igla (1994) who state that the language is extinct. Notice that Caló has also been used for non-Romani slang and cant varieties, also in the south-western USA (e.g. Rosensweig 1973, Polkinhorn et al. 1983). These slang or cant varieties are not considered in this section.

from 13 different European Romani groups suggests that the various Roma groups of Europe descend from one single founder population and tentatively places the origin of this founder population in the India-Pakistani border area (roughly the area of Rajasthan, Punjab and Jammu & Kashmir; this is also in accordance with numerous linguistic and anthropological studies, cf. Matras 2002); the genomic data further indicates that the founder population left the area of origin about 1,500 years ago and arrived in the Balkans about 900 years ago (possibly via present-day Iran and Turkey; linguistically this is supported, as evidenced by loans from languages spoken in these areas), from where they spread to the rest of Europe (Mendizabal et al. 2012). Historical sources, however, do not mention Roma in the Balkans until the 14th century (Samer 2003).

It seems as if the Roma arrived in Spain in the early 1400s; the earliest certain reference to Roma in Spain is from 1425, when Alfonso V of Aragon granted a safe-conduct for the pilgrims under one 'Don Juan de Egipte Menor' (Fraser 1995:76).[227] The Roma population in Spain is today estimated at about 650,000–800,000,[228] residing in both rural and urban areas, especially in and around Madrid and Andalusia (Bakker 1995). Most Spanish Roma, or Kalé, have Spanish (especially Andalusian Spanish) as their mother tongue (Bakker 1995).

The Roma have suffered centuries of stigmatization and aggressive persecution; negative attitudes and bigotry still prevail against them in most societies, with some countries engaging in open and outright discrimination. Roma are in many cases put under great pressure to assimilate to the mainstream society, while at the same time being severely marginalized. Language shift to the language of the host society has been one effect of this pressure. However, a number of Roma societies have developed so-called Para-Romani languages, that is, mixed languages between the host languages and the Romani of the community. While there is considerable debate as to how these languages emerged (see Matras 2002:247ff for a concise overview and further references), it does not seem farfetched to assume that identity played a role. For a severely marginalized population, the mixed language might serve as a way of maintaining a sense of continuity with the origins of the population, as well as flagging a separate identity from the host population. Furthermore, it seems as if many Para-Romani languages, including Caló, were or are used as in-group languages for secret communication and for the exclusion of others (cf. Mulcahy 1979:15ff and Leigh 1998 on Caló specifically):

> Caló serves as a 'secret language' which can be spoken if the necessity should arise that a third party (presumably a Gentile [i.e. a non-Roma – VV]) should be kept in the dark. Perhaps more importantly it serves as a marker of ethnic identification – a symbol both of solidarity and separation. Caló therefore has to do primarily with boundaries: with process of access and closure.
> (Mulcahy 1979:16)

227. The Roma were often referred to as 'Egyptians' in early European sources, whence the word *Gypsy*.

228. According to Minority Rights Group (*sv* Spain at http://www.minorityrights.org/1527/spain/spain-overview.html, accessed 13 February 2015)

It is not possible to determine exactly when Caló may have emerged, but the archaic nature of the Spanish elements in Caló as well as archival data point to a relatively early development, possibly as early as the 16th century (Bakker 1995, Buzek 2011).

The steady shift to Spanish has led Caló to be labelled endangered, and, in some sources, even extinct (e.g. Boretzky & Igla 1994, Bakker 1995, Buzek 2011). However, language revitalization programs have been initiated, notably by Juan de Dios Ramírez-Heredia who is promoting what he calls *romanó-kaló*, which is essentially an attempt to make Caló more like the older Iberian Romani (cf., for example, Hancock 1990, Ramírez-Heredia 1993; see also the site Unión Romaní at http://www.unionromani.org/, accessed 13 February 2015). Sociolinguistic attitudinal studies indicate that there is a strong possibility that such revitalization projects may succeed (Andersson 2011).

14.4.3.2 *A short linguistic sketch of Caló*

Caló can be described as a G-L mixed language, with a predominantly Spanish grammar and an essentially Romani lexicon.

The phonemes of Caló are taken over from Andalusian Spanish (Bakker 1995), with 17 consonants, /p, b, m, f, t, d, n, s, ɾ, r, l, ʧ, ɲ, j, k, g, x/, and five vowels, /i, e, a, u, o/. Those Romani phonemes that were not represented in Andalusian Spanish were lost, for example the aspirated consonants became nonaspirated (/pʰ, kʰ, ʧʰ/ > /p, k, ʧ/, except that /tʰ/ became /ʧ/) and /v/ became /b/. As in Andalusian Spanish, there seems to be free variation between /r/ and /l/, and /s/ and /θ/. However, the stress pattern of Caló differs from Spanish and resembles Romani in that ultimate stress is common.

Both Spanish and Romani allow various synthetic morphological strategies, and this has carried over to Caló. Both derivation and inflection is carried out through affixation. Most of the derivational and affixational affixes are Spanish, though some are Romani, such as the gender agreement suffixes *-i* (feminine) and *-o* (masculine), the noun forming *-pen* and in some instances the plural markers *-ia* (feminine nouns) and *-e* (nominalized adjectives). However, in the latter case the Romani plural suffixes are followed by the Spanish plural *-s*, yielding a double marking. There are instances of frozen Romani case forms and the Romani verbal person markers *-av* (1st person singular)[229] and *-el* (3rd person singular) before the Spanish person markers. The latter has been claimed to have acquired a derivational function, which would in that case represent an innovation in Caló, in that verbs with *-el* denote a more intense action, as in *ʧin-ar* 'to cut' versus *ʧin-el-ar* 'to harvest', *ker-ar* 'to do' versus *ker-el-ar* 'to execute, work, perform' or *ʧib-ar* 'to put, place' versus *ʧib-el-ar* 'to include, insert' (Mayo 1870: 61). However, this has been contested by, for example Adiego (2005) and Clavería (1962); for a summary of arguments, see Adiego (2005: 73ff).

There are two genders, masculine (words ending in a consonant or in *-e, -ó, -o*, or *-u*) and feminine (words ending in *-í* or *-a*). Plural is indicated with the Spanish *-(e)s* for all nouns (cf. the masculine *pelé* 'egg' and the feminine *ʧaʧumí* 'truth' in Example (471a and b)), irrespective of gender; nouns ending in *-i or -í* may take the plural marker *-as* (as in (471c)). Case is not relevant.

229. Though *-av* could also be the Romani *-av-* 'CAUSative' (Anthony Grant, p.c.).

(471) a. mang-ó dui pelé-s axeriz-ao-s pa bufete-ar[230]
request-1SG.PST.PFV two egg-PL fry-PTCP-PL for lunch-INF
'I requested two fried eggs to eat for lunch.'
b. sinan ʧorrí-as as kiribí-s pur pen-an as ʧatʃumí-s
be-3PL.PRES evil-PL DEF.F.PL midwife-PL when speak-3PL.PRES DEF.F.PL truth-PL
'The midwives are bad when they speak the truth.'
c. as panʧe angustí-as ja bae
DEF.F.PL five finger-PL of.DEF.F.SG hand
'The five fingers of the hand.' (Quindale 1867: 2, 5, 22)

There are the indefinite articles *(j)ek(e)* (masculine), which is identical with the numeral 'one', and *ondola* (feminine), both of Romani origin.

(472) a. jeki diɲí terel-a xobedeke xara-s
one pound have-3SG.PRES 16 ounce-PL
'One pound is 16 ounces.'
b. ʧit-aron jes trixul e pateran
put-3PL.PST.PFV one cross of signpost
'They placed a cross as a signpost.' (Quindale 1867: 29, 57)

The definite article, essentially of Spanish origin, inflects for gender and number. The definite article may contract with the preposition *de* 'of'.

			contracted with *de*	
	SINGULAR	PLURAL	SINGULAR	PLURAL
MASCULINE	*o(r)*	*le(r)*	*je*	*es*
FEMININE	*a/i*	*as/ar/le(r)*	*ja*	*jas*

There are the demonstratives, of Romani origin, *okona/okono* 'this' (plural *okonas* 'these') and *okola/okolo* 'that' (plural *okolas* 'those').

(473) okona sinel-a dekeró ʧaboro, y okola deskerí
DEM.PROX.SG be-3SG.PRES 3SG.POSS.M.SG son and DEM.DIST.SG 3SG.POSS.F.SG
ʧabori: a os dui ʧindó
daughter to 3PL.M.O two give.birth-PST
'This is her son and that is her daughter: she gave birth to them two (i.e. both).'
(Quindale 1867: 28)

The demonstratives may also be used as a third person singular pronoun:

(474) a. sáta pinʧ-aré okono?
how know-1SG.FUT this
'How will I know it?' (Mayo 1870: 59)
b. rand-a okono andré tiró lel
write-2SG.IMP this in 2SG.POSS.M.SG note.book
'Write it in your notebook.' (Quindale 1867: 63)

230. In all the examples of this section the orthography of the source has been altered to an IPA transcription.

The pronominal system (of Romani origin) differentiates between three persons and two numbers. The third person has gender differentiation.

	SUBJECT	OBJECT
1SG	*menda/man*	*mange/nu/me*
2SG	*tuke/tute/tue*	*tuke/tute/tue*
3SG.M	*ó*	*o*
3SG.F	*siró*	*a*
1PL	*amange, mu*	*amange/mu*
2PL	*sange/bros*	*sange*
3PL.M	*xunós*	*os*
3PL.F	*sirás*	*as*

Possessive pronouns appear prenominally and agree with the noun in gender and number. Notice that the same word is used for both 'his' and 'her' (cf. Spanish *su*).

	SINGULAR	PLURAL	
1SG.M/1SG.F	*minrió/minrí* or *men*	*minrés/minrias*	'my'
2SG.M/2SG.F	*tiró/tirí* or *tun*	*tirés/tirías*	'your.SG'
3SG.M/3SG.F	*deskeró/deskerí* or *sun*	*deskerés/deskerías*	'his, her'
1PL.M/1PL.F	*amaró/amarí* or *nonrio/nonria*	*amarés/amarías* or *nonrios/nonrias*	'our'
2PL.M/2PL.F	*xiré/xirí or bos*	*xirés/xirías* or *bruas*	'your.PL'
3PL.M/3PL.F	*deskeró/deskerí*	*deskerés/deskerías*	'their'

Nominal possession is expressed analytically with the preposition *e* 'of':

(475) os deke ditʃabanelo-s ja lirí e undebel
DEF.PL.M 10 commandment-PL of.DEF.F.SG law of God
'The ten commandments of God's law.' (Quindale 1867:28)

Adjectives agree with the nouns they modify in gender and number (some adjectives may get double plural marking; see above):

(476) sin-aban hambré-s baribú latʃo-s
be-3PL.PST.IPFV person-PL much good-PL
'They were very good people.' (Quindale 1867:37)

Comparison is expressed analytically with *bus/buter* 'more' and *but* 'very' or post-adjectival *baribú* 'much', as in *latʃo* 'good' versus *bus latʃo* 'better' versus *but latʃo/ latʃo baribú* 'best'.

Verbal inflection is taken over from Spanish. However, all verbs have regularized to only one conjugation (*-ar*). Since the verb inflects for person, subject pronouns are not obligatory to the clause (so-called "pro-drop"):

(477) xamel-emos amarí pirría e cata tʃibé
eat-1PL.PRES 1PL.POSS.F.SG pot of each day
'We eat our stew every day.' (Quindale 1867:59)

There are two moods, the indicative and the subjunctive. The indicative has a present tense, a past imperfective, a past perfective, a future tense, a conditional and an imperative. The subjunctive has a present, a past and a future tense. Colloquial Caló has only the present tense (used as a nonpast to express both present and future events) and only one aspect-neutral past tense in both the indicative and the subjunctive (Mayo 1870: 64ff). There are a number of modal verbs.

The word order is predominantly subject-verb-object:

(478) yeké-s durotun-és sin-aban nak-ando as okana-s ja
one-PL shepherd-PL be-3PL.PST.IPFV pass-GER DEF.PL.F hour-PL of.DEF.F.SG
ratʃí opré deskerías braxí-as
night on.top 3PL.POSS.F.PL cattle-PL
'Some shepherds were passing the hours of the night on their livestock.'
(Quindale 1867: 14)

Negation is expressed with the invariant *na(nai)*. Polar questions are formed through intonation only; in content questions the interrogative phrase is fronted:

(479) a. terel-ais akoi butʃi e xam-ar?
have-2PL.PRES here something of eat-INF
'Do you have something to eat here?'
b. kitʃí mol-a okono?
how.much be.worth-3SG.PRES this
'How much is this worth?'
(Quindale 1867: 38, 63)

There is a copula *sinar/sinelar* 'to be', which is obligatory and inflects for three persons and two numbers:

	SINGULAR		PLURAL	
1	*sis*	I am	*simo*	we are
2	*sisle*	you are	*sai*	you are
3	*sin*	s/he/it is	*sen*	they are

The copula can also be conjugated in the Spanish manner. There is no existential.

There are the coordinating conjunctions *y/ta* 'and', *o* 'or' and *tami* 'but'. There are the relativizers *koin* (which functions as the interrogative 'who?'; plural *koines*), used primarily with human referents, as well as *sos* and *ma*.

(480) a. koin girel-a á mange, girel-a á sos mange bitʃab-ó
who scorn-3SG.PRES to 1SG.O scorn-3SG.PRES to REL 1SG.O send-3SG.PST.PFV
'Whoever scorns me, scorns the one who sent me.'
b. xamel-a ma tuke tʃild-aren anglal
eat-2SG.IMP REL 2SG prepare-3PL.FUT.SUB in.front
'Eat what they put in front of you.'
(Quindale 1867: 24, 35)

Like many other secret languages, Caló makes use of cryptolalic forms, where glosses are replaced according to various principles. This helps keep the language unintelligible to outsiders. For example, the Spanish word for March is *marzo*, the initial syllable of which is identical to the Spanish word for 'sea' (*mar*). The Caló word for 'sea' is *loria* and so a cryptolalic form for 'March' becomes *Loriazo* (attaching the *-zo* of *marzo* to the Caló word for 'sea'; Bakker 1995: 134).

14.4.3.3 *Short text*

(Excerpt from a rhyme of the months of the year, from Coelho 1892. The Spanish orthography has been changed to IPA. Unaltered Spanish words appear in italics. Translation and glossing by me.)

Agoustuntʃo.	*En*	*la*	huertisara	sin-a	*el*	xulaj;	solt-ó	se
august	in	DEF.F.SG	garden	be-3SG.PRES	DEF.M.SG	master	fall.asleep-3SG.PST.PFV	REL

ja;	*los*	tʃukel-es	*me*	ladrisarel-an,	*jo*	manró	le	tʃubel-o,	*ja*	le
already	DEF.M.PL	dog-PL	1SG.O	bark-3PL.PRES	1SG.S	bread	3PL	give-1SG.PRES	already	DEF.M.PL

tʃikubel-o	*dos*	petí-s	ke	bari-ás	*son*	*ja*.
steal-1SG.PRES	two	beast-PL	that	big-F.PL	be.3PL.PRES	already

Setembruntʃo.	*komo*	mikel-as	*las*	tʃorí-s	*en*	*los*	palonolaré-s,	*siendo*	*el*
September.	how	leave-2SG.PRES	DEF.F.PL	mule-PL	in	DEF.M.PL	pen-PL	be.PTCP	DEF.M.SG

mesuntʃo	*más*	kontrasiuntʃo	*de*	*los*	gustipeɲí-s?	*Dexaste=las*	tʃori-ar,
month	more	contrary	of	DEF.M.PL	robbery-PL	leave.2SG.IMP=DEF.F.PL	rob-INF

biene	*un*	kaló	*y*	*te*	*las*	nikob-a.
come.3SG.PRES	one	Cale	and	2SG.O	DEF.F.PL	steal-3SG.PRES

'**August**. The farmer is in the field. He has already fallen asleep. The dogs bark at me, I give them bread, quickly I steal the two beasts that are big already. // **September**. How (can you) leave the mules in the pen, (it) being the most contrary of months of the thieves? Let them be stolen, a Kale comes and steals them from you.'

14.4.3.4 *Some sources of data*

There is not much primary data available for Caló, especially not recent data. Mayo published a grammar (1870) and an extensive dictionary (under the pseudonym Quindale 1867), which also contains a number of phrases and sentences, unfortunately only accessible to those who read Spanish. Coelho (1892) gives a number of sentences and some texts, unfortunately only accessible to those who read Portuguese. Borrow (1841) gives a few New Testament texts with translations to English. George Borrow's translation of the Gospel according to Luke is available online at http://www.gutenberg.org/ebooks/29470 (accessed 13 February 2015).

14.5 Summary

Pidgins seem to have a slight tendency for not marking a relative clause with any relative particle. However, they do not seem more likely than non-pidgins to lack an overt expression for the head in subject relative clauses. It does not seem uncommon for pidgins to have directional serial verb constructions.

Most of the extended pidgins have a relative particle to indicate a relative clause. It seems roughly equally common for extended pidgins to have a resumptive pronoun or to have a gap for the head in subject relative clauses. Directional serial verb constructions seem very common for extended pidgins.

Creole languages seem to tend to have a relative particle to indicate a relative clause. As with non-creoles, it is much more common for creoles to have a gap for the head in subject relative clauses. However, creole languages are possibly less likely to have a non-reduction strategy for the head in subject relative clauses than non-creoles. While it is not uncommon for creoles to have directional serial verb constructions, it is also not uncommon for creoles to lack them; that is, creole languages do not seem particularly prone to having directional serial verb constructions.

G-L mixed languages seem to adopt the relative clause strategies of the input language that provided most of the grammar, while N-V mixed languages seem to adopt the relative clause strategy from the input language that provided most of the verb phrase structure. Directional serial verb constructions do not seem to be attested for mixed languages.

14.6 Key points

- **Pidgins are not especially likely to lack relative particles and do not differ from non-pidgins with respect to subject relativization strategy.**
- **Extended pidgins (pidgincreoles) tend to have relative particles and are not especially prone to have a gap for subject relativization.**
- **Creoles tend to have relative particles and a gap for subject relativization.**
- **Mixed languages seem to take the relative clause strategies from the language(s) which has provided the bulk of the grammatical or verb phrase structure.**
- **Directional serial verb constructions are neither common nor uncommon for pidgins.**
- **English-lexified extended pidgins (pidgincreoles) have directional serial verb constructions.**
- **Directional serial verb constructions are neither common nor uncommon for creoles.**

14.7 Exercises

1. How do the findings on relativization strategies in creole languages relate to the notion of creoles as typologically unique?
2. What are the implications of the findings on the relativization strategies of extended pidgins (pidgincreoles)?
3. How do the findings on relativization strategies in creoles relate to the notion of the pidgin-to-creole life cycle?
4. Does it seem possible to predict with reasonable accuracy from which language the relativization strategy of a given mixed language will originate? Motivate your answer and give examples.
5. What are the implications of the findings on directional serial verb constructions in creoles?

Languages cited in Chapter 15

Chapter 15

Pragmatics

Pidgins and creoles are often described as having an invariant negative particle to negate declarative clauses, as forming polar questions through intonation only and as lacking politeness distinctions in the pronominal system. Section 15.1 in this chapter tests whether pidgins and creoles differ from non-pidgins and non-creoles with respect to the negative morpheme used, and discusses negative morphemes in extended pidgins and mixed languages. Section 15.2 checks whether pidgins and creoles differ from non-pidgins and non-creole with respect to the formation of polar questions, and brings up polar questions in extended pidgins and mixed languages. Section 15.3 discusses politeness distinctions in second person pronouns in pidgin and creole languages and compares them to non-pidgins and non-creoles, as well as discusses politeness distinctions in second person pronouns in extended pidgins and mixed languages. Section 15.4 gives short sketches of three languages mentioned in the chapter: Juba Arabic (an Arabic-lexified extended pidgin in Sudan), Papiá Kristang (a Portuguese-lexified creole in Malaysia) and Angloromani (an English/Romani mixed language in the UK).

15.1 Negation

Negation reverses the truth of a proposition. For example, the declarative sentence *John is baking a cake* states the fact (the actuality) that John is baking a cake. If we add a negative marker to the declarative, we reverse this actual fact: *John is not baking a cake* states that whatever John may be doing, he is not baking a cake. There are different types and scopes of negation. With **clausal negation** a whole clause is negated, producing a negative counterpart to the affirmative declarative clause, as in *John is not baking a cake*. With constituent negation only a particular constituent of a clause is negated, as in the noun phrase negation <u>*No cake*</u> *was baked* (the negator refers to the noun phrase *cake* only and not the entire clause). Languages may also have **negative pronouns**, as in <u>*Nobody*</u> *baked a cake*, or **negative adverbs**, as in *John* <u>*never*</u> *bakes cakes*.

Scope refers to that section of the utterance which is affected by a particular form. In English, negation usually has scope over everything that comes after it, as in *I deliberately didn't finish the cake* versus *I didn't deliberately finish the cake*. In the former sentence I consciously saw to it that I didn't finish the cake, while in the second I did finish it, but it was not intentional.

This section will compare clausal negation in pidgins and creoles with non-pidgins and non-creoles, as well as discuss clausal negation in extended pidgins and mixed languages. For the purpose of comparison, a language has here been coded for its dominant strategy only. It is beyond the scope of this section to properly discuss negation in the languages of the world. For a very accessible typological overview, see Miestamo (2007), as well as Givón (2001a: 369ff).

15.1.1 Negation in pidgin languages

Pidgins are usually described as having one invariant negative marker (cf. e.g. Winford 2003: 276). This is, for example, the case in KiSetla where the Swahili negated existential *ha-pana* ('NEGative-EXISTential') has become a general negative particle:

KiSetla (Pidgin (Swahili-lexified): Kenya)

(481) a. mimi hapana anguka
1SG NEG fall
'I will not fall.'
b. yeye hapana oe
3SG NEG marry
'He hasn't gotten married.' (Vitale 1980: 57)

To have a negative particle as the main strategy for negating declarative sentences is, in fact, the by far most common strategy in the current pidgin sample, as shown in Table 15.1. In fact, only three languages have other strategies: Pidgin A70 (Bantu-lexified: Cameroon) has the negative prefixes *ke-* or *teke-* (Alexandre 1963) and Island Carib Men's Language (Carib-lexified: Lesser Antilles Islands) has the negative affixes *-pa* or *i-...-pa* (if the verb starts with a consonant; Taylor & Hoff 1980), while Chinese Pidgin Russian has either the negative prefix *ne-* or the auxiliary verb *netu* (Perekhvalskaya 2013b: feature 100).

As the figures in Table 15.1 show, languages with a negative particle are more common in the current pidgin sample than in Dryer's (2013e) sample. It thus seems as if pidgins are more likely than non-pidgins to have negative particles as their main strategy for negating declarative sentences.[231]

231. The languages with negative particles remain highly overrepresented in the pidgin sample compared to the WALS sample even if the comparison only involves the two largest groups in the WALS sample (negative particles and negative affixes).

Table 15.1 Negative morphemes in the current pidgin sample and in WALS (Dryer 2013e). For a full legend of the languages in the pidgin sample, see http://dx.doi.org/10.1075/cll.48.additional.

	Pidgin sample		WALS	
	N	%	N	%
Negative affix	2	5.9	395	31.4
Negative particle	31	91.2	502	43.4
Negative auxiliary verb	–	–	47	4.1
Negative word, unclear if verb or particle	–	–	73	6.3
Variation negative word / affix	–	–	21	1.8
Double negation	–	–	119	10.3
Mixed	1	2.9	–	
Total	34		1157	

($\chi^2 = 66.44$; $df = 6$; $p_{sim} < 0.001$*** (B = 10,000))
($G = 22.83$; $df = 6$; $p_{two\text{-}tailed} < 0.001$***)

15.1.2 Negation in extended pidgins (pidgincreoles)

Eight of nine extended pidgins have a negative particle as their dominant or only strategy for negated declarative sentences. For all English-lexified languages the negator is *no*, such as in Nigerian Pidgin:

Nigerian Pidgin (Extended pidgin (English-lexified): Nigeria)

(482) à no bay nyam
1SG.S NEG buy yam
'I didn't buy yams.' (Faraclas 1996: 89)

It should be noticed, however, that Nigerian Pidgin (as well as Cameroon Pidgin English) also has an auxiliary verb form *neva* which is specifically a negator for the past, though that form seems to be less frequent than the general and tenseless negator *no*. The Juba Arabic negator is *ma* (Manfredi & Petrollino 2013b), while the Sango negator is *ape* (Samarin 2013b).

Nagamese has a negative prefix *no-* for all nonpast forms and a negative auxiliary form *nai* for past tense negation specifically (Bhattacharjya 2001). For more on Nagamese, see 8.3.1.

15.1.3 Negation in creole languages

Creoles are usually assumed to have a negative particle as the only or dominant strategy for negating declarative sentences (cf. e.g. Holm 2000: 194ff), as is the case in Papiá Kristang:

Papiá Kristang (Creole (Portuguese-lexified): Malaysia)

(483) Maria ńgka kumí mangga
PN NEG eat mangoe
'Maria doesn't eat / is not eating mangoes.' (Baxter 2013b: feature 100)

In (483) the negator is the invariant form *ńgka*. For more on Papiá Kristang, see 15.4.2.

A few languages have double negation (or a bipartite negative marker), where two forms have to occur simultaneously for the negative clause to be grammatical, as in, for example, Fa d'Ambô:

Fa d'Ambô (Creole (Portuguese-lexified): Equatorial Guinea)

(484) amu na po fe-f
1SG NEG can make-NEG
'I am not able to do it.' (Post 2013a: feature 100)

In (484) the negator *na … -f* is composed of two parts, both of which have to appear for the clause to be grammatical. For more on Fa d'Ambô, see 13.4.2.

Some of the languages in the current creole sample have a specific negator for the past tense, which is analyzed as a negative auxiliary verb in APiCS because it "is inherently tense-marked and occurs in an auxiliary slot" (Haspelmath et al. 2013: 399). This is, for example, the case in Belizean Creole:

Belizean Creole (Creole (English-lexified): Belize)

(485) a. yu no waak da ridj de
2SG NEG walk that ridge there
'You don't walk along that ridge.'

b. yu neva ivn memba dat if a neva kum ya kum
2SG NEG.PST even remember that if 1SG NEG.PST come here come
tɛl yu
tell 2SG
'You would not even have remembered if I had not come to tell you'
(Escure 2013b: feature 100)

In (485a) the negator is *no*, while in (485b) the negator is *neva*, a portmanteau form that specifically indicates negation in the past. Languages with this system have here been coded as "mixed" (negative particle / auxiliary verb). In Saramaccan and Sri Lanka Portuguese a negative affix and a negative particle is equally dominant, while in Palenquero it is equally common to have double negation and a negative particle (for more on Palenquero, see 12.4.3). These languages have also been coded as "mixed". The figures are summarized in Table 15.2:

Table 15.2 Negative morphemes in the current creole sample and in WALS (Dryer 2013e). For a full legend of the languages in the creole sample, see http://dx.doi.org/10.1075/cll.48.additional.

	Creole sample		WALS*	
	N	%	N	%
Negative affix	–		395	34.2
Negative particle	39	76.5	502	43.4
Negative auxiliary verb	–		47	4.1
Negative word, unclear if verb or particle	–		72	6.2
Variation negative word / affix	–		21	1.8
Double negation	3	5.9	119	10.3
Mixed	9	17.6	–	
Total	51		1156	

($\chi^2 = 240.44$; $df = 6$; $p_{sim} < .001$*** (B = 10,000))
($G = 100.53$; $df = 6$; $p_{two\text{-}tailed} < 0.001$***)
* Ndyuka (= Nengee) has been taken out to avoid overlap

The figures in Table 15.2 show that it is more common for the languages in the creole sample than in Dryer's (2013e) sample to have a negative particle as the dominant (or only strategy) for negating declarative sentences. Based on these figures it thus seems as if creoles are more likely than non-creoles to have a negative particle.[232]

15.1.4 Negation in mixed languages

Mixed languages are typically described as having adopted the system of one of the input languages or to represent a blend of the input languages. For example, Petjo, a G-L mixed language, has taken over the negative particle of Dutch, the language which provided the bulk of the structure:

Petjo (Mixed language (Dutch/Bazaar Malay): Indonesia)

(486) djangkriek hij laat niet los
grasshopper 3SG let NEG loose
'The grasshopper didn't let go.' (van Rheeden 1995: 117)

Shelta and Angloromani are examples of G-L mixed languages which have taken over the negator from the language which provided the bulk of the content words, namely Irish and Romani respectively. The Shelta *ni:dʲeʃ* derives from the Irish negative existential *ni h-eadh* 'it is not', while the Angloromani *kek* derives from the Romani indefinite *kek* 'nothing'.

232. The dominance of negative particles in the creole sample is highly significant even if the values are merged to "Negative particle" versus "Other" for the two databases.

Angloromani (Mixed language (English/Romani): UK)

(487) mush kek juns chichi
man NEG knows nothing
'The man doesn't know anything.' (Matras 2009: 25)

Mednyj Aleut, an Aleut/Russian N-V mixed language, has inherited the Russian negative prefix *ni-* (Sekerina 1994), while Gurindji Kriol, an N-V Gurindji/Kriol mixed language, has inherited the Kriol negative particles *neba* and *kaan* (Meakins 2011). In both cases the strategy for negation thus seems to be inherited from the language that provided the bulk of the verb phrase structure.

Media Lengua could be argued to represent a blend of the two input languages (Spanish and Quechua), in that the strategy for expressing negative declaratives involved a double negation, *no ... -chu*, where *no* is inherited from Spanish and *-chu* from Quechua:

Media Lengua (Mixed Language (Quechua/Spanish): Ecuador)

(488) llubi-xu-kpi mañana no i-sha-chu
rain-PROG-SUBORD tomorrow NEG go-1SG.FUT-NEG
'If it rains tomorrow I won't go.' (Muysken 2013b)

Wutun, an F-S mixed language could also be argued to represent a blend of the two input languages (Amdo Tibetan and Mandarin) in that the negative prefix *be-* has inherited its form from Mandarin *bu*, but appears as a prefix rather than a particle, in accordance with the Amdo Tibetan structure:

Wutun (Mixed language (Amdo Tibetan/Mandarin): China)

(489) be-jedo-li
NEG-know-OBJPER
'S/he does not know.' (Janhunen et al. 2008: 100)

15.2 Polar questions

Interrogative clauses are those formed with the purpose of gleaning information. There are two main types of interrogatives or **questions: polar questions** (also called **yes-no questions**) where the information requested is only the confirmation or disconfirmation of the truth value of a given answer (through the answers *Yes* or *No*) and **content questions**, where more elaborate information is requested (meaning that the answers *Yes* or *No* are insufficient or inadequate). An example of a polar question is *Will you bake a cake?* where the answers *Yes* or *No*, are appropriate (as well as various intermediate answers such as *Maybe* or *I don't know*). An example of a content question is *How do you bake a cake?* where more elaborate information is required to answer the question appropriately.

Languages differ with respect to the strategies they use to form polar questions. Most commonly a distinctive intonation pattern (typically rising) is used in combination with some other strategy. This section will empirically check what the dominant strategies for forming polar questions are in pidgin and creoles languages, as well as compare the strategies with non-pidgins and non-creoles. The section will also discuss strategies for forming polar questions in extended pidgins (pidgincreoles) and mixed languages. It is important to note that for the comparison with the languages in WALS, the coding principles used in Dryer (2013g) have been followed:

> If there is no evidence of any grammatical device other than intonation being used to indicate a neutral polar question in a language, the language is shown on the map as having interrogative intonation only. In some languages, intonation may be the most common means of indicating a polar question, but if some other method is used a minority of the time, then the language is shown on the map according to that method. (Dryer 2013g)

In other words, the languages in the pidgin and creole samples have been coded twice for this section: once for their dominant strategy and once according to the principles in Dryer (2013g), to make the samples compatible with that in WALS.

15.2.1 Polar questions in pidgin languages

Pidgins are often described as forming polar question through intonation only (cf. Sebba 1997: 41) as is the case in Fanakalo:

Fanakalo (Pidgin (Zulu-lexified): South Africa)

(490) yena khon-a lo gane?
she have-V ART child
'Does she have children?' (Mesthrie 2013: feature 103)

In (490) the clause has the same word order as a declarative clause, and lacks any overt marker to indicate that the clause is a question, except for the fact that the intonation differs from a declarative clause. As shown in Table 15.3, this is the dominant strategy for most of the languages in the pidgin sample. However, for some languages the dominant strategy is to have a question particle, as, for example in Broome Pearling Lugger Pidgin:

Broome Pearling Lugger Pidgin (Pidgin (Malay-lexified): Australia)

(491) yu kam burrum japang-ka: sau?
2SG come from Japan-Q south
'Did you come from Japan or from the south (i.e. Perth)?' (Hosokawa 1987: 292)

In (491) the question particle *-ka:* (as well as rising intonation) indicates that the clause is a polar question.

Table 15.3 Dominant strategy for polar questions in the current pidgin sample. For a full legend of the languages in the pidgin sample, see http://dx.doi.org/10.1075/cll.48.additional.

	N	%
Interrogative intonation only	20	83.3
Question particle	4	16.7
Total	24	

($\chi^2 = 10.67$; $df = 1$; $p_{two\text{-}tailed} = 0.0011^{**}$; $p_{sim} = 0.0016^{**}$ (B = 10,000))
($G = 11.41$; $df = 1$; $p_{two\text{-}tailed} < 0.001^{***}$)

As the figures in Table 15.3 show, the absolute majority of the languages in the pidgin sample have (rising) intonation as the only indication that a clause is a polar question. In order to compare whether the languages in the pidgin sample differ from the languages in Dryer's (2013g) sample, the coding was altered to match the principles of Dryer's codings (see above). With the altered codings, the number of languages that mark polar questions through intonation only decreased, since seven of the languages make use of some other strategy a minority of the time. However, this group remains dominant in the pidgin sample, as opposed to Dryer's sample. The figures are summarized in Table 15.4:

Table 15.4 Polar questions in the current pidgin sample and in WALS (Dryer 2013g). For a full legend of the languages in the pidgin sample, see http://dx.doi.org/10.1075/cll.48.additional.

	Pidgin sample		**WALS**	
	N	%	N	%
Question particle	6	26.1	585	61.3
Interrogative verb morphology	–	–	164	17.2
Mixture of previous two types	–	–	15	1.6
Interrogative word order	1	4.3	13	1.4
Absence of declarative morphemes	–	–	4	0.4
Interrogative intonation only	14	60.9	173	18.1
No interrogative-declarative distinction	–	–	1	0.1
A-not-A construction[233]	2	8.7	–	–
Total	23		955	

($\chi^2 = 114.61$; $df = 7$; $p_{sim} < 0.001^{***}$ (B = 10,000))
($G = 16.36$; $df = 7$; $p_{two\text{-}tailed} = 0.022^{*}$)

233. An **A-not-A construction** (also called a **disjunctive-negative structure**) is when a polar question is formed by repeating the verb twice, once in its positive form and once in its negative form, something like *You eat don't eat cakes?* for *Do you eat cakes?*

As shown in Table 15.4, question particles represent the most common strategy for forming polar questions in WALS, while interrogative intonation only is the most common strategy in the pidgin sample.[234] These figures thus suggest that pidgins seem more likely than non-pidgins to form polar questions through intonation only.

15.2.2 Polar questions in extended pidgins (pidgincreoles)

Seven of nine extended pidgins in the small sample have as the dominant strategy to indicate polar questions through intonation only, as for example, Bislama:

Bislama (Extended pidgin (English-lexified): Vanuatu)

(492) yu save ronron bitim mi?
2SG can run beat 1SG
'Can you run faster than me?' (Meyerhoff 2013b: feature 103)

In (492) the word order remains the same as in a declarative clause and there is no overt marker to indicate that this is a polar question, except for the (rising) intonation. While intonation is the dominant strategy, Nigerian Pidgin and Sango also make use of question particles for polar questions:

Nigerian Pidgin (Extended pidgin (English-lexified): Nigeria)

(493) Àbì yù go make̱t?
Q 2SG.S go market
'Did you go to the market?' (Faraclas 1996: 9)

Sango (Extended pidgin (Ngbandi-lexified): Central African Republic)

(494) esi mama ti mo a-ga ge so a-kwi?
Q mother of 2SG PM-come here thus PM-die
'Did your mother who came here die?' (Samarin 2013b: feature 103)

Tok Pisin makes equal use of interrogative intonation only and question particles to indicate polar questions (Smith & Siegel 2013b), while Nagamese only makes use of the question particle *niki* (plus rising intonation; Bhattacharjya 2001). For more on Tok Pisin and Nagamese, see 1.4.3 and 8.3.1 respectively.

234. The overrepresentation of interrogative intonation as a polar question strategy and underrepresentation of any other strategy in the pidgin sample remains statistically significant even if the comparison is trimmed down to only those values that represent more than 5% of the languages in Dryer's (2013g) sample, i.e. if the values "Mixture of previous two types", "Interrogative word order", "Absence of declarative morphemes", "No interrogative-declarative distinction" and "A-not-A question" are grouped into a category "Other".

15.2.3 Polar questions in creole languages

Creole languages are also often described as indicating polar questions by way of (rising) intonation only (cf. Sebba 1997: 41), as is the case in Lingala:

Lingala (Creole (Bobangi-lexified): Congo, DR Congo)

(495) a-zal-ákí na ndáko?
3SG-be-PST in house
'Was she home?' (Meeuwis 2013b: feature 103)

In (495) the clause has the same structure as it would have in an affirmative declarative clause (*She is at home*), except for the (rising) intonation. Hawai'i Creole English is rare cross-linguistically in that while the strategy for marking polar questions is through interrogative intonation only, the intonation is falling rather than rising. For more on Hawai'i Creole English, see 6.4.1.

A fair number of languages in the sample have a question particle as the dominant strategy for marking polar questions, such as Saramaccan:

Saramaccan (Creole (English-lexified): Suriname)

(496) I ké woóko, no?
2SG want work Q.TAG
'Do you want to work?' (Aboh et al. 2013b: feature 103 citing Veenstra 1996: 18)

In (496) the question tag *no* is added to the declarative sentence to form a polar question. Some of the languages in the creole sample, such as Papiá Kristang, make equal use of a question particle and intonation only to mark polar questions. The figures are summarized in Table 15.5 (ND stands for 'no dominant order'):

Table 15.5 Dominant strategy for polar questions in the current creole sample. For a full legend of the languages in the creole sample, see http://dx.doi.org/10.1075/cll.48.additional.

	N	%
Interrogative intonation only	36	69.2
Question particle	10	19.2
Interrogative intonation / question particle: ND	6	11.5
Total	52	

($\chi^2 = 30.62$; $df = 2$; $p_{\text{two-tailed}} < 0.001$***; $p_{\text{sim}} < 0.001$*** (B = 10,000))
($G = 28.53$; $df = 2$; $p_{\text{two-tailed}} < 0.001$***)

As indicated by the figures in Table 15.5, the absolute majority of the languages have as their dominant strategy to mark polar questions through intonation only. In order to compare whether the languages in the creole sample differ from the languages in Dryer's (2013g) sample, the coding was altered to match the principles of Dryer's coding (see above). With the altered coding, the number of languages that mark polar questions through intonation only decreased, since 27 of the languages make use of some other strategy a minority of the time.[235] The figures are summarized in Table 15.6:

Table 15.6 Polar questions in the current creole sample and in WALS (Dryer 2013g). For a full legend of the languages in the creole sample, see http://dx.doi.org/10.1075/cll.48.additional.

	Creole sample		WALS*	
	N	%	N	%
Question particle	26	50	585	61.3
Interrogative verb morphology	–	–	164	17.2
Mixture of previous two types	–	–	15	1.6
Interrogative word order	1	1.9	13	1.4
Absence of declarative morphemes	–	–	4	0.4
Interrogative intonation only	25	48.1	172	18
No interrogative-declarative distinction	–	–	1	0.1
Total	52		954	

($\chi^2 = 33.92$; $df = 6$; $p_{sim} = 0.0027$** (B = 10,000))
($G = 21.21$; $df = 6$; $p_{two\text{-}tailed} = 0.0017$**)
* Ndyuka (=Nengee) has been removed from the WALS sample to avoid overlap.

The figures in Table 15.6 show that the 'Interrogative intonation only' strategy for forming polar questions is more common in the creole sample than in Dryer's sample, though with the altered figures the 'Question particle' strategy is not significantly different between the two samples.[236] These figures suggest that creole languages seem more likely than non-creoles to have interrogative intonation and less likely than non-creoles to have interrogative verb morphology to form polar questions.

235. Gullah makes use of an interrogative word order or a question particle in addition to the 'intonation only' strategy (Klein 2013b: feature 103); the language has here arbitrarily been coded for the value 'Interrogative word order', but could equally well have been coded for the value 'Question particle'. The statistical significance of the distribution between the two samples is not noticeably affected by altering the value of Gullah to 'Question particle'. For more on Gullah, see 4.3.1.

236. The overrepresentation of 'Interrogative intonation only' as a polar question strategy and underrepresentation of 'Interrogative verb morphology' in the creole sample remains statistically significant even if the comparison is trimmed down to only those values that represent more than 5% of the languages in Dryer's (2013g) sample, i.e. if the values 'Mixture of previous two types', 'Interrogative word order', 'Absence of declarative morphemes' and 'No interrogative-declarative distinction' are grouped into a category 'Other'.

15.2.4 Polar questions in mixed languages

Mixed languages are typically described as having adopted the system of one of the input languages or to represent a blend of the input languages. In the G-L mixed language Javindo, for example, the dominant strategy was to have an interrogative intonation only, but a question particle (inherited from Javanese) or an inverted word order (inherited from Dutch) was also possible:

Javindo (Mixed language (Dutch/Javanese): Indonesia)

(497) a. je sie-t proempie-nja?
2SG see-2SG.PRES plum-DEM
'Do you see that plum?'

b. apa loe kira goewa andjing?
Q 2SG think 1SG dog
'Do you think I'm a dog?'

c. wil-t je proev-en
want-2SG.PRES 2SG try-INF
'Do you want to try?' (van Rheeden 1995: 113)

In (497a), which represents the most frequent strategy in Javindo (van Rheeden 1995) there is no overt marking to indicate that the clause is a polar question, except for the rising intonation, while in (497b) the question particle *apa* and in (497c) the inverted word order (placing the auxiliary clause-initially) mark the clauses as polar questions.

Hezhou, an F-S mixed language, has inherited the question particle from Uyghur, as has Ejnu, a G-L mixed language:

Hezhou (Mixed language (Mandarin/Uyghur): China)

(498) fatsɪxa kɛ vɛ̃lli-mu?
house.O build finished-Q
'Is the house built?' (Lee-Smith 1996b: 866)

Ejnu (Mixed language (Uyghur/Persian): China)

(499) χanida mikɛ hɛs-mu nist mu?
home.LOC goat EXIST-Q NEG.EXIST Q
'Are the goats at home?' (Lee-Smith 1996a: 860)

Example (498) shows how Hezhou uses the Uyghur question particle =*mu*, while Example (499) shows how Ejnu uses the question particle *mu* to form an A-not-A question, which might represent an innovation in Ejnu.

15.3 Politeness

A central concept in pragmatics is the notion of **face**, which can be described as the public self-image that any given person wants to maintain (a term derived from the English expression 'to lose face', see Brown & Levinson (1987 [1978]: 61). There are two main aspects to the notion of face, the **negative face**, which basically denotes the need to be independent and free from imposition, and the **positive face**, which, very simplified, denotes the need to belong and be accepted. **Politeness** is a way of interaction which shows awareness of and respect for someone else's face. One way of expressing politeness is to adjust the linguistic form used to refer to something or someone when talking to or about it (so-called **referent honorifics**). This is particularly well-known for personal pronouns, where the choice of pronominal form depends on the level of familiarity with the person addressed. Most well-known is to have a binary distinction (often called **T/V pronouns** after the Latin *tu* 'you.SINGular.NOMinative' and *vos* 'you.PLural.NOMinative'), but languages may also have more than two distinctions (here called 'Multiple politeness distinctions'). Yet another way of indicating politeness when addressing someone is to avoid the use of pronouns altogether and use either a name or some other noun, something like *Would John like some more cake?* (when addressing John) or *Would Sir like some more cake?* (again addressed directly to someone), a strategy sometimes termed **pronoun avoidance**.

This section will look at whether pidgins and creoles differ from non-pidgins and non-creoles with respect to politeness distinctions in second person pronouns, as well as bring up politeness distinctions in second person pronouns in extended pidgins (pidgincreoles) and mixed languages. It is beyond the scope of the section to adequately discuss the various politeness strategies employed by the languages of the world. For a very accessible introduction to the topic of linguistic politeness, see Watts (2003) and the classic Brown & Levinson (1987 [1978]).

15.3.1 Politeness in pidgin languages

In a small sample of pidgin languages, the absolute majority do not make any politeness distinctions in second person pronouns, as for example, in Lingua Franca.

Lingua Franca (Pidgin (Romance-lexified): Mediterranean Basin)

(500) mi poudir servir per ti per qoualké cosa?
1SG can serve OBJ 2SG OBJ some thing
'Can I serve you anything?' (Anonymous 1830: 94)

In (500) the second person singular pronoun is used in a situation where other Romance languages would have used the polite pronoun – in fact the French translation of this sentence in the source is *Puis-je vous servis en quelque chose?*, where the polite *vous* is used instead of the familiar *tu*. For more on Lingua Franca, see 5.3.1.

Three of the languages, however, namely Chinese Pidgin Russian, Singapore Bazaar Malay and Tây Bòy, have a binary politeness distinction.

Chinese Pidgin Russian (Pidgin (Russian-lexified): Russia/China border)

(501) Kapitána, váša ni kasájsia!
captain 2PL NEG concern
'It is none of your business, sir.'
(Perekhvalskaya 2013b: feature 18 citing Jabłońska 1957: 167)

In (501) the second person plural form is used as a polite address form to a single referent.

In order to compare whether pidgins differ from non-pidgin with respect to politeness distinctions in second person pronouns, I compared the current pidgin sample with Helmbrecht's (2013) sample. It should be noticed that the values in the pidgin sample are highly tentative at best, based on very scanty data. It could therefore be that the group coded as having no politeness distinction is overrepresented in the pidgin sample. The figures are summarized in Table 15.7:

Table 15.7 Politeness distinctions in second person pronouns in the current pidgin sample and in WALS (Helmbrecht 2013). For a full legend of the languages in the pidgin sample, see http://dx.doi.org/10.1075/cll.48.additional.

	Pidgin sample		WALS	
	N	%	N	%
No politeness distinction	19	86.4	136	65.7
Binary politeness distinction	3	13.6	49	23.7
Multiple politeness distinction	–	–	15	7.2
Pronoun avoidance	–	–	7	3.4
Total	22		207	

($\chi^2 = 4.47$; $df = 3$; $p_{sim} = 0.20$ (B = 10,000))
($G = 5.84$; $df = 3$; $p_{two\text{-}tailed} = 0.12$)

As shown in Table 15.7 most languages in the pidgin sample lack politeness distinctions in second person pronouns, as is also the case in the WALS sample. In fact the difference in distribution between the two samples is not statistically significant.

15.3.2 Politeness in extended pidgins (pidgincreoles)

Six of eight extended pidgins in the small sample do not have any politeness distinctions in second person pronouns, such as Nigerian Pidgin:

Nigerian Pidgin (Extended pidgin (English-lexified): Nigeria)

(502) Yù dè tek ègúsí prìpyár sup
2SG.S NCOMPL take ègúsí prepare soup
'You (both polite and informal) prepare soup with ègúsí (a vegetable).'
(Faraclas 2013b: feature 18)

In (502) the same form (*yù*) is used in both polite and informal contexts. Two languages, Bislama and Sango, have binary politeness distinctions in second person pronouns. In Bislama the second person plural, *yufala*, is used in certain traditional respect relationships for a single addressee (Meyerhoff 2013b: feature 18), and in Sango the second plural *ala* may be used as a polite form for single referents, both for second ('you.sinGular') and third (s/he) persons:

Sango (Extended pidgin (Ngbandi-lexified): Central African Republic)

(503) mama, ala de ti lango ape?!
mother 2PL continue of sleep NEG
'Mother, haven't you fallen asleep yet?!' (Samarin 2013b: feature 18)

15.3.3 Politeness in creole languages

The majority of the languages in the creole sample do not have any politeness distinction in second person pronouns, as is the case in, for example, Jamaican.

Jamaican (Creole (English-lexified): Jamaica)

(504) Misa Broun, yu no nuo a wa dem a du.
Mr. Brown 2SG NEG know FOC what 3PL PROG do
'Mr. Brown, you don't know what they're doing.' (Farquharson 2013b)

In (504) the second singular pronoun (and not, for example the plural *unu*) is used even if the context is not informal.

A number of languages in the creole sample have a binary politeness distinction for second person pronouns, such as, for example, Nengee:

Nengee (Creole (English-lexified): Suriname, French Guyana)

(505) gaanman, u mu yeepi den sama ya
paramount.chief 2PL must help DET.PL person DEM
'Chief, you should help these people.' (Migge 2013b: feature 18)

In (505) the second person plural form *u* is used as a polite form for a single addressee; the second person singular *i* would not have been appropriate. For more on Nengee, see 2.4.2.

Some languages have more than two distinctions for second person pronouns, such as Cavite Chabacano, which has an intimate form (*bo*), a familiar form (*tu*) and a polite form (*uste(d)*) (Sippola 2013a).

A fair number of languages make use of a pronoun avoidance strategy, where some noun is used as a title instead of actually using a pronominal form. For example, titles such as 'Uncle', 'Friend' or 'Sir' may be used in direct interlocution with the referee, such as in Sri Lanka Portuguese:

Sri Lanka Portuguese (Creole (Portuguese-lexified): Sri Lanka)

(506) etus siɲoor juuntu ta-papiyaae lingvaay siɲoor-pa lo-intinda?
3PL.HON gentleman with PRES-speak language gentleman-DAT FUT-understand
'Do you understand the language they speak to you?' (Smith 2013b: feature 18)

In (506) the title *siɲoor* 'gentleman' instead of a second person pronoun is used as a polite form when directly addressing someone.

In order to compare whether creoles differ from non-creoles with respect to politeness distinctions in second person pronouns, I compared the current creole sample with Helmbrecht's (2013) sample. The figures are summarized in Table 15.8:

Table 15.8 Politeness distinctions in second person pronouns in the current creole sample and in WALS (Helmbrecht 2013). For a full legend of the languages in the creole sample, see http://dx.doi.org/10.1075/cll.48.additional.

	Creole sample		WALS*	
	N	%	N	%
No politeness distinction	29	58	136	66
Binary politeness distinction	11	22	48	23.3
Multiple politeness distinction	3	6	15	7.3
Pronoun avoidance	7	14	7	3.4
Total	50		206	

($\chi^2 = 8.79$; $df = 3$; $p_{\text{two-tailed}} = 0.032$*; $p_{sim} = 0.032$* (B = 10,000))
($G = 6.74$; $df = 3$; $p_{\text{two-tailed}} = 0.081$)
* Angolar has been removed from the WALS sample to avoid overlap

As shown in Table 15.8 the proportions of the first three categories differ very little between the two samples, while more languages in the creole sample make use of pronoun avoidance. The fact that the overall difference between the two samples is statistically significant is actually due to the overrepresentation of creole languages that make use of a pronoun avoidance strategy.[237]

15.3.4 Politeness in mixed languages

The politeness systems of mixed languages are still not well studied, but mixed languages are typically assumed to represent a compromise between the contributing languages or to essentially represent the system of one of the contributing languages. Gurindji Kriol, for example, does not have any politeness distinctions for the second person pronoun, essentially reflecting the system of Kriol (Meakins 2013b, Schultze-Berndt & Angelo 2013). Sri Lankan Malay, on the other hand, has a binary politeness distinction in the second person pronouns:

Sri Lankan Malay (Mixed Language (Malay/Sinhala/Tamil): Sri Lanka)

(507) lu / lorang e-biilang (aða) attu buttul
2SG.FAM 2SG.POL ASP-say (AUX) one correct
'What you (familiar/polite) have said is correct.' (Slomanson 2013b: feature 18)

Example (507) shows the binary politeness distinction in Sri Lankan Malay, which could be considered an innovation, since Malay makes use of a pronoun avoidance strategy in direct addresses (Prentice 1990: 930), while both Sinhala and Tamil have multiple politeness distinctions for second person pronouns (Chandralal 2010: 267 and Brown & Levinson 1987 [1978]: 293 respectively).

Media Lengua could also be argued to show an innovation in that there are no politeness distinctions in second person pronouns (Muysken 2013b), as opposed to the binary distinction in both Spanish and Quechua (cf. Helmbrecht 2013).

15.4 Snapshots

Pidgins are expected to have an invariant negator, to mark polar questions with rising intonation only and to lack politeness distinctions. Extended pidgins are often assumed to be more similar to creoles than to pidgins. Juba Arabic is an example of an extended pidgin which has a negative particle and which marks polar questions through intonation only.

237. Although the actual number of occurrences compared to the expected number of occurrences is as such not statistically significant. These figures were generated with the HCFA 3.2 script provided by Stefan Th. Gries, the use of which is here gratefully acknowledged. See further <http://www.linguistics.ucsb.edu/faculty/stgries/>.

Creoles are also often expected have an invariant negator, to mark polar questions with rising intonation only and to lack politeness distinctions. Papiá Kristang is an example of a creole language which has a negative particle, which marks polar questions either through intonation only or with a question particle, and which lacks politeness distinctions in second person pronouns.

Mixed languages are expected to represent the system of one of the input languages or to represent a blend of both input languages. Angloromani is an example of a mixed language which has taken over the negative particle from Romani, but forms polar questions as in English and which lacks politeness distinctions in the second person pronoun, as in English.

15.4.1 Juba Arabic: An Arabic-lexified extended pidgin (pidgincreole) in Sudan[238]

15.4.1.1 *A brief background sketch of Juba Arabic*

Juba Arabic is spoken as a first, second or third language in South Sudan and in diaspora communities in Sudan, Egypt, the UK, USA, Canada and Australia and is called *arabi juba, ʕarabi juba, árabi ta Júba* or *Juba Arabic* by the speakers themselves. The language derives its name from the city of Juba, the capital of South Sudan, where the largest number of speakers is concentrated. The total number of speakers is not known. It is mutually intelligible with the Arabic-lexified creole Kinubi.

The Arab conquest, by way of the Upper Nile, of what is now the Sudan, started in the 12th century and peaked in the 15th century (Manfredi & Petrollino 2013a). With the establishment of various strong states that replaced the previous Christian Nubian kingdoms, Arabic became the *lingua franca* of the area. A military expedition from Egypt in 1820 eventually conquered a large part of present-day Sudan. This in turn opened up Sudan for trade in ivory, and permanent traders' camps were established, so-called *zarāʾibs* (lit. 'cattle enclosures'), throughout the White Nile Basin, the Bahr al-Ghazal and the Equatorial Province. Within twenty years the camps had developed into slaving camps (Owens 2001). The camps were inhabited by a small but dominant minority of Arabic speakers and a large majority of various indigenous people, who had been "forcibly drawn from various Nilotic tribes (Mundu, Lugbara, Dinka, Shilluk, Bari)" (Manfredi & Petrollino 2013a: 55) and who occupied different social roles (interpreters, soldiers, slaves).

These traders' camps soon gradually turned into military camps and the *zarāʾib* private troops were incorporated into the Egyptian government army. At the same time the locals of various linguistic backgrounds started to join the camps by choice. In this multilingual setting a pidginized Arabic arose.

By the last quarter of the 19th century the *zarāʾibs* had grown so powerful that they were "in effect dominating the economy and politics of the south" (Manfredi & Petrollino 2013a: 55), which led the Egyptian government to assign the different provinces to various chosen governors. However, the Mahdi revolt of 1882 led to the capture of Khartoum and the occupation of a number of provinces, considerably weakening the Egyptian government, which by then was

238. This section is based predominantly on Manfredi & Petrollino (2013a).

effectively occupied by the British. This in turn led to a number of local revolts as well as army desertions, which eventually led the Egyptian forces to withdraw from the south. The British established control over the area in 1998 and eventually came to an Anglo-Egyptian agreement, whereby an Egyptian governor-general was appointed with British consent; in practice Sudan was under British rule (Kramer et al. 2013: 14). The withdrawal of the Egyptian forces led to a hiatus of Arabic influence in what is now South Sudan. The pidginized Arabic that had arisen in the camps was thus largely left to develop without very little or no superstrate (Arabic) influence during the remainder of the British colonial era (Miller 1991b, Owens 2001). With the declaration of independence in 1956 a new Arabization policy was opened up, once again increasing the influence of Sudanese Arabic.

After the Addis Ababa peace agreement was signed in 1972, South Sudan acquired more administrative autonomy, which in turn strengthened the position of Juba Arabic as a *lingua franca* as a super-tribal South Sudanese identity marker (Miller 1991b, Luffin 2011). This expanded the range of domains Juba Arabic was used in, bringing it into such areas as formal communicative settings, religious settings (for example in missionary churches), courts, broadcasting media and – despite the lack of an established orthography – in written form (Latin script) for personal correspondence, songs, poetry and theatre as well as for written religious texts, such as Christian missionary prayer books (Luffin 2011). The latter has been a considerable factor in spreading Juba Arabic in South Sudan.

In the last thirty years Juba Arabic has also started to be acquired as a mother tongue. There is a continuum of lects ranging from basilectal, predominantly in the rural areas, via mesolectal to acrolectal, predominantly in urban areas, where adstratal contact with the prestigious Sudanese Arabic is more intense.

15.4.1.2 *A short linguistic sketch of Juba Arabic*

Juba Arabic has 18 consonants, /b, m, w, f, t, d, s, z, n, r, l, ʤ, ʈ, ʃ, j, k, g, h/, and five vowels, /i, e, a, o, u/. There is allophonic but not contrastive vowel length. Stress is contrastive. Syllables may be moderately complex with up to one consonant in the onset and up to two consonants in the coda. Tone is not relevant. Though there is no established orthography, conventions typically use <j, y, š> for /ʤ, j, ʃ/ respectively. An accent (´) marks stress.

The morphology is predominantly analytic, though there is suffixation as well as cliticization. In some instances pluralization is indicated non-linearly, through ablaut. There is also reduplication, which essentially denotes intensification. Serialized verbs may also be reduplicated as one entity (see below).

Nouns inflect for number, typically with the plural suffix *-át*:

(508) a. Wani ayinú bagará
PN see cow
'Wani saw the cow.' (Vincent 1986: 77)

b. ána kan bi=šílu bagar-at de fi=tehet máŋa
1SG ANT IRR=bring cow-PL DEM.PROX.SG in=under mangoes
'I used to herd these cows to the mango trees.'
(Manfredi & Petrollino 2013a: 61 citing Manfredi 2005: 188)

Collective plurals are expressed with prenominal *nas* 'people', as in *nas gazál* '(the group of) gazelles' or *nas ajús* '(the group of) the elders' (Manfredi & Petrollino 2013a: 56). Gender and case are not relevant.

There are no articles, and definiteness or indefiniteness is typically inferred from context, though definiteness may be indicated through personal or relative pronouns or with demonstratives, and indefiniteness may optionally be emphasized by the numeral *wáhid* 'one'.

(509) a. ínna der árufu šunú fi fi sénter
1PL want know what EXIST in centre
'We want to know what is happening in the town centre.' (Tosco 1995: 425)

b. ána wedi le úo gurús de
1SG give to 3SG money DEM.PROX.SG
'I gave him the money.' (Manfredi & Petrollino 2013a: 61 citing Manfredi 2005: 140)

There are the proximate demonstrative *de/da* 'this' (plural *dol/del* 'those') and the distal demonstrative *dak* 'that' (no plural form).

(510) a. anína bi=ágder árif hája de batál wa hája dak kwes
1PL IRR=can know thing DEM.PROX.SG bad and thing DEM.DIST good
'We can know that this is bad and that is good.'

b. ána gum šílu bagar-át del
1SG stand.up bring cow-PL DEM.PROX.PL
'I began to herd these cows.' (Manfredi & Petrollino 2013a: 60 citing Manfredi 2005: 104)

The pronominal system distinguishes between three persons and two numbers. There are no specific object pronouns. Notice that the third persons do no distinguish for gender. The possessive pronouns are lexicalized forms involving the possessive marker *ta* 'of' (except for the first and second singular forms).

	PERSONAL	POSSESSIVE
1SG	*ána*	*tái*
2SG	*íta/éta*	*táki*
3SG	*úo*	*to*
1PL	*(a)nína/ánna*	*tanína/tánna*
2PL	*ítakum/étakum*	*tákum*
3PL	*úmon*	*tómon*

Possession is expressed analytically with the possessive marker *ta/bitá* (the latter form being more acrolectal):

(511) ínna báda ŋákama lám ta jemús
1PL begin cut meat POSS buffalo
'We begin cutting the buffalo meat.' (Tosco 1995: 428)

Adjectives are postnominal and agree with the noun in number. Plurality is either indicated through the plural suffix *-ín* or through stem ablaut. Comparison is either formed analytically with the preposition *min* 'from' or, much less commonly, with *fāta* 'pass, surpass':

(512) a. zaráf towíl min fil
giraffe tall from elephant
'The giraffe is taller than the elephant.'
(Manfredi & Petrollino 2013a: 58 citing Manfredi 2005: 207)

b. úo kebír fútu íta
3SG big pass 2SG
'He is bigger than you.' (Miller 1993: 167)

There is the preverbal anterior tense marker *kan*, the progressive aspect proclitic *ge=* and the preverbal irrealis proclitic *bi=*; the latter two may co-occur with *kan*, though *bi=* and *ge=* cannot co-occur. The lexical aspect of the verb affects the reading of the clause in that stative verbs get a present tense reading in the base form and a past tense reading with the anterior marker *kan*, while dynamic verbs get a perfective reading in the base form and a past-before-past reading with the anterior marker *kan*. There are also the auxiliary verbs *bíga* 'become' (denoting inchoative), *gum* 'get up' (denoting inchoative in narratives), *bíji* < Arabic 'he is coming/will come' (denoting resultative) and *biréwa* < Arabic 'he is leaving/will leave' (denoting the near future). There are a number of modal verbs.

The passive is most commonly formed by fronting the object to subject position and demoting the subject to adjunct position, indicated by the preposition *ma* 'with'. Compare the following:

(513) a. jes de kútu John géni fi síjin
army DEM.PROX.SG put PN stay in prison
'The army imprisoned John.'

b. John kutú géni fi síjin (ma jes)
PN put stay in prison with army
'John was imprisoned (be the army).' (Manfredi & Petrollino 2013a: 61)

The word order is typically subject-verb-object, though objective topics may be fronted. Negation is expressed with the invariant preverbal *ma*.

(514) ána fikir ombári Obóma ma rúa fi suk
1SG think yesterday PN NEG go in market
'I think that yesterday Oboma didn't go to the market.' (Tosco 1995: 426)

There is a negative existential *mafi*:

(515) máfi mile
NEG.EXIST salt
'There is no salt.' (Manfredi & Petrollino 2013a: 61)

Polar questions are indicated through intonation only.

(516) ána bi=ákulu naárde wa búkra ána ma bi=ákulu?
1SG IRR=eat today and tomorrow 1SG NEG IRR=eat
'Today I eat, and tomorrow I don't?'
(Manfredi & Petrollino 2013b: feature 103 citing Manfredi 2005: 197)

In content questions the interrogative phrase remains *in situ*.

There is no copula:

(517) a. Marísa tamám
PN good
'Marisa is good' (Manfredi & Petrollino 2013a: 57)

b. Ládo kan mudéris
PN ANT teacher
'Lado was a teacher.' (Tosco 1995: 443)

Complement clauses are often introduced by the verb *gal(e)* 'say':

(518) úo fékir gále imkin assét de awuju ákulu úo
3SG think say maybe lion DEM.PROX.SG want eat 3SG
'He thinks that the lion might want to eat him.' (Miller 1991a: 464)

There is the relative particle *al* 'who, which, that', which may be omitted in basilectal speech. If the head noun is animate, the relative clause may optionally be introduced by *abú* (< Arabic *abū* 'father').

(519) zol al ámulu háfra hófra, al úo xabír de, al
person REL do dig hole REL 3SG expert DEM.PROX.SG REL
áruf kalám ta grínti de, b=odí lo láham al kefáya
know problem POSS hippo DEM.PROX.SG IRR=give to meat REL enough
'The man who did the digging of the trap, who is the expert, who knows the problem of hippo(-hunting), is given a good portion of meat.' (Tosco 1995: 427)

15.4.1.3 *Short text*

(This is an excerpt of a text in Manfredi & Petrollino 2013a: 63f. It was narrated by a 35-year old speaker from Juba, living in Cairo.)

Fi=yom kéda ána kan ge=rówa fi=táraf báhar. Ána rówa ya ána wósulu fi=téhet
in=day like.this 1SG ANT PROG=go in=bank river 1SG go then 1SG arrive in=under

máŋa. Ána ge=dóru máŋa ya bolis ja min henák. Pólis gum dúgu ána.
mangoes 1SG PROG=turn mangoes then police come in bank police get.up beat 1SG

Wa gum šílu ána dákalu ána fi=sijin. Úmon gum dúgu~dúgu ána šedíd ya
and get.up carry 1SG put.in 1SG in=prison 3PL get.up beat~RED 1SG strong then

ána bíga tabán. Úmon lissa kamán úmon dúgu~dúgu ána.
1SG become ill 3PL still also 3PL beat~RED 1SG

'Some time ago I was going to the bank of the river (Nile). I walked until I arrived under the mango trees. I was walking (under) the mango trees when the police came. The police started to beat me. (The police) took me away and brought me to prison. They started to beat me hard until I succumbed. They continued to beat me.'

15.4.1.4 *Some sources of data*

There is some primary data available for Juba Arabic. Manfredi & Petrollino (2013a) contains a number of glossed and translated examples, as well as a longer text. Manfredi (2005) and Watson & Ola (1984) are full grammars and contain numerous examples. There are a number of podcasts available in Juba Arabic, accessible via http://www.podcastdirectory.com/ (accessed 13 February 2015).

15.4.2 Papiá Kristang: A Portuguese-lexified creole in Malaysia[239]

15.4.2.1 *A brief background sketch of Papiá Kristang*

Papiá Kristang, by scholars also called *Kristang, Malaccan, Malayo-Portuguese, Malaysian Creole Portuguese, Luso-Malay, Portuguese Patois* or *Malacca(n) (Creole) Portuguese* in English, and *Malaqueiro, Malaquenho, Malaquense, Malaquês, Papia Cristao*, or *dialecto português de Malaca* in Portuguese, or *Bahasa Serani* (from *Nazarene*, i.e. 'Christian language'), *Serani* or *Bahasa Geragu* (disparaging, lit. 'prawn language' due to a type of prawn that is popular with the Kristang population) in Malay, is spoken by about 800 people in Malacca (West Malaysian), as well as in small diaspora communities in Kuala Lumpur and Singapore. The language is called *(Papiá) Kristang* by the speakers themselves.

The Portuguese first landed at Malacca in 1509 with five ships under Admiral Diogo Lopes de Sequeira's command (Hancock 1964). Two years later, in 1511, Alfonso de Albuquerque landed with 19 ships, bringing 800 Portuguese and 600 Indian soldiers (Hancock 1964), and built the fort that was to remain a key Portuguese trade and administrative port until it was taken by the Dutch in 1642. By then Malacca had a population of about 20,000, of which about one third were Portuguese descendants (Hancock 1964). With the Dutch take-over, most of the Portuguese and those of Portuguese ancestry left Malacca.

Malacca was one in a network of Portuguese trade ports stretching from Goa in India to the Moluccas in Insular South-East Asia and further to Macau. There was intense contact between these ports, with settlers and their entourage posted at different ports at different times. The languages of the various ports and the surrounding areas are thus likely to have influenced each other. Furthermore, constant contact with non-Portuguese ports would have been likely.

The Dutch rule lasted until 1795, when the British took over and Malaya, including Malacca, was a British colony until independence in 1957, at which point it was renamed Malaysia.

Papiá Kristang survived despite the fact that the Portuguese left the area some 370 years ago. This is in part due to the fact that the Kristang community was Roman Catholic, as opposed to the Protestant Dutch and Anglican British. Religious identity thus strengthened the Kristang cultural community bond (Baxter 2005). Religion is also likely to have "provided linguistic reinforcement through pastoral and liturgical use of 'Portuguese', and partially, through education" (Baxter 2005: 12). Furthermore, education was given in some form of Portuguese in the 19th century by the Portuguese Mission and the Malacca Free School, and, later, by the London Missionary Society (Baxter 2005). A second factor that may have led to the maintenance of the language is

239. This section is based almost exclusively on Baxter (2013a).

the socioeconomic history of the community. At the time of the Dutch take-over, the Portuguese speaking community dominated, both in numbers and in economic power. By the end of the 19th century that had reversed, with the Kristang community having dwindled to a small minority primarily engaged in the fishing trade. However, in collaboration between the Catholic Church and the British Administration in 1933, the *Padri sa Chang* ('the priest's land') or Portuguese Settlement was created, to which socially disadvantaged Kristang from central town areas were resettled to an area that had traditionally been the core of the Kristang residence (Baxter 2005). This created a large Papiá Kristang speech community, which "displayed strong inward focussing in kinship and friendship relations, a high degree of intramarriage, and a high proportion of extended families with elderly Kristang speakers present" (Baxter 2005: 15), all of which are factors that support language maintenance.

Since the mid-19th century, the position of English has been dominant, due to schools and the language of administration. English was (and remains) a prestige language, which Papiá Kristang was not, and was the key to socioeconomic advancement, leading to a growing Kristang middle class which has steadily been shifting to English. Most of the fluent speakers are above 40 years of age and most age-groups are shifting to English in the intimate (family and friends) domains. Despite the stigmatizing attitudes towards Papiá Kristang, the speech community nowadays takes pride in their language and culture. The language has now been granted a special status and the Kristangs of the *Padri sa Chang* community have a positive attitude towards the language (Baxter 2005). However, the language is not taught in minority language schools, and the transmission to children is weak. The pressure of Malay, which all Papiá Kristang speakers are bilingual in, is also very strong. While the language is endangered, the prospects for a potential revitalization program seem possible (Baxter 2005), if the levels of awareness for the language situation are raised (cf. Maros et al. 2014).

15.4.2.2 *A short linguistic sketch of Papiá Kristang*

Papiá Kristang has 18 consonants, /p, b, m, f, v, t, d, n, r, s, z, l, ɲ, ʧ, ʤ, k, g, ŋ/ and eight vowels, /i, e, ɛ, ə, a, ɔ, o, u/. Stress most commonly falls on the ultimate or penultimate syllable. It is a syllable-timed language. Syllables may be complex with up to three consonants in the onset and one in the coda. The orthography used here follows that proposed in Baxter (1988), where /ɲ, ʧ, ʤ, ŋ/ are represented by <ny, ch, j, ng> respectively, both /e/ and /ɛ/ by <e>, both /ɔ/ and /o/ by <o> and /ə/ by <ĕ>.

The morphology is predominantly analytic, though there is reduplication, which indicates intensification or pluralization.

Noun phrases are invariant. Gender is irrelevant, though natural gender may be indicated by *femi* 'female' and *machu* 'male', as in *baka fami* 'she-goat' and *baka machu* 'billy goat' (Baxter 2013a: 125). Human syntactic objects are case marked with the prenominal objective particle *ku*. There is no specific plural marker, though plurality may be indicated through reduplication.

(520) aké kren~krensa ta fazé amoku
that child~RED PROG make noise
'The children are making noise.' (Baxter 2013b: feature 26 citing Baxter 1988: 102)

There is no definite article, though demonstratives may be used as such. The numeral *ńgua* 'one' may be used as an indefinite article.

(521) a. fémi já kazá ku kristang
girl PRF marry OBJ Kristang
'The girl married a Kristang.' (Baxter 2013b: feature 28 28 citing Baxter 1988: 90)

b. aké prau pezadu
that boat heavy
'The boat is heavy.' (Baxter 2013b: feature 28 citing Baxter 1988: 87)

c. eli ja olá ńgua mulé brangku mbés
3SG PFV see one woman white very
'He saw a woman who was very white.' (Baxter 2013b: feature 29 citing Baxter 1988: 87)

d. eli teng justu ńgua prau, ńgka dos prau
3SG have just one boat NEG two boat
'He has only one boat, not two boats.' (Baxter 2013b: feature 29)

There are the demonstratives *ís(t)i* 'this' and *aké(li)* 'that'.

Personal pronouns distinguish between two numbers and three persons. They are identical for subject and object functions.

	SINGULAR	PLURAL
1	*yo*	*nus*
2	*bos*	*bolotu*
3	*eli*	*olotu*

The third person forms are used only with animate (mainly human) referents. The possessive pronouns are formed by adding *sa* to the personal pronouns.

Nominal possession is indicated with the possessive particles *sa* or *di*, as in *káza sa janéla* 'the window of the house', *chapéu di Juáng* 'John's hat' or *Chang di Padri* '(the) Priest's ground' (Hancock 1964: 301).

Adjectives are postnominal. Comparatives and superlatives are formed with *más* … *di* 'more … than':

(522) a. eli más altu di Pio
3SG more tall than PN
'He is taller than Pio.' (Baxter 2013a: 124 citing Baxter 1988: 184)

b. Maira más altu di tudu mbes aké femi femi
PN more tall of all once DEM female female
'Maria is the tallest of all the girls.' (Baxter 2013a: 124)

There are three overt tense and aspect markers: *ja* (perfective aspect), *ta* (imperfective aspect) and *lo(gu)* (irrealis). The bare form indicates the habitual past or present for dynamic verbs, and normal past or present for stative verbs; the lexical aspect of the verb may thus affect the tense/aspect reading of the clause.

(523) a. yo sa pai fai sibrisu na municipal
1SG POSS father do work LOC municipal
'My father works/used to work in the Municipal.' (Baxter 2013a: 124 citing Baxter 1988: 134)

b. eli sabé bos ta beng
3SG know 2SG IPFV come
'S/he knows/knew (that) you are/were coming.'
(Baxter 2013a: 124f citing Baxter 1988: 134f)

c. Taté ja olá ku bela Rozil
PN PFV see OBJ old PN
'Taté saw old Rozil.' (Baxter 2013b: feature 51 citing Baxter 1988: 176)

d. Diego ta les buku
PN IPFV read book
'Diego is/was reading a book.' (Baxter 2013a: 125)

e. amiang otu dia, eli logu nai mar
tomorrow other day 3SG IRR go sea
'The day after tomorrow, he will go fishing.' (Baxter 2013a: 125 citing Baxter 1988: 126)

f. kantu yo teng doi, yo lo komprá kareta
if 1SG have money 1SG IRR buy car
'If I have/had money I will/would buy a car.' (Baxter 2013a: 126 citing Baxter 1988: 126)

There are the modal auxiliaries *toká* 'be obliged to', *miste* 'must, should', *prěsizu* 'need, should', *podi* 'can', *sabé* 'can' and *kére* 'want'.

The word order is typically subject-verb-object. Negation is tense and aspect sensitive: *ńgka* negates verbs in the perfective or imperfective aspect, *nadi* negates verbs in the irrealis, and *nang* negates imperatives.

Polar questions may either be indicated through intonation only, or be formed with the question particle *ka*, or with the tags *seng* 'yes', *ńgka* 'no', or with the confirmation particle *ná*. In content questions the interrogative phrase may be fronted or remain *in situ*.

Though the copula is usually omitted in both nominal and adjectival predication, there is the rare and archaic copula *teng*, which is more commonly used for locative expressions:

(524) a. yo teng ńgua jenti di otru mundu
1SG COP INDEF person of other world
'I am a person from another world.'

b. eli teng na bangsal
3SG COP LOC fisherman's.hut
'He is at the fisherman's hut.' (Baxter 2013a: 126)

There are the coordinating conjunctions *ku* 'with, and', *kě* 'or' and *mas* 'but'. Subordination is usually indicated by juxtaposition only:

(525) yo abé eli teng aki
1SG know 3SG COP here
'I know (that) he is here.' (Baxter 2013a: 128 citing Baxter 1988: 201)

Relative clauses are indicated with the particle *ki* 'what, who' or may remain unmarked. Serial verb constructions are common, especially with the verbs *bai* 'go', *beng* 'come' and *dá* 'give'.

(526) a. eli ja kuré bai kaza.
3SG PFV run go home
'He ran home.'

b. nu lo da kumí ku olotu
1PL IRR give eat OBJ 3PL
'We will feed them.' (Baxter 2013a: 126 citing Baxter 1988: 212, 214)

15.4.2.3 *Short text*

(Excerpt from Baxter 2013a: 129, oral narration of the story of The Snake Prince.)

Di numinti teng ńgua bairu, teng dos kaza; ńgua riku, ńgua pobri. Jenti riku sa
at beginning COP a village COP two house one rich one poor person rich POSS

fila sa nomi Maria; jenti pobri sa fila sa nomi Luzia. Kada dia ki
daughter POSS name PN people poor POSS daughter POSS name PN every day REL

Deus da, jenti pobri lo falá ku sa fila ku Luzia: "Bai matu buska lenya
God give people poor IRR say OBJ POSS daughter OBJ PN go jungle seek firewood

ke kuzinyá." Kada dia isti Luzia bai matu Maria lo sigí. Ki kauzu? Maria mbezu
want cook each day DEM PN go jungle PN IRR follow what cause PN envious

ku Luzia.
with PN

'At the beginning, there was a village, there were two houses; one rich, one poor. The name of the rich people's daughter was Maria; the name of the poor people's daughter was Luzia. Every day, the poor parents would say to their daughter, to Luzia: "Go to the forest and look for firewood for cooking." Every day, Luzia would go to the forest, and Maria would follow her. Why? Maria was jealous of Luzia.'

15.4.2.4 *Some sources of data*

There is a fair amount of primary data available for Papiá Kristang. Baxter (1988) is a full grammar, with numerous examples. Baxter & de Silva (2004) is a dictionary. Joan Marbeck (see http://joanmarbeck.com/, accessed 13 February 2015) has published a number of works on and in Papiá Kristang.

15.4.3 Angloromani: An English/Romani mixed language in Great Britain[240]

15.4.3.1 *A brief background sketch of Angloromani*

Angloromani, also called *Gypsy*, *Romany*, *Romani*, *Romani English*, *English Romani*, *English Romanes* or *Anglo-Romani* by scholars, and called *Romanes*, *Romnis*, *Romani*, *Pogadi Chib* ('broken language'), *posh-ta-posh* ('half-and-half') or, pejoratively, *Pikey talk* ('tramps' talk') by the speakers themselves (Bakker & Kenrick 2008). The exact number of speakers is not known, though estimates have been made at just under 200,000 (Lewis et al. 2014), half of whom live in Great Britain, while the other half is spread around the Anglophone world. While people of Roma descent are often referred to as Roma, this is not the commonly used term as a self-ascription among the English and Welsh Roma; some use the term *Romanichals*, but nowadays most use the terms *Gypsy* or *Romani Gypsy* to refer to themselves (Matras et al. 2007), a practice that will therefore be followed in this section.

240. This section is based primarily on Hancock (1984b) and Matras (2010). I am very grateful to Ian Hancock and Vijay John for their helpful comments on this snapshot.

The many varieties of Romani spoken in the world all descend from a Proto-Romani, which was an Indo-Aryan language. Genomic as well as linguistic and anthropological studies place the origin of the European Roma in the India-Pakistani border area (roughly the area of Rajasthan, Punjab and Jammu & Kashmir), but when they emigrated from India and how their migration path evolved is debated. For a concise and accessible overview, with numerous further references, see Matras (2002: 14ff). A recent genomic study with data from different European Romani suggests that the founder population left the area of origin about 1,500 years ago and arrived in the Balkans about 900 years ago (possibly via present-day Iran and Turkey), from where they spread to the rest of Europe (Mendizabal et al. 2012). However, historical sources do not mention Roma in the Balkans until the 14th century (Samer 2003).

The Gypsies, referred to as 'Egyptian pilgrims' in early sources, have been part of Great Britain since 1506 at the latest, when they asked protection from the Scottish king en route to Denmark, though they might have settled already in 1460 (Matras 2010).

Exactly when Angloromani emerged and what the causes involved were remains debated (for a concise overview of various positions, see Grant 1998 and Matras et al. 2007). The earliest known record of Romani in Great Britain is the thirteen phrases of the 'Egipt speche' noted down by Andrew Borde, which he apparently learned from some far-away people he encountered in a tavern (Bakker & Kenrick 2008). In his *The fyrst boke of the introduction of knowledge made by Andrew Borde, of physycke doctor*, published in 1547, he has a chapter that *treteth of Egypt, and of theyr mony and of theyr speche* ('is about Egypt, and of their money and of their speech'):

> The people of the cou[n]try be swarte, and doth go disgisyd in theyr apparel, contrary to other nacyons: they be lyght fyngerd, and vse pyking; they haue litle maner, and euyl loggyng & yet they be pleasunt daunsers.[241] (Borde 1870 [1547]: 217)

Borde goes on to claim that few 'Egyptians' now live in Egypt and then gives the sample sentences. The small sample suggests that this was Romani (or 'inflected Romani', that is, "unmixed" Romani) and the sentences are still intelligible to most Romani speaking people (Bakker & Kenrick 2008). A possible very early reference to Angloromani "as a newly devised speech" (Hancock 1984b: 90) could be what Thomas Harman describes in his *A caveat or warning for common cursetors, vulgarly called vagabonds* published in 1573, where he mentions the speech of these so-called 'vagabonds' "whiche language they terme Peddelers Frenche, an unknown toungue onely, but to these bold beastly bawdy beggers, and vayne vacabonds, being halfe myngled with Englishe, when it is familiarly talked"[242] (Harman 1814 [1573]: 64). Harman states that this language, which he says is spoken by a number of these 'vagabonds', "began but within these XXX. yeres or little aboue" ('began within these 30 years or a little more') (*ibid.*: vi). The *Winchester confessions*

241. "The people of the country are swarthy, and go disguised in their apparel, contrary to other nations: they are light fingered, and go picking; they have little manners, and evil longing & yet they are pleasant dancers."

242. "which language they term Peddlers French, an unknown tongue, except to these bold beastly bawdy beggars, and vain vagabonds, being half mingled with English, when it is familiarly talked."

1615–1616, an appendix to a criminal proceedings record, gives Romani vocabulary and phrases apparently used by a group of outlaws (McGowan 1996). In this source the Romani is no longer inflected, and in some phrases there are Romani words embedded in an English matrix, such as *Swisht with a sayster in the end* '(a) staff with a pike in the end'; it has thus been argued to be the first evidence of the mixed language that we now know as Angloromani (Bakker 2002).

Given the centuries of stigmatization and discrimination that Roma and those of Roma descent have suffered, as well as the heavy pressure to assimilate to the mainstream society, including shifting to the language of the host society, while at the same time being severely marginalized, it seems fair to assume that the emergence of so-called Para-Romani varieties (i.e. mixed languages between Romani and the host community language) at least partially had to do with identity (see Matras 2002:247ff for a concise overview and further references on the development of Para-Romani languages). For a severely marginalized population, the mixed language might serve as a way of maintaining a sense of continuity with the origins of the population, as well as flagging a separate identity from the host population, a discourse device that may be termed an 'emotive mode' (Matras et al. 2007). Furthermore, it seems as if many Para-Romani languages, including Angloromani, were or are used as in-group languages for secret communication and for the exclusion of others (cf. Hancock 1984b, Bakker & Kenrick 2008, Matras 2010).

15.4.3.2 *A short linguistic sketch of Angloromani*

Angloromani has taken over the phonemes of English, thus has 23 consonants, /p, b, m, f, v, w, t, d, n, s, z, l, r, θ, ð, ʃ, ʒ, ʧ, ʤ, j, k, g, ŋ/ and 12 vowels, /i, ɪ, e, ɜ, ə, æ, ɑ, ɒ, ʌ, ɔ, ʊ, u/. It is a rhotic language, with a rolling /r/. Some speakers have kept the historic uvular fricative /χ/, though for most speakers it has become /h/ or /k/. The historic aspirated stops /p^h, t^h, k^h/ have been lost (though in some cases this has become a voiced/unvoiced contrast, as in *t^hud* > *tud* 'milk' versus *tud* > *dud* 'light'; Hancock 1984b:102). The phonemes /θ, ð, ʃ, ʒ, ʧ, ʤ, j, ŋ/ are here represented by <th, th, sh, zh, ch, j, y, ng>. Since Angloromani functions in an English matrix, syllables may be as complex as in English, i.e. with up to three consonants in the onset and three in the coda. Tone is not relevant.

The morphology is, like in English (and unlike Romani), predominantly analytic, though the few English inflectional affixes have been retained. Apart from various English-derived derivation affixes, there are also Romani-derived ones, such as the nominalizer *-(m)engr-* < Romani *-engr-* 'GENitive.PLural' (lit. 'thing(s) belonging or pertaining to'),[243] as in *dikka-mengr-i* 'mirror' (lit. 'see-GENitive.PLural-Feminine') < *dik-* 'to see', *pi-mengr-a* 'coffee, tea' (lit. 'drink-GENitive. PLural-Masculine') < *pi-* 'to drink' or *waffa-ta-mengr-a* 'foreigner' (lit. 'other-country-GENitive. PLural-Masculine') < *vaver them* 'other country' (Matras 2010:104) and the nominalizer *-bən*, as in *jinəbən* 'knowledge' < *jin* 'to know' or *kɔːnibən* 'blindness' < *kɔːni* 'blind' (Hancock 1984b:103). Reduplication is used to express intensification.

---

243. It should be noted that while this *-(m)engr* is a productive derivational affix in Angloromani, it is not productive in e.g. Vlax Romani (Vijay John, p.c.).

Number is typically indicated with the English plural *-(e)s*, as in *mush* 'man' / *mush-es* 'men' (Matras 2010: 118) though a Romani plural *-a* may also be used, as in *yɔk* 'eye' / *yɔk-a* 'eye-PLural' (Hancock 1984b: 102). Double plural marking may occur, as in *vast* 'hand' / *vast-a-s* 'hand-PLural-PLural' (Matras 2010: 118). Gender and case is not relevant; historic Romani cases appear only in fossilized forms.

The articles derive from English and are optional:

(527) a. mush kek jun-s chichi
man NEG know-PRES nothing
'(The) man doesn't know anything.' (Matras 2010: 120)

b. maw be rokker-ing in front of the mush and rakli!
NEG be talk-PROG in front of DEF man and girl
'Don't be talking in front of the man and (the) girl!' (Matras 2010: 120)

c. mush akai
man here
'(A) man (is) here.' (Matras 2010: 120)

d. man=ll ja te la a piben
1SG=FUT go COMP take a drink
'I'll go and take a drink.' (Matras et al. 2007: 157)

There are the demonstratives *duvva* 'this' and *kuvva* 'that', which may also function as definite articles.

The pronominal system distinguishes between three persons and two numbers. Most forms are Romani derived. Notice that there is a male/female distinction in the third person singular, but no specifically neutral form.

	SINGULAR	PLURAL
1	*mandi/me(i)/mi*	*mendi/we*
2	*tutti/tu(t)*	*you*
3.M	*lesti/yo(y)*	*lendi/lengi*
3.F	*latti/yo(y)*	

Notice that English pronouns may also be used. Possessive pronouns are formed by adding the English possessive marker *=s* to the personal pronoun forms:

(528) tutti=s ruzlibən an' mandi=s gʌzəl-əs
2SG=POSS strength and 1SG=POSS brain-PL
'your strength and my brains' (Hancock 1984b: 105)

Subject pronouns may be omitted:

(529) a. mandi kom dovva chavvi but kek kom dovva chavvi
1SG like this child but NEG like this child
'I like this child but (I) don't like that child.'

b. kek jel there, lel the otchaben
NEG go there get the veneral.desease
'Don't go there, (you'll) get VD!' (Matras 2010: 120)

Nominal possession is indicated with the English possessive marker *=s*.

Adjectives are prenominal and invariant. Comparison is formed as in English, with the suffixes *-er* and *-est*, as in *yɔky* 'intelligent' / *yɔki-er* 'more intelligent' / *yɔki-est* 'most intelligent' (Hancock 1984b: 108), unless the word has more than two syllables, in which case comparison is expressed analytically with *more* and *most*, as in *wafədi* 'bad' / *more wafədi* / 'worse' / *(the) most wafədi* 'worst' (*ibid*).

Verbs are inflected as in English and thus take the past tense marker *-ed*, the future tense marker *will* (VERB) and the progressive aspect marker *-ing*, though any of these markers may optionally be omitted. The present tense marker *-s* is commonly generalized to all persons:

(530) a. mandi jin-s
1SG know-PRES
'I know.'

b. tutti jin-s
2SG know-PRES
'You know.'

c. mandi pukkere-d the rakli
1SG say-PST the woman
'I told the woman.'

d. lesti=s savv-ing at mandi
3SG.M=PRES laugh-PROG at 1SG
'He's laughing at me.'

e. I=ll do some hobben
1SG=FUT do some food
'I'll make some food.'

f. foki jel akai
people come here
'People (are) com(ing) here.' (Matras 2010: 14, 20, 121f)

The passive may be formed as an English *get*-passive:

(531) lɛdi=ll get mɔ:-d
3PL=FUT get kill-PTCP
'They'll get killed.' (Hancock 1984b: 107)

The word order is subject-verb-object. Negation is commonly expressed with the invariant preverbal negator *kek(ka)*. The prohibitive may be expressed by the English *don't* or a double form *kek(ka) don't*:

(532) a. mush kek jun-s
man NEG know-PRES
'(The) man doesn't know.'

b. kekka rokker romanes up the gav
NEG talk Romanes up the town
'Don't talk Romanes in the town.'

c. kek don't mang no kushti in her, she=s chikli this rakli is!
NEG do.NEG look no good in her she=PRES dirty this girl is
'Don't look for no good in her, she's dirty this girl is!' (Matras 2010: 115f)

Polar questions may be formed through inverted word order, like in English. In content questions the interrogative phrase may be fronted, as in English, or may be omitted.

(533) a. did you lel some luvva?
did 2SG make some money
'Did you make some money?' (Matras 2010: 114)

b. how doevee ankee devus
how far travel day
'How far have you travelled today?' (Matras et al. 2007: 153)

c. pen your naave
say 2SG.POSS name
'What is your name?' (Matras et al. 2007: 152)

The copula may be omitted, also when it functions as an existential:

(534) a. mandi boktalo, del mandi obben
1SG hungry give 1SG food
'I (am) hungry, give me food.'

b. divya chavvi akai
wild child here
'(There are) wild children here.' (Matras 2010: 120)

Coordinating constructions are formed with the English coordinators *and*, *but* and *or*.

There is the Romani derived relative particle *kon/kun*, though relative clauses may also be formed as in English:

(535) the poor fowki that haven't got a poshaera to their name
the poor people REL have.NEG got a half.penny to 3PL.POSS name
and want to take money off=em they haven't got chichi
and want to take money off=3PL.O 3PL.S have.NEG got nothing
'The poor people that haven't got a half-penny to their name and want to take money off'em they haven't got anything.' (Matras 2010: 115)

15.4.3.3 *Short text*

(From Ian Hancock (p.c.), a personal letter sent by a speaker of Angloromani to Ian Hancock. The English forms appear in italics.)

Mandi sikker-*ed it to the* godgo. *He* penn-*ed that* miro tickno lil sas kushti, *but*
1SG show-PST it to the non.Gypsy he say-PST that 1SG.POSS small book COP good but

I=d kerr-*ed some* bongo wafedi lav-s *in it. Then with his* kokoro vast *he* chinn-*ed*
I=PST make-PST some wrong bad word-PL in it then with his own hand he write-PST

mandi *a translation* adre Romanes *of an* angitrakeri gill, *but* mandi=s *a*-trash-*ed as*
1SG a translation in Romanes of an English song but 1SG=PRES a-fear-PST as

it=s kek but kushti.
it=PRES NEG but good

'I showed it to the non-Gypsy. He said that my small book was fine, but that I'd made some mistakes in it. Then with his own hand, he wrote me a translation in Romani of an English song, but I'm afraid that it's not very good.'

15.4.3.4 *Some sources of data*

There is a fair amount of primary data available for Angloromani. Matras (2010) is a very thorough description of the language, containing numerous examples as well as an appendix lexicon. The Manchester Romani Project (http://romani.humanities.manchester.ac.uk/, accessed 13 February 2015) gives a wealth of information of various Romani dialects, as well as various Para-Romani languages, including a bibliography on Angloromani topics (http://romani.humanities.manchester.ac.uk/db/bibliography/index.html?cat=1, accessed 13 February 2015) and an Angloromani dictionary (http://romani.humanities.manchester.ac.uk/angloromani/, accessed 13 February 2015).

15.5 Summary

Pidgins seem more likely than non-pidgins to make use of a negative particle to negate declarative clauses. Pidgins also seem more likely than non-pidgins to indicate polar questions through intonation only. However, pidgins do not seem more likely than non-pidgins to lack politeness distinctions for second person pronouns.

Almost all extended pidgins (pidgincreoles) make use of a negative particle for negated declarative sentences and indicate polar questions through rising intonation only. Furthermore, the majority of the extended pidgins lack politeness distinctions for second person pronouns.

Creoles seem more likely than non-creoles to use a negative particle for negative declarative sentences. Creoles also seem more likely than non-creoles to mark polar questions through rising intonation only and less likely than non-creoles to mark polar questions though verbal morphology. However, creoles are not more likely than non-creoles to lack politeness distinctions in second person pronouns.

Mixed languages seem to take strategies of one of the input languages, or to represent a blend of the input languages with respect to negation, polar questions as well as politeness distinctions in the second person pronouns, though language-specific innovations may also occur.

15.6 Key points

- **Pidgins are more likely than non-pidgins to have a negative particle and to form polar questions through intonation only.**
- **Extended pidgins tend to have negative particles, to form polar questions through intonation only and to lack politeness distinctions in second person pronouns.**
- **Creoles are more likely than non-creoles to have negative particles and to form polar questions through intonation only.**
- **The negation and polar question strategies in mixed languages seem inherited from one of the input languages or to represent a blend of the input languages.**
- **Pidgins are as likely as non-pidgins to lack politeness distinctions in second person pronouns.**

- **Creoles are as likely as non-creoles to lack politeness distinctions in second person pronouns.**
- **Mixed languages may exhibit innovations with respect to politeness strategies in second person pronouns.**

15.7 Exercises

1. Do extended pidgins (pidgincreoles) align more closely with pidgins than with creoles with respect to negative marking, polar question formation and politeness in second person pronouns?
2. What are the implications of the findings on negation and polar question strategies in creole languages?
3. Is the following statement true or false? Motivate your answer.
   The negation strategy in a mixed language is always derived from the input language which provided the grammatical structure.
4. How do the findings with respect to politeness strategies in second person pronouns relate to the notion of creoles as simple languages?
5. Give examples of what may represent innovations with respect to politeness strategies in second person pronouns in mixed languages.

Glossary

absolute tense Tense where the event is placed before, after or simultaneous to the speech moment on a time line.

accommodation The process by which speakers modify their language or accent away from or towards that of their interlocutors.

acrolect The variety most similar to the standard language.

actionality See **lexical aspect**.

active voice Grammatical subcategory which announces that the grammatical subject of a clause is also the semantic agent of the clause.

adjectival predication See **predicative adjective**.

adjective clause See **relative clause**.

adjunct (also **peripheral participant**) Non-obligatory clause participant.

adstrate language Language or variety which has influenced some other language or variety of roughly equal prestige.

affix Bound morpheme that does not carry any lexemic information.

Afrogenesis Theory that postulates that all Atlantic creoles ultimately descend from one West African pidgin.

Aktionsart See **lexical aspect**.

allopatric speciation Evolutionary process where a population evolves into separate species due to geographic isolation.

analytic construction (also **periphrastic construction**) Morphological construction by way of free morphemes.

animacy Classification of nouns according to how animate or inanimate they are.

A-not-A construction (also a **disjunctive-negative structure**) Polar question formed by giving the verb twice, once in its positive form and once in its negative form.

argument (also **core participant**) Obligatory clause participant.

article Marker (free or bound) used to signal whether the noun phrase referred to is identifiable or not.

aspect Grammatical device indicating the perspective taken on an event.

autoglossonym The name by which speakers refer to their own language.

auxiliary verb Semantically more or less empty verb used to express grammatical information.

baby-talk See **child-directed speech**.

banya song and dance Type of song and dance performed by the slave population and descendants of the slave population in Suriname.

basilect The variety least similar to the standard language.

bilingual Person with two L1s.

blackbirding Recruitment of labourers by coercion through trickery or kidnapping.

borrowing When a language or variety takes over a linguistic form from another language or variety.

bound morpheme Morpheme which cannot function as its own word but has to attach to a host.

Bozal Slave that was born in Africa and brought to the (Caribbean) colonies.

bridge language See ***lingua franca***.

broken language See **interlanguage**.

categorical data Data that is sorted in discrete, mutually exclusive, categories.

child-directed speech (also **baby-talk**) Speech register used by caretakers when addressing small children.

chi-square goodness-of-fit test (also **a one-dimensional chi-square test**) Chi-square test applied to unpaired categorical data.

chi-square test (also **Pearson Chi-Square Test**) Statistical test applied to categorical data to estimate how probable it is that the given distribution arose by chance.

chi-square value (χ) The test statistical value arrived at when applying a chi-square test. The higher the value, the less likely it is that the observed result came about by chance.

chi-squared contingency table test Chi-square test applied to binomial (i.e. consisting of two groups) or multinomial (i.e. consisting of more than two groups) categorical data.

circumfix Type of bound morpheme involving at least a prefix and a suffix simultaneously.

clausal negation Negation that negates an entire clause producing the counterpart of an affirmative declarative.

clitic Bound morpheme that is syntactically independent from its host.

coda That part of a syllable which appears after the nucleus.

code-mixing The mixing of two or more languages or varieties in the same utterance. Sometimes used interchangeably with code-switching.

code-switching The switching between two or more languages or varieties in the same utterance. Sometimes used interchangeably with code-mixing.

codification The process of setting up a linguistic norm.

Common Core theory Theory which proposes that the structure of a given contact language derives from those parts of the input languages that overlap.

common noun Noun not referring to a specific individual or place.

complex clause Clause consisting of several clauses.

concatenative marker Bound morphological marker.

consonant Segment formed by creating some kind of obstacle as the air passes from the lungs through the mouth.

contact language Cover term for languages that arose in situations of extreme contact.

content question Question formed with an interrogative phrase. Demands an answer that contains more information than just confirmation or disconfirmation.

contingency table Table of frequencies in matrix format that displays the cross-classification relationship between two or more categorical data variables.

continuum A non-discrete range of variation where there are no sharp borders.

contrastive segment Minimal meaning distinguishing unit.

convergence Process by which speakers make their speech and behaviour more similar to that of their interlocutors.

converted language Language which has adopted the structure of another language or other languages without changing its lexicon.

coordination Process where linguistic units of the same status are linked together.

copula Semantically empty formative that serves as a link between a noun phrase and a predicate.

core participant See **argument**.

corpus planning The process of implementing codification, language cultivation and language planning.

correlative Relative clause where the head occurs inside the relative clause but also has an overt reference in the matrix clause.

cosubordination Complex clause where the units are neither embedded in each other nor independent from each other.

count noun Noun denoting a discrete entity that can be counted.

covert prestige Implicit prestige attached to non-prestigious language or variety forms, the use of which emphasizes group identity and solidarity.

creole continuum Gradation of closeness between a creole and its lexifier language.

Creole exceptionalism See **Creole Prototype**.

creole Language which emerged in situation of intense contact and which has become the mother tongue of an entire speech community.

Creole Prototype (also **Creole exceptionalism**) Theory which proposes that a given set of features can be identified as unique for creole languages.

creolization Process by which a language becomes a creole.

definite article Marker (free or bound) which codes specificity and indicates that the noun phrase referred to is identifiable.

definiteness Grammatical device used to indicate whether an entity is identifiable or not.

degrees of freedom (*df*) The number of units that are free to vary.

dependent clause A clause which cannot function independently but which is embedded in main clause.

depidginization Process by which a pidgin gradually assimilates to the lexifier through continued contact.

derivational aspect See **lexical aspect**.

dialect (also **regional dialect**) Variety of language that is distinctive to a certain region.

dialect levelling (also **koineization**) The process by which dialects become more similar to each other.

diathesis See **voice**.

diffusion The gradual spread of an item.

diglossia Situation where two distinct varieties with distinct functional ranges are used in a speech community.

disjunctive-negative structure See **A-not-A construction.**

ditransitive verb Verb which takes two objects, thus has three participants.

divergence Process by which speakers make their speech and behaviour more different from that of their interlocutors.

Domestic Origin Hypothesis Theory for Afrogenesis specifically for the English-lexified Atlantic creoles.

domestic workforce pidgin Pidgin that arose in the interaction between domestic staff and their employers, where each of them had different linguistic origins.

du form Form of dramatization of banya songs.

dual Number value referring to two entities exactly.

dynamic verb A verb where the lexical aspect implies an inherent element of change.

E(xternal)-languages The communal norm of a language understood independently of the properties of the mind.

early pidgin See **jargon.**

embedded clause Clause which is a dependent component of a main clause.

endogenous creole Creole which developed through contact between immigrant settlers and indigenous population groups.

equative clause Clause which describes that the subject is the same as the entity of the predication.

etymological orthography Orthography which retains earlier spellings despite changes in pronunciation.

European expansion European exploration starting in the 15th century which led to trade with and colonization of different parts of the world.

Event 0 Point in time when a colony was founded.

Event 1 Point in time when the number of substrate speakers surpassed the number of superstrate speakers.

Event 2 Point in time when the number of locally-born substrate speakers surpassed the number of superstrate speakers.

Event 3 Point in time when mass immigration to a colony stops.

Event X Point in time when the number of locally-born substrate speakers surpassed the foreign-born substrate speakers.

evolutionary account Theory of creole formation proposing that creoles emerged in an environment of language competition meaning that the given structure of a creole is dependent on the particular linguistic ecology of the situation.

exogenous creole Creoles which developed through contact between different linguistic groups, none of which were indigenous to the area where the creole emerged.

expanded pidgin See **extended pidgin.**

expected result In statistics, the result that, all things being equal, would be obtained in an experiment.

extended pidgin (also **expanded pidgin, stable pidgin** or **pidgincreole**) Pidgin that has become a main means of interethnic communication and is used in a potentially unlimited range of domains.

face The public image a person wishes to maintain.

factor See **variable.**

feature pool Linguistic equivalent of gene pool; the sum of every individual's linguistic system in any given situation.

foreigner talk Register used by native speakers when addressing non-native speakers.

Foreigner Talk theory Theory which proposes that the structure of pidgin languages came about because the target model input was foreigner talk.

fort creoles Type of endogenous creole proposed to have emerged around the trading ports set up by the European explorers and colonizers.

founder effect Phenomenon where genetic variability is lost when a new population is established by a small group of individuals from the original population.

founder event The occasion when a small group of individuals break away from a larger ancestral population group.

Founder Principle The principle of the founder effect by which the structure of a language in a contact situation is determined by the founder population.

free morpheme Morpheme which functions on its own as a word.

full reduplication Reduplication where the entire base is copied.

gap Strategy for relative clauses where (1) there is no overt element in the relative clause which is coreferential with the head noun, or (2) where there is neither any overt reference which is coreferential with the head noun, nor any relative particle.

gene pool The sum of every individual's genetic information in a given population.
genealogical balance See **genetic balance**.
genealogical bias See **genetic bias**.
genetic (or genealogical) balance Balance of a cross-linguistic sample where different genetic branches are represented by the same number of languages.
genetic (or genealogical) bias Bias to a cross-linguistic sample where some language families or genera are over- or underrepresented.
G-L mixed language Mixed language that has its structure from one input language and its vocabulary from another input language.
gloss The analytical explanation of a linguistic unit.
glossary "A collection of grossly inaccurate definitions (written late at night when you really ought to be asleep) of things that you thought you understood" (Field et al. 2012: 918).
Gradualist Model Theory on the emergence of creoles proposing that they evolved gradually over several generations through a combination of L1 and L2 acquisition.
graphization The selection of a script and orthographic convention.
G-test (or **likelihood ratio test**) Statistical test applied to categorical data to estimate how probable it is that the given distribution arose by chance.
G-test value (*G*) The test statistic value arrived at when applying a G-test. The higher the value, the less likely it is that the observed result came about by chance.
head The main unit of a construction.
high variety (H) The prestigious variety in a diglossic situation.
homestead Small(er) semi-isolated farms.
hybrid The offspring of genetically distinct parents.
Hybridization When a hybrid is produced through the interbreeding of two species.
I(nternal)-languages The system of linguistic knowledge in any individual's brain.
imperfective Aspectual category indicating that an event is viewed from within its course.
implicational pattern Pattern of variation that is systematic and predictable.
incipient pidgin See **jargon**.
indefinite article Marker (free or bound) used to indicate that the noun phrase referred to is not identifiable.
indentured labour Form of contract labour where an individual is bound to work for an employer for a set amount of time (usually to pay off debts, most commonly debts for the travel costs).
infix Affix which places itself inside a morpheme.
input language Language that was part of a contact situation and is proposed to have contributed to the contact language that emerged from that situation.
interlanguage (also **broken language**) The linguistic system of someone who is in the process of acquiring a foreign language.
Interlanguage Hypothesis See **Interlanguage theory**.
Interlanguage theory (also **Interlanguage Hypothesis**) Theory which proposes that the structure of pidgins reflect the fact that they emerged as incompletely learned versions of the model language.
interlinearization (also **interlinearized morpheme translation** or **interlinearized glossing**) Morpheme-by-morpheme analysis and glossing from one language to another.
interlinearized glossing See **interlinearization**.
interlinearized morpheme translation See **interlinearization**.
interlingua See ***lingua franca***.
interrogative Type of speech act forming a request for information.
intertwined language Language that is composed of two or a few mutually dependent components that form a unique whole.
intransitive verb Verb that has only one participant (the subject).
irrealis Mood used to denote that the speaker is not able to assert that a proposition is true.
isolating marker Free morpheme marker.
jargon (also **unstable/early/primitive/incipient/rudimentary pidgin** or **pre-pidgin**) Individual *ad hoc* solutions in individual contact situations leading to a highly variable and unstable contact language.
koineization See **dialect levelling**.
L1 (also **mother tongue, native language**) The language that a speaker has acquired naturally as a child.
L2 (also **second language**) A language learned in addition to a person's L1.
language attitudes The positive or negative feelings that people have about their own language or the language(s) of others.
Language Bioprogram Hypothesis (LBH) Theory that proposes that creoles emerged as a result of the

inadequate linguistic input that the pidgin-speaking parents provided the first generation of mixed heritage children, causing these children resort to an innate human blueprint for language in order to create a fully equipped and functional language for themselves. The implication is thus that creoles give an indication of the nature of the human language faculty.

language competition An evolutionary approach to the development of and change in languages following the principles of biological replication whereby in a pool of linguistic features, some are selected and propagated due to their higher competitive value.

language family The highest node of a group of affiliated languages.

language genus A level of genetic language classification which is proposed to be globally comparable in time depth between different language families.

language intertwining A non-directional process where speakers combine aspects of two or a few languages and form a new language.

language planning The conscious efforts to influence or change the language use in a given community.

language policy (also **status planning**) The allocation of languages or varieties to different societal domains.

language shift (also **language transfer/assimilation/replacement**) The process in which a population abandons one language in favour of another.

lect Any distinct variety of a language, whether based on regional, social or any other factors.

lectal diversity The assortment of different language lects within one language situation.

lexical aspect (also ***Aktionsart***, **actionality** or **derivational aspect**) Semantic specification of the inner structure of an event.

lexical reservoir The collected vocabulary available to a given speaker.

lexical verb The verb which carries the semantic content of the verbal construction.

lexifier language That language from which a contact language derives most of its vocabulary.

likelihood ratio test See **G-test**.

lingua franca (also a **bridge/vehicular language** or an **interlingua**) A language systematically used to enable communication between groups of people who have different L1s.

lingueme (also **linguistic genotype**) The linguistic structure produced by speakers each time they make an utterance.

linguistic ecology The specific makeup of any given linguistic situation.

linguistic genotype See **lingueme**.

lobisingi Special type of love songs sung especially by the descendants of the slave population in Suriname.

low variety (L) The non-prestigious variety in a diglossic situation.

main clause (also **superordinate clause**) An independent clause. Sometimes called a matrix clause.

maritime pidgin See **nautical pidgin**.

Maroon creole Creole spoken by Maroon communities.

mass noun Noun denoting a non-discrete entity, i.e. which is not in units that can be counted.

matched guise Technique used to obtain information about unconsciously held language attitudes, whereby the same speaker uses different guises (different languages or varieties) presented to listeners who then rate the speech according to different criteria.

matrix clause A clause which contains an embedded subordinate clause. Sometimes also used to signify main clause.

mercantilism Economic theory which holds that wealth can only be measured in gold and silver.

mesolect The variety which lies somewhere between the basi- and the acrolect.

Middle Passage The journey of the slaves from West Africa to the Caribbean.

military pidgin A pidgin that arose among troops of different linguistic backgrounds.

mine pidgin A pidgin that arose between mine workers and/or their employers where the various groups had different linguistic backgrounds.

mixed language A language that arose primarily due to expressive needs in community bi- or multilingualism and which has a limited amount of identifiable source languages.

modality (1) Grammatical category coding the attitude a speaker has towards a given proposition. (2) If differentiated from mood: the semantic label of attitudes towards events.

monogenetic Having a single origin.

Monogenetic theory Theory which proposes that all pidgins (and creoles) ultimately descend from one original pidgin.

mood (1) Grammatical category coding the attitude a speaker has towards a given proposition. (2) If differentiated from modality: the higher level clausal distinction of realis/irrealis.

morpheme The abstract notion of the smallest meaningful unit.

morphemic principle Orthographic principle where the spelling has a fixed form for each morpheme.

morphosyntax The way morphemes are put together to form words, phrases and sentences.

mother tongue See **L1**.

multilingual (1) Person with more than two L1s. (2) Person who is proficient in more than two languages, not all necessarily L1s.

native language See **L1**.

nativization The process whereby a pidgin becomes the L1 of an entire community.

Nautical Jargon theory Theory which proposes that the structure of pidgins derives from the role of the jargons that were used on ships.

nautical pidgin A pidgin that emerged as a result of interethnic communication between seamen on board or between ships, or between seamen and coastal people.

negation Device used to reverse the truth of a proposition.

negative adverb Adverb negating a clause.

negative face The public image of a person which maintains his/her independence and freedom from imposition.

negative pronoun Pronoun referring to a non-existing entity.

nominal predication See **predicative noun phrase**.

non-linear marker Morphological marker which involves some kind of modification of the host.

non-restrictive relative clause Relative clause which only adds information about the head noun but does not restrict the potential referents to any specific noun phrase.

noun Part of speech usually referring to concrete or abstract entities.

noun phrase (NP) The unit which functions as an argument and has a noun or a pronoun as its head.

nucleus The core of a syllable.

number Grammatical device for expressing how many entities are being referred to.

observed results In statistics, the result that was obtained in a given survey or experiment.

one-dimensional chi-square test See **chi-square goodness-of-fit test**.

onset That part of a syllable which comes before the nucleus.

oral literature (also **orature**) Any body of literature that is preserved and transmitted orally.

orature See **oral literature**.

overt prestige Explicit prestige attached to prestigious language or variety forms.

paralexification The phenomenon where a speech community has access to two parallel lexicons.

parapatric speciation Evolutionary process where a small part of the original population forms its own niche, but remains in limited contact with the ancestor population.

partial reduplication Reduplication where a set part of the base is copied.

passive voice Grammatical subcategory which announces that the grammatical subject of a clause is also the semantic patient of the clause.

paucal Number value referring to a small group of entities.

Pearson Chi-Square Test See **chi-square test**.

perfective Aspectual category indicating that an event is viewed as a bounded whole.

peripatric speciation Evolutionary process where a small part of the original population gets isolated from the ancestor population and evolves into a new species.

peripheral participant See **adjunct**.

periphrastic construction See **analytic construction**.

phoneme The abstract notion of the smallest meaning distinguishing unit.

phonemic orthography (also **phonological orthography**) Orthographic principle by which each phoneme has its own symbol.

phonological orthography See **phonemic orthography**.

pidgin (also **stable pidgin**) A secondary language with a set structure which emerged in a situation where speakers of mutually unintelligible languages needed to communicate with each other, typically used only in a limited set of contexts.

pidgincreole See **extended pidgin**.

Pidginization Index (*PI*) A proposed method of quantifying the extent to which an eventual creole in a contact situation will have to rely on the bioprogram.

pidginization The process by which a pidgin arises.

pidgin-to-creole life cycle The idea that a creole has emerged through a predictable route: a contact situation leads to a jargon, the jargon stabilizes and becomes a pidgin, which gradually comes to be used in wider contexts and becomes an expanded pidgin, which nativizes and becomes a creole.

plantation creole Creole that arose in the context of a plantation economy.

plantation Large-scale agricultural units that produce goods for commercial purposes in industrial like conditions.

plantation pidgin Pidgin that arose in the context of a plantation economy.

plural Number value referring to more than one entity.

polar question (also **yes-no question**) Interrogative where the answer is expected to be either a confirmation or disconfirmation.

politeness A form of interaction which shows awareness and respect for someone else's face.

polygenetic Having many origins.

polylectal Of a person: competent in more than one lects.

positive face The public self-image of a person which maintains his/her acceptance and group belonging.

post-creole continuum The process of a proposed final stage in a creole life-cycle, where the creole gradually merges with the lexifier through continued contact.

post-pidgin continuum The process of a proposed final stage in a creole life-cycle, where the pidgin gradually merges with the lexifier through continued contact.

predicate adjective See **predicative adjective**.

predicate nominal See **predicative noun phrase**.

predicate That part of the clause which asserts something about the subject.

predicative adjective (also **adjectival predication** or **predicate adjective**) Adjective which functions as a predicate to a subject.

predicative noun phrase (also **nominal predication** or **predicate nominal**) Noun phrase which functions as a predicate to a subject.

prefix Affix which places itself at the beginning of its host.

pre-pidgin See **jargon**.

primitive pidgin See **jargon**.

pronoun avoidance Politeness strategy where the speaker avoids using pronouns to refer to someone.

proper noun Noun referring to a specific individual or place.

prosodic feature See **suprasegmental feature**.

proverb A saying that expresses common sense world wisdom.

***p*-value** In statistical significance testing, the probability of obtaining the same or a very similar test statistic result as the observed result if the survey or experiment was done again with a different sample.

questions See **interrogative**.

realis Mood used to indicate that the speaker is very sure that a proposition is true.

recreolization The phenomenon of a speech community shifting to a more basilectal form of a creole.

reduplication Morphological process where a set amount of phonological material is copied from a base and fused with it to form a stem.

referent honorific Politeness strategy where the linguistic form chosen depends on what or whom is being referred to.

regional dialect See **dialect**.

register Language variety defined according to the social situations in which it is used.

relative clause (also **adjective clause**) Clause which modifies a noun phrase by marking out a particular antecedent of which a certain proposition is true.

relative particle (also **relativizer**) Morphological marker indicating a relative clause.

relative pronoun Pronoun used to introduce a relative clause and which is coreferential with the head noun.

relative tense Tense where an event is placed before, after or simultaneous to a given reference point on the time line.

Relexification Hypothesis Theory which proposes that creoles emerged as adult workers relexified their ancestor languages with the superstrate language in a colonial situation.

relexification The phenomenon where a language replaces most of its lexicon with that of another language.

repidginization The phenomenon of a creole being used as a lingua franca and in the process undergoing various changes.

restrictive relative clause Relative clause which restricts the potential referents in the matrix clause to a specific noun phrase out of several.

resumptive pronoun Personal (not relative) pronoun in relative clause that is coreferential with the head noun.

riddle An amusing word game that displays conventional wisdom.

rudimentary pidgin See **jargon**.

sample A set of data selected from a population by a defined procedure.

scope That section which is affected by the meaning of a particular form.

second language See **L2**.

serial verb construction (also **serial verb**) Cosubordinate construction where a string of verbs jointly act as a single predicate.

serial verb See **serial verb construction**.

singular Number value referring to one entity exactly.

slavery A system where human beings are treated as goods that can be bought and sold, and that are forced to work.

social dialect See **sociolect**.

sociolect (also **social dialect**). Variety of language defined according to social criteria.

speciation Evolutionary process by which new species are formed.

stable pidgin 1. See **pidgin** 2. See **extended pidgin**.

standardization The process by which a language or variety becomes the standard norm.

statistically significant A cut-off point in statistical testing where the test result indicates that the risk is low enough that the result came about by chance for it to be acceptable to reject the null hypothesis (which assumes that there is no relationship between the measured phenomena).

stative verb A verb where the lexical aspect implies that there is no element of change, merely a constant state.

status planning See **language policy**.

subordination Construction which contains a dependent clause embedded within a main clause.

substrate language (1) Language or variety which is already established for a person and which may influence the outcome of the acquisition of another language. (2) That language or variety which has influenced the structure or use of a more dominant language or variety in a community.

suffix Affix which places itself at the end of a host.

superordinate clause See **main clause**.

superstrate language Language or variety which has influenced the structure and use of a less dominant language or variety in a community.

suprasegmental feature (also **prosodic feature**) Contrastive feature which can carry over across segments.

syllable Unit of speech sound(s) which can be produced in isolation.

symbiotic mixed language Mixed language which exists alongside one or more of its source languages and which is not the only language of its speakers.

sympatric speciation Evolutionary process where a new species evolves within the original population while inhabiting the same geographical region.

synthesis The level of accumulated information a word can hold.

synthetic construction Morphological construction containing affixation.

T/V pronoun Binary pronoun distinction used as referent honorifics.

target language The language that an individual is aiming to acquire.

tense Grammatical device which places an event on a time line.

tertiary hybridization Proposed stage in a contact situation when a contact language is used by parties, none of whom speak the lexifier language natively.

tone Prosodic property of pitch variation.

tourist pidgin Pidgin that emerged in a contact situation involving a domestic workforce and regularly returning tourists, both parties of which have different linguistic backgrounds.

trade pidgin Pidgin that emerged in situations of trade, where the trading parties have different linguistic backgrounds.

transfer In L2 acquisition, the influence of the person's L1 on the language being acquired.

transitive verb Verb which only takes one object, i.e. has two participants.

translation The closest idiomatic rendering in language B of an expression in language A. Not to be confused with analysis.

trial Number value referring to three entities exactly.

triangular trade Trade among three ports or regions; here specifically the trade between Europe, West Africa and the New World.

unstable pidgin See **jargon**.

urban pidgin Pidgin that evolved in an urban setting among speakers of different linguistic backgrounds.

variable Something that can be measured and that can differ across units or time.

vehicular language See ***lingua franca***.

verb Part of speech usually referring to actions and processes.

verb phrase (VP) The unit composed of at least one verb and its dependents.

voice (also **diathesis**) Grammatical category which states the semantic role of the subject in the clause.

vowel Segment formed by letting air flow freely from the lungs through the mouth.

yes-no question See **polar question**.

References

Aboh, E. O. 2009. Competition and selection. That's all! In Aboh & Smith (eds), 317–44.

Aboh, E. O. & Ansaldo, U. 2007. The role of typology in language creation. A descriptive take. In Ansaldo et al. (eds), 39–66.

Aboh, E. O. & Smith, N. (eds). 2009. *Complex Processes in New Languages* [Creole Language Library 35]. Amsterdam: John Benjamins. DOI: 10.1075/cll.35

Aboh, E. O., Smith, N. & Veenstra, T. 2013a. Saramaccan. In Michaelis et al. (eds), 2013c, 27–38.

Aboh, E. O., Veenstra, T. & Smith, N. 2013b. Saramaccan structure dataset. In Michaelis et al. (eds), 2013a. http://apics-online.info/contributions/3 (13 February 2015)

Acar, K. 2004. Globalization and language. English in Turkey. *Sosyal Bilimler* 2(1): 1–10.

Adamson, L. & Smith, N. 1994. Sranan. In Arends et al. (eds), 219–232.

Adamson, L. & Smith, N. 2003. Productive derivational predicate reduplication in Sranan. In Kouwenberg (ed.), 83–92.

Adamson, L. & van Rossem, C. 1994. Creole literature. In Arends et al. (eds), 75–84.

Adelaar, K. A. & Prentice, D. J. 1996. Malay. Its history, role and spread. In Wurm, et al. (eds), 673–693.

Adiego, I.-X. 2002. *Un vocabulario español-gitano del Marqués de Sentmenat (1697–1762). Edición y estudio lingüístico*. Barcelona: Edicions Univesitat de Barcelona.

Adiego, I.-X. 2005. The vestiges of Caló today. In *General and Applied Romani linguistics. Proceedings from the 6th International Conference on Romani Linguistics*, B. Schrammel, D. W. Halwachs & G. Ambrosch (eds), 60–78. Munich: Lincom.

Aikhenvald, A. Y. 2006a. Grammars in contact. A cross-linguistic perspective. In *Grammars in Contact. A Cross-linguistic Typology*, A. Y. Aikhenvald & R. M. Dixon (eds), 1–66. Oxford: OUP.

Aikhenvald, A. Y. 2006b. Serial verb constructions in typological perspective. In Aikhenvald & Dixon (eds), 1–68.

Aikhenvald, A. Y. & Dixon, R. M. (eds). 2006. *Serial Verb Constructions. A Cross-Linguistic Typology*. Oxford: OUP.

Alexandre, P. 1963. Aperçu sommaire sur le Pidgin A 70 du Cameroun. *Cahiers d'Études Africaines* 3(12): 577–82.

Alleyne, M. 1971. Acculturation and the cultural matrix of creolization. In Hymes (ed.), 169–86.

Andersson, P. 2011. Actitudes hacia la variedad caló. Un estudio sociolingüistico de adolescentes andaluces. PhD dissertation, Göteborgs Universitet.

Andrews, A. D. 2007. Relative clauses. In *Language Typology and Syntactic Description, Vol. II: Grammatical Categories and the Lexicon*, 2. edn, T. Shopen (ed.), 206–236. Cambridge: CUP.

Anonymous. 1684. *The Indian Interpreter*. Trenton: Salem Town Records book B.64–68, State Archives of New Jersey.

Anonymous. 1830. *Dictionnaire de la langue franque ou petit mauresque*. Marseilles: Typographie de Feissat Ainé et Demonchy.

Anonymous. 1860. *The Englishman in China*. London: Saunders, Otley and Co.

Anonymous. 1916. *Le français tel que le parlent nos tirailleurs sénégalais*. Paris: Imprimerie Militaire Universelle L. Fournier.

Anonymous. 1980. *Bord la mer*. Port Louis: Port Louis Harbour and Docks Workers Union.

Ansaldo, U. 2008. Sri Lanka Malay revisited. Genesis and classification. In *Lessons from Documented Endangered Languages* [Typological Studies in Language 78], K.D. Harrison, D.S. Rood & A. Dwyer (eds), 13–42. Amsterdam: John Benjamins. DOI: 10.1075/tsl.78.02ans

Ansaldo, U. 2009. *Contact Languages. Ecology and Evolution in Asia*. Cambridge: CUP. DOI: 10.1017/CBO9780511642203

Ansaldo, U. (ed.). 2012. *Pidgins and Creoles in Asia* [Benjamins Current Topics 38]. Amsterdam: John Benjamins. DOI: 10.1075/bct.38

Ansaldo, U. & Matthews, S. 2007. Deconstructing creole. The rationale. In Ansaldo, et al. (eds), 1–18.

Ansaldo, U., Matthews, S. & Lim, L. (eds). 2007. *Deconstructing Creole* [Typological Studies in Language 73]. Amsterdam: John Benjamins. DOI: 10.1075/tsl.73

Ansaldo, U., Matthews, S. & Smith, G.P. 2012. China Coast Pidgin. Texts and contexts. In Ansaldo (ed.), 59–90.

Appel, R. & Verhoeven, L. 1994. Decolonization, language planning and education. In Arends et al. (eds), 65–74.

Arends, J. 1989. Syntactic Developments in Sranan. Creolization as a Gradual Process. PhD dissertation, University of Nijmegen.

Arends, J. 1992. Towards a gradualist model of creolization. In Byrne & Holm (eds), 371–80.

Arends, J. 1994a. The African-born slave child and creolization (a postscript to the Bickerton-Singler debate on nativization). *Journal of Pidgin and Creole Languages* 9(1): 115–9. DOI: 10.1075/jpcl.9.1.14jac

Arends, J. 1994b. The socio-historical background of creoles. In Arends et al. (eds), 15–24.

Arends, J. 1995. Demographic factors in the formation of Sranan. In *The Early Stages of Creolization* [Creole Language Library 13], J. Arends (ed.), 333–385. Amsterdam: John Benjamins. DOI: 10.1075/cll.13.11are

Arends, J. 2005. Lingua Franca. In *Encyclopedia of Linguistics*, P. Strazny (ed.), 625–626. New York NY: Taylor & Francis.

Arends, J. 2008. A demographic perspective on creole formation. In Kouwenberg & Singler (eds), 309–331.

Arends, J. & Bruyn, A. 1994. Gradualist and developmental hypotheses. In Arends et al. (eds), 111–120.

Arends, J. & Carlin, E.B. (eds) 2002. *Atlas of the Languages of Suriname*. Leiden: KITLV Press.

Arends, J. & Muysken, P.C. 1992. Demografische modellen in de creolistiek. *Gamma/TTT, Tijdschrift voor Taalkunde* 1(1): 41–55.

Arends, J., Muysken, P.C. & Smith, N. (eds) 1994b. *Pidgins and Creoles. An Introduction* [Creole Language Library 15]. Amsterdam: John Benjamins. DOI: 10.1075/cll.15

Arends, J., Muysken, P.C. & Smith, N. 1994a. Conclusions. In Arends et al. (eds), 319–30.

Arnold, A.J. (ed.). 1997. *A History of Literature in the Caribbean, Vol. III: Cross-cultural Studies* [Comparative History of Literatures in European Languages XII]. Amsterdam: John Benjamins. DOI: 10.1075/chlel.xii

Arnold, A.J., Rodríguez-Luis, J. & Dash, J.M. (eds). 1994. *A History of Literature in the Caribbean, Vol. I: Hispanic and Francophone Regions* [Comparative History of Literatures in European Languages X]. Amsterdam: John Benjamins. DOI: 10.1075/chlel.x

Arnold, A.J., Rodríguez-Luis, J. & Dash, J.M. (eds) 2001. *A History of Literature in the Caribbean, Vol. II: English- and Dutch-speaking Countries* [Comparative History of Literatures in European Languages XV]. Amsterdam: John Benjamins. DOI: 10.1075/chlel.xv

Arnold, F.S. 1898. Our old poets and tinkers. *The Journal of American Folklore* 11(42): 210–220. DOI: 10.2307/533264

Auer, P. (ed.) 1998a. *Code-switching in Conversation. Language, Interaction and Identity*. London: Routledge.

Auer, P. 1998b. Introduction. In Auer (ed.), 1–24.

Auer, P. 1999. From codeswitching via language mixing to fused lects. Toward a dynamic typology of bilingual speech. *International Journal of Bilingualism* 3(4): 309–32. DOI: 10.1177/13670069990030040101

van den Avenne, C. 2005. Bambara et français-tirailleur. Une analyse de la politique linguistique de l'armée coloniale française: La Grande Guerre et après. *Société Internationale pour l'Histoire du Français Langue Étrangère ou Seconde* 35: 123–50.

Avram, A.A. 2010. An outline of Romanian Pidgin Arabic. *Journal of Language Contact – VARIA* 3(1): 20–38. DOI: 10.1163/19552629-90000018

Aye, D.K.K. 2005. Bazaar Malay. History, Grammar and Contact. PhD dissertation, National University of Singapore.

Aye, D.K.K. 2013. Singapore Bazaar Malay structure dataset. In Michaelis et al. (eds), 2013a. http://apics-online.info/contributions/67 (13 February 2015)

Baayen, R.H. 2008. *Analyzing Linguistic Data. A Practical Introduction to Statistics using R*. Cambridge: CUP. DOI: 10.1017/CBO9780511801686

Bailey, B.L. 1966. *Jamaican Creole Syntax. A Transformational Approach*. Cambridge: CUP.

Bailey, C.-J. 1971. Trying to talk in the new paradigm. *Working Papers in Linguistics, University of Hawai'i at Manoa* 4(2): 312–339.

Baissac, C. 1887. *Le folklore de l'Ile Maurice*. Paris: Maisonneuve et Larose.

Baker, P. 1972. *Kriol. A Description of Mauritian Creole*. London: C. Hurst & Co.

Baker, P. 1982. The Contribution of Non-Francophone Immigrants to the Lexicon of Mauritian Creole. PhD dissertation, University of London.

Baker, P. 1990. Off target? *Journal of Pidgin and Creole Languages* 5(1): 107–119. DOI: 10.1075/jpcl.5.1.07bak

Baker, P. 1994. Creativity in creole genesis. In *Creolization and Language Change*, D. Adone & I. Plag (eds), 65–84. Tübingen: Max Niemeyer.

Baker, P. 1995. Motivation in creole genesis. In *From Contact to Creole and Beyond*, P. Baker (ed.), 3–15. London: University of Westminster Press.

Baker, P. 1998. Investigating the origin and diffusion of shared features among the Atlantic English Creoles. In *St. Kitts and the Atlantic Creoles. The Texts of Samuel Augustus Matthews in Perspective*, P. Baker & A. Bruyn (eds), 315–364. London: University of Westminster Press.

Baker, P. 2000. Theories of creolization and the degree and nature of restructuring. In Neumann-Holzschuh & Schneider (eds), 41–63.

Baker, P. 2002. No creolisation without prior pidginisation? *Te Reo* 44: 31–50.

Baker, P. 2003a. CPE1. Corpus of Chinese Pidgin English as attested in English language sources (1721–1842). Ms.

Baker, P. 2003b. CPE2. Corpus of Chinese Pidgin English as attested in English language sources (1843–1990). Ms.

Baker, P. & Corne, C. 1986. Universals, substrata and the Indian Ocean creoles. In Muysken & Smith (eds), 163–184.

Baker, P. & Fon Sing, G. 2007. *The Making of Mauritian Creole. Analyses diachroniques à partir des textes anciens*. London: Battlebridge.

Baker, P. & Hookoomsing, V. Y. 1987. *Diksyoner kreol morisyen*. Paris: L'Harmattan.

Baker, P. & Huber, M. 2001. Atlantic, Pacific, and world-wide features in English-lexicon contact languages. *English World-Wide* 22(2): 157–208. DOI: 10.1075/eww.22.2.02bak

Baker, P. & Kriegel, S. 2013. Mauritian Creole. In Michaelis et al. (eds), 2013d, 250–260.

Baker, P. & Mühlhäusler, P. 1990. From business to Pidgin. *Journal of Asian Pacific Communication* 1: 87–115.

Bakker, D. 2010. Language sampling. In *The Oxford Handbook of Linguistic Typology* J. J. Song (ed.), 100–27. Oxford: OUP.

Bakker, P. 1989. 'The language of the coast tribes is half Basque'. A Basque-American Indian Pidgin in use between Europeans and Native Americans in North America, ca. 1540-ca. 1640. *Anthropological Linguistics* 31(3-4): 117–47.

Bakker, P. 1994. Pidgins. In Arends et al. (eds), 25–40.

Bakker, P. 1995. Notes on the genesis of Caló and other Iberian Para-Romani varieties. In *Romani in Contact. The History, Structure and Sociology of a Language*, Y. Matras (ed.), 125–150. Amsterdam: John Benjamins. DOI: 10.1075/cilt.126.07bak

Bakker, P. 1997a. *A Language of Our Own. The Genesis of Michif, the Mixed Cree-French Language of the Canadian Métis*. Oxford: OUP.

Bakker, P. 1997b. Michif. A mixed language based on Cree and French. In Thomason (ed.), 295–363.

Bakker, P. 2000. Convergence intertwining. An alternative way towards the genesis of mixed languages. In *Languages in Contact*, D. G. Gilbers, J. Nerbonne & J. Schaeken (eds), 29–35. Amsterdam: Rodopi.

Bakker, P. 2002. An early vocabulary of British Romani (1616). A linguistic analysis. *Romani Studies.* 12(2): 75–101. DOI: 10.3828/rs.2002.4

Bakker, P. 2003a. Mixed languages as autonomous systems. In Matras & Bakker (eds), 107–150.

Bakker, P. 2003b. Pidgin inflectional morphology and its implications for creole morphology. In *Yearbook of Morphology 2002*, G. E. Booij & J. van Marle (eds), 3–34. Dordrecht: Kluwer. DOI: 10.1007/0-306-48223-1_2

Bakker, P. 2003c. The absence of reduplication in pidgins. In Kouwenberg (ed.), 37–46.

Bakker, P. 2008. Pidgins versus creoles and pidgincreoles. In Kouwenberg & Singler (eds), 130–157.

Bakker, P. 2009. Phonological complexity in pidgins. In Faraclas & Klein (eds), 7–27.

Bakker, P. 2013a. Michif. In Michaelis et al. (eds), 2013e. 158–165.

Bakker, P. 2013b. Michif structure dataset. In Michaelis et al. (eds), 2013a. http://apics-online.info/contributions/75 (13 February 2015)

Bakker, P., Daval-Markussen, A., Parkvall, M. & Plag, I. 2011. Creoles are typologically distinct from non-creoles. *Journal of Pidgin and Creole Languages* 26(1): 5–42. DOI: 10.1075/jpcl.26.1.02bak

Bakker, P. & Daval-Markussen, A. In press. Creole typology. Are there typical creole features? *Language and Linguistics Compass.*

Bakker, P. & Fleury, N. 2004. *Learn Michif by Listening*. Audio CD with accompanying text. Manitoba Metis Federation: Michif Language Program.

Bakker, P. & Kenrick, D. 2008. Angloromani. In *Language in the British Isles*, D. Britain (ed.), 368–374. Cambridge: CUP.

Bakker, P. & Mous, M. (eds). 1994. *Mixed Languages. 15 Case Studies in Language Intertwining.* Amsterdam: IFOTT.

Bakker, P. & Muysken, P.C. 1994. Mixed languages and language intertwining. In Arends, et al. (eds), 41–52.

Baku, K. 2011. African agency, forts and castles and the African slave trade in the Gold Coast. Paper delivered at the *Society for Pidgin and Creole Linguistics*, Accra, Ghana, 2–6 August 2011.

Bamgbose, A. 1991. *Language and the Nation. The Language Question in Sub-saharan Africa.* Edinburgh: EUP.

Baptista, M. 2002. *The Syntax of Cape Verdean Creole. The Sotavento Varieties* [Linguistik Aktuell/Linguistics Today 54]. Amsterdam: John Benjamins. DOI: 10.1075/la.54

Baptista, M. 2010. Cape Verdean in education. A linguistic and human right. In Migge et al. (eds), 273–296.

Baptista, M. 2013. Cape Verdean Creole of Brava. In Michaelis et al. (eds), 2013d, 12–19.

Baptista, M. & Guéron, J. (eds). 2007. *Noun Phrases in Creole Languages. A Multi-faceted Approach* [Creole Language Library 31]. Amsterdam: John Benjamins. DOI: 10.1075/cll.31

Bartens, A. 2013a. Creole languages. In Bakker & Matras (eds), 65–158.

Bartens, A. 2013b. Nicaraguan Creole English. In Michaelis et al. (eds), 2013c, 115–126.

Bascom, W.R. 1992. *African Folktales in the New World.* Bloomington IN: Indiana University Press.

Batie, R.C. 1991. Why sugar? Economic cycles and the changing of staples on the English and French Antilles 1624–54. In *Caribbean Slave Society and Economy. A Student Reader*, H. Beckles & V. Shepherd (eds), 37–55. New York NY: New Press.

Bauer, L. 2003. *Introducing Linguistic Morphology*, 2nd edn. Edinburgh: EUP.

Baxter, A.N. & de Silva, P. 2004. *A Dictionary of Kristang-English (with an English-Kristang Concordance).* Canberra: Pacific Linguistics.

Baxter, A.N. 1988. *A Grammar of Kristang (Malacca Creole Portuguese).* Canberra: Pacific Linguistics.

Baxter, A.N. 2005. Kristang (Malacca Creole Portuguese) – a long-time survivor seriously endangered. *Estudios de Sociolingüística* 6(1): 1–37.

Baxter, A.N. 2013a. Papía Kristang. In Michaelis et al. (eds), 2013d, 122–130.

Baxter, A.N. 2013b. Papiá Kristang structure dataset. In Michaelis et al. (eds), 2013a. http://apics-online.info/contributions/42 (13 February 2015)

Beckwith, M.W. 1924. *Jamaica Anansi Stories.* New York NY: G.E. Stechert.

Benítez-Torres, C.M. 2009. Inflections vs. derivational morphology in Tagdal. A mixed language. In *Selected proceedings of the 38th Annual Conference of African Linguistics.*, M. Masangu, F. McLaughin & E. Potsdam (eds), 69–83. Somerset MA: Cascadilla Proceedings Project.

Bergman, G. 1984. *Kortfattad svensk språkhistoria.* Stockholm: Prisma.

Berndt, C. & Berndt, R. 1948. Pastoral stations in the Northern Territory and native welfare. *Aborigines Protector* 2(4): 13–16.

Berndt, R.M. & Berndt, C.H. 1987. *End of an Era. Aboriginal Labour in the Northern Territory.* Canberra: Australian Institute of Aboriginal Studies.

Berry-Haseth, L., Broek, A. & Joubert, S.M. 1988. *Pa saka kara. Antologia di literatura papiamentu.* Curaçao: Fundashon Pierre Lauffer.

Bhattacharjya, D. 2001. The Genesis and Development of Nagamese. Its Social History and Linguistic Structure. PhD dissertation, the City University of New York.

Bhattacharjya, D. 2007. Nagamese (Restructured Assamese). In Holm & Patrick (eds), 237–54.

Biagui, N.B. & Quint, N. 2013. Casamancese Creole. In Michaelis et al. (eds), 2013d, 40–49.

Biber, D. & Conrad, S. 2009. *Register, Genre, and Style*. Cambridge: CUP. DOI: 10.1017/CBO9780511814358

Bichsel-Stettler, A. 1989. Aspects of the Sri Lanka Malay Community and its Language. MA thesis, Universität Bern.

Bickel, B. & Nichols, J. 2007. Inflectional morphology. In *Language Typology and Syntactic Description, Vol. III: Grammatical Categories and the Lexicon*, 2nd edn, T. Shopen (ed.), 169–240. Cambridge: CUP.

Bickerton, D. 1973. On the nature of the creole continuum. *Language* 49(3): 640–69. DOI: 10.2307/412355

Bickerton, D. 1974. Creolization, linguistic universals, natural semantax and the brain. *University of Hawaii Working Papers in Linguistics* 6: 125–41.

Bickerton, D. 1975. *Dynamics of a Creole System*. Cambridge: CUP.

Bickerton, D. 1977. *Change and Variation in Hawaiian English, Vol. II: Creole Syntax*. Final Report on national Science Foundation Grant No. GS-39748. Honolulu: Social Sciences and Linguistics Institute, University of Hawaii.

Bickerton, D. 1980a. Creolization, linguistic universals, natural semantax and the brain. In *Issues in English Creoles*, R. Day (ed.), 1–18. Heidelberg: Groos. DOI: 10.1075/veaw.g2.03bic

Bickerton, D. 1980b. Decreolisation and the creole continuum. In *Theoretical Orientations in Creole Studies*, A. Valdman & A. R. Highfield (eds), 109–127. New York NY: Academic Press.

Bickerton, D. 1981. *Roots of Language*. Ann Arbor MI: Karoma.

Bickerton, D. 1984. The language bioprogram hypothesis. *Behavioral and Brain Sciences* 7: 212–218. DOI: 10.1017/S0140525X00044393

Bickerton, D. 1988. Creole languages and the bioprogram. In *Linguistics. The Cambridge Survey*, Vol. 2, F. Newmeyer (ed.), 267–84. Cambridge: CUP. DOI: 10.1017/CBO9780511621055.015

Bickerton, D. & Wilson, W. H. 1987. Pidgin Hawaiian. In *Pidgin and Creole Languages. Essays in Memory of John E. Reinecke*, G. G. Gilbert (ed.), 61–76. Honolulu HI: University of Hawaii Press.

Bilby, K. M. 1983. How the "older heads" talk. A Jamaican Maroon spirit possession language and its relationship to the creoles of Suriname and Sierra Leone. *New West Indian Guide* 57(1-2): 37–88. DOI: 10.1163/13822373-90002097

Bisang, W. 2009. Serial verb constructions. *Language and Linguistics Compass* 3(3): 792–814. DOI: 10.1111/j.1749-818X.2009.00128.x

Bizri, F. 2009. Sinhala in contact with Arabic. The birth of a new pidgin in the Middle East. In *Annual Review of South Asian Languages and Linguistics 2009*, R. Singh (ed.), 135–49. Berlin: De Gruyter.

Bizri, F. 2010. *Pidgin Madame. Un grammaire de la servitude*. Paris: Geuther.

Blanco Barros, J. A. 1971–72. Noticia Historial de la provincia de Cartagena de las Indias, año 1772. Por Diego de Peredo. *Anuario* 6-7: 119–154.

Bloomfield, L. 1933. *Language*. New York NY: Holt, Reinehart & Winston.

Bobyleva, E. 2013. *The Development of the Nominal Domain in Creole Languages. A Comparative-Typological Approach*. Utrecht: LOT.

Bolton, K. 2003. *Chinese Englishes. A Sociolinguistic History*. Cambridge: CUP.

Bonnefoey, A. 1916. Journal of Antoine Bonnefoy, 1741–1742. Transl. Dr. J. Franklin Jameson. In *Travels in the American Colonies*, N. D. Mereness (ed.), 137–255. New York NY: Macmillan.

Borde, A. 1870[1547]. *The Fyrst Boke of the Introduction of Knowledge Made by Andrew Borde of Physycke Doctor*, ed. by F. J. Furnivall. London: N. Trübner & Co.

Boretzky, N. & Igla, B. 1994. Romani mixed dialects. In Bakker & Mous (eds), 35–68.

Borges, R. D. 2013. *The Life of Language. Dynamics of Language Contact in Suriname*. Utrecht: LOT.

Borrow, G. H. 1841. *The Zincali. An Account of the Gypsies of Spain*. London: John Murray.

Boruah, B. K. 1993. *Nagamese. The Language of Nagaland*. New Delhi: Mittal.

Bourhis, R. Y. & Giles, H. 1977. The language of intergroup distinctiveness. In *Language, Ethnicity and Intergroup Relations*, H. Giles (ed.), 119–135. London: Academic Press.

Bradley, D. 1996. Burmese as a lingua franca. In Wurm et al. (eds), 745–747.

Bradley, D. 2008. Mainland Southeast Asia / Südostasiatisches Festland. In *Sociolinguistics / Soziolinguistik. An International Handbook of the Science of Language and Society / Ein internationales Handbuch zur Wissenschaft von Sprache un Gesellschaft*, 2nd edn, U. Ammon, N. Dittmar, K. J. Mattheier & P. Trudgill (eds), 2007–2013. Berlin: De Gruyter.

Bradshaw, J. 2007. Tok Pisin ia-bracketing. Neither substrate nor syntax. In *Language Description, History and Development. Linguistic Indulgence in Memory of Terry Crowley* [Creole Language Library 30], J. Siegel, J. Lynch & D. Eades (eds), 159–167. Amsterdam: John Benjamins. DOI: 10.1075/cll.30.18bra

Braun, M. 2009. *Word-formation and Creolisation. The Case of Early Sranan*. Tübingen: Niemeyer. DOI: 10.1515/9783484970229

Brenzinger, M. 1987. Die sprachliche und kulturelle Stellung der Mbugu (Ma'a). MA thesis, Universität zu Köln.

Britannica. 2011a. Jamaica. In *Encyclopædia Britannica Ultimate Reference Suite*. Chicago IL: Encyclopædia Britannica. *sv*.

Britannica. 2011b. Philippines. In *Encyclopædia Britannica Ultimate Reference Suite*. Chicago IL: Encyclopædia Britannica. *sv*.

Britannica. 2011c. Suriname. In *Encyclopædia Britannica Ultimate Reference Suite*. Chicago IL: Encyclopædia Britannica. *sv*.

Britannica. 2011d. Vietnam. In *Encyclopædia Britannica Ultimate Reference Suite*. Chicago IL: Encyclopædia Britannica. *sv*.

Broch, I. & Jahr, E. H. 1984a. *Russenorsk. Et pidginspråk i Norge*, 2nd, rev. edn. Oslo: Novus.

Broch, I. & Jahr, E. H. 1984b. Russenorsk. A new look at the Russo-Norwegian pidgin in northern Norway. In *Scandinavian Language Contacts*, P. S. Ureland & I. Clarkson (eds), 21–65. Cambridge: CUP.

Broch, O. 1930. Russenorsk tekstmateriale. *Maal og Minne* 4: 113–140.

Brown, L. 2007. 'A most irregular traffic'. The Oceanic passages of the Melanesian labour trade. In *Many Middle Passages. Forced Migration and the Making of the Modern World*, E. Christopher, C. Pybus & M. Rediker (eds), 184–203. Berkeley CA: University of California Press.

Brown, P. & Levinson, S. C. 1987[1978]. *Politeness. Some Universals in Language Usage*, Cambridge: CUP.

Brown-Blake, C. & Devonish, H. 2012. Planning for language rights in the Caribbean. The birth of the Charter on Language Policy and Language Rights in the Creole-speaking Caribbean. In *Language Rights and Language Policy in the Caribbean*, C. Brown-Blake & D. E. Walicek (eds), 3–21.

Brüser, M., dos Reis Santos, André, Dengler, E. & Blum, A. 2002. *Dicionário do crioulo da ilha de Santiago (Cabo Verde), sob a direcção de Jürgen Lang*. Tübingen: Günter Narr.

Bruyn, A. 1995. *Grammaticalization in Creoles. The Development of Determiners and Relative Clauses in Sranan*. Amsterdam: IFOTT.

Bruyn, A. 2007. Bare nouns and articles in Sranan. In Baptista & Guéron (eds), 339–381.

Bryant, G.A. & Barrett, C. 2007. Recognizing intentions in infant-directed speech. Evidence for universals. *Psychological Science* 18(8): 746–751. DOI: 10.1111/j.1467-9280.2007.01970.x

Bryant, G.A., Liénard, P. & Barrett, C. 2012. Recognizing infant-directed speech across distant cultures. Evidence from Africa. *Journal of Evolutionaly Psychology* 10(2): 47–59. DOI: 10.1556/JEP.10.2012.2.1

Buchner, M. 1887. *Kamerun. Skizzen und Beratungen*. Leipzig: Duncker & Humblot.

Burdon, J.A. 1935. *Archives of British Honduras*. London: Sifton Praed & Co.

Buzek, I. 2011. *Historia crítica de la lexicografía gitano-española*. Brno: Muni Press.

Buzelin, H. & Winer, L.S. 2008. Literary representations of creole languages. Cross-linguistic perspectives from the Caribbean. In Kouwenberg & Singler (eds), 637–665.

Byrne, F. & Holm, J.A. (eds). 1992. *Atlantic meets Pacific. A Global View of Pidgnization and Creolization* [Creole Language Library 11]. Amsterdam: John Benjamins. DOI: 10.1075/cll.11

Campanius, J. 1696. *Lutheri Catechismus Öfwersatt på American-Virginske Språket*. Stockholm: Burchardi.

Carden, G. & Stewart, W.A. 1988. Binding theory, bioprogram, and creolization. Evidence from Haitian Creole. *Journal of Pidgin and Creole Languages* 3(1): 1–67. DOI: 10.1075/jpcl.3.1.02car

Cardoso, H.C. 2009a. Jacques Arends' model of gradual creolization. In Selbach et al. (eds), 13–23.

Cardoso, H.C. 2009b. *The Indo-Portuguese language of Diu*. Utrecht: LOT.

Cardoso, H.C. 2010. African slave population of Portuguese India. Demographics and impact on Indo-Portuguese. *Journal of Pidgin and Creole Languages* 25(1): 95–119. DOI: 10.1075/jpcl.25.1.04car

Cardoso, H.C. 2012. Oral traditions of the Luso-Asian communities. Local, regional and continental. In *Portuguese and Luso-Asian legacies, 1511–2011, Vol. 2: Culture and Identity in the Luso-Asian world: Tenacities and Plasticities*, L. Jarnagin (ed.), 143–166. Singapore: Institute of Southeast Asian Studies.

Cardoso, H.C. 2013. Diu Indo-Portuguese. In Michaelis et al. (eds), 2013d, 90–101.

Carlin, E.B. & Boven, K. 2002. The native population. Migrations and identities. In *Atlas of the Languages of Suriname*, J. Arends & E.B. Carlin (eds), 11–46. Leiden: KITLV Press.

Carnie, A. 2002. *Syntax. A Generative Introduction*, 2nd edn. Malden MA: Blackwell.

Carr, E.B. 1972. *Da Kine Talk. From Pidgin to Standard English in Hawaii*. Honolulu HI: University Press of Hawaii.

Cash, A. 1977. The language of the Maguires. *Journal of the Gypsy Lore Society* 1(3): 177–180.

Cassidy, F.G. & Le Page, R.B. 1980. *Dictionary of Jamaican English*, 2nd edn. Cambridge: CUP.

Cassidy, F.G. 1980. The place of Gullah. *American Speech* 55(1): 3–16. DOI: 10.2307/455386

Chambers, J.K. & Trudgill, P. 1998. *Dialectology*, 2nd edn. Cambridge: CUP. DOI: 10.1017/CBO9780511805103

Chandralal, D. 2010. *Sinhala* [London Oriental and African Language Library 15]. Amsterdam: John Benjamins. DOI: 10.1075/loall.15

Charry, E., Koefoed, G. & Muysken, P.C. (eds) 1983. *De Talen van Suriname*. Muiderberg: Dick Coutinho.

Chaudenson, R. 1977. Toward the reconstruction of the social matrix of creole language. In Valdman (ed.), 259–276.

Chaudenson, R. 1992. *Des îles, des hommes, des langues*. Paris: L'Harmattan.

Chaudenson, R. 2001. *Creolization of Language and Culture*. London: Routledge.

Christiansen-Bolli, R. 2010. A Grammar of Tadaksahak. A Northern Songhay Language of Mali. PhD dissertation, Universiteit Leiden.

Christofoletti Silveira, A., dos Santos Agostinho, A. L., Bandeira, M., Freitas, S. & Antunes de Araujo, G. 2013. Fa d'ambô. Língua crioula de Ano Bom. *Cadernos de Estudos Lingüísticos* 55(2): 25–44.

Cifoletti, G. 2004. *La lingua franca barbaresca*. Rome: Il Calamo.

Clark, R. 1977. *In Search of Beach-la-Mar. Historical Relations among Pacific Pidgins and Creoles*. Auckland: Department of Anthropology University of Auckland.

Clark, R. 1990. Pidgin English and Pidgin Maori in New Zealand. In *New Zealand Ways of Speaking English*, A. Bell & J. Holmes (eds), 97–114. Wellington: Victoria University Press.

Clavería, C. 1962. Notas sobre el gitano español. In *Strenae estudios de filología e historia dedicados al profesor Manuel García Blanco*, C. J. Cela (ed.), 109–119. Salamanca: Universidad de Salamanca.

Clements, C. 2013. Korlai. In Michaelis et al. (eds), 2013d, 102–110.

Coelho, A. 1881. *Os dialectos romanicos ou neo-latinos na Africa, Asia e America*. Lisbon: Casa da Sociedade de Geographia.

Coelho, A. 1892. *Os ciganos de Portugal. Com um estudio sobre o calão*. Lisbon: Imprensa Nacional.

Cole, P. 1982. *Imbabura Quechua*. Amsterdam: North-Holland.

Colot, S. & Ludwig, R. 2013a. Guadeloupean Creole and Martinican Creole. In Michaelis et al. (eds), 2013d, 205–219.

Colot, S. & Ludwig, R. 2013b. Guadeloupean Creole structure dataset. In Michaelis et al. (eds), 2013a. http://apics-online.info/contributions/50 (13 February 2015)

Colot, S. & Ludwig, R. 2013c. Martinican Creole structure dataset. In Michaelis et al. (eds), 2013a. http://apics-online.info/contributions/51 (13 February 2015)

Comrie, B. 1976. *Aspect*. Cambridge: CUP.

Comrie, B. 1985. *Tense*. Cambridge: CUP. DOI: 10.1017/CBO9781139165815

Comrie, B. 1989. *Language Universals and Linguistic Typology. Syntax and Morphology*, 2nd edn. Oxford: Blackwell.

Comrie, B. & Kuteva, T. 2013. Relativization on subjects. In Dryer & Haspelmath (eds), Ch. 122. http://wals.info/chapter/122 (13 February 2015)

Corbett, G. G. 2000. *Number*. Cambridge: CUP. DOI: 10.1017/CBO9781139164344

Correa de Faria, F. R. 1858. Compendio da Língua Indígena Brasilica. *Annaes da Bibliotheca e Archivo Público do Pará* 2: 293–332.

Cousturier, L. 1920. *Des inconnus chez moi*. Paris: Éditions de la Sirène.

Couto de Magalhães, J. V. 1876. *O Selvagem*. Rio de Janeiro: Typographia da Reforma.

Couto, H. H. 1994. *O crioulo português da Guiné-Bissau*. Hamburg: Buske.

Craig, D. 2008. Pidgins/creoles and education. In Kouwenberg & Singler (eds), 593–614.

Crawford, J. M. 1978. *The Mobilian Trade Language*. Knoxville TN: The University of Tennessee Press.

Crevaux, J. 1883. *Voyages dans l'Amérique du Sud*. Paris: Librairie Hachette.

Croft, W. 2000. *Explaining Language Change. An Evolutionary Approach*. Harlow: Longman.

Croft, W. 2003. Mixed languages and acts of identity. An evolutionary approach. In Matras & Bakker (eds), 41–72.

Crowley, T. 2008. Pidgin and creole morphology. In Kouwenberg & Singler (eds), 74–97.

Cummins, J. 2001. *Negotiating Identities. Education for Empowerment in a Diverse Society*, 2nd edn. Los Angeles CA: California Association for Bilingual Education.

Cummins, J. 2009. Fundamental psycholinguistic and sociological principles underlying educational success for linguistic minority students. In *Social Justice through Multilingual Education*, T. Skutnabb-Kangas, R. Phillipson, A. K. Mohanty & M. Panda (eds), 19–35. Bristol: Multilingual Matters.

Curnow, T. J. 2001. What language features can be 'borrowed'? In *Areal Diffusion and Genetic Inheritance. Problems in Comparative Linguistics*, A. Y. Aikhenvald & R. M. Dixon (eds), 412–36. Oxford: OUP.

da Cruz, A. 2011. *Fonologia e gramática do Nheengatú. A língua geral falada pelos povos Baré, Warekena e Baniwa*. Utrecht: LOT.

Da Jesus Book. 2000. Orlando FL: Wycliffe Bible Translators.

Dahl, Ö. 1985. *Tense and Aspect Systems*. Oxford: Blackwell.

Dahl, Ö. 2004. *The Growth and Maintenance of Linguistic Complexity* [Studies in Language Companion Series 71]. Amsterdam: John Benjamins. DOI: 10.1075/slcs.71

Dakhlia, J. 2008. *Lingua franca. Histoire d'une langua métisse en Méditerranée*. Arles: Actes Sud.

Dance, D. C. 1986. *Fifty Caribbean Writers. A Bio-bibliographical Critical Sourcebook*. New York NY: Greenwood Press.

d'Ans, A.-M. 1987. *Haïti. Paysage et société*. Paris: Éditions Karthala.

de Anchieta, J. 1595. *Arte de Grammatica da Lingua mais Usada na costa do Brasil*. Coimbra: Antonio Mariz.

de Friedemann, N. S. & Patiño Rosselli, C. 1983. *Lengua y sociedad en el Palenque de San Brasilio*. Bogotá: Instituto Caro y Cuervo.

de Goeje, C. H. 1908. *Verslag der Toemoekhoemak-expeditie (Tumuc-Humac-expeditie)*. Leiden: E. J. Brill.

de Gruiter, M. 1994. Javindo, a contact language in pre-war Semarang. In Bakker & Mous (eds), 151–159.

de Gruiter, V. E. 1990. *Het Javindo. De Verboden Taal*. Den Haag: Moesson.

de Josselin de Jong, J. P. 1926. Het huidige Negerhollandsch. Texten en woordenlijst. *Verhandelingen der Koniklijke Academie van Wetenschappen te Amsterdam, Nieuwe Reeks* 26(1).

de Laet, J. 1633. *Novvs Orbis. Seu descriptionis indiae occidentalis libri XVIII*. Leiden: Elzeviers.

de Mishaegen, A. 1946. *Dans la forêt canadienne*. Brussels: La Renaissance du Livre.

de Rooij, V. A. 1994a. Shaba Swahili. In Arends, et al. (eds), 179–190.

de Rooij, V. A. 1994b. Variation. In Arends et al(eds), 53–64.

de Smit, M. 2010. Modelling mixed languages. Some remarks on the case of Old Helsinki Slang. *Journal of Language Contact – VARIA* 3: 1–19. DOI: 10.1163/19552629-90000017

DeCamp, D. 1971. Toward a generative analysis of a post-creole speech continuum. In Hymes (ed.), 349–370.

DeCamp, D. 1977. The deveopment of pidgin and creole studies. In Valdman (ed.), 3–20.

Decker, K. 2006. *The Song of Kriol. A Grammar of the Kriol Language of Belize*. Dallas TX: SIL International.

Decker, T. 1988. *Juliohs Siza*. Umeå: Department of English, Umeå University.

Decker, T. 2010. *Boss Coker befo St. Peter*. Heinge: Heingeborgen Press.

Defoe, D. & Roberts, G. 1726. *The Four Years Voyages of Capt. George Roberts*. London: A. Bettesworth.

DeGraff, M. 2001. Morphology in creole genesis. Linguistics and ideology. In *Ken Hale. A Life in Language*, M. Kenstowicz (ed.), 53–121. Cambridge MA: The MIT Press.

DeGraff, M. 2003. Against creole exceptionalism. *Language* 79(2): 391–410. DOI: 10.1353/lan.2003.0114

DeGraff, M. 2007. Kreyòl Ayisyen or Haitian Creole (Creole French). In Holm & Patrick (eds), 101–126.

DeGraff, M. 2009. Language acquisition in creolization and, thus, language change. Some Cartesian-Uniformitarian boundary conditions. *Language and Linguistics Compass* 3(4): 888–971. DOI: 10.1111/j.1749-818X.2009.00135.x

Dejean, Y. 1993. An overview of the language situation in Haiti. *International Journal of the Sociology of Language* 102: 73–83.

Dejean, Y. 2012. Identifying the standards for Haitian Creole. In *Sargasso: Language Rights and Language Policy in the Caribbean*, C. Brown-Blake & D. E. Walicek (eds), 83–95.

Delafosse, M. 1904. *Vocabulaires comparatifs de plus de 60 langues ou dialectes parlés à la Côte d'Ivoire et dans les régions limitrophes. Avec des notes linguistiques et ethnologiques, une bibliographie et une carte*. Paris: Leroux.

Delaney, J. 2010. Strait through. Magellan to Cook & the Pacific, Princeton University Library. http://libweb5.princeton.edu/visual_materials/maps/websites/pacific/contents.html (13 February 2015)

Dench, A. 1998. Pidgin Ngarluma. An indigenous contact language in North Western Australia. *Journal of Pidgin and Creole Languages* 13(1): 1–62. DOI: 10.1075/jpcl.13.1.02den

Denny, E. 1860. Military journal of Major Ebenezer Denny. In *Memoirs of the Historical Society of Pennsylvania*, Vol. 7, 237–485. Philadelphia PA: J. B. Lippincott & Co.

Denwood, P. 1999. *Tibetan* [London Oriental and African Language Library 3]. Amsterdam: John Benjamins. DOI: 10.1075/loall.3

Denzin, N. K. 2009. *The Research Act. A Theoretical Introduction to Sociological Methods*. New Brunswick NJ: AldineTransaction.

Devonish, H. 2008. Language planning in pidgins and creoles. In Kouwenberg & Singler (eds), 615–636.

Devonish, H. & Harry, O. G. 2004. Jamaican Creole and Jamaican English. Phonology. In Schneider et al. (eds), 450–80.

Devonish, H. & Thompson, D. 2013a. Creolese. In Michaelis et al. (eds), 2013c, 49–60.

Devonish, H. & Thompson, D. 2013b. Creolese structure dataset. In Michaelis et al. (eds), 2013a. http://apics-online.info/contributions/5 (13 February 2015)

do Couto, H. H. 2002. *A língua franca mediterrânea. Histórico, textos e interpretação*. Brasília: Editora Plano: Oficina Editorial Instituto de Letras UnB.

Donicie, A. 1954. *De Creolentaal van Suriname: Spraakkunst*, 2nd edn. Paramaribo: Radhakishun.

Downing, C. T. 1838. *The Fan-qui in China in 1836–7*, Vol.1. London: Henry Colburn.

Doyle, A. 2001. *Irish*. Munich: Lincom.

Drechsel, E. J. 1996. An integrated vocabulary of Mobilian Jargon, a Native American pidgin of the Mississippi Valley. *Anthropological Linguistics* 38(2): 248–54.

Drechsel, E. J. 1997. *Mobilian Jargon. Linguistic and Sociohistorical Aspects of a Native American Pidgin*. Oxford: Clarendon.

Drechsel, E. J. 1999. Language contact in the early colonial Pacific. Evidence for a maritime Polynesian jargon or pidgin. In Rickford & Romaine (eds), 71–96.

Dryer, M. S. & Haspelmath, M. (eds). 2013.*The World Atlas of Language Structures Online*. Leipzig: Max Planck Institute for Evolutionary Anthropology. <http://wals.info/

Dryer, M. S. 1989. Large linguistic areas and language sampling. *Studies in Language* 13(2): 257–292. DOI: 10.1075/sl.13.2.03dry

Dryer, M. S. 2013a. Coding of nominal plurality. In Dryer & Haspelmath (eds), Ch. 33. http://wals.info/chapter/33 (13 February 2015)

Dryer, M. S. 2013b. Definite articles. In Dryer & Haspelmath (eds), Ch. 37. http://wals.info/chapter/37 (13 February 2015)

Dryer, M. S. 2013c. Genealogical language list. In Dryer & Haspelmath (eds), supplement 4. http://wals.info/supplement/4 (13 February 2015)

Dryer, M.S. 2013d. Indefinite articles. In Dryer & Haspelmath (eds), Ch. 38. http://wals.info/chapter/38 (13 February 2015)

Dryer, M.S. 2013e. Negative morphemes. In Dryer & Haspelmath (eds), Ch. 112. http://wals.info/chapter/112 (13 February 2015)

Dryer, M.S. 2013f. Order of subject, object, and verb. In Dryer & Haspelmath (eds), feature 81A. http://wals.info/feature/81A (13 February 2015)

Dryer, M.S. 2013g. Polar questions. In Dryer & Haspelmath (eds), Ch. 116. http://wals.info/chapter/116 (13 February 2015)

Du Ru, P. 1700. Journal D'un Voyage fait avec Mr. d'Iberville de la Rade de Bilocchis dans le haut de Mississipi avec un detail de tout ce qui s est fait depuis ce temps jusquau depart du vaisseau. Ms, Edward E. Ayer Collection, Newberry Library, Chicago IL.

Dutton, T.E. 1983. Birds of a feather. A pair of rare pidgins from the Gulf of Papua. In *The Social Context of Creolization*, E. Woolford & W. Washabaugh (eds), 77–105. Ann Arbor MI: Karoma.

Dutton, T.E. 1985. *A New Course in Tok Pisin (New Guinea Pidgin)*. Canberra: Australian National University.

Dutton, T.E. 1997. Hiri Motu. In Thomason (ed.), 9–41.

Eades, D. 1999. News from Da Pidgin Coup in Hawai'i. *Pidgins and Creoles in Education* 10: 5–7.

Eckkrammer, E.M. 1999. The standardization of Papiamentu. New trends, problems and perspectives. *Bulletin VALS-ASLA* 69(1): 59–74.

Ehrhart, S. & Revis, M. 2013. Tayo. In Michaelis et al. (eds), 2013d, 271–282.

Eltis, D., Behrendt, S.D., Richardson, D. & Klein, H.S. 1999. *The Transatlantic Slave Trade, 1562–1867. A Database on CD-ROM*. Cambridge: CUP.

Embéo e Majaró Lucas (The Gospel according to Luke), transl. George Barrow 1837: British and Foreign Bible Society.

Ennes, E. 1948. The Palmares "republic" of Pernambuco. Its final destruction, 1694. *The Americas* 5(2): 200–216. DOI: 10.2307/977806

Escure, G. 1982a. Belizean Creole. In *Central American English*, J.A. Holm (ed.), 29–70. Heidelberg: Julius Groos.

Escure, G. 1982b. Contrastive patterns of intergroup interaction in the creole continuum of Belize. *Language in Society* 11(2): 239–64. DOI: 10.1017/S0047404500009210

Escure, G. 1997. *Creole and Dialect Continua. Standard Acquisition Processes in Belize and China (PRC)* [Creole Language Library 18]. Amsterdam: John Benjamins. DOI: 10.1075/cll.18

Escure, G. 2004. Garifuna in Belize and Honduras. In Escure & Schwegler (eds), 35–65.

Escure, G. & Schwegler, A. (eds). 2004. *Creoles, Contact, and Language Change. Linguistics and Social Implications* [Creole Language Library 27]. Amsterdam: John Benjamins. DOI: 10.1075/cll.27

Escure, G. 2011. African substratal influence on the counterfactual in Belizean Creole. In Lefebvre (ed.), 181–200.

Escure, G. 2013a. Belizean Creole. In Michaelis et al. (eds), 2013c, 92–100.

Escure, G. 2013b. Belizean Creole structure dataset. In Michaelis et al. (eds), 2013a. http://apics-online.info/contributions/9 (13 February 2015)

Ethnolingüistica 2014. Nheengatú. http://www.etnolinguistica.org/lingua:nheengatu (13 February 2015).

Faine, J. 1939. *Le créole dans l'univers. Étude comparative des parlers français-créoles*. Port-au-Prince: Imprimerie de l'Etat.

Faraclas, N. 1996. *Nigerian Pidgin*. London: Routledge. DOI: 10.4324/9780203192801

Faraclas, N. 2007. Tok Pisin (Pidgin/Creole English). In Holm & Patrick (eds), 355–372.

Faraclas, N. 2013a. Nigerian Pidgin. In Michaelis et al. (eds), 2013c, 176–184.

Faraclas, N. 2013b. Nigerian Pidgin structure dataset. In Michaelis et al. (eds), 2013a. http://apics-online.info/contributions/17 (13 February 2015)

Faraclas, N. & Klein, T.B. (eds). 2009. *Simplicity and Complexity in Creoles and Pidgins*. London: Battlebridge.

Faraclas, N., Walicek, D.E., Alleyne, M., Geigel, W. & Ortiz, L. 2007. The complexity that really matters. The role of political economy in creole genesis. In Ansaldo et al. (eds), 227–264.

Farquharson, J.T. 2013a. Jamaican. In Michaelis et al. (eds), 2013c, 81–91.

Farquharson, J.T. 2013b. Jamaican structure dataset. In Michaelis et al. (eds), 2013a. http://apics-online.info/contributions/8 (13 February 2015)

Fattier, D. 2013. Haitian Creole. In Michaelis et al. (eds), 2013d, 195–204.

Ferguson, C.A. 1959. Diglossia. *Word* 151: 325–340.

Ferguson, C.A. 1971. Absence of copula and the notion of simplicity. A study of normal speech, baby talk, foreigner talk, and pidgins. In Hymes (ed.), 141–50.

Ferguson, C.A. 1972. *Language Structure and Language Use. Essays*. Stanford CA: Stanford University Press.

Ferguson, C.A. 1975. Toward a characterization of English Foreigner Talk. *Anthropological Linguistics*. 17(1): 1–4.

Ferguson, G. 2006. *Language Planning and Education*. Edinburgh: EUP.

Ferguson, J.A. 2011. Haiti. In *Encyclopædia Britannica Ultimate Reference Suite*. Chicago IL: Encyclopædia Britannica. *sv*.

Fernández, M.A. 2012. Leyenda e historia del chabacano de Ermita (Manila). *UniverSOS* 9: 9–46.

Fernández-Armesto, F. 1987. *Before Columbus. Exploration and Colonisation from the Mediterranean to the Atlantic*, 1229–1492. Philadelphia PA: University of Pennsylvania Press.

Field, A., Miles, J. & Field, Z. 2012. *Discovering statistics using R*. London: Sage.

Field, J. 2004. *Psycholinguistics. The Key Concepts*. London: Routledge.

Figueira, L. 1621. *Arte da Língua Brasilica*. Lisbon: Manoel da Silva.

Finney, M.A. 2013a. Krio. In Michaelis et al. (eds), 2013c, 157–166.

Finney, M.A. 2013b. Krio structure dataset. In Michaelis et al. (eds), 2013a. http://apics-online.info/contributions/15 (13 February 2015)

Foley, W.A. 2013a. Yimas-Arafundi Pidgin. In Michaelis et al. (eds), 2013e, 105–13.

Foley, W.A. 2013b. Yimas-Arafundi Pidgin structure dataset. In Michaelis et al. (eds), 2013a. http://apics-online.info/contributions/69 (13 February 2015)

Fraser, A. 1995. *The Gypsies*. Oxford: Blackwell.

Frazier, F.N. 2001. *The True Story of Kaluaikoolau. As Told by his Wife, Piilani*. Lihue, Honolulu HI: Kauai Historical Society; Distributed by University of Hawaiʻi Press.

Fyle, C.N. & Jones, E.D. 1980. *A Krio-English Dictionary*. Oxford: OUP.

Fyle, C.N. 2010. *Lɛ wi rayt Krio*. Heinge: Heingeborgen Press.

Garrett, P. 2010. *Attitudes to Language*. Cambridge: CUP. DOI: 10.1017/CBO9780511844713

Gass, S.M. 2003. Input and interaction. In *The Handbook of Second Language Acquisition*, C.J. Doughty & M.H. Long (eds), 224–255. Oxford: Blackwell. DOI: 10.1002/9780470756492.ch9

Gass, S.M. 2013. *Second Language Acquisition. An Introductory Course*, 4th edn. New York NY: Routledge.

Gass, S.M. & Selinker, L. 2008. *Second Language Acquisition. An Introductory Course*, 3rd edn. New York NY: Routledge.

Gautier, A. 1985. *Les soers de solitude. La condition féminine dans l'esclavage aux Antilles du XVIIe au XIXe siècle*. Paris: Editions Caribéennes.

Geggus, D. 1997. The naming of Haiti. *NWIG: New West Indian Guide / Nieuwe West-Indische Gids* 71(1-2): 43–68. DOI: 10.1163/13822373-90002615

Gessi, R. 1892. *Seven Years in the Soudan. Being a Record of Explorations, Adventures, and Campaigns against the Arab Slave Hunters*. London: Sampson Low & Marston Company.

Gibson, K. 1992. Tense and aspect in Guyanese Creole with reference to Jamaican and Carriacouan. *International Journal of American Linguistics* 58(1): 49–95.

Gil, D. 2001. Creoles, complexity and Riau Indonesian. *Lingustic Typology* 5: 325–371.

Giles, H. & Powesland, P. F. 1975. *Speech Style and Social Evaluation*. London: Academic Press.

Givón, T. 2001a. *Syntax. An Introduction*, Vol. I, 2nd edn. Amsterdam: John Benjamins.

Givón, T. 2001b. *Syntax. An introduction*. Vol. II. 2nd edn. Amsterdam: John Benjamins.

Glick, C. E. 1938. *The Chinese Migrant in Hawaii. A Study in Accommodation*. Chicago IL: University of Chicago.

Goddard, I. 1997. Pidgin Delaware. In Thomason (ed.), 43–98.

Golovko, E. 1994. Copper Island Aleut. In Bakker & Mous (eds), 113–121.

Golovko, E. 1996. A case of nongenetic development in the Arctic area. The contribution of Aleut and Russian to the formation of Copper Island Aleut. In Jahr & Broch (eds), 63–77.

Golovko, E. & Vakhtin, N. 1990. Aleut in contact. The CIA enigma. *Acta Linguistica Hafniensia* 22(1): 97–125. DOI: 10.1080/03740463.1990.10411524

Gómez Rendón, J. A. 2008. *Mestizaje lingüístico en los Andes. Génesis y estructura de una lengua mixta*. Quito: Abya-Yala.

Gonzalez, A. 1998. The language planning situation in the Philippines. *Journal of Multilingual and Multicultural Development* 19(5-6): 487–525. DOI: 10.1080/01434639808666365

Gonzalez, A. 2003. Language planning in multilingual countries. The case of the Philippines. Plenary talk held at the *Conference on Language Development, Language Revitalization and Multilingual Education in Minority Communities in Asia*, 6–8 November 2003, Bangkok. http://www-01.sil.org/asia/ldc/plenary_papers/andrew_gonzales.pdf (13 February 2015)

Good, J. 2012. Typologizing grammatical complexities. Or why creoles may be paradigmatically simple but syntagmatically average. *Journal of Pidgin and Creole Languages* 27(1): 1–47. DOI: 10.1075/jpcl.27.1.01goo

Gooden, S. 2003. The Phonology and Phonetics of Jamaican Reduplication. PhD dissertation, Ohio State University.

Goodman, M. 1964. *A Comparative Study of Creole French Dialects*. The Hague: Mouton.

Goodman, M. 1985. The origin of Virgin Island Creole Dutch. *Amsterdam Creole Studies* 8(48): 67–106.

Gor, K. & Long, M. H. 2004. Input and second language processing. In *The New Handbook of Bilingualism*, T. K. Bhatia & W. C. Ritchie (eds), 445–472. Malden MA: Blackwell.

Grant, A. 1994. Shelta. The secret language of Irish Travellers viewed as a mixed language. In Bakker & Mous (eds), 123–50.

Grant, A. 1998. Romani words in non-standard British English and the development of Angloromani. In *The Romani Element in Non-standard Speech*, Y. Matras (ed.), 165–191. Wiesbaden: Harrassowitz.

Grant, A. 2013a. Chinuk Wawa. In Michaelis et al. (eds), 2013e, 149–57.

Grant, A. 2013b. Chinuk Wawa structure dataset. In Michaelis et al. (eds), 2013a. http://apics-online.info/contributions/74 (13 February 2015)

Gries, S. T. 2013. *Statistics for Linguists with R. A Practical Introduction*, 2nd edn. Berlin: De Gruyter. DOI: 10.1515/9783110307474

Grimes, C. E. 1996. Indonesian – The official language of a multilingual nation. In Wurm et al. (eds), 719–727.

Guha, A. 1983. The Ahom political system. An enquiry into the state formation process in medieval Assam (1228–1714). *Social Scientist* 11(12): 3–34. DOI: 10.2307/3516963

Guttman, L. 1944. A basis for scaling qualitative data. *American Sociological Review* 9(2): 139–150. DOI: 10.2307/2086306

Hackert, S. 2013. Bahamian Creole. In Michaelis et al. (eds), 2013c, 127–138.

de Haedo, D. 1612. *Topographia e historia general de Argel*. Valladolid: Diego Fernandez de Cordonay Ouiedo.

Hagemeijer, T. 2013a. Santome. In Michaelis et al. (eds), 2013d, 50–58.

Hagemeijer, T. 2013b. The Gulf of Guinea creoles. Genetic and typological relations. In *Creole Languages and Linguistic Typology* [Benjamins Current Topics 57], P. Bhatt & T. Veenstra (eds), 163–205. Amsterdam: John Benjamins. DOI: 10.1075/bct.57.06hag

Hahn, R. F. 1998. Uyghur. In *The Turkic Languages*, L. Johanson & É. Á. Csató (eds), 379–396. London: Routledge.

Hall, R. A. 1961. How Pidgin English has evolved. *New Scientist* 9: 413–415.

Hall, R. A. 1962. The life cycle of pidgin languages. *Lingua* 11: 151–156. DOI: 10.1016/0024-3841(62)90021-9

Hall, R. A. 1966. *Pidgin and Creole Languages*. Ithaca NY: Cornell University Press.

Hamilton, M. B. 2009. *Population Genetics*. Oxford: Wiley-Blackwell.

Han, Z. & Odlin, T. (eds). 2006. *Studies of Fossilization in Second Language Acquisition*. Clevedon: Multilingual Matters.

Hancock, I. 1964. The Portuguese Creoles of Malacca. *Linguistics* 6: 39–71.

Hancock, I. 1969. A provisional comparison of the English-based Atlantic creoles. *African Language Review* 8: 7–72.

Hancock, I. 1972. *A List of Place Names in the Pacific North-West Derived from the Chinook Jargon with a Word-list of the Language*. Vancouver: Vancouver Public Library.

Hancock, I. 1977. Repertory of pidgin and creole languages. In Valdman (ed.), 362–391.

Hancock, I. 1979. On the origins of the term pidgin. In *Readings on Creole Studies*, I. Hancock, E. Polomé, M. Goodman & B. Heine (eds), 81–86. Ghent: Story-scientia. DOI: 10.1075/ssls.2.05han

Hancock, I. 1984a. Shelta and Polari. In *Language in the British Isles*, P. Trudgill (ed.), 384–403. Cambridge: CUP.

Hancock, I. 1984b. The social and linguistic development of Angloromani. In *Romani rokkeripen to-divvus. The English Romani Dialect and its Contemporary Social, Educational and Linguistic Standing*, T. A. Acton & D. Kenrick (eds), 89–122. London: Romanestan Publications.

Hancock, I. 1986a. The cryptolectal speech of the American roads. Traveller Cant and American Angloromani. *American Speech* 61(3): 206–220. DOI: 10.2307/454664

Hancock, I. 1986b. The Domestic Hypothesis, diffusion and componentiality. An account of Atlantic Anglophone creole origins. In Muysken & Smith (eds), 71–102.

Hancock, I. 1987. A preliminary classification of the Anglophone Atlantic creoles, with syntactic data from thirty-three representative dialects. In *Pidgin and Creole Languages. Essays in Memory of John E. Reinecke*, G. G. Gilbert (ed.), 264–333. Honolulu HI: University of Hawaii Press.

Hancock, I. 1990. The Romani speech community. In *Multilingualism in the British Isles*, V. Edwards & S. Alladina (eds), 96–97. London: Longman.

Hancock, I. 1992. The social and linguistic development of Scandoromani. In *Language Contact. Theoretical and Empirical Studies*, E. H. Jahr (ed.), 37–52. Berlin: De Gruyter.

Harman, T. 1814[1573]. *A Caveat of Warning for Common Cursetors Vulgarly Called Vagabonds*. London: T. Bensley.

Harry, O. G. 2006. Illustrations of the IPA. Jamaican Creole. *Journal of the International Phonetic Association* 36(1): 125–131. DOI: 10.1017/S002510030600243X

Haspelmath, M. 2002. *Understanding Morphology*. London: Arnold.

Haspelmath, M. 2013. The occurrence of nominal plurality. In Dryer & Haspelmath (eds), Ch. 34. <http://wals.info/chapter/34 (13 February 2015)

Haspelmath, M. & the APiCS Consortium 2013a. Functions of reduplication. In Michaelis et al. (eds), 2013a, http://apics-online.info/parameters/26 (13 February 2015)

Haspelmath, M. & the APiCS Consortium 2013b. Passive constructions. In Michaelis et al. (eds), 2013f, 358–361.

Haspelmath, M., Dryer, M. S., Gil, D. & Comrie, B. (eds) 2005. *The World Alas of Language Structures*. Oxford: OUP.

Haspelmath, M., Michaelis, S. M. & the APiCS Consortium 2013. Negative morpheme types. In Michaelis et al. (eds), 2013f, 398–401.

Hatch, E. M. 1983. *Psycholinguistics. A Second Language Perspective*. Rowley MA: Newbury House.

Hearn, L. 1885. *Gombo zhèbes. Little Dictionary of Creole Proverbs, Selected from Six Creole Dialects*. New York NY: W. H. Coleman.

Hedrick, P. W. 2011. *Genetics of Populations*, 4th edn. Sudbury MA: Jones and Bartlett.

Helleiner, J. 2003. *Irish Travellers. Racism and the Politics of Culture*. Toronto: University of Toronto Press.

Helmbrecht, J. 2013. Politeness distinctions in pronouns. In Dryer & Haspelmath (eds), Ch. 45. http://wals.info/chapter/45 (13 February 2015)

Hesseling, D. C. 1897. Het Hollandsch in Zuid Afrika. *De Gids* 61: 138–162.

Hesseling, D. C. 1933. Hoe onstond de eigenaardige vorm van het Kreools? *Neophilologus* 18: 209–215. DOI: 10.1007/BF01514474

Hesseling, D. C. 1979a. Dutch in South Africa. In *On the Origin and Formation of Creoles. A Miscellany of Articles by Dirk Christiaan Hesseling*, T. L. Markey & P. T. Roberge (eds), 1–23. Ann Arbor MI: Karoma.

Hesseling, D. C. 1979b. How creoles originate? In *On the Origin and Formation of Creoles. A Miscellany of Articles by Dirk Christiaan Hesseling*, T. L. Markey & P. T. Roberge (eds), 62–71. Ann Arbor MI: Karoma.

Higman, B. W. 2000. The sugar revolution. *The Economic History Review* 53(2): 213–236. DOI: 10.1111/1468-0289.00158

Hinnenkamp, V. 1982. *Foreigner Talk und Tarzanisch. Eine vergleichende Studie über die Sprechweise gegenüber Ausländern am Beispiel der Deutschen und der Türken*. Hamburg: Buske.

Högström, P. 1747. *Beskrifning öfwer de til Sweriges krona lydande lapmarker*. Stockholm: Lars Salvius.

Holm, J. A. 1988. *Pidgins and Creoles, Vol. I: Theory and Structure; Vol. II: Reference Survey*. Cambridge: CUP.

Holm, J. A. 2000. *An Introduction to Pidgin and Creoles*. Cambridge: CUP. DOI: 10.1017/CBO9781139164153

Holm, J. A. & Kepiou, C. 1992. Tok Pisin i kamap pisin gen? Is Tok Pisin repidginizing? In Byrne & Holm (eds), 341–354.

Holm, J. A. & Patrick, P. L. (eds). 2007. *Comparative Creole Syntax. Parallel Outlines of 18 Creole Grammars*. London: Battlebridge.

Holman, E. W., Brown, C. B., Wichmann, S., Müller, A., Velupillai, V., Hammarström, H., Sauppe, S., Jung, H., Bakker, D., Brown, P., Belayev, O., Urban, M., Mailhammer, R., List, J.-M. & Egorov, D. 2011. Automated dating of the world's language families based on lexical similarity. *Current Anthropology* 52(6): 841–875. DOI: 10.1086/662127

Holman, J. 1834. *A Voyage Round the World. Including Travels in Africa, Asia, Australasia, America, etc. etc. from MDCCCXXVII to MDCCCXXXII*. London: Smith, Elder, and Co.

Hosali, P. 2000. *Butler English. Form and Function*. Delhi: B. R. Publishing Corporation.

Hosali, P. 2004. Butler English. Morphology and syntax. In Kortmann & Schneider (eds), 1031–1044.

Hosokawa, K. 1987. Malay Talk on boat. An account of Broome Pearling Lugger Pidgin. In *A World of Language. Papers Presented to Professor S. A. Wurm on his 65th Birthday*, D. C. Laycock & W. Winter (eds), 287–296. Canberra: Pacific Linguistics.

Hough, J. 2011. DNA study. Travellers a distinct ethnicity. *Irish Examiner* 31 May. http://www.irishexaminer.com/ireland/dna-study-travellers-a-distinct-ethnicity-156324.html

Hualde, J. I. & Schwegler, A. 2008. Intonation in Palenquero. *Journal of Pidgin and Creole Languages* 23(1): 1–31. DOI: 10.1075/jpcl.23.1.02hua

Huber, M. 1999a. Atlantic English Creoles and the Lower Guinea Coast. A case against Afrogenesis. In *Spreading the Word. The Issue of Diffusion among the Atlantic Creoles*, M. Huber & M. Parkvall (eds), 81–110. London: University of Westminster Press.

Huber, M. 1999b. *Ghanaian Pidgin English in its West African Context. A Sociohistorical and Structural Analysis* [Varieties of English around the World G24]. Amsterdam: John Benjamins. DOI: 10.1075/veaw.g24

Huber, M. 2000. Restructuring in vitro? Evidence from early Krio. In Neumann-Holzschuh & Schneider (eds), 275–307.

Huber, M. 2004. The Nova-Scotia-Sierra Leone connection. New evidence on an early variety of African American Vernacular English in the diaspora. In Escure & Schwegler (eds), 67–95.

Huber, M. 2013a. Ghanaian Pidgin English. In Michaelis et al. (eds), 2013c, 167–175.

Huber, M. 2013b. Ghanaian Pidgin English structure dataset. In Michaelis et al. (eds), 2013a. http://apics-online.info/contributions/16 (13 February 2015)

Huber, M. & the APiCS Consortium 2013a. Pequenino. In Michaelis, et al. (eds), 2013f, 435–439.

Huber, M. & the APiCS Consortium 2013b. Savvy. In Michaelis, et al. (eds), 2013f, 440–443.

Huber, M. & Velupillai, V. 2009. German colonial sources and the history of Pidgin English. A first analysis of the material relating to German New Guinea in the Deutsche Kolonialbibliothek. Paper delivered at the *7th International Conference on Missionary Linguistics*, Bremen, Germany, 28 February–2 March 2012.

Huber, M. & Velupillai, V. 2015+a. Das Pidginenglische in den deutschen Kolonien. Quellen, Methoden und Erkenntnisse. In *Studienbuch Sprache und Kolonialismus*, T. Stolz, I. H. Warnke & D. Schmidt-Brücken (eds.). Berlin: de Gruyter.

Huber, M. & Velupillai, V. 2015+b. Die Database of Early Pidgin and Creole Texts: Sprachplanung und Sprachattitüden gegenüber dem Pidginenglisch in Deutsch-Neuguinea. In *Sprachgebrauch, Sprachkonzepte und Sprachenpolitik in kolonialen und postkolonialen Kontexten* [working title], B. Kellermeier-Rehbein, M. Schulz & D. Stolberg (eds.). Berlin: de Gruyter.

Hudson, R. A. 1996. *Sociolinguistics*, 2nd edn. Cambridge: CUP. DOI: 10.1017/CBO9781139166843

Hull, A. 1968. The origins of New World French phonology. *Word* 24: 255–269.

Hurford, J. R. 2012a. Linguistics from an evolutionary point of view. In *Philosophy of Linguistics*, R. M. Kempson, T. Fernando & N. Asher (eds), 473–498. Oxford: North Holland.

Hurford, J. R. 2012b. *The Origins of Grammar. Language in the Light of Evolution*. Oxford: OUP.

Huttar, G. L. 1983. A Creole-Amerindian pidgin of Suriname. Ms. http://www.sil.org/resources/archives/6318 (13 February 2015)

Huttar, G. L. & Huttar, M. 1988. A humorous Paramaccan text. *Southwest Journal of Linguistics* 8(2): 34–50.

Huttar, G. L. & Velantie, F. J. 1997. Ndyuka-Trio Pidgin. In Thomason (ed.), 99–124.

Hutton, J. H. 1921. *The Angami Nagas. With Some Notes on Neighbouring Tribes*. London: Macmillan.

Hymes, D. (ed.). 1971. *Pidginization and Creolization of Languages*. Cambridge: CUP.

ICCLR 2011. Charter. Brief history. http://caribbeanlanguagepolicy.weebly.com/charter.html (13 February 2015)

Inoue, A. 2007. Grammatical features of Yokohama Pidgin Japanese. Common characteristics of restricted pidgins. *Japanese/Korean Linguistics* 15: 55–66.

International Phonetic Association 1999. *Handbook of the International Phonetic Association. A Guide to the Use of the International Phonetic Alphabet*. Cambridge: CUP.

Intumbo, I., Inverno, L. & Holm, J. A. 2013. Guinea-Bissau Kriyol. In Michaelis et al. (eds), 2013d, 31–39.

Ishmael, O. 2010. *The Magic Pot*. Nansi Stories from the Caribbean: Xlibris Corporation.

Jabłońska, A. 1957. Język mieszany chińsko-rosyjski w Mandżurii (The Sino-Russian mixed language in Manchuria). *Przegląd Orientalistyczny* 21: 157–168.

Jackson, K. D. 1990. *Sing Without Shame. Oral Traditions in Indo-Portuguese Creole Verse* [Creole Language Library 5]. Amsterdam: John Benjamins. DOI: 10.1075/cll.5

Jacobs, B. 2012. *Origins of a Creole. The History of Papiamentu and its African Ties*. Berlin: De Gruyter. DOI: 10.1515/9781614511076

Jahr, E. H. 1996. On the pidgin status of Russenorsk. In Jahr & Broch (eds), 107–22.

Jahr, E. H. & Broch, I. (eds). 1996. *Language Contact in the Arctic. Northern Pidgins and Contact Languages*. Berlin: De Gruyter. DOI: 10.1515/9783110813302

Janhunen, J., Peltomaa, M., Sandman, E. & Dongzhoug, X. 2008. *Wutun*. Munich: Lincom.

Janssen, D. P., Bickel, B. & Zúñiga, F. 2006. Randomization tests in language typology. *Linguistic Typology* 10: 419–440. DOI: 10.1515/LINGTY.2006.013

Jarva, V. 2008. Old Helsinki Slang and language mixing. *Journal of Language Contact – VARIA* 1: 52–80. DOI: 10.1163/000000008792512547

Jennings, W. 2009. Demographic factors in the formation of French Guianese Creole. In Selbach et al. (eds), 373–387.

Johanson, L. 2001. *Discoveries on the Turkic Linguistic Map*. Uppsala: Universitetstryckeriet.

Johanson, L. 2008. Remodeling grammar. Copying, conventionalization, grammaticalization. In *Language Contact and Contact Languages* [Hamburg Studies on Multilingualism 7], P. Siemund & N. Kintana (eds), 61–79. Amsterdam: John Benjamins. DOI: 10.1075/hsm.7.05joh

Johnson, A. C. 1992. Varieties of Krio and Standard Krio. In *Reading and Writing Krio. A Workshop Held at the Institute of Public Administration and Management, University of Sierra Leone, Freetown, 29–31 January, 1990*, E. D. Jones, K. I. Sandred & N. Schrimpton (eds), 21–30. Uppsala: Almqvist & Wiksell.

Joint Select Committee 2001. Report of the Joint Select Committee on its deliberations on the bill entitled 'An act to ament the constitution of Jamaica to provide for a Charter of Rights and for connected matters'. Kingston.

Jones, E.D. & Shrimpton, N. (eds) 1995. *Ridinbuk fɔ makituman*. Umeå: Department of English, Umeå University.

Jones, S.M. 1942. *Study of Kauai*. Honolulu HI: University of Hawaii Press.

Jourdan, C. 1991. Pidgins and creoles. The blurring of categories. *Annual Review of Anthropology* 20: 187–209. DOI: 10.1146/annurev.an.20.100191.001155

Jourdan, C. 2002. *Pijin. A Trilingual Cultural Dictionary*. Canberra: Pacific Linguistics.

Jourdan, C. 2004. Solomons Island Pijin. Morphology and syntax. In Kortmann & Schneider (eds), 702–719.

Jourdan, C. 2008. The cultural in pidgin genesis. In Kouwenberg & Singler (eds), 359–381.

Jourdan, C. 2009. Bilingualism and creolization in the Solomon Islands. In Selbach et al. (eds), 245–256.

Jourdan, C. & Angeli, J. 2014. Pijin and shifting language ideologies in urban Solomon Islands. *Language in Society* 43(3): 265–285. DOI: 10.1017/S0047404514000190

Jourdan, C. & Keesing, R. 1997. From Fisin to Pijin. Creolization in process in the Solomon Islands. *Language in Society* 26(3): 401–420. DOI: 10.1017/S0047404500019527

Jourdan, C. & Selbach, R. 2004. Solomon Islands Pijin. Phonetics and phonology. In Schneider et al. (eds), 690–709.

Juliana, E. 1970. *Echa cuenta*. Amsterdam: De Bezige Bij.

Kapanga, A. 1998. Impact of language variation and accommodation theory on language maintenance. An analysis of Shaba Swahili. In *Endangered Languages. Language Loss and Community Response*. L.A. Grenoble & L.J. Whaley (eds), 261–89. Cambridge: CUP. DOI: 10.1017/CBO9781139166959.012

Kaplan, R.B. & Baldauf, R.B. 1997. *Language Planning from Practice to Theory*. Clevedon: Multilingual Matters.

Kaye, A.S. & Tosco, M. 2003. *Pidgin and Creole Languages. A Basic Introduction*. Munich: Lincom.

Keenan, E.L. & Dryer, M.S. 2007. Passive in the world's languages. In *Language Typology and Syntactic Description, Vol. I: Clause Structure*, 2. edn, T. Shopen (ed.), 325–361. Cambridge: CUP.

Keesing, R. 1991. The expansion of Melanesian Pidgin. Further early evidence from the Solomons. *Journal of Pidgin and Creole Languages* 6(2): 215–229. DOI: 10.1075/jpcl.6.2.03kee

Kent, R.K. 1996. *Palmares. An African state in Brazil. In Maroon Societies. Rebel Slave Communities in the Americas*, 3rd edn, 170–190. Baltimore MD: Johns Hopkins University Press.

Kerswill, P. 2002. Koineization and accommodation. In *The Handbook of Language Variation and Change*, J.K. Chambers, P. Trudgill & N. Schilling-Estes (eds), 669–702. Malden MA: Blackwell.

Klaiman, M.H. 1991. *Grammatical Voice*. Cambridge: CUP.

Klein, H.S. 1999. *The Atlantic Slave Trade*. Cambridge: CUP.

Klein, T.B. 2011. Typology of creole phonology. Phoneme inventories and syllable templates. *Journal of Pidgin and Creole Languages* 26(1): 155–193. DOI: 10.1075/jpcl.26.1.06kle

Klein, T.B. 2013a. Gullah. In Michaelis et al. (eds), 2013c, 139–147.

Klein, T.B. 2013b. Gullah structure dataset. In Michaelis et al. (eds), 2013a. http://apics-online.info/contributions/13 (13 February 2015)

Klein, T.B. 2013c. Typology of creole phonology. Phoneme inventories and syllable templates. In *Creole Languages and Linguistic Typology* [Benjamins Current Topics 57], P. Bhatt & T. Veenstra (eds), 207–44. Amsterdam: John Benjamins. DOI: 10.1075/bct.57.07kle

Kleinecke, D. 1959. An etymology for "Pidgin". *International Journal of Applied Linguistics* 25: 271–272.

Kloss, H. 1967. 'Abstand' languages and 'Ausbau' languages. *Anthropological Linguistics* 9(7): 29–41.

Kloss, H. 1969. *Research Possibilities on Group Bilingualism*. Quebec: International Center for Research on Bilingualism.

Knauft, B. M. 1999. *From Primitive to Postcolonial in Melanesia & Anthropology*. Ann Arbor MI: University of Michigan Press.

Knight, V. J. J. 1990. Social organization and the evolution of hierarchy in southeastern chiefdoms. *Journal of Anthropological Research* 46(1): 1–23.

Kortmann, B. & Schneider, E. W. (eds). 2004. *A Handbook of Varieties of English, Vol. 2: Morphology & Syntax*. Berlin: De Gruyter. DOI: 10.1515/9783110197181

Koskinen, A. 2010. Kriol in Caribbean Nicaragua schools. In Migge et al. (eds), 133–165.

Kotsinas, U.-B. 1989. Stockholmsspråk genom 100 år (The language of Stockholm over 100 years). *Tijdschrift voor Skandinavistiek* 10(1-2): 14–37.

Kouwenberg, S. 1994. *A Grammar of Berbice Dutch Creole*. Berlin: De Gruyter. DOI: 10.1515/9783110885705

Kouwenberg, S. (ed.). 2003. *Twice as Meaningful. Reduplication in Pidgins, Creoles and Other Contact Languages*. London: Battlebridge.

Kouwenberg, S. 2007. Berbice Dutch (Creole Dutch). In Holm & Patrick (eds), 25–52.

Kouwenberg, S. 2009a. The demographic context of creolization in early English Jamaica, 1655–1700. In Selbach et al. (eds), 327–48.

Kouwenberg, S. 2009b. The invisible hand in creole genesis. Reanalysis in the formation of Berbice Dutch. In Aboh & Smith (eds), 115–158.

Kouwenberg, S. 2011. Berbice Dutch. *Sprogmuseet* 29 December. http://sprogmuseet.dk/kreolsprog/berbice-dutch/ (13 February 2015)

Kouwenberg, S. 2013a. Berbice Dutch. In Michaelis et al. (eds), 2013c, 275–284.

Kouwenberg, S. 2013b. Berbice Dutch structure dataset. In Michaelis et al. (eds), 2013a. http://apics-online.info/contributions/28 (13 February 2015)

Kouwenberg, S. & Murray, E. 1994. *Papiamentu*. Munich: Lincom.

Kouwenberg, S. & Ramos-Michel, A. 2007. Papiamentu (Creole Spanish/Portuguese). In Holm & Patrick (eds), 307–332.

Kouwenberg, S. & Singler, J. V. (eds). 2008. *The Handbook of Pidgin and Creole Studies*. Oxford: Blackwell. DOI: 10.1002/9781444305982

Kouwenberg, S. & Singler, J. V. 2008. Introduction. In Kouwenberg & Singler (eds), 1–16.

Kramer, K. 1991. Plantation development in Berbice from 1753 to 1779. The shift from the interior to the coast. *New West Indian Guide*, 65(1-2): 51–65. DOI: 10.1163/13822373-90002016

Kramer, R. S., Lobban, R. A. & Fluehr-Lobban, C. 2013. *Historical Dictionary of the Sudan*, 4th edn. Lanham MD: Scarecrow Press.

Kroon, S. & Yağmur, K. 2012. *Meertaligheid in het Onderwijs in Suriname. Een Onderzoek naar Praktijken, Ervaringen en Opvattingen van Leerlingen en Leerkrachten als Basis voor de Ontwikkeling van een Taalbeleid voor het Onderwijs in Suriname*. The Hague: Nederlandse Taalunie.

Kuykendall, R. S. 1968. *The Hawaiian Kingdom, I. 1778–1854. Foundation and Transformation*. Honolulu HI: University of Hawaii Press.

Labov, W. 1994. *Principles of Linguistic Change, Vol. I: Internal Factors*. Oxford: Blackwell.

Labov, W. 2001. *Principles of Linguistic Change, Vol. II: Social Factors*. Oxford: Blackwell.

Labov, W. 2010. *Principles of Linguistic Change, Vol. III: Cognitive and Cultural Factors*. Oxford: Blackwell. DOI: 10.1002/9781444327496

Ladefoged, P. 2005. *Vowels and Consonants. An Introduction to the Sounds of Languages*, 2. edn. Oxford: Blackwell.

Ladefoged, P. & Johnson, K. 2010. *A Course in Phonetics*, 6th edn. Boston MA: Wadsworth/Cengage Learning.

LaHaye, L. 2008. Mercantilism. In *The Concise Encyclopedia of Economics* [Library of Economics and Liberty]. http://www.econlib.org/library/Enc/Mercantilism.html (13 February 2015)

Lalla, B. & D'Costa, J. 1990. *Language in Exile. Three Hundred Years of Jamaican Creole*. Tuscaloosa AL: The University of Alabama Press.

Lâm, T. B. 2010. *A Story of Việt Nam*, 3rd edn. Denver CO: Outskirts Press.

Lambert, W. E., Hodgson, R. C., Gardner, R. C. & Fillenbaum, S. 1960. Evaluational reactions to spoken languages. *The Journal of Abnormal and Social Psychology* 60(1): 44–51. DOI: 10.1037/h0044430

Lane, D. M. 2014. Online statistics education. A multimedia course of study. http://onlinestatbook.com/2/index.html (13 February 2015)

Lang, J. 2006. L'influence des Wolof et du wolof sur la formation du créole santiagais. In *Cabo Verde. Origens da sua sociedade e do seu crioulo*, J. Lang, J. A. Holm, J.-L. Rougé & M. J. Soares (eds), 53–62. Tübingen: Günter Narr.

Lang, J. 2013a. Cape Verdean Creole of Santiago. In Michaelis et al. (eds), 2013d, 3–11.

Lang, J. 2013b. Cape Verdean Creole of Santiago structure dataset. In Michaelis et al. (eds), 2013a, http://apics-online.info/contributions/30 (13 February 2015)

Larson-Hall, J. 2010a. *A Guide to Doing Statistics in Second Language Research Using SPSS*. London: Routledge.

Larson-Hall, J. 2010b. *A Guide to Doing Statistics in Second Language Research Using R*. London: Routledge. http://cw.routledge.com/textbooks/9780805861853/guide-to-R.asp (11 February 2015)

Laverdure, P., Allard, I. R. & Crawford, J. C. 1983. *The Michif Dictionary. Turtle Mountain Chippewa Cree*. Winnipeg: Pemmican publications.

Lawes, W. G. 1888. *Grammar and Vocabulary of Language Spoken by Motu Tribe (New Guinea)*, 2nd rev. edn. Sydney: Charles Potter, Government.

Lawton, D. 1980. Language attitude, discreteness and code shifting in Jamaican Creole. *English World-Wide* 1(2): 221–226. DOI: 10.1075/eww.1.2.04law

Laycock, D. C. 1985. Phonology. Substratum elements in Tok Pisin phonology. In *Handbook of Tok Pisin (New Guinea Pidgin)*, S. A. Wurm & P. Mühlhäusler (eds), 295–307. Canberra: Australian National University.

Le Page, R. B. 1977. *De-creolization and Re-creolization. A Preliminary Report on the Sociolinguistic Survey of Multilingual Communities Stage II*: St. *Lucia*. York: York Papers in Linguistics.

Le Page, R. B. & Tabouret-Keller, A. 1985a. *Acts of Identity. Creole-based Approaches to Language and Ethnicity*. Cambridge: CUP.

Le Page, R. B. & Tabouret-Keller, A. 1985b. *Acts of Identity. Creole-based Approaches to Language and Ethnicity*. Cambridge: CUP.

Lee-Smith, M. W. 1996a. The Ejnu language. In Wurm et al. (eds), 851–863.

Lee-Smith, M. W. 1996b. The Hezhou language. In Wurm et al. (eds), 865–873.

Lee-Smith, M. W. 1996c. The Tangwang language. In Wurm et al. (eds), 875–882.

Lefebvre, C. 1998. *Creole Genesis and the Acquisition of Grammar. The Case of Haitian Creole*. Cambridge: CUP.

Lefebvre, C. 2004. *Issues in the Study of Pidgin and Creole Languages* [Studies in Language Colmpanion Series 70]. Amsterdam: John Benjamins. DOI: 10.1075/slcs.70

Lefebvre, C. (ed.). 2011. *Creoles, their Substrates, and Language Typology* [Typological Studies in Language 95]. Amsterdam: John Benjamins. DOI: 10.1075/tsl.95

Lehmann, C. & Moravcsik, E. 2000. Noun. In *An International Handbook on Inflection and Word-Formation*, G.E. Booij, C. Lehmann, J. Mugdan, S. Skopeteas & W. Kesselheim (eds), 732–757. Berlin: De Gruyter.

Lehmann, T. 1993. *A Grammar of Modern Tamil*, 2nd edn. Pondicherry: Pondicherry Institute of Linguistics and Culture.

Leigh, K. 1998. Romani elements in present-day Caló. In *The Romani Element in Non-standard Speech*, Y. Matras (ed.), 243–282. Wiesbaden: Harrassowitz.

Leland, C.G. 1876. *Pidgin-English Sing-song. Songs and Stories in the China-English Dialect. With a Vocabulary*. London: Trübner & co.

Leland, C.G. 1882. *The Gypsies*. Boston MA: Houghton, Mifflin & Co.

Lesho, M. & Sippola, E. 2013. The sociolinguistic situation of the Manila Bay Chabacano-speaking communities. *Language Documentation & Conservation* 7: 1–30.

Levelt, C.C. & van de Vijver, R. 2004. Syllable types in cross-linguistic and developmental grammars. In *Constraints in Phonological Acquisition*, R. Kager, J. Pater & W. Zonneveld (eds), 204–218. Cambridge: CUP.

Levin, H., Giles, H. & Garrett, P. 1994. The effects of lexical formality and accent on trait attributions. *Language & Communication* 14(3): 265–274. DOI: 10.1016/0271-5309(94)90004-3

Lewis, P., Simons, G.F. & Fennig, C.D. 2014. *Ethnologue. Languages of the World*, 17th edn. Dallas TX: SIL International. http://www.ethnologue.com (13 February 2015)

Li, C.N. & Thompson, S.A. 1981. *Mandarin Chinese. A Functional Reference Grammar*. Berkeley CA: University of California Press.

Li, M. & Matthews, S. 2013. Chinese Pidgin English structure dataset. In Michaelis et al. (eds), 2013a. http://apics-online.info/contributions/20 (13 February 2015)

Li, M., Matthews, S. & Smith, G.P. 2005. Pidgin English texts from The Chinese and English Instructor. *Hong Kong Journal of Applied Linguistics* 10(1): 79–167.

Lindstedt, J. 2006. Native Esperanto as a test case for natural language. In *A Man of Measure. Festschrift in Honour of Fred Karlsson on his 60th Birthday*, M. Suominen, A. Arppe, A. Airola, O. Heinämäki, M. Miestamo, U. Määttä, J. Niemi, K.K. Pitkänen & K. Sinnemäki (eds). Special supplement to *SKY Journal of Linguistics* 19: 47–55.

Linnekin, J. 1991. Hawaiians. In *Encyclopedia of World Cultures, Vol. 2: Oceania*, T.E. Hays (ed.), 95–97. Boston MA: GK Hall.

Lipski, J.M. 1996. Spanish in the Pacific. In Wurm et al. (eds), 271–98.

Lipski, J.M. 2012. The "new" Palenquero. Revitalization and re-creolization. In *Colombian Varieties of Spanish*, R.J. File-Muriel & R. Orozco (eds), 21–41. Madrid: Iberoamericana.

Love, R.S. 2006. *Maritime Exploration in the Age of Discovery*, 1415–1800. Westport CT: Greenwood Press.

Lowry, R. 2013. Concepts and applications of inferential statistics. http://vassarstats.net/textbook/ (13 February 2015)

Luffin, X. 2005. *Un créole arabe. Le kinubi de Mombasa*. Munich: Lincom.

Luffin, X. 2011. Arabic-based pidgins and creoles. In *The Semitic Languages. An International Handbook*, S. Weninger (ed.), 990–1001. München: De Gruyter.

Luffin, X. 2013a. Kinubi. In Michaelis et al. (eds), 2013e, 50–53.

Luffin, X. 2013b. Kinubi structure dataset. In Michaelis et al. (eds), 2013a. http://apics-online.info/contributions/63 (13 February 2015)

Lum, D. H. 1990. *Pass on, no pass back!* Honolulu HI: Bamboo Ridge Press.

Lunn, J. 1988. *Memoirs of the Maelstrom. A Senegalese Oral History of the First World War*. Oxford: Heinemann.

Macalister, R. A. S. 1937. *The Secret Languages of Ireland. With Special Reference to the Origin and Nature of the Shelta Language Partly Based upon Collections and Manuscripts of the late John Sampson*. Cambridge: CUP.

MacDonald, L. 1990. *A grammar of Tauya*. Berlin: De Gruyter. DOI: 10.1515/9783110846027

Maddieson, I. 2013a. Consonant inventories. In Dryer & Haspelmath (eds), Ch. 1. http://wals.info/chapter/1 (13 February 2015)

Maddieson, I. 2013b. Front rounded vowels. In Dryer & Haspelmath (eds), Ch. 11. http://wals.info/chapter/11 (13 February 2015)

Maddieson, I. 2013c. Syllable structure. In Dryer & Haspelmath (eds), Ch. 12. http://wals.info/chapter/12 (13 February 2015)

Maddieson, I. 2013d. Tone. In Dryer & Haspelmath (eds), Ch. 13. http://wals.info/chapter/13 (13 February 2015)

Maddieson, I. 2013e. Vowel quality inventories. In Dryer & Haspelmath (eds), Ch. 2. http://wals.info/chapter/2 (13 February 2015)

Magnusson, L. G. 2003. Mercantilism. In *A Companion to the History of Economic Thought*, W. J. Samuels, J. Biddle & J. B. Davis (eds), 46–60. Malden MA: Blackwell. DOI: 10.1002/9780470999059.ch4

Makhudu, K. D. 2002. An introduction to Flaaitaal (or Tsotsitaal). In R. Mesthrie (ed.), *Language in South Africa*, 398–406. Cambridge: CUP.

Manfredi, S. 2005. Descrizione grammaticale dell'arabo Juba con riferimenti sociolinguistici alla comunità del Cairo. MA thesis, Università degli Studi di Napoli L'Orientale.

Manfredi, S. & Petrollino, S. 2013a. Juba Arabic. In Michaelis et al. (eds), 2013e, 54–66.

Manfredi, S. & Petrollino, S. 2013b. Juba Arabic structure dataset. In Michaelis et al. (eds). 2013a. http://apics-online.info/contributions/64 (13 February 2015)

Marantz, A. 1982. Re reduplication. *Linguistic Inquiry* 13(3): 435–482.

Marcos, H.-M. 1976. Italian. In *Language in Ethiopia*, M. L. Bender, J. D. Bowen, R. L. Cooper & C. A. Ferguson (eds), 170–80. Oxford: OUP.

Maros, M., Halim, Nurul Alia Abdul, Zaki, Norfarhana Fadila MOhd, Rahman, Anis Nadiah Che Abdul, Razak, S. S., Kaswandi, S. S. & Rosmidi, Wan Fadli Hazilan Wan 2014. Portuguese Settlement community's awareness and response to Papia Kristang language shift. *Procedia* 118: 273–81.

Maschler, Y. 1998. On the transition from code switching to a mixed code. In Auer (ed.), 125–149.

Matras, Y. 2002. *Romani. A Linguistic Introduction*. Cambridge: CUP. DOI: 10.1017/CBO9780511486791

Matras, Y. 2003. Mixed languages. Re-examining the structural prototype. In Matras & Bakker (eds), 151–76.

Matras, Y. 2009. *Language Contact*. Cambridge: CUP. DOI: 10.1017/CBO9780511809873

Matras, Y. 2010. *Romani in Britain. The Afterlife of a Language*. Edinburgh: EUP. DOI: 10.3366/edinburgh/9780748639045.001.0001

Matras, Y. & Bakker, P. (eds). 2003. *The Mixed Language Debate. Theoretical and Empirical Advances*. Berlin: De Gruyter. DOI: 10.1515/9783110197242

Matras, Y., Gardner, H., Jones, C. & Schulman, V. 2007. Angloromani. A different kind of language? *Anthropological Linguistics* 49(2): 142–84.

Matras, Y. & Sakel, J. (eds). 2007. *Grammatical Borrowing in Cross-linguistic Perspective*. Berlin: De Gruyter.

Matthews, S. & Li, M. 2013. Chinese Pidgin English. In Michaelis et al. (eds), 2013c, 206–213.

Matthews, S. & Yip, V. 1994. *Cantonese. A Comprehensive Grammar*. London: Routledge.

Matthews, W. 1935. Sailors' pronunciation in the second half of the seventeenth century. *Anglia – Zeitschrift für englische Philologie* 59: 193–251.

Matzel, K. 1966. *Einführung in die singhalesische Sprache*. Wiesbaden: Harrassowitz.

Maurer, P. 2011. *The Former Portuguese Creole of Batavia and Tugu (Indonesia)*. London: Battlebridge.

Maurer, P. 2013a. Angolar. In Michaelis et al. (eds), 2013d, 59–71.

Maurer, P. 2013b. Angolar structure dataset. In Michaelis et al. (eds), 2013a. http://apics-online.info/contributions/36 (13 February 2015)

Maurer, P. 2013c. Papiamentu. In Michaelis et al. (eds), 2013d, 163–181.

Maurer, P. 2013d. Principense. In Michaelis et al. (eds), 2013d, 72–80.

Maurer, P. & the APiCS Consortium 2013. Tone. In Michaelis et al. (eds), 2013f, 480–483.

Maurer, P., Michaelis, S.M. & the APiCS Consortium 2013. Directional serial verb constructions with 'come' and 'go'. In Michaelis et al. (eds), 2013f, 334–337.

Mayo, F. d. S. 1870. *El gitanismo. Historia, costumbres y dialecto de los gitanos*. Madrid: Libreria de Victoriano Suarez.

McConvell, P. 1985. Domains and codeswitching among bilingual Aborigines. In *Australia. Meeting Place of Languages*, M.G. Clyne (ed.), 95–125. Canberra: Pacific Linguistics.

McConvell, P. 1988. Mix-im-up. Aboriginal codeswitching old and new. In *Codeswitching. Anthropological and Sociolinguistic Perspectives*, M. Heller (ed.), 97–124. Berlin: De Gruyter.

McConvell, P. & Meakins, F. 2005. Gurindji Kriol. A mixed language emerges from code-switching. *Australian Journal of Linguistics* 25(1): 9–30. DOI: 10.1080/07268600500110456

McDonough, J. 2003. *The Navajo Sound System*. Dordrecht: Kluwer. DOI: 10.1007/978-94-010-0207-3

McGowan, A. 1996. *The Winchester Confessions, 1615–1616. Depositions of Travellers, Gypsies, Fraudsters, and Makers of Counterfeit Documents, Including a Vocabulary of the Romany Language*. South Chailley: Romany and Traveller Family History Society.

McWhorter, J.H. 1995. Sisters under the skin. A case for genetic relationship between the Atlantic English-based creoles. *Journal of Pidgin and Creole Languages* 10(2): 289–333. DOI: 10.1075/jpcl.10.2.04mcw

McWhorter, J.H. 1997. It happened at Cormantin. Locating the origin of the Atlantic English-based creoles. *Journal of Pidgin and Creole Languages* 12(1): 59–102. DOI: 10.1075/jpcl.12.1.03mcw

McWhorter, J.H. 2000. *The Missing Spanish Creoles. Recovering the Birth of Plantation Contact Languages*. Berkeley CA: University of California Press.

McWhorter, J.H. 2002. The rest of the story. Restoring pidginization to creole genesis theory. *Journal of Pidgin and Creole Languages* 17(1): 1–48. DOI: 10.1075/jpcl.17.1.02mcw

McWhorter, J.H. 2005. *Defining Creole*. Oxford: OUP.

McWhorter, J.H. 2011. *Linguistic Simplicity and Complexity. Why Do Languages Undress?* Berlin: De Gruyter. DOI: 10.1515/9781934078402

Meakins, F. 2008. Land, language and identity. The socio-political origins of Gurindji Kriol. In *Social Lives in Language - Sociolinguistics and Multilingual Speech Communities. Celebrating the Work of Gillian Sankoff* [Impact: Studies in Language and Society 24], M. Meyerhoff & N. Nagy (eds), 69–94. Amsterdam: John Benjamins. DOI: 10.1075/impact.24.08mea

Meakins, F. 2010. The development of asymmetrical serial verb constructions in an Australian mixed language. *Lingustic Typology* 14: 1–38. DOI: 10.1515/lity.2010.001

Meakins, F. 2011. *Case-marking in Contact. The Development and Function of Case Morphology in Gurindji Kriol* [Creole Language Library 39]. Amsterdam: John Benjamins. DOI: 10.1075/cll.39

Meakins, F. 2013a. Gurindji Kriol. In Michaelis et al. (eds), 2013e, 131–40.

Meakins, F. 2013b. Gurindji Kriol structure dataset. In Michaelis et al. (eds), 2013a. http://apics-online.info/contributions/72 (13 February 2015)

Meakins, F. 2013c. Mixed languages. In Bakker & Matras (eds), 159–228.

Meeuwis, M. 2013a. Lingala. In Michaelis et al. (eds), 2013e, 25–33.

Meeuwis, M. 2013b. Lingala structure dataset. In Michaelis et al. (eds), 2013a. http://apics-online.info/contributions/60 (13 February 2015)

Meijer, G. & Muysken, P.C. 1977. On the beginnings of pidgin and creole studies. Schuchardt and Hesseling. In Valdman (ed.), 21–45.

Menang, T. 2004. Cameroon Pidgin English (Kamtok). Phonology. In Schneider et al. (eds), 902–17.

Mendizabal, I., Lao, O., Marigorta, U.M., Wollstein, A., Gusmão, L., Ferak, V., Ioana, M., Jordanova, A., Kaneva, R., Kouvatsi, A., Kučinskas, V., Makukh, H., Metspalu, A., Netea, M.G., Pablo, R. de, Pamjav, H., Radojkovic, D., Rolleston, S.J., Sertic, J., Macek, M., JR, Comas, D. & Kayser, M. 2012. Reconstructing the population history of European Romani from genome-wide data. *Current Biology* 22(24): 2342–2349. DOI: 10.1016/j.cub.2012.10.039

Mesthrie, R. 2008. 'I've been speaking Tsotsitaal all my life without knowing it'. Towards a unified account of Tsotsitaals in South Africa. In *Social Lives in Language – Sociolinguistics and Multilingual Speech Communities. Celebrating the Work of Gillian Sankoff* [Impact: Studies in Language and Society 24], M. Meyerhoff & N. Nagy (eds), 95–110. Amsterdam: John Benjamins. DOI: 10.1075/impact.24.09mes

Mesthrie, R. 2013. Fanakalo structure dataset. In Michaelis et al. (eds), 2013a. http://apics-online.info/contributions/61 (13 February 2015)

Mesthrie, R. & Surek-Clark, C. 2013. Fanakalo. In Michaelis et al. (eds), 2013e, 34–41.

Meyerhoff, M. 2003. Reduplication in Bislama. An overview of phonological and semantic factors. In Kouwenberg (ed.), 231–8.

Meyerhoff, M. 2006. *Introducing Sociolinguistics*. London: Routledge.

Meyerhoff, M. 2013a. Bislama. In Michaelis et al. (eds), 2013c, 223–231.

Meyerhoff, M. 2013b. Bislama structure dataset. In Michaelis et al. (eds), 2013a. http://apics-online.info/contributions/23 (13 February 2015)

Michaelis, S.M. & Rosalie, M. 2013. Seychelles Creole. In Michaelis et al. (eds), 2013d, 261–270.

Michaelis, S.M., Maurer, P., Haspelmath, M. & Huber, M. (eds). 2013a. *Atlas of Pidgin and Creole Language Structures Online*. Munich: Max Planck Digital Library.

Michaelis, S.M., Maurer, P., Haspelmath, M. & Huber, M. (eds). 2013b. *The Atlas and Survey of Pidgin & Creole Languages*, 4 Vols. Oxford: OUP.

Michaelis, S.M., Maurer, P., Haspelmath, M. & Huber, M. (eds). 2013c. *Survey of Pidgin and Creole Languages, Vol. I: English-based and Dutch-based Languages*. Oxford: OUP.

Michaelis, S.M., Maurer, P., Haspelmath, M. & Huber, M. (eds). 2013d. *Survey of Pidgin and Creole Languages, Vol. II: Portuguese-based, Spanish-based and French-based Languages*. Oxford: OUP.

Michaelis, S.M., Maurer, P., Haspelmath, M. & Huber, M. (eds). 2013e. *Survey of Pidgin and Creole Languages, Vol. III: Pidgins, Creoles and Mixed Languages Based on Languages from Africa, Asia, Australia and the Americas*. Oxford: OUP.

Michaelis, S. M., Maurer, P., Haspelmath, M. & Huber, M. (eds). 2013f. *The Atlas of Pidgin and Creole Language Structures*. Oxford: OUP.

Michaëlius, J. 1909. Letter of Reverend Jonas Michaëlius, 1628. In *Narratives of New Netherland, 1609–1664*, J. F. Jameson (ed.), 117–133. New York NY: Scribner.

Miestamo, M. 2007. Negation. An overview of typological research. *Language and Linguistics Compass* 1(5): 552–570. DOI: 10.1111/j.1749-818X.2007.00026.x

Migge, B. 2013a. Nengee. In Michaelis et al. (eds), 2013c, 39–48.

Migge, B. 2013b. Nengee structure dataset. In Michaelis et al. (eds), 2013a. http://apics-online.info/contributions/4 (13 February 2015)

Migge, B. & Léglise, I. 2012. *Exploring Language in a Multilingual Context. Variation, Interaction and Ideology in Language Documentation*. Cambridge: CUP. DOI: 10.1017/CBO9780511979002

Migge, B., Léglise, I. & Bartens, A. 2010a. Creoles in education. A discussion of pertinent issues. In Migge, et al. (eds), 1–30.

Migge, B., Léglise, I. & Bartens, A. (eds). 2010b. *Creoles in Education. An Appraisal of Current Programs and Projects* [Creole Language Library 36]. Amsterdam: John Benjamins. DOI: 10.1075/cll.36

Mihalic, F. 1971. *The Jacaranda Dictionary and Grammar of Melanesian Pidgin*. Milton Queensland: Jacaranda.

Miller, C. 1991a. Grammaticalisation du verbe gale "dire" et subordination en Juba -Arabic. In *Leçons d'Afrique. Filiation, rupture et reconstitution des langues: Un hommage à G. Manessy*, R. Nicolaï (ed.), 455–482. Leuven: Peeters.

Miller, C. 1991b. Le changement linguistique à Juba et à Khartoum. In *Sudan. History, Identity, Ideology / Historire, Identités, Ideologies*, H. Bleuchot, C. Delmet & D. Hopwood (eds), 153–80. Ithaca NY: Ithaca Press.

Miller, C. 1993. Restructuration morpho-syntaxique en Juba-arabic et Ki-nubi. À propos du débat universaux/substrat et superstrat dans les études creoles. *Materiaux Arabes et Sudarabiques* 5: 137–74.

Milroy, L. 1987. *Language and Social Networks*, 2nd edn. Oxford: Blackwell.

Milroy, L. 2002. Social networks. In *The Handbook of Language Variation and Change*, J. K. Chambers, P. Trudgill & N. Schilling-Estes (eds), 549–72. Malden MA: Blackwell.

Minks, A. 2013. *Voices of Play. Miskitu Children's Speech and Song on the Atlantic Coast of Nicaragua*. Tucson AZ: University of Arizona Press.

Moitt, B. 2001. *Women and Slavery in the French Antilles*, 1635–1848. Bloomington IN: Indiana University Press.

Molony, C. 1973. Sound changes in Chabacano. In *Parangal Kay Cecilio Lopez*, A. Gonzales (ed.), 38–50. Quezon City: Linguistic Society of the Philippines.

Moore, C. R. 1981. Kanaka Maratta. A History of Melanesian Mackay. PhD dissertation, James Cook University of North Queensland.

Moore, D., Facundes, S. & Pires, N. 1993. Nheengatu (Língua Geral Amazonica), its history, and the effect of language contact. In Report 8. Survey of California and Other Indian Languages. *Proceedings of the Meeting for the Society for the Study of the Indigenous languages of the Americas July 2–4, 1993 and the Hokan-Penutian Workshop July 3, 1993*, M. Langdon (ed.), 93–118. Berkeley CA: University of California, Dept. of Linguistics.

Morisseau-Leroy, F. 1953. *Wa Kreyon (Antigone)*: Culture.

Morrison, R. 1807. Unpublished journal. Council for World Mission Archives, School of Oriental and African Studies, University of London.

Mortensen, R. 2000. Slaving in Australian courts. Blackbirding cases, 1869–1871. *Journal of South Pacific Law* 4: 1–22.

Mosel, U. & Mühlhäusler, P. 1982. New evidence of a Samoan Origin of New Guinea Tok Pisin (New Guinea Pidgin English). *The Journal of Pacific History* 17(3): 166–175. DOI: 10.1080/00223348208572445

Moser, G. M. 1969. African literature in Portuguese: The first written, the last discovered. *African Forum* 2(4): 78–96.

Mous, M. 2001. *Paralexification in langauge intertwining*. In *Creolization and Contact* [Creole Language Library 23], 113–123. Amsterdam: John Benjamins. DOI: 10.1075/cll.23.05mou

Mous, M. 2003a. The linguistic properties of lexical manipulation and its relevance for Ma'á. In Matras & Bakker (eds), 209–236.

Mous, M. 2003b. *The Making of a Mixed Language. The Case of Ma'a/Mbugu* [Creole Language Library 26]. Amsterdam: John Benjamins. DOI: 10.1075/cll.26

Mous, M. 2013. Mixed Ma'a/Mbugu. In Michaelis et al. (eds), 2013e, 42–49.

Mufwene, S. S. 1996. The founder principle in creole genesis. *Diachronica* 13(1): 83–134. DOI: 10.1075/dia.13.1.05muf

Mufwene, S. S. 1997. Jargons, pidgins, creoles, and koines. What are they? In *The Structure and Status of Pidgins and Creoles* [Creole Language Library 19], A. K. Spears & D. Winford (eds), 35–70. Amsterdam: John Benjamins. DOI: 10.1075/cll.19.05muf

Mufwene, S. S. 2000. Creolization is a social, not a structural, process. In Neumann-Holzschuh & Schneider (eds), 64–84.

Mufwene, S. S. 2001. *The Ecology of Language Evolution*. Cambridge: CUP. DOI: 10.1017/CBO9780511612862

Mufwene, S. S. 2004. Gullah. Morphology and syntax. In Kortmann & Schneider (eds), 356–373.

Mufwene, S. S. 2013. Kikongo-Kituba. In Michaelis et al. (eds), 2013e, 3–12.

Mühleisen, S. 2013a. Trinidad English Creole. In Michaelis et al. (eds), 2013c, 61–9.

Mühleisen, S. 2013b. Trinidad English Creole structure dataset. In Michaelis et al. (eds), 2013a. http://apics-online.info/contributions/6 (13 February 2015)

Mühlhäusler, P. 1976. Samoan Plantation Pidgin English and the origins of New Guinea Pidgin. An introduction. *The Journal of Pacific History* 11(2): 122–125. DOI: 10.1080/00223347608572295

Mühlhäusler, P. 1983. Samoan Plantation Pidgin English and the origin of New Guinea Pidgin. In *The Social Context of Creolization*, E. Woolford & W. Washabaugh (eds), 28–76. Ann Arbor MI: Karoma.

Mühlhäusler, P. 1984. Tracing the roots of Pidgin German. *Language & Communication* 4(1): 27–57. DOI: 10.1016/0271-5309(84)90018-1

Mühlhäusler, P. 1997. *Pidgin and Creole Linguistics*, Rev. and expanded edn. London: University of Westminster Press.

Mulcahy, F. D. 1979. Studies in Gitano social ecology. Linguistic performance and ethnicity. *International Journal of the Sociology of Language* 19: 11–28.

Muraz, G. 1931. *Vocabulaire du patois arabe tchadien ou Tourkou et des dialectes sara-madjinngaye et sara-m'baye (s.-o. du Tchad). Suivi de conversations et d'un essai de classification des tribus saras, les superstitions locales, les coutumes et les pratiques de la medecine indigene dans la race sara.* Paris: C. Lavauzelle.

Murillo Velarde, P. 1749. *Historia de la provincia de Philipinas de la Compañía de Jesús*. Manila: Imprenta de la Compañía de Iesús.

Muysken, P. C. 1981. Halfway between Quechua and Spanish. The case for relexification. In Valdman, A. & Highfield, A. R. (eds). *Historicity and variation in creole studies*. Ann Arbor: Karoma. 52–78.
Muysken, P. C. 1988. Lexical restructuring and creole genesis. In Boretzky, N., Enninger, W. & Stoltz, T. (eds). *Beiträge zum 4. Essener Kolloquium über "Sprach-kontakt, Sprachwandel, Sprachwechsel, Sprachtod" vom 9.10–10.10.1987 an der Universität Essen*. Bochum: Brockmeyer. 193–210.
Muysken, P. C. 1994. Callahuaya. In Bakker & Mous (eds), 201–5.
Muysken, P. C. 1997a. Callahuaya. In Thomason (ed.), 427–47.
Muysken, P. C. 1997b. Media Lengua. In Thomason (ed.), 365–426.
Muysken, P. C. 2000. *Bilingual Speech. A Typology of Code-mixing*. Cambridge: CUP.
Muysken, P. C. 2008. Creole studies and multilingualism. In Kouwenberg & Singler (eds), 287–308.
Muysken, P. C. 2013a. Media Lengua. In Michaelis et al. (eds), 2013e, 143–148.
Muysken, P. C. 2013b. Media Lengua structure dataset. In Michaelis et al. (eds), 2013a. http://apics-online.info/contributions/73 (13 February 2015)
Muysken, P. C. & Smith, N. (eds). 1986. *Substrata Versus Universals in Creole Genesis* [Creole Language Library 1]. Amsterdam: John Benjamins. DOI: 10.1075/cll.1
Muysken, P. C. & Veenstra, T. 1994. Universalist approaches. In Arends et al. (eds), 121–134.
Myers-Scotton, C. 1993. *Duelling Languages. Grammatical Structure in Codeswitching*. Oxford: Clarendon.
Myers-Scotton, C. 2002. *Contact Linguistics. Bilingual Encounters and Grammatical Outcomes*. Oxford: OUP.
Myers-Scotton, C. 2003. What lies beneath. Split (mixed) languages as contact phenomena. In Matras & Bakker (eds), 73–106.
Naro, A. J. 1978. A study on the origins of pidginization. *Language* 54(2): 314–47. DOI: 10.2307/412950
Navarrete, M. C. 2001. Cimarrones y palenques en el nuevo reino de Granada. *Tzintzun: Revista de Estudios Históricos* 33: 117–47.
Navarrete, M. C. 2008. 'Por haber todos concebido ser General la libertad para los de su color'. Construyendo el pasado del palenque de Matudere. *Historia Caribe* 13: 7–45.
Neumann-Holzschuh, I. & Klingler, T. A. 2013. Louisiana Creole structure dataset. In Michaelis et al. (eds), 2013a. http://apics-online.info/contributions/53 (13 February 2015)
Neumann-Holzschuh, I. & Schneider, E. W. (eds). 2000. *Degrees of Restructuring in Creole Languages* [Varieties of English around the World G22]. Amsterdam: John Benjamins. DOI: 10.1075/eww.25.1.09ace
Nguyễn, Đ.-H. 1995. *NTC's Vietnamese-English Dictionary*. New updated edn. Lincolnwood: NTC/Contemporary Publishing Group.
Nichols, J. D. 1995. The Ojibwe verb in "Broken Oghibbeway". *Amsterdam Creole Studies* 12: 1–18.
Nickel, M. & Wilner, J. 1984. A sketch of Sranan Tongo. In *Papers on Sranan Tongo*, P. Willem (ed.), 8–123. Paramaribo: Instituut voor Taalwetenschap.
Nicolaï, R. 1979. Les dialectes du songhay. (Contribution à lètude des changements linguistiques). PhD dissertation, University of Nice.
Nicolaï, R. & Zima, P. 1997. *Songhay*. Munich: Lincom.
Nigoza, E. 2007. *Bahra. The History, Legends, Customs and Traditions of Ternate, Cavite. Bahra. Manga historia, alamat, custumbre y tradiciong di Bahra*. Cavite: Cavite Historical Society.
Ninio, A. 2011. *Syntactic Development, its Input and Output*. Oxford: OUP. DOI: 10.1093/acprof:oso/9780199565962.001.0001

Noguera, M.C., Schwegler, A., Gomes, V., Briceño, I., Alvarez, L., Uricoechea, D., Amorim, A., Benavides, E., Silvera, C., Charris, M., Bernal, J.E. & Gusmão, L. 2013. Colombia's racial crucible. Y chromosome evidence from six admixed communities in the Department of Bolivar. *Annals of Human Biology* 1–7.

Nordhoff, S. 2009. *A Grammar of Upcountry Sri Lanka Malay*. Utrecht: LOT.

Northrup, D. 1995. *Indentured Labor in the Age of Imperialism, 1838–1914*. Cambridge: CUP.

Noss, R.B. 1971. Politics and language policy in Southeast Asia. *Language Sciences* 16: 25–32.

Odo, C. 1975. Phonological Processes in the English Dialect of Hawaiʻi. PhD dissertation, University of Hawaiʻi at Mānoa.

Odo, C. 1977. Phonological representation in Hawaiian English. *University of Hawaii Working Papers in Linguistics* 9(3): 77–85.

Okrand, M. 1992. *Klingon Dictionary. Official Guide to Klingon Words and Phrases*. New York NY: Simon & Schuster.

Ortega, L. 2009. *Understanding Second Language Acquisition*. London: Hodder Education.

Owens, J. 2001. Arabic sociolinguistics. *Arabica* 48(4): 419–469. DOI: 10.1163/1570058013231638l6

Oxford English Dictionary. 2013. Oxford: OUP. http://www.oed.com/ (13 February 2015)

Paauw, S. 2008. The Malay Contact Varieties of Eastern Indonesia. A Typological Comparison. PhD dissertation, The State University of New York at Buffalo.

Paauw, S. 2013a. Ambon Malay. In Michaelis et al. (eds), 2013e, 94–104.

Paauw, S. 2013b. Ambon Malay structure dataset. In Michaelis, et al. (eds), 2013a. http://apics-online.info/contributions/68 (13 February 2015)

Palmer, F.R. 2001. *Mood and Modality*, 2. edn. Cambridge: CUP. DOI: 10.1017/CBO9781139167178

Papen, R. 2003. Michif. One phonology or two? *University of British Columbia Working Papers in Linguistics* 12: 57–70.

Parkinson, B. 1995. Aw fɔ arenj yu biznɛs mek i fayn ɛn bɛtɛ. In Ridinbuk fɔ makituman, E.D. Jones & N. Shrimpton (eds), 1–3. Umeå: Department of English, Umeå University.

Parkvall, M. 1998. A short note on the peopling of English St. Kitts. In *St. Kitts and the Atlantic Creoles. The Texts of Samuel Augustus Matthews in Perspective*, P. Baker & A. Bruyn (eds), 63–74. London: University of Westminster Press.

Parkvall, M. 1999. On the possibility of Afrogenesis in the case of French Creoles. In Rickford & Romaine (eds). 187–214.

Parkvall, M. & Bakker, P. 2013. Pidgins. In Bakker & Matras (eds), 15–64.

Patrick, P.L. 1999. *Urban Jamaican Creole. Variation in the Mesolect* [Varieties of English around the World G17]. Amsterdam: John Benjamins. DOI: 10.1075/veaw.g17

Patrick, P.L. 2004. Jamaican Creole. Morphology and syntax. In Kortmann & Schneider (eds), 407–38.

Patrick, P.L. 2007. Jamaican Patwa (Creole English). In Holm & Patrick (eds), 127–52.

Patrick, P.L. 2008. Pidgins, creoles and variation. In Kouwenberg & Singler (eds), 461–87.

Paulo, P.A. 2000. *Misa andi lengua ri palenge*. Cartagena.

Payne, T.E. 1997. *Describing Morphosyntax. A Guide for Field Linguists*. Cambridge: CUP.

Perekhvalskaya, E. 2013a. Chinese Pidgin Russian. In Michaelis et al. (eds), 2013e, 69–76.

Perekhvalskaya, E. 2013b. Chinese Pidgin Russian structure dataset. In Michaelis et al. (eds), 2013a. http://apics-online.info/contributions/65 (13 February 2015)

Petitjean-Roget, J. 1980. *La societé d'habitation à la Martinique. Un demi-siècle de formation 1634–1685*. Lille: Atelier de Reproduction des Thèses.

Pfänder, S. 2013a. Guyanais. In Michaelis et al. (eds), 2013d, 220–228.

Pfänder, S. 2013b. Guyanais structure dataset. In Michaelis et al. (eds), 2013a. http://apics-online.info/contributions/52 (13 February 2015)

Plag, I. 2008a. Creoles as interlanguages. Inflectional morphology. *Journal of Pidgin and Creole Languages* 23(1): 114–35. DOI: 10.1075/jpcl.23.1.06pla

Plag, I. 2008b. Creoles as interlanguages. Syntactic structures. *Journal of Pidgin and Creole Languages* 23(2): 307–28. DOI: 10.1075/jpcl.23.2.06pla

Plag, I. 2009a. Creoles as interlanguages. Phonology. *Journal of Pidgin and Creole Languages* 24(1): 119–38. DOI: 10.1075/jpcl.24.1.06pla

Plag, I. 2009b. Creoles as interlanguages. Word-formation. *Journal of Pidgin and Creole Languages* 24(2): 339–62. DOI: 10.1075/jpcl.24.2.05pla

Polkinhorn, H., Velasco, A. & Lambert, M. 1983. *El libro de caló*. San Diego CA: Atticus Press.

Pontoppidan, E. 1881. Einige Notizen über die Kreolensprache der dänischwestindischen Inseln. *Zeitschrift für Ethnologie* 13: 130–138.

Poplack, S. 2001. Code-switching (linguistic). In *International Encyclopedia of the Social and Behavioral Sciences*, N.J. Smelser & P.B. Baltes (eds), 2062–2065. Amsterdam: Elsevier. DOI: 10.1016/B0-08-043076-7/03031-X

Post, M. 1994. Fa d'Ambu. In Arends, et al. (eds), 191–204.

Post, M. 2013a. Fa d'Ambô structure dataset. In Michaelis et al. (eds), 2013a. http://apics-online.info/contributions/38 (13 February 2015)

Post, M. 2013b. Fa d'Ambô. In Michaelis et al. (eds), 2013d, 81–89.

Postma, J. 1990. *The Dutch in the Atlantic Slave Trade*, 1600–1815. Cambridge: CUP.

Prentice, D.J. 1990. Malay (Indonesian and Malaysian). In *The World's Major Languages, 1*, B. Comrie (ed.), 913–35. Oxford: OUP.

Prescod, P. 2009. On -self and reflexivity in English-lexified pidgins and creoles. In Faraclas & Klein (eds), 153–74.

Prichard, H. & Shwayder, K. 2013. Against a split phonology of Michif. The 37th Penn Linguistics Colloquium.

Prince, J.D. 1912. An ancient New Jersey Indian jargon. *American Anthropologist* 14(3): 508–524. DOI: 10.1525/aa.1912.14.3.02a00060

Prokosch, E. 1986. *Arabische Kontaktsprachen. Pidgin- und Kreolsprachen in Afrika*. Graz: Institut für Sprachwissenschaft der Universität Graz.

Quindale, F. [. d.S. M. 1867. *Diccionario gitano*. Madrid: Oficina Tipográfica del Hospicio.

Ramírez-Heredia, J. d. D. 1993. La recuperación del romanó-kaló. *I Tchatchipen* 2: 35–40.

Ravindranath, M. 2009. Language Shift and the Speech Community. Sociolinguistic Change in a Garifuna Community in Belize. PhD dissertation, University of Pennsylvania.

Rawley, J.A. 2005. *The Transatlantic Slave Trade. A History*, rev. edn. Lincoln NB: University of Nebraska Press.

Reinecke, J.E. 1937. Marginal Languages. A Sociological Survey of the Creole Languages and Trade Jargons. PhD dissertation, Yale University.

Reinecke, J.E. 1938. Trade jargons and creole dialects as marginal languages. *Social Forces* 17(1): 107–18. DOI: 10.2307/2571156

Reinecke, J.E. 1971. Tây Bòi. Notes on the Pidgin French of Vietnam. In Hymes (ed.), 47–56.

Reinecke, J.E., Tsuzaki, S., DeCamp, D., Hancock, I. & Wood, R. 1975. *A Bibliography of Pidgin and Creole Languages*. Honolulu HI: University of Hawaii Press.

Relethford, J. 2012. *Human Population Genetics*. Hoboken NJ: Wiley-Blackwell. DOI: 10.1002/9781118181652

Reusch, H. H. 1895. *Folk og natur i Finmarken*. Oslo: T. O. Brøgger.

Rickford, J. R. 1987. *Dimensions of a Creole Continuum. History, Texts & Linguistic Analysis of Guyanese Creole*. Stanford CA: Stanford University Press.

Rickford, J. R. 1991. Variation theory. Implicational scaling and critical age limits in models of linguistic variation, acquisition and change. In *Crosscurrents in Second Language Acquisition and Linguistic Theories* [Language Acquisition and Language Disorders 2], T. Huebner & C. A. Ferguson (eds), 225–246. Amsterdam: John Benjamins. DOI: 10.1075/lald.2.13ric

Rickford, J. R. & Romaine, S. (eds). 1999. *Creole Genesis, Attitudes and Discourse. Studies celebrating Charlene J. Sato* [Creole Language Library 20]. Amsterdam: John Benjamins. DOI: 10.1075/cll.20

Ricklefs, M. C. 2001. *A History of Modern Indonesia Since c. 1200*, 3rd edn. Houndmills: Palgrave Macmillan.

Rittner, D. & McCabe, T. L. 2004. *Encyclopedia of Biology*. New York NY: Facts On File.

Roberts, S. J. 1999. Grammatical development in Hawaiian Creole and the role of substrate languages. Paper presented at the *Society of Pidgin and Creole Languages Annual Meeting*, Los Angeles, California.

Roberts, S. J. 2000. Nativization and the genesis of Hawaiian Creole. In *Language Change and Language Contact in Pidgins and Creoles* [Creole Language Library 21], J. H. McWhorter (ed.). Amsterdam: John Benjamins. DOI: 10.1075/cll.21.10rob

Roberts, S. J. 2005. The Emergence of Hawaiʻi Creole English in the Early 20th Century. The Sociohistorical Context of Creole Genesis. PhD dissertation, Stanford University.

Roberts, S. J. 2013a. Pidgin Hawaiian. In Michaelis et al. (eds), 2013e, 119–127.

Roberts, S. J. 2013b. Pidgin Hawaiian structure dataset. In Michaelis et al. (eds), 2013a. http://apics-online.info/contributions/71 (13 February 2015)

Roberts, S. J. 2013c. The development of Hawaiʻi Creole English. A reassessment. Paper delivered at *ICHL21* Oslo, Norway, 5–9 August 2013.

Roberts, S. J. & Bresnan, J. 2008. Retained inflectional morphology in pidgins. A typological study. *Lingustic Typology* 12: 269–302.

Romaine, S. 1988. *Pidgin and Creole Languages*. London: Longman.

Romaine, S. 1992. *Language, Education and Development. Urban and Rural Tok Pisin in Papua New Guinea*. Oxford: OUP.

Rosen, N. 2006. Language contact and Michif stress assignment. *STUF-Sprachtypologie und Universalienforschung* 59(2): 170–90.

Rosen, N. 2007. Domains in Michif Phonology. PhD dissertation, University of Toronto.

Rosensweig, J. B. 1973. *Caló. Gutter Spanish*. New York NY: E. P. Dutton.

Rouse, I. 1992. *The Tainos. Rise and Decline of the People Who Greeted Columbus*. New Haven CT: Yale University Press.

Rubino, C. R. 2013. Reduplication. In Dryer & Haspelmath (eds), Ch. 27. http://wals.info/chapter/27 (13 February 2015)

Sabino, R. 1990. *Towards a Phonology of Negerhollands. An Analysis of Phonological Variation*. PhD dissertation, University of Pennsylvania.

Sakoda, K. & Siegel, J. 2003. *Pidgin Grammar. An Introduction to the Creole Language of Hawaiʻi*. Honolulu HI: Bess press.

Samarin, W. J. 1967. *A Grammar of Sango*. The Hague: De Gruyter.

Samarin, W. J. 2013a. Sango. In Michaelis et al. (eds), 2013e, 13–24.

Samarin, W.J. 2013b. Sango structure dataset. In Michaelis et al. (eds), 2013a. http://apics-online.info/contributions/59 (13 February 2015)

Samer, H. 2003. *ROMBASE. Didactically Edited Information on Roma.* http://romani.uni-graz.at/rombase/index.html (13 February 2015)

Sankoff, G. & Brown, P. 1976. On the origins of syntax in discourse. A case study in Tok Pisin relatives. *Language* 52(3): 631–666. DOI: 10.2307/412723

Sato, C. 1985. Linguistic inequality in Hawaii. The post-creole dilemma. In *Language of Inequality*, J. Manes & N. Wolfson (eds), 256–272. Berlin: De Gruyter.

Saville-Troike, M. 2012. *Introducing Second Language Acquisition*, 2nd edn. Cambridge: CUP. DOI: 10.1017/CBO9780511888830

Schaengold, C. 2003. The emergence of Bilingual Navajo. English and Navajo languages in contact regardless of everyone's best intentions. In *When Languages Collide. Perspectives on Language Conflict, Language Competition, and Language Coexistence*, B.D. Joseph, J. Destafano, N.G. Jacobs & I. Lehiste (eds), 235–254. Columbus OH: Ohio State University Press.

Schaengold, C. 2004. Bilingual Navajo. Mixed Codes, Bilingualism, and Language Maintenance. PhD dissertation, The Ohio State University.

Schellong, O. 1934. *Alte Dokuments aus der Südsee. Zur Geschichte der Gründung einer Kolonie. Erlebtes und Eingeborenenstudien.* Königsberg: Gräfe und Unzer.

Schieffelin, B.B. & Doucet, R.C. 1994. The "real" Haitian Creole. Ideology, metalinguistics, and orthographic choice. *American Ethnologist* 21(1): 176–200. DOI: 10.1525/ae.1994.21.1.02a00090

Schneider, E.W., Burridge, K., Kortmann, B., Mesthrie, R. & Upton, C. (eds). 2004. *A Handbook of Varieties of English, Vol. I: Phonology*. Berlin: De Gruyter.

Schröder, A. 2013a. Cameroon Pidgin English. In Michaelis et al. (eds), 2013c, 185–194.

Schröder, A. 2013b. Cameroon Pidgin English structure dataset. In Michaelis et al. (eds), 2013a. http://apics-online.info/contributions/18 (13 February 2015)

Schuchardt, H. 1884. Kreolische Studien IV. Über das Malaiospanische der Philippinen. *Sitzungsberichte der philosophisch-historischen Classe der Kaiserlichen Akademie der Wissenschaften, Wien* 105(1): 111–50.

Schuchardt, H. 1885. Kreolistische Studien III. Über das Indoportugiesische von Diu. *Sitzungsberichte der philosophisch-historischen Classe der Kaiserlichen Akademie der Wissenschaften, Wien* 103: 3–18.

Schuchardt, H. 1888a. Beiträge zur Kenntnis des kreolischen Romanisch I. Allgemeineres über das Negerportugiesische. *Zeitschrift für Romanische Philologie* 12: 242–254. DOI: 10.1515/zrph.1888.12.1-4.242

Schuchardt, H. 1888b. Kreolische Studien VII. Über das Negerportugiesische von Annobon. *Sitzungsberichte der philosophisch-historischen Classe der Kaiserlichen Akademie der Wissenschaften, Wien* 116(1): 193–226.

Schuchardt, H. 1888c. Kreolistische Studien VIII. Über das Annamito-französische. *Sitzungsberichte der philosophisch-historischen Classe der Kaiserlichen Akademie der Wissenschaften, Wien* 116: 227–34.

Schuchardt, H. 1890. Kreolische Studien IX. Über das Malaioportugiesische von Batavia und Tugu. *Sitzungsberichte der philosophisch-historischen Classe der Kaiserlichen Akademie der Wissenschaften, Wien* 122: 1–256.

Schuchardt, H. 1909. Die Lingua Franca. *Zeitschrift für Romanische Philologie* 33: 441–461.

Schuchardt, H. 1914. *Die Sprache der Saramakkaneger in Surinam*. Amsterdam: Johannes Müller.

Schuchardt, H. 1987. Kreolische Studien X. Über das Negerenglische in Westafrika, ed. by W. Viereck. Anglia. *Zeitschrift für englische Philologie* 105(1/2): 2–27.

Schultze-Berndt, E. & Angelo, D. 2013. Kriol structure dataset. In Michaelis, et al. (eds), 2013a. http://apics-online.info/contributions/25 (13 February 2015)

Schultze-Berndt, E., Meakins, F. & Angelo, D. 2013. Kriol. In Michaelis, et al. (eds), 2013c, 241–250.

Schütz, A. 1994. *The Voices of Eden. A History of Hawaiian Language Studies*. Honolulu HI: University of Hawaii Press.

Schwegler, A. 2000. The myth of decreolization. The anomalous case of Palenquero. In Neumann-Holzschuh & Schneider (eds), 409–36.

Schwegler, A. 2007. Bare nouns in Palenquero. A fresh consensus in the making. In Baptista & Guéron (eds), 205–22.

Schwegler, A. 2011. Palenque(ro). The search for its African substrate. In Lefebvre (ed.), 225–249.

Schwegler, A. 2013a. Palenquero. In Michaelis, et al. (eds), 2013d, 182–192.

Schwegler, A. 2013b. Palenquero structure dataset. In Michaelis, et al. (eds), 2013a. http://apics-online.info/contributions/48 (13 February 2015)

Schwegler, A. 2015+. Combining population genetics (DNA) with historical linguistics. On the African origins of Latin America's Black populations. In *Spanish Language and Sociolinguistic Analysis*, S. Sessarego & F. Tejedo (eds). Amsterdam: John Benjamins.

Schwegler, A. & Green, K. 2007. Palenquero (Creole Spanish). In Holm & Patrick (eds), 273–306.

Sea Island Translation Team 2005. *De Nyew Testament. The New Testament in Gullah Sea Island Creole with marginal text of the King James Version*. New York NY: American Bible Society.

Sebba, M. 1987. *The Syntax of Serial Verbs. An Investigation into Serialisation in Sranan and Other Languages* [Creole Language Library 2]. Amsterdam: John Benjamins. DOI: 10.1075/cll.2

Sebba, M. 1993. *London Jamaican. Language Systems in Interaction*. London: Longman.

Sebba, M. 1997. *Contact Languages. Pidgins and Creoles*. London: Macmillan.

Sebba, M. 1998. Meaningful choices in creole orthography. "Experts" and "users". In *Making Meaningful Choices in English. On Dimensions, Perspectives, Methodology and Evidence*, R. Schulze (ed.), 223–233.Tübingen: Günter Narr.

Sekerina, I. A. 1994. Copper Island (Mednyj) Aleut (CIA). A mixed language. *Languages of the World* 8: 14–31.

Selbach, R. 2008. The superstrate is not always the lexifier. Lingua Franca in the Barbary Coast 1530–1830. In *Roots of Creole Structures. Weighing the Contribution of Substrates and Superstrates* [Creole Language Library 33], S. M. Michaelis (ed.), 29–58. Amsterdam: John Benjamins. DOI: 10.1075/cll.33.05sel

Selbach, R., Cardoso, H. C. & van den Berg, M. (eds). 2009. *Gradual Creolization. Studies Celebrating Jacques Arends* [Creole Language Library 34]. Amsterdam: John Benjamins. DOI: 10.1075/cll.34

Shapiro, R. 2012. Chinese Pidgin Russian. In Ansaldo (ed.), 1–58.

Shi, D. 1992. On the etymology of pidgin. *Journal of Pidgin and Creole Languages* 7(2): 343–7. DOI: 10.1075/jpcl.7.2.11din

Shibatani, M. 1990. *The Languages of Japan*. Cambridge: CUP.

Shohamy, E. G. 2006. *Language Policy. Hidden Agendas and New Approaches*. Abingdon: Routledge.

Shosted, R. K. 2006. Correlating complexity. A typological approach. *Lingustic Typology* 10: 1–40. DOI: 10.1515/LINGTY.2006.001

Siegel, J. 1985. Origins of Pacific Island labourers in Fiji. *The Journal of Pacific History* 20(1): 42–54. DOI: 10.1080/00223348508572504

Siegel, J. 2000. Substrate influence in Hawai'i Creole English. *Language in Society* 29: 197–236. DOI: 10.1017/S0047404500002025

Siegel, J. 2008a. Pidgins/creoles, and second language acquisition. In Kouwenberg & Singler (eds), 189–218.

Siegel, J. 2008b. *The Emergence of Pidgin and Creole Languages*. Oxford: OUP.

Siegel, J., Szmrecsanyi, B. & Kortmann, B. 2014. Measuring analyticity and syntheticity in creoles. *Journal of Pidgin and Creole Languages* 29(1): 49–85. DOI: 10.1075/jpcl.29.1.02sie

Siewierska, A. 1984. *The Passive. A Comparative Linguistic Analysis*. London: Croom Helm.

Siewierska, A. 2013. Passive constructions. In Dryer & Haspelmath (eds), Ch. 107. http://wals.info/chapter/107 (13 February 2015)

Silverstein, M. 1972. Goodbye Columbus. Language and Speech Community in Indian-European Contact Situations. Ms.

Singler, J. V. 1984. Variation in Tense-aspect-modality in Liberian English. PhD dissertation, University of California, Los Angeles.

Singler, J. V. 1990a. On the use of sociohistorical criteria in the comparison of creoles. In *Issues in Creole Linguistics*, P. A. Seuren & S. S. Mufwene (eds), 645–659. Berlin: De Gruyter.

Singler, J. V. 1990b. *Pidgin and Creole Tense-Mood-Aspect Systems* [Creole Language Library 6]. Amsterdam: John Benjamins. DOI: 10.1075/cll.6

Singler, J. V. 1992. Nativization and pidgin/creole genesis. A reply to Bickerton. *Journal of Pidgin and Creole Languages* 7(2): 319–33. DOI: 10.1075/jpcl.7.2.07sin

Singler, J. V. 1995. The demographics of creole genesis in the Caribbean. A comparison of Martinique and Haiti. In *The Early Stages of Creolization* [Creole Language Library 13], J. Arends (ed.), 203–232. Amsterdam: John Benjamins. DOI: 10.1075/cll.13.10sinb

Singler, J. V. 2008. The sociohistorical context of creole genesis. In Kouwenberg & Singler (eds), 332–358.

Sippola, E. 2011. *Una gramática descriptiva del chabacano de Ternate*. Helsinki: University of Helsinki.

Sippola, E. 2013a. Cavite Chabacano structure dataset. In Michaelis et al. (eds), 2013a. http://apics-online.info/contributions/45 (13 February 2015)

Sippola, E. 2013b. Ternate Chabacano. In Michaelis et al. (eds), 2013d, 143–148.

Sippola, E. 2013c. Ternate Chabacano structure dataset. In Michaelis et al. (eds), 2013a. http://apics-online.info/contributions/44 (13 February 2015)

Sistren 2005. *Lionheart gal. Life Stories of Jamaican Women*. Kingston: University of the West Indies Press.

Slabbert, S. & Myers-Scotton, C. 1996. The structure of Tsotsitaal and Iscamtho. Code switching and in-group identity in South African townships. *Linguistics* 34: 317–342.

Slomanson, P. 2013a. Sri Lankan Malay. In Michaelis et al. (eds), 2013e, 77–85.

Slomanson, P. 2013b. Sri Lankan Malay structure dataset. In Michaelis et al. (eds), 2013a. http://apics-online.info/contributions/66 (13 February 2015)

Smart, J. R. 1990. Pidginization in Gulf Arabic. A first report. *Anthropological Linguistics* 32(1-2): 83–119.

Smith, G. P. 2002. *Growing up with Tok Pisin. Contact, Creolization, and Change in Papua New Guinea's National Language*. London: Battlebridge.

Smith, G. P. 2004. Tok Pisin in Papua New Guinea. Phonology. In Schneider et al. (eds), 710–728.

Smith, G. P. & Siegel, J. 2013a. Tok Pisin. In Michaelis et al. (eds), 2013c, 214–222.

Smith, G.P. & Siegel, J. 2013b. Tok Pisin structure dataset. In Michaelis et al. (eds), 2013a. http://apics-online.info/contributions/22 (13 February 2015)

Smith, I.R. 2013a. Sri Lanka Portuguese. In Michaelis et al. (eds), 2013d, 111–121.

Smith, I.R. 2013b. Sri Lanka Portuguese structure dataset. In Michaelis et al. (eds), 2013a. http://apics-online.info/contributions/41 (13 February 2015)

Smith, I.R. & Paauw, S. 2006. Sri Lanka Malay. Creole or convert? In *Structure and Variation in Language Contact*, A. Deumert & S. Durrleman (eds), 159–181. Amsterdam: John Benjamins. DOI: 10.1075/cll.29.09smi

Smith, N. 1987. The Genesis of the Creole Languages of Suriname. PhD dissertation, University of Amsterdam.

Smith, N. 1994. An annotated list of creoles, pidgins, and mixed languages. In Arends, et al. (eds), 331–74.

Smith, N. 1999. Pernambuco to Surinam 1654–1665? The Jewish slave controversy. In *Spreading the Word. The Issue of Diffusion among the Atlantic Creoles*, M. Huber & M. Parkvall(eds), 251–298. London: University of Westminster Press.

Smith, N. 2000. Symbiotic mixed languages. A question of terminology. *Bilingualism: Language and Cognition* 3(2): 122–123. DOI: 10.1017/S1366728900290214

Smith, N. 2008. Creole phonology. In Kouwenberg & Singler (eds), 98–129.

Smith, N., Robertson, I. & Williamson, K. 1987. The Ijo element in Berbice Dutch. *Language in Society* 16: 49–90. DOI: 10.1017/S0047404500012124

Smith, N. & Adamson, L. 2006. Tonal phenomena in Sranan. *STUF-Sprachtypologie und Universalienforschung* 59(2): 211–218.

Smith, R.T. 2000[1962]. *British Guiana*. London: OUP.

Snow, C.E., van Eeden, R. & Muysken, P.C. 1981. The interactional origins of foreigner talk. Municipal employees and foreign workers. *International Journal of the Sociology of Language* 28: 81–92.

Song, J.J. 2001. *Linguistic Typology. Morphology and Syntax*. Harlow: Longman.

Song, J.J. 2009. Word order patterns and principles. *An overview. Language and Linguistics Compass* 3(5): 1328–1341. DOI: 10.1111/j.1749-818X.2009.00153.x

Song, J.J. 2010. Word order typology. In *The Oxford Handbook of Linguistic Typology*, J.J. Song (ed.), 253–279. Oxford: OUP.

Speedy, K. 2007. Reunion Creole in New Caledonia. *What influence on Tayo? Journal of Pidgin and Creole Languages* 22(2): 193–230. DOI: 10.1075/jpcl.22.2.02spe

Spencer, A. & Zwicky, A.M. (eds). 1998. *The Handbook of Morphology*. Oxford: Blackwell.

Spencer, A. 1996. *Phonology. Theory and Description*. Oxford: Blackwell.

Spolsky, B. (ed.). 2012. *The Cambridge Handbook of Language Policy*. Cambridge: CUP. DOI: 10.1017/CBO9780511979026

Sreedhar, M.V. 1976. Standardization of Naga Pidgin. *Anthropological Linguistics* 18(8): 371–379.

Sreedhar, M.V. 1985. *Standardized Grammar of Naga Pidgin*. Mysore: Central Institute of Indian Languages.

Stageberg, N.C. 1956. Pidgin French grammar. A sketch. *The Modern Language Journal* 40(4): 167–169. DOI: 10.1111/j.1540-4781.1956.tb02112.x

Stassen, L. 2013a. Predicative adjectives. In Dryer & Haspelmath (eds), Ch. 118. http://wals.info/chapter/118 (13 February 2015)

Stassen, L. 2013b. Zero copula for predicate nominals. In Dryer & Haspelmath (eds), Ch. 120. http://wals.info/chapter/120 (13 February 2015)

StatSoft, I. 2013. *Electronic Statistics Textbook*. Tulsa OK: StatSoft. <http://www.statsoft.com/textbook/

Stefánsson, V. 1909. The Eskimo trade jargon of Herschel Island. *American Anthropologist* 11(2): 217–232. DOI: 10.1525/aa.1909.11.2.02a00050

Steinkrüger, P.O. 2013. Zamboanga Chabacano. In Michaelis et al. (eds), 2013d, 156–162.

Stewart, J. 2011. A Brief Descriptive Grammar of Pijal Media Lengua and an Acoustic Vowel Space Analysis of Pijal Media Lengua and Imbabura Quichua. MA thesis, University of Manitoba.

Stewart, M.M. 2007. Aspects of the syntax and semantics of bare nouns in Jamaican Creole. In Baptista & Guéron (eds), 383–399.

Stewart, W.A. 1965. Urban negro speech. Sociolinguistic factors affecting English teaching. In *Social Dialects and Language Learning. Proceedings of the Bloomington, Indiana, Conference, 1964*, R.W. Shuy (ed.), 10–18. Champaign IL: National Council of Teachers of English.

Strommer, M.A. 2013. Creating secret pidgin languages as an act of indigenous resistance? A case study from Papua New Guinea. Paper delivered at the *Society for Pidgin and Creole Linguistics*, Boston, USA, 4–5 January 2013.

Stuchtey, B. 2011. Colonialism and imperialism, 1450–1950. In *European History Online (EGO)*. Mainz: Institute of European History (IEG). http://www.ieg-ego.eu/stuchteyb-2010-en (13 February 2015)

Suvorov, E.K. 1912. *Komandorskie ostrova i pusnoj promysel na nix* (Commander Islands and the fur trade there). St. Petersburg.

Swolkien, D. 2013a. Cape Verdean Creole of São Vicente. In Michaelis et al. (eds), 2013d, 20–30.

Swolkien, D. 2013b. Cape Verdean Creole of São Vicente structure dataset. In Michaelis et al. (eds), 2013a. http://apics-online.info/contributions/32 (13 February 2015)

Syea, A. 2013. *The Syntax of Mauritian Creole*. London: Bloomsbury.

Tate, S. 1984. Jamaican Creole Approximation by Second-generation Dominicans? The Use of Agreement Tokens. MA thesis, University of York.

Taylor, A.J. 1978. Evidence of a Pidgin Motu in the earliest written Motu materials. In *Proceedings of the Second International Conference on Austronesian Linguistics*, S.A. Wurm & L. Carrington (eds), 1325–1350. Canberra: Pacific Linguistics.

Taylor, D.R. & Hoff, B.J. 1980. The linguistic repertory of the Island-Carib in the seventeenth century. *The Men's Language: A Carib pidgin? International Journal of American Linguistics* 46(4): 301–12.

Taylor, D.R. 1961. New languages for old in the West Indies. *Comparative Studies in Society and History* 3(3): 277–88. DOI: 10.1017/S0010417500012238

Taylor, D.R. 1963. The origin of West Indian creole languages. Evidence from grammatical categories. *American Anthropologist* 65: 800–814. DOI: 10.1525/aa.1963.65.4.02a00020

Taylor, D.R. 1971. Grammatical and lexical affinities of creoles. In Hymes (ed.), 293–296.

Taylor-Pearce, E. 1984. *Queen Esther*. Umeå: Department of English, Umeå University.

The Baba Diarra Letter. 1927. *La Race Nègre* 1(1): 2.

Thomason, S.G. 1980. On interpreting 'The Indian Interpreter'. *Language in Society* 9: 167–93. DOI: 10.1017/S0047404500008046

Thomason, S.G. 1993. On identifying the sources of creole structures. A discussion of Singler's and Lefebvre's papers. In *Africanisms in Afro-American Language Varieties*, S.S. Mufwene (ed.), 280–295. Athens GA: University of Georgia Press.

Thomason, S.G. 1997a. Ma'a (Mbugu). In Thomason (ed.), 469–487.

Thomason, S.G. 1997b. Mednyj Aleut. In Thomason (ed.), 449–468.

Thomason, S. G. 2001. *Language Contact. An Introduction*. Edinburgh: EUP.
Thomason, S. G. 2003. Social factors and linguistic processes in the emergence of stable mixed languages. In Matras & Bakker (eds), 21–39.
Thomason, S. G. & Elgibali, A. 1986. Before Lingua Franca. Pidginized Arabic in the eleventh century A. D. *Lingua* 68: 317–349. DOI: 10.1016/0024-3841(86)90015-X
Thomason, S. G. & Kaufman, T. 1988. *Language Contact, Creolization, and Genetic Linguistics*. Berkeley CA: University of California Press.
Thomason, S. G. (ed.). 1997. *Contact Languages. A Wider Perspective* [Creole Language Library 17]. Amsterdam: John Benjamins. DOI: 10.1075/cll.17
Thometz, K. 2001. *Life Turns Man Up and Down. High Life, Useful Advice, and Mad English: African Market Literature*, 1st edn. New York NY: Pantheon Books.
Thompson, R. W. 1961. A note on some possible affinities between the Creole dialects of the Old World and those of the New. In *Proceedings of the Conference on Creole Language Studies*, R. B. Le Page (ed.), 107–113. London: Macmillan.
Timberlake, A. 2004. *A Reference Grammar of Russian*. Cambridge: CUP.
Tirona, T. T. 1924. *An Account of the Ternate Dialect (of Cavite P. I.)*. Tagalog Paper 487 of the Beyer' Collection, Philippine National Library.
Tjon Sie Fat, P. B. 2009. *Chinese New Immigrants in Suriname. The Inevitability of Ethnic Preforming*. Amsterdam: Amsterdam University Press. DOI: 10.5117/9789056295981
Todd, L. 1974. *Pidgins and Creoles*. London: Routledge and Kegan Paul. DOI: 10.4324/9780203381199
Todd, L. 1990. *Pidgins and Creoles*, 2nd rev. edn. London: Routledge.
Tong, T. K. 1862. *The Chinese and English Instructor*. Guangzhou.
Tosco, M. 1995. A pidgin verbal system. The case of Juba Arabic. *Anthropological Linguistics* 37(4): 423–459.
Tosco, M. & Owens, J. 1993. Turku. A descriptive and comparative study. *Sprache und Geschichte in Afrika* 14: 177–267.
Turner, L. D. 2002[1949]. *Africanisms in the Gullah dialect*. Columbia SC: University of South Carolina Press.
Uffmann, C. 2009. Creole consonant inventories. How simple? In Faraclas & Klein (eds), 81–106.
UNESCO 1953. *The Use of Vernacular Languages in Education*. Paris: UNESCO. http://unesdoc.unesco.org/images/0000/000028/002897eb.pdf (15 December 2013).
Vakhtin, N. 1998. Copper Island Aleut. A case of language "resurrection". In *Endangered Languages. Language Loss and Community Response*, L. A. Grenoble & L. J. Whaley (eds), 317–27. Cambridge: CUP. DOI: 10.1017/CBO9781139166959.014
Valdman, A. (ed.). 1977. *Pidgin and Creole Linguistics*. Bloomington IN: Indiana University Press.
van den Berg, M. 2007. A Grammar of Early Sranan. PhD dissertation, Radboud University of Nijmegen.
van den Berg, M. & Smith, N. 2013. Early Sranan. In Michaelis et al. (eds), 2013c, 3–14.
van der Voort, H. 1996. Eskimo pidgin in West Greenland. In Jahr & Broch (eds), 157–258.
van der Voort, H. 2013. Eskimo Pidgin. In Michaelis et al. (eds), 2013e, 166–174.
van Lier, R. A. 1971. *Frontier Society. A Social Analysis of the History of Surinam*. The Hague: Martinus Nijhoff.
van Minde, D. 1997. *Malayu Ambong. Phonology, morphology, syntax*. Leiden: CNWS.
van Name, A. 1869–1870. Contributions to creole grammar. *Transactions of the American Philological Association*. 1. 123–67. DOI: 10.2307/310229

van Rheeden, H. 1994. Petjo. The mixed language of the Indos in Batavia. In Bakker & Mous (eds), 223–237.

van Rheeden, H. 1995. *Het Petjo van Batavia. Onstaan en Structuur ven de Taal van de Indo's.* Amsterdam: Universiteit van Amsterdam.

van Rossem, C. & van der Voort, H. 1996. *Die Creol Taal. 250 Years of Negerhollands Texts.* Amsterdam: Amsterdam University Press. DOI: 10.5117/9789053561348

van Sluijs, R. 2013a. Afrikaans. In Michaelis et al. (eds), 2013c, 285–296.

van Sluijs, R. 2013b. Negerhollands. In Michaelis et al. (eds), 2013c, 265–274.

Veenstra, T. 1996. *Serial Verbs in Saramaccan. Predication and Creole Genesis.* Dordrecht: ICG Printing.

Veenstra, T. 2008. Creole genesis. The impact of the Language Bioprogram Hypothesis. In Kouwenberg & Singler (eds), 219–241.

Velupillai, V. 2003a. *Hawai'i Creole English. A Typological Analysis of the Tense-Mood-Aspect System.* Houndmills: Palgrave Macmillan.

Velupillai, V. 2003b. The absence of reduplication in Hawai'i Creole English. In Kouwenberg (ed.), 245–9.

Velupillai, V. 2012. *An Introduction to Linguistic Typology.* Amsterdam: John Benjamins. DOI: 10.1075/z.176

Velupillai, V. 2014. There's a time for everything, except in some languages. A global study of tense. Guest Lecture at the *Collegium generale "'lles hat seine Zeit': Konzepte der Zeit in Wissenschaft und Gesellschaft"*, Universität Bern, 7 May 2014.

Vincent, G. B. 1986. Juba Arabic from a Bari perspective. *Current approaches to African linguistics* 3: 71–78.

Vitale, A. J. 1980. Kisetla. Linguistic and sociolinguistic aspects of a Pidgin Swahili of Kenya. *Anthropological Linguistics* 22(2): 47–65.

Volker, C. A. 1982. An Introduction to Rabaul Creole German (Unserdeutsch). MA thesis, University of Queensland.

Volker, C. A. 1989a. Rabaul Creole German syntax. *Working Papers in Linguistics, University of Hawai'i at Manoa* 21(1): 153–189.

Volker, C. A. 1989b. The relationship between traditional secret languages and two school-based pidgin languages in Papua New Guinea. *Horizons – Journal of Asia-Pacific Issues* 3: 19–24.

Volker, C. A. 1991. The birth and decline of Rabaul Creole German. *Language and Linguistics in Melanesia* 22: 143–156.

Volker, C. A. 2008. *Papua New Guinea Tok Pisin English dictionary.* Melbourne: OUP.

Vollbehr, E. 1912. *Mit Pinsel und Palette durch Kamerun. Tagebuchaufzeichnungen und Bilder.* Leipzig: List & von Bressensdorf.

von Beck, C. 1903. Neu-Guinea. In *Das überseeische Deutschland. Die deutschen Kolonien in Wort und Bild*, F. K. Hutter, R. Büttner, K. Dove, A. Seidel, C. von Beck, H. Seidel, F. Reinecke & B. von Deimling (eds), 485–566. Suttgart: Union.

Voorhoeve, J. 1971. Varieties of creole in Suriname. Church Creole and Pagan cult languages. In Hymes (ed.), 305–16.

Voorhoeve, J. & Lichtveld, U. M. 1975. *Creole Drum. An Anthology of Creole Literature in Surinam.* New Haven CT: Yale University Press.

Voorhoeve, J. & Lichtveld, U. M. 1980. *Suriname. Spiegel der Vaderlandse Kooplieden*, 2nd rev. edn. Den Haag: Martinus Nijhoff.

Ward, E. 1927[1698–1703]. *The London-Spy. The Vanities and Vices of the Town Exposed to View*, ed. with notes by A. L. Hayward. New York NY: George H. Doran Co.

Wardhaugh, R. 2006. *An Introduction to Sociolinguistics*, 5th edn. Malden MA: Blackwell.

Watson, R. L. & Ola, L. B. 1984. *Juba Arabic for Beginners*. Juba: Summer Institute of Linguistics.

Watts, R. J. 2003. *Politeness*. Cambridge: CUP. DOI: 10.1017/CBO9780511615184

Webb, E. R. 2009. Neither simpler nor more complex. Optimality and creole grammars. In Faraclas & Klein (eds), 67–80.

Webster, A. K. 2008. "Plaza 'góó and before he can respond...". Language ideology, bilingual Navajo, and Navajo poetry. *Pragmatics* 18(3): 511–541.

Wedel Jarlsberg, F. V. 1887. Nogle meterialier til beskrivelse over Finmarkens Amt. *Illustreret Familielæsning* 6.

Wessén, E. 1992. *Svensk språkhistoria, III: Grundlinjer till en historisk syntax*. Edsbruk: Akademitryck.

Wetzer, H. 1996. *The Typology of Adjectival Predication*. Berlin: de Gruyter. DOI: 10.1515/9783110813586

Whinnom, K. 1956. *Spanish Contact Vernaculars in the Philippine Islands*. Hong Kong: Hong Kong University Press.

Whinnom, K. 1965. Contacts de langues et emprunts lexicaux. The origin of European-based creoles and pidgins. *Orbis* 14: 509–527.

Whinnom, K. 1971. Linguistic hybridization and the 'special case' of pidgins and creoles. In Hymes (ed.), 91–115.

Whinnom, K. 1977. Lingua Franca. Historical problems. In *Pidgin and Creole Linguistics*, A. Valdman (ed.), 295–312. Bloomington IN: Indiana University Press.

Williams, F., Whitehead, J. L. & Miller, L. M. 1971. *Attitudinal Correlates of Children's Speech Characteristics* [OSOE Research Report Project No. 0-0336]. Washington DC: United States Office of Education.

Williams, J. P. 2000. Yimas-Alamblak Tanim Tok. An indigenous trade pidgin of New Guinea. *Journal of Pidgin and Creole Languages* 15(1) 37–62. DOI: 10.1075/jpcl.15.1.03wil

Williams, S. W. 1836. Jargon spoken at Canton. How it originated and has grown into use; mode in which the Chinese learn English; examples of the language in common use between foreigners and Chinese. *The Chinese Repository* 4: 428–35.

Wilson, J. 1625. The relation of Master John Wilson of Wanstead in Essex, one of the last ten that returned into England from Wiapoco in Guinea 1606. In *Purchas his Pilgrimes*. London: William Stansby.

Wilson, M. 1999. Français tirailleur. The Pidgin French of France's African Troops. MA thesis, University of Auckland.

Winer, L. S. 1993. *Trinidad and Tobago* [Varieties of English around the World T6]. Amsterdam: John Benjamins. DOI: 10.1075/veaw.t6

Winford, D. 1985. The concept of "diglossia" in Caribbean Creole situations. *Language in Society* 14: 345–356. DOI: 10.1017/S0047404500011301

Winford, D. 1993. *Predication in Caribbean English Creoles* [Creole Language Library 10]. Amsterdam: John Benjamins. DOI: 10.1075/cll.10

Winford, D. 2000. Irrealis in Sranan. Mood and modality in a radical creole. *Journal of Pidgin and Creole Languages* 15(1): 63–125. DOI: 10.1075/jpcl.15.1.04win

Winford, D. 2003. *An Introduction to Contact Linguistics*. Oxford: Blackwell.

Winford, D. & Migge, B. 2004. Surinamese creoles. Morphology and syntax. In Kortmann & Schneider (eds), 482–516.

Winford, D. & Plag, I. 2013. Sranan. In Michaelis et al. (eds), 2013c, 15–26.

Winterstein, F. 1908. *Die Verkehrs-Sprachen der Erde*. Berlin: Diesterweg Verlag.

Wood, P.H. 1974. *Black Majority. Negroes in Colonial South Carolina from 1670 through the Stono Rebellion*. New York NY: Norton.

Woods, D.L. 2006. *The Philippines. A Global Studies Handbook*. Santa Barbara CA: ABC-Clio.

Wright, F. 1984. A Sociolinguistic Study of Passivization amongst Black Adolescents in Britain. PhD dissertation, University of Birmingham.

Wright, S. 2003. *Language Policy and Language Planning. From Nationalism to Globalisation*. Houndmills: Palgrave Macmillan. DOI: 10.1057/9780230597037

Wurm, S.A. 1992. Some contact languages and pidgin and creole languages in the Siberian region. *Language Sciences* 14(3): 249–285. DOI: 10.1016/0388-0001(92)90007-2

Wurm, S.A. & Harris, J.B. 1963. *Police Motu. An Introduction to the Trade Language of Papua (New Guinea) for Anthropologists and Other Fieldworkers*. Canberra: Pacific Linguistics.

Wurm, S.A., Mühlhäusler, P. & Tryon, D.T. (eds). 1996. *Atlas of Languages of Intercultural Communication in the Pacific, Asia, and the Americas*. Berlin: De Gruyter. DOI: 10.1515/9783110819724

Wyse, A. 1989. *The Krio of Sierra Leone. An Interpretative History*. London: C. Hurst.

Yakpo, K. 2013. Pichi structure dataset. In Michaelis et al. (eds), 2013a. http://apics-online.info/contributions/19 (13 February 2015)

Yamanaka, L.-A. 1993. *Saturday Night at the Pahala Theatre*. Honolulu HI: Bamboo Ridge Press.

Yamanaka, L.-A. 1996. *Wild Meat and the Bully Burgers*. New York NY: Farrar Straus Giroux.

Yillah, S.M. & Corcoran, C. 2007. Krio (Creole English), or Sierra Leonean. In Holm & Patrick (eds), 175–98.

Yip, M. 2002. *Tone*. Cambridge: CUP. DOI: 10.1017/CBO9781139164559

Index

O

P

Pidgin Hindustani 462, 473

Pidgin Ngarluma 14, 28, 294, 298–299